Judicial Review: Law and Practice

General Editor
Frances Patterson QC

Assistant Editor
Sam Karim

Contributors
Simon Burrows

Colin Crawford

Jonathan Easton

Anthony Gill

David Hercock

Sam Karim

Frances Patterson QC

Hugh Southey QC

Matthew Stockwell

Amanda Weston

JORDANS

Published by
Jordan Publishing Limited
21 St Thomas Street
Bristol BS1 6JS

British Library Cataloguing-in-Publication Data

A catalogue record for this book is available from the British Library.

ISBN 978 1 84661 176 6

Typeset by Letterpart Ltd, Reigate, Surrey

Printed in Great Britain by CPI Antony Rowe, Chippenham and Eastbourne

CONTRIBUTORS

Simon Burrows

Barrister, Kings Chambers

Chapter 4 The Tribunal System;
Chapter 8 Mental Health

Colin Crawford

Barrister, Kings Chambers

Chapter 2 Remedies (section on
Mediation and Alternative
Remedies); Chapter 13 Central/Local
Government

Jonathan Easton

Barrister, Kings Chambers

Chapter 7 Housing

Anthony Gill

Barrister, Kings Chambers

Chapter 2 Remedies; Chapter 3
Practice and Procedure

David Hercock

Barrister, Kings Chambers

Chapter 11 Consumer Protection;
Chapter 12 Licensing

Sam Karim

Barrister, Kings Chambers

Chapter 1 Grounds of Judicial
Review; Chapter 2 Remedies;
Chapter 3 Practice and Procedure;
Chapter 6 Community Care

Frances Patterson QC

*Public Law Commissioner; Deputy
High Court Judge*

Chapter 2 Remedies; Chapter 3
Practice and Procedure; Chapter 5
Planning and Environment

Hugh Southey QC

Tooks Chambers

Chapter 9 Criminal Law

Matthew Stockwell

Barrister, India Buildings Chambers

Chapter 10 Education

Amanda Weston

Barrister, Tooks Chambers

Chapter 14 Immigration Law

PREFACE

The advent of the regionalisation project of the Administrative Court was the catalyst for the development of this book. Whilst we were discussing the embryonic stages of establishing the Northern Administrative Law Association at Kings Chambers in Manchester in 2008 it appeared to us, having regard to other texts, that there was a potential gap in the market: for a book that provided a concise and comprehensive introduction to the law and practice of judicial review proceedings together with in depth analysis of areas where judicial review is readily used as a mean of redress, including town and country planning, community care and social welfare, immigration, housing, mental health, education and licensing. This book, therefore, provides a wide-ranging coverage of administrative law and its niche practice areas including essential procedural rules, forms and guidance issued by the Administrative Court.

The Administrative Court in London will remain the centre for most of the work of the Administrative Court but with the two-year anniversary of the regionalisation of the Administrative Court approaching it is important to remember the rationale for the establishment of the Court in the regions. The report of the Judicial Working Group convened by then Vice-President of the Queen's Bench Division (now President), May LJ in January 2007 stated, 'The present system discriminates against those who are not in the South of England. Nearly all judicial review and other claims in the Administrative Court have to be brought in London, with the obvious inconvenience and additional expense that this causes for claimants, defendants, interested parties and their lawyers. Proper access to justice is not achieved if those in the regions can only bring judicial review and other claims in the Administrative Court in London.'

There is no doubt that the regionalisation of the Administrative Court has been a success in terms of access to justice, costs and speed of resolution.[1] Political debate has been littered with reference to public sector cuts, but amid the gloom of recession was a sensible implementation about which the court system should, justifiably, be proud.

---

[1] See *Beholding Court*, The Lawyer, 17 March 2010 where Langstaff J (liaison Judge to the Northern Circuit) stated how successful he considered the process of devolution has been: 'The workload of the regional Administrative Courts has exceeded our expectations and we are now dealing with developing plans to cope with the ever-increasing caseload over the forthcoming years. Most importantly, however, there is evidence that claimants have instigated claims in the regional centres when under the previous regime they would not have availed themselves of seeking a remedy if the court was still just present in London... the regional centres have shown that they are able to dispose of cases at a far greater speed, in some cases up to 75 per cent faster than London.'

We wish to thank the co-authors for their dedicated contributions, each being highly experienced in the topics that they have covered. We have endeavoured to state the law as at 1 March 2011. We hope that this book provides an indispensable source of reference and a guide to the burgeoning practice area of judicial review throughout England and Wales.

Frances Patterson QC
Sam Karim
March 2011

CONTENTS

Part 2
Specific Areas

Chapter 5
Planning and Environment

Chapter 6
Community Care

Part 3
Appendices

TABLE OF CASES

References are to paragraph numbers.

TABLE OF STATUTES

References are to paragraph numbers.

TABLE OF STATUTORY INSTRUMENTS

References are to paragraph numbers.

INTRODUCTION

This book is designed to provide a source for public law practitioners who practise across the broad spectrum of laws in which judicial review is used as an avenue of redress. It may be of value to others who appear less frequently in judicial review cases but need a convenient reference point. Part 1 seeks to concentrate primarily on the central subject matter, namely, judicial review. Part 2 considers how judicial review is currently utilised to review the lawfulness of the powers and duties of those exercising public function in various areas. Because of the evolving nature of judicial review and administrative law this work does not seek to be a comprehensive Encyclopaedia on Judicial Review. Indeed, it is hard to think that any work could be so. What this work does is to cover the main subject areas where judicial review claims are brought.

WHAT IS JUDICIAL REVIEW?

The Bowman Report[1] summarised judicial review as, 'the means by which those with a "sufficient interest" can challenge the exercise or non-exercise of powers by public bodies on the grounds of illegality, irrationality or procedural impropriety.'

Although originally a cause of action against central or local government, judicial review now extends to cover many non-governmental organisations and the commercial world. Put another way, administrative law determines the powers and duties of administrative authorities. As said by Sir Ivor Jennings, administrative law should be defined according to its subject matter: the law of public administrative or administrative law.[2] Carnwath LJ has said recently 'Judicial review is the court's response to allegations of abuse of power adversely affecting the rights or interests of those bringing the claim. The starting point must therefore be to identify the legal source of the power in question and the practical consequences of its exercise'.[3]

The importance of the Administrative Court and its function cannot be understated. Sir Thomas Bingham MR (as he then was) in *R v Ministry of*

---

[1]   Review of Crown Office work carried out by Sir Jeffrey Bowman who reported to the Lord Chancellor in 2000. The Crown Office was the predecessor of the Administrative Court.
[2]   Jennings, *The Law and the Constitution*, 5th edn, p 217.
[3]   *R (Hillingdon BC) v SS for Transport* [2010] EWHC 626.

Justice ex p Smith described this Court as having, '...the constitutional role and duty of ensuring that the rights of citizens are not abused by the unlawful exercise of executive power...'.[4]

At the Administrative Court an individual seeks to challenge a decision of an administrative body by way of achieving one or more of the various remedies that are potentially available, namely: (a) a quashing order (formerly known as certiorari); (b) a prohibiting order (formerly known as prohibition); (c) a mandatory order (formerly know as mandamus); (d) a declaration; (e) an interim declaration; (f) an injunction; and (g) a substitutionary remedy.

Judicial review, therefore, is a process by which the above remedies may be applied for at a specialist part of the High Court (Queens Bench Division), which considers public law and administrative law cases, the Administrative Court. The supervisory jurisdiction has been noted by commentators as unique because, '...the question is not whether the judge disagrees with what the public body has done, but whether there is some recognisable public law wrong...'. Professor Paul Craig explained the conceptual justification for judicial intervention within the context of the supervisory role as:

'It is readily apparent that the execution of legislation may require the grant of discretionary power to a minister or an agency. Parliament may not be able to foresee all the eventualities and flexibility may be required to implement the legislation. The legislature will of necessity grant power subject to conditions [...] Herein lies the modern conceptual justification for judicial intervention. It was designed to ensure that those to whom such grants of power were made did not transgress the sovereign will of Parliament.'[5]

The 2000 edition of the Treasury Solicitors' publication, *The Judge Over Your Shoulder* provides a useful description of who is affected by administrative law stating that:

'1.2 "Administrative" or "public" law governs the acts of public bodies and the exercise of public functions. Public bodies include "non-departmental public bodies", such as the Committee on Standards in Public Life, and Next Steps Agencies like HM Prison Service.

1.3 Private sector bodies may also be subject to administrative law when they exercise a public function. Generally, bodies exercise public functions when they act and have authority to act for the

---

4   [1996] 2 WLR 305 at 338.
5   Professor PP Craig, *Administrative Law*, 5th edn, 2003, Sweet & Maxwell, p 5.

collective benefit of the general public. The activities of City institutions with market regulatory functions, like the London Stock Exchange, are a good example'.[6]

The Fourth Edition of the publication provides that:

'The Human Rights Act 1998 is part of administrative law because it governs the exercise of statutory powers by public authorities. For example, the Act has an important bearing on the way in which those powers are to be interpreted. The devolution legislation is part of administrative law for the same reason. Likewise European Community (EC) law may be relevant to the exercise of statutory powers.'[7]

HISTORY

The present jurisdiction of the High Court extends the continuous lineage from the earliest periods of the English common law initiated by the separation of the King's Council around 1200 into the King's Bench (which grew out of the King's Court or *Curia Regis*) that was also granted jurisdiction to supervise and correct the actions of inferior courts and officials.[8] At some unknown stage, a Court independent of the King's personal presence grew out of the Curia Regis, consisting of a number of Royal judges who would hear cases themselves around the country. However, in 1215 the King's Court was formally recognised by way of the Magna Carta, as was the Common Bench (later Court of Common Pleas). At this stage, the King's Bench was theoretically a *movable* Court.[9] Increasingly, however, the King's Bench became a fixed Court, even though it could in theory meet anywhere in England, and from 1421 it appears not to have moved from Westminster Hall. The Court of Queen's Bench became the Queen's Bench Division of the High Court of Justice in 1873.

The growth of judicial review is a relatively recent phenomenon:

'...the extension of judicial control of the administrative process has provided over the 30 years the most striking feature of the development of common law in those countries of whose legal systems it provides the source; and although it is a development that has already gone a long way towards providing a system of administrative law as comprehensive in its content as the droit

---

[6]   Treasury Solicitor, *The Judge Over Your Shoulder, A Guide to Judicial Review for UK Government Administrators*, 3rd edn, 2000.

[7]   Treasury Solicitor, *The Judge Over Your Shoulder, A Guide to Judicial Review for UK Government Administrators*, 4th edn, 2006.

[8]   Pollard, Parpworth & Hughes, *Constititional and Administrative Law*, 4th edn, Oxford, p 461.

[9]   One may argue, therefore, that there is historical underpinning to the recent regionalisation of the Administrative Court that occurred in April 2009.

administrative of countries of the civil law, albeit differing in procedural approach, it is a development that is still continuing.'[10]

This assertion by Lord Diplock in 1984 regarding the organic development of administrative law remains accurate in the contemporary usage of the Administrative Court. Prior to this 'striking development' since the Second World War, administrative law was an unknown specialism. Lord Reid stated in *Ridge v Baldwin* [1964] AC 40, HL that, '...we do not have a developed system of administrative law – perhaps because until fairly recently we did not need it' This view was clearly reflected by Mr Maudling (Secretary of State for the Home Department) when in 1971 he said, in debating the Immigration Bill 1971, that, '...I have never seen the sense of administrative law in our country, because it merely means someone else taking the Government's decision for them...'.[11] It is clear that matters have since moved on!

There have been three milestones in the development of this area of law, namely: (i) the introduction in the Rules of the Supreme Court in 1977 of a codified process by which to challenge the decision of a administrative body (subsequently giving legislative effect to the new procedure contained in the RSC Order 53 by the Supreme Court Act 1981, section 31); (ii) the House of Lords decision of *Mahon*[12] which defined that actions or powers exercised by a administrative body must be categorised as raising questions of 'public law' and its distinction with 'private law'; and (iii) the explosion of government after the Second World War.[13] Lord Diplock described the development in *R v Inland Revenue* [1982] AC 617 at 641C-D as, '...that progress towards a comprehensive system of administrative law that I regard as having been the greatest achievement of the English courts in my judicial lifetime...'. In equal terms, Lord Geoff stated in *Kleinwort Benson Ltd v Lincoln City Council* [1999] AC 349 at 378E that:

> 'Occasionally, a judicial development of the law will be of a more radical nature, constituting a departure, even a major departure, from what has previously been considered to be established principle, and leading to a realignment of subsidiary principles within that branch of the law. Perhaps the most remarkable example of such a development is to be found in the decisions of this House in the middle of this century which led to the creation of our modern system of administrative law. It is into this category that the present case falls; but it must nevertheless be seen as a development of the law, and treated as such.'

Finally, it is worth noting the impact of the Labour government and its policies between 1997 and 2010 and the increase of litigation in the Administrative

---

10 Lord Diplock in *Mahon v Air New Zealand* [1984] AC 808.
11 Official Report, Standing Committee B, 25 May 1971, col 1508.
12 *Mahon v Air New Zealand* [1984] AC 808.
13 See Bradley & Ewing, *Constitutional & Administrative Law*, 14th edn, pp 662 to 664 'reform of the administrative law' for more information.

Court with the introduction of a major package of constitutional reform such as devolution, human rights, reform of the House of Lords and freedom of information. As a result, there has been an expansion of judicial influence. As stated by Professor Robert Stevens:

> '[T]he most obvious and public change concerned the expansion of judicial review to provide an extensive power for the courts to intervene in procedural due process over a wide range of public and quasi public matter[s].'[14]

The 2000 edition of *The Judge Over Your Shoulder* indicated that judicial review was, '...[A] growth industry. In 1974 there were 160 applications for leave to seek judicial review in England and Wales. By 1998 the figure was 4,539...'.[15] As set out in paragraph 3.0 in 2010 there were over 13,000 applications for permission lodged: a figure which could not have been anticipated just over ten years ago.

De Smith, Woolf and Jowell described the changes from the 1970s, stating that:

> '...From the 1970s onwards a number of pressure groups consciously adopted "test case strategies" in which judicial review, in conjunction with other forms of legal proceedings and together with conventional forms of political action, was used to seek changes in government policy [...] Success, however, was often temporary, limited and indirect: judicial review generated publicity and was capable of inflicting political embarrassment on ministers. The response of government however, was often to nullify or sidestep the effects of an unpalatable judicial decision by enacting primary legislation [...]'.[16]

THE PRESENT DAY

The Administrative Court and Administrative Court Office were established on 2 October 2000. The changes were introduced after a review of the Crown Office by Sir Jeffrey Bowman which was submitted to the Lord Chancellor in March 2000. It recommended that the Crown Office and the Crown Office List be renamed as the Administrative Court to emphasise the principal work of the Court.

The Bowman review had been instigated after the rapid expansion of administrative law and consequential growth of judicial review during the 1980s and 1990s. As a result there was increasing concern about how cases

---

[14] Robert Stevens, *The English Judges – Their role in the changing constitution*, Hart Publishing, 2002.

[15] Treasury Solicitor, *The Judge Over Your Shoulder, A Guide to Judicial Review for UK Government Administrators*, 3rd edn, 2000.

[16] De Smith, Woolf and Jowell, *Judicial Review of Administrative Action*, 5th edn, 1995.

were dealt with and delays in dealing with cases. The Law Commission had recommended in 1994[17] that the procedure and remedies for judicial review be reformed and observed that there was a public interest in the prompt adjudication of disputes through the courts.

The Bowman Report hoped that its recommendations would achieve such a solution. It said, 'We believe that its work would be dealt with more efficiently and effectively by a smaller number of nominated judges working in the Crown Office List for a majority of the year in a similar fashion to the Commercial Court.'

The Report could not have foreseen the explosion of work in the Administrative Court during the 2000s which at one time threatened the efficient and effective running of the court with which Bowman was concerned. The delays before cases reached any substantive hearing were the subject of widespread concern and complaint.

A series of significant steps have been taken to relieve the pressure on the Administrative Court. First, most of the immigration cases have been transferred to the Upper Tribunal. Secondly, more specialist judges have been appointed (there are currently 50 nominated High Court judges for Administrative Court work and significant numbers of suitable qualified Deputy High Court judges). Thirdly, as a result of the implementation of the recommendations of the Report of the Judicial Working Group headed by Lord Justice May (President of the Queen's Bench Division)[18] looking at Justice Outside London the Administrative Court has opened in regional centres. From 21 April 2009 public law cases arising in the regions can be tried at the venue most local to them (Birmingham, Leeds, Liverpool and Manchester)[19] thus spreading the work from London, relieving pressure on the Administrative Court List in London and making the Administrative Court more accessible to all. Further, there is the ability on the part of the judge at the permission stage to transfer the case to a more convenient venue or the

---

[17]   *Administrative Law: Judicial Review and Statutory Appeals* (Law Commission No 226).

[18]   Report of the Judicial Working Group in January 2007 ('report'). In a News Release dated 17 November 2007, The Working Group in their report, *Justice Outside of London*, said: 'Nearly all judicial review and other claims in the Administrative Court have to be brought in London, with the obvious inconvenience and additional expense that this causes for claimants, defendants, interested parties and their lawyers. The essential point is proper access to justice is not achieved if those in the regions can only bring judicial review and other claims in the Administrative Court in London. The present system discriminates against those who are not in the South of England.' Lord Justice May, President of the Queen's Bench Division also has said in a interview, 'The move is not just a pragmatic one...It is also that it is right, in itself, for these cases to be heard locally...the important thing is that claimants based in the regions will be able to have their cases dealt with at the centre that they regard as most convenient, instructing – if they wish – lawyers also based in the region.' (*Times*, 9 April 2009, 'Administrative Court takes asylum cases out to the regions'.)

[19]   Manchester (Civil Justice Centre, 12th Floor, 1 Bridge Street, Manchester, M3 3FX), Leeds (Leeds Combined Court, 1 Oxford Row, Leeds, LS1 3BG), Birmingham (Civil Justice Centre, Priory Courts, 5th Floor, 33 Bull Street, Birmingham, B4 6DS) and Cardiff (Civil Justice Centre, 2 Park Street, Cardiff, CF10 1ET).

option for the parties to apply that proceedings be transferred to the venue most proximate and convenient in accordance with PD 53D which deals with venue. All of these initiatives mean that there is now a framework in place for the Administrative Court to resume its role as a specialist court able to work expeditiously and effectively.[20]

Even so the number of applications for permission to bring judicial review proceedings lodged with the Administrative Court in 2010 was 13,088. That illustrates the scale of the problem that the Administrative Court has to tackle. Some 15 per cent of that total were lodged in the four regional centres of Birmingham, Cardiff, Leeds and Manchester. The regional courts are thus providing, as was anticipated, much needed relief to the Administrative Court in London. The total figures are somewhat deceptive as judicial review is a two stage process with permission to proceed required to be able to proceed to the full hearing. Sunkin and Bondy in their study, *The Dynamics of Judicial Review Litigation: the Resolution of Public Law Challenges before Final Hearing*[21] found that increasing numbers of judicial review claims are settled in favour of claimants without the need for trial in the Administrative Court.

The Court operates under a lead nominated judge with overall responsibility for the speed, efficiency and economy with which the work of the Administrative Court is undertaken.[22] The Administrative Court Office is responsible for the running of the Administrative Court. In London there are a team of lawyers responsible for different areas of work. Each of the regional centres has its own dedicated office and all Administrative Court centres are linked to a central computer system so that each Administrative Court centre is aware of proceedings in other centres to secure efficiency and to avoid 'forum shopping'.[23]

---

[20]   Paragraph 5.2 of the 53D Practice Direction (Venue) provides the following guidance: 'The general expectation is that proceedings will be administered and determined in the region with which the claimant has the closest connection, subject to the following considerations as applicable: (a) any reason expressed by any party for preferring a particular venue; (b) the region in which the defendants or any relevant office or department where the defendant is based; (c) the region in which the claimant's legal representatives are based; (d) the ease and cost of travel to a hearing; (e) the availability and suitability of alternative means of attending a hearing (for example by video link); (f) the extent and nature of media interest in the proceedings in any particular locality; (g) the time within which it is appropriate for the proceedings to be determined; (h) whether it is desirable to administer or determine the claim in another region in the light of the volume of claims issued at, and the capacity, resources and workload of, the court at which it is issued; (i) whether the claim issued is sufficiently similar to those in another outstanding claim to make it desirable that they should be determined together with, or immediately following the other claim; and (j) whether the claim raises devolution issues and for that reason whether it should more appropriately be determined in London or Cardiff.'

[21]   Public Law Project: 2009.

[22]   Currently Ouseley J.

[23]   All four regional centres have their own dedicated administrative staff, including an Administrative Court Office lawyer. In addition, all regional centres (including London) use the same computer network system, COINS. This is a confidential and secure system, which enables all five centres to act cohesively. As such, the system prevents the possibility of two or more of the same claims being issued more than once in the respective regional centre.

Parallel with changes to the way the Administrative Court is administered amendments have been made to what was RSC O53. Those changes are now encompassed in RSC O54 which in turn modifies Part 8 of the Civil Procedure Rules. Together, and read with the Practice Directions that accompany RSC O54 and section 31 of the Senior Courts Act 1981, they provide the procedural rules for judicial review. These are dealt with in greater detail later in this work.

WORK OF THE ADMINISTRATIVE COURT

The work of the Administrative Court is described by the Court itself as:

> 'varied, consisting of the administrative law jurisdiction of England and Wales as well as a supervisory jurisdiction over inferior courts and tribunals. The supervisory jurisdiction, exercised in the main through the procedure of Judicial Review, covers persons or bodies exercising a public law function – a wide and still growing field'.[24]

Annex A to the HMCS website lists the work of the Administrative Court as follows:

> 'Judicial review – of decisions of inferior courts and tribunals, public bodies and persons exercising a public function. Criminal cases may arise from decisions of magistrates' courts or the Crown Court when it is acting in its appellate capacity.
>
> Statutory appeals and applications – the right given by certain statutes to challenge decisions of eg Ministers, Local Government, Tribunals.
>
> Statutory review challenge to decisions of the IAT to refuse leave to appeal.
>
> Appeals by way of case stated – appeals against decisions of magistrates' courts and the Crown Court (predominantly criminal cases).
>
> Applications for habeas corpus.
>
> Applications for committal for contempt.
>
> Applications for an order preventing a vexatious litigant from instituting or continuing proceedings without the leave of a judge.
>
> Applications under the Coroners Act 1988.

---

[24] HMCS website.

Some matters are required by statute or rules of Court to be heard by a Divisional Court (ie a court of two or more judges):

1. Applications for committal for contempt where the contempt: (a) is committed in connection with: (i) proceedings before a Q.B. Divisional Court, (ii) criminal proceedings (except where it is in the face of the court or disobedience to an order), (iii) proceedings in an inferior court, or (b) is committed otherwise than in any proceedings.

2. Appeals from the Law Society Disciplinary Tribunal. Such appeals are heard by a three judge court unless the Lord Chief Justice otherwise directs. By convention these appeals are heard by a Court presided over by the Lord Chief Justice.

3. Applications under s 13 of the Coroners Act 1988 (with fiat of the Attorney General).

4. Applications for vexatious litigant orders under s 42 of the Supreme Court Act 1981.

5. Applications relating to parliamentary and local government elections under the Representation of the People Acts (unless exercisable by a single judge by express statutory provision).

Others can be, and usually are, heard by a Divisional Court:

1. Applications for judicial review in a criminal cause or matter.

2. Applications for leave to apply for judicial review in a criminal cause or matter, after refusal by a single judge (whether on paper or after oral argument).

3. Appeals by way of case stated in a criminal cause or matter, whether from the Crown Court or from a magistrates court.

The remaining matters in the Administrative Court List will generally be heard by a single judge.'

Part 1

GENERAL PRINCIPLES

Chapter 1

GROUNDS OF JUDICIAL REVIEW

INTRODUCTION

1.1   It would not be possible to consider the grounds of judicial review without reference to the immortal maxim of Lord Diplock in the case of *Council of Civil Service Unions v Minister for the Civil Service*[1] ('GCHQ case'):

> 'Judicial review has I think developed to a stage today when, without reiterating any analysis of the steps by which the development has come about, one can conveniently classify under three heads the grounds on which administrative action is subject to control by judicial review. The first ground I would call "illegality", the second "irrationality" and the third "procedural impropriety". That is not to say that further development on a case by case basis may not in the course of time add further grounds. I have in mind particularly the possible adoption in the future of the principle of "proportionality" which is recognised in the administrative law of several of our fellow members of the European Economic Community [...].'[2]

1.2   This quotation provides a useful boundary to consider the modern structure of challenging decisions by way of judicial review. Lord Diplock referred to a decision falling foul of 'illegality' when the decision maker misunderstood and/or incorrectly applied the relevant law. 'Irrationality' was described as a decision, which was so outrageous in its defiance of logic or accepted moral standards that no sensible person could have arrived at that same decision. 'Procedural impropriety' was described as covering those situations where there has been: (i) a breach of procedural rules laid down by the relevant legislation; (ii) a breach of the common law rules of natural justice; and/or (iii) where there had been procedural unfairness.

1.3   The grounds of judicial review are analysed in this chapter under the general conceptual headings of 'ultra vires', 'reasonableness' and 'fairness' (although not in that order). There is also the ground of proportionality, considered under the guise of human rights jurisprudence. There is an obvious degree of overlap between the various grounds of review.

IRRATIONALITY/UNREASONABLENESS

1.4   At the centre of the ground of 'reasonableness' is an acknowledgment that the decision-maker enjoys a considerable discretion when making a particular decision. Traditionally the Administrative Court would intervene only where a public body had used a power for a purpose not permitted by a statutory provision (acting *ultra vires*), or alternatively when the decision was obviously unreasonable or irrational. In situations

---

[1]   [1985] AC 374.
[2]   Ibid, para 410.

where there was a real unfairness, the Court intervened when the decision maker had made a serious factual error in reaching its decision.[3]

1.5 Lord Greene formulated the concept of reasonableness in *Associated Provincial Picture Houses Ltd v Wednesbury Corporation*[4] when he said:

> '... we have heard in this case a great deal about the meaning of the word "unreasonable". It is true the discretion must be exercised reasonably. Now what does that mean? Lawyers familiar with the phraseology commonly used in relation to exercise of statutory discretions often use the word "unreasonable" in a rather comprehensive sense. It has frequently been used and is frequently used as a general description of the things that must not be done. For instance, a person entrusted with a discretion must, so to speak, direct himself properly in law. He must call his own attention to the matters which he is bound to consider. He must exclude from his consideration matters which are irrelevant to what he has to consider. If he does not obey those rules, he may truly be said, and often is said, to be acting "unreasonably". Similarly, there may be something so absurd that no sensible person could ever dream that it lay within the powers of the authority. Warrington LJ in *Short v Poole Corporation* [1926] Ch 66, 90, 91 gave the example of the red-haired teacher, dismissed because she had red hair. That is unreasonable in one sense. In another sense it is taking into consideration extraneous matters. It is so unreasonable that it might almost be described as being done in bad faith; and, in fact, all these things run into one another.'

1.6 This has been famously coined as '*Wednesbury* unreasonableness'. In the GCHQ case Lord Diplock stated that:[5]

> 'By "irrationality" I mean what can now be succinctly referred to as "*Wednesbury* unreasonableness" ... It applies to a decision which is so outrageous in its defiance of logic or of accepted moral standards that no sensible person who had applied his mind to the question to be decided could have arrived at it. Whether a decision falls within this category is a question that judges by their training and experience should be well equipped to answer, or else there would be something badly wrong with our judicial system.'

1.7 Some examples of such unreasonableness include where a decision was so absurd that the decision maker must have taken leave of his senses;[6] a decision that looked at objectively is so devoid of any plausible justification that no reasonable body of persons could have reached it;[7] 'a criterion so nebulous as to be unlikely to produce any result other than one which is quixotic, or arbitrary or whimsical would be *Wednesbury* unreasonable';[8] an approach that lacks logic to such a degree as to be unreasonable;[9] and that oppressive decisions may be held to be repugnant to compulsory public law standards.[10]

1.8 In *R v Secretary of State for the Environment, ex p Nottinghamshire County Council*[11] Lord Scarman explicitly indicated that Wednesbury unreasonableness was not an exhaustive statement of the law, noting that:

---

3   *E v Secretary of State for the Home Department* [2004] QB 1044.
4   [1947] 2 All ER 680.
5   At para 410G to H.
6   *R v Secretary of State for the Environment, ex p Nottingham County Council* [1986] AC 240, Lord Scarman at 247H and 248D.
7   *Bromley LBC v Greater London Council* [1983] 1 AC 768, Lord Diplock at 821B.
8   *R v Bradford MBC, ex p Skiandar Ali* [1994] ELR 299 at 308E.
9   *R (A) v Liverpool CC* [2007] EWHC 1477 (Admin) at 39.
10 *R (Khatun) v LB Newham* [2004] EWCA Civ 55 at 37 to 41.
11 [1986] AC 240.

'"*Wednesbury* principles" is a convenient legal "shorthand" used by lawyers to refer to the classical review by Lord Greene MR in the *Wednesbury* case of the circumstances in which the courts will intervene to quash as being illegal the exercise of an administrative discretion. No question of constitutional propriety arose in the case, and the Master of the Rolls was not concerned with the constitutional limits to the exercise of judicial power in our parliamentary democracy. There is a risk, however, that the judgment of the Master of the Rolls may be treated as a complete, exhaustive, definitive statement of the law.'

1.9   In *R v Parliamentary Commissioner for Administration, ex p Balchin*,[12] Sedley J (as he then was) held that a decision would be *Wednesbury* unreasonable if it disclosed an error of reasoning which robbed the decision of its logical integrity. This apparent 'loosening' of Lord Greene's formula was supported by Lord Cooke in *R v Chief Constable of Sussex, ex p International Trader's Ferry Ltd*[13] where he regarded the formulation by Lord Greene as 'tautologous and exaggerated'.[14] Lord Cooke advocated a simple test, namely: was the decision one which a reasonable authority could reach?

1.10   Contemporary principal considerations in respect of *unreasonable decision making* include:

(i)   an error of reasoning which robbed the decision of its logical integrity;[15]

(ii)   the test of whether a reasonable decision maker made the right decision by directing himself in law, seized of the relevant facts and taking into account considerations which he was bound to take into account, as applied by Lord Bingham in *Re Duffy*;[16]

(iii)   the determination of the 'reasonableness' of a decision must be based upon an objective analysis;[17]

(iv)   the principles of *Wednesbury* unreasonableness can be applied with various degrees of intensity depending upon the subject matter,[18] and as such, it has been

---

[12]   [1996] EWHC Admin 152.

[13]   [1999] 1 All ER 129 at 157.

[14]   Above at para 549.

[15]   Sedley J in *R v Parliamentary Commission for Administration, ex p Balchin* [1997] COD 146.

[16]   [2008] UKHL 4 at 28. This case is a scarce example of a successful judicial review claim brought on irrationality grounds. The Appellants appealed against a decision upholding the appointment of two new members of the Parades Commission for Northern Ireland, both of whom were prominent loyalist proponents of a parade down the Garvaghy Road, arguably the most contentious of all parades in Northern Ireland. The House of Lords held that role of the Commission was to resolve contentious disputes by mediation or, if this was not possible, by decisions that balanced the interests of those who wished to march and those who were opposed to the marches. These tasks could only satisfactorily be performed by a body that was seen to be objective, independent and impartial. Another example of such a case is *R (Rogers) v Swindon NHS PCT* which involved the policy of the PCT which was to refuse funding for treatment with the unlicensed drug Herceptin save where exceptional personal or clinical circumstances could be shown. The Court found that there was no rational basis for distinguishing between patients within the eligible group on the basis of exceptional clinical circumstances any more than there was on the basis of personal circumstances. The Court found that, once the PCT had decided to fund Herceptin for some patients and that cost was irrelevant, the only reasonable approach was to focus on the clinical needs of the individual patient and to fund patients within the eligible group who had been properly prescribed Herceptin by their physicians. The Court of Appeal therefore found that the policy was irrational and unlawful.

[17]   See *R v Secretary of State for the Environment, ex p Hammersmith & Fulham LBC* [1991] 1 AC 521 per Lord Bridge at p 593E and *R v Department for Education and Employment, ex p Begbie* [2000] 1 WLR 1115 at 1130B.

[18]   Ibid at pp 546–549.

held that the greater the interference with human rights the more the Court will require by way of justification. As aptly stated by Lord Bingham in *R v MOD, ex p Smith & Others*:[19]

> 'The court may not interfere with the exercise of an administrative discretion save where the court is satisfied that the decision is unreasonable in the sense that it is beyond the range of responses open to a reasonable decision-maker. But in judging whether the decision-maker has exceeded the margin of appreciation the human rights context is important. The more substantial the interference with human rights the more the court will require by way of justification before it is satisfied that the decision is reasonable in the sense outlined above.'

(v) irrationality may be inferred from an absence of reasons;[20]

(vi) in relation to expert opinion and irrationality, in *R (Campaign to End All Animal Experiments t/a British Union for the Abolition of Vivisection) v SSHD*[21] the Court of Appeal overturned the decision of a Chief Inspector appointed by the defendant under the Animals (Scientific Procedures) Act 1986 who had misconstrued statutory guidance in a report on research on non-human primates at Cambridge University. May LJ said that '… the court must be careful not to substitute is own inexpert view of the science for a tenable expert opinion. … In my view, absent material misconstruction, the court should be very slow to conclude that this expert and experienced Chief Inspection reached a perverse scientific conclusion';[22] and

(vii) the case of *R (Bradley & Ors) v Secretary of State for Work and Pensions*[23] is a good example in relation to Ombudsman recommendations. The Ombudsman found that there had been maladministration on the part of the Secretary of State.[24] The Secretary of State rejected all but one of the Ombudsman's findings and recommendations. At first instance Bean J, concluded that, absent a successful application for judicial review on the part of the Secretary of State, the findings of the Ombudsman are binding on him, subject only to exceptions where the findings are objectively shown to be flawed or irrational or peripheral, or where there is genuine fresh evidence to be considered.[25] The Court found that, on the facts, no reasonable Secretary of State could disagree with the Ombudsman's finding of maladministration in relation to the information issued to the public about the security of pension schemes. Bean J did, however, decline to quash any of the other rejections, in part because he found the Ombudsman's conclusions to have been logically flawed in some key respects. The Court of Appeal[26] stated that the relevant question for the judge was whether the Secretary of State had acted rationally in rejecting the ombudsman's findings. As such, the decision of the Secretary of State to reject the third finding of maladministration could not be held to be irrational.[27]

---

[19] [1996] QB 517. See also the case of *Sheffield City Council v Smart* [2002] EWCA Civ 4 at 42.

[20] *R v Civil Service Appeal Board, ex p Cunningham* [1991] 4 All ER 310.

[21] [2008] EWCA Civ 417.

[22] Ibid at para 1.

[23] [2007] EWHC 242 (Comm).

[24] In particular in respect of the advice and information provided to workers as to the security to pensions provided by the Pensions Act 1995.

[25] Adopting the reasoning of a case concerning the Local Government Ombudsman, *R (Eastleigh Borough Council) v Local Commissioner for Administration* [1988] 1 QB 855.

[26] [2009] QB 114.

[27] Note that the appeal was dismissed, cross-appeal allowed in part. The Court concluded that there was force

1.11   In summary, this ground is best described with reference to the following cases.

1.12   Firstly, in *R v Teignmouth DC, ex p Teignmouth Quay Co Ltd*[28] the Court stated that '… the question whether to quash this decision is not answered simply by asking whether the council behaved "unreasonably" in the general sense … [but] … whether they behaved "unreasonably" in the way they purported to exercise the powers granted and limited by statute'; and secondly, *HMB Holding Ltd v Antigua and Barbuda*[29] when the Court adopted the time honoured approach by defining this ground as one '… which no sensible person who had applied his mind to the question to be decided could have arrived at ….'

1.13   The test is, therefore, a very high one. As a result, few practitioners instigate judicial review proceedings simply relying on an 'unreasonableness' argument. There has, however, been a general 'loosening' of the *Wednesbury* principle.[30]

ILLEGALITY

1.14   The law binds public bodies who are vested with powers under statute, statutory provisions or otherwise. The primordial purpose of judicial review is to regulate the exercise of such powers, and to ensure that they are used in accordance with the rule of law. When a public body acts in a way, which goes beyond the limits of its own powers, it is said to be acting 'ultra vires'. In the GCHQ case Lord Diplock defined illegality as meaning that, '… the decision-maker must understand correctly the law that regulates his decision-making power and must give effect to it ….'[31]

Ultra vires[32]

1.15   The classic theoretical example of a public body acting 'ultra vires' is when the body acts outside its powers vested in statute. *In R (Bancoult) v Secretary of State for Foreign & Commonwealth Affairs*[33] Sedley LJ defined this head of review as:

'The concept of ultra vires acts was borrowed during the 19th century by public law from company law, where powers are spelt out in articles of association and acts can be measured against them. The same is frequently the case in public law: hence the transferability of the concept.'

---

in the argument that the judge erred in treating the ombudsman's finding as only a finding that the maladministration was a significant contributory factor in the creation of financial losses suffered by individuals. There was nothing to suggest that the secretary of state questioned the ombudsman's conclusion that, if there was maladministration, that caused injustice in the forms of outrage, distress, anxiety and uncertainty. Neither the secretary of state nor the judge challenged the ombudsman's view that the concept of injustice was wide enough to cover a sense of outrage, distress, anxiety and uncertainty, nor that the concept would cover the loss of opportunities to make informed choices or to take remedial action. There could be no answer to say that there was no real prospect that remedial action would avoid financial loss.

[28]   [1995] 2 PLR 1 at 10D.
[29]   UKPC 37 at 31.
[30]   See for example cases of *Congreve v Home Office* [1976] QB 629, *R v Lord Saville of Newdigate, ex p A* [1999] 4 All ER 860 and *R v Parliamentary Commissioner for Administration, ex p Balchin* [1997] COD 146.
[31]   [1985] AC 374 at 410F.
[32]   A Latin phrase meaning 'beyond the power'.
[33]   [2008] QB 365 at 59.

1.16   In practice, however, the questions of 'principle' and 'construction' of a particular statute are fundamental, ie whether or not the particular statute permits an action/omission. Examples include:

(a)   *R v Secretary of State for Health ex p Hammersmith & Fulham*:[34] where asylum seekers could not be provided with cash under the National Assistance Act 1948 as the Act provides that local authorities must themselves make arrangements for services, and 'providing cash' did not fall within that definition.

(b)   *R v Thames Magistrates Court, ex p Clapton Cash & Carry*[35] where magistrates had the power to order the destruction of food that was unfit for human consumption.

(c)   *R v Secretary of State for the Home Department, ex p Anderson*[36] where Anderson was a prisoner who applied for judicial review of prison standing orders restricting prisoners' access to legal advice prior to the making of an internal complaint. It was held that the standing orders were ultra vires. There were no clear words in the enabling relevant Act allowing such an impediment to the prisoner's access to the courts.

(d)   *R v Criminal Injuries Compensation Board, ex p Barrett*[37] where judicial review was granted of the CICB's apportionment of damages between a parent and his two children. Apportionment was ultra vires (in this instance) because in effect it reduced the children's compensation by the value of insurance payments made to the parent.

(e)   *Credit Suisse v Allerdale Borough Council*.[38] A bank brought a claim to enforce a contract of guarantee entered into by the council, as security for monies loaned by the bank to a company set up by the council. The action failed. The contract was ultra vires. Schedule 13 of the Local Government Act 1972 provided a comprehensive code defining and limiting a local authority's borrowing powers, from which section 111 (incidental powers) could provide no escape route.

(f)   *R v London Borough of Southwark, ex p Dagou*.[39] Following the necessary inquiries, Southwark made a decision under section 64 of the Housing Act 1985 proposing to refer the application to Newham but gave no reasons. Following representations made by Newham, Southwark reversed its decision as to intentionality and decided to lock the applicant out of her temporary accommodation. The application was granted on the basis: (1) once inquiries under section 62 were complete and the decision notified to the applicant, that decision was final, so that any further inquiry or determination was ultra vires; and (2) the Council was in breach of its statutory obligation to give reasons for the section 64 notice.

---

34   1 CCLR 96, QBD.
35   [1989] COD 518, QBD.
36   [1984] QB 778 DC.
37   [1994] COD 234.
38   [1997] QB 306 CA.
39   (1996) 28 HLR 72.

(g) *R v Secretary of State for the Home Department, ex p Saleem.*[40] The Court of Appeal granted the appeal of the IAT's[41] refusal to entertain an application for leave to appeal. Rule 42(1)(a) of the Asylum Appeals (Procedure) Rules 1996[42] was ultra vires the enabling Act, since the rule went beyond regulating rights of appeal and was destructive of such rights. The rule was not expressly authorised by the Act; nor did it arise by necessary implication; nor was it reasonable.

(h) *Rochester City Council v Kent County Council.*[43] In proceedings for restitution, Rochester City Council were entitled to recover £2m, which it had contributed towards Kent County Council's Medway road scheme. The contributions were ultra vires, since section 274 of the Highways Act 1980 could not be used to contribute towards an existing scheme. Alternatively, Kent County Council had been unjustly enriched given government funding, which had become available.

1.17 Not only must a public authority's action be lawful; so must its purpose. A decision made with the improper purpose of, for example, punishment, or of improperly extracting cash, can be judicially reviewed even if the resulting decision is itself formally one that is otherwise within a decision-maker's available powers.[44] Difficulties in this area can arise where a body is using a statutory power for a collateral purpose (namely one which is alien to the purpose for which it was granted).[45]

Unlawfully delegating power or fettering discretion

1.18 A public body is not entitled either to improperly delegate its powers, or to act under a completely inflexible policy. In particular, while it is accepted that Ministers cannot personally make every decision issued in their name where legislation confers a power on a specified individual or body, the power cannot be delegated to another person or body. Moreover, a body or tribunal is not entitled blindly to follow policy guidelines. Neither is it entitled to fetter the exercise of its discretion. In the case of *Port of London Authority, ex p Kynoch Ltd*[46] Banks LJ observed that:

> 'There are on the one hand, cases where a tribunal in the honest exercise of its discretion has adopted a policy, and without refusing to hear an applicant intimates what its policy is, and that after hearing him it will in accordance with its policy decide against him, unless there is something exceptional in his case [...] On the other hand there are cases where a tribunal has passed a rule, or come to a determination, not to hear any application of a particular character by whomsoever made.'

1.19 This latter course of action is not acceptable. In the more recent case of *R v Secretary of State for the Home Department, ex p Venables*,[47] Lord Browne-Wilkinson observed that:

> 'When Parliament confers a discretionary power exercisable from time to time over a period, such a power must be exercised on each occasion in the light of the circumstances at that

---

40 [2001] 1 WLR 443 CA.
41 Immigration Asylum Tribunal.
42 Which provided that notice of a special adjudicator's determination was deemed to have been received two days after posting regardless of whether or when actually received.
43 *The Times*, 5 March 1998.
44 *Padfield v Minister of Agriculture Fisheries and Food* [1968] AC 997.
45 *Bromley LBC v Greater London Council* [1983] 1 AC 768.
46 [1919] 1 KB 176.
47 [1998] AC 407.

time. In consequence, the person on whom the power is conferred cannot fetter the future exercise of his discretion by committing himself now as to the way he will exercise the power in the future [...] By the same token, the person on whom the power has been conferred cannot fetter the way he will use that power by ruling out of consideration on the future exercise of that power factors which may then be relevant to such an exercise. These considerations do not preclude the person on whom the power is conferred from developing and applying a policy as to the approach which he will adopt in the generality of case [...] But the position is different if the policy adopted is such as to preclude the person on whom the power is conferred from departing from the policy or from taking into account circumstances which are relevant to the particular case [...] If such an inflexible and invariable policy is adopted, both the policy and the decision taken pursuant to it will be unlawful.'

Taking into account irrelevant considerations

1.20   A claim for judicial review can lie where a body or tribunal has either disregarded a relevant consideration, or taken into account an irrelevant consideration when reaching a decision. In the case of *R (on the application of Alconbury Developments Ltd) v Secretary of State for the Environment, Transport and the Regions*[48] Lord Slynn observed that:

'It has long been established that if the Secretary of State [...] takes into account matters irrelevant to his decision or refuses or fails to take account of matters relevant to his decision, or reaches a perverse decision, the court may set his decision aside.'

Error of law

1.21   A public body can also act illegally when it acts contrary to some higher legal authority,[49] or it makes a material error of law. In such circumstances, a ground of redress is available where a public body reaches a decision that is materially flawed by reason of misdirection in law. As aptly stated by Lord Diplock in the GCHQ case, '... the decision-maker must understand correctly the law that regulates his decision-making power and must give effect to it ....'[50]

1.22   In *R (Razgar) v Secretary of State for the Home Department*[51] an asylum seeker claimed that to remove him to Germany would breach his rights under Article 8 of the Convention to a private and family life. The Secretary of State 'certified' this claim.[52] The Secretary of State's reasoning was, bluntly, that the interests of immigration control always trumped the Article 8 rights of individuals. The House of Lords held in effect that this was a misdirection of law. Article 8 might be engaged and might be violated by deporting a person (even if he was not a refugee and had no formal right reside in the UK). The judgment of whether Article 8 was violated would depend on the facts. It could not be said in this particular case that the claim was 'manifestly unfounded'.

---

[48]   [2001] UKHL 23.
[49]   Such as: (i) EC law, or (ii) human rights.
[50]   [1985] AC 374, 410F.
[51]   [2004] 2 AC 368.
[52]   Which meant that as well as rejecting it, he declared it to be 'manifestly unfounded', with the consequence that the asylum seeker had no right to the normal statutory appeal through the immigration system – he had to go to Court by way of judicial review.

Reasons

1.23   A perennial question in 'reasons' challenges is the extent to which it is appropriate for the decision-maker to rely upon reasons not fully articulated at the time of the decision. There is no general common law principle that requires reasons to be provided.[53] However, there is a clear impetus towards such a general duty.[54] This question arose in stark terms in *R (London Fire and Emergency Planning Authority) v Secretary of State for Communities and Local Government* [2007] EWHC 1176 (Admin). The Secretary of State had decided to substitute her own decision for that of the disciplinary tribunal in the case of two fire-fighters dismissed for breaching their conditions of service (and, in particular, for their role in a fire-consultancy business they ran alongside their regular employment). The reasons in each case noted the fire fighter's record in the Fire Service and indicated that 'in the interests of justice' the Secretary of State considered that dismissal was too harsh a penalty. When the authority applied for judicial review on the ground that the Secretary of State's reasons were insufficient, the Secretary of State subsequently provided extended reasons. Stanley Burnton J quashed the decision on a number of grounds, inter alia, the deficiency in the reasoning. He considered that:

'[t]he invocation of "the interests of justice" is wholly uninformative, no more than a formula suggestive of the absence or concealment of specific reasons. It is evident from the reduction in the sanctions itself that the Secretary of State thought dismissal was too harsh, and ... to state that a sanction is too harsh is, or certainly should be, a statement of the obvious. Why the penalty was too harsh is unexplained ... The Authority was left entirely in the dark.'[55]

1.24   He considered that the expanded reasons should not be accepted, in so far as they justified the original decisions:

'[t]hey were produced a year after the decisions were taken, without the benefit of any contemporaneous record of the reasons given at the meeting of 12 January 2006 for rejecting the original recommendation, and well after the Authority had formulated its challenge to the original reasons. I do not question the honesty of the maker of the belated witness statement, but it seems to me that in these circumstances the Court cannot and should not be assured that the reasons put forward in the expanded reasons were in fact the reasons and, what is equally important, that they represent a comprehensive summary of the salient reasons for the Secretary of State's decision to reject the unanimous recommendations of his [sic] officials and to allow the appeals'.[56]

1.25   In *R v Westminster County Council, ex p Ermakov*,[57] Hutchinson LJ made some general observations about elucidation of letters of refusal. In particular, at page 316(e) he said:

'Whilst it is true that judicial review is a discretionary remedy, and that relief may be refused even where the ground of challenge is made good, it is clear that on reconsideration the decision would be the same, I agree with Rose J's comments in *ex p Carpenter* that in cases where the reasons stated in the decision letter have been shown to be manifestly flawed, it should only be in very exceptional cases that relief should be refused on the strength of

---

53   *R v Kensington & Chelsea Royal London Borough Council, ex p Grillo* (1996) 28 HLR 94 at 105 the Court said that at present there is no 'general obligation on administrative authorities to give reasons for their decisions'.
54   See para 62.1.2 of *Judicial Review Handbook*, Michael Fordham QC, 5th Edition, Hart Publishing.
55   Para 64.
56   Para 66.
57   [1996] 2 All ER 302.

reasons adduced in evidence after the commencement of proceedings. Accordingly, efforts to secure a discretionary refusal of relief by introducing evidence of true reasons significantly different from the stated reasons are unlikely to succeed'.

1.26   In *R v Hereford Council, ex p Hereford Waste Watchers Ltd*[58] the Court set out the central propositions for considering late reasons at paragraph 34 when it stated:

'In my judgment, the following propositions appear from the above authorities:

(i)   Where there is a statutory duty to give reasons as part of the notification of the decision, so that (as Laws J put it in *Northamptonshire County Council ex p D*) "the adequacy of the reasons is itself made a condition of the legality of the decision", only in exceptional circumstances if at all will the Court accept subsequent evidence of the reasons.

(ii)   In other cases, the Court will be cautious about accepting late reasons. The relevant considerations include the following, which to a significant degree overlap:

(a)   Whether the new reasons are consistent with the original reasons.

(b)   Whether it is clear that the new reasons are indeed the original reasons of the whole committee.

(c)   Whether there is a real risk that the later reasons have been composed subsequently in order to support the tribunal's decision, or are a retrospective justification of the original decision. This consideration is really an aspect of (b).

(d)   The delay before the later reasons were put forward.

(e)   The circumstances in which the later reasons were put forward. In particular, reasons put forward after the commencement of proceedings must be treated especially carefully. Conversely, reasons put forward during correspondence in which the parties are seeking to elucidate the decision should be approached more tolerantly.'

1.27   Most recently the position was succinctly summarised by Nicol J in *R v Law Society, ex p Keane*[59] at paragraph 28:

'A court must be cautious in relying on a decision-maker's supplemental reasons that are given for the first time in response to a judicial review challenge. The reasons are obvious: there is a risk of *ex post facto* rationalisation or justification even where the evidence is given in good faith – see for instance *R v Westminster City Council ex parte Ermakov* [1996] 2 All ER 302 CA and *R (Nash) v Chelsea College of Art and Design* [2001] EWHC 538 (Admin).'

PROCEDURAL IMPROPRIETY

1.28   As outlined above, this concept covers issues of fairness, both substantive and procedural. It includes both the duty to act according to common law rules of natural justice and procedural fairness, and failure to follow procedural requirements. Where a dispute requires resolution, the body responsible for deciding the matter is expected to act according to the rules of natural justice. As stated by Lord Denning:

'The rule against bias is one thing. The right to be heard is another. These two rules are the essential characteristics of what is often called natural justice. They are the twin pillars supporting it. The Romans put them in the two maxims: *nemo judex in causa sau*, and *audi*

---

[58]   [2005] EWHC 191 (Admin).
[59]   [2009] EWHC 783 (Admin).

alteram partem. They have recently been put in the two words, impartiality and fairness. But they are separate concepts and are governed by separate considerations.'

Bias

1.29 Actual bias is rare. In the majority of cases the Court will be seeking to examine whether there has been an appearance of bias. The case of *Magill v Porter* [2001] UKHL 67 provides a good example of the test to be used. Lord Hope observed that the, '... The question is whether the fair minded observer, having considered the facts, would conclude that there was a real possibility that the tribunal was biased ....' The rule is often seen as an aspect of procedural fairness.

1.30 It is helpful to start with a passage from *Flaherty v National Greyhound Racing Club Ltd* [2005] EWCA Civ 1117. The Court was concerned with a tribunal hearing, but the principles applied are generic. Having referred to the basic test stated by Lord Hope in *Porter* (cited above), Scott Baker LJ continued:

> 'The test for apparent bias involves a two stage process. First, the Court must ascertain all the circumstances which have a bearing on the suggestion that the tribunal was biased. Secondly, it must ask itself whether those circumstances would lead a fair minded and informed observer to conclude that there was a real possibility that the tribunal was biased .... An allegation of apparent bias must be decided on the facts and circumstances of the individual case .... The relevant circumstances are those apparent to the court upon investigation; they are not restricted to the circumstances available to the hypothetical observer at the original hearing ....'[60]

1.31 Further guidance is to be found in the judgment of Lord Hope in *Gillies v Secretary of State for Work and Pensions* [2006] UKHL 2. The claim of apparent bias in that case was directed towards the medical member of a disability appeal tribunal, Dr Armstrong. Lord Hope stated:[61]

> 'The critical issue is whether the fair-minded and informed observer would conclude, having considered the facts, that there was a real possibility that Dr Armstrong would not evaluate reports by other doctors who acted as [examining medical practitioners] objectively and impartially against the other evidence. The fair-minded and informed observer can be assumed to have access to all the facts that are capable of being known by members of the public generally, bearing in mind that it is the appearance that these facts give rise to that matters, not what is in the mind of the particular judge or tribunal member who is under scrutiny. It is to be assumed ... that the observer is neither complacent nor unduly sensitive or suspicious when he examines the facts that he can look at. It is to be assumed too that he is able to distinguish between what is relevant and what is irrelevant, and that he is able when exercising his judgment to decide what weight should be given to the facts that are relevant.'

1.32 In the recent case of *Persimmon Homes v Vale of Glamorgan Council* [2010] EWHC 535 (Admin) Beatson J adopted that test in determining whether a local planning authority officer was biased or predisposed against a development proposal when she had adopted the policy of the Welsh Assembly against the proposed settlement and against the interests of the company employing her husband. He concluded that she was not.

---

[60] Para 27.
[61] Para 17.

1.33   Allegations of bias can originate in various forms including:[62]

(a)   Direct interest[63] in the outcome, otherwise known as 'being judge in one's own cause'. An example includes *R v Bow Street Metropolitan Stipendiary Magistrate, ex p Pinochet Ugarte* (No 2) [2000] 1 AC 119 where the House of Lords had to set aside one of its own decisions, having realised that one of the Law Lords had been closely related to a party intervening in the appeal;

(b)   Actual bias. This is difficult to prove, and consequently rare. It involves a judge actually being predisposed to one party's case; and

(c)   Apparent bias. The question is whether the fair-minded and informed observer would conclude in all the circumstances that there is a real possibility that the decision-maker is in fact biased.[64] Problems can arise, for example, where barristers in independent practice also sit as part-time judges with other judges, and so might act as advocates in front of their own judicial colleagues.[65]

1.34   Examples include *R (Brooke & Ors) v Parole Board* [2007] EWHC 2036 (Admin), in which the independence of the Parole Board was challenged under both the provisions of the common law regarding apparent bias and Article 5(4) of the ECHR. Although two previous – and recent – Strasbourg challenges to the ECtHR had rejected the Board's independence,[66] the Court found that the full evidence had not been before the Strasbourg court in either decision. The Court held that the relationship of sponsorship between the Ministry of Justice ('MOJ') and the Parole Board was such, as to create what 'objectively appeared to be a lack of independence'. The Court stated:

> '[w]hat was a perfectly appropriate, if not essential relationship with the Secretary of State when the Board existed to advise him upon decision making which was his statutory responsibility is no longer appropriate once the Board has been entrusted by Parliament with the duty of making the decisions itself, as a court, and those decisions are binding upon him'.[67]

1.35   The Court of Appeal case of *National Assembly for Wales v Condron* [2006] EWCA Civ 1573 is also worthy of some consideration. The perception of bias arose from an alleged remark made in a meeting between the Chair of the Planning Decision Committee, and one of the objectors to a highly controversial opencast mining scheme. The application had received a favourable recommendation from an Inspector and the Assembly's Committee was to debate the report the following day. The Chair said that he was 'going to go with the Inspector's Report'. The Committee then resolved that it was minded to grant the application and the planning permission, the subject of the challenge, was formally issued in due course. It was found at first instance that the Chair was biased. Before the Court of Appeal, however, the view was taken that the attributed words went no further than indicating a predisposition to follow the inspector's report and not a closed mind. It did not matter how the person to whom those words were addressed had interpreted them. The question was whether the fears expressed by the

---

[62]   The Courts, however, have continually expressed the view that a party should not make allegations of bias unless there is satisfactory prima facie material upon which it is proper to do so.

[63]   Pecuniary or otherwise.

[64]   *Porter v Magill (No 2)* [2002] 2 AC 357.

[65]   *Lawal v Northern Spirit Ltd* [2003] ICR 856.

[66]   *Weeks v United Kingdom* (1988) 10 EHRR 293 and *Hirst v United Kingdom* (Application 40787/98) *The Times*, 3 August 2001.

[67]   Para 63.

complainant were objectively justified. Accordingly, the Court made it clear that the judge must look at all the circumstances as they appear from the material before it, not just at the facts known to the objectors or available to the hypothetical observer at the time of the decision. Richards LJ said that:

> 'The conclusion I have reached is that a fair-minded and informed observer, having considered all the facts as they are now known, would *not* conclude that there was a real possibility that Carwyn Jones himself or the PDC as a whole was biased when reaching the decision to grant planning permission. Viewed in its wider context, the brief remark by Carwyn Jones that is at the centre of the case provides an insufficient basis for the suggestion that the decision was approached with a closed mind and without impartial consideration of all relevant planning issues.'

1.36　In *Persimmon Homes Teeside Limited v R (Kevin Paul Lewis)*[68] the Court of Appeal overturned the decision of Jackson J to quash the politically sensitive decision of Redcar and Cleveland Borough Council taken during 2007 between the notice of election and the election itself. While Pill LJ delivered the main judgment in the Court of Appeal, all three judges (Pill LJ, Rix LJ and Longmore LJ) delivered substantive concurring judgments.

1.37　Relevant considerations from this case are thus:

(a)　in *Condron* Lord Justice Richards had conducted a lengthy analysis of all the relevant facts and circumstances. The court placed itself in the shoes of the classic 'fair-minded and informed observer and made its own assessment of the real possibility of predetermination'. Pill LJ in *Redcar* agreed that it was, 'the appropriate approach in these circumstances'.[69] It is for the court with its expertise to 'take on the responsibility of deciding whether there is a real risk that minds were closed';[70]

(b)　it was for the court to assess whether committee members did make the decision with closed minds or whether the circumstances indicate such a real risk of closed minds that the decision ought not, in the public interest, to be upheld.[71] However, both Pill LJ and Rix LJ took the view that the importance of appearances is 'generally more limited in this context than in a judicial context',[72] ie that there was 'no escaping the fact that a decision-maker in the planning context is not acting in a judicial or quasi-judicial role but in a situation of democratic accountability';[73]

(c)　in relation to planning decisions, the Court did not say that the decision in *Georgiou v Enfield London Borough Council* [2004] LGR 497 was wrong. Planning decision makers are not required to be impartial but to address the planning issues before them 'fairly and on their merits, even though they may approach them with a predisposition in favour of one side of the argument or the other';[74]

---

[68]　[2008] EWCA Civ 746.
[69]　Ibid at para 65.
[70]　Ibid.
[71]　Ibid at para 71.
[72]　Ibid at paras 71 and 98.
[73]　Ibid at para 94.
[74]　Ibid at para 95.

(d)   in considering whether or not there has been predetermination, evidence of political affiliation or of the adoption of policies towards a planning proposal will not be sufficient. Something more would be required which 'goes to the appearance of a predetermined, closed mind in the decision-making itself';[75]

(e)   Collins J was approved in *R (Island Farm Development Ltd) v Bridgend County Borough Council* [2006] EWHC Admin 2189 where he stated, 'The reality is that Councillors must be trusted to abide by the rules which the law lays down, namely that, whatever their views, they must approach their decision-making with an open mind in the sense that they must have regard to all material considerations and be prepared to change their views if persuaded that they should .... So it is with Councillors and, unless there is positive evidence to show that there was indeed a closed mind, I do not think that prior observations or apparent favouring of a particular decision will suffice to persuade a court to quash the decision';[76] and

(f)   Rix LJ cited with approval a passage in De Smith's Judicial Review (6th edition, 2007, at paras 10-065ff) and headed: Policy and Bias, which noted that decision-makers are entitled 'to exhibit certain kinds of bias in the exercise of their judgment or discretion on matters of public policy'[77] and while ordinary members of legislative bodies are 'entitled, and sometimes expected, to show political bias'[78] they of course ought not to show personal bias or participate in decisions on a matter in which they have a private pecuniary or proprietary interest. The following principles of public law remain applicable: the duty not to fetter discretion; keeping within the statutory purpose; adhering to procedural requirements; and procedural fairness.

1.38   The modern approach is that, for the generality of decision-makers governed by public law (and not just judicial decision makers), the dividing line between predisposition and predetermination is to be assessed by reference to whether a fair-minded and informed observer would conclude, having considered all the facts as appear when the Court determines the matter, that there was a real possibility of bias, *Condron*.[79] As aptly stated by Pill LJ, something more is required which 'goes to the appearance of a predetermined, closed mind in the decision-making itself'.[80]

Fairness

1.39   This concept covers all aspects of what Lord Diplock described as 'procedural impropriety'. It includes both the duty to act according to common law rules of natural justice and procedural fairness. Where a dispute requires resolution, the decision maker is expected to act according to the rules of natural justice, ie to act fairly between the parties, allowing all sides to be heard, and taking a decision impartially.

---

[75]   Ibid at para 96.
[76]   Ibid at paras 59 and 96.
[77]   Ibid at para 99.
[78]   Ibid.
[79]   See paras 40 and 57.
[80]   Ibid at para 96.

1.40   A public body might act 'unfairly' in either of two manners:

(a)   it has decided to do something which is inherently unfair ('substantive unfairness') which has developed in law principally through the doctrine of 'legitimate expectation' (see below); or

(b)   the actual decision making process has been unfair ('procedural unfairness').

1.41   A recent example of where the Secretary of State has consulted on an unfair basis such that 'the decisions taken by the Secretary of State and Minister simply made a mockery of the consultation process' and were so unfair as to be unlawful is the case of *Devon County Council, Norfolk County Council v Secretary of State for Communities and Local Government & Exeter City Council and Norwich City Council* [2010] EWHC 1456 (Admin). The Secretary of State had invited proposals for unitary councils in England which contained a set of criteria which a proposal had to meet in order to be eligible for consideration. He took his decision on a different basis from the one that he had said that he would adopt and which had been the basis of consultation and changed his approach without warning.

1.42   Another example of when the 'fairness' argument has been deployed is *R (Eisai Ltd) v National Institute for Health and Clinical Excellence* [2008] EWCA Civ 438 where the Court of Appeal held that NICE had acted unfairly in failing to allow the appellant pharmaceutical company access to a fully executable version of an economic model used to assess the cost-effectiveness of a medicine the appellant supplied, use of which had been recommended by NICE in only a limited group of patients. The court noted that, 'whether or not consultation is a legal requirement, if it is embarked upon it must be carried out properly',[81] and relied on established principles of procedural fairness in deciding the matter in favour of the appellant.

1.43   In *Abbey Mine Ltd v Coal Authority* [2008] EWCA Civ 353 the claimant appealed against the dismissal of a claim for judicial review relating to a decision of the defendant authority to offer a coal mining licence to a company (Corus) other than the claimant. The claimant's principal complaint was that Corus' application should, as a matter of fairness, have been disclosed to it. The Court emphasised that what fairness demands varies according to context and that it is for the court in the exercise of its responsibility to set procedural standards for public decision-making to determine the reach of the duty of fairness. It acknowledged that there are cases in which it is of the essence of fair procedure that material or information belonging to one party has to be disclosed to another (in particular, cases where a party faces an adverse allegation, or where a right or privilege is being withdrawn). Here, however, the signal feature of the context was that it concerned rival applications for a licence to undertake a commercial venture and there was a distinction to be drawn between a right to know the decision-maker's concern about one's own case and the right to know the details of the rival's case. Whilst it would obviously be unfair if one applicant saw his opponent's bid, and the opponent did not see his, here both were treated equally. But if every applicant saw every other's bid and was entitled to comment, challenge and criticise, 'the resulting prolongation and complexity of the decision-making process can scarcely be exaggerated'.[82] The Court emphasised that fairness always takes place in a practical setting and that in a competition case such as the present there were two broad requirements imposed by the

---

81   Para 24.
82   Para 33.

duty to act fairly: (1) that an applicant be told the substance of the decision-maker's concerns about his own case, and (2) that each applicant be treated like any other. There was no obligation, however, on the authority to disclose Corus' application to Abbey Mine.

Legitimate expectation

1.44

> 'The doctrine of "legitimate expectations" is much in vogue where allegedly unreasonable administrative decisions of the executive are under challenge and if ever there were a case in which a complaint based on legitimate expectations could be justifiably raised this seems to me to be that case.'[83]

> 'the protection of legitimate expectations is at the root of the constitutional principle of the rule of law, which requires regularity, predictability, and certainty in the government's dealings with the public'.[84]

1.45   The well established rule of legitimate expectation is thus: where a public authority represents[85] that it will conduct itself in a particular way, that representation may give rise to a legitimate expectation that the public authority will so act, and the public authority may have to give effect to that expectation. In *Coughlan* Lord Woolf MR described this doctrine as 'still a developing field of law'.[86]

1.46   In *R (Bhatt Murphy) v Independent Assessor*[87] Laws LJ stated:

> '28. Legitimate expectation of either kind may (not must) arise in circumstances where a public decision-maker changes, or proposes to change, an existing policy or practice. The doctrine will apply in circumstances where the change or proposed change of policy or practice is held to be unfair or an abuse of power: see for example *Ex p Coughlan* paragraphs 67 ff, *Ex p Begbie* [2000] 1 WLR 1115, 1129F – H. The court is generally the first, not the last, judge of what is unfair or abusive; its role is not confined to a back-stop review of the primary decision-maker's stance or perception: see in particular *Ex p Guinness Plc* [1990] 1 QB 146. Unfairness and abuse of power march together: see (in addition to *Coughlan* and *Begbie*) *Preston* [1985] AC 835, *Ex p Unilever* [1996] STC 681, 695 and *Rashid* [2005] INLR 550 paragraph 34. But these are ills expressed in very general terms; and it is notorious (and obvious) that the ascertainment of what is or is not fair depends on the circumstances of the case. The excoriation of these vices no doubt shows that the law's heart is in the right place, but it provides little guidance for the resolution of specific instances.'

1.47   Such legitimate expectations are commonly divided into procedural legitimate expectations, where the expectation is of a procedural benefit such as notice or consultation before any change of tack on the part of the public authority, and substantive legitimate expectations, where the expectation is that the public authority will act in accordance with its representation as a matter of substance.

---

[83]   *EB Kosovo (FC) v Secretary of State for the Home Department* [2008] 3 WLR 178, para 31 *per* Lord Scott.
[84]   *DeSmith's Judicial Review* (6th edn, 2007), para 12-001. See also Craig and Schønberg, *Substantive Legitimate Expectations after Coughlan* [2000] PL 684, 696–697.
[85]   Either by way of an express promise or implicitly by way of past practice.
[86]   Para 56.
[87]   [2008] EWCA Civ 755.

Procedural legitimate expectation

1.48 Procedural unfairness is often referred to as the breach of the requirements of natural justice. Those requirements typically include:

(a)   a fair opportunity for a person to learn what is alleged against him ('the right to be informed') before any decision is made;

(b)   a fair opportunity to present a case to the person making the relevant decision ('the right to be heard'), including having sufficient time to prepare if necessary;

(c)   due process;

(d)   adequate consultation;

(e)   a hearing and/or decision within a reasonable time; and

(f)   adequate reasoning (at least enough to see whether the decision itself is challengeable).

1.49 Where a decision is procedurally unfair, but an appeal right is available, the fairness of the appeal procedure may be such as to 'cure' the first instance decision of any public law defect. Put another way, the Court will tend to look at the overall decision (including what happened at the appeal stage) in order to determine whether there was any unfairness. The fact that Stage 1 of a decision-making process was unfair might be irrelevant, if Stages 1 and 2 taken together were fair.

1.50 The specific procedural standards will vary with the context. Not every type of decision, for example, carries with it the right to make oral representations, or to cross-examine one's opponent. A particular result of the above principles is that the executive is under a legal duty to set up fair systems in certain important areas of its practice. The asylum process is one such area: see *R (Q) v Secretary of State for the Home Department* [2004] QB 36 at para 69.

1.51   Laws LJ in *Bhatt Murphy* explained that:

> '29 ... The paradigm case arises where a public authority has provided an unequivocal assurance, whether by means of an express promise or an established practice, that it will give notice or embark upon consultation before it changes an existing substantive policy: see *CCSU* [1985] AC 374 at 408G – H (Lord Diplock's category (b)(ii)), *Ex p Baker* [1995] 1 All ER 73 at 89 (Simon Brown LJ's category 4, acknowledged by him to equate with Lord Diplock's category (b)(ii): see p 90), *Ex p Coughlan* at paragraph 57, p.242A – C: Lord Woolf's category (b)). I need not for present purposes set out these taxonomies.'

Consultation

1.52   Where a public body undertakes a consultation exercise, it must be conducted properly. In the case of *R v North and East Devon Health Authority, ex p Coughlan*[88] the Court of Appeal determined that:

---

[88]   (1999) LGR 703.

'To be proper, consultation must be undertaken at a time when proposals are still at a formative stage; it must include sufficient reasons for particular proposals to allow those consulted to give intelligent consideration and an intelligent response; adequate time must be given for this purpose; and the product of consultation must be consciously taken into account when the ultimate decision is taken.'

1.53   The proper starting point for any analysis of rules governing consultation is with the 'Sedley requirements' which remain the standard of proper consultation applied by the Courts.[89] The Sedley requirements are fourfold:

(1)   That consultation must be at a time when proposals are still at a formative stage. This means a public authority cannot wait until it has identified a settled solution, *R v North & East Devon HA, ex p Pow* (1998) 1 CCLR 280. It must engage the consultation process prepared to change direction if required, *R v Barnet LBC, ex p B* [1994] ELR 357.[90] It cannot make the decision in principle and then consult, *R (Sardar) v Watford BC* [2006] EWHC 1590 (Admin). Nor can it start by excluding an option and so denying any real opportunity to present a case on it *R (Medway Council) v SS Transport* [2002] EWHC 2516 (Admin).[91]

(2)   Those undertaking the consultation must give sufficient reasons for any proposal to permit of 'intelligent consideration' and 'response'. The reasons must not be incorrect or misleading, *R (Madden) v Bury MBC* [2002] EWHC 1882 (Admin). Those engaged with the process should be informed of the criteria to be considered, *R (Capenhurst) v Leicester CC* [2004] EWHC 2124 (Admin).[92] Documentary advice ought not to be withheld from those involved, *R (Edwards) v Environment Agency* [2006] EWCA Civ 877.[93] It is not necessary to set out the arguments against the proposal (*R (Beale) v Camden LBC* [2004] EWHC 6 (Admin) [2004] LGR 291).

(3)   Adequate and sufficient time must be given for the consideration and response even in cases of urgency, *R (Westminster CC) v Mayor of London* [2002] EWHC 2440.

(4)   Finally, the outcome of the consultation must be thoroughly taken into account when completing the proposal.

1.54   In addition, relevant considerations include:

(i)   a statutory scheme may impose a consultation duty such as section 11 of the Health and Social Care Act 2001, *R (Morris) v Trafford Healthcare NHS Trust* [2006] EWHC 2334 (Admin);

(ii)   there could be a procedural legitimate expectation of consultation arising from a promise, see *R (Montpeliers & Trevors Association) v City of Westminster* [2005] EWHC 16 (Admin) and *R v Birmingham CC, ex p Dredger* (1994) 6 Admin LR 553;

---

[89]   *R v Barnet LBC, ex p B* [1994] ELR 357, 372G, referring to *R v Brent LBC, ex p Gunning* (1985) 84 LGR 168.
[90]   See para 375C.
[91]   See para 32.
[92]   Para 46.
[93]   See also *R v SS Health, ex p US Tobacco* [1992] 1 QB 353.

(iii)   consultation may be necessary as a matter of simple fairness or due process, (*R (Carton) v Coventry City Council* [2001] ACD 445);

(iv)   the significance of the impact of any possible change may be such to give rise to a right to be consulted, *R (Sporting Options Plc) v Horserace Betting Levy Board* [2003] EWHC 1943 (Admin);[94] and

(v)   it can be unfair not to allow further representations on a newly emergent live issue, *R (Elmbridge BC) v SS Environment* [2002] Env LR 1.[95]

1.55   In *R (Greenpeace Limited) v Secretary of State for Trade & Industry* [2007] EWHC 311 Sullivan J held that a consultation process carried out by the Department of Trade and Industry on the use of new build nuclear power plants for electricity production was procedurally unfair and a breach of a legitimate expectation that there would be the fullest consultation on that particular matter.[96] The Court summarised that the starting point to be taken was that where a public authority had issued a promise or adopted a practice, which represented how it was proposed to act in a given area, the law would require the promise or practice to be honoured unless there was a good reason not to do so.[97] The consultation process was very seriously flawed, procedurally unfair and a breach of Greenpeace's legitimate expectation that there would be the fullest consultation. The purpose of the consultation document was unclear. There was effectively no discussion of the public considerations that would apply to nuclear new build. The period given for consultation was inadequate and it could not be said that following the consultation period the decision made by the Secretary of State would have been reasonably foreseeable by those consultees who took the consultation document at face value and relied upon it.

1.56   The Court of Appeal decision of *R (Fudge) v SW Strategic Health Authority* [2007] EWCA Civ 803 arose out of a challenge to an alleged failure to consult under section 11 of the Health and Social Care Act 2001.[98] At first instance the High Court refused to grant a declaration that either the strategic health authority or PCT had been obliged to involve the public in or consult about the process by which the Department of Health had proposed to introduce an Independent Sector Treatment Centre.[99] The Court of Appeal, applying the strict wording of section 11, found that the obligation to consult only arose where the relevant body was actually providing health services (rather than where it was to provide services in the future). The Court of Appeal found that the

---

94   Consultation may be unnecessary if relevant views can be taken as being engaged through an alternative mechanism such as an external review, see *R (Legal Remedy UK Ltd) v SS Health* [2007] EWHC 1252 (Admin). A public authority which chooses to consult must do so properly *R (British Waterways Board) v First SS* [2006] EWHC 1019 (Admin).

95   See also *R (Wandsworth LBC) v SS Transport* [2005] EWHC 20 (Admin).

96   In 2003, the Government published a White Paper on the future of energy production in the UK. That addressed the possible use of new nuclear power plants to produce electricity. It indicated that there was to be 'the fullest public consultation' before the Government reached any decision to change its policy. In 2006 the Secretary of State announced a review of the White Paper and issued a consultation paper for an energy review. A consultation period of 12 weeks was used and it was finally decided to support nuclear new build as part of the UK's future electricity generating mix. Greenpeace contended that, given the express promise that there would be the fullest public consultation before the Government reached any decision to change its policy not to support new nuclear build it and other members of the public had a legitimate expectation in view of the White paper which provided a contrary view.

97   *Nadarajah v Secretary of State for the Home Department* [2005] EWCA Civ 1363 was applied.

98   Section 11 imposed an obligation on bodies identified in the section to make arrangements to secure public involvement in and consultation on proposals relating to national health services.

99   [2007] EWHC 1195 (Admin).

PCT did not escape the obligation on the basis that it was not responsible for making any decision. However, the Court refused to grant a declaration because it would accomplish nothing, especially in circumstances where the claimant had – very late in the day – acknowledged that there was no question of such a declaration actually changing matters. The Court expressed the strong view that:

> '... in those cases where the obligation under s 11 may be limited, very little will be achieved by bringing proceedings for judicial review ... [that] ... these proceedings were wholly disproportionate to the limited utility of the result achieved.'

Substantive legitimate expectation

1.57   A substantive legitimate expectation arises where the Court allows a claim to enforce the continued enjoyment of an existing practice or policy, in the face of the decision-maker's ambition to change or abolish it. Thus it is to be distinguished from a merely procedural right. It has been expressed by Simon Brown LJ in *ex p Baker*[100] as:

> '1. Sometimes the phrase [sc. legitimate expectation] is used to denote a substantive right: an entitlement that the claimant asserts cannot be denied him ... [Various] authorities show that the claimant's right will only be found established when there is a clear and unambiguous representation upon which it was reasonable for him to rely. Then the administrator or other public body will be held bound in fairness by the representation made unless only its promise or undertaking as to how its power would be exercised is inconsistent with the statutory duties imposed upon it. The doctrine employed in this sense is akin to an estoppel.'

1.58   This formed part of the judgment of the court delivered by Lord Woolf in *Coughlan* at paragraph 57 (242C) when he stated:

> '(c) Where the court considers that a lawful promise or practice has induced a legitimate expectation of a *benefit which is substantive*, not simply procedural, authority now establishes that here too the court will in a proper case decide whether to frustrate the expectation is so unfair that to take a new and different course will amount to an abuse of power. Here, once the legitimacy of the expectation is established, the court will have the task of weighing the requirements of fairness against any overriding interest relied upon for the change of policy.'

1.59   Laws LJ further provided that:

> 'The doctrine of substantive legitimate expectation plainly cannot apply to every case where a public authority operates a policy over an appreciable period. That would expand the doctrine far beyond its proper limits .... The concept of substantive legitimate expectation therefore poses a question: what are the conditions under which a prior representation, promise or practice by a public decision-maker will give rise to an enforceable expectation of a substantive benefit?'[101]

1.60   In *Niazi*[102] the Court considered the circumstances in which the mere fact of a settled policy or practice could give rise to a legitimate expectation. In relation to procedural legitimate expectations, Laws LJ drew a distinction between what he referred to as 'the paradigm case' of procedural legitimate expectation, where a public authority has provided an unequivocal assurance of giving notice or consulting before it changes

---

[100]   [1995] 1 All ER 73.
[101]   *Niazi* paras 35 and 36.
[102]   [2008] EWCA Civ 755.

an existing substantive policy,[103] and what he called 'the secondary case' of procedural legitimate expectation, where the procedural legitimate expectation arises out of a benefit or advantage that the claimant has in the past enjoyed.[104]

1.61   Laws LJ went on to hold that substantive legitimate expectations and secondary cases of procedural legitimate expectation are concerned only with 'exceptional situations'.[105] In relation to substantive legitimate expectations, he held that such a legitimate expectation will only arise where there has been a specific undertaking, which is 'pressing and focussed' in nature and which is directed at a particular individual or group, by which the continuation of the relevant policy is assured.[106] In relation to secondary cases of legitimate expectation, he held that for such a legitimate expectation to arise, the impact of the public authority's past conduct on the claimant must be similarly 'pressing and focussed', such that the relevant individual or group could in reason have substantial grounds to expect that the substance of the policy will continue to inure for their particular benefit.[107]

1.62   Similarly in *Bhatt Murphy* Laws LJ said:

> '33. Here I have set out the reasoning in the cases because it is in this area of substantive legitimate expectation that the subject's first uncertainty arises. It concerns the references in *Ex p Baker* to "a clear and unambiguous representation" and in *Ex p Coughlan* to "a lawful promise or practice". These citations do not explain the content of the putative representation, promise or practice. It must, however, surely go to the enjoyment of the substance of the policy in question. Presumably there will either be an authoritative representation of what the relevant policy is and will continue to be, or else simply the fact of a policy's being settled and established in practice. A promise or practice: but not the kind of promise or practice found in the paradigm case of procedural legitimate expectation. In the procedural case we find a promise or practice of *notice* or *consultation* in the event of a contemplated change. In the substantive case we have a promise or practice of present and future *substantive policy*. This difference is at the core of the distinction between procedural and substantive legitimate expectation.'

1.63   In *Coughlan* the claimant (a very severely disabled lady) and seven comparably disabled patients had been given a clear promise by the health authority that a particular facility, Mardon House, would be their home for life. But the health authority decided to close Mardon House, which had ceased to be financially viable. The Court said at paragraph 86:

> '[The health authority's promise of a home for life] was an express promise or representation made on a number of occasions in precise terms. It was made to a small group of severely disabled individuals who had been housed and cared for over a substantial period in the Health Authority's predecessor's premises at Newcourt. It specifically related to identified premises, which it was represented, would be their home for as long as they chose. It was in unqualified terms. It was repeated and confirmed to reassure the residents. It was made by the Health Authority's predecessor for its own purposes, namely to encourage Miss Coughlan and her fellow residents to move out of Newcourt and into Mardon House, a specially built substitute home in which they would continue to receive nursing care. Miss Coughlan relied on the promise. Strong reasons are required to justify resiling from a

---

[103]   Ibid, para 29.
[104]   Ibid, paras 37–39. This is the second category of legitimate expectation referred to by Simon Brown LJ in *R v Devon County Council, ex p Baker* [1995] 1 All ER 73, 88–89.
[105]   *Niazi*, para 41.
[106]   Ibid, paras 43, 46.
[107]   Ibid, para 49.

promise given in those circumstances. This is not a case where the Health Authority would, in keeping the promise, be acting inconsistently with its statutory or other public law duties. A decision not to honour it would be equivalent to a breach of contract in private law.'

1.64   Laws LJ has summarised the present position as follows:

'A very broad summary of the place of legitimate expectations in public law might be expressed as follows. The power of public authorities to change policy is constrained by the legal duty to be fair (and other constraints which the law imposes). A change of policy, which would otherwise be legally unexceptionable, may be held unfair by reason of prior action, or inaction, by the authority. If it has distinctly promised to consult those affected or potentially affected, then ordinarily it must consult (the paradigm case of procedural expectation). If it has distinctly promised to preserve existing policy for a specific person or group who would be substantially affected by the change, then ordinarily it must keep its promise (substantive expectation). If, without any promise, it has established a policy distinctly and substantially affecting a specific person or group who in the circumstances was in reason entitled to rely on its continuance and did so, then ordinarily it must consult before effecting any change (the secondary case of procedural expectation). To do otherwise, in any of these instances, would be to act so unfairly as to perpetrate an abuse of power.'[108]

1.65   Other recent cases based on claims of breach of substantive legitimate expectations include:

- *R (HSMP Forum Ltd) v SSHD* [2008] EWHC 664 (Admin) which involved a successful challenge to SSHD's attempt to introduce retrospective revisions to the Highly Skilled Migrant Programme).

- *Slough Borough Council and Corby Borough Council v Secretary of State for Communities and Local Government* [2008] EWHC 1977 (Admin) an unsuccessful challenge to the Local Authority Business Growth Incentives Scheme.

- *R (Bath) v North Somerset Council* [2008] EWHC 630 (Admin), a Council had not made a clear and unequivocal representation concerning the use of funds generated by the transfer of housing stock.

- *Staff Side of Police Negotiating Board v Secretary of State for the Home Department* [2008] EWHC 1173 (Admin) concerned a challenge by the claimant to the defendant's decision not to implement in full at the recommended date a pay award for the year 2007–8 for police officers. The main focus of the claim was that the police officers had a legitimate expectation in respect of pay increases recommended by the PNB which had been flouted by the defendant's decision. The court rejected the challenge, concluding that well before the time of the decision in issue the legitimate expectation that had been established was that the PNB recommendations/PAT awards on pay 'would be carefully considered, would not be lightly set aside and would only be departed from for good reasons'. There was no legitimate expectation, however, that reasons of grave or serious national importance would be required for such a departure, as the claimants contended.

- *R (Wheeler) v Office of the Prime Minister* [2008] EWHC 1409 (Admin), challenge to decision not to hold a referendum on the Treaty of Lisbon dismissed, the court observing that even if ministerial statements had had the effect of a

---

[108]   Ibid, para 50.

promise to hold a referendum – which the court did not accept – they would not give rise to a legitimate expectation enforceable in public law.

- *R (Grimsby Institute of Further and Higher Education) v Chief Executive of Skills Funding (Formerly Learning and Skills Council)* [2010] EWHC 2134 Admin where a challenge to the decision on the part of the Learning and Skills Council's refusal to 'grant approval in detail' for a building scheme for a new college based upon two legitimate expectations that: (i) once approval in principle had been given that the application would be dealt with according to L's usual and known procedures; (ii) that L would be funded and organised in a manner that enabled it to meet its commitments given at the approval in principle stage. Approval in detail was not given as L had run out of funds. The Court found that legitimate expectations based upon a representation had to be clear and unambiguous and there was nothing in L's handbook that made the availability of funds irrelevant and that there had been no departure from L's practice or procedure.

HUMAN RIGHTS

Background

1.66   The Human Rights Act 1998 ('HRA') was enacted a decade ago. It is now a well-established part of the English legal backdrop.

1.67   The key provisions include:

(a)   Section 2 requires a Court or Tribunal determining a question under the HRA in connection with a Convention right to take account of any jurisprudence or decision of the Strasbourg institutions.

(b)   Section 3 sets out the interpretative obligation requiring the Courts to read, and give effect to, legislation in a way which is compatible with those Convention rights, so far as it is possible to do so.

(c)   Section 4 outlines the ability to seek and obtain a declaration of incompatibility if legislation cannot be interpreted compatibly with Convention.

(d)   Section 6 makes it unlawful for a public authority to act in a way which is incompatible with a Convention right unless it could not have acted differently as a result of a statutory provision.

1.68   The 'rights and fundamental freedoms' which are protected by the European Convention of Human Rights ('ECHR') as enshrined by the HRA include:

- Article 2: the right to life.

- Article 3: prohibition of torture.

- Article 5: the right to liberty and security.

- Article 6: the right to a fair trial.

- Article 8: the right to respect for private and family life, the home and correspondence.

- Article 9: the right to thought, conscience and religion.

- Article 10: freedom of expression.

- Article 11: freedom of assembly and association.

- Article 12: the right to marry.

- Article 14: the prohibition of discrimination in respect of Article rights.

- Article 1, 1st Protocol: the protection of property.

The interpretative obligation

1.69   The Administrative Court considering a claim that a public authority has acted unlawfully by breaching a Convention right is required to take into account the Strasbourg jurisprudence. At present where there is established Strasbourg jurisprudence on an Article right, the Court will effectively be required to adopt that interpretation. The House of Lords (as it was previously known) in a succession of cases have explained the nature of the obligations pursuant to section 2 of the HRA:

(a)   *R (Ullah) v Special Adjudicator* [2004] UKHL 26, Lord Bingham of Cornhill stated at [20] that:

> 'It is of course open to member states to provide for rights more generous than those guaranteed by the Convention, but such provision should not be the product of interpretation of the Convention by national courts, since the meaning of the Convention should be uniform throughout the states party to it. The duty of national courts is to keep pace with the Strasbourg jurisprudence as it evolves over time: no more, but certainly no less.'

(b)   *R v Chief Constable of South Yorkshire Police, ex p LS and Marper* [2004] UKHL 39. Lord Steyn stated at [27]:

> 'While I would not wish to subscribe to all the generalisations in the Court of Appeal about cultural traditions in the United Kingdom, in comparison with other European states, I do accept that when one moves on to consider the question of objective justification under article 8(2) the cultural traditions in the United Kingdom are material. With great respect to Lord Woolf CJ the same is not true under article 8(1). [Lord Steyn then set out Lord Bingham's speech above in *Ullah*] ... The question whether the retention of fingerprints and samples engages article 8(1) should receive a uniform interpretation throughout member states, unaffected by different cultural traditions. And the current Strasbourg view, as reflected in decisions of the Commission, ought to be taken into account.'

(c)   *R (Animal Defenders International) v Secretary of State for Culture, Media and Sport* [2008] UKHL 15. Lord Scott expressed his opinion that it would be possible for the domestic courts to have a divergence of view from the ECtHR on the meaning of Article rights. He stated at [44]:

'The result of the present appeal to this House shows, therefore, no more than the possibility of a divergence between the opinion of the European Court as to the application of art 10 in relation to the statutory prohibition of which ADI complains and the opinion of this House. The possibility of such a divergence is contemplated, implicitly at least, by the 1998 Act. The 1998 Act incorporated into domestic law the articles of the Convention and of the Protocols set out in Sch 1 to the Act. So the articles became part of domestic law. But the incorporated articles are not merely part of domestic law. They remain, as they were before the 1998 Act, articles of a Convention binding on the United Kingdom under international law. In so far as the articles are part of domestic law, this House is, and, when this House is eventually replaced by a Supreme Court, that court will be, the court of final appeal whose interpretation of the incorporated articles will, subject only to legislative intervention, be binding in domestic law. In so far as the articles are part of international law they are binding on the United Kingdom as a signatory of the Convention and the European Court is, for the purposes of international law, the final arbiter of their meaning and effect. Section 2 of the 1998 Act requires any domestic court determining a question which has arisen in connection with a Convention right to take into account, inter alia, "any judgment, decision, declaration or advisory opinion of the European Court of Human Rights" (ss (1)(a)). The judgments of the European Court are, therefore, not binding on domestic courts. They constitute material, very important material, that must be taken into account, but domestic courts are nonetheless not bound by the European Court's interpretation of an incorporated article.'

(d) *R (Pretty) v Director of Public Prosecutions (Secretary of State for the Home Department Intervening)* [2002] 1 AC 800, where the House of Lords held Article 8 was directed to the protection of personal autonomy while the person was alive but did not confer a right to decide when or how to die. The European Court of Human Rights in *Pretty v United Kingdom* (2002) 35 EHRR 1 disagreed. At paragraphs 65 and 67 the Court said that:

'The very essence of the Convention is respect for human dignity and human freedom. Without in any way negating the principle of sanctity of life protected under the Convention, the Court considers that it is under article 8 that notions of the quality of life take on significance. In an era of growing medical sophistication combined with longer life expectancies, many people are concerned that they should not be forced to linger on in old age or in states of advanced physical or mental decrepitude which conflict with strongly held ideas of self and personal identity .... The applicant in this case is prevented by law from exercising her choice to avoid what she considers will be an undignified and distressing end to her life. The Court is not prepared to exclude that this constitutes an interference with her right to respect for private life as guaranteed under article 8(1) of the Convention. It considers below whether this interference conforms with the requirements of the second paragraph of article 8.'

(e) *R (on the application of Purdy) (Appellant) v Director of Public Prosecutions (Respondent)* [2009] EWCA Civ 92 the Court of Appeal held that it was bound to follow the decision of the House of Lords and was not at liberty to apply the ruling of the Strasbourg court; and

(f) In the House of Lords in *R (on the application of Purdy) (Appellant) v Director of Public Prosecutions (Respondent)* [2009] UKHL 45, Lord Hope said at paragraph 34 that:

'The House is, of course, free to depart from its earlier decision and to follow that of the Strasbourg court. As Lord Bingham said in *R (Ullah) v Special Adjudicator* [2004] UKHL 26, [2004] 2 AC 323, para 20, it is ordinarily the clear duty of our domestic courts to give practical recognition to the principles laid down by the Strasbourg court as governing the Convention rights as the effectiveness of the Convention as an international instrument depends on the loyal acceptance by member states of the principles that, as the highest authority on the interpretation of those rights, it lays down .... But it is obvious that the interests of human rights law would not be well served if the House were to regard itself as bound by a previous decision as to the meaning or effect of a Convention right which was shown to be inconsistent with a subsequent decision in Strasbourg. Otherwise the House would be at risk of endorsing decisions which are incompatible with Convention rights.'

Public authority

1.70 The duty under section 6 which makes it unlawful to act incompatibly with Convention rights only applies to a 'public authority'. Section 6(3) of the HRA 1998 provides that a 'public authority' includes not only a court or tribunal under section 6(3)(a), but also, '(b) any person certain of whose functions are functions of a public nature'. What is a public authority has been the subject of litigation and the interface of public authorities and private providers remains a live topic.

1.71 In *YL v Birmingham City Council* [2007] UKHL 27 the majority of the House of Lords[109] concluded that an independent provider of health and social care services housing an 84 year old woman with Alzheimer's disease in a nursing home was not a public authority for the purposes of the HRA. The Court was particularly influenced by the fact that Southern Cross, the nursing home provider was a private, profit-earning company, acting for private and commercial gain, and merely contracting with a local authority to provide a service.[110] The Court reinforced that it was necessary to examine the context in which a contractor was acting, and the basis upon which the contractor was acting, and the key focus had to be on the nature of the functions it was undertaking.[111]

1.72 This case has plain consequences. Individuals placed in privately run-care homes by a local authority pursuant to the National Assistance Act cannot directly invoke the provisions of the Convention against the care home provider itself. Such providers are not public authorities for the purposes of the HRA.[112]

1.73 The case of *London & Quadrant Housing Trust v R on the application of Weaver and the Equality and Human Rights Commission* [2009] EWCA Civ 587 applied YL and found that the termination of a tenancy and the seeking of possession on the ground of non payment of rent in respect of social housing could not properly be categorised as an exercise of a public nature. Rather it was a private act arising out of a contract. Whether the landlord as a registered social landlord was a public authority so that when terminating the tenancy of someone in social housing that act was subject to human rights principles and properly a public law challenge was rejected in the circumstances of the case. Again, the importance of context was emphasised.

---

[109] Lord Bingham and Baroness Hale dissenting.

[110] The majority view in this case was consistent with the earlier decision in *Cameron v Network Rail (Infrastructure Ltd)* [2007] 1 WLR 163.

[111] In contrast, both Lord Bingham and Baroness Hale concluded that the type of situation Southern Cross was in was precisely that designed to be covered by section 6(3)(b), where a private body was performing an important public function of the provision of care, albeit pursuant to contractual arrangements.

[112] Individuals do, however, have an arguable course of action against a local authority if they fail to enforce the terms of the contract between themselves and private care home. Those terms ought to include that they ought to abide by the HRA.

Convention rights

1.74 What follows is a brief outline of the Convention rights which are frequently used in judicial review claims:

(a) Article 2: in *R (L) (A Patient) v Secretary of State for the Home Department* [2007] EWCA Civ 767 the Court of Appeal confirmed that the rights under Article 2 extended not only to accountability of the state for the death of a person or serious injury while in state custody, but also to an investigation of the facts and explanation of how the death or serious injury occurred.[113] An internal prison investigation of the attempted suicide of a young person held on remand in Feltham was insufficient to comply with Article 2. Recently in *R (Smith) v Oxfordshire Assistant Deputy Coroner* [2009] EWCA Civ 441 the Court of Appeal held that the State was bound to conduct an investigation into the death of a conscript to satisfy Article 2.

(b) Article 3 is well known. Recently in *R (AM) v SOSHD* [2009] EWCA Civ 219 the Court of Appeal indicated that the possibility of inmates at the privately run immigration detention centre having suffered inhuman and degrading treatment triggered the State's duties of investigation under Article 3 and that such duties were not affected by the possibility of a criminal investigation or the bringing of civil proceedings.

(c) Article 5 is no better exemplified than in the recent control order litigation. In *Secretary of State for the Home Department v JJ* [2007] UKHL 45 control orders were imposed on individuals resulting in an effective curfew upon them for 18 hours a day and exclusion of visitors. The House of Lords dismissed the SSHD's appeal against the quashing of those orders and concluded that the overall effect of the orders did amount to a deprivation of liberty for the purposes of Article 5.[114] See also *Secretary of State for the Home Department v E* [2007] UKHL 47 where a 12 hour curfew was held to be insufficiently stringent to infringe Article 5. More recently, in *R (James) v SOSOJ* [2009] UKHL 22 the House of Lords held that Article 5(4) was only engaged in public protection sentences so as to ensure that a Court (the Parole Board) should speedily decide whether a prisoner continued to be lawfully detained: that would continue to be the case unless and until it was satisfied of his safety for release or that so long had elapsed without any effective review of his dangerousness that there was a breach of Article 5(1).

(d) Article 6: in *R (Wright) v Secretary of State for Health* [2007] EWCA Civ 999, the Court of Appeal held that the denial of a right to make representations before a care worker[115] was in breach of a care worker's rights under Article 6. Moreover, that breach was not cured by the fact that the care worker had an opportunity to seek to persuade the Secretary of State to remove him/her from the list, to seek judicial review of the decision to include the worker on the list, or to appeal under

---

[113] The mere fact of such a death or serious injury obliged the state to commence an independent investigation, and in cases of serious injury, the necessity for a further public hearing would depend on whether it appeared to the independent investigator that the state or its agents potentially bore responsibility for the injury.

[114] Lord Brown made clear his view that a curfew of 16 hours a day was the maximum permitted before Article 5 was infringed.

[115] Which is provisionally included on a list of persons considered unsuitable to work with children, held by the Secretary of State under section 82 of the Care Standards Act.

section 86 of the CSA. May LJ stated at paragraph 37 that, '... Article 6 is infringed because the worker does not get any hearing, let alone a fair and public one within a reasonable time. Possibilities of judicial review are not sufficient to achieve compliance with Article 6 ....'

(e) Article 8: the right to respect for private and family life, home and correspondence has a broad application.[116] Lord Bingham has provided that:

> 'The content of this right has been described as "elusive" and does not lend itself to exhaustive definition. This may help to explain why the right is expressed as one to respect, as contrasted with the more categorical language used in other articles. But the purpose of the article is in my view clear. It is to protect the individual against intrusion by agents of the state, unless for good reason, into the private sphere within which individuals expect to be left alone to conduct their personal affairs and live their personal lives as they choose.'[117]

English courts have been more reluctant than the European Court of Human Rights to interpret Strasbourg jurisprudence as extending the scope of Article 8. See *R v Attorney General & Anor, ex p Countryside Alliance* [2007] UKHL 52 where the House of Lords refused to find a breach of Article 8.[118] See also the House of Lords 2009 decision in *Purdy*. Note the recent case of *R (G) v Nottinghamshire Healthcare NHS Trust* [2009] EWCA Civ 795 (CA) where the Court of Appeal concluded that a smoking ban at a special hospital did not have a sufficiently adverse effect on a patient's physical or mental integrity as to engage Article 8. Even if Article 8 has been engaged, the Court indicated that the ban was justified under Article 8(2).

(f) Article 10: in *R (Animal Defenders International) v Secretary of State for Culture, Media and Sport* [2008] UKHL 15. Lord Bingham stated at [33]:

> 'The weight to be accorded to the judgment of Parliament depends on the circumstances and the subject matter. In the present context it should in my opinion be given great weight, for three main reasons. First, it is reasonable to expect that our democratically-elected politicians will be peculiarly sensitive to the measures necessary to safeguard the integrity of our democracy. It cannot be supposed that others,

---

[116] In *Société Colas Est v France* (2002) 39 EHRR 17 the Court accepted that raids carried out by official inspectors on company premises were capable of engaging the company's rights to a 'home' within the meaning of Article 8(1). This was reinforced in *Buck v Germany* [2005] ECHR 41604/98 at [31] and *Kent Pharmaceuticals Ltd v UK* no 9355/03, 11 October 2005. See also *Wieser and Bicos Beteiligungen GMBH v Austria* App no 74336/01 (16 October 2007) [2007] ECHR 815, when the Court found violations of Article 8 in respect of the search and seizure of data belonging both to a lawyer and a company.

[117] *R (Countryside Alliance)* (above) per Lord Bingham at [10].

[118] The claimant argued: (i) infringement of private life and autonomy in reliance on *Pretty v UK* (2002) 35 EHRR and the ECtHR's finding that private life is a broad term not susceptible to exhaustive definition, but covering the physical and psychological integrity of a person, sometimes embracing aspects of an individual's physical and social identity, protecting a right to personal development and the right to establish relations with others in the outside world and extending to matters within the personal and private sphere, where personal autonomy is an important principle; (ii) cultural lifestyle relying on *G and E v Norway* (1983) 35 DR 30, *Buckley v UK* (1996) 23 EHRR 101 and *Chapman v UK* (2001) 33 EHRR 399; (iii) use of home relying on Strasbourg case law extending the concept of 'home' to business premises and a professional person's office; and (iv) loss of livelihood/home relying on *Sidabras v Lithuania* (2004) 42 EHRR 104 concerning two former KGB officers who were dismissed from their jobs and debarred from a wide range of public and private sector employments because of their former employment. The ECtHR found that a far-reaching ban on taking up private sector employment did affect private life (although it did not determine whether Article 8 had been infringed in that case, instead finding a breach of Article 14). None of these arguments succeeded before the House of Lords.

including judges, will be more so. Secondly, Parliament has resolved, uniquely since the 1998 Act came into force in October 2000, that the prohibition of political advertising on television and radio may possibly, although improbably, infringe art. 10 but has nonetheless resolved to proceed under s 19(1)(b) of the Act. It has done so, while properly recognising the interpretative supremacy of the European Court, because of the importance which it attaches to maintenance of this prohibition. The judgment of Parliament on such an issue should not be lightly overridden. Thirdly, legislation cannot be framed so as to address particular cases. It must lay down general rules .... A general rule means that a line must be drawn, and it is for Parliament to decide where. The drawing of a line inevitably means that hard cases will arise falling on the wrong side of it, but that should not be held to invalidate the rule if, judged in the round, it is beneficial.'

(g) Article 12: in *R (Baiai) v Secretary of State for the Home Department (Nos 1 and 2)* [2007] EWCA Civ 478, the Court of Appeal considered a regime requiring a person subject to immigration control who wished to enter into a civil marriage in the UK to seek a certificate of approval from the Secretary of State. The Court found the particular regime created to be incompatible with the right to marry under Article 12.

(h) Article 14 provides that:

> 'The enjoyment of the rights and freedoms set forth in this Convention shall be secured without discrimination on any ground such as sex, race, colour, language, political or other opinion, national or social origin, association with a national minority, property, birth or other status.'

This is not a free-standing provision. It prohibits discrimination only in the enjoyment of the rights and freedoms in the Convention. Equally, it is does not require any other Article to be violated. In relation to the term 'other status' note *Kjeldsen, Busk Madsen and Pedersen v Denmark* (1976) 1 EHRR 711, para 56, the ECtHR referred to 'discriminatory treatment having as its basis or reason a personal characteristic ("status") by which persons or groups of persons are distinguishable from each other'. In *R(S) v Chief Constable of the South Yorkshire Police* [2004] UKHL 39 the House of Lords adopted the requirement to identify a 'personal characteristic', and not to treat the list as open-ended.[119] The 'personal characteristic' requirement has also been applied by the Court of Appeal in *R(RJM) v Secretary of State for Work and Pensions* [2007] EWCA Civ 614. The Court also concluded that 'other status' in Article 14 depended upon a personal characteristic, but rejected the notion that the nature of the personal characteristic must necessarily be involuntary.

(i) Article 1, 1st Protocol: in *R (Malik) v Waltham Forest NHS Primary Care Trust* [2007] 1 WLR 2092, the Court of Appeal found that inclusion of a doctor's name on a list of those qualified to work locally for the NHS was effectively a licence to render services to the public. As it was not transferable or marketable, it was found not to be a possession for the purposes of Art 1, 1st Protocol. The mere prospect of future loss could not amount to a possession for that purpose where such clientele/goodwill did not exist. An individual's monetary loss of future livelihood could not, on its own, constitute a possession.

---

[119] The case is being appealed to the European Court of Human Rights. In any event, this was applied again in *R (Clift) v Secretary of State for the Home Department* [2007] 1 AC 484 [27]–[28].

Chapter 2

REMEDIES

INTRODUCTION

2.1   This chapter considers public law remedies, both interim and final, that may be available on a claim for judicial review. The Administrative Court has a wide range of powers available which originate from statutory and common law sources. All remedies in judicial review though are discretionary.

2.2   In summary the remedies are:

- Interim orders, including injunctions, declarations and stays of proceedings: Senior Courts Act 1981, s 37 and the Civil Procedure Rules (CPR) parts 25 and 54.

- The prerogative orders of quashing, prohibition, and mandatory, injunctions and declarations which may be granted in combination or together: Senior Courts Act 1981, ss 29 and 31 and CPR part 54.

- Under common law there may be a right to restitution or damages if the claimant can show a recognised tort or breach of contract.

- Under the Human Rights Act 1998 declarations of incompatibility (s 4) and damages for an action breaching Convention Rights (s 8).

- Under EC Law there is full protection of Community Law rights, which may require additional and modified remedies to be available.

INTERIM RELIEF

2.3   At any time in judicial review proceedings the court may grant interim relief as provided for in part 25 CPR. This includes interim injunctions,[1] interim declarations[2] and the jurisdiction to grant a stay.[3]

Procedure

2.4   Typically, interim remedies are sought when the claim is lodged. CPR 54.6 states that the claimant must specify any remedy (including interim) that is being claimed. Interim relief, however, may be sought at any stage of the proceedings.[4] It can also be granted before a claim has been made if the matter is urgent or it is necessary to do so in

---

[1]   CPR r 25.1(1)(a) – including against the Crown: *Re M* [1994] 1 AC 377.
[2]   CPR r 25.1(1)(b).
[3]   CPR r 54.10(2).
[4]   CPR 25.2(1).

the interests of justice.[5] A Practice Direction[6] sets out the procedure to be followed. Although it only refers to interim injunctions the procedure which it sets out is appropriate for other forms of interim relief.

2.5 The most common form of interim relief is an interim injunction and stay of proceedings but the full orders listed in CPR 25.1(1) are available.

2.6 In cases of real urgency an application can be made to the out of hours judge. Where an interim application is refused on the papers it can be renewed at an oral hearing.

2.7 In practice it is not uncommon for the Administrative Court to deal with a claim for interim relief in an urgent case by ordering an expedited substantive hearing or a rolled up hearing. That enables it to be able to provide a remedy and to resolve the prospect of lengthy and contested satellite litigation.

Actions against the Crown

2.8 The interim power includes the ability on the part of the court to grant injunctions against ministers of the Crown on claims for judicial review. Initially it was thought that Part II of the Crown Proceedings Act 1947 restricted the court's powers. However, the House of Lords have held that the court has power to make coercive orders, prohibitory and mandatory against ministers of the Crown: see *M v Home Office* [1994] 1 AC 377. That includes the power to grant interim injunctions against ministers where it is necessary to protect rights under EC law. The only occasion now where such a power could not be used is where the power was entirely internal to the state, as then Community law has no application.[7] Such occasions are likely to be increasingly few.

2.9 Further, in *M v Home Office* [1994] 1 AC 377 and *Davidson v Scottish Ministers* [2005] UKHL 74 the House of Lords has held that Part II of the 1947 Act applies only to 'civil proceedings' as defined in s 38(2) of the Act and which do not include claims for judicial review. Despite that the most appropriate remedy against the Crown in both interim and final form is that of a declaration. Although the power to grant injunctions against the Crown exists in practice, it is used sparingly.

Principles on interim relief

2.10 The principles that a court will follow on interim remedies have been heavily influenced by private law.[8] In essence it is an approach of a modified 'balance of convenience'. It is modified to take into account the wider public interest that arises in public law cases. In short, what is required is firstly, an arguable case for the grant of judicial review and, secondly, the avoidance of the greater risk of injustice. The court will consider the overall case, taking into account the strength of the claim, the status quo, the wider public interest and, if relevant, which will be rare in public law cases, the prospect of any monetary order providing an adequate ultimate remedy. Where a public

---

5   CPR 25.2(2).
6   Practice Statement (Administrative Court: Listings and Urgent Cases) [2002] 1 WLR 810.
7   *R v Ministry of Agriculture, Fisheries and Food, ex p First City Trading Ltd* [1997] 1 CMLR 250 where Community principles could not be used to review the UK's Beef Transfer Scheme which granted emergency aid to abattoirs after the BSE crisis.
8   *American Cyanamid Co v Ethicon Ltd* [1975] AC 396 HL – a balance of convenience is the right approach.

authority is involved 'the balance of convenience has to be looked at more widely and take into account the interests of the public in general to whom these duties are owed.'[9]

Cross undertaking in damages

2.11   The claimant's cross undertaking in damages is clearly more difficult in a public law case. In the case of *Huddleston v Durham County Council* [1999] EWHC Admin 757 a cross undertaking was not required because of the wider public interest. 'The consequences of work starting without such an environmental assessment may, in my judgment, be such as to make irreversible any harm that might be caused. In those circumstances, it seems to me that there is probably a much wider issue than the narrow one between the applicant and the second respondent in relation to the immediate effect upon the applicant and his family. That wider issue is one that the Court can properly have regard to and have regard to notwithstanding the fact that the applicant is not in a position to offer any undertaking as to any financial loss. It may well be, and in my judgment it is likely, that the second respondent could fairly readily satisfy the court that steps will be taken that will prevent any great harm of the kind that is spoken of by English Nature and by the Environment Agency.' Interim relief was granted. It has been said that the requirement for a cross undertaking is essentially a matter for the judge in the exercise of his discretion: *R v Inspectorate of Pollution, ex p Greenpeace* [1993] EWCA Civ 9.

Injunctions

2.12   The leading authority on interim relief in public law cases remains *R v Transport Secretary, ex p Factortame (No 2)* [1991] 1 AC 603. The House of Lords adopted a two stage approach. First, there should be a consideration as to the adequacy of damages as a remedy. There, when the Crown was seeking to enforce the law it may not be appropriate to impose upon the Crown the usual undertaking in respect of damages. The same would apply to a local authority. Second, if there is doubt as to the adequacy of either or both of the respective remedies in damages, then the court proceeds to what is usually called the balance of convenience, and for that purpose will consider 'all the circumstances of the case'. 'In this context, particular stress should be placed upon the importance of upholding the law of the land, in the public interest, bearing in mind the need for stability in our society, and the duty placed upon certain authorities to enforce the law in the public interest. This is, of itself, an important factor to be weighed in the balance when assessing the balance of convenience. So, if a public authority seeks to enforce what is on its face the law of the land, and the person against whom such action is taken challenges the validity of that law, matters of considerable weight have to be put into the balance to outweigh the desirability of enforcing, in the public interest, what is on its face the law, and so to justify the refusal of an interim injunction in favour of the authority, or to render it just or convenient to restrain the authority for the time being from enforcing the law.'

2.13   In *R v Environment Agency, ex p Mayer Parry* [2000] EWHC Admin 388 the court applied the principles set out in *R v Transport Secretary, ex p Factortame (No 2)* even when the issue was 'what is the law of the land?'[10] The court was asked to grant a

---

[9]   *Smith v Inner London Education Authority* [1978] 1 All ER 411 – a dispute between parents and the LEA over whether to go to comprehensive schooling where the claimant parents had no real prospect of success at full trial.

[10]   The court had earlier referred to the ECJ questions on the meaning of recycling under EC Directives on waste and the packaging of waste.

mandatory injunction and other interim remedies by way of interim relief. Taking into account the interests of the public to whom a duty was owed the court refused an application for interim relief where the public interest in the receipt of revenue from Packaging Waste Recovery Notes (PRNs) enabling the Secretary of State to meet his obligations under the EC Directive was a forceful consideration and to allow the accreditation of PRNs was likely to lead to administrative difficulties. The court refused to declare or direct alternative payment prior to the substantive hearing and took the view that the public interest was in maintaining the status quo.

2.14   Inevitably, the courts will be more reluctant to grant an interim mandatory injunction compelling a public body to take specific action rather than grant an interim injunction that has the effect of preventing a public body from doing something. The court has said that a claimant seeking an interim mandatory injunction needs to establish a very strong case since an order of that kind is 'one stage removed' from the interim relief that is normally granted.[11] It has been done to keep a residential home open pending appeal.[12]

2.15   Examples of where interim injunctions have been granted are in immigration removal cases,[13] housing/welfare cases, restraining the designation of a protected site on the basis of a claim for incompatibility with primary legislation,[14] and to continue funding for a college placement in a special educational needs case.[15]

The European dimension

2.16   There is a difference between the test for interim relief as a matter of European law and as a matter of domestic law. The differences were explored in *R v Secretary of State for Health, ex p Imperial Tobacco Ltd* [2002] QB 161. Various tobacco companies applied to the court for interim relief pending a ruling from the European court on the validity of a directive. The Court of Appeal refused interim relief and held that the appropriate test was one of European law. The House of Lords held that had they been required to determine the matter they would have referred the issues raised to the European Court. As it was, the issue had been rendered redundant as a result of an opinion on the part of the Advocate General finding the directive invalid.

Interim declarations

2.17   This is a comparatively recent power since the introduction of the CPR. In *R v Environment Agency, ex p Mayer Parry Recycling Ltd* [2000] EWHC Admin 388 an interim declaration was considered by reference to the balance of convenience. In *R (Ashworth Hospital Authority) v Mental Health Review Tribunal for West Midlands and the North West Region* [2001] EWHC Admin 901 'the Court should not deprive a person of liberty by injunction or compel him to submit to treatment, except in the most exceptional cases' by way of interim relief.

---

[11]   *R v Westminster City Council, ex p Augustin* [1993] 1 WLR 730.
[12]   *R v Service Houses and Wandsworth London Borough Council, ex p Goldsmith* [2000] 3 CCLR 354 (granted by the Court of Appeal).
[13]   *R (Pharis) v Secretary for State for the Home Department* [2004] EWCA Civ 654.
[14]   *William Sinclair v English Nature* [2001] EWHC Admin 408.
[15]   *R (S) v Norfolk County Council* [2004] EWHC Admin 404.

Stays

2.18 CPR 54.10(2) makes it clear that where permission to proceed is given the court can also give directions, including ones that relate to a stay of proceedings to which the claim relates.

2.19 A wide interpretation is given by the courts to proceedings. Proceedings will include not only judicial proceedings, but administrative decisions and the process of arriving at such decisions.[16, 17] 'The purpose of a stay in a judicial review is clear. It is to suspend the "proceedings" that are under challenge pending the determination of the challenge. It preserves the status quo. This will aid the judicial review process and make it more effective. It will ensure, so far as possible, that, if a party is ultimately successful in his challenge, he will not be denied the full benefit of his success', see *R (on the application of H) v Ashworth Hospital and others* [2002] EWCA Civ 923. The court made it clear that a stay would apply against all orders, even those which have been fully implemented due to the fact that a successful judicial review challenge does in some sense re-write history.

Bail

2.20 Both the High Court and the Court of Appeal have the power to grant bail in judicial review on the basis of the power 'to make ancillary orders temporarily releasing an applicant from detention and that on an appeal in those proceedings this court by virtue of s 15(3) of the 1981 Act can make the like order': *R v Secretary of State for the Home Department, ex p Sezek* [2001] EWCA Civ 795.

THE PREROGATIVE REMEDIES: MANDATORY, PROHIBITING AND QUASHING ORDERS

Mandatory order

2.21 A mandatory order exists to compel the performance of a public duty. It will not be granted to enforce a private law duty, such as restitution of money owing.[18] A mandatory order issues from the High Court and is directed to any person, corporation or inferior tribunal requiring him, or it, to do something specified in the order which relates to an office and is in the nature of a public duty.[19]

2.22 The modern mandatory order is used to compel the performance of a public duty on the part of a public authority or decision maker. It may compel a court or tribunal to exercise its jurisdiction to determine a case or, where a body has discretion, it

---

[16] *R v Secretary of State for Education and Science, ex p Avon* [1991] 2 WLR 702 including a stay on the 'process by which the challenged decision has been reached, including the decision itself'.

[17] *Cala Homes (South) v Secretary of State for Communities and Local Government* [2010] EWHC 3278 for a recent example of where the balance of convenience favoured that an earlier stay be lifted as agreement on an early date, for an expedited 'rolled up' hearing had been reached and the Secretary of State had given appropriate undertakings.

[18] *R v Barnet Magistrates' Court, ex p Cantor* [1998] 2 All ER 333. Here the court quashed a finding by the magistrates' court that the claimant, who was a beneficiary of a discretionary trust, should pay prosecution costs. The claimant's mother had paid the costs on the claimant's behalf and the court recognised that the claimant had a claim for the repayment of the costs. However, the court would not make a mandatory order and instead made a declaration that the money had been paid as a result of an unlawful order.

[19] *Padfield v Minister of Agriculture, Fisheries and Food* [1968] AC 997 per Lord Reid at 1034, HL.

may require the body to consider the exercise of the discretion when the occasion arises.[20] A public body may have declined to exercise a jurisdiction on a misconstruction of its statutory remit. In that event, the court will usually order the body to hear and determine the matter according to law.[21]

2.23	A mandatory order can require a public authority to perform a specific act if a statute imposes a clear and unqualified duty to carry it out. In practice such cases are rare. The courts have granted a mandatory order requiring a local authority to pay sums specified by a statutory instrument.[22] Where the statutory duty is on the face of it absolute, the court may read into it an implied exception on public policy grounds. The courts will not grant a mandatory order which will facilitate the commission of a criminal act[23] or allow a person to profit from a criminal act.[24]

2.24	In the case of housing provision a public law duty may give rise to a private law right. In such a case the House of Lords has considered whether the remedy should come through JR or an ordinary claim.[25] It found that no private law right arose as the Housing Act which enabled the power was a programme of social benefit of a public nature. Therefore, the court found that the appropriate path was to seek a remedy in Judicial Review. Lewis considers that the principle is likely to be applied generally.[26]

2.25	The court is more willing to grant a mandatory order to compel a public body to take an action of a procedural nature. It will not order a public body to exercise a discretion, still less to exercise a discretion in a particular way. In *Padfield v Minister of Agriculture, Fisheries and Food*[27] the court indicated that the minister should exercise his power to refer a complaint to a committee of investigation. Even in that case the mandatory order required the minister only to consider whether to make the reference. It did not order the minister to make it.

2.26	In *R v Secretary of State for Trade and Industry, ex p Lonrho*[28] the Divisional Court required the minister to make a reference to the Monopolies and Mergers Commission. The Divisional Court was reversed by the Court of Appeal whose decision was upheld by the House of Lords. The House of Lords found that the Divisional Court decision would have the effect of transforming a discretion into a duty.

2.27	In the consideration of European Law the courts will be more willing to take positive action to protect enforceable rights of the individual in domestic courts. In such cases the courts may be required to determine what action must be taken to allow enjoyment of those rights.[29]

---

[20]	*R v Tower Hamlets LBC, ex p Chetnik Developments* [1988] AC 858.

[21]	Eg *R v Nottingham County Court, ex p Byers* [1985] 1 WLR 403 at 407.

[22]	*R v Liverpool City Council, ex p Coade, The Times*, 10 October 1986. The wages owed to the claimant by the education authority could be claimed in JR under SCA 1981, s 31(4).

[23]	*R v Registrar-General, ex p Smith* [1990] 2 WLR 782. The court refused the claimant's application for JR of the Registrar's refusal to release the details of his biological mother where there was a risk the claimant might attack his mother when he tracked her down.

[24]	*R v Chief National Insurance Cssr, ex p Connor* [1981] QB 758. A widow was not allowed to profit by a widow's benefit where she had murdered her husband.

[25]	*O'Rourke v London Borough of Camden* [1998] AC 188.

[26]	Lewis, 4th edn, 6-052.

[27]	[1968] AC 997.

[28]	DC in *The Times*, 18 January 1989, CA in (1989) New LJ 150 and HL in [1989] 1 WLR 525.

[29]	*R v Secretary of State for Transport, ex p Factortame Ltd (No 2)* [1991] 1 AC 603 at 643–645, paras 18–19.

2.28   In cases where statutes impose an obligation on a public body to provide services the courts must be careful not to intrude upon the administrative role of a public body by determining the allocation of public funds and finite resources. The courts have refrained from making such orders and instead have construed such obligations: to include a discretion as to how to perform such a duty;[30] or to be a 'target duty';[31] or to be a duty to make reasonable effort or best endeavours,[32] or to be read with a gloss that a body which fails to act may have a just cause or excuse, so that the failure will not constitute a breach.[33]

2.29   The courts will often make a declaration rather than resort to a mandatory order on the basis that the public body may be relied on to comply with the duty set out in the declaration without the need for a coercive order.[34] Where a declaration is made the court may give the claimant liberty to apply for further relief if the respondent does not act upon it.[35]

2.30   As with all the JR remedies, the grant of a mandatory order is within the discretion of the court. It may be sought where there is an alternative remedy but the remedy is less beneficial and effective.[36] Disobedience of a mandatory order is a contempt of court and is punishable by fine or imprisonment.[37]

2.31   In the case of a corporate body the order should be addressed to each member of the body, and the individuals who have control of the body should be named in the writ of attachment.[38] Findings of contempt can be made against a government department or a minister acting in his official capacity.[39] In such cases the finding of contempt will not be enforced punitively against the minister. The finding of contempt is considered to be sufficient in itself to force the department or minister to act to obey the order. RSC Order 53, r.10 provided that no action or prosecution might be begun against any person

---

30   *R v Lancashire CC, ex p Guyer* [1980] 1 WLR 1024 at 1033 per Stephenson LJ – a discretion found in how a local authority performed its duty to protect a right of way. Lancashire CC had only to act to protect a right of way where there was no serious dispute over the status of the highway.

31   *R v Inner London Education Authority, ex p Ali* (1990) 2 Admin LR 822. Where an education authority fails to meet required education provision through no fault of its own no breach of duty occurs.

32   *R v Bristol Corpn, ex p Hendy* [1974] 1 WLR 498 at 501 per Lord Denning MR. The local authority 'have only to do the best they can'.

33   *R v Inner London Education Authority, ex p Ali* (1990) 2 Admin LR 822; *Meade v Haringey LBC* [1979] 1 WLR 637 at 650 per Eveleigh LJ. Provided the Council (as education authority) have a 'just and reasonable excuse' for their action there would be no breach of duty.

34   Eg *R v Secretary of State for Home Dept, ex p Anderson* [1984] QB 778 at 795 per Robert Goff LJ and *R (van Hoogstraten) v Governor of Belmarsh Prison* [2003] 1 WLR 263 at para 47. The prison authorities refused to let an individual (Di S) visit Mr van Hoogstraten in prison. Di S was an Italian advocate who Mr van Hoogstraten claimed had a right to visit him as a legal advisor. The court made a declaration that Mr van Hoogstraten's visitor should be allowed access to him but refused to make a mandatory order in case the prison found grounds to refuse Di S access on grounds of his character.

35   *R v Liverpool City Corps, ex p Ferguson and Ferguson* [1985] IRLR 501. The court quashed a decision of the education authority not to pay teachers who could not work because schools were closed due to strike action by janitorial staff. The court set a date by which the authority should pay the arrears to the teachers and gave them liberty to apply for further relief.

36   *R v Thomas* [1892] 1 QB 426 at 431 per Wills J, DC, 'under which circumstances the remedy by appeal would not be as satisfactory and effectual as the remedy by mandamus'.

37   *R v Poplar MBC, ex p Metropolitan Asylums Board (No 2)* [1922] 1 KB 95 at 105 per Lord Sterndale MR, CA.

38   *R v Poplar MBC, ex p Metropolitan Asylums Board (No 2)* [1922] 1 KB 95 at 105–106 per Lord Sterndale MR, CA.

39   *M v Home Office* [1994] 1 AC 377 at 427 per Lord Woolf.

in respect of actions taken to obey a mandatory order. It is thought that this principle still applies following the introduction of the CPR although there is no longer any express provision to that effect.

2.32   The CPR makes no provision for the awarding of an interim remedy where the claimant seeks a mandatory order; but a mandatory interim injunction can now be granted in a claim for JR.[40]

2.33   Mandatory orders will not lie to compel the performance of a moral duty[41] or order anything contrary to law. According to De Smith[42] the narrow technicalities that once applied to the grant of mandamus no longer restrict the remedy of a mandatory order.[43] It is desirable that the claimant should be able to show that he has demanded performance of a duty and that that duty has been refused by the authority obliged to discharge it. Before applying for JR the claimant should address a specific demand or request to the defendant that he perform the duty imputed to him.[44] The Pre-Action Protocol for Judicial Review obliges a claimant to take this step by writing a letter to the defendant before claim.

Prohibiting order

2.34   A prohibiting order is an order issuing from the High Court and directed to an inferior court, tribunal, public authority or other body whose decisions are justifiable which forbids that body to act in excess of its jurisdiction or contrary to law. Whereas quashing orders exist to quash a decision already made, prohibiting orders are used to prevent the respondent from acting or continuing to act in such a way as to exceed or abuse its jurisdiction.[45]

Examples of when a prohibiting order has been granted

2.35   These have included against magistrates to prevent them exceeding their jurisdiction;[46] a prison board of visitors seeking to hear a charge that they had no power to deal with;[47] a local authority to prohibit it acting on a licensing resolution regarding taxis;[48] a minister to prevent him making an invalid clearance order;[49] a rent tribunal seeking to proceed with a case outside its jurisdiction;[50] Electricity Commissioners

---

[40]   *R v Kensington and Chelsea Royal LBC, ex p Hammell* [1989] QB 518 at 529–531.
[41]   Eg to make good an officer's pay: *ex p Napier* (1852) 18 QB 692.
[42]   6th edn of De Smith.
[43]   Lewis, 4th edn, at 6-066.
[44]   *R v Horsham DC, ex p Wenman* [1995] 1 WLR 680 at 709 per Brooke J: 'Lawyers acting for a party should not regard it as unnecessary to write a letter before action merely because they believe it to be inevitable that the response will deny their clients' claim'.
[45]   *R v Horseferry Road Justices, ex p Independent Broadcasting Authority* [1987] QB 54. The court quashed a summons by the magistrates' court where the court found no criminal offence was intended to be created by s 4(3) of the Broadcasting Act 1981. An informant (Norris McWhirter) alleged that ITV had committed an offence under the Act by inserting a single frame into an edition of Spitting Image, which showed a puppet of the informant in an unflattering light.
[46]   *R v Horseferry Road Justices, ex p Independent Broadcasting Authority* [1987] QB 54.
[47]   *R v Board of Visitors of Dartmoor Prison, ex p Smith* [1987] QB 106 at 127.
[48]   *R v Liverpool Corps, ex p Liverpool Taxi Fleet Operators' Assoc* [1972] 2 QB 299 at 309 per Lord Denning MR.
[49]   *R v Minister of Health, ex p Davis* [1929] 1 KB 619 at 628, CA.
[50]   *R v Tottenham and District Rent Tribunal, ex p Northfield (Highgate) Ltd* [1957] 1 QB 103 at 107 per Lord Goddard CJ DC

seeking to hold an inquiry in order to bring into force an *ultra vires* scheme of supply;[51] and a chief medical officer likely to act with bias.[52]

Earliest time for application

2.36   An application for JR seeking a prohibiting order may be made as soon as the complete absence of jurisdiction is apparent on the record of the inferior court,[53] and without the question of jurisdiction having been raised in the inferior court.[54] The applicant will not have to raise an objection before the inferior court even when the defect is not clear upon the record in cases: (i) where the question is one of law not dependent on disputed facts;[55] or (ii) when he contends that the tribunal is so constituted such that there is a likelihood of bias.[56]

2.37   A prohibiting order must be invoked at an early stage when there remains something to be done that the court can prohibit. Similarly a quashing order will not lie unless a decision has been made that a court can quash. However, sometimes both are pursued where a quashing is required to quash an order made in excess of a tribunal or court's jurisdiction, and a prohibiting order is required to prevent the tribunal or court from continuing to exceed its jurisdiction.

Quashing orders

2.38   A quashing order is an order of the High Court by which it quashes a decision of an inferior court or tribunal, public authority or other body, which is susceptible to judicial review.

2.39   In order to found a claim for a quashing order a decision must exist to be quashed.[57] A quashing order is not available against a view expressed in correspondence or against a recommendation.[58] It can lie against a preliminary decision (*R v Postmaster General, ex p Carmichael* [1928] 1 KB 291). The form of the decision is immaterial. The decision can be in the form of a report or even of inactivity.[59] The decision must have had some legal effect and must affect identifiable 'subjects'.[60]

---

[51]   *R v Electricity Cssrs, ex p London Electricity Joint Committee Co* (1920) Ltd [1924] 1 KB 171 at 197 per Bankes LJ, CA.

[52]   *R v Kent Police Authority, ex p Godden* [1971] 2 QB 662 at 670, [1971] 3 All ER 20, CA: prohibition against a chief medical officer examining a police officer to determine whether the officer was to be compulsorily retired when the doctor was likely to be biased having recently examined the officer for another purpose.

[53]   *London Corps v Cox* (1867) LR 2 HL 239: 'Where ... it is apparent on the record that the [court] never had jurisdiction ... the case is ripe for decision without waiting for any further pleading' per Lord Cranworth at 293.

[54]   *London Corps v Cox* (1867) LR 2 HL 239 at 291 per Willes J.

[55]   *R v Tottenham and District Rent Tribunal, ex p Northfield (Highgate) Ltd* [1957] 1 QB 103 at 108, [1956] 2 All ER 863, DC.

[56]   *R v Kent Police Authority, ex p Godden* [1971] 2 QB 662 at 670, [1971] 3 All ER 20, CA. *R (Al-Hasan) v Secretary of State for the Home Department* [2005] UKHL 13 [2005] 1 WLR 688 where a deputy prison governor conducted a disciplinary hearing relating to disobeying an order given when he was present.

[57]   *R v St Lawrence's Hospital Statutory Visitors, ex p Pritchard* [1953] 1 WLR 1158 at 1166 per Parker J: 'this motion fails on the ground that there is no decision or determination to be quashed'.

[58]   *R v Secretary of State for Employment, ex p Equal Opportunities Commission* [1995] 1 AC 1 at 25 per Lord Keith. In that case a declaration was appropriate remedy at 37 per Lord Browne-Wilkinson.

[59]   *R v Hillingdon LBC, ex p Streeting* [1980] 1 WLR 1425 at 1432: The director of housing at the authority wrote to the claimant 'I do not propose to notify any other housing authority that your application for assistance in obtaining accommodation has been made'.

[60]   *R v Criminal Injuries Compensation Board, ex p Lain* [1967] 2 QB 864 at 892 per Lord Parker CJ.

2.40   The primary role of the quashing order in modern public law is to quash an *ultra vires* decision. The order is technically an order bringing the decision of the decision making body to the High Court so that the court may decide whether the decision is valid. Where the decision is found to be ultra vires a quashing order may be issued that will quash the decision. By quashing the decision the order confirms that the decision is a nullity to be deprived of legal effect. The House of Lords has said that a quashing order is the primary and most appropriate remedy for achieving the nullification of a public law decision.

2.41   If, on an application for JR, the High Court quashes the decision to which the application relates, it may remit the matter to the court, tribunal or authority which made the decision with a direction to reconsider the matter and reach a decision in accordance with the findings of the High Court.[61] On some occasions the High Court may substitute its own decision for the decision challenged in the application. This course is open to the court only if: (i) the decision in question was made by a court or tribunal; (ii) the decision quashed was quashed on the ground of an error of law; and (iii) without the error of law there would have been only one decision that the original court or tribunal could have reached.[62] Unless the High Court otherwise directs, a decision substituted under s 31(5A) of the SCA 1981 has effect as if it were the decision of the original court[63] or tribunal.[64]

2.42   A quashing order lies to quash any decision of a public law body exercising public law powers. A quashing order can quash a licence,[65] directions to remove an immigrant,[66] the resolution of a local authority to adopt a particular policy,[67] a grant of planning permission[68] or a grant of a tenancy.[69]

2.43   A quashing order can be twinned with a declaration. This is useful where the precise consequences of quashing a decision need to be made clear. It may be paired with other JR remedies where appropriate. The judicial review jurisdiction and the prerogative remedies lay against any body exercising public law powers, whether derived from statute, the prerogative[70] or other non-statutory sources.[71]

---

61   Senior Courts Act 1981 s 31(5) (s 31(5) subsequently substituted by s 31(5), (5A), (5B) of the Tribunals, Courts and Enforcement Act 2007, s 141).

62   Senior Courts Act 1981, s 31(5A) as substituted.

63   Senior Courts Act, s 31(5B) as substituted.

64   CPR 54.19 (3) – the CPR enables the court not only to reverse the decision but also to require what is just to be done in an particular case, see *R v Northumberland Compensation Appeal Tribunal, ex p Shaw* [1952] 1 KB 338 at 347, [1952] 1 All ER 122 at 127–128, CA per Denning LJ. But where certain facts have been admitted by counsel during the JR proceedings the court will not make a direction based on such admissions: *R v Vaccine Damage Tribunal, ex p Loveday* (1985) *The Times*, 20 April, CA.

65   *R v North Hertfordshire DC, ex p Cobbold* [1985] 3 All ER 486. A licence to hold an open-air concert was quashed as the condition requiring agreement on policing levels could not be met and could not be severed from the licence as a whole (Mann J).

66   *R v Immigration Officer, ex p Shah* [1982] 1 WLR 544 at 550 per Woolf J.

67   *R v Liverpool City Council, ex p Secretary of State for Employment* [1989] COD 404. The decision of the Council to withhold grants from an organisation wishing to join an Employment Training Scheme in order to put pressure on the organisation was unlawful.

68   *R v Great Yarmouth BC, ex p Botton Bros Arcades Ltd* (1988) 56 P&CR 99. No duty existed to hear objectors but fairness required they be heard and so certiorari would issue to quash the decision (Otton J).

69   *R v Port Talbot BC, ex p Jones* [1988] 2 All ER 207 (1987) 20 HLR 265 at 277 per Nolan J. A decision of the Council to allocate a council house to a member of the council outside the ordinary criteria for allocation was quashed. The applicant was the leader of the council, which made the wrongful allocation.

70   *R v Secretary of State for Foreign and Commonwealth Affairs, ex p Everett* [1989] QB 811 at 817 per O'Connor LJ: whether an act under the prerogative was amenable to JR was a question of the nature of the act. The issuing of a passport was an administrative act affecting an individual's freedom to travel and was not likely to raise issues of foreign policy and thus was amenable to Judicial Review.

2.44   It was thought quashing orders could not lie against non-binding acts, such as advisory opinions and reports, of those exercising public law powers;[72] but it is now clear that a quashing order may be issued in appropriate circumstances to quash a recommendation.[73] The courts may grant a declaration that a non-binding advisory circular is *ultra vires*,[74] and that a report is void.[75] There does not appear to be any reason now why a quashing order would not be available in similar circumstances. A hypothetical order would confirm that an unlawful act had occurred and confirm that the circular or report should not be relied upon.

2.45   It is sometimes suggested that quashing orders serve no purpose in the case of nullities, since a nullity is without a legal effect for the order to quash. However, the quashing order serves a purpose in this respect, that it establishes the invalidity of the act and makes clear that it is a nullity without legal effect. The quashing order clarifies the position and allows parties to act, confident that the court recognises the lack of legal effect of the challenged decision.

2.46   The Divisional Court has held that a quashing order is available to quash a decision which is a nullity.[76] The Court held that an unlawful acquittal was a nullity which did not allow the acquitted person to rely upon the concept of 'double jeopardy' or autrefois acquit to resist a fresh prosecution. The Court found that the quashing order was a 'convenient way of preventing the continuance of an ostensible effect'.[77] However, the Court indicated that the more suitable remedy to force the continuation of the trial by the Justices was for the DPP to seek a mandatory order compelling the trial to continue.

2.47   The Court of Appeal held that judicial review was available to determine whether a draft order in council which was laid before Parliament for approval but was not yet submitted to Her Majesty in Council was within the powers conferred in the enabling

---

[71]   *Reg v Criminal Injuries Compensation Board, ex p Lain* [1967] 2 QB 864; *R v Panel on Take-overs and Mergers, ex p Datafin plc* [1987] QB 815 at 835–836, 846–849; The panel considered itself to be a body deriving its authority entirely from the consent of parties but the court found that in fact it carried on public law duties with public law sanctions and was thus amenable to JR. *R v Norfolk CC, ex p M* [1989] QB 619 at 628 per Waite J: the register of sex offenders and suspected sex offenders operated by the Council was, despite its administrative character, available to a significant enough part of the public to impose a duty upon the Council to act fairly in its operation. M (against whom two complaints had been made but no charges preferred) was added to the register without prior consultation or details of the reasons for the Council's decision to add him. The Council's decision to add him to the register was quashed.

[72]   *R v Statutory Visitors to St Lawrance's Hospital Caterham, ex p Pritchard* [1953] 1 WLR 1158. The report of a board of visitors to a hospital was found not to be amenable to Judicial Review. This DC decision is now considered qualified.

[73]   *R v Agricultural Dwelling-House Advisory Committee for Bedfordshire Cambridgeshire and Northamptonshire, ex p Brough* (1986) 19 HLR 367. The advisory report of a committee advising a local housing authority on an application for a dwelling by an agricultural worker was found to be amenable to JR and was quashed, as the opinion was likely to be followed by the housing authority.

[74]   *Gillick v West Norfolk and Wisbech Area Health Authority* [1986] AC 112 at 193–194 per Lord Bridge: 'But the occasions of a departmental non-statutory publication raising ... a clearly defined issue of law, unclouded by political, social or moral overtones, will be rare. In cases where any proposition of law implicit in a departmental advisory document is interwoven with questions of social and ethical controversy, the court should, in my opinion, exercise its jurisdiction with the utmost restraint ...'.

[75]   *Grunwick Processing Laboratories v Advisory, Conciliation and Arbitration Service* [1978] AC 655 at 705 per Lord Keith. A recommendation by ACAS that a union should be recognised was based upon insufficient consultation of the relevant workforce (only one third were consulted) and thus was void.

[76]   *R v Hendon Justices, ex p DPP* [1994] QB 167 at 178 per Mann LJ.

[77]   *R v Hendon Justices, ex p DPP* [1994] QB 167 at 178 per Mann LJ: 'We recognise the defiance of logic in stating that the order can go, but in practice decisions which are nullities are quashed as a convenient way of preventing the continuance of any ostensible effect'.

Act.[78] The appropriate remedy was considered to be a declaration as a quashing order might be perceived as an attempt to restrain Parliament in its discussions.

2.48   A quashing order may be insufficient in cases where the claimant is challenging a decision to refuse to exercise a discretionary power. In such a case a quashing order would merely establish that the decision maker has acted unlawfully, but would not of itself compel the public body to consider exercising the discretionary power. In such a case the quashing order may need to be coupled with a mandatory order compelling the authority to consider exercising its discretion or to hear the case according to law.[79]

2.49   The court may grant a quashing order with leave to apply for further relief in case the public authority does not act according to law.[80] The court has the power to quash the decision and remit the matter to the original decision maker with a direction to decide the matter in accordance with the court's judgment.[81]

2.50   Where a public body is under a duty to act and has refused to act the court may, instead of making a mandatory order, make a quashing order and accompany it with a declaration setting out the extent of the public body's obligations. In a case where a local health authority refused to provide psychiatric care services, the court quashed the refusal, and made a declaration clarifying the extent of the health authority's duties and invited the health authority to reconsider the claimant's case in light of the judgment.[82]

2.51   Where a public authority misconstrues its jurisdiction and threatens to exceed it the appropriate remedy is a prohibiting order, or injunction, sometimes in conjunction with a quashing order to quash the decision to act beyond its powers.[83] However, the court may simply issue a quashing order to quash the decision to act on the basis that the public authority is unlikely to continue to act unlawfully when the quashing order has established the illegality.[84]

Severance

2.52   Where only part of a decision is invalid, and that part can be separated from the valid part of the decision, the court may grant a quashing order to quash the invalid part whilst leaving the valid part untouched.[85]

2.53   In *DPP v Hutchinson*[86] the House of Lords held that there were two aspects to the test of severance in public law: the ability to sever the act textually and in its substance. A legislative act was severable textually if the offending clause, phrase,

---

[78]   *R v HM Treasury, ex p Smedley* [1985] QB 657 at 666–667.

[79]   *R v Tower Hamlets LBC, ex p Chetnik Developments Ltd* [1987] 1 WLR 593 at 605–606 (affirmed by the HoL [1988] AC 858 – a quashing order was granted to quash the Council's decision to refuse a discretionary refund and a mandatory order was made to make the Council hear and determine the matter according to law).

[80]   *R v Police Complaints Board, ex p Madden* [1987] 1 WLR 447 at 472; *R v Hillingdon LBC, ex p Royco Homes Ltd* [1974] 2 QB 720 at 732.

[81]   Senior Courts Act 1981 s 31(5); CPR r 54.19(2).

[82]   *R v Ealing Local Health Authority, ex p Fox* [1993] 1 WLR 373 at 387.

[83]   *R v Horseferry Road Justices, ex p Independent Broadcasting Authority* [1986] 3 WLR 132, [1987] QB 54 at 73 per Lloyd LJ.

[84]   *R v Commission for Racial Equality, ex p Hillingdon BC* [1982] AC 779 at 793.

[85]   The same principles apply as in declarations; *R v Secretary of State for Transport, ex p GLC* [1986] QB 556.

[86]   [1990] 2 AC 783 – byelaw imposed by the Secretary of State for Defence relating to the military base at Greenham Common took away the rights of commoners which rights he was not allowed to limit by the terms of the enabling Act.

sentence or word could be removed from the text without compromising the coherence or grammar of the provision. The act was severable in substance if what remained was unchanged in its legislative purpose, operation and effect. If both tests were satisfied, the act could be severed. In certain cases an act would not be textually severable but would be severable in substance. The court might in such cases still be able to sever the act and find it only partially invalid.

2.54 In *Hutchinson* the byelaw was not severable and was, therefore, found to be invalid in its entirety. *Hutchinson* related to delegated legislation but it is thought that it can be extended to other public law acts and decisions. In *R v IRC, ex p Woolwich Equitable Building Society*[87] a regulation imposing income tax liability could be altered by severing the paragraph that was *ultra vires*. However, the offending paragraph specified the rate of tax to be paid as being that in the 1985–86 tax year. The paragraph could not be severed in substance, since its removal would require the substitution of another tax rate from another year which would change the purpose and effect of the regulation. In *Woolwich* the entire regulation had to be quashed.

2.55 The test of severability has been used in determining whether conditions attached to licences or planning permissions can be severed leaving a functioning licence or permission intact without having to quash the whole decision. The courts have considered whether the condition can be removed without altering the character of the licence or permission. If the licence or provision would be fundamentally different, it has to be quashed.[88]

2.56 In *Hutchinson* Lord Bridge considered that severance might not be applicable to the resolution of a public authority to appropriate land where the power of the authority did not extend to all of the land.[89] In such cases Lord Bridge considered the language of severance to be inappropriate. Instead the resolution should be construed to determine which land was affected.

Restrictions on quashing orders

2.57 Some restrictions remain upon quashing orders. Quashing orders may not lie against superior courts.[90] Superior courts include the Supreme Court, the Court of Appeal, the High Court, Masters of the Supreme Court,[91] and the Courts-Martial Appeal Court.[92] The Supreme Court (as constituted prior to the Constitutional Reform Act 2005) was the Court of Appeal, the High Court of Justice and the Crown Court.[93]

---

[87] [1990] 1 WLR 1400.
[88] *R v North Hertfordshire DC, ex p Cobbold* [1985] 3 All ER 486; *Hall v Shoreham-by-Sea Urban DC* [1964] 1 WLR 240.
[89] *DPP v Hutchinson* [1990] 2 AC 783 at 810.
[90] *R v Oxenden* (1691) 89 ER 545; *Suratt and others v Att-Gen of Trinidad and Tobago* [2008] 2 WLR 262 at para 49.
[91] *Murrell v British Leyland Tees* [1989] COD 389.
[92] Section 1 of the Court-Martial (Appeals) Act 1968. Courts martial in times of martial law operate entirely outside the law and are not subject to JR: *Re Clifford and O'Sullivan* [1921] 2 AC 570.
[93] Section 1 of the Senior Courts Act 1981.

Examples of where quashing orders have been granted

2.58   These have included orders against a department of state,[94] an individual minister's order,[95] a local authority's grant of planning permission[96] or a licence,[97] a valuation officer,[98] an immigration officer,[99] licensing justices,[100] the Gaming Board (as was, now the Gambling Commission),[101] the Police Complaints Board,[102] an election court,[103] rent tribunals,[104] a medical appeal tribunal,[105] a diary produce quotas tribunal,[106] the Health and Safety Commission,[107] a prison board of visitors,[108] a prison governor in respect of a disciplinary award,[109] the Commission for Racial Equality[110] (as was), and the mental health commissioners.[111]

---

[94]   *Board of Education v Rice* [1911] AC 179 at 182 per Lord Loreburn LC, HL.

[95]   *R v Secretary of State for the Environment, ex p Brent LBC* [1982] QB 593 at 646–647 per Ackner LJ [1982] 2 WLR 693: the Secretary of State had fettered his discretion when making an order under the Local Govt, Planning and Land Act 1980; *R v Secretary of State for Home Dept, ex p Dannenberg* [1984] QB 766 at 777 per Dunn LJ [1984] 2 All ER 481, CA: the deportation order made by the Secretary of State failed to give reasons and was invalid on its face and had to be quashed; *R v Secretary of State for the Environment, ex p Binney* (1983) *The Times*, 8 October: Where there were two large groups of residents, one opposing and one supporting a road scheme, no reasonable minister could find an inquiry was unnecessary.

[96]   *R v Hillingdon LBC, ex p Royco Homes Ltd* [1974] QB 720, [1974] 2 All ER 643 at 732 per Lord Widgery CJ, DC.

[97]   *R v London CC, ex p Entertainments Protection Association* [1931] 2 KB 215 at 234 per Scrutton LJ, CA: a council granted a cinema licence beyond its jurisdiction contrary to the Sunday Observance Act 1780.

[98]   *R v Paddington Valuation Officer, ex p Peachey Property Corps Ltd* [1966] 1 QB 380 at 400–401 per Lord Denning MR, [1965] 2 All ER 836, CA.

[99]   *R v Chief Immigration Officer, Lympne Airport, ex p Amrik Singh* [1969] 1 QB 333 at 342 per Lord Parker CJ, [1968] 3 WLR 945, DC; *R v Chief Immigration Officer, Gatwick Airport, ex p Kharrazi* [1980] 1 WLR 1396 at 1404 per Lord Denning MR, CA.

[100] *R v Dudley Justices, ex p Curlett* [1974] 1 WLR 457 at 460 per Lord Widgery CJ, [1974] 1 WLR 457, DC: the granting of an alcohol license with a condition unknown to law, *R v Barnsley MBC, ex p Hook* [1976] 1 WLR 1052 at 1058 per Lord Denning MR, CA: the decision of the Council to revoke a street trader's license offended the principles of natural justice.

[101] *R v Gaming Board for Great Britain, ex p Benaim and Khaida* [1970] 2 QB 417 at 430–432 per Lord Denning MR, [1970] 2 WLR 1009, CA (relief refused on the facts).

[102] *R v Police Complaints Board, ex p Madden* [1983] 1 WLR 447 at 471 per McNeill J.

[103] *R v Cripps, ex p Muldoon* [1984] QB 68 at 89 per Robert Goff LJ, DC; affirmed [1984] QB 686, [1984] 2 All ER 705, CA.

[104] *R v Fulham, Hammersmith and Kensington Rent Tribunal, ex p Zerek* [1951] 2 KB 1 at 13 per Lord Goddard CJ, DC.

[105] *R v Medical Appeal Tribunal, ex p Gilmore* [1957] 1 QB 574 at 585 per Denning LJ, CA.

[106] *R v Dairy Produce Quotas Tribunal, ex p S Dimelow Farms* (1988) *The Times*, 7 November.

[107] *R v Health and Safety Commission, ex p Spelthorne BC* (1983) *The Times*, 18 July.

[108] *R v Blundeston Prison Board of Visitors, ex p Fox-Taylor* [1982] 1 All ER 646. Where the board of visitors were aware of evidence to aid a prisoner in his disciplinary hearing but did not inform the prisoner of the existence of the witness there was a breach of natural justice. The court quashed the finding of the board.

[109] *Leech v Deputy Governor of Parkhurst Prison* [1988] AC 533 at 568 per Lord Bridge, [1988] 1 All ER 485, HL, 'it can hardly be doubted that governors and deputy governors dealing with offences against discipline may occasionally fall short of the standards of fairness which are called for in the performance of any judicial function. Nothing, I believe, is so likely to generate unrest among ordinary prisoners as a sense that they have been treated unfairly and have no effective means of redress'.

[110] *R v Commission for Racial Equality, ex p Hillingdon LBC* [1982] QB 276 at 289 per Lord Denning MR, CA (affirmed [1982] AC 779, HL), 'the Commission for Racial Equality is a public body, its proceedings can be challenged by judicial review, no matter whether they are regarded as judicial or administrative. There is no need to go into the many cases on the subject. We have had them so often. The central principle is that a public body must exercise its powers and carry out its duties in accordance with the intentions of Parliament, express or implied. It must not go beyond the bounds. If it does, its conduct is ultra vires and the courts can interfere to put it right'.

[111] *R v Mental Health Commission, ex p W* (1988) *The Times*, 27 May. The Commissioners had no power to refuse a course of treatment to a patient diagnosed with a sexual perversion.

Injunctions to restrain a person from acting in office

2.59   The High Court may grant an injunction to restrain a person from acting in certain public offices[112] in which he is not entitled to act[113] and, where necessary, declare the office vacant.[114]

2.60   The order must be sought by way of JR.[115] The conduct of the applicant may be considered before the awarding of an injunction.[116]

DECLARATIONS AND INJUNCTIONS

2.61   An application for a declaration or an injunction[117] may be made by way of an application for JR.[118] In such a case the court may grant the declaration or injunction if it considers that it would be just and convenient to grant it having regard to the factors in SCA 1981, s 31(2)(a)–(c).

2.62   The jurisdiction to grant declaratory or injunctive relief is concurrent with the jurisdiction to grant these remedies in private law claims.[119] However, a person seeking to establish that a public authority has by its decision infringed his rights that are protected under public law should pursue a remedy through JR and not by way of an ordinary claim.[120]

Injunction

2.63   An injunction is a discretionary, equitable remedy awarded by superior courts or, with some limitations, by a county court judge, to restrain an imminent threat or the commission or continuance of, an unlawful act or to compel the taking of steps to repair an unlawful omission or to restore the damage inflicted by an unlawful act. An injunction can therefore be prohibitory or mandatory.[121]

2.64   An injunction will not be issued to secure the provision of services which the court cannot effectively supervise,[122] or where damages are an adequate remedy.

---

[112]   A substantive office of a public nature and permanent character which is held under the Crown or which has been created by a statutory provision or royal charter: Senior Courts Act 1981, s 30(2).

[113]   Senior Courts Act 1981, s 30(1)(a).

[114]   Senior Courts Act 1981, s 30(1)(b).

[115]   Senior Courts Act, s 31(1)(c), CPR 54.2(d).

[116]   *Everett v Griffiths* [1924] 1 KB 941 at 958 per McCardie J.

[117]   Not including an injunction under Senior Courts Act 1981, s 30 to restrain a person from acting in an office in which he is not entitled to act: CPR 54.2.

[118]   Senior Courts Act 1981, s 31(1)(b) and s 31(2) and CPR 54.3.

[119]   Eg *Gillick v West Norfolk and Wisbech Area Health Authority* [1986] AC 112, [1985] 3 All ER 402, HL.

[120]   *O'Reilly v Mackman* [1983] 2 AC 237, [1982] 3 All ER 1124, HL.

[121]   On mandatory injunctions see *Redland Bricks Ltd v Morris* [1970] AC 652, [1969] 2 All ER 576, HL.

[122]   *Attorney-General v Colchester Corporation* [1955] 2 QB 207, [1955] 2 All ER 124 (no mandatory injunction to order continuance of a ferry service); *Dowty Boulton Paul Ltd v Wolverhampton Corps* [1971] 2 All ER 277, [1971] 1 WLR 204 (no injunction to order maintenance of an airfield); Cf. Unusual case in *Warwickshire CC v British Railways Board* [1969] 3 All ER 631, [1969] 1 WLR 1117, CA (prohibitory injunction to restrain invalid closure of a railway line).

2.65   Injunctions, both final and interim, may be granted against an officer of the Crown and he may be held in contempt if he breaches an injunction.[123] An injunction can be granted by a court even though compliance with the injunction may lead to practical difficulties.[124]

2.66   An injunction will not be granted to restrain proceedings in Parliament[125] but it seems that a body can be restrained from spending public money to introduce or oppose a private Bill in Parliament.[126] The courts may issue an injunction in relation to a statutory instrument even when that instrument has been laid before both Houses of Parliament.[127]

Declarations

2.67   The court may grant an injunction or make a declaration instead of, or in addition to, one of the prerogative orders if it is just to do so and considering: (i) the nature of the matter in which the prerogative remedies may be granted; (ii) the nature of the persons and/or bodies against whom relief may be granted by the prerogative orders; and (iii) all the circumstances of the case.[128]

2.68   An injunction or declaration can be sought as the sole remedy in a JR claim.[129] The court's jurisdiction to award such a remedy is no longer confined to cases where the prerogative orders would be available.[130]

2.69   A declaration can be granted by the court in the exercise of its discretion instead of one of the prerogative remedies where, for example, the applicant has delayed in applying for JR[131] or where the award of another remedy would be disruptive and lead to uncertainty and delay.[132] Declarations are often issued against Ministers instead of prerogative orders as they are expected to observe the decision of the court and comply with declaratory judgements.[133] Declarations have been used to resolve disputes between

---

[123]   *M v Home Office* [1994] 1 AC 377, [1993] 3 All ER 537, HL.

[124]   *Bradbury v Enfield LBC* [1967] 3 All ER 434 at 441, [1969] 1 WLR 1311 at 1324, CA, per Lord Denning MR ('even if chaos should result, still the law must be obeyed').

[125]   The Bill of Rights (1689) 'the freedom of speech and debates or proceedings in Parliament ought not to be impeached or questioned in any court or place out of Parliament'.

[126]   *Attorney-General v London and Home Counties Joint Electricity Authority* [1929] 1 Ch 513; but see *Bilston Corporations v Wolverhampton Corps* [1942] Ch 391, [1942] 2 All ER 447.

[127]   *Hoffman-La Roche & Co AG v Secretary of State for Trade and Industry* [1975] AC 295, [1974] 2 All ER 1128, HL.

[128]   Section 31(2) of the Senior Courts Act 1981.

[129]   *R v Secretary of State for Employment, ex p Equal Opportunities Commission* [1995] 1 AC 1, HL; *R v Bromley LBC, ex p Lambeth LBC, The Times*, 16 June 1984. Local authorities applied for, and received, a declaration that their contributions to Association of London Authorities were intra vires.

[130]   *R v Bromley LBC, ex p Lambeth LBC, The Times*, 16 June 1984 and the dicta of the Court of Appeal in *Law v National Greyhound Racing Club* [1983] 1 WLR 1302 at 1310.

[131]   *R v Rochdale MBC, ex p Schemet* [1994] ELR 89, 91 LGR 425. The court found that the council's change of policy on school transport was unlawful but delay by the Schemet family meant certiorari would not be granted as the council had already budgeted in line with the new policy.

[132]   *R v Secretary of State for Social Services, ex p Assoc. of Metropolitan Authorities* [1986] 1 All ER 164, [1986] 1 WLR 1. The Minister had failed to consult the Association as mandated before making regulations regarding public housing. The Association sought a quashing order in JR but were not granted one. A declaration was made.

[133]   *M v Home Office* [1994] 1 AC 377 at 397, [1993] 3 All ER 537 at 543, HL, per Lord Woolf.

two public authorities;[134] to decide whether advice contained in departmental circulars was correct in law;[135] and to direct a tribunal as to the decision it should reach.[136]

2.70 A declaration cannot be merely academic. It must be effective at the time of the hearing or it must be certain to have effect in the future.[137] To ignore a declaratory judgement does not constitute a contempt of court but if a declaration is ignored the court may enforce it by way of injunction.

2.71 The cases, therefore, where a declaration or injunction is available in public law but the prerogative remedies of quashing, prohibiting or mandatory orders are not are narrow and limited. In *R v Bromley LBC, ex p Lambeth LBC*[138] the court considered that a prerogative order would not be available as the applicant was not affected by the decision of the respondent. Lambeth LBC simply wanted a declaration that payments to a particular organisation would be lawful under the Local Government Act 1972. JR was pursued against Bromley LBC because it had earlier brought JR proceedings against a different local authority to stop payment to the same organisation when it was operating under a different constitution.

2.72 Hodgson J held that the declaratory jurisdiction lay within the realm of public law, although prerogative remedies were unavailable, since it extended to the powers of statutory bodies. Woolf J (as he then was) also held that the court had a jurisdiction to grant declaratory relief on some public law point of general importance even if no decision yet existed against which a prerogative remedy could be sought.[139]

2.73 Quashing orders can lie against administrative acts[140] and in particular against delegated legislation.[141]

2.74 The order might be used to quash normative acts and is not confined to decisions affecting only specified individuals.[142] Since the power to make delegated legislation is derived from statute, public law principles apply to the use of such powers. Lewis

---

[134] Eg *R v London Transport Exec, ex p GLC* [1983] QB 484, [1983] 2 All ER 262. The GLC was granted declarations confirming that instructions from the GLC to the London Transport Executive were lawful and could be lawfully implemented.

[135] *Royal College of Nursing of the United Kingdom v Dept of Health and Social Security* [1981] AC 800, [1981] 1 All ER 545, HL. The Royal College sought a declaration that DHSS guidance on a new method of abortion administered by nurses rather than doctors, as required in the Abortion Act 1967, was wrong in law. The DHSS sought a declaration to the contrary. Held: the DHSS's declaration was granted and the Royal College's refused; *Gillick v West Norfolk and Wisbech Area Health Authority* [1986] AC 112, [1985] 3 All ER 402, HL. Declarations were sought that a DHSS Memorandum of Guidance on contraceptive advice and treatment was unlawful. Declarations were refused.

[136] Eg *Barty-King v Ministry of Defence* [1979] 2 All ER 80.

[137] *Nottinghamshire CC v Secretary of State for the Environment* [1986] AC 240, [1986] 1 All ER 199, HL.

[138] *The Times*, 16 June 1984.

[139] *R v Secretary of State for the Environment, ex p Greater London Council* [1985] JPL 868. Appeal against a Queen's Bench Master's decision to strike out the GLC's application. Although the Master accepted that the GLC was not a 'person aggrieved' there were special circumstances that made it desirable that the approach of the planning inspector be tested by way of Judicial Review (Woolf J).

[140] Eg *R (Javed) v Secretary of State for the Home Dept* [2001] EWCA Civ 789, [2002] QB 129. The Asylum (Designated Countries etc) Order 1996 was reviewable in JR.

[141] *R v Secretary of State for Health, ex p United States Tobacco Intl Inc* [1991] 3 WLR 529. United States Tobacco had regulations banning oral snuff quashed on the basis of one of five grounds (unfairness).

[142] *Minister for Health v King (on the Prosecution of Yaffe)* [1931] AC 494.

considers that the need for a separate public law procedure with shorter time limits in order to protect certainty relating to the decisions of public authorities, applies with 'especial force to legislative measures'.[143]

2.75 Another case where the declaratory remedy is available and a quashing order is not is in proceedings against the Crown. A quashing order lies against a Minster of the Crown and a minister exercising power derived from the prerogative[144] but not against the Crown itself. Section 21(1) of the Crown Proceedings Act 1947 provides that the courts have power to make certain orders, including declarations, against the Crown in civil proceedings; but, as set out earlier, JR is not included in the definition of civil proceedings in the Act.[145] Strictly, there is no power to make a declaration in JR against the Crown itself and the appropriate route to be followed to obtain one would be through an ordinary action. The occasions when a declaration would be needed against the Crown personally are likely to be very limited and concern the personal exercise by the Crown of prerogative powers. It is not a matter of great practical importance as statutory powers are usually vested in Ministers of the Crown and their exercise of those powers is challengeable through judicial review.

Orders against the Crown

2.76 No court can compel the Sovereign to perform any duty: so a mandatory order cannot lie against the Crown.[146] Where it is sought to establish a right against the Crown the appropriate procedure is that in accordance with the Crown Proceedings Act 1947. No order will lie against any person acting as an agent of the Crown and discharging duties on behalf of the Crown.[147] This exception is of limited practical importance[148] because a mandatory order can be made where the government official has a particular duty in relation to subjects.[149] If a statute requires 'the minister' to do something, a mandatory order can be made to force the minister to act.[150] This remedy is preserved in the Crown Proceedings Act 1947, s 40(5).[151]

DAMAGES AND RESTITUTION

Damages

2.77 A claim for damages may be attached to a claim for JR.[152] The court may award damages to the applicant if he has joined a claim for damages with his JR claim[153] and

---

[143] Clive Lewis, *Judicial Remedies in Public Law*, 4th edn 2-175.
[144] Lewis (supra) 6-015, *Council of Civil Service Unions v Minister of Civil Service* [1985] AC 374, *R v Secretary of State for Foreign and Commonwealth Affairs, ex p Everett* [1989] EHRR 52.
[145] Section 38(2) of the CPA 1947.
[146] *R v Powell* (1841) 1 QB 352 at 361 per Lord Denman CJ and *R v Treasury Lords Cssrs* (1872) LR 7 QB 387 at 394 per Cockburn CJ: 'Court cannot claim even in appearance to have any power to command the Crown; the thing is out of the question'.
[147] *R v Customs Cssrs* (1836) 5 Ad & El 380 at 383 per Littledale J; *R v Secretary of State for War* [1891] 2 QB 326, CA.
[148] *M v Home Office* [1994] 1 AC 377 at 417, [1993] 3 All ER 537 at 560, HL, per Lord Woolf.
[149] The distinction was drawn in *R v Secretary of State for War* [1891] 2 QB 326 at 334, CA, Charles J.
[150] *R v Customs and Excise Cssrs, ex p Cooke and Stevenson* [1970] 1 All ER 1068 at 1072–1073.
[151] The CPA does not limit the discretion of the court to grant relief by way of mandatory order in cases where the relief might have been granted before the commencement of the Act, notwithstanding that by reason of its provisions some other and further remedy is available.
[152] Senior Courts Act 1981, s 31(4); CPR r 54.3(2).
[153] Senior Courts Act 1981, s 31(4)(a).

the court is satisfied that if the claim had been made in an action begun by the claimant at the time of his making the JR claim he would have been awarded damages.[154]

2.78	Section 31(4) of the SCA 1981 is not intended to create a new right but rather to remove the need for duplicate proceedings under Part 7 and Part 54. A claim under section 31(4) can be made only in conjunction with a claim for the prerogative remedies or for a declaration or injunction. It cannot be made in isolation. Damages can be awarded only if they would have been available in an ordinary claim where there was a right to damages in private law or under the HRA 1998. The change allows, for convenience, the rolling into a public law claim of a claim for damages under private law or the HRA 1998.

2.79	That an act of a public body is found to be *ultra vires* does not entitle an individual to damages for loss *per se*. The claimant must demonstrate that the unlawful act is identifiable as a recognised tort or as a breach of contract.[155] The general principles relating to tortious and contractual liability apply to public bodies exercising public law powers and powers derived from private law rights in contract and property.

2.80	When considering tortious acts committed by public bodies the courts will consider the special context of public administration.[156] The imposition of a duty of care is intended to lead to an improvement in the standard of care observed by a public authority in providing services.[157] The court will be mindful of cases where the imposition of a duty may make an authority unduly cautious in the exercise of its powers, or where a duty might lead to unproductive litigation which would distract the authority from its duty to provide the relevant service.[158]

2.81	In deciding whether to impose a duty upon a public authority the court will consider the availability of alternative remedies such as a statutory right of appeal.[159] In

---

[154]	Senior Courts Act 1981, s 31(4)(b).

[155]	*X v Bedfordshire County Council* [1995] 2 AC 633 at 730 per Lord Browne-Wilkinson: 'the breach of a public law right by itself gives rise to no claim for damages. A claim for damages must be based on a private law cause of action'; *R v Knowsley Metropolitan Borough Council, ex p Maguire* (1992) 90 LGR 653: there is no general right to damages for maladministration. The claimant had no right to damages due to the authority's unlawful refusal to issue him with a taxi license.

[156]	*X v Bedfordshire County Council* [1995] AC 633 per Lord Browne-Wilkinson at 739. The court will not hold a public authority vicariously liable for the actions of an employee where to do so would interfere with or 'discourage' the performance of the authority's duties. However occasions here vicarious liability will not be found will be rare: per Lord Slynn in *Phelps v Hillingdon LBC* [2001] 2 AC 619 at 653.

[157]	*Phelps v Hillingdon LBC* [2001] 2 AC 619 at 672 per Lord Clyde the imposition of a duty 'may have the healthy effect of securing that high standards are sought and secured'; *Barrett v Enfield London Borough* [2001] 2 AC 550 at 568 per Lord Slynn approving Sir Thomas Bingham MR (as was).

[158]	*X v Bedfordshire County Council* [1995] AC 633.

[159]	*Rowley v Secretary of State for Work and Pensions* [2007] 1 WLR 2861 at para 73 per Dyson LJ: 'I accept, of course, that the mere fact that there is an alternative remedy is not necessarily a reason for denying the existence of a common law duty of care. It is important to see how comprehensive a remedy is provided and to consider it in the context of the statutory scheme as a whole. Ultimately, what has to be decided is whether, having regard to the purpose of the legislation, Parliament is to be taken as having intended that there should be a right to damages for negligence. The more comprehensive the remedy provided by Parliament, the less likely it is that Parliament is to be taken as having had that intention'. *Jain v Trent Strategic Health Authority* [2009] UKHL 4 per Lord Scott at para 28 'This line of authority demonstrates, in my opinion, that where action is taken by a State authority under statutory powers designed for the benefit or protection of a particular class of persons, a tortious duty of care will not be held to be owed by the State authority to others whose interests may be adversely affected by an exercise of the statutory power. The reason is that the imposition of such a duty would or might inhibit the exercise of the statutory powers and be potentially adverse to the interests of the class of persons the powers were designed to benefit or protect, thereby putting at risk the achievement of their statutory purpose'.

Jones v Department of Employment[160] the existence of a statutory right of appeal was a factor in the court's decision that an adjudication officer owed no duty of care to a claimant in processing a claim.

2.82   In *X v Bedfordshire County Council* the House of Lords found that a statutory complaints procedure and a reference to the local government ombudsman were more appropriate remedies than a negligence action in relation to maladministration in dealing with children at risk or with special educational needs.[161]

2.83   Article 6 of the European Convention on Human Rights guarantees the individual's access to the courts. The European Court has found that the failure of UK courts to find a duty of care in domestic law in a particular context does not infringe an individual's article 6 rights;[162] but, an individual may allege the infringement of other rights, such as the article 8 right to family and private life, which may go into the balance against policy considerations.[163]

2.84   In *Chief Constable of Hertfordshire Police v Van Colle, Smith v Chief Constable of Sussex*[164] the possibility of such a claim was not sufficient to set aside the rule that the police do not owe a common law duty in relation to their investigative functions.

2.85   In relation to statutory duties there is the problem that not all statutory duties give rise to a claim in damages. The issue becomes whether Parliament intended to confer a right to sue for damages where there has been a breach of a duty imposed by statute.[165] By a process of considering statutory construction the court will try to discern if an intention to create a private law remedy in damages can be found. As part of that process the relevant considerations include 'the object and scope of the provisions, the class (if any) intended to be protected by them, and the means of redress open to a member of such a class if the statutory duty is not performed'.[166] The difficulty in discerning an intention is such that the value of the exercise has been doubted. However, the intention of Parliament remains a cogent consideration in the courts' conclusions.

---

[160]   [1989] QB 1 at 19 per Glidewell LJ Cf. *R v HM Treasury, ex p Petch* [1990] COD 19 where a duty in negligence could lie in parallel with a duty under the Superannuation Act 1972. Although Popplewell J held it was not negligence in its ordinary sense.

[161]   *X v Bedfordshire County Council* [1995] AC 633 at 751 and 762 per Lord Browne-Wilkinson: 'In my judgment ... the courts should hesitate long before imposing a common law duty of care ... The statute [Education Act 1981] provides its own detailed machinery for securing that the statutory purpose is performed. If, despite the complex machinery for consultation and appeals contained in the Act, the scheme fails to provide the benefit intended that is a matter more appropriately remedied by way of the Ombudsman looking into the administrative failure than by way of litigation. For these reasons I reach the conclusion that an education authority owes no common law duty of care in the exercise of the powers and discretions relating to children with special educational needs specifically conferred on them by the Act of 1981'.

[162]   *TP and KM v United Kingdom* (2002) 34 EHRR 2 at paragraphs 92–103; *Z v United Kingdom* (2002) 34 EHRR 97 at 87–104

[163]   *CA in D v East Berkshire Community NHS Trust* [2004] QB 558 at paras 78–85.

[164]   [2008] 3 WLR 593 at 136–139.

[165]   *R v Deputy Governor of Parkhurst Prison, ex p Hague* [1992] 1 AC 58 at 159 per Lord Bridge: 'the fundamental question: "Did the legislature intend to confer on the plaintiff a cause of action for breach of statutory duty?"'; *X v Bedfordshire County Council* [1995] 2 AC 633 at 731 per Lord Browne-Wilkinson: 'The basic proposition is that in the ordinary case a breach of statutory duty does not, by itself, give rise to any private law cause of action. However, a private law cause of action will arise if it can be shown, as a matter of construction of the statute, that the statutory duty was imposed for the protection of a limited class of the public and that Parliament intended to confer on members of that class a private right of action for breach of the duty'; *Cullen v Chief Constable* [2003] 1 WLR 1763 at 41.

[166]   Per Bingham LCJ in *Olotu v Home Office* [1997] 1 WLR 328 at 336.

2.86   Public bodies are also liable for the tort of misfeasance in public office. The tort consists of a deliberate and dishonest abuse of power by a public officer or body.[167] It may be committed maliciously; or where it acted in the knowledge that the action was *ultra vires* and that where the public body acted the claimant or a class of persons[168] would probably suffer loss. To establish the tort the victim must show some special damage suffered. A prisoner whose correspondence was inspected in bad faith by prison officers was unable to demonstrate loss.[169] A prisoner moved from the open prison estate to the closed estate established such restraint of freedom caused him to sustain special damage.[170]

2.87   Claims for restitution, or the recovery of sums paid can also be attached to a claim for JR.[171]

Restitution

2.88   A restitutionary claim may be pursued by or against a public body where sums have been collected or paid out in pursuance of a power found to be *ultra vires*. Where a citizen pays monies to a public authority in the form of taxes or other dues, and the demand by the public authority is *ultra vires*, those sums are recoverable as of right.[172]

2.89   In *Woolwich v IRC No 2* the Inland Revenue repaid tax levied pursuant to regulations found to be *ultra vires* and paid interest on the taxes from the date of judgement; but refused to pay interest for the period from the date of payment to the date of judgement. The building society sought to show it was entitled to recover the money and so was entitled to the interest for the whole period. The majority of the House of Lords decided that the building society was entitled to recover money paid pursuant to a demand that was narrowly *ultra vires* in that there was no authority for the demand once the regulations were quashed. Two members of the majority in the House of Lords also expressed the view that the same principle applied where the tax was not due for some other reason such as misconstruction of the regulations or statute.[173]

2.90   In cases where money was paid under an agreement that was later found to be *ultra vires* the law has been changed by House of Lords decisions. Previously the law was thought to be that money paid under a mistake of law was not recoverable.[174] In *Kleinwort Benson Ltd v Lincoln City Council*[175] the House of Lords overruled *Bilbie v Lumley*[176] and found that the previous rule was not part of English law.

2.91   A person who pays money under a mistake is *prima facie* entitled to recover it on the ground of unjust enrichment. Money is paid under a mistake of law even where the

---

167   See *Three Rivers DC v Governors of the Bank of England* [2003] 1 AC 1.
168   The claimant or class of persons need not be identifiable. In *Akenzua v Secretary of State for the Home Department* [2003] 1 WLR 741 the fact that the murder victim of a released individual, or a group of potential victims, was unidentifiable was not a reason to strike out the claim.
169   *Watkins v Home Office* [2006] 2 AC 395 at 23 per Lord Bingham.
170   *Karagozlu v Commissioner of Police for the Metropolis* [2007] 1 WLR 1881 at 45 per Sir Anthony Clarke MR.
171   Senior Courts Act 1981, s 31(4) as amended by the Civil Procedure (Modification of Supreme Court Act 1981) Order 2004 – as of 1 May 2004 a restitutionary claim can be included in a Judicial Review claim.
172   *Woolwich Building Society v Inland Revenue Cssrs (No 2)* [1993] AC 70.
173   *Woolwich Building Society v Inland Revenue Cssrs (No 2)* [1993] AC 70, per Lord Goff at 177 and per Lord Slynn at 205.
174   See *Bilbie v Lumley* (1802) 2 East 469.
175   [1999] 2 AC 349.
176   Supra.

parties were unaware of the ultra vires status of the agreement or where the settled view of the law was that such agreements were lawful. There appears to be no limitation on claiming money paid under a settled understanding of the law when that understanding is later departed from by a decision of the court.[177] In *Sempra Metals Ltd (formerly Metallgesellschaft Ltd) v Inland Revenue Cssrs*[178] it was found that interest, including compound interest, may be awarded.

2.92   The courts have recognised some defences to a claim for recovery of money paid through a mistake of law. Where the recipient of the money has changed his position in reliance on the payment so that repayment would be inequitable, the court will not order restitution.[179] It is likely that where the money was paid under a compromise agreement or in settlement of a legal claim, there will be a defence.[180] It is not a defence that the defendant honestly believed that he was entitled to retain the money or that the money was paid under a fully performed void contract.[181]

2.93   In *Woolwich v IRC*[182] the court left open the possibility of a defence where the taxpaying company passed on the cost of an *ultra vires* tax demand to its customers.[183] In the case of *ultra vires* tax demands a public policy defence may develop,[184] since an error of law on the part of a public authority may result in it being liable to repay large sums of tax which may already have been spent. Such a situation could have a severe effect on a local authority's budget. Some statutory provisions deal with this problem by precluding repayment where the error was based on a general practice.[185]

2.94   A claim for restitution can be pursued through JR under SCA 1981, s 31 (4) where it is subordinate to a public law claim, which seeks to determine whether an action was *ultra vires*.[186]

HRA damages

2.95   Damages are also available under s 8 of the Human Rights Act 1998 where they 'afford just satisfaction' to a claimant[187] who has suffered loss as a result of a public authority infringing his human rights under the European Convention on Human Rights adopted into UK law by the HRA 1998 Schedule 1.[188] The court must take account of any other remedy granted in respect of the infringement.[189] The court must also take into account the principles applied by the European Court of Human Rights in finding a right to damages and in quantifying such damages.[190]

---

[177]   *Kleinwort Benson Ltd v Lincoln City Council* [1999] 2 AC 349 (Lords Browne-Wilkinson and Lloyd dissenting on this point).
[178]   [2008] 1 AC 561.
[179]   *Lipkin Gorman (a firm) v Karpnale Ltd* [1991] 2 AC 548.
[180]   *Kleinwort Benson Ltd v Lincoln City Council* [1999] 2 AC 349 at 1112.
[181]   *Kleinwort Benson Ltd v Lincoln City Council* [1999] 2 AC 349 at 1112.
[182]   Supra.
[183]   *Woolwich Building Society v Inland Revenue Cssrs (No 2)* [1993] AC 70.
[184]   Lord Goff in *Kleinwort Benson Ltd v Lincoln City Council* [1999] 2 AC 349 at 1122 and Lord Goff again in *R v Tower Hamlets LBC, ex p Chetnik Developments Ltd* [1988] AC 858 at 882.
[185]   Taxes Management Act 1970, s 33(2A)(a).
[186]   Senior Courts Act 1981, s 31(4) as amended by the Civil Procedure (Modification of Supreme Court Act 1981) Order 2004 – as of 1 May 2004 a restitutionary claim can be included in a Judicial Review claim.
[187]   Human Rights Act 1998, s 8(3).
[188]   Human Rights Act 1998, Sch 1 – The Articles.
[189]   Section 8(3) of the Human Rights Act 1998 and see *Anufrijeva v Southwark LBC* [2004] 2 WLR 603 at para 55.
[190]   Section 8(4) of the Human Rights Act 1998.

2.96   In *A v Essex County Council UKSC* [2010] UKSC 33 a claim was made for damages under s 8 of the HRA as a result of a severely autistic claimant being asked to leave school in January 2002 but no replacement school placement was made available to him until July 2003. It was argued that that was a breach of the claimant's right to education under article 2 of Protocol 1 of ECHR. The court dismissed the claim on the factual basis that it stood no realistic prospect of success as there was no minimum right to education but there was no issue about the availability if damages had the claim been established.

2.97   In the giving of 'just satisfaction' damages will not always be necessary. Remedies in judicial review may be enough to give just satisfaction by guaranteeing an end to the violation.[191] In considering the right to damages in relation to the HRA 1998 the purpose of the Act should be considered. It is not a tort statute. It exists to protect Human Rights and not merely to provide compensation. The award of damages would not normally be necessary to secure a high degree of compliance with the statute by public bodies.

2.98   In considering quantum in HRA damages claims, the court should be guided by the approach of the European Court of Human Rights where damages awards are those considered equitable to the individual without precise calculation. UK courts should follow ECtHR principles and should not draw parallels with damages awarded in comparable domestic torts.[192] In the case of *R (Bernard) v Enfield Borough Council* [2002] EWHC 2282 the court took as its guide awards made by the Local Government Ombudsman.

2.99   In determining whether damages should be awarded the court may have regard to the gravity or severity of the violation, the manner in which the violation occurred and its impact on the individual.[193] Where anxiety and frustration are the harm suffered, it is unlikely that an award of damages will be justified.[194] Where a significant monetary loss has been suffered, for example where unlawful discrimination has caused the loss of employment, an award of damages is likely and the court will be able to assess such compensation.[195]

2.100   In a HRA JR and damages claim and in JR damages claim generally the court may deal with the substantive JR claim first and defer the consideration of damages to a separate occasion.[196]

2.101   Interest on damages is also recoverable.[197] Interest, whether from statute,[198] or in damages,[199] cannot be recovered on an application for judicial review where the unlawful decision successfully challenged had resulted in the late payment of a grant by the

---

[191]   *Anufrijeva v Southwark LBC* [2004] 2 WLR 603 at para 53; *R (Bernard) v Enfield LBC* [2002] EWHC 2282 at para 39 (damages awarded where a family were forced to live in substandard conditions for a period of 20 months).

[192]   *R (Greenfield) v Secretary of State for the Home Department* [2005] 1 WLR 673 at paras 18–19.

[193]   *Anufrijeva v Southwark LBC* [2004] 2 WLR 603 at paras 66–70.

[194]   *Anufrijeva v Southwark LBC* [2004] 2 WLR 603 at paras 65 and 75.

[195]   *Anufrijeva v Southwark LBC* [2004] 2 WLR 603 at 59; *R (Hooper) v Secretary of State for Work and Pensions* [2003] 1 WLR 2623 at para 147.

[196]   *Anufrijeva v Southwark LBC* [2004] 2 WLR 603.

[197]   *R v Liverpool City Council, ex p Coade, The Times*, October 10, 1986.

[198]   Senior Courts Act 1981, s 35A (added).

[199]   Unless there is an express or implied contractual provision to this effect which sounds in damages.

respondent authority.[200] The private law claim and its attendant damages are usually such that the practice is to deal with the public law claim first before dealing with the private law rights and the claim to damages.[201]

DISCRETION

2.102 Prerogative orders, declaratory orders and injunctions are discretionary remedies. The court has a wide discretion whether to grant relief at all and in what form to grant it.[202] The principles affecting the exercise of discretion are common to all the JR remedies. In deciding whether to exercise its discretion the court will take account of the conduct of the party applying for relief.

Conduct of the claimant

2.103 A taxpayer was refused relief amounting to quashing an authority's refusal to refund rates because of his previous unwarranted refusal to pay rates owed and because the authority was not being unjustly enriched.[203] In *Windsor and Maidenhead Royal Borough Council v Brandrose Investments Ltd*[204] the Council was refused relief where the litigation was found to be pointless. An authority was refused relief where it sought to challenge ministerial confirmation of its own policy based on the authority's own procedural error.[205]

2.104 The court will refuse to exercise its discretion in JR on the ground of the claimant's misconduct. Misconduct may consist in a failure to disclose material facts[206] and even in an inadvertent mis-statement of facts.[207]

Delay

2.105 Delay is a ground of refusal to exercise discretion in JR. Delay is governed by the Senior Courts Act 1981 and the CPR 54.5. A claim for JR must be commenced promptly, and in any event not later than three months after the grounds relied on arose.[208] A finding at the permission stage that a claim was not made promptly is conclusive. It cannot be reopened at the full hearing.[209]

2.106 The court may allow a claim to proceed, even if was not made promptly, if the claimant can show a good reason.[210] However, by s 31(6) of the SCA 1981, if the court

---

200 *R v Secretary of State for Transport, ex p Sherriff & Sons* (1988) *Independent*, 12 January. The claimants had taken out a loan relying on the making of a grant by the minister to pay off the loan. The grant was delayed and interest accrued on the loan. The court found that the grant could not be construed as a debt.

201 *R v Governor of Brockhill Prison, ex p Evans (No 2)* [1998] 4 All ER 993 (lawfulness of detention dealt with before claim for damages for false imprisonment); *R v Coventry CC, ex p Phoenix Aviation* [1995] 3 All ER 37 (court dealt with ultra vires claim before claim for breach of contract); *R v Chief Constable of Lancashire, ex p Parker* [1993] QB 577 (claim over validity of search warrant before claim for damages for trespass and aggravated damages).

202 See *R (Edwards) v Environment Agency* [2008] UKHL 22 at para 63.

203 *Dorot Properties Ltd v London Borough of Brent* [1990] COD 378.

204 [1983] 1 WLR 509.

205 *R v Secretary of State for Education and Science, ex p Birmingham City Council* (1984) 83 LGR 79.

206 *R v Kensington Income Tax Cssrs, ex p Princess Edmond de Polignac* [1917] 1 KB 486.

207 *R v North East Thames Regional Health Authority, ex p De Groot* [1988] COD 25.

208 CPR r 54.5(1).

209 *R v Criminal Injuries Compensation Board, ex p A* [1999] 2 WLR 974.

210 CPR r 3.1(2)(a).

considers there has been 'undue delay' in the making of an application it may refuse to grant leave to make the application or refuse any relief if it considers that such relief would cause 'substantial hardship' or 'substantially prejudice' the rights of another or would be 'detrimental to good administration'.

2.107 In *R v Dairy Produce Quota Tribunal for England and Wales, ex p Caswell*[211] Lord Goff, giving the judgement of the House of Lords, held that 'detrimental to good administration' must be different from case to case as the need for finality would differ. Relevant factors in assessing detriment would be: the length of delay, the extent and effect of the decision under challenge, and the impact if the decision were to be reopened.

2.108 In *Caswell* the decision related to the fixing of the claimant's dairy quota. The reopening of the decision would lead to other challenges which, if successful, would require the reopening of quota allocation decisions for the previous four years as the quotas were derived from a national capped quota.

2.109 In *R v Swale Borough Council, ex p RSPB*[212] the court refused to exercise its discretion on the basis of 'substantial prejudice to others' in the RSPB's challenge to the grant of planning permission to reclaim mudflats on the River Medway. The Society's challenge came out of time. The port authority had already entered into a dredging contract with another party. If relief were granted to the RSPB, the spoil already dredged would have to be dumped at sea or otherwise than upon the mudflats. There would be greater expense and the overall scheme would be delayed, with further losses.

2.110 In *R (Gavin) v London Borough of Haringey* the court refused to quash a planning permission when there was prolonged delay in bringing the claim as the developer had already made substantial financial commitments to get the development under way. The court refused to quash the planning permission but gave a declaratory judgement that there had been a failure to comply with the relevant procedural requirements.[213]

2.111 The court's discretion is so broad that the court may refuse to grant relief even where the claim is within time. In *R v Brent LBC, ex p O'Malley*[214] the claimant challenged the decision of a local authority to dispose of housing stock on the basis that it had failed to follow the appropriate consultation procedures. Despite the illegality of the decision the court would not grant relief as the third party interests of the majority of the tenants, who supported the disposal scheme, and good administration would be prejudiced if relief were to be granted.

2.112 Undue delay,[215] unreasonable[216] or unmeritorious[217] conduct, acquiescence in the irregularity complained of[218] or waiver of the right to object[219] may all result in the court's declining to grant relief.

---

[211] [1990] AC 738.
[212] (1991) 2 Admin L.Rep 790.
[213] *R (Gavin) v London Borough of Haringey* [2004] 2 P & CR 13.
[214] (1997) 10 Admin L.Rep 265.
[215] *Hanson v Church Cssrs for England* [1978] QB 823 at 831, [1977] 3 All ER 404 at 408, CA, per Lord Denning MR; *R v Rochdale MBC, ex p Schemet* [1994] ELR 89, 91 LGR 425 – delay resulted in the court making a declaration rather than a quashing order.
[216] *R v Crown Court at Knightsbridge, ex p Marcrest Ltd* [1983] 1 All ER 1148, [1983] 1 WLR 300, CA; *Fullbrook v Berkshire Magistrates' Court Committee* (1970) 69 LGR 75; *ex p Fry* [1954] 2 All ER 118 at 120, [1954] 1 WLR 730 at 734, AC, per Hallett J.

2.113 The effect of granting relief is a further consideration.[220] The court would not grant relief the effect of which would be to facilitate unlawful activity.[221]

2.114 The court may refuse to exercise its discretion where the grant of the remedy is unnecessary[222] or futile.[223] The court refused a declaration that the Inner London Education Authority was in breach of its statutory duty when the authority was to be abolished a few weeks after the date of the judgement.[224] However, the House of Lords has held that a quashing order should be granted to quash a deportation order on specified dates which were long past the date of judgement.[225]

2.115 Cases arise where prerogative relief will be of no use to the claimant but the court nevertheless issues a declaratory judgement to clarify the law for decision makers in the future.[226] Such cases would mean that pursuit of judicial review would not be merely an academic exercise. The court may give guidance as to the state of the law without making a formal declaration.[227]

2.116 Other relevant considerations include whether practical problems,[228] including administrative confusion or inconvenience[229] to the public and the effects on third parties,[230] would result from the order or whether the form of the order would require

---

[217] *R v Chief National Insurance Cssr, ex p Connor* [1981] QB 758, [1981] 1 All ER 769, DC. The denial of a widow's allowance where the individual had stabbed her husband to death; *Goordin v Secretary of State for the Home Dept* (1981) 125 Sol Jo 624, *The Times*, 11 August, CA. It is wrong to apply for a judicial remedy 'when political capital is sought to be made ... out of judicial review': *R v GLC, ex p Royal Borough of Kensington and Chelsea* (1982) *The Times*, 7 April (precept issued by the GLC).

[218] *R v Secretary of State for Education and Science, ex p Birmingham CC* (1984) 83 LGR 79 cf. *R v Port Talbot BC, ex p Jones* [1988] 2 All ER 207. A councillor who acquiesced in a decision was allowed to challenge it in JR as leader of the council acting on behalf of the wider community.

[219] *Whelan v R* [1921] 2 IR 310; *R v Williams, ex p Phillips* [1914] 1 KB 608; *R v Nailsworth Licensing Justices, ex p Bird* [1953] 1 WLR 1046.

[220] *R v Brent Health Authority, ex p Francis* [1985] QB 869, [1985] 1 All ER 74, DC; *R v Hillingdon Health Authority, ex p Goodwin* [1984] ICR 800.

[221] *R v Hereford and Worcester County Council, ex p Smith (Tommy)* [1994] COD 129, CA. A gypsy sought JR of an authority restricting access to lay bys. JR was refused on three grounds including that JR should not be granted to further the unlawful camping overnight on lay bys.

[222] *R v Boundary Commission for England, ex p Foot* [1983] QB 600, [1983] 1 All ER 1099, CA.

[223] *R v Commonwealth Public Services Commission, ex p Killeen* (1914) 18 CLR 586 (Aust); *Secretary of State for Social Services, ex p Assoc. Metropolitan Authorities* [1986] 1 All ER 164, [1986] 1 WLR 1 (certiorari refused but declaration given since challenged regulations had since been consolidated in regulations which were not challenged. *R v Ministry of Agric. Fisheries and Ford, ex p Live Sheep Traders Ltd* [1995] COD 297, DC (the court will not make declaration that repealed legislation is unlawful. Cf. *R v Northavon DC, ex p Palmer* (1993) 25 HLR 674 at 6 Admin LR 195, Sedley J granted permission to apply for JR even though the declaration sought was academic in order that the claimant might attach a claim for damages. 'Procedurally debatable' but not to grant permission would be 'a denial of justice' Sedley J at 679 and 200.

[224] *R v Inner London Education Authority, ex p Ali and Murshid* [1990] COD 317.

[225] *R v Secretary of State for the Home Dept, ex p Bugdaycay* [1987] AC 514.

[226] See section on Declarations.

[227] *R v Bromley Licensing Justices, ex p Bromley Licensed Victuallers* [1984] 1 WLR 585; *R v Bromley Magistrates' Court, ex p Smith* [1995] 1 WLR 944 and *R (Sacupima) v Newham LBC* [2001] 1 WLR 563 at 565G–H.

[228] *Chief Constable of North Wales Police v Evans* [1982] 3 All ER 141, [1982] 1 WLR 1155. The court had the power to order the CC to reinstate a probationary constable but Lord Brightman, at 156 and 1176, felt to do so would 'border on usurpation of the powers of the chief constable' and a declaration was made.

[229] *R v Paddington Valuation Officer, ex p Peachey Property Corps Ltd* [1964] 1 WLR 1186 at 1195, DC per Widgery J: 'administrative chaos and public inconvenience ... would follow the quashing of a valuation list' (later affirmed by the CA in [1966] 1 QB 380 at 418; *R v Rochdale MBC, ex p Schemet* (1992) 91 LGR 425, Roch J refused to quash an unlawful policy as it would affect two years of Rochdale's education budget and instead made a declaration to prevent the authority pursuing the unlawful policy into the future.

[230] *R v Panel on Take-overs and Mergers, ex p Datafin plc* [1987] QB 815 at 842 per Sir John Donaldson MR: 'I

the close supervision of the court or be practically incapable of performance.[231] The court may refuse to grant relief where the claimant has suffered no injustice or prejudice, for instance where a breach of natural justice had not prevented a claimant from receiving a fair hearing.[232] Similarly, where a technical breach of procedural requirements has occurred the court may refuse to exercise its discretion where the claimant has not suffered any prejudice.[233] The court will assess the degree of prejudice suffered by looking to the underlying purpose of the statutory requirements that have been breached.

2.117 The court may not quash a decision, despite an error of law[234] or failure to consider relevant, matters[235] where the decision maker would have reached the same conclusion if he had been correctly informed of the law or had been fully aware of the relevant considerations. Similarly a decision in breach of natural justice may not be quashed if the same decision would have been reached if natural justice had been observed.[236] The obvious risk with this approach is that the court might assume that the decision maker would see the same merits in the case as the court.

2.118 The courts will not refuse a remedy where there might be any doubt about whether the decision maker would have come to the same decision if he had not been in error.[237] Also, there is a public interest in holding public bodies to account when they do not observe the appropriate public law principles in exercising their discretionary powers. Quashing orders in these cases emphasise to public authorities the need to take care to act lawfully.

2.119 Courts should refuse to grant relief only where the decision would undoubtedly have been the same without the error and the granting of relief would be contrary to the public interest.[238]

---

wish to make it clear beyond a peradventure that in the light of the special nature of the panel, its functions, the market in which it is operating, the time scales which are inherent in that market and the need to safeguard the position of third parties, who may be numbered in thousands, all of whom are entitled to continue to trade upon an assumption of the validity of the panel's rules and decisions, unless and until they are quashed by the court, I should expect the relationship between the panel and the court to be historic rather than contemporaneous'.

231 *R v Peak Park Joint Planning Board* (1976) 74 LGR 376 at 380, DC, per Lord Widgery CJ 'the court does not allow mandamus to go if the form of the order may require day to day supervision and the detailed examination of circumstances'.

232 *R v Monopolies and Mergers Commission, ex p Brown (Matthew)* [1987] 1 WLR 1235 at 1247; *R v Secretary of State for Foreign and Commonwealth Affairs, ex p Everett* [1989] QB 811 at 819.

233 *R v Cornwall County Council, ex p Nicholls* [1989] COD 507. That the report before an education authority was not in the form specified in the Education Act 1944 did not prejudice its decision.

234 *R v Deputy Governor of Parkhurst Prison, ex p Hague* [1992] 1 AC 58 (the HoL reversed the CA decision on a separate issue; *R v Knightsbridge Crown Court, ex p Marcrest Properties* [1983] 1 WLR 300.

235 *R v Mansfield Justices, ex p Sharkey* [1985] QB 613 at 630. The court refused to exercise its discretion, as the decision would remain unchanged in a case where the magistrates' court had not considered all the relevant factors in the case of bail conditions imposed upon miners involved in disorder during strikes.

236 Eg *Glynn v Keele University* [1971] 1 WLR 487 at 495–496. A student who stripped in the students union at Keele University was not given an opportunity to make a plea in mitigation to the Vice-Chancellor before being excluded from University residences but the facts were not disputed and even if the claimant had had an opportunity to mitigate the penalty would have been the same. In this case the Vice-Chancellor of the Chancery Division applied JR principles in the court of Chancery.

237 *Berkeley v Secretary of State for the Environment* [2001] 2 AC 603 at 616 at para 8. Per Lord Hoffman in a case where the decision maker had filed to take account of an Environmental Impact Assessment.

238 *R v Bacon's School Governors, ex p Inner London Education Authority* [1990] COD 414, *The Independent*, 29 March 1990. A school board of governors voted to close the school, one of the governors had an indirect monetary interest in the decision. The decision was confirmed by a second vote excluding the disqualified

2.120 The court has complete discretion whether to take action on a decision and may decline to do so in the interest of the wider public even though it declares the decision to be unlawful.[239] In the *Argyll Group* decision the Master of the Rolls made clear the need to consider wider public policy implications over the interests of the claimant.

2.121 In balancing the various factors in determining whether to exercise its discretion to grant a remedy the court will base its decision upon the circumstances applying at the time of the hearing and not those operating at the time of the decision.[240] Discretion must be exercised consistently and on clear principles if JR discretion is not to become arbitrary and unpredictable.

THE ROLE OF MEDIATION AND OTHER ALTERNATIVE REMEDIES IN JUDICIAL REVIEW

2.122 The term ADR is a familiar one. However, this acronym is used for two related but different ideas.

2.123 The first, *alternative dispute resolution*, focuses on processes which are seen as alternatives to dispute resolution by the courts. The alternative is often seen as being necessary because of the costs of litigation. In many areas governed by public law the particular matter in dispute may be of a relatively small financial amount, while nevertheless important for the claimant, and the costs involved in a full judicial review may be seen as disproportionate. Indeed, even for cases where the matter is of greater financial significance there is pressure to reduce costs, particularly to the public purse. For alternative dispute resolution, the primary aim is, therefore, to provide the equivalent of court justice, but delivered more cheaply and in an accessible manner. This, it is often argued will result in greater access to justice for the more disadvantaged and less articulate members of society.

2.124 The second, *appropriate dispute resolution*, focuses more on the nature of the process and the remedy which can be obtained. It is often argued that an adversarial process, where one side wins and the other loses as a result of the application of judicial principles, is less appropriate than a more flexible process which applies wider principles or standards designed to achieve a fair result in the particular circumstances of the case. It is also argued that a more comprehensible and accessible system is needed for claimants for whom the legal process and judicial review is not only impenetrable but also a positive deterrent to seeking a remedy.

2.125 Any particular system of dispute resolution outside of the courts can seek to further either or both of these ideas, and can have advantages and disadvantages accordingly. Both are part of what has been termed 'proportionate dispute resolution'

---

governor. The second decision was allowed to stand as administratively necessary and it was unlikely the disqualified governor had any influence on the second vote.

[239] *R v Monopolies and Mergers Commission, ex p Argyll Group plc* [1986] 1 WLR 763 at 774–775 where Sir John Donaldson MR listed relevant factors in consideration of good public administration, CA; *R v Secretary of State for Social Services, ex p Assoc. of Metropolitan Authorities* (1992) 25 HLR 131 at 139–140 (Tucker J declined to quash regulations whose quashing would lead to uncertainty and delay; a declaration was made instead). *R v Restormel BC, ex p Corbett* [2001] EWCA Civ 330, [2001] 1 PLR 108 at 27 per Schiemann LJ (court declined to quash an unlawful grant of planning permission where to do so would unjustly deprive the landowner of compensation).

[240] *R v Secretary of State for Foreign and Commonwealth Affairs, ex p Everett* [1989] QB 811 at 818 per O'Connor LJ.

which seeks to reduce the number of administrative errors and provide an appropriate range of mechanisms to resolve the different type of disputes effectively, fairly and efficiently.[241]

2.126 The remainder of this chapter provides a brief explanation of the more prominent alternatives to judicial review.

MEDIATION

Introduction

2.127 Mediation has now become a feature of the legal landscape in many areas of law. For example, it is a well-known and useful tool in family law areas and is often invoked in commercial disputes. However, it has been less well used in public law areas. This is, however, changing as pressure on the public purse increases and there are calls for disputes, such as appeals in relation to planning permissions, to be resolved more quickly.

2.128 Mediation is not adjudication or arbitration. Instead, it is a flexible process where the aim is to provide a solution acceptable to all parties. The mediator can facilitate this negotiated process by utilising various techniques, but control of the process remains with the parties and the mediator must remain neutral.

2.129 Certainly, the process may be cheaper by producing a quicker outcome, and with less formal processes and representation, than an action in the courts. However, if the parties are represented as they would be in court, which may well be necessary to redress a power imbalance, and the mediator must also be paid for, the cost advantage may be less significant. Much will depend on the type of legal action involved. The main advantage is that the process provides a different solution or remedy acceptable to both or all sides.[242] While the solution may involve some compromise, it can also be a constructive process finding an alternative way of achieving the aims of the parties. As with cost, the possible advantage of a speedier outcome will depend on the type of public law action involved.

2.130 Previously mediation was not part of mainstream tools for public law. However, there has been increasing recognition of its value, not least from policy makers concerned with reducing costs and delay in public administration. However, it is still limited in its actual use, and the policy advice remains just that – largely advisory and the process is not yet compulsory. Indeed, despite formal schemes, for example in the Court of Appeal, and various trials having taken place and, as seen below, the threat of adverse costs implications, the evidence is that it is very rare for mediation to be suggested by judges in the Administrative Court.[243]

---

[241] *Transforming Public Services: Complaints Redress and Tribunals*, Cm 6243, 2004.
[242] A conclusion supported by empirical study, see Bondy and Mulcahy, *Mediation and Judicial Review: An empirical research study, The Public Law Project*, 2009, p 86.
[243] Ibid, p 5.

Support for mediation

2.131 Support for mediation processes can be drawn from the general literature on its use in relation to disputes and legal processes generally. It is not the intention to repeat this here. However, support for its use in public law processes can also be drawn from some more specific sources.

General

2.132 In *Cowl v Plymouth City Council*,[244] Woolf CJ stated that:

> '1.   The importance of this appeal is that it illustrates that, even in disputes between public authorities and the members of the public for whom they are responsible, insufficient attention is paid to the paramount importance of avoiding litigation whenever this is possible. Particularly in the case of these disputes both sides must by now be acutely conscious of the contribution alternative dispute resolution can make to resolving disputes in a manner which both meets the needs of the parties and the public and saves time, expense and stress.
>
> 2.   The appeal also demonstrates that courts should scrutinise extremely carefully applications for judicial review in the case of applications of the class with which this appeal is concerned. The courts should then make appropriate use of their ample powers under the CPR to ensure that the parties try to resolve the dispute with the minimum involvement of the courts. The legal aid authorities should co-operate in support of this approach.
>
> 3.   To achieve this objective the court may have to hold, on its own initiative, an inter partes hearing at which the parties can explain what steps they have taken to resolve the dispute without the involvement of the courts. In particular the parties should be asked why a complaints procedure or some other form of ADR has not been used or adapted to resolve or reduce the issues which are in dispute. If litigation is necessary the courts should deter the parties from adopting an unnecessarily confrontational approach to the litigation. If this had happened in this case many thousands of pounds in costs could have been saved and considerable stress to the parties could have been avoided.'

2.133 The case arose out of a proposal to close a residential home. The Council had an internal complaints procedure which it had, in a letter to the court, indicated its willingness to use and it undertook not to move the claimants from the home for a period of six weeks. Nevertheless, the judicial review hearing was expedited because the claimants contended that they were in urgent need of protection. As the Court of Appeal noted,

> '14.   It appears that one reason why the wheels of the litigation may have continued to roll is that both parties were under the impression that unless they agreed otherwise the complainants were *entitled* to proceed with their application for judicial review unless the complaints procedure on offer technically constituted an "alternative remedy" which would fulfil all the functions of judicial review. This is too narrow an approach to adopt when considering whether an application to judicial review should be stayed. The parties do not today, under the CPR, have a right to have a resolution of their respective contentions by judicial review in the absence of an alternative procedure which would cover exactly the same ground as judicial review. The courts should not permit, except for good reason, proceedings for judicial review to proceed if a significant part of the issues between the parties could be resolved outside the litigation process. The disadvantages of doing so are limited. If subsequently it

---

244   [2001] EWCA Civ 1935; [2002] 1 WLR 803.

becomes apparent that there is a legal issue to be resolved, that can thereafter be examined by the courts which may be considerably assisted by the findings made by the complaints panel.'

2.134 The issue of closure of residential homes is of course subject to established legal principles, and so was amenable to resolution by litigation. Nevertheless, the Court of Appeal rejected robustly the suggestion that an alternative resolution method was not appropriate.

'15.   … the claimants prepared a supplemental skeleton argument which set out ten reasons why the complaint procedure is not a suitable alternative remedy to judicial review. We have examined each of those reasons carefully and in our judgement they establish no basis on which the claimants could reasonably object to the matters in issue being dealt with by the complaints procedure, as modified at the hearing before us. As an alternative, they certainly could have been the subject of mediation.'

2.135 This comment emphasises the utility of mediation even where the matter may be the subject of legal rights, contrary to the view held by traditionalists. Indeed, the Court of Appeal returned to this theme and emphasised further their stringent views.

'25.   We do not single out either side's lawyers for particular criticism. What followed was due to the unfortunate culture in litigation of this nature of over-judicialising the processes which are involved. It is indeed unfortunate that, that process having started, instead of the parties focussing on the future they insisted on arguing about what had occurred in the past. So far as the claimants were concerned, that was of no value since Plymouth were prepared, as they ultimately made clear was their position, to re-consider the whole issue. Without the need for the vast costs which must have been incurred in this case already being incurred, the parties should have been able to come to a sensible conclusion as to how to dispose the issues which divided them. If they could not do this without help, then an independent mediator should have been recruited to assist. That would have been a far cheaper course to adopt. Today sufficient should be known about ADR to make the failure to adopt it, in particular when public money is involved, indefensible.'

2.136 The Court concluded with an exhortation to practitioners.

'27.   This case will have served some purpose if it makes it clear that the lawyers acting on both sides of a dispute of this sort are under a heavy obligation to resort to litigation only if it is really unavoidable. If they cannot resolve the whole of the dispute by the use of the complaints procedure they should resolve the dispute so far as is practicable without involving litigation. At least in this way some of the expense and delay will be avoided. We hope that the highly skilled and caring practitioners who practise in this area will learn from what we regard as the very unfortunate history of this case.'

2.137 Of course such exhortations, while they may be influential in supporting a culture change, are unlikely to be effective in the short term unless backed up by a sanction. The immediate sanction can bite at two stages.

2.138 First, at the permission stage. In *R (on the application of S) v Hampshire County Council*,[245] following a core assessment report the local authority refused to provide services for S, a child with behavioural difficulties. It was contended that the assessment had been unlawful, procedurally unfair and discriminatory. The local authority

---

245   [2009] EWHC 2537 (Admin).

submitted that S should be refused permission to apply for judicial review because there was an adequate alternative remedy which had not been pursued, in that the covering letter accompanying the report had invited discussion if any concerns as to S's needs had been raised, but S's mother had not complained or taken issue with the contents of the assessment at all. The court held that the existence of an alternative remedy enabled the court to conclude that permission should be refused; that the complaints procedure for core assessment reports was there to provide a speedy, informal and cheap method of resolving disputes; and that was the appropriate route by which to notify the local authority of points of dispute and to seek to have them resolved. This approach was endorsed by the Court of Appeal in *R (on the application of C & ANR) v Nottingham City Council*,[246] where in refusing permission on appeal, Jackson LJ stated that:

> 'For my part, I would echo in this case all of the sentiments which Lord Woolf CJ expressed in *Cowl*. In this case also, the parties are under a heavy obligation to resort to litigation – and, I would add, to continue with litigation – only if that is really unavoidable. In the present case litigation is far from unavoidable.'

2.139 Secondly, in the award of costs. The effect of the *Cowl* case is that when dealing with costs the courts will take into account whether ADR was considered or used, so a litigant who refuses to engage in more appropriate procedures runs the risk of not recovering the costs even if successful in the litigation.

2.140 However, the costs sanction will only be successful where one party seeks to invoke the alternative process. If both simply proceed with litigation in the normal way then this principle is unlikely to be invoked. In addition, a failure to engage in the alternative process is not necessarily fatal to recovery of costs. In *Hurst v Leeming*,[247] the claimant submitted that no such order should be made because both before and after the commencement of these proceedings he invited the defendant to proceed to mediation but this was refused. In awarding the costs to the defendant, Lightman J held that:

(a)   the fact that heavy costs had already been incurred was not a justification for refusing to mediate, but it was a factor to be taken into account in the mediation process;

(b)   the fact that a party believed he had a watertight case was no justification for refusing mediation;

(c)   the fact that a full and detailed refutation of the opposite party's case had already been supplied was also not a sufficient justification for refusing mediation;

(d)   nevertheless, the defendant was justified, on the facts of this case, in taking the view that mediation was not appropriate because it had no realistic prospect of success, by reason of the character and attitude of the claimant.

It was stressed that a litigant would normally be taking a great risk by refusing mediation on this ground. However, this was an exceptional decision and reflected how seriously disturbed the claimant's judgment was in relation to his case.

---

[246]   [2010] EWCA Civ 790.
[247]   [2002] EWHC 1051(Ch).

The pre-action protocol for judicial review

2.141 As explained in Chapter 3, Practice and Procedure, when judicial review proceedings are instituted, it is necessary to indicate whether there has been compliance with the pre-action protocol. The aim of it is to allow both parties to understand the complaint and justification for the decision, and thereby allow the opportunity for settling the issue or narrowing down the areas of dispute.

2.142 Mediation can be seen as a logical extension of this process. Again, the sanction for failure to comply with the protocol applies at two stages.

2.143 First, at the permission stage. In *R (on the application of S) v Hampshire County Council*,[248] not only was the existence of an alternative remedy sufficient to enable the court to conclude that permission should be refused, but it was also held that the complete failure on S's part to comply with the pre-action protocol in relation to the assessment, meant there was no attempt whatsoever to seek to avoid litigation and so this also warranted refusal of permission. There was never any adequate opportunity for the local authority to consider and respond to points of dispute before the proceedings were launched, and *Cowl* was applied.

2.144 Secondly, a failure to comply may be taken into account in decisions on costs.

The view in The Judge Over Your Shoulder

2.145 This document was published by the Treasury Solicitor to warn government departments and advise how to avoid judicial challenge. It advises that ADR avoids confrontation, encourages reconciliation, and is usually cheaper and less public than judicial review, and that:

> 'Whether mediation or some other form of ADR is appropriate to the case will depend on the nature of the decision being challenged, whether there is any room for manoeuvre, what other parties are affected and so on. The point to remember, however, is that the pre-action protocol is intended to offer opportunities, including ADR, for settling disputes without recourse to litigation. It will be to your advantage as decision-maker to grasp those opportunities.'

2.146 That advantage also extends to those challenging the decision in most circumstances. It is perhaps understandable that those being challenged may, in the hope that it will simply 'go away', be tempted to forget about the dispute until it is listed for hearing, by which time it is too late to engage in effective mediation. It is less understandable for those challenging the decision to allow the opportunity for earlier resolution to pass. They should seek to encourage mediation, except of course where the aim of the challenge is to achieve delay, for example in regard to the implementation of a decision.

Current suggestions that courts and ombudsman should have power to require mediation

2.147 As noted above, in considering whether to grant permission to seek judicial review, and in awarding costs, the courts can take into account whether or not

---

[248] [2009] EWHC 2537 (Admin).

alternative remedies were attempted. They do not at present have powers to require mediation or other alternative remedies to be attempted before litigation proceeds. Nevertheless, there are calls from some quarters that such a change should be made to the CPR to permit judges to direct such attempts before judicial review proceeds.

2.148 Equally, although the use of ombudsmen is, as explained below, seen as itself being an alternative to litigation, there are now powers for the Ombudsmen to appoint and pay a mediator or other appropriate person to assist in the conduct of an investigation.[249] Again, some consider that this should be extended to require such mediation.

Particular advantages in public law

2.149 There are a number of reasons why mediation could be particularly beneficial in public law matters:

(a) **Cost** – while this is normally split between the parties, there may be an advantage for the private sector/applicant to have a prompt decision by meeting the cost of the mediator, with the other costs borne by each side. Not only will this result in less delay for some matters, but it may result in a lower overall cost than if the matter proceeded to litigation. It is also more likely to encourage the public body to engage in mediation rather than incur further legal costs. Of course, much will depend on the particular matter. There may not be a saving for a short simple judicial review matter. In other matters it may appear to increase costs. For example, in planning disputes, it has been suggested that the additional cost of paying for a mediator when an Inspector is provided free of charge will act as a barrier to mediation. However, significant savings may well be made by the applicant in relation to the other costs of delay, attendance at the inquiry, etc.

(b) **Speed** – again much will depend on the particular matter at issue, but a binding decision may be achieved in advance of the time by which it would be reached by the litigation or appeal process. Even if the mediation is not completely successful, it may well narrow down the issues and thereby reduce the time taken in the litigation or appeal process.

(c) **Control** – an important aspect of the mediation process is that the parties keep control of the outcome. That may well be important in terms of the meaning and limits of policy for public authorities. For example, rather than risking an adverse decision from an Inspector as to the meaning or implementation of a policy, which will then be invoked in subsequent applications, a local planning authority may well prefer to accept a mediated outcome which, while not ideal, is nevertheless an acceptable application of the policy. Similarly, an applicant can use the process to obtain a permission which, while not identical to that applied for, is nevertheless acceptable.

(d) **Relationships** – avoiding confrontation is important in any continuing relationship and for the image created by public bodies, so the mediation process is perfectly suited to avoiding developing a confrontational relationship.

---

[249] The Parliamentary Commissioner Act 1967, s 3; the Local Government Act 1974, s 29; and the Health Service Commissioners Act 1993, para 1A of Sch 2; as amended by the Regulatory Reform (Collaboration etc between Ombudsmen) Order 2007 (SI 2007/1889).

(e) **Creative solutions** – mediation has the clear advantage of permitting a fresh look at the aims of all parties and developing a more creative outcome, rather than simply having a yes/no decision. It also avoids the rigidity of legal principles and even the precedent value of ombudsmen's and Inspectors' decisions.

(f) **Confidentiality** – while much of the business of public authorities will be public in any event, there is nevertheless often a need for confidentiality, *eg* planning obligations which are dealt with very unsatisfactorily in the current inquiry process, and the mediation process is again particularly suited to maintaining confidentiality.

(g) **Discipline and focus** – in the financially overstretched public sector context, and with competing demands on the time and resources available, mediation provides a compact and focussed productive process.

(h) **Satisfaction and compliance** – the essence of successful mediation is that the outcome is acceptable to both/all sides.

(i) **Search for consensus in public sector** – in public administration at present the language and policy is one of seeking partnership, agreements, involving stakeholders etc. The mediation process is ideally placed to achieve that.

Objections to the use of mediation in public law

2.150 There are various objections to the use of mediation in any legal dispute. Again, this is not the place to engage in a long exposition of the general literature as to the objections to mediation processes in relation to disputes and legal processes generally. However, some more specific objections to its use in public law processes can be identified.

2.151 Indeed, the relative lack of use, despite the exhortations identified above, raises the issue of whether there is good reason for this. It has been argued that the use of mediation in the public law context is more problematic for various reasons and that public law is different.

It is wrong to consider public law as a single category

2.152 It is often said that public law is too wide a term, and that the substantive issues covered by public law differ widely. At one level, both assertions are correct. However, in so far as both seek to establish that public law is essentially different from private law and not amenable to mediation, the only valid justification is that we must be sensitive to whether the subject matter is amenable to mediation.

2.153 Of course a dispute over two rival interpretations of the meaning of a statutory provision, or a policy in national guidance or a development plan, ultimately requires a court or similar process to decide which is correct. But only a relatively few disputes in public law are actually about such interpretation or matters of enforcement of absolute rights. Most are concerned with particular decisions within a well understood, if flexible, legal and policy framework.

Duties and discretions

2.154 A related point which is often raised is that there is an important difference between statutory duties and discretion. For the former, it is said that only litigation is appropriate since this is a matter of legal right, not to be undermined by a settlement or negotiation, however consensual.

2.155 Of course mediation is easier to operate in regard to discretionary powers where there is a choice between a range of legitimate decisions. Clearly this category accounts for many decisions made by public authorities.

2.156 Nevertheless, mediation can still have a role to play in matters of statutory duty, in relation to resolution of disputes of fact; what constitutes satisfactory compliance with the duty in terms of good use of resources; and in clarifying areas of continuing dispute. It is also wrong to think that duties are always absolute – much depends on the context.

2.157 Equally, there will be matters where discretion is being exercised but mediation is not appropriate such as where there are simply two conflicting aims and no scope for either a third way or a compromise.

Not just two parties but the public as well

2.158 Equally, it is often argued that mediation is not appropriate because the dispute does not, as in most commercial disputes, concern simply two parties – the complainant and the public authority – but also involves the public. That is misconceived as a general objection because:

(a)   a 'normal' mediation can be multi-party;

(b)   while the public authority represents the 'public interest', it can nevertheless be recognised that there are separate third party interests to be taken into account;

(c)   it may actually assist third parties to understand the issues or have their narrow/specific interest dealt with discretely;

(d)   in relation to local government, if the mediation process can be in advance of the local planning authority decision on a controversial application, it may reduce the practice of elected members refusing planning applications in order to allow third parties to object at an appeal, and the strength and weakness of the third parties' position properly understood by all sides;

(e)   it is the experience of some that the public inquiry, the main alternative to resolving disputes in planning matters, is all but incomprehensible to most of the lay public.

2.159 It can also be noted that in 1997 the Government stated in a consultation paper on planning that:

> 'Successful mediation would obviate the need for an appeal or inquiry, but openness and fairness, and the law, demand that a fresh application and decision should be made, in the normal way, in respect of any amended scheme emerging from mediation. Third parties

would not normally be involved directly in mediation, but would have the opportunity to comment on the revised scheme. When mediation narrows, but does not dispose of, an appeal then third parties can still make representations to the Inspector.'

2.160 This of course represents a view where the mediation involves only the applicant and the local planning authority. However, it is certainly possible and indeed desirable in some circumstances, to involve clearly identified third party interests in the mediation process, since this can introduce more certainty and faster decision-making into the process.

2.161 In both circumstances, the normal rules as to what is a significant amendment requiring re-consultation apply.

Authority to settle

2.162 Most mediators consider it an essential part of the process that the participants have authority to settle the matter in the course of the mediation.

2.163 It is normally regarded as essential that those attending the mediation have the power to settle, so that it makes the process meaningful and minimises the chance of a party apparently reaching an agreement and then reneging on it or seeking further concessions.

2.164 It is often thought that this causes problems for the public authority. For example a leading textbook notes:[250]

> 'Complications may well arise with public bodies. Given the decision-making structures of national or local government, it is unlikely that any individuals will be able to attend a mediation with completely unfettered authority to settle. More likely, those who attend will be authorised to agree settlement terms subject to obtaining final approval from the appropriate committee .... Although not ideal ... mediation can and does still operate effectively in these circumstances. It may, however, be helpful to obtain a commitment in advance that the appropriate committee will meet within a specified and short period following the mediation so that the matter is not left unresolved for too long.'

2.165 While that shows that the issue is not insuperable, the difficulty may in any event be overstated. It is an objection which is thought to have greater force in regard to local government than for other public bodies. As far as local government is concerned, because:

(a) it is already the case that those officers involved in the proceedings are already delegated to take the relevant decision as to any settlement of modification of the authority's position, eg in relation to the conduct of legal proceedings or planning appeals;

(b) delegated authority is usually given in general terms;

(c) where it is not done, or the issue is recognised to be sensitive politically, then it is usually structured as an officer decision after consultation with the appropriate Chair or Cabinet member;

---

[250] Mackie, Miles, Marsh and Allen, *The ADR Practice Guide*, pp 95–96.

(d)   the trend in local government law generally is to have executive decision-making so that not only the officer but also the relevant elected member with authority could attend the mediation, although this does not of course apply in the regulatory controls such as planning.

Other tailor-made processes / remedies

2.166 It may be thought that other tailor made and designed alternatives to the courts would be more appropriate – such as public inquiries and/or Ombudsmen. However, not only do they also have disadvantages, often in terms of control, costs, speed and effectiveness, but it is instructive that not only the ombudsmen, through 'informal settlements' and recent powers to finance mediation described above, but also the Planning Inspectorate are both actively encouraging mediation as a cost effective alternative to their own procedures.

Summary

2.167 Despite the strong exhortations from the courts and policymakers to use mediation, it is by no means the case that mediation is suitable for all public law issues.

2.168 Certainly, it is suitable for any functional area where discretion exists, or finding agreed facts is important. It has been widely used in relation to neighbour/tenancy issues, and could also be used in some social services issues as it is in matrimonial disputes.

2.169 In recent years there has been much encouragement in planning, environmental and compulsory purchase matters. This has included a pilot project and repeated exhortations in reports and adopted policy.[251] However, this has failed to deliver much activity, and Sir Henry Brooke has characterised the policy guidance as 'pious incantations' and the Government's response to the Barker Report's suggestion to promote mediation as 'a thoroughly flaccid response'.[252]

2.170 There are a number of possible reasons why it has not been utilised more. One clear barrier is what is perceived as an additional cost, since the cost of an appeal, as opposed to representation, is met by the public purse, but not the cost of mediation. However, it is capable of reducing overall costs, and the issue is on whom the costs should fall.

2.171 Another reason may be that it is seen purely as an alternative to a final dispute resolution and it is judged solely on that basis. However, it is a technique which can be used to produce useful results in a number of situations, and can be a success in relation to appeals even if it fails to resolve the matter conclusively and simply narrows down issues, in a more formal and rigorous way than, for example, the statement of common ground which it is necessary to provide in advance of a planning appeal.[253]

---

[251]   For example, see consultation documents in 1997, 2001and 2002; Major Infrastructure Inquiry Rules 2002; Planning and Access for Disabled Circulars 2002 and 2005; Compulsory Purchase Circular 02/2003; Crichel Down Rules Circular 06/2004; PPS 11 Regional Planning (2004); PPS 12 Development Plans (2004); Planning Obligations Circular 05/2005; Planning Policy Wales; the Barker Report (2006).

[252]   Sir Henry Brooke, 'Mediation and Planning: The Role of Mediation in Planning and Environmental Disputes', [2008] JPEL 1390.

[253]   Andy Grossman, 'Mediation in Planning – from talking the Talk to Walking the Walk', [2009] JPEL Occ Paper 24.

2.172 It is an issue which will not go away, and the relevance and utility of mediation is all the greater given the reality of resourcing of the public sector today. It is capable of reducing costs, while it has the similar advantage of allowing an independent expert to be involved but with control remaining with the parties.

OTHER ALTERNATIVE REMEDIES

2.173 Alternative remedies for disputes or complaints may be provided in different ways. In a work on judicial review it is not the place to provide a full account of the policy background and practice in relation to each of these. Instead, the main elements will be briefly explained and the relationship with judicial review outlined.

2.174 Three important themes throughout these alternatives are:

(a)   the extent to which they deal with individual grievances or with more general systemic or administrative faults;

(b)   the extent to which they concentrate on merits or simply the legality of decisions;

(c)   the relationship of the principles applied to those applied by the courts.

Tribunals

2.175 Tribunals can now be viewed not so much as an alternative to the courts, which they were originally, but as specialised courts with their own procedures. They have developed from an ad hoc system of specialist supervisory and adjudicative bodies. Depending on the terms of reference of the particular tribunal, it reviews the legality and/or the merits of decisions. They concentrate on individual grievances. Tribunals are dealt with in detail in Chapter 4.

Inquiries

2.176 Inquiries take two forms. The first is the ad hoc inquiry into a single event or issue. The second is the mechanism by which appeals against adverse decision or proposals are made.

2.177 The first is usually a fact-finding exercise, although recommendations can be made to ministers or those establishing the inquiry.[254] These do not usually provide a specific remedy to an aggrieved individual, and are usually concerned with the merits of particular decision or with more general issues. The inquiries, and the decisions, are themselves amenable to judicial review.

2.178 The second is most often used in the areas of planning, highways, compulsory purchase, and other environmental matters. While originally these were also conceived as fact-finding exercises, and the Inspector reported to the minister who made the decision, now the vast majority of such appeals are determined by the Inspector.

---

[254]   Inquiries Act 2005.

2.179 Partly as a result of the search for speedier and cheaper determination of such appeals, the vast majority are determined without an actual formal inquiry, with cross-examination of the evidence. Most are dealt with by informal hearing or written representations.

2.180 These inquiries are therefore concerned with merits and not usually with more general policy issues. Again, these inquiries or determinations are subject to either statutory appeal to the court or judicial review.

2.181 As noted above, there are calls for mediation to be used in appropriate cases to deal with an appeal, instead of an inquiry or another mechanism, and successful pilot projects have been promoted by the Planning Inspectorate.

Internal complaints systems

2.182 Internal complaints systems were not previously regarded as effective mechanisms, largely because they were perceived to lack the necessary independence and impartiality. Nevertheless they have become an established part of the dispute landscape for four main reasons:

(1) First, from a more general management and audit perspective it is considered that organisations can learn from the mistakes highlighted by the complaints process, and so improve performance generally and minimise future errors.

(2) Secondly, external review by ombudsmen has resulted not only in exhortations from public bodies to have such internal systems to minimise external complaints, but has also increased the use of 'local settlements' by means of internal review when the external complaint is notified to the public body.

(3) Thirdly, clearly influenced by considerations of relative cost and speed, there has been strong policy support for such mechanisms, although of course a tension exists between these aims if the internal complaints system rejects the complaints and it nevertheless proceeds to external review.

(4) Fourthly, this policy has been given statutory force in some instances and the processes given formal recognition, such as for local authority standards committees, explained below, or for the National Health Service or under the Housing Act 1996.[255]

2.183 Such internal review is of course usually concerned with the merits of individual complaints but it may, if properly used, spill over into more general policy and administrative reviews. Other than in special cases such as local Standards Committees, such internal procedures are not usually concerned with enforcing legal principles, or have an independent element.

Standards

2.184 While grievances or complaints usually relate to a decision which affects an individual complainant and the purpose of the complaint is to seek redress, there is

---

[255] Local Authority Social Services and National Health Service Complaints (England) Regulations 2009 (SI 2009/309); Housing Act 1996, s 202.

another area where the aim is essentially holding to account those who made errors. The mechanism can be used to assist in a wider complaint process, or can be considered a sufficient remedy itself.

2.185 The issue of standards of conduct of elected members and public officials is wider than simply the principles of judicial review. Much of it is concerned with rules appropriate to the operation of Parliament, or the relations between Ministers and civil servants. Nevertheless, the two overlap in that the principles of natural justice relating to bias overlap with the regime governing interests and participation in decisions; the principles of fettering discretion and predetermination also overlaps with interests and the public perceptions of these; and legal principles relating to relevant considerations and proper purposes overlap with the general principles contained in codes of conduct.

2.186 Although issues of sleaze, expenses and improper conduct have recently had a higher profile in relation to Westminster, this issue has a longer history of legislative intervention in relation to local government. The result is a regime which is more accessible to complainants. The old National Code of Local Government Conduct, adopted under the Local Government and Housing Act 1989, was subject to review by the Nolan Committee on Standards in Public Life which dealt with the Standards of Conduct in Local Government.[256]

2.187 The same general principles of public life as apply elsewhere in the public sector were applied to local government but these were to be made more specific, and it was recommended that the old Code should be replaced by a Code that would in part be prescribed nationally and part determined by local discretion. The recommendation of the report was that observance of the Code would be enforced by council's standards committees with disciplinary powers, subject to a right of appeal to an independent tribunal. Much of the new Code is concerned with personal and prejudicial interests and restrictions on participation in decision-making.

2.188 The Government responded to the Nolan Committee's report,[257] and the main difference was that the Government preferred to entrust serious member misconduct to an Independent Standards Board in England, and kept a role for the Ombudsman in Wales.

2.189 The Local Government Act 2000 requires every council to adopt a code of conduct for members, based upon a model code and general principles to be specified by the Secretary of State by order. In practice, all parts of the model code are mandatory.[258] Every authority must also establish a standards committee to promote and maintain high standards of conduct within the authority and to monitor the operation of the code. The Standards Committee must contain some independent members.[259]

---

[256] Third Report, published in July 1997 (Cm. 3702-1).

[257] In two papers – 'Modernising Local Government in Wales; a New Ethical Framework' published by the Welsh Office in June 1998; and for England 'Modernising Local Government; a New Ethical Framework', published in April 1998.

[258] Local Authorities (Model Code of Conduct) Order 2007 (SI 2007/1159); Local Authorities (Model Code of Conduct) (Wales) Order 2008 (SI 2008/788 (W.82)).

[259] For England this is 25 per cent, see Standards Committee (England) Regulations 2008 (SI 2008/1085); for Wales, the minimum is 50 per cent, see Standards Committee (Wales) Regulations 2001 (SI 2001/2283 (W.172)), as amended.

2.190 The 2000 Act provided that alleged breaches of codes of conduct by members would be investigated by the Commissioner for Local Administration in Wales or Ethical Standards Officers of the Standards Board for England. Following an investigation, the Local Commissioner/ethical standards officer could refer the alleged breach of the code of conduct to the Adjudication Panel for adjudication by a case tribunal, or to the monitoring officer, or decide that there is no breach or no action need be taken. As a result of the Local Government and Public Involvement in Health Act 2007, in England there is now more local investigation and determination and Standards for England, as it is now called, deals only with the most serious allegations.

2.191 Members of the Adjudication Panel for Wales are appointed by the National Assembly in Wales. In England, from January 2010 the Adjudication Panel for England became the First-tier Tribunal (Local Government Standards in England) as part of the General Regulatory Chamber. A person who is brought before a case tribunal may be represented by counsel, a solicitor, or any other person they would like to represent them. Among other sanctions, a full case tribunal may suspend or disqualify someone from being a member or becoming a member of any relevant authority for up to five years.

2.192 The role of the monitoring officer was also enhanced, and is crucial to the operation of the system.

2.193 The system is therefore designed for two purposes. First, and foremost, to maintain public confidence in local government.[260] Secondly, to promote good practice and to discipline councillors who breach the Code. It thus does not provide a direct remedy for an individual aggrieved by any decision or action.

2.194 Nevertheless, it may provide an effective remedy in two ways. First, if the matter is raised with the monitoring officer, this may result in a review of the actual decision if it is also alleged that the decision is also legally defective. Secondly, if the complainant is seeking 'vindication' rather than a specific individual outcome, this can provide a cost free route. One of the 'main elements' of the Localism Bill introduced to Parliament in December 2010 is the proposal to 'abolish the Standards Board regime'. The Bill seeks to leave most standards issues to the individual local authority, but this may well continue to provide these two alternative remedies.

Audit

2.195 Audit is a term usually associated with financial reporting and management analysis. As with the private sector, this plays an important role across the whole public sector. Standard financial reporting has always been necessary to ensure probity, and more recent developments such as economy and impact studies, Best Value, performance indicators etc are intended to not only to deliver value for money but also to ensure that the implementation of policy is delivered properly and effectively.

2.196 Such accountability is of course at a general level and may be valuable for those with a specific interest in a policy or issue being audited. However, in relation to local government there are also long established powers relating to the legality of decisions which are available to the auditor and which members of the public may request to be

---

[260]   *Richardson & Orme v North Yorkshire County Council, the First Secretary of State & Brown & Potter Ltd* [2004] 2 All ER 31.

used. This has the following advantages for anyone thinking about instituting a judicial challenge: the reaction of the auditor may be a good guide to how successful an independent challenge would be; if the auditor accepts the complaint then the authority may reverse the decision to avoid an audit challenge or adverse report; and it would pass the costs of any eventual court action on to the auditor.

2.197 In England responsibility for audit arrangements in governed by the Audit Commission Act 1998 and is undertaken by the Audit Commission for Local Authorities and the National Health Service in England. In Wales, the Auditor General for Wales[261] has responsibility under the Public Audit (Wales) Act 2004. Private sector firms may be appointed by the Commission or the Auditor General as auditors for any authority. In August 2010 the Government announced that the Audit Commission would be scrapped, and that from 2012, local authorities would be able to appoint their own external auditors. At the time of this work going to press, this is still being considered but it is unlikely to alter the detailed powers of the auditor.

2.198 The duties of the auditor, historically called the district auditor, in respect of the legality of decisions were described as follows:[262]

> 'The district auditor holds a position of much responsibility. In some respects he is like a company auditor, he is a watchdog to see that the accounts are properly kept and that no one is making off with the funds. ... In other respects, however, the duties of a district auditor go far beyond those of a company auditor. He must see whether, on the financial side, the councillors and their officers have discharged their duties according to law. He must listen to any elector who makes objection to the accounts. He must make his own investigation also. If he finds that the councillors or the officers, or any of them, have expended money improperly, or unreasonably, or allowed it to be so expended, it is his duty to surcharge them ....'

2.199 The surcharge provisions, by which individual councillors could be forced to repay unlawful sums, were controversial and were eventually repealed by the Local Government Act 2003, but the rest of this description remains good.

2.200 The public can raise issues with the auditor who must consider whether in the public interest he should make a report on any matter in order that it may be considered by the body concerned or brought to the attention of the public.[263] He is also to consider whether the public interest requires an immediate report rather than a report at the conclusion of the audit. The authority is then under a duty to give consideration to it.

2.201 Where it appears to the auditor that an item of account is 'contrary to law' he may apply to the court for a declaration to that effect.[264] Essentially this means if the action represented by the item of account is unlawful and in principle includes a breach of the fiduciary duty a court can declare that is the position.[265]

2.202 The threat of such action on the part of the auditor is clearly very important, and where the auditor expresses a view in a report, as opposed to actually seeking a

---

[261] Originally established under the Government of Wales Act 1998, s 90.
[262] *Asher v Secretary of State for the Environment* [1974] Ch 208 at 219, Lord Denning M.R.
[263] Audit Commission Act 1998, s 8 and the Public Audit (Wales) Act 2004, s 22.
[264] Audit Commission Act 1998, s 17(1); Public Audit (Wales) Act 2004, s 32.
[265] For an explanation of the fiduciary duty, see para **13.104**.

declaration, it is open to an authority to seek judicial review of that view and itself ask for a declaration.[266] While the court had reservations about using judicial review in this way, as opposed to waiting for an application for a declaration by the district auditor, the auditor acquiesced on the basis that the matter should be determined quickly so the court proceeded to hear the applications.

2.203 As a further power, the auditor may issue an advisory notice if he has reason to believe that the body or an officer of the body is about to make or has made a decision, or is about to take or has begun to take a course of action, which involves or would involve the body incurring expenditure which is unlawful.[267] Such a notice requires the authority to give the auditor not less than a maximum of 21 days' notice in writing before taking that decision or action.

2.204 The auditor is also a useful tool for obtaining information, since he has a right of access to all documents relating to an audited body which appear to him to be necessary for the purposes of his statutory functions.

2.205 In addition, all persons interested may inspect the accounts to be audited and all books, deeds, contracts, bills, vouchers and receipts relating thereto, and they may make copies of them.[268] Indeed, in *Veolia*,[269] an environmental activist claimed to be entitled to inspect and take copies of schedules to the waste management contract between the authority and the company. The company asked the local authority not to disclose the documents on the ground of commercial confidentiality and brought proceedings to compel the authority to keep the documents confidential. The High Court held that the legislative materials supported a broad approach, and that Parliament's intention in using the words 'relating to' was simply that there should be an enquiry as to the factual connection between the limited category of documents mentioned on the one hand and the accounts to be audited on the other. The contract itself, and any invoice paid under it, related to the accounts. The Court found that the concern about commercial confidentiality was understandable, but there was no duty to keep commercial confidentiality under the statutory provision. This permits wider access to information than would be possible under the Freedom of Information Act 2000.

Ombudsmen

2.206 While the auditor is primarily concerned with general issues of financial and management accountability, but have a more minor role for individual grievances, the ombudsmen are the opposite. Established primarily as an individual grievance remedying institution, they have developed a more general administrative audit role and promote good administrative practice. Nevertheless, they remain primarily concerned with providing a remedy where appropriate for an individual who has suffered injustice.

2.207 Since the Parliamentary Commissioner for Administration was created in 1967, there has been a proliferation of Ombudsmen. This term 'ombudsman' does not appear in the formal statutory title of the three main Ombudsmen – the Parliamentary Commissioner,[270] the Health Services Commissioner,[271] and the Commission for Local

---

266 *R v District Auditor, ex p West Yorkshire Metropolitan CC* [1985] RVR 191; and *R v District Auditor, ex p Leicester City Council* [1985] RVR 191.
267 Audit Commission Act 1998, s 19A; Public Audit (Wales) Act 2004, s 33.
268 Audit Commission Act 1998, s 15(1); Public Audit (Wales) Act 2004, s 30(1).
269 *Veolia ES Nottinghamshire Ltd v Nottinghamshire County Council* [2009] EWHC 2382 (Admin).
270 Parliamentary Commissioner Act 1967.

Administration.[272] However, these are known generally as the Parliamentary Ombudsman, the Health Services Ombudsman and the Local Government Ombudsman.

2.208 The term 'ombudsman' is now becoming more widely understood and is given statutory recognition in some instances, such as the Public Services Ombudsman for Wales,[273] and the Housing Ombudsman.[274] Indeed the general concept has been widely accepted and, while these and various other bodies are statutory bodies with a formal remit to deal with public sector bodies, there are numerous other non-statutory ombudsmen dealing with the public and private sectors,[275] and statutory ombudsmen dealing with the private sectors.[276]

2.209 The detailed remit, and exclusions from jurisdiction, of each of these bodies is beyond the scope of this work. Indeed, each scheme has its own detailed rules relating to jurisdiction, exclusions, access, procedure, and remedies. However, the following comments can be made about the three main Ombudsmen schemes.

2.210 Their remit is to investigate allegations of injustice through maladministration, although the Health Services Ombudsman has a wider jurisdiction to also include clinical judgement.

2.211 The term maladministration has never been defined by statute but has been left deliberately flexible. In the second reading debate on the Parliamentary Commissioner Bill, the Minister stated that the characteristics of maladministration include 'bias, neglect, inattention, delay, incompetence, ineptitude, perversity, turpitude, arbitrariness and so on', and this has become known as the 'Crossman catalogue'.[277] It remains a flexible concept to deal with different and changing situations. It is thus wider than, but overlaps with, judicial principles and although it is largely about how decisions are reached it can involve the merits of 'bad rules'.

2.212 This overlap raises the issue of what the relationship between the courts and the Ombudsmen should be, and the main issue is whether it should be cheaper, more accessible justice in accordance with legal principles, or a different concept. Clearly it is different in the sense that it is a wider concept, but where they do overlap the issue is whether authorities should be subjected to two regimes and the complainant should be allowed to choose between two different mechanisms with different remedies available.

2.213 This issue involves three issues – the statutory position; the judicial approach; and the respective remedies.

2.214 First, for all three of the main Ombudsmen, there is a statutory exclusion to the effect that they should not investigate where the person aggrieved has or had a right of appeal or review to a tribunal, or where the person has or had a remedy in any court of law. However, this is subject to the qualification that an investigation may be undertaken if the ombudsman is satisfied that in the circumstances of the case it is not reasonable to

---

[271] Health Services Commissioner Act 2003.
[272] Local Government Act 1974.
[273] Public Services Ombudsman (Wales) Act 2005.
[274] Housing Act 1996.
[275] For example the Waterways Ombudsman.
[276] For example the Pensions Ombudsman.
[277] HC Deb Vol 754, c 51 (1966).

expect the complainant to resort to that remedy. This has been interpreted liberally by the ombudsmen not only on the basis that the cost of challenges to the courts are a sufficient reason, but also on the basis that since 1967 the principles of judicial review have expanded and so the overlap is now much greater than it was thought to be.

2.215 Secondly, this approach to the wide discretion has been supported by the courts.[278] In addition, as with the approach to mediation described above, the courts have encouraged the use of this alternative to judicial review.[279] This approach raises two main issues.

(1) Given the respective time scales, where complaints to the ombudsmen can be made after the three months period for judicial review has expired, and any investigation is unlikely to be completed within that time scale in any event, such an approach relies either on the courts extending the three month period for bringing an action, which is risky, or proceedings must be commenced and then stayed, which undermines the cost advantages.

(2) The objection that this means that authorities which are acting in a manner which the courts define as lawful, may nevertheless be told they should not act in that way, is rejected not only on the basis that this must be is what Parliament intended by enacting this system, but also because the remedies provided by the two systems are different.

2.216 Thirdly, the remedies provided under the ombudsmen schemes appear less effective. The schemes rely on persuasion in that the ombudsmen have power only to recommend particular redress. Again the substance of this is not defined and is left very flexible. It may range from recommending a formal apology to a substantial award of financial compensation. There is, however, no formal power to impose a particular remedy or to quash or overturn decisions which have been made.

2.217 In practice, the public bodies do comply in the vast majority of cases. Where there is non-compliance then additional powers are given to issue a special or further report. This will be raised in Parliament in the case of the Parliamentary Ombudsman, and in the case of the Local Ombudsman additional publicity for it and the response, at the expense of the authority, can be required by the Ombudsman.

2.218 Over the years there have been calls for judicial enforcement of Ombudsmen's decisions, particularly in the case of the Local Government Ombudsmen, on the basis that any non-compliance, however infrequent, undermines the authority of the institution and deprives the complainant of what an independent body thinks appropriate. These calls, however, have been resisted largely on the basis that it would undermine the flexibility and informality of investigations.

2.219 The Ombudsman, therefore, is both an alternative dispute resolution mechanism in that the principles applied overlap with those of the courts but a remedy can be provided more cheaply, and also an appropriate dispute resolution mechanism in that

---

[278] See e g *R v Local Commissioner for Local Government for North and North East England, ex p Liverpool City Council* [2001] 1 All ER 462.

[279] See *R v Lambeth London Borough Council, ex p Crookes* (1995) 29 HLR 28; R (on the application of *Scholarastica UMO v Commissioner for Local Administration* [2003] EWHC 3202 (Admin).

the more flexible investigatory procedure is more appropriate to the issues at stake and the principles of maladministration are not restricted to existing legal principles but can be tailored to the particular situation.

2.220 Nevertheless, while this is itself a valuable alternative to litigation, it is instructive to note that, in the search for speed, economy and more flexible dispute resolution, there are now powers for the Ombudsmen to appoint and pay a mediator or other appropriate person to assist in the conduct of an investigation.[280]

2.221 This is a clear reminder that no one mechanism is appropriate for all public law disputes or grievances. Judicial review is certainly a valuable and important tool, but a range of alternatives exist which may provide cheaper and more appropriate solutions.

---

[280] Parliamentary Commissioner Act 1967, s 3; Local Government Act 1974, s 29; and the Health Service Commissioners Act 1993, para 1A of Sch 2; as amended by the Regulatory Reform (Collaboration etc between Ombudsmen) Order 2007 (SI 2007/1889).

Chapter 3

PRACTICE AND PROCEDURE

JUDICIAL REVIEW IN THE ADMINISTRATIVE COURT

3.1   The procedure for bringing a judicial review claim is governed by CPR part 54 backed up with reference to Practice Direction 54. They need to be read with part 8 CPR and section 31 of the Senior Courts Act 1981 which tied an application to the High Court for prerogative relief as well as an application for a declaration and/or an injunction to an application for judicial review. Part 54 develops judicial review further in that it makes it clear that it does not depend only on the prerogative remedies but also on the nature and the functions of the body that is subject to challenge.

Pre-Action Protocol

3.2   Prior to bringing a claim for JR a claimant should first comply with the Pre-Action Protocol for Judicial Review.[1]

3.3   The Pre-Action Protocol requires a letter to be sent by the claimant to the defendant before making a claim for JR.[2] A standard form of the letter is to be found in Annex A to the Protocol and should be used in normal circumstances.[3] Relevant factors include:

- The letter should contain the date and details of the decision, act or omission being challenged, a summary of the facts and an outline of the alleged unlawfulness.[4]

- If the claimant seeks particular information, which he considers relevant to the claim, the details of the information sought should be contained in the letter.[5]

- A copy of the letter before claim should be sent to any interested parties.[6]

- A claim should not normally be made until after the proposed reply date given in the letter before claim unless the circumstances of the case require the claim be made more sooner.[7]

---

[1]   See http://www.justice.gov.uk/civil/procrules_fin/contents/protocols/prot_jev/htm.
[2]   Para 8 of Pre-Action Protocol.
[3]   Para 9 of Pre-Action Protocol.
[4]   Para 10 of Pre-Action Protocol.
[5]   Para 10 of Pre-Action Protocol.
[6]   Para 11 of Pre-Action Protocol.
[7]   Para 12 of Pre-Action Protocol.

- The letter of claim should set out the details of the actions which it is desired the defendant should take, ie what remedy is sought.[8]

- The letter before claim should specify a proposed reply date, usually 14 days.[9]

- The reply to the letter before claim should also be made in a standard form in most cases.[10] The reply should set out the public body's response to the claim and whether the claim will be resisted in whole or in part.[11]

- The protocol does not suspend the time limits for making a claim for JR. As such the Protocol is not appropriate where a claim would become out of time if the Protocol was followed. In such cases the claim should be filed and the claim form used to explain why the Pre-Action Protocol was not followed.

- Neither is the Protocol appropriate in 'urgent cases' where there is a need for an interim order to compel or prohibit a public body from acting. The Protocol gives examples of urgent cases such as an immigration claim where the claimant is due to be removed from the UK and a housing claim where a local authority has failed to secure interim accommodation for a homeless claimant.

- Failure to comply with the pre-action protocol may affect prospects of recovering costs. In *R (Kemp) v Denbighshire Local Health Board* [2006] EWHC 181 (Admin) the claimant had succeeded in obtaining funding relating to his nursing home costs but because he failed to comply with the pre-action protocol, no order for costs was made given that there was no evidence that the defendant would not have offered a review had a pre-action protocol letter been written. In addition, in *R (Ewing v Office of the Deputy Prime Minister)* [2006] 1 WLR 1260, Lord Justice Brooke stated at paragraph 54 that, '... Needless to say, if the claimant skips the pre-action protocol stage, he must expect to put his opponents to greater expense in preparing the summary of their grounds for contesting the claim, and this may be reflected in the greater order for costs that may be made against him if permission is refused ....'

3.4   Judicial Review is a two-stage process. The claimant must first obtain permission to apply for JR.

PRE-ISSUE CONSIDERATIONS

3.5   Applications for Judicial Review fall within the jurisdiction of the Administrative Court.[12] The JR procedure under Part 54 must[13] be used in a claim for JR where the claimant is seeking one of the prerogative orders[14] or an injunction restraining a person

---

8   See model letter at Annex A to Pre-Action Protocol.
9   Para 13 and model letter at Annex A of Pre-Action Protocol.
10   See model letter at Annex B to Pre-Action Protocol.
11   See model letter at Annex B to Pre-Action Protocol.
12   *Practice Direction – Judicial Review* (2000) PD 54, para 2.1.
13   CPR 54.2 is prescriptive and mandatory but CPR 3.10 gives the court general power to rectify procedural errors and the court will always seek to advance the overriding objective in preference to procedural formalism and technicalities.
14   CPR 54.2(a)–(c).

from acting in any office in which he is not entitled to act.[15] The JR procedure may be used in a claim for JR where the claimant is seeking either an injunction or a declaration.[16] A claim for JR may include a claim for damages but may not seek damages alone.[17]

Standing

3.6   Whether a claimant had sufficient standing to bring proceedings used to be a significant issue. Now the approach to standing is sufficiently generous that it is rarely an issue. Fundamentally, however, the court should not grant permission unless it considers that the claimant has sufficient interest (Senior Courts Act 1981, s 31(3)). The standing question at the permission stage is whether the claimant is a 'busybody' with 'no interest whatsoever', *R (Dixon) v Somerset CC* [1998] Env LR 111, 116–117, 330–331. Short of an abuse of process, the court will not refuse permission for an otherwise arguable challenge but will take care to satisfy itself that the claim genuinely reveals an arguable point. Auld LJ stated in *R (Noble) v Thanet DC* [2005] EWCA Civ 782:

> 'In [dismissing the appeal] I add a note of dissatisfaction at the way the availability of the remedy of judicial review can be exploited – some might say abused – as a commercial weapon by rival potential developers to frustrate and delay their competitors' approved developments, rather than for any demonstrated concern about potential environmental or other planning harm .... However seemingly complicated the issues are, or how sophisticated and technical the statement of facts and grounds supporting the initial claim for judicial review, they should be subject to rigorous examination by the single judge at the permission stage of a claim for judicial review'.

Duty of candour/disclosure

3.7   A claimant is under a duty to disclose all material facts in the claim form.[18] These include all facts known to the claimant at the time he applies for permission. The court may take account of those facts that he would have known had he made the proper and necessary inquiries before applying for permission.[19] The extent of inquiries the claimant should have made will depend on the circumstances of the case, including the nature of the case, the order for which the applicant is applying, the degree of legitimate urgency and the time available for making inquiries.[20] Non-disclosure is sufficient for the court to refuse the remedy sought,[21] to set aside permission[22] or refuse permission, and the claimant may be penalised in costs.

3.8   When setting out the facts and issues of law which demonstrate that the public body's action was unlawful the claimant should disclose any outstanding appeals against

---

[15]   CPR 54.2(d).

[16]   CPR 54.3.

[17]   CPR 54.3(2), a claim seeking only damages will be transferred out of the Administrative Court under CPR 54.20.

[18]   *R v Lloyds Corpn, ex p Briggs* [1993] 1 Lloyd's L Rep 176; *R v Jockey Club Licensing Committee, ex p Wright (Barrie John)* [1991] COD 306 and *R (Burkett) v Hammersmith and Fulham LBC* [2002] 1 WLR 1593 at para 50.

[19]   *R v Jockey Club Licensing Committee, ex p Wright (Barrie John)* [1991] COD 306.

[20]   *R v Jockey Club Licensing Committee, ex p Wright (Barrie John)* [1991] COD 306.

[21]   *R v Kensington General Cssrs, ex p Polignac (Princess)* [1917] 1 KB 486.

[22]   *R v SoS Home, ex p Sholola* [1992] Imm AR 135; *R v SoS Home, ex p Chinoy* (1991) 4 Admin LR 457, [1991] COD 381, DC; applications to set aside permission may now only be made rarely.

the decision,[23] or any rights of appeal that exist but have not been pursued and set out why judicial review is, in the circumstances, appropriate. The claim should identify any legislative provisions which purport to oust the court's jurisdiction and explain why the claimant contends the jurisdiction is not ousted.[24]

3.9   Equally, a defendant is required to satisfy the requirement of the duty of candour which applies from the outset and which applies to all information relevant to the issues of the case, not just documents. The point was explained by Lord Donaldson MR in *R v Lancashire County Council, ex p Huddleston* [1986] ALL ER 941 when he said this:

> 'This development [ie the remedy of judicial review and the evolution of a specialist administrative or public law court] has created a new relationship between the courts and those who derive their authority from public law, one of partnership based on a common aim, namely the maintenance of the highest standards of public administration ... The analogy is not exact, but just as the judges of the inferior courts when challenged on the exercise of their jurisdiction traditionally explain fully what they have done and why they have done it, but are not partisan in their own defence, so should be the public authorities. It is not discreditable to get it wrong. What is discreditable is a reluctance to explain fully what has occurred and why ... Certainly it is for the applicant to satisfy the court of his entitlement to judicial review and it is for the respondent to resist his application, if it considers it to be unjustified. But it is a process which falls to be conducted with all the cards face upwards on the table and the vast majority of the cards will start in the authority's hands.'

3.10   The Practice Direction to CPR Part 54 states (at para 12) that 'disclosure is not required unless
the court orders otherwise'. What this means is that CPR Part 31 (which sets out the rules applicable on standard disclosure) will not ordinarily apply on an application for judicial review unless the Court orders otherwise (CPR, PD 54A, para 12.1). One occasion when a court will order otherwise is when cross-examination is necessary to enable the court to establish the facts of a case for itself; *R (N) v M and others* [2003] 1 WLR 562, *R (Wilkinson) v Broadmoor Special Hospital Authority* [2002] 1 WLR 419. Disclosure is required to enable proper and effective cross-examination to take place.

3.11   In that exceptional category of judicial review involving inquiry into issues of fact, where disclosure has to be given, it is suggested that the best practice is to do so in accordance with the principles set out in CPR 31:

- the parties are required to help the court further the overriding objective which is to deal with cases justly. Dealing with a case justly includes dealing with the case in ways which are proportionate, CPR 3, s 1(2)(c);

- parties are required to disclose only the documents which:

  (i)   they rely upon;
  (ii)   adversely affect their own, or another party's, case;
  (iii)   support another party's case;

---

[23]   *R v Humberside CC, ex p Bogdal* [1992] COD 467; *R v Mid-Worcestershire Justices, ex p Hart* [1989] COD 397.

[24]   *R v Cornwall CC, ex p Huntingdon* [1992] 3 All ER 566 (substantive decision affirmed by CA at [1994] 1 All ER 694).

- document means anything in which information of any description is recorded. It will include, for example, not only letters and emails, but drafts, calendars, manuscript and post-it notes, voicemails, computer disks, documents stored on servers and back-up systems and documents that have been deleted and blogs;

- disclosure is required if a party has or at any time has had a document so that the existence of destroyed or lost documents or documents which have been passed on must be disclosed; and

- parties are required to undertake a reasonable search for disclosable documents.

3.12 In *R (Al Sweady) v Secretary of State for Defence* [2009] EWHC 2387 (Admin) the court emphasised that legal representatives have a duty to ensure that proper disclosure is given where there is to be cross-examination or in any case where the court makes findings of fact. The court made it plain that any infringements of the three basic human rights (Articles 2, 3 and 5) would be subject to intense scrutiny and that in such a case the duty of disclosure is 'even more acute'.

Time limits for bringing a claim

3.13 The claim form must be filed promptly and in any event within three months of the date when the grounds for the claim arose.[25] The court has jurisdiction to grant an extension of time.[26] An extension cannot be agreed between the parties without the court's consent.[27] The time limits run from the date the grounds for JR arose, not when the claimant became aware of the decision being challenged. That the claimant was delayed in becoming aware of the grounds for challenge is a factor which may be relevant to the question of whether there is good reason to extend the time limit.

3.14 Claims must be brought 'promptly' and the courts have emphasised that a claim will not necessarily be prompt merely because it has been made within the three-month period.[28] Promptness has not been tested as a test for delay with regard to European Convention or EU law but is likely to be compatible. The ECtHR rejected a challenge to the former provisions dealing with time-limits which are materially identical to the current provisions of the CPR as it considered the requirement was proportionate in pursuit of a legitimate end of ensuring claimants acted quickly to avoid prejudicing the rights of others.[29] The ECJ has held that it is compatible with EU law for domestic law to lay down reasonable time-limits[30] and has not challenged a similar rule to the JR time-limit.[31]

3.15 Where the court considers there has been undue delay it may refuse to grant permission or decide that it would be inappropriate to grant relief sought on the application[32] if it considers the granting of relief would cause substantial hardship, or

---

[25] CPR 54.5.
[26] CPR 3.2(a). Where a shorter time-limit is provided by statute or subordinate legislation that shorter time-limit applies: CPR 54.5(3).
[27] CPR 54.2. That a defendant does not object to a claim being brought out of time may be relevant to the court exercising its discretion.
[28] Eg *R v Independent Television Cssrs, ex p TV NI Ltd, The Times*, 20 December 1991.
[29] Application no. 4167/98 *Lam v UK*.
[30] Case 33/76 *Rewe v Landwirtschaftskammer Saarland* [1976] ECR 1989 at para 5.
[31] Case C-208/90 *Emmot v Minister for Social Welfare and the Att-Gen* [1991] ECR I-4269.
[32] *R v Swansea City Council, ex p Main* (1981), *The Times*, 23 December.

prejudice the rights of any person or be detrimental to good administration.[33] The court may consider delay even when the defendant indicates that no point would be taken on delay.[34] In *R (Law Society) v LSC* [2010] EWHC 2550 (Admin) Moses LJ stated at paragraph 116 that:

> 'The need for promptness in judicial review is well-known. Good public administration requires finality. This is because public authorities need to have certainty as to the legal validity of their decisions and actions, and third parties need to be able to rely on those decisions and actions. Promptness has been recognised to be particularly important where the interest of other parties is concerned: see for example *R v Monopolies and Mergers Commission, ex parte Argyll Group plc* [1986] 1 WLR 763 at 782–783; *R v Independent Television Commission, ex parte TVNI Limited* [1996] JR 60; and the authorities cited in *Fordham's Judicial Review Handbook*, Fifth Edition, 26.2.2.'

3.16   The court may grant an extension of time for the bringing of a claim.[35] Any extension granted may be subject to any conditions which the court considers appropriate.[36] Undue delay should be determined once and for all and should not be an issue at both the permission stage and the substantive hearing.[37]

Alternative remedy[38]

3.17   It is worthy of note that a claim in judicial review should be a last resort, see *Cowl v Plymouth City Council* [2002] 1 WLR 803. The courts cannot compel an Alternative Dispute Resolution ('ADR') but a failure to provide or pursue an alternative remedy may affect the grant of permission and/or the grant of relief to an otherwise successful claim and/or the award of costs. Differing methods of ADR include complaints procedures, mediation, complaint to a relevant Ombudsman and round table meetings.[39]

3.18   The Court of Appeal has emphasised the importance of using alternative administrative means, such as an internal complaints procedure.[40] In its discretion the court may refuse to grant a remedy at the substantive hearing if an alternative remedy exists or existed and should have been used.[41] However, it has been indicated that to refuse a remedy after a full substantive hearing and costs would not be in line with the overriding objective.[42]

3.19   The claim form should state whether an alternative remedy exists and whether or not the claimant is pursuing it.[43] Reasons should be given as to why JR is the appropriate remedy instead of the alternative remedies.[44]

---

[33]   SCA 1981, s 31(6).
[34]   *R v Dairy Produce Quota Tribunal, ex p Wynn Jones* [1987] 2 EGLR 9.
[35]   CPR 3.1(2)(a).
[36]   CPR 3.1(3).
[37]   *R v CICB, ex p A* [1999] 2 AC 330 per Lord Slynn at 341, HL.
[38]   Where an alternative remedy exists: *R v SoS for the Home Dept, ex p Swati* [1986] 1 WLR 477; or existed and should have been used: *R (Carnell) v Regents Park College and Conference of Colleges Appeal Tribunal* [2008] ELR 268 at paras 31–33.
[39]   See Chapter 2 from para 2.122.
[40]   *R (Cowl) v Plymouth CC* [2002] 1 WLR 803.
[41]   *R v Brentford General Cssrs, ex p Chan* [1986] STC 46; *R v Birmingham CC, ex p Ferrero Ltd* [1993] 1 All ER 539.
[42]   *R v Chief Constable of Merseyside Police, ex p Bennion* [2001] ACD 114.
[43]   *R v Humberside CC, ex p Bogdal* [1992] COD 467.
[44]   *R v SoS for the Home Dept, ex p Swati* [1986] 1 WLR 477 at 483 per Sir John Donaldson MR (as was), CA.

Academic challenges

3.20   It is well established that although the Administrative Court has a discretion to entertain claims that have become academic, such discretion should be exercised cautiously and only where there are good public interest reasons for doing so. Recently in *R (Raw) v London Borough of Lambeth* [2010] EWHC 507 (Admin), Stadlen J stated at paragraph 68 that:

> 'I have given anxious consideration to whether that is a course which I should follow in this case. I have come to the conclusion that it is not. My first concern is that as a matter of first principle given that part of the policy lying behind the general rule against entertaining academic claims is to discourage the proliferation of such claims, it seems to me that there is a risk of defeating that objective if, having declined to adjudicate upon a claim on the ground that it is academic the court proceeds to set out what its views would have been if it had adjudicated on it. Albeit such views would be of no binding effect, the fact that the court might be prepared to express them in the form of obiter dicta might nonetheless encourage future claims. Allied to this is the related consideration that on one view expressions of view by the court in the form of obiter dicta, after it has declined to entertain a hypothetical claim, are potentially even more unsatisfactory than obiter dicta in the form of views expressed as part of such an adjudication. Such obiter dicta may place the losing party in the invidious position of deciding whether to ignore the court's views on the ground that they are obiter dicta, to implement them even though they consider them to be wrong or to incur the expense of seeking permission to appeal against them even though the outcome of such an appeal, even if favourable to that party, would still take the form of further obiter dicta.'

THE CLAIM FORM AND SERVICE

3.21   The court's permission to proceed is required in a claim for JR.[45] The claimant must file a claim form in the Administrative Court Office.[46] Since the regionalisation of the Administrative Court in April 2009 a claim can be filed in London, Cardiff, Manchester, Birmingham or Leeds. Further, Form N464 allows an application to be made for transfer of the judicial review hearing to a more convenient local court centre if the requirements set out in PD 54D 5.2 are met. The requirements include the reason for the preference, the region in which both parties and their representatives are based, the ease and cost of travel, the speed within which the decision is sought, whether it is desirable to administer or determine the claim in another reason. Venue is also something that the judge determining the permission application needs to consider in appropriate cases. The claim is brought in the name of the Crown on the application of the claimant against the public body.[47]

Issuing the claim

3.22   A claim for JR is made using the JR claim form (N461) with the additional information prescribed in CPR 54.6, PD 16 para 15 and PD 54.

3.23   The Claim must state:

(a)   the claimant and claimant's solicitor;

---

[45]   CPR 54.4.
[46]   PD 54, para. 2.1.
[47]   PD Administrative Court [2000] 1 WLR 1654.

(b) the decision, act or omission challenged;

(c) the name and address of any person the claimant considers an interested person. Where the JR relates to ongoing proceedings all other parties to the original proceedings must be named as interested persons (CPR 54.6(1) and PD 54, para 5.1);

(d) that the claimant is pursuing JR (CPR 54.6(1)(b);

(e) any remedy sought, (including any interim remedy) that is being claimed (CPR 54.6(1)(c)) and any relief sought under the HRA 1998 (PD 16, para 15.1(2));

(f) a detailed statement of grounds for seeking JR, which should be set out on the Claim Form or accompany it;[48]

(g) a statement of the facts relied upon;

(h) an application for extending the time to file the claim form if necessary;

(i) any directions sought; and

(j) a statement of truth.

3.24 If the Human Rights Act 1998 is engaged further requirements arise:

(a) the form must state any relief sought under the HRA 1998 (PD 16, para 15.1(2));

(b) where the HRA is raised as an issue or a remedy under the HRA is sought precise details of the infringement alleged and the Convention right relied upon must be given (PD 16, 15.1(2)(a));

(c) where a declaration of incompatibility under section 4 of the HRA is sought, precise details of the legislative provisions and the alleged incompatibility (PD 16, 15.1(2)(d));

(d) where a HRA claim is founded on the finding of another court of tribunal, the details of that other court's finding (PD 16, 15.1(2)(e)); and

(e) where a HRA claim is founded on a judicial act which is alleged to have infringed a Convention right as provided by section 9 of the HRA, details of the judicial act and of the court in question (PD 16, 15.1(2)(f)).

3.25 Similarly if the claim raises a devolution issue, the claim form must specify that fact, and give a summary of the facts, circumstances and points of law on the basis of which it is alleged a devolution issue arises.[49]

---

[48] See PD 54, para 5.6 and also for (g), (h), and (i).
[49] PD 54, para 5.4.

3.26 PD 54, para 5.7 provides that the claim form must be accompanied by:

(a) any written evidence in support of the claim or any application to extend time;

(b) a copy of any order that the claimant seeks to have quashed;

(c) where the claim relates to the decision of a lower court or tribunal, an approved copy of the reasons for that decision;

(d) copies of any document relied upon by the claimant;

(e) copies of any relevant statutory material; and

(f) a list of the essential documents for advance reading by the court, with page references for the passages relied upon.

3.27 Two copies of a paginated and indexed bundle containing all the documents required under PD 54, paras 5.6 and 5.7 must be filed when the claim is issued (para 5.9 and CPR, r 54.6(2)).

Service

3.28 The claim form and the other documentation described above (see CPR, r 54.6(2)) must be served on the defendant and the other interested parties within seven days after the date of issue (CPR, r 54.7). Service must be by the parties and will not be completed by the court. An interested party is any person (other than the claimant and defendant) who is directly affected by the claim.[50] A person is directly affected if he would be affected by the grant of a remedy.[51] Any person may apply for permission to file evidence or make representations at the hearing of a Judicial Review.[52]

Acknowledgement of service

3.29 The defendant (and anyone else served with a claim form) must file an acknowledgement of service.[53] The acknowledgement of service must be filed not more than 21 days after service of the claim form.[54] The acknowledgment must be served on the claimant and any other person named in the claim[55] as soon as practicable, and no later than seven days after it is filed.[56] These time limits cannot be extended by agreement between the parties.[57] A party who fails to file an acknowledgement may be precluded from taking part in any permission hearing.[58] That party will not be excluded from the substantive hearing as long as he complies with CPR 54.14 or any other

---

[50] CPR 54.1(2)(f).
[51] *R v Rent Officer Service, ex p Muldoon* [1996] 3 All ER 498, [1996] 1 WLR 1103 at 1105, HL. *R v MMC, ex p Milk Marque Ltd and NFU* [2000] COD 329 at para 5 per Moses J – that a decision is of 'the utmost significance and importance' does not necessarily mean that the person is 'directly affected'.
[52] CPR 54.17.
[53] In accordance with CPR 54.8 – the correct form is N462 (as of April 2009). The acknowledgement should specifically deal with any argument to be advanced on grounds of delay since delay is an issue to be determined at the permission stage: *R v CICB, ex p A* [1999] 2 AC 330, [1999] 2 WLR 974, HL.
[54] CPR 54.8(2)(a).
[55] CPR 54.7(b).
[56] CPR 54.8(2)(b).
[57] CPR 54.8(3) and CPR 54.8(5) excludes CPR 10.3(2).
[58] CPR 54.9(1)(a).

directions made by the court.[59] Where a person takes part in the substantive JR the court may take his failure to file an acknowledgement of service into account when deciding what order to make as to costs.[60]

3.30 The acknowledgement of service must: (i) set out the summary grounds for contesting the claim (if contested); and (ii) the name and address of any person the filing party considers to be an interested party.[61] The acknowledgement may include an application for directions.[62] The Court of Appeal has given guidance as to what the summary grounds of defence should contain. In *Ewing v Office of the Deputy Prime Minister*[63] Carnwath LJ stated, at para 34:

> 'Neither the rules nor the practice direction expand on what is meant by "summary grounds". However, the "summary" required under this rule must be contrasted with the "detailed grounds for contesting the claim" and the supporting "written evidence", which are required following the grant of permission (CPR 54.14). In construing the rule, it is necessary also to have regard to its purpose, and place in the procedural scheme ... The purpose of the "summary of grounds" is not to provide the basis for full argument of the substantive merits, but rather ... to assist the judge in deciding whether to grant permission, and if so on what terms ... It should be possible to do what is required without incurring "substantial expense at this stage".'

3.31 Brooke LJ added, at paras 52–54:

> 'If they [the defendants] wish to incur greater expense in preparing a document that is more elaborate than the rules require at this stage, they should not expect to recover the extra expense from a claimant whose application is dismissed at the permission stage ... Needless to say, if the claimant skips the Pre-Action Protocol stage, he must expect to put his opponents to greater expense in preparing the summary of their grounds for contesting the claim, and this may be reflected in the greater order for costs that is made against him if permission is refused'.

URGENT CASES

3.32 The Administrative Court has introduced a procedure for urgent cases.[64] Claimants should complete a form requesting their case be considered urgently. The form requires the claimant to state: (a) the need for urgency; (b) the timescale sought for the consideration off the permission application; and (c) the date by which the substantive hearing should take place.[65] Where an interim injunction is sought, a claimant must, in addition, provide: (a) a draft order; and (b) the grounds for the injunction.[66]

3.33 The claimant must serve (by fax and post) the claim form and application for urgency on the defendant and interested parties, advising them of the application and

---

[59] CPR 54.9(1)(b).
[60] CPR 54.9(2).
[61] CPR 54.8(4)(a)(i) and (ii) – there is no requirement for the defendant to file evidence but there is nothing to stop a defendant filing evidence in an appropriate case.
[62] CPR 54.8(4)(b).
[63] [2005] EWCA Civ 1583.
[64] Practice Statement (Administrative Courts: Listing and Urgent Cases) [2002] 1 WLR 810.
[65] Ibid.
[66] Ibid.

that they may make representations. Those additional items are required where an interim injunction is sought which must be served by the claimant on the defendant in the same manner.[67]

3.34 The application for urgent consideration will be considered by a judge who, within the time requested, will make such orders as he considers appropriate.[68] Applications can be made and are dealt with out of hours in cases of real urgency.

3.35 In applications for interim relief where the claimant is about to be removed from the UK the Court of Appeal has given specific guidance.[69] Specific guidance has also been issued in relation to asylum seekers who have been refused support because they did not make their claims as soon as reasonably practicable (see s 55 of the Nationality, Immigration and Asylum Act 2002).[70]

3.36 In cases where the matter is so urgent that the JR would be moribund without an immediate hearing the judge may order what is known as a 'rolled up' hearing with the permission application to be heard orally with a substantive hearing immediately thereafter. Equally a rolled up hearing can be ordered if a speedy resolution to the dispute is needed. The judge will then set an accelerated timetable for the case to proceed including tight timetables for the production of evidence from the defendant and any interested parties and abridgement of time for the production of skeleton arguments.

INTERIM ORDERS

Directions

3.37 In addition to the case management directions given at the permission stage there can be occasions when it is necessary to seek further directions from the court either before or after the permission stage. Directions may be required either due to some additional information becoming available or thought to be available but not being released by the other side, circumstances that make an expedited hearing need to be sought or a case where the nature of factual dispute is such as to require the cross examination of a witness. Although the latter is a rare occasion it can occur. The Administrative Court has the power to deal with all such applications where the interests of justice require it.

3.38 Until the substantive judicial review hearing interim orders should normally be able to be dealt with on the papers. All parties are under a duty to be candid. Under CPR 54.16 no written evidence may be relied upon unless it has been served in accordance with the rules or in accordance with the directions of the court or the court gives permission. Although Rule 8.6(1) which deals with written evidence is expressly disapplied under CPR 54.16 the other provisions of Rule 8.6 that deal with requiring or permitting a party to give oral evidence or to attend for cross examination are available. Although cross examination is rarely sought or permitted and should be treated as the exception in judicial review cases if the interests of justice in an individual case require it

---

[67]   Ibid.
[68]   Ibid.
[69]   *R (Madan) v SoS Home* [2007] 1 WLR 2891.
[70]   *R (Q, D, KH, OK, JK H, T and S) v SoS Home* [2003] EWHC 2507 (Admin) Maurice Kay J and Practice Statement (Judicial Review: Asylum Support) [2004] 1 WLR 644 Collins J.

cross-examination can be ordered and does occur.[71] The same principles apply to disclosure.[72] It follows that neither disclosure nor cross examination is automatic.

3.39   Expedition may be ordered if the individual circumstances of the case require it. Most judicial review cases can be said to be urgent so the circumstances would have to take the case out of the ordinary queue. Examples of when expedition may be ordered include cases involving the liberty of an individual, the removal of an asylum seeker from the jurisdiction and cases where expedition is necessary in the interests of good public administration.

3.40   There is also the power to stay proceedings under CPR 54.10(2). If granted the stay would operate to restrain a public body from acting.[73] In effect it suspends the proceedings. It cannot be used to compel a public body to act.

Interim relief

3.41   Applications for interim relief will also be considered at the permission stage. Where there is an application for interim relief the judge may order a hearing for interim relief and permission. The court can grant interim relief pending the oral hearing or for a fixed period. The court can at the same time grant leave to the defendant to apply to discharge the interim injunction.[74] Interim relief can be granted before permission to proceed with the claim is given.[75]

3.42   Any applications for interim relief should be set out clearly in the claim form.[76] It does not automatically follow that if permission is granted that any interim relief sought will be forthcoming.[77] In most cases, if not all, interim relief will only be considered at a hearing where all the affected parties are present. The grant of interim relief in JR proceedings will normally follow the same principles as interim remedies in general proceedings.[78]

PERMISSION

3.43   The court will consider whether to grant permission without an oral hearing on the papers[79] when it will make an order either granting or refusing permission and giving any directions to the parties for the future course of the proceedings.[80] The judge's order and the reasons for his decision are then served upon the claimant,

---

71   *R (on the application of the Friends of Basildon Golf Course) v Basildon District Council* [2009] EWHC 66 – overturned by the Court of Appeal but not on the judicial review procedure followed where a witness gave oral evidence and was cross examined about the processes that he had followed as part of an EIA screening opinion. See also earlier paras **3.10** to **3.12** inclusive.

72   *R v Inland Revenue Commissioners, ex p National Federation of Self Employed and Small Businesses* [1982] AC 617 'Upon general principles, [disclosure] should not be ordered unless and until the court is satisfied that the evidence reveals grounds for believing that there has been a breach of public duty; and it should be strictly limited to documents relevant to the issue which emerges from the affidavits.' Lord Scarman at 654E–F.

73   *R v Secretary of State for Education, ex p Avon CC* [1991] 1 QB 558.

74   *R (Lawer) v Restormel BC* [2007] EWHC 2299 (Admin), [2008] HLR 20.

75   *M v Home Office* [1994] 1 AC 377 at 423.

76   CPR 54.6(1)(c).

77   *R v SoS Home Dept, ex p Doorga* [1990] COD 109, [1990] Imm AR 98, CA.

78   CPR 25 and the principles in *American Cyanamid Co v Ethicon Ltd* [1975] AC 396, [1975] 1 All ER 504, HL.

79   PD 54, para 8.4.

80   CPR 54.10(1). The court may direct a stay of the originating proceedings CPR 54.10(2).

defendant and any other person who filed an acknowledgement of service.[81] Where the court refuses permission on the papers or gives permission to proceed subject to conditions or on certain grounds only,[82] the claimant may not appeal but may request the decision be reconsidered at an oral hearing.[83] The request for such a hearing must be filed within seven days of the service of the reason for the decision.[84] The claimant, defendant and any other person who filed an acknowledgement will be given at least two days' notice of the hearing date. No party other than the claimant need attend a permission hearing unless the court directs otherwise.[85] If other parties attend the court is unlikely to make a costs order against the claimant.[86]

3.44 Permission should be granted if, on material before the court, without inquiring in depth, there is an *arguable* case for granting the relief the claimant seeks.[87] This initial filter exists 'to prevent the time of the court being wasted by busybodies with misguided or trivial complaints of administrative error and to remove the uncertainty in which public authorities might be left …'.[88] The granting of permission is within the court's discretion. The Court of Appeal has indicated that permission should be granted where a point exists which merits investigation on a full hearing, with both parties represented and with all relevant evidence and arguments on the law.[89] Initially it was thought the permission procedure would be used to filter out only the weakest of cases and permission would be granted if from the papers there appeared to be a point which might turn out to be an arguable case.[90] In short, permission should only be granted where the court is satisfied that the papers actually disclose that there is an arguable point (not merely that an arguable point might emerge on further consideration of the papers). Though permission will not necessarily be determined on a brief review of the papers an in-depth examination is inappropriate.[91]

3.45 In granting permission for JR the court may limit the grounds which the claimant may argue. This was the position prior to the introduction of the CPR and remains the case after its introduction.[92] Even if a ground has been refused at the permission stage it is within the court's discretion to allow the issue to be argued at the substantive hearing if it is in the interests of justice and the overriding objective.[93]

3.46 It is within the court's discretion to direct that there be an oral hearing of the application for permission and a claimant can ask to have any refusal of permission reconsidered at an oral hearing.[94]

---

[81] CPR 54.11.
[82] CPR 54.12(1).
[83] CPR 54.12(3).
[84] CPR 54.12(4).
[85] PD 54, para 8.5.
[86] *R (Mount Cook Land Ltd et al v Westminster CC)* [2003] EWCA Civ 1346.
[87] *IRC v Nat Fed of Self-Employed and Small Businesses Ltd* [1982] AC 617 at 644, HL, per Lord Diplock; *R v SoS for the Home Dept, ex p Swati* [1986] 1 All ER 717, [1986] 1 WLR 477, CA.
[88] Per Lord Diplock in *R v IRC, ex p National Federation of Self-Employed and Small Businesses Ltd* [1982] AC 617 at 643.
[89] *R v SoS Home, ex p Begum* [1990] COD 107; [1990] Imm AR 1.
[90] Lord Diplock in *R v IRC, ex p Nat Fed of Self-Employed and Small Businesses Ltd* [1982] AC 617 at 644a.
[91] *R (Davey) v Aylesbury Vale DC* [2008] 1 WLR 878 at para 12 per Sedley LJ 'While there may be cases in which it is necessary or helpful to explore issues in depth at this stage, such cases must be quite exceptional. The proper place for a full exploration of evidence and argument is at the hearing of a claim which has been shown at the permission stage to be arguable.'
[92] *R v Staffordshire CC, ex p Ashworth* (1996) 4 Admin L Rep 373; *R v Advertising Standards Authority, ex p City Trading* [1997] COD 202 (Pre-CPR). CPR 54.12(1)(b)(ii).
[93] *R (Smith) v Parole Board* [2003] 1 WLR 2548 at para 12–16 and CPR 54.15.
[94] CPR 54.12.

3.47 The court retains its inherent jurisdiction to set aside orders, including orders to grant permission to apply for JR.[95] The inherent jurisdiction of the court to set aside permission will be used sparingly, for instance where permission has been granted before the defendant has put in an acknowledgement of service.[96]

3.48 On granting permission for JR the court may give any appropriate directions for the future conduct of the claim.[97] The court can order a stay of the proceedings to which the JR claim relates.[98]

RENEWAL OF THE APPLICATION FOR PERMISSION

3.49 If permission is refused or the scope of the claim is limited to only certain of the grounds raised, a claimant is entitled to request an oral hearing by renewing his application (CPR 54.12(3)). The Notice of Renewal (form 86b) must be filed within seven days of the service of the decision (CPR 54.12(4)). The renewal form should set out grounds for renewal in light of the judge's reasons for refusing permission on the papers (*Practice Statement* [2002] 1 All ER 633, 636d). Although not granted as of right, it is extremely rare for a request for an oral hearing to be refused.

The oral hearing

3.50 An oral hearing will be listed for a 30 minute hearing and all parties will be given at least two days notice of the hearing date (CPR 54.12(5)). Where it is believed that 30 minutes will be insufficient for the permission hearing, a written estimate of the predicted time and a request for a special fixture should be made to the Listing Office, see the ACO Notes for Guidance [2005] JR 5 at 10.4. Whilst generally neither the defendant nor any interested party is needed to attend – PD54, para 8.5 – the court may require them to do so if it considers it necessary, and in any event, they may often wish to do so. Oral permission hearings should be short and not a full-scale dress rehearsal of the substantive hearing, *R (Mount Cook) v Westminster CC* [2003] EWCA Civ 1346, at [71] per Auld LJ.

Appeal on permission

3.51 The procedure for applying for permission is the same in the High Court in both civil and criminal matters. However, if permission is refused in the High Court the appeal process is different for criminal and civil matters. The refusal of permission to apply for JR in civil matters may be appealed to the Court of Appeal. The same right does not exist in criminal matters.[99] 'Criminal matters' are those that arise in the context of criminal proceedings where, if the proceedings were carried to their conclusion, they might result in the conviction of a person.[100] If the High Court considers that the claim raises an important point of law but that the claim would fail it may grant permission and then dismiss the substantive claim and certify that the claim raises a point of law of general public importance.[101] The claimant may then petition the Supreme Court for

---

[95]   *R v SoS Home, ex p Chinoy* (1991) 4 Admin LR 457, [1991] COD 381, DC.
[96]   *R (Webb) v Bristol CC* [2001] EWHC 696 (Admin).
[97]   CPR 54.10.
[98]   CPR 54.10(1).
[99]   SCA 1981, s 18(1).
[100]   *Amand v Home Secretary* [1943] AC 147.
[101]   *R v DPP, ex p Camelot plc* (1998) 10 Admin L Rep 93.

permission to appeal against the dismissal of the substantive claim where he could not petition against the refusal to grant permission for judicial review.

3.52   Where permission is refused in a civil matter, after an oral hearing, the claimant may apply to the Court of Appeal for permission to appeal against that refusal.[102] The claimant must make the application for permission to appeal within seven days of the decision of the High Court.[103] The claimant must lodge:

(a)   an appellant's notice;

(b)   an additional copy of the notice and additional copies to be sealed and returned for the defendant and any interested parties;

(c)   the order of the High Court refusing permission;

(d)   the claim form;

(e)   a copy of the original decision being challenged;

(f)   any written evidence in support of the applicant's application;

(g)   a copy of the High Court bundle; and

(h)   a transcript of the High Court judgement.

3.53   The Court of Appeal will usually grant permission for JR rather than granting permission to appeal.[104] The JR will then proceed in the High Court unless the Court of Appeal orders otherwise.[105] In exceptional circumstances the Court of Appeal may decide to hear the substantive JR itself rather than return it to the High Court.

3.54   Where the Court of Appeal refuses permission to appeal against the High Court's refusal to grant permission there is no further appeal.[106] When the Court of Appeal grants permission to appeal and then hears the appeal but refuses permission to apply for JR then the Supreme Court does have jurisdiction to entertain a petition for leave to appeal and if permission is granted the appeal itself.[107]

SUBSTANTIVE HEARING

3.55   Where permission is granted, the court will give case management directions (CPR 54.10). These directions may include provisions about serving the claim form and evidence on other persons. Where a claim is made under the HRA, a direction may be made for giving notice to the Crown or for joining the Crown as a party (see PD 54,

---

[102]   CPR 52.15.
[103]   CPR 52.15(2).
[104]   CPR 52.15(3).
[105]   CPR 52.15(4).
[106]   *R v SoS Trade and Industry, ex p Eastaway* [2000] 1 WLR 2222 at 2226 per Lord Bingham, see *R (Burkett) v Hammersmith and Fulham LBC* [2002] 1 WLR 1593 at para 12.
[107]   *R (Burkett) v Hammersmith and Fulham LBC* [2002] 1 WLR 1593 at para 13.

para 8.2). Once permission has been granted, other parties cannot apply to have permission set aside (CPR 54.13) although the court can use its inherent jurisdiction to do so.[108]

3.56 If permission is granted, a defendant or any other person served with the claim form who wishes to contest the claim (or support it on additional grounds) must file and serve detailed grounds and any written evidence relied upon within 35 days after service of the order giving permission (CPR 54.14). A party relying upon any documents not already filed must file a paginated bundle of those additional documents with his detailed grounds (PD 54, para 10.1). Claimants and their legal advisors are under an obligation to reconsider the merits of the claim in the light of written evidence served by other parties.

3.57 Any person may apply to file evidence or make representations at the hearing (CPR 54.17). Prior to the CPR a person was regarded as sufficiently affected to justify being joined only if they were affected without the intervention of an intermediate agency: *R v Liverpool CC, ex p Muldoon* [1996] 1 WLR 1103, HL. If permission to be joined is granted to a third party, it may be given with conditions and the court may make directions (PD 54, para 13.2).

3.58 It is possible to determine the application for judicial review without a hearing where all parties agree (CPR 54.18).

Additional grounds

3.59 Where a claimant seeks to rely on additional grounds beyond those for which permission was given, notice must be given to the court and to the other persons who have been served with the claim form no later than seven clear days before the substantive hearing (or the warned date for the hearing) (PD 54, para 11.1). Permission must be sought for the additional grounds (CPR 54.15). The hearing on whether new grounds can be added will either be at the commencement of the substantive judicial review or by way of a further interim hearing. In considering whether to allow amendments to the grounds of JR the court will consider the general issues of whether any injustice will be caused to the defendant and whether the defendant can be compensated in costs. Generally new grounds are more likely to be allowed where issues of law are raised which do not require new evidence. If new grounds are allowed to be added but new evidence is required the court is likely to adjourn the hearing to allow the defendant to provide new evidence. In such circumstances the claimant is likely to be liable in costs for the additional work at the end of the substantive hearing whatever its outcome.

Skeleton arguments

3.60 The claimant must file and serve a skeleton argument not less than 21 working days before the hearing date (or warned date).[109] Other parties must file and serve their skeleton arguments not less than 14 working days before the hearing or warned date.[110]

---

[108] *R v Commissioner for Local Administration, ex p Field* [2000] COD 58.
[109] PD 54, para 15.1.
[110] PD 54, para 15.2.

The claimant's skeleton argument must be accompanied by a paginated and indexed bundle of all the relevant documentation.[111] Skeleton arguments must contain:

(a)   a time estimate for the complete hearing, including delivery of the judgement;

(b)   a list of issues;

(c)   a list of legal points to be taken (together with relevant authorities and page references for passages relied upon);

(d)   a chronology (with page references to the bundle of documents);

(e)   a list of the essential documents for advance reading by the judge; and

(f)   a list of persons referred to.[112]

The hearing

3.61   Hearings are conducted in public, subject to general principles justifying a hearing in private. The hearing is conducted on the basis of written material and legal submissions to the court. There are rare cases where the court will require witnesses to attend for cross-examination.[113] In addition to the materials before the decision maker, it was held in *R v SoS for the Environment, ex p Powis*[114] that the court will consider the following categories of fresh evidence:

(a)   evidence bearing on any question of fact as to whether the decision maker had jurisdiction;

(b)   evidence on whether any procedural requirements were observed; and

(c)   evidence to prove misconduct – examples are bias on the part of the decision maker, and fraud or perjury by a party.

3.62   The court considers whether the grounds for seeking JR are made out, and whether, in its discretion, it ought to grant relief.

3.63   The position where the decision-making authority has expressed more than one reason for a decision and the claimant successfully impugns/challenges one or some of them arose in *R v Broadcasting Complaints Commission, ex p Owen*.[115] May LJ said that where the reasons could be separated, and the court is satisfied that, despite one reason being bad in law, the same decision would have been reached for the valid reasons, then, within its discretion, the High Court would not intervene by way of JR.

---

[111]   PD 54, para 16.1.
[112]   PD 54, para 15.3.
[113]   *R (Wilkinson) v Responsible Medical Officer Broadmoor Hospital* [2002] 1 WLR 419.
[114]   [1981] 1 WLR 584 at 595 per Dunn LJ.
[115]   [1985] QB 1153 at 1177.

CONVERSION TO A COMMON LAW CLAIM

3.64 The court has power under CPR 54.20 to order JR proceedings to continue as proceedings brought under CPR Part 7. This power maybe exercised where the relief claimed is a declaration, an injunction, or damages, and the court considers that such relief should not be granted on an application for JR but might be granted in an ordinary claim. The purpose underlying the CPR, and this power of conversion, is to provide 'a framework which is sufficiently flexible to enable all issues between the parties to be determined'.[116]

CONSENT ORDERS

3.65 Where the parties come to an agreement to dispose of the application it is possible to obtain an order from the court to put that agreement into effect without needing to attend at court. The procedure is in PD54, para 17. A document setting out the proposed order and containing a short statement of the matters relied on as justifying the making of the order, quoting the authorities and statutory provisions relied on, should be signed by all the parties. The original of this document, together with two copies, should be handed into the appropriate Administrative Court Office, which will put it before the judge. If the judge is satisfied that an order can be made, the proceedings will be listed for a public hearing where the order will be pronounced without the parties needing to attend. If the judge is not satisfied that it would be proper to make the order, the proceedings will be listed in the usual way.

APPEALS

3.66 Appeals against a decision of the court granting or refusing the JR claim may only be appealed to the Court of Appeal with permission.[117] Permission will only be given where there is a real prospect of success or there is some compelling reason why the appeal should be heard.[118] An issue of general public importance would be one such compelling reason.

3.67 Permission should be sought from the court of first instance (the High Court) initially.[119] If permission is refused by the court of first instance, an application for permission to appeal may be made to the Court of Appeal by filing an appellant's notice setting out the grounds for appeal and including the application for permission to appeal within 21 days of the decision of the lower court or within such time as directed by the lower court.[120] The applicant for permission must serve the appellant's notice on each respondent within seven days of filing the notice.[121] The respondent is not required to take any action until permission to appeal is granted unless directed to take some action by the court.[122]

---

[116] Per Lord Woolf in *R (Heather) v Leonard Cheshire* [2002] HRLR 30 at para 39.
[117] CPR 52.3.
[118] CPR 52.3(6).
[119] CPR 52.2.
[120] CPR 52.3(3) and 52.4.
[121] CPR 52.4(3) and PD 52, para 21.
[122] PD 52, para 22.

3.68 The applicant must file in the Court of Appeal office:

(a) an appellant's notice with two additional copies for the court and one copy for each respondent;

(b) a skeleton argument;

(c) a sealed copy of the order being appealed;

(d) the order of the court below refusing permission to appeal and the reasons;

(e) any written evidence in support of the application to appeal; and

(f) those parts of the bundle in the JR below which are reasonably necessary to deal with the appeal (including the claim form, written evidence, any decision letter and the key documents).[123]

3.69 The documents required to be included in the appeal bundle are set out at PD52, para 19. The appellant does not need to serve the appeal bundle on the respondents at this stage. He must serve the appellant's notice and his skeleton argument on the respondent unless the court directs otherwise.[124]

3.70 The application for permission to appeal is usually dealt with on the papers by a Lord Justice of Appeal, though the court may direct that an oral permission hearing be held with or without the respondent present. Where permission is refused, the applicant can, within seven days, apply for an oral hearing to reconsider the refusal.[125] If permission is granted the applicant must serve the appeal bundle (already filed with the Court of Appeal) on the respondents within seven days of the order giving permission to appeal.[126]

3.71 If permission to appeal was given in the lower court the appellant's notice and bundle should be filed within 14 days of the lower court's decision and should be served within seven days of filing. The respondent may file a notice asking the Court of Appeal to uphold the decision of the court below on different or additional grounds.[127] The respondent must file a skeleton argument in the Court of Appeal and serve it on the other parties.[128]

3.72 If permission is granted, the appeal is a review of the decision of the court below[129] and the appeal will be allowed only where the court below was wrong or the decision unjust because of some procedural irregularity.[130] No party may rely on any matter not contained within the appeal notice unless the court gives permission.[131] The Court of Appeal will not allow grounds to be argued that were not raised in the lower

---

[123] PD 52, para 5.6.
[124] PD 52, para 5.24.
[125] CPR 52.3(4).
[126] PD 52, para 6.2.
[127] CPR 52.5(2)(b).
[128] PD 52, para 7.7 and 7.7B.
[129] CPR 52.11(1).
[130] CPR 52.11(3).
[131] CPR 52.11(5).

court.[132] Nor will fresh evidence usually be admitted.[133] The Court of Appeal retains the discretion to depart from these limitations where the justice of the case requires it.[134]

3.73   There is a further appeal to the Supreme Court where permission is given either by the Court of Appeal or the Supreme Court.

COSTS

3.74   The most important provision in relation to costs is section 51 of the Senior Courts Act 1981, which provides the court with full discretion to determine the issue of costs, subject to enactments and rules of court. CPR 44.3 confirms that the court has discretion to order one party to pay the costs, the amount of those costs and when they are to be paid.

The permission stage

3.75   Paragraphs 8.5 and 8.6 of the Part 54 Practice Direction relate to the permission hearing and state that the defendant or other interested party need not attend a hearing on the question of permission unless the court directs otherwise. Additionally, where the defendant or any interested party does attend a permission hearing, the court will not make an order for costs against the claimant in cases where the defendant has attended and argued successfully that permission should not be granted save that: (1) the court will order that the claimant pays the costs of the preparation and filing of the acknowledgement of service, and (2) in exceptional circumstances: *Mount Cook Land and Another v Westminster City Council* [2003] EWCA Civ 1346 where Auld LJ sets out a non-exhaustive list of exceptions.[135] The rationale for ordering the claimant to pay the costs associated with the acknowledgement of service is because the defendant is obliged to file one.

3.76   Costs are usually not awarded to the claimant when the Administrative Court decides that permission should be granted. That applies both to a decision on the papers and after an oral hearing. This is because the costs issue can be dealt with at the substantive hearing, but more likely because the order is silent in relation to costs it is deemed to contain an order for costs in the case. Exceptionally, if the claimant has followed the pre-action protocol and receives no response from the defendant so that the claimant is obliged to issue proceedings and at that stage the defendant springs to life and files an acknowledgement of service that reveals the hopelessness of the claimant's case the defendant may not obtain any order for costs and the claimant may receive his even though he decided to discontinue after receipt of the acknowledgement of service from the defendant. Where permission is refused on consideration of the papers, if the defendant expressly asks for costs, the claimant will usually pay the costs of preparation and filing of the acknowledgement of service unless there are exceptional circumstances.[136]

---

[132]   *R (H) v SoS Home* [2002] 3 WLR 967 at para 47.
[133]   CPR 52.11(2).
[134]   *E v SoS Home* [2004] QB 1044 at paras 81–82.
[135]   See para 76(5) and (6).
[136]   *Mount Cook Land Limited v Westminster City Council* [2003] EWCA Civ 1346.

Substantive hearing

3.77 The general rule in costs provides that the unsuccessful party will be ordered to pay the costs of the successful party. However, the court may decide to make a different order having regard to all the circumstances of the case, but, in particular, to the conduct of the parties and whether a party has succeeded in part of the claim. The conduct in this context means whether the parties have followed any relevant pre-action protocol to try to settle the proceedings and the manner in which they have pursued or defended the case. For many judicial review hearings the court will want to conduct a summary assessment of costs 44 PD 7 (paragraph 13.2 (2)). The Court will normally do so in any case lasting less than one day. A schedule of costs must be served not less than 24 hours before the hearing. The court will not make a summary assessment of the costs of a publicly funded litigant but so assess the costs payable by them. In all other cases the issue of costs is likely to go off for detailed consideration by the costs judge.

3.78 Other relevant considerations include:

- Discontinuance. This falls into two parts:

  (1) before permission is considered. In those cases the general rule is that no order for costs is made. The exception is where there is a plain and obvious case: *R v Royal Borough of Kensington and Chelsea, ex p Ghrebregiosis* (1994) 27 HLR 602 and see the example given in paragraph **3.76**, and

  (2) discontinuance after permission is granted but before a substantive hearing. In *R v Liverpool City Council,l ex p Newman* (1993) 5 Admin LR 669 it was held that there was a general rule that the defendant would recover his costs where it could be shown that the discontinuance was as a result of the claimant's recognition of the likely failure of his challenge but the situation was different where some step had been taken by the defendant which rendered the claim unnecessary to be continued. In *R v Boxall v Mayor and Burgess of Waltham Forest London Borough Council* (2001) 4 CCLR 258 the court said:

  > 'The over-riding objective is to do justice between the parties without incurring unnecessary Court time and consequently additional costs. At each end of the spectrum there will be cases where it is obvious which side would have won had the substantive issues been fought to a conclusion. In between, the position will, in differing degrees, be less clear. How far the Court will be prepared to look into the previously unresolved substantive issues will depend on the circumstances of the particular case, not least the amount of costs at stake and the conduct of the parties. In the absence of a good reason to make any other order the fall-back is to make no order as to costs.'

  The Court should take care to ensure that it does not discourage parties from settling judicial review proceedings, for example, by a local authority making a concession at an early stage.

- Partial success. In *PR (Bateman) v Legal Services Commission* [2001] EWHC Admin 797 the claimants succeeded in quashing a decision of the Legal Services Commission but were deprived of 25 per cent and 15 per cent of their costs respectively of the issues on which they failed. CPR 44.3 can 'properly and where appropriate should be applied in such a way as positively to encourage litigants to be selective as to the points they take and positively to discourage litigants taking a multiplicity of bad points', see Munby J at para 18.

- Sanctions. The ordinary costs orders can be departed from because of a party's conduct. The conduct does not have to be causative of the loss (contrast wasted costs orders). In *Aegis Group PLC v Commissioners Inland Revenue* [2005] EWCH 1468 (Ch), a late response to a judicial review pre-action protocol letter with no adequate explanation for the delay resulted in the defendant recovering only 85 per cent of his costs. Conduct can include refusing ADR. In practice this means mediation or failure to follow a complaints procedure, see *Halsey v Milton Keynes General NHS Trust* [2004] EWCA Civ 576, [2004] 1 WLR 3002 [2004] 4 All ER 920.

- Indemnity. Costs can be awarded on an indemnity basis where there has been 'unreasonable behaviour of such a high degree that it can be characterised as exceptional', *Terry v LB Tower Hamlets* 15 Dec 2003 QBD. Examples include taking 'almost every possible point under the sun', see *R v Costwold DC, ex p Kissel* February 28 1997 unreported, or failure to give proper disclosure – *R (Banks) v SSEFRA* [2004] EWHC 416 (Admin).

- Under section 51 of the Senior Courts Act 1981 the Court has power to award costs against a non-party. This is an exceptional power but will ordinarily be exercised where the third party has controlled the proceedings or hopes to benefit from them so as to be the real party *Dymocks Franchise Systems (NSW) Pty Ltd v Todd* [2004] UKPC 39, [2004] 1 WLR 2807.

- Legal Aid. The fact that a party is in receipt of public funding is not to be taken into account in deciding whether and what costs order to make, see section 22 of the Access to Justice Act 1999. Lord Justice Kay in a report of a working party entitled 'Litigating the Public Interest' stated at paragraphs 36–8 and 103 (http://www.liberty-human-rights.org.uk/publications/6-reports/litigating-the-public-interest.pdf):

    'The view was also expressed that many members of the judiciary are not sufficiently aware of the difference that not ordering costs *inter partes* makes both to lawyers doing legal aid work and to the CLS. For lawyers the rates of pay that their work will attract are considerably higher where the work is paid by their client's opponent. Just as the success fee in CFA cases is used to subsidise those CFA cases that the lawyer does not win, so cases paid at *inter partes* rates effectively subsidise cases paid at legal aid rates. For the CLS an *inter partes* costs order made on a legally-aided matter means that they are likely to have to pay out little themselves on the case and therefore have more funds available for other cases. An order that the lawyers in a legally-aided matter be paid by the CLS is a straight drain on the Commission's funds. Making an *inter partes* costs order against a public authority on a legally-aided matter is not a simple matter of robbing Peter to pay Paul.'

- In terms of assessment, the commonly used formula now is that there be 'detailed assessment of the claimant's [or other assisted party's] publicly funded costs'. The SCCO costs guide suggests 'there be detailed assessment of the costs of the claimant which are payable out of the Community Legal Service Fund' [annex to the SCCO Costs Guide 2006].[137]

---

[137] Appendix A6 to the Supreme Court Costs Office Guide 2006.

- A successful defendant or interested party defending a claim against a publicly funded client may in certain situations apply to have their costs paid by the LSC where they will not recover them against the client. The requirements are that it must be 'just' and 'equitable' for the Order to be made. The application *must* be made within three months of the making of the relevant costs order.

Protective costs order

3.79   Certain public law cases have issues of broader public interest which are unlikely to be resolved unless the claimant's exposure to liability to pay the defendant's costs is capped. An unsuccessful publicly funded litigant is entitled to a 'costs protection' on the basis that they can only be required to pay more than the amount 'which is a reasonable one' for them to pay having regard to their means and their conduct in relation to the dispute (Access to Justice Act 1999, s 11). This is known as a Protective Costs Order (PCO). There has been a growth of litigation concerning Protective Costs Orders. The principles were stated by Lord Phillips in *R (Corner House Research) v Secretary of State for Trade and Industry* [2005] 1 WLR 2600 at 74.

> 'We would therefore restate the governing principles in these terms:
>
> 1.   A protective costs order may be made at any stage of the proceedings, on such conditions as the court thinks fit, provided that the court is satisfied that:
>   i)   the issues raised are of general public importance;
>   ii)   the public interest requires that those issues should be resolved;
>   iii) the applicant has no private interest in the outcome of the case;
>   iv)   having regard to the financial resources of the applicant and the respondent(s) and to the amount of costs that are likely to be involved it is fair and just to make the order;
>   v)   if the order is not made the applicant will probably discontinue the proceedings and will be acting reasonably in so doing.
> 2.   If those acting for the applicant are doing so pro bono this will be likely to enhance the merits of the application for a PCO.
> 3.   It is for the court, in its discretion, to decide whether it is fair and just to make the order in the light of the considerations set out above.'

3.80   Certain of the principles have been controversial, in particular in environmental cases. In the case *of R (on the application of Buglife) v Thurrock Thames Gateway Development Corporation and others* [2008] EWCA Civ 1209 the Court of Appeal upheld an order capping the amount that the claimant charity would have to pay if it lost the case at £10,000. This was in a challenge to a planning permission granted for a distribution hub which was likely to destroy/affect nationally valuable invertebrates. The Master of the Rolls said that there was 'no difference in principle between the approach to PCOs in cases which raise environmental issues and the approach in cases which raise other serious issues and *vice versa*' (para 17).

3.81   However in *R (on the application of Garner) v Elmbridge BC, Gladedale Group and Network Rail Infrastructure* [2010] EWCA Civ 1006 the Court of Appeal considered an appeal by Mr Garner, an architect whose practice specialised in historic building conservation, who sought to challenge a grant of planning permission for the redevelopment of Hampton Court Station opposite to and in the setting of the grade 1 Hampton Court Palace. The Aarhus Convention and an EU Directive were directly engaged. Mr Garner sought a PCO. Sullivan LJ said[138] 'Turning then to the two

---

[138]   Para 39.

grounds on which Nicol J refused a PCO, I accept the appellant's submission that in an Article 10a[139] case there is no justification for the application of the issues of "general public importance/public interest requiring resolution of those issues" in the *Corner House* conditions. Both Aarhus and the directive are based on the premise that it is in the public interest that there should be effective public participation in the decision-making process in significant environmental cases (those cases that are covered by the EIA and IPPC directives); and an important component of that public participation is that the public should be able to ensure, through an effective review procedure that is not prohibitively expensive, that such important environmental decisions are lawfully taken. In summary, under community law it is a matter of general public importance that those environmental decisions subject to the directive are taken in a lawful manner, and, if there is an issue as to that, the general public interest does require that that issue be resolved in an effective review process. The *Corner House* principles are judge-made law and in accordance with the *Marleasing* principle those judge-made rules for PCOs must be interpreted and applied in such a way as to secure conformity with the directive.' On the second ground which was whether the costs of the proceedings were to be considered on subjective or objective bases Sullivan LJ continued 'Even if it is either permissible or necessary to have some regard to the financial circumstances of the individual claimant, the underlying purpose of the directive to ensure that members of the public concerned having a sufficient interest should have access to a review procedure which is not prohibitively expensive would be frustrated if the court was entitled to consider the matter solely by reference to the means of the claimant who happened to come forward, without having to consider whether the potential costs would be prohibitively expensive for an ordinary member of "the public concerned"'.[140]

3.82   On 15 November 2010 the Ministry of Justice published proposals for Consultation in response to Lord Justice Jackson's report on costs, 'Reform of Civil Litigation Funding in England and Wales'. The consultation period ends on 14 February 2011. Lord Justice Jackson had proposed a system of qualified one way costs shifting in certain cases including environmental judicial reviews. His proposal was that:

> 'Costs ordered against the claimant in any claim [covered by QOCS] shall not exceed the amount (if any) which is a reasonable one for him to pay having regard to all the circumstances including:
>
> (a)   the financial resources of all the parties to the proceedings, and
> (b)   their conduct in connection with the dispute to which the proceedings relate.'

3.83   Under this arrangement, in most cases unsuccessful defendants would continue to be liable for claimants' costs, but unsuccessful claimants would only be liable for defendants' costs if and to the extent that it would be reasonable. The Ministry of Justice, through its Consultation Paper, is seeking views on whether qualified one-way costs shifting should only be available in judicial review cases where the claimant is an individual, or whether it should extend to cases brought by non-commercial organisations in the public interest. It considers (as Jackson LJ did) that the existing 'loser pays' rule will continue to apply to commercial claimants.

3.84   The government makes clear in its consultation paper that it is working to codify the Civil Procedure Rules to codify the law on PCOs in environmental judicial reviews so

---

[139]   Directive 83/337/EEC which was directly applicable.
[140]   Para 46.

as to make the law more certain and transparent. The amended Rules will encourage applications for PCOs early in the proceedings alongside the consideration of permission. The amendments are expected to come into effect in April 2011.

Chapter 4

THE TRIBUNAL SYSTEM

INTRODUCTION

4.1   The passing of the Tribunals, Courts and Enforcement Act 2007 has brought about a change in the framework of administrative law tribunals. The changes that it has brought about and is bringing about will alter the nature of the cases brought in the Administrative Court. In the circumstances it is appropriate to explain what is still a relatively new Tribunal system first of all in this chapter.

THE ROLE OF THE TRIBUNAL SYSTEM

Background

4.2   In May 2000 the Government asked Sir Andrew Leggatt to investigate and report on the delivery of justice through the Tribunals to ensure that Tribunals were 'fair, timely proportionate and effective', that the 'administrative and practical arrangements for supporting those decision-making procedures' were human rights compliant by being fair and impartial, that there were 'adequate arrangements' for improving people's knowledge and understanding of those rights in relations to disputes, and that tribunals functioned in such a way that made those rights and responsibilities a reality.

4.3   Leggatt was also asked to ensure that the arrangements for the funding and management of the tribunals and other bodies by Government Departments 'are efficient, effective and economical' whilst paying 'due regard both to judicial independence, and to ministerial responsibility for the administration of public funds'. Finally, that 'performance standards for tribunals are coherent, consistent and public; and effective measures for monitoring and enforcing those standards are established' and that 'Tribunals overall constitute a coherent structure for the delivery of administrative justice'.[1] Leggatt's Report, Tribunals for Users: One System – One Service, made a large number of criticisms of the present system and a correspondingly large number of recommendations. The main focus of his criticisms of administrative tribunals was their lack of independence from the departments they were intended to review, and the lack of uniformity in their structure.

4.4   The Government's response to Leggatt was a White Paper in July 2004,[2] in which the Government spelled out its five-year strategy around the following principles:

(a)   developing **policies that help empower citizens** and communities to manage their own problems, protecting them from crime and anti-social behaviour, and narrowing the justice gap;

---

[1]   See Leggatt's final report: 'Tribunals for Users – One System, One Service'.
[2]   'Transforming Public Service: Complaints, Redress and Tribunals' (Cm 6243).

(b)   moving out of courts and tribunals disputes that could be resolved elsewhere through better use of **education, information, advice** and **proportionate dispute resolution**;

(c)   **changing radically the way we deliver services** so that the courts, tribunals, legal services and constitutional arrangements are fit for purpose and cost effective; and

(d)   **re-shaping the Department of Constitutional Affairs' organisation and infrastructure** so that it is aligned structurally to meet the needs of the public and works well with the rest of government.[3]

4.5   The resulting legislation, the Tribunals, Courts and Enforcement Act 2007 (TCEA), has far-reaching implications for all those involved with the Tribunals, whether as individual applicants or government departments or agencies, or those who sit on the various Tribunals. The policy intent behind Part 1 (which deals with the new structure of Tribunals) is to 'create a new, simplified statutory framework from tribunals, bringing existing tribunal jurisdictions together and providing a structure for new jurisdictions and new appeal rights'.[4]

LEGISLATION

4.6   The TCEA creates the new role of Senior President of Tribunals (SPT) (TCEA 2007, s 2(1)).[5] To reflect the history leading up to the creation of the new system the SPT must, in carrying out the functions of that office have regard to: (a) the need for the Tribunals to be accessible, and (b) the need for proceedings before the Tribunals to be fair as well as being handled quickly and efficiently (s 2(3)). The members of the Tribunals must be 'experts in the subject matter of the law to be applied in which they decide matters' (s 2(3)(c)). Furthermore, the SPT must recognise 'the need to develop innovative methods of resolving disputes that are of a type that maybe brought before tribunals' (s 2(3)(d)).

4.7   The term 'tribunal' refers to the First-tier Tribunal (FTT), the Upper Tribunal (UT), the employment tribunal (ET), the Employment Appeals Tribunal (EAT) and the Asylum and Immigration Tribunal (AIT) (TCEA 2007, s 2(4)). The two new tribunals (FTT and UT) are to be divided into a number of Chambers each containing a certain limited number of jurisdictions, to reflect the specialist expertise of those sitting (s 7). In November 2008 the first two Chambers of the FTT came into existence.

4.8   At the time of writing the structure is as follows:

First-tier Tribunal:

• Social Entitlement Chamber: Asylum Control, Social Security and Child Support, and Criminal Injuries Compensation.

• Health, Education and Social Care: Care Standards, Mental Health, Special Educational Needs and Disability, Primary Care Lists.

---

3   White Papers, p 5.
4   Explanatory Notes, p 2.
5   The first holder being Sir Robert Carnwath, a Court of Appeal Judge.

- War Pensions and Armed Forces Compensation Chamber: War Pensions and Armed Forces Compensation.

- The General Regulatory Chamber: Charity, Claims Management Services, Consumer Credit, Environment, Environment, Estate Agents, Gambling Appeals, Immigration Services, Information Rights, Local Government Standards in England, and Transport.

- Immigration and Asylum Chamber: Immigration and Asylum

Tax Chamber:

- Tax

Upper Tribunal:

- Administrative Appeals

- Tax and Chancery

- Lands

- Immigration and Asylum.

4.9   The SPT presides over both the UT and the FTT. This means that the Tribunals are headed by an independent member of the judiciary. Furthermore, the UT is a superior court of record (TCEA 2007, s 3(5)), which allows the expert tribunal to develop its own case law where appropriate. The appointment of judges (the legal members) and members (experts, like medical practitioners and lay people) is subject to s 4 and Schedule 2 of the TCEA. Judges may be appointed if they satisfy the eligibility criteria (five years' legal experience or, if not, exceptionally, if the Lord Chancellor considers them to be suitable).[6] By s 31(2) certain judges are transferred-in – ie these are members of existing tribunals who automatically became FTT Judges when that tribunal's functions are assumed by the FTT. Similar provisions apply to the UT: s 5 and Schedule 3. Under s 6 certain judges automatically become judges of both FTT and UT: these include judges of the Appeal Courts in England and Wales, as well as Scotland and Northern Ireland, High Court Judges, Circuit Judges and District Judges.

4.10   Most of the present tribunals, some of them already part of the FTT, were appealed to the High Court whether by way of statutory appeal (for instance in the case of the Care Standards Tribunal) or judicial review (JR) (for instance, the Mental Health Review Tribunal). The new system is intended radically to reduce the number of judicial reviews through three specific provisions:

Review of decisions

4.11   First, each FTT is empowered to review its own decision whether by its own initiative or on an application by a person with a right of appeal: TCEA 2007, s 9(1) and (2)(a) and (b). This is subject to the exception of 'excluded decisions' which cannot be

---

6   The appointment is subject to a competition held by the Judicial Appointments Commission.

reviewed.[7] This power has been incorporated into the Rules so far brought into force in the Social Entitlement Chamber (SEC) and Health Education and Social Care Chamber (HESC). By way of illustration, the HESC Rules[8] deal with the issue of reviews in Part 5. Under rule 45, the Tribunal 'may set-aside a decision which disposes of proceedings, or part of such a decision and re-make the decision or relevant part of it, if: (a) the Tribunal considers it in the interests of justice to do so; and (b) one or more of the conditions in paragraph (2) are satisfied. These conditions are: (a) a document relating to the proceedings was not sent to, or was not received at an appropriate time by a party or a party's representative; (b) a document relating to the proceedings was not sent to the Tribunal at an appropriate time; (c) a party or a party's representative, was not present at a hearing related to the proceedings; or (d) there has been some other procedural irregularity in the proceedings'.

4.12   A party wishing for a decision (or part of a decision) to be set-aside must make a written application which must be received not later than 28 days 'after the date on which the Tribunal sent notice of the decision to the party' (Rule 45(3)). An application for permission to appeal to the UT under Rule 46 of the HESC Rules gives the Tribunal an opportunity under Rule 47(1) to consider whether the decision that is the subject of the proposed appeal should be reviewed. However, this power is subject to Rule 49(1)(a) which allows the Tribunal to review a decision under Rule 47(1) if, and presumably, only if, 'it is satisfied that there was an error of law in the decision'. In special education needs cases an application for a review of a decision may be made 'if circumstances relevant to the decision have changed since the decision was made' (Rule 48(2)).

4.13   The net effect of the right to review has yet to be seen. However, those dealing with reviews are likely to be the more senior members of the FTT judiciary. Some decisions will be easy: for instance, in the mental health jurisdiction the failure to notify a nearest relative of a hearing will be reviewable since it will be both a failure to serve a document and a procedural irregularity. Equally, making an order that is plainly unlawful – for instance, adjourning a hearing to ensure that a non-statutory recommendation is complied with – will also be easily reviewable. However, more difficulty arises where there is a challenge to the adequacy of the reasons given by the Tribunal, and/or where the coherence of the decision is challenged. If the reviewing Judge considers the reasons given to be inadequate or incoherent he will be obliged to review the decision on the grounds that it is in the interests of justice to do so and the inadequacy of the reasons constitutes some other procedural irregularity. In reaching his decision the reviewing Judge will have to consider whether the decision of the Tribunal was obviously wrong in law or whether the decision made was unreasonable on *Wednesbury* principles. The Explanatory Notes to the TCEA, ss 9 and 10 state that the power to review is 'intended to capture decisions that are clearly wrong, so avoiding the need for an appeal. The power has been provided in the form of a discretionary power for the Tribunal so that only appropriate decisions are reviewed. This contrasts with cases where an appeal on a point of law is made, because, for instance, it is important to have an authoritative ruling'.[9] This makes perfect sense in the context of the new Tribunal system where there is a desire for the UT to create its own case law. This point was emphasised the first time the UT was called upon to judicially review a case in which the FTT had reviewed itself. In *R (RB) v The First Tier Tribunal* [2010] UKUT 160 (ACC) in which the Senior President presided, the UT observed: 'The power to

---

[7]   These 'excluded decisions' are listed at Tribunals, Courts and Enforcement Act (TCEA) 2007, s 11(5).

[8]   The Tribunal Procedure (First Tier Tribunal) (Health, Education and Social Care Chamber) Rules 2008 (SI 2008/2699).

[9]   Taken from the Explanatory Notes to the Tribunals, Courts and Enforcement Act 2007.

review decisions is an important and valuable one. It is common ground that the powers of review on a point of law are intended, among other things, to provide an alternative remedy to an appeal. In a case where the appeal would be bound to succeed, a review will enable appropriate corrective action to be taken without delay'.[10] It could not have been intended that the power of review should enable the FTT to usurp the UT's function of determining appeals on contentious points of law. Nor could it have been intended to enable a later FTT panel (or the same Judge on a later occasion) to take a different view of the law from an earlier FTT decision where both views are tenable. '[I]f a power of review is to be exercised to set aside the original decision because of perceived error of law, this should only be done in clear cases'.[11] One critical observation the UT made concerned the length and detail of the FTT's review decision. The UT took the view that if an error is clear it should be possible to give reasons in a couple of paragraphs, drawing attention to an overlooked authority or statutory provision, or to agree with a ground of appeal.

4.14   Under the TCEA 2007, s 9(4), once the FTT has reviewed a decision, it <u>may</u> in the light of the review either: (a) correct accidental errors in the decision or in a record of the decision, (b) amend reasons given for the decision, or (c) set the decision aside. Where the decision is set-aside the FTT <u>must</u> either: (a) re-decide the matter concerned, or (b) refer the matter to the UT.[12] There is nothing in the Act that requires the renewed decision to be made by the individual Judge reviewing the decision. The Act simply requires the FTT to re-decide or refer the matter. The reviewing Judge may, for instance, quite properly set aside a plainly wrong decision, but consider it necessary for the new decision to be made by a full Tribunal having heard evidence from witnesses. In those circumstances, the reviewing Judge will remit the case.

Appeals to the Upper Tribunal

4.15   Under the TCEA 2007, s 11, any party to a case before the FTT has a right of appeal[13] to the UT 'on any point of law arising from a decision made by the First-tier Tribunal other than an excluded decision'.[14] That right may only be exercised with permission,[15] such permission may be given by either the FTT or the UT on an application by a party.[16] The excluded decisions are listed at s 11(5), and include: (a) an appeal against a FTT decision which itself was an appeal under the Criminal Injuries Compensation Act 1995, appeals against national security certificates under (b) the Data Protection Act 1998, and (c) the Freedom of Information Act 2000, and (f) 'any decision of the First-tier Tribunal that it is of a description specified in any order made by the Lord Chancellor'. Importantly, a decision made by the FTT under s 9 of the Act (ie to review or not to review, actions taken or not taken if a review is carried out, setting aside an earlier decision of the FTT or referring or not referring a matter to the UT) is excluded under (d) and (e).

4.16   If a case is brought before the UT the proceedings are governed by the Tribunals, Courts and Enforcement Act (TCEA) 2007, s 12 and the Rules.[17] Section 12 provides

---

10   RB at para 22.
11   RB at para 24.
12   TCEA 2007, s 9(5)(a) and (b).
13   TCEA 2007, s 11(2) subject to (8).
14   TCEA 2007, s 11(1).
15   TCEA 2007, s 11(3).
16   TCEA 2007, s 11(4)(a) and (b).
17   Tribunal Procedure (Upper Tribunal) Rules 2008 (SI 2008/2698).

that if the UT, in deciding an appeal, finds that the making of the decision concerned involved the making of an error on a point of law, the UT may (but need not) set aside the decision of the FTT and, if it does it must either remit the case to the FTT with directions for its reconsideration or remake the decision. If the UT remits the decision it may direct that the members of the FTT who are chosen to reconsider the case are not to be the same as those who made the decision that has been set-aside and can give procedural directions in connection with the reconsideration of the case by the FTT.[18] If the UT decides to re-make the decision, it may: (a) make any decision which the FTT could make if the FTT were remaking the decision, and (b) may make such findings of fact as it considers appropriate. The application for permission to appeal to the UT itself must be in writing and, generally, the application must be received by the UT no later than one month after the FTT that made the decision under challenge sent its notice of refusal of permission to appeal or refused to admit the application for permission to appeal.[19] In the case of an application under the Safeguarding Vulnerable Groups Act 2006, s 4 (ie from a decision of the Independent Barring Board) the period is three months from the date the decision challenged was sent to the appellant.[20] Rule 21(4) and (5) specify the formalities for the application. Rule 21(6) concerns the extension of time for making the application if it was made out of time (the applicant must give a reason). Rule 21(7) concerns the situation where the application was made too late to the tribunal below and it refused to admit the application; again the reason must be given and the UT '*must only admit the application*' if it is satisfied that it is in the interests of justice to do so.[21]

4.17 If the UT refuses permission to appeal it is obliged to send written notice of the refusal and written reasons for it.[22] These decisions will generally be made without a hearing (see Rule 34). However, where an application for appeal is refused or where permission is given, but only on limited grounds or subject to conditions,[23] without a hearing, and the case is a HESC mental health or special educational needs case or a safeguarding of vulnerable groups case, the appellant may apply for the decision to be reconsidered at a hearing.[24] Interestingly, as with the FTT, the UT has express powers to correct, set-aside and review its own decisions.[25] Under Rule 45 the UT may review its decision when a party applies for permission to appeal. However, the UT may do so if, and only if: (a) when making the decision the UT has overlooked a legislative provision or binding authority which could have had a material effect on the decision; or (b) since the UT's decision a court has made a decision that is binding on the UT and which could have had a material effect on the UT's decision had it been made before that decision. The obvious purpose, once again, is to ensure that obvious mistakes at the UT can be rectified without the additional delay and expense of an appeal to the Court of Appeal.

Judicial Review in the UT

4.18 Section 15 of the Tribunals, Courts and Enforcement Act 2007 grants the UT the powers to grant the following kinds of relief, ie: (a) a mandatory order, (b) a prohibiting

---

18 TCEA 2007, s 12(3).
19 Rule 21(3)(b).
20 Rule 21(3)(a). Until 3 November 2008 the appeal was to the Care Standards Tribunal.
21 Rule 21(7)(b).
22 Rule 22(1).
23 Under Rule 22(1)(2).
24 Rule 22(3) and (4).
25 Section 10 of the TCEA 2007, and Rules 41 to 43 which are similar to those discussed above in relation to the FTT.

order, (c) a quashing order, (d) a declaration, and (e) injunctions. There are two routes by which a judicial review case will come before the UT. An application may be made to the UT, which the UT can consider if, but only if, the conditions under s 18 of the Act are met or if the UT is authorised to proceed even though all the conditions have not been met. The restrictions on the judicial reviews powers, under s 18 are four in number: (1) the UT can only be asked to grant a remedy it has the power to grant; (2) the application must not call into question anything done by the Crown Court; (3) the case falls within a class specified in a direction given in accordance with the Constitutional Reform Act 2005, Part 1 of Schedule 2, ie the Lord Chief Justice (or someone to whom he delegates the power) may, with the agreement of the Lord Chancellor, specify a class of case which the UT may deal with, rather than the High Court;[26] (4) the Judge presiding at the hearing is required to be a High Court Judge in England and Wales, or a Judge of the Court of Appeal, or 'such other persons as may be agreed from time to time between the Lord Chief Justice and the SPT'.[27] If the UT does not have the function of deciding the application (ie any of conditions 1 to 4 are not met) then it must order the transfer of the application to the High Court.[28] The other route for a judicial review case to the UT is under the Tribunals, Courts and Enforcement Act 2007, s 19, which amends the Senior Courts Act 1981, s 31[29] to provide that where an application is made to the High Court for judicial review or for permission to apply for judicial review and all four of the following conditions are met the High Court must transfer the application to the UT.[30]

4.19   The conditions are: (1) the application includes nothing other than relief or permission to apply for relief under the Tribunals, Courts and Enforcement Act 2007, s 31(1), an award under s 31(4), or interest or costs, (2) the application does not call into question anything done by the Crown Court, (3) the application must fall within the Tribunals, Courts and Enforcement Act 2007, s 18(6), ie within a case directed by the Lord Chief Justice and the Lord Chancellor, and (4) that the application does not call into question any decision made under the Immigration Acts, British Nationality Act 1981, or any instrument under those Acts, or any other nationality law provision. However, if conditions 1, 2 and 4 are met, but not 3, the High Court may order a transfer to the UT if it appears to it to be just and convenient to do so.[31]

4.20   The UT Rules now contain provisions concerning judicial review.[32] It is not expected that there will be many judicial review cases in the UT. In one of the first reported decisions of the UT one of the issues before the tribunal was whether it had jurisdiction to hear an appeal against the FTT's decision not to review an earlier decision on the disclosure of documents. The UT stated 'In the circumstances of this case, this issue could not entirely deprive us of jurisdiction in any event because, if there is no right of appeal, we could treat the appeal as an application for permission to apply for judicial review and waive the requirement to serve the First-tier Tribunal'.[33]

---

[26]   This has been done for all cases the UT will hear, barring the excluded categories in the Lord Chief Justice's Practice Direction Classes of Cases Specified under the Tribunals, Courts and Enforcement Act 2007, s 18(6), 31 October 2008.

[27]   TCEA 2007, s 18(8)(a) and (b). In Scotland the Judge must be one of the Court of Session, and in Northern Ireland a High Court Judge or Appeal Court Judge. In those jurisdictions the agreement in (b) must be between the Lord President or the Lord Chief Justice of Northern Ireland and the SPT.

[28]   TCEA 2007, s 18(3).

[29]   Now the Senior Courts Act 1981, s 31A.

[30]   TCEA 2007, s 19 inserting s 31A(1) and (2).

[31]   TCEA 2007, s 19(3).

[32]   SI 2008/2698, Part 4.

[33]   *Dorset Healthcare NHS Trust v MH* [2009] UKUT 4 (Administrative Appeals Chamber).

The UT as a 'superior court of record'

4.21   Section 3(5) of the Tribunals, Courts and Enforcement Act 2007 declares that the UT is a superior court of record. Does this mean that it is not amenable to judicial review, and, if it is, to what extent and under what circumstances? This was the question that concerned the Divisional Court and the Court of Appeal in *R (Rex Cart) v The Upper Tribunal and others*.[34] The substantive issue in the case arose out of an application to revise a variation direction given by the Secretary of State under the Child Support Act 1991.[35] The UT refused to grant permission to the applicant to appeal on the grounds that the Secretary of State had failed to give written notice of variation. That was challenged by way of judicial review to the High Court. The Divisional Court held that the UT is amenable to judicial review but only on the pre-Anisminic grounds of jurisdictional error[36] or a denial of the right to a fair hearing. That decision was upheld on Appeal by the Court of Appeal, albeit for different reasons.

4.22   The judgments of the Court of Appeal are important not only for answering the important question posed in the proceedings, but also in the way that they make valuable authoritative statements about the structure, purpose and constitutional significance of the new Tribunal system. The important features of the decision are:

(a)   The UT does not have a status equivalent to the High Court. Ad hoc authority is needed if it is to exercise any such powers (paragraph 13).

(b)   The UT's appellate function in itself does not give it immunity from judicial review.

(c)   In Leggatt's Report the author had thought that by making the UT a superior court of record it would avoid being liable to JR, but he thought that such immunity ought to contained in an express statutory provision.[37] This was never done.

(d)   The term 'superior Court of record' has no meaning in Scotland and in England and Wales is 'in truth a concept of uncertain import' (paragraph 16). Quoting Laws, LJ 'the designation is not a reliable guide, let alone a definiens of courts which are immune from judicial review' (paragraph 17).

(e)   The UT is subject to the supervisory jurisdiction of the High Court through judicial review.

(f)   However, the extent of judicial review is not the same as in other inferior Courts and Tribunals. Judicial review is itself 'an artefact of the common law'. Since Anisminic any denial of procedural justice had been justiciable. But this was subject always to the principle that judicial review is a remedy of last resort and errors of law within jurisdiction have to be corrected, if they can be, by appeal (see paragraph 24 of the judgment of Sedley LJ).

---

[34]   In the Court of Appeal [2010] EWCA Civ 859. In the Queen's Bench Divisional Court at [2009] EWHC 3052 (Admin) and at [2010] 2 WLR 1012. This includes an excellent outline of the new Tribunal system by Laws, LJ.

[35]   The facts of the case are summarised in the High Court decision at paras 26 and 27. The original decision is [2009] UKUT 62.

[36]   *Anisminic Ltd v Foreign Compensation Commission* [1969] 2 AC 147.

[37]   See Leggatt Tribunals for Users (2001) at paras 6.33 and 6.44.

(g) The scope of judicial review available in relation to any amenable decision-making body is necessarily a matter of law. The rules of standing in judicial review were made by judges and 'by judges they could be changed when necessary to meet the need to preserve the integrity of the rule of law despite changes in the social structure, methods of government and the extent to which the activities of private citizens are controlled by governmental authorities'.[38] The complete reordering of administrative justice brought about by Leggatt and his reforms is such a change and calls for a reconsideration of the principles of law (see paragraph 28 of the judgment of Sedley LJ).

(h) Two principles need to be reconciled: the relative autonomy Parliament intended for the Tribunals in general and the UT in particular on the one hand, and the High Court as the guardian of standards of legality and due process, from which the UT is not exempt, on the other (see paragraph 35 of the judgment of Sedley LJ).

(i) 'It seems to us that there is a true jurisprudential difference between an error of law made in the course of an adjudication which a tribunal is authorised to conduct and the conducting of adjudication without lawful authority. Both are justiciable before the UT if committed by the FTT, but if committed by the UT will go uncorrected unless judicial review lies. The same course is true of errors of law within jurisdiction: but these, in our judgment, reside within the principle that a system of law, while it can guarantee to be fair, cannot guarantee to be infallible. Outright excess of jurisdiction by the UT and denial by it of fundamental justice, should they ever occur, are in a different class: they represent the doing by the UT of something that Parliament cannot possibly have authorised them to do' (see paragraph 36 of the judgment of Sedley LJ).

4.23 Save in the restricted circumstances of outright excess of jurisdiction or denial of procedural justice the decision clarifies that recourse to judicial review of decisions of the Upper Tribunal will not lie.

THE TRIBUNAL SYSTEM: AN OVERVIEW OF APPEALS[39]

Onward Appeals – pre and post transfer

4.24 The following is a useful overview of the system of appeals reproduced from the Appendix to the judgments in *Cart*:

---

[38] Quoting Lord Diplock in *R v IRC, ex parte National Federation of the Self-Employed* [1982] AC 617, 639–40.
[39] Table taken from *R (C) v The Upper Tribunal* [2010] EWCA Civ 859.

First-tier Tribunal

4.25 War Pensions and Armed Forces Compensation Chamber (established November 2008)

Tribunal	Previous onward appeal	New onward appeal	Basis of appeal to UT
Pension Appeals Tribunal (England and Wales)	Pensions Appeal Tribunal (War Pensions Administrative Provisions Act 1919, s 8(2))	Administrative Appeals Chamber (UT)	Point of law (right of appeal to UT extended to include appeal against assessment of award. Previous appeal only against entitlement decision with JR against assessment)

Health, Education and Social Care Chamber (established November 2008)

Tribunal	Previous onward appeal	New onward appeal	Basis of appeal to UT
Care Standards Tribunal (except appeals under the Safeguarding Vulnerable Groups Act 2006, s 4)	High Court (Protection of Children Act 1999, s 9(6))	Administrative Appeals Chambers (UT)	Point of law
Mental Health Review Tribunals for England	No right of appeal; case stated procedure or judicial review by High Court	Administrative Appeals Chambers (UT)	Point of Law
Special Educational Needs and Disability Tribunal	High Court (Tribunals and Inquiries Act 1992, s 11)	Administrative Appeals Chamber (UT)	Point of law
Family Health Services Authority	High Court (Tribunals and Inquiries Act 1992, s 11)	Administrative Appeals Chambers (UT)	Point of Law

General Regulatory Chamber (established September 2009)

Tribunal	Previous onward appeal	New onward appeal	Basis of appeal to UT
Charity Tribunal	High Court (Charities Act 1993, s 2(c))	Tax and Chancery Chamber (UT)	Point of Law
Consumer Credit Appeals Tribunal	Court of Appeal (Consumer Credit Act 1974, s 41A)	Administrative Appeals Chamber (UT)	Point of law
Estate Agents Appeals Panel	High Court (Estate Agents Act 1979, s 7)	Administrative Appeals Chamber (UT)	Point of law
Transport Tribunal (appeals against decisions of the Driving Standards Agency)	Court of Appeal (Transport Act 1985, para 14 of Sch 4)	Administrative Appeals Chambers (UT)	Point of law
Gambling Appeals Tribunal – transfer date January 2010	High Court (Gambling Act 2005, s 143)	Administrative Appeals Chamber (UT)	Point of Law
Claims Management Services Tribunal – transfer date January 2010	Court of Appeal (Compensation Act 2006, s 13)	Administrative Appeals Chamber (UT)	Point of law
Information Tribunal (except appeals against national security certificates – transfer date January 2010	High Court (Data Protection Act 1998, s 49)	Administrative Appeals Chamber (UT)	Point of law
Immigration Services Tribunal – transfer date January 2010	No right of appeal: JR to High Court	Administrative Appeals Chamber (UT)	Point of law

Tribunal	Previous onward appeal	New onward appeal	Basis of appeal to UT
Adjudication Panel for England – transfer date January 2010	High Court (Local Government Act 2000, ss 78–79)	Administrative Appeals Chambers (UT)	Point of law and wider appeal rights for a person penalised by a decision

Tax Chamber (established April 2009 at the same time as other changes to the tax appeals system by HMRC)

Tribunal	Previous onward appeal	New onward appeal	Basis of appeal to UT
General Commissioners of Income Tax	High Court (Taxes and Management Act 1970, s 56)	Tax and Chancery Chamber (UT)	Point of law, and wider appeal rights against amount of certain penalties
Special Commissioners of Income Tax	(Taxes and Management Act 1970, s 56)		
VAT and Duties Tribunals	(Tribunals and Inquiries 1992, s 11)		
Section 706 Tribunal Section 704 Tribunal	(Tribunals and Inquiries Act 1992, s 11)		

Social Entitlement Chamber (established November 2008)

Tribunal	Previous onward appeal	New onward appeal	Basis of appeal to UT
Social Security and Child Support Appeal Tribunals	Social Security/Child Support Commissioners (Social Security Act 1998, s 14/Child Support Act 1991, s 24)	Administrative Appeals Chamber (UT)	Point of Law Under Tax Credit Act 2002, para 2(2) or 4(1) of Sch 2; Child Trust Funds Act 2004, s 21(10)

Tribunal	Previous onward appeal	New onward appeal	Basis of appeal to UT
Criminal Injuries Compensation Panel	No right of appeal: JR by High Court	No right of appeal: JR by Administrative Appeals Chamber (UT)	Point of law
Asylum Support Tribunal	No right of appeal: JR by High Court	No right of appeal: JR by the High Court	

Immigration and Asylum Chamber (established February 2010)

Tribunal	Previous onward appeal	New onward appeal	Basis of appeal to UT
Asylum and Immigration Tribunal	Reconsideration by AIT and review by High Court (Nationality Immigration and Asylum Act 2002, s 103A)	Immigration and Asylum Chamber (UT)	Point of law

Upper Tribunal

4.26   Administrative Appeals Tribunal (established November 2008)

Tribunal	Previous onward appeal	New onward appeal	Basis of onward appeal
Social security/Child Support Commissioners	Court of Appeal (Social Security Act 1998 s 15; Child Support Act 1991, s 25)	Court of Appeal	Point of law
Care Standards Tribunal (appeals under Safeguarding Vulnerable Groups Act 2006, s 4)	Court of Appeal (Safeguarding Vulnerable Groups Act 2006, s 4)	Court of Appeal	Point of Law
Transport Tribunal (appeals against decisions of Traffic Commissioners)	Court of Appeal (Transport Act 1985, para 14 of Sch 4)	Court of Appeal	Law and fact

Tribunal	Previous onward appeal	New onward appeal	Basis of onward appeal
Information Tribunal: appeals against national security certificates under Data Protection Act 1998, s 28 and Freedom of Information Act 2000, s 60 – transfer date January 2010	No onward appeal	No onward appeal (excluded decision under TCEA 2007, s 13(8))	n/a

Tax and Chancery (established April 2009)

Tribunal	Previous onward appeal	New onward appeal	Basis of onward appeal
Financial Services and Markets Tribunal	Court of Appeal (Financial services and Markets Act 2000, s 137)	Court of Appeal	Point of law
Pensions Regulator Tribunal	Court of Appeal (Pensions Act 2004, s 104)	Court of Appeal	Point of Law

Lands Chambers (established April 2009)

Tribunal	Previous onward appeal	New onward appeal	Basis of onward appeal
Lands Tribunal	Court of Appeal (Lands Tribunal Act 1949, s 3(4))	Court of Appeal	Point of Law

Immigration and Asylum Chambers (established February 2010)

Tribunal	Previous onward appeal	New onward appeal	Basis of onward appeal
Asylum and Immigration Tribunal – reconsiderations	Court of Appeal (Nationality, Immigration and Asylum Act 2002, s 103)	Court of Appeal	Point of law

Part 2

SPECIFIC AREAS

Chapter 5

PLANNING AND ENVIRONMENT

INTRODUCTION

5.1   Planning law provides a range of measures to regulate the development and use of land in the public interest. The Town and Country Planning Act 1947 removed the right to develop land without official planning permission. Much contained in that Act has been the foundation of the present modern system. A decision on the part of a local planning authority to grant planning permission is susceptible to challenge by judicial review.[1] Although that has been accepted for a long time there has been an increased use of judicial review to challenge planning decisions in recent years. The obvious reason is that whereas applicants for planning permission have the right to appeal to the Secretary of State, third parties do not. The remedy of judicial review is thus the only remedy open to third parties in those circumstances.

5.2   It has been said that the statutory framework contained within the Town and Country Planning Act 1990 (TCPA) (an act of consolidation) provides a comprehensive statutory code.[2] Planning law has developed since 1947 with alterations made to the statutory provisions to reflect changes in society, policy, EU influence and the public interest in development.

5.3   The planning system has become more front loaded, with the policy objective being to involve third parties as much as possible in consultation before the planning decision is made. Proposals in the Localism Bill cement that approach with amendments to ss 61 and 62 of the TCPA proposed to require prospective developers to consult local communities before submitting planning applications for certain developments. The developer is then required to take account of any responses generated during the consultation process and has to decide whether to make changes to the proposals as a consequence before submitting the planning application. Given the increased statutory weight to be attached to third party views from the outset of the planning process, the absence of a right of appeal on the part of third parties can be seen as being increasingly anachronistic. That, coupled with enhanced environmental awareness, has meant that third parties are becoming more active in bringing challenges to a planning permission granted by a local planning authority. Subject to obtaining favourable advice such proceedings can be funded by the Legal Services Commission. In certain cases it can, therefore, be less costly to a third party to bring judicial review proceedings than to be represented and appear at a lengthy public inquiry although a deliberate decision not to be involved in the earlier inquiry process can affect the issue of whether the claimant has sufficient standing to bring judicial review proceedings (which is dealt with below).[3]

---

[1]   *R v Sheffield City Council, ex p Mansfield* (1978) 37 P & CR 1.
[2]   *Pioneer Aggregates* [1985] 1 AC 132.
[3]   See para **5.25** and the case of *Ashton v Secretary of State for Communities and Local Government* [2011] 1 P & CR 117.

5.4   Before going on to look at the various areas of challenge, an outline review of the statutory framework is necessary.[4] Both the Town and Country Planning Act 1990, as amended,[5] and the Acquisition of Land Act 1981 provide statutory grounds of challenge to planning decisions and compulsory purchase orders. The availability of an alternative remedy would be a powerful reason for not allowing a challenge to the grant of planning permission to proceed. The same preclusive effect would apply to the statutory provisions relating to a Compulsory Purchase Order. It is important to record that only a person aggrieved can use the route of statutory challenge to a planning decision. Thus it is not infrequently the case, that a party can receive a decision in their favour but be fearful that the reasoning used (which is flawed) to reach the decision will be used by others against them in later decisions or appeals. Such cases cannot be the subject of a statutory challenge.

STATUTORY FRAMEWORK

Planning decisions

5.5   All planning applications for development or use of land are to be determined in accordance with the Development Plan unless material considerations indicate otherwise: see s 38(6) of the Planning and Compulsory Purchase Act 2004. The consequence is that there is a plan led, but not plan determined, system of development control. The definition of development is set out in s 55 of the TCPA 1990. The headline definition in s 55(1) is that development is 'the carrying out of any mining, building, engineering or other operations or the making of a material change of use of land'. The following sub-sections make express provision for inclusion or exclusion of certain categories within the description of development. Planning permission is required for all development unless otherwise stated: see s 57. If there is a breach of planning control and the local planning authority consider it to be expedient to do so, having regard to the provisions of the development plan and to any other material considerations, then it may issue an enforcement notice to remedy the breach: see TCPA, s 172.

5.6   Section 70 of the TCPA provides that where an application for planning permission is made to the local planning authority in dealing with that application the local planning authority shall have regard to the Development Plan, so far as material to that application, and to any other material considerations. The role of material considerations can be critical in taking a planning decision. What is or is not a material consideration is a matter of law and ultimately for the court.[6] There is no statutory definition of what a material consideration is. To be material the consideration has to relate to planning. Otherwise, the parameters of materiality have been defined by the courts[7] and a broad approach has been approved.[8] 'Any consideration which relates to the use and development of land is capable of being a material consideration … it

---

[4]   For a comprehensive work on Town and Country Planning see the *Planning Encyclopaedia*.

[5]   Mainly by the Planning and Compulsory Purchase Act 2004.

[6]   *Bolton MBC v Secretary of State for the Environment* [1991] JPL 241.

[7]   *Stringer v Minister of Housing and Local Government* [1971] 1 All ER 65, *Great Portland Estates plc v Westminster City Council* [1985] AC 661.

[8]   *R (Rank) v East Cambridgeshire District Council* [2003] JPL 454 – a consideration is material for the purposes of s 70(2) if it was not irrelevant to the determination and if it might make a difference to the way in which the authority dealt with the application. See also *R (Hillingdon and others) v Secretary of State for Transport* [2010] EWHC 626 where the court accepted that the issue of climate change was a material consideration on a challenge to the Secretary of State's confirmation of support for the proposal of a third runway and new passenger facilities at Heathrow Airport.

follows that financial consequences are capable of amounting to a material consideration in so far as they relate to the use and development of land.'[9] The category of material considerations is not fixed or final as evidenced in the case of *HSE v Wolverhampton City Council and Victoria Hall Ltd* [2010] EWCA Civ 892 which found that the payment of compensation on a revocation or discontinuance order could be a material consideration to be taken into account by the local planning authority contrary to an earlier decision of the High Court in *Alnwick District Council v Secretary of State for the Environment, Transport and the Regions* [2000] 79 P & CR 130. Another recent example of a new material consideration is in *R (Copeland) v London Borough of Tower Hamlets* [2010] EWHC 1845 where the proximity of a hot food take away shop to a school following a healthy eating policy was held to be a material consideration. Other examples include Planning Policy Statements and Circulars, statements of government policy, consultation responses on a planning application from departments other than planning, economic and, in certain circumstances, financial considerations. As planning and environmental matters are concerned with the development and use of land in the public interest personal considerations are generally (but not always) immaterial.

5.7   Once something is established as a material consideration the weight to be attached to it is entirely a matter for the decision-maker.[10] If the decision-maker takes into account something which is not a material consideration, the decision-taker is vulnerable to having his decision quashed. Likewise, if the decision-maker fails to take into account a material consideration he is similarly vulnerable to a challenge to the legality of the decision taken. What is important is that the material consideration is such as would be likely to make a real possibility of difference to the decision taken. Either stance on the part of a decision-maker would be illegal ie the omission of a material consideration or the inclusion in the decision making process of an immaterial consideration. Depending on the circumstances the omission of a material consideration or the converse may also be irrational.

5.8   Further, what is a material consideration can change between the resolution to grant planning permission and the issue of the planning permission. In *Kides v South Cambridgeshire District Council* [2002] EWCA Civ 1370 where there was a period of five years between the resolution to grant permission and its issue the court held 'In practical terms, therefore, where since the passing of the resolution some new factor has arisen of which the delegated officer is aware, and which might rationally be regarded as a "material consideration" for the purposes of section 70(2), it must be a counsel of prudence for the delegated officer to err on the side of caution and refer the application back to the authority for specific reconsideration in the light of that new factor. In such circumstances the delegated officer can only safely proceed to issue the decision notice if he is satisfied: (a) that the authority is aware of the new factor, (b) that it has considered it with the application in mind, and (c) that on a reconsideration the authority would reach (not might reach) the same decision' (para 126). In the case of *R (Dry) v West Oxfordshire District Council* [2010] EWCA Civ 1143 the court upheld that approach although remarked that it would depend on the particular circumstances of the case and dismissed an appeal that the change in a flood zone from zone 1 to zone 2 was such a comparable change in material consideration.

---

9   *Alnwick District Council v Secretary of State for the Environment, Transport and the Regions* [2000] 79 P & CR 130 per Richards J which although disapproved in the Court of Appeal in *HSE v Wolverhampton City Council and Victoria Hall* [2010] EWCA Civ 892 not on the definition of 'material considerations'.

10   *Tesco Stores Ltd v Secretary of State for the Environment* [1995] 1 WLR 759.

5.9   There are statutory grounds of appeal under sections 287, 288 and 289 of the Town and Country Planning Act which are dealt with in greater detail below. They are, however, only available for a 'person aggrieved' by the decision and who is able to show that he has been substantially prejudiced by the decision taken. Section 284 of the Town and Country Planning Act 1990 is a preclusive section. It precludes a challenge to the High Court on revocation or modification[11] of a planning permission, a discontinuance order, a tree preservation order,[12] an order made under s 221(5),[13] certain orders under Schedule 9[14] and any decision by the Secretary of State on appeal under s 77 or under s 78 other than by s 287 and s 288 of the Act. Section 289 provides the right of statutory challenge to the High Court in respect of a decision on an enforcement notice appeal. Section 285 of the Act precludes an enforcement notice being challenged in any other way.

5.10   There are certain exceptions to the preclusive provisions. Where the preclusive provisions apply, the usual process of judicial review is applicable. For a recent example of this see *Trim v North Dorset District Council* [2010] EWCA Civ 1406 where the court held that a breach of condition notice was a pure public law act and only challengeable by judicial review. The exclusivity principle applied such that it was an abuse of process to challenge the validity of public law actions or decisions other than by judicial review. The exceptions to the preclusive provision include the decision-making process of the local planning authority in determining a planning application when a third party wants to challenge that process or decision, an order confirmed by special parliamentary procedure, interim orders by the Secretary of State during the course of proceedings[15] and costs orders.[16]

5.11   There are other preclusive provisions which prevent the challenge to the validity of planning permissions or decisions in certain circumstances: see s 286,[17] decisions on the part of the Secretary of State under s 22 of the Planning (Hazardous Substances) Act 1990, and various orders in relation to the listed buildings and conservation areas under ss 62–65 of the Planning (Listed Buildings and Conservation Areas) Act 1990, and notices under s 215 requiring the proper maintenance of land. The time limits in the various ouster clauses are strictly enforced by the courts.[18]

5.12   Unlike an application for judicial review challenges under s 287 and s 288 are not subject to any sift on the merits of the claim. Despite judicial dicta[19] urging the

---

[11]   Sections 97 and 102.
[12]   Section 198.
[13]   Advertisement regulation orders.
[14]   Discontinuance of mineral workings under paras 1, 2, 5 or 6 of Sch 9.
[15]   Such as a refusal to adjourn an inquiry.
[16]   *Balogh v Secretary of State for the Environment* [1996] 1 PLR 32 where the Court held that remained the case even where there was another appeal against the merits of the decision proceedings under s 288 although the two proceeding could be heard together.
[17]   Which prohibits a challenge to the decision on the basis that it should have been made by some other local planning authority.
[18]   *Khan v Newport Borough Council* [1991] COD 157 – CA refused permission on the basis of a six week time period within which to challenge a TPO, *R v Dacorum District Council, ex p Cannon* [1996] 2 PLR 45 – JR refused of listed building enforcement notice because statutory appeal was available with full alternative remedy.
[19]   *R on the application of Linda Davies v Secretary of State for Communities and Local Government* [2008] EWHC 2223 per Sullivan J at 56. 'Challenges under section 288 have the potential to delay much needed development, even though the grounds of challenge may well be devoid of merit. Moreover, the need to have a full hearing in respect of all challenges under section 288, regardless of whether or not the grounds of challenge are arguable, greatly increases the costs for all of the parties involved, and occupies the time of the court unnecessarily.'

introduction of a comparable sift to that which exists for applications under s 289 where permission from the court has to be obtained to proceed before the substantive hearing and akin to the requirement to obtain permission to bring judicial review proceedings no such procedure has yet been introduced. The case of *Bovale v Secretary of State for Communities and Local Government* [2009] EWCA Civ 171 dealt with a claim under s 288 where the Secretary of State as defendant had been ordered to file and serve any evidence and additional grounds to those relied upon by the local authority at an early stage in the proceedings as opposed to the current practice where a defendant may serve additional evidence but is not obliged to do so and so the case being run may not be known until receipt of the defendant's skeleton argument. The Court of Appeal held that 'a judge has no power to alter the Civil Procedure Rules either by a judgment or practice direction or to vary or alter any practice direction which was binding on the court to which it was directed'. At the time of writing the procedure thus remains as it has for some time.

5.13   An application under the statutory challenge provisions to decisions other than enforcement notice appeals has to be made within a six-week period under s 287(4). That is calculated from the day following publication of the order in question. That means that the proceedings have to be filed and served within the six-week period. The time period is absolute.

5.14   The basis for challenge to a planning decision, order or direction under s 288 of the Town and Country Planning Act is that:

(i)   the decision is outside the powers conferred by the Act; or

(ii)   any of the relevant requirements of the Act have not been complied with.[20]

5.15   Under s 288(3) there is the same six-week period within which to challenge a relevant order under that section. That is, in the case of a decision letter, from the date on which it is date stamped by the Secretary of State and signed on his behalf. The time limit is absolute.

5.16   The grounds of challenge are broadly the same as those under s 287 dealing with questioning the validity of development plans. In practice 'It is well established that s 288(1)(b) is broadly speaking a provision enabling the normal grounds of judicial review to be relied upon, often described as *Wednesbury* grounds of challenge: see *Ashbridge Investments Limited v Minster of Housing and Local Government* [1965] 1 WLR 1320; *Seddon Properties Limited v Secretary of State for the Environment* [1978] JPL 835; *R (Alconbury Developments Ltd) v Secretary of State for the Environment* [2003] 2 AC 295' per Keene LJ in *First Secretary of State, West End Green (Properties) Limited v Sainsbury's Supermarkets Limited* [2007] EWCA Civ 1083.

5.17   As a result a planning decision is frequently challenged on the basis of illegality in the form of inadequate reasons, irrationality and procedural impropriety. The law on the adequacy of reasons for a planning decision was set out in *South Bucks DC v Porter (No 2)* [2004] UKHL 33:

> 'The reasons for a decision must be intelligible and they must be adequate. They must enable the reader to understand why the matter was decided as it was and what conclusions were

---

[20]   See s 288(1)(b).

reached on the "principal important controversial issues", disclosing how any issue of law or fact was resolved. Reasons can be briefly stated, the degree of particularity required depending entirely on the nature of the issues falling for decision. The reasoning must not give rise to a substantial doubt as to whether the decision-maker erred in law, for example by misunderstanding some relevant policy or some other important matter or by failing to reach a rational decision on relevant grounds. But such adverse inference will not readily be drawn. The reasons need refer only to the main issues in the dispute, not to every material consideration. They should enable disappointed developers to assess their prospects of obtaining some alternative development permission, or, as the case may be, their unsuccessful opponents to understand how the policy or approach underlying the grant of permission may impact upon future such applications. Decision letters must be read in a straightforward manner, recognising that they are addressed to parties well aware of the issues involved and the arguments advanced. A reasons challenge will only succeed if the party aggrieved can satisfy the court that he has genuinely been substantially prejudiced by the failure to provide an adequately reasoned decision.'[21]

5.18   Even if the grounds of challenge are made out at the substantive hearing there remains a residual discretion with the court in a case where the Secretary of State has failed to take into account a domestic material consideration on the part of the Court as to whether to quash the decision. 'If the matter was fundamental to the decision' or the judge concludes that there is a real possibility that the consideration is a matter that would have made a difference to the decision then the impugned decision will be quashed: *Bolton MBC v Secretary of State for the Environment* (1990) 61 P & CR 343. If a party seeks to argue that the decision taken would have been the same regardless the test is that 'the defendants would have to show that the decision would inevitably have been the same and the court must not unconsciously stray from its proper province of reviewing the propriety of the decision making process into the forbidden territory of evaluating the substantial merits of the decision ...'. See *Smith v NE Derbyshire PCT and others* [2006] EWCA Civ 1291.[22]

5.19   The discretion to quash is even narrower where there is a breach of European legislation as set out below.

5.20   Under s 289 there is the right to challenge an enforcement notice decision. That proceeds differently to challenges brought under ss 287 and 288 of the TCPA.

5.21   First, the decision challenged under s 289 can be brought on a point of law only: s 289(1). The challenge has to be brought within a period of 28 days, although, unlike the position under s 288, there is power to extend time.[23]

5.22   Secondly, permission has to be sought from the court to bring the proceedings. There are procedural requirements to be followed as to which documents to file when seeking permission.[24] The test is whether there is an arguable case to proceed. There is no further right of appeal to the Court of Appeal.

---

[21]   Per Lord Brown at para 36.

[22]   May LJ at para 10, applied in *Copeland v London Borough of Tower Hamlets* [2010] EWHC 1845.

[23]   *R v Wandsworth BC v Secretary of State for Transport, Local Government and the Regions* [2004] P & CR 32 where time was extended by two weeks where there was no question of delay being used as an attempt to string proceedings out, CPR r 3.1(2).

[24]   They are the use of Form TCP(L) to make the initial application for permission accompanied by a draft appellant's notice and if permission is granted use of an appellant's notice which is form N161. The procedure is set out in RSC O94.

5.23 Once permission is granted in a challenge under s 289 the matter proceeds to a substantive hearing in a way similar to a substantive judicial review hearing. If successful, the matter is remitted to the Secretary of State for redetermination.

5.24 All of this is relevant as not only are the principles of challenge the same despite different terminology, judicial review is a remedy of the last resort. If there is a suitable alternative remedy that can give appropriate relief that should be used before taking any judicial review proceedings. If the issue of alternative remedy is to be raised in judicial review proceedings by a defendant then it should be in the Summary Grounds of Resistance so that it can be addressed at the permission stage.[25]

'A person aggrieved'

5.25 The right to bring the statutory challenge is only exercisable by 'a person aggrieved'. The threshold for a 'person aggrieved' is higher than 'having a sufficient interest' which is required to bring judicial review proceedings. In *Historic Buildings and Monuments Commission (English Heritage) v Secretary of State for Communities and Local Government* [2009] EWHC 2287 Admin the court remarked that 'the right of statutory challenge comes at the end of a complex and formal series of opportunities for consultation, objection and hearing. It is understandable that Parliament should intend to limit the right of appeal to those who have played an active part in the process that is designed to ensure that the important issues are identified and properly examined as early in the process as possible ...'. That means considering whether the person claiming to be aggrieved has played a substantial role in the process, for example as an active objector or possibly as an active interested person. Whether a challenger will meet that test will always be a matter of fact and degree depending upon the circumstances. On appeal in *Ashton v Secretary of State for Communities and Local Government* [2010] EWCA Civ 600 the Court of Appeal considered the principles to be applied in deciding whether a person was 'aggrieved'. The Court held that there were two factors for consideration, namely, the extent to which the person seeking to challenge the decision had taken part in the planning procedures and the extent to which it is necessary for the person to demonstrate that the order had an adverse effect on him. On the facts they found that an individual whose involvement had been as a member of an action group opposed to the development which had made representations to a public inquiry into the proposed development but had not participated personally was not an 'aggrieved' person.[26]

5.26 Procedure is dealt with in an earlier chapter but the following procedural points from recent cases are particularly pertinent in planning and environmental cases due to the amount of paper that the cases can generate. First, time estimates for the hearing should be realistic: *Wiltshire Council v Secretary of State for Communities and Local Government* [2010] EWHC 1009,[27] court bundles should be properly prepared: *Leeds*

---

[25]   *R v Falmouth and Truro Health Authority, ex p South West Water Ltd* [2001] QB 445 'the critical decision in an alternative remedy case certainly one that requires a stay, is the one taken at the grant of permission stage'.

[26]   See para 53 in the judgement of Pill LJ where the principles are set out. On the facts in that case see para 54: 'His participation in the planning process was insufficient in the circumstances to acquire standing. He was not an objector to the proposal in any formal sense and did not make representations, either oral or written, at the properly constituted Public Inquiry. Mere attendance at parts of the hearing and membership of WCDG, which has not brought proceedings in this court, were insufficient.'

[27]   'Accurate and agreed time estimates are essential if the Administrative Court is to function properly and in

City Council v SSCLG [2010] EWHC 1412[28] and skeleton arguments should not be excessive: *Khader and Aziz v Lyons* [2010] EWCA Civ 716 'the court will not for ever tolerate the time and cost of *both* excessive written submission *and* oral argument of commensurate length'.[29] The issue of costs and, in particular, protective costs orders is dealt with in the chapter on Practice and Procedure. Otherwise the general principles are stated shortly below.

Compulsory purchase decisions

5.27   A compulsory purchase order can be made under a variety of authorising statutory provisions such as the Highways Act 1980, the Housing Act 1996 and the Town and Country Planning Act 1990 to name but a few. In terms of challenging a compulsory purchase order provision is made by the Acquisition of Land Act 1981 s 23 for 'any person aggrieved'[30] by a compulsory purchase order or a certificate under Part III or Schedule 3 to make an application to the High Court on the basis that any relevant requirement has not been complied with.

5.28   An application to the High Court has to be made within six weeks from the date on which the order under challenge becomes operative.[31] The calculation of the period of time is carried out[32] as for proceedings to be brought under the TCPA. The time period is similarly absolute both in terms of its commencement[33] and end.

5.29   The Court may grant an interim order suspending the CPO[34] or at the final hearing quash the compulsory purchase order or any provision within it or the certificate either generally or as it affects the property of the applicant.[35]

5.30   Apart from the statutory remedies under s 24, s 25 of the Acquisition of Land Act restricts the questioning of a confirmed compulsory purchase order in any other legal proceedings.

5.31   What the Acquisition of Land Act, however, does not do is to preclude judicial review proceedings being brought in relation to the issue of the General Vesting

---

the interest of litigants. If unrealistic estimates are given to the listing office, those responsible may find that cases are removed from the list, to the general inconvenience of the parties, and that other sanctions may be imposed'. Simon J at para 42.

28   See Keith J at paras 60/61.

29   May P at para 37, skeleton arguments should 'not kill oral advocacy unintentionally'.

30   *Lomax and Others v Secretary of State for Transport, Local Government and the Regions and Rochdale Metropolitan Borough Council* (2002) 21 EG 143 where Richards J was satisfied that an objector who had withdrawn his objection to the CPO inquiry was still a person aggrieved and able to challenge confirmation of the decision under s 23.

31   That is if the Statutory Order (Special Procedure) Act 1945 applies, or if it does not, six weeks from when the notice of confirmation of the order or making of the order is first published in accordance with the Acquisition of Land Act 1981, or if it is a certificate the date on which notice of the giving of the certificate is first published: see s 23(4).

32   *Okolo v Secretary of State for the Environment* [1997] 4 All ER 242.

33   *Enterprise Inns plc v Secretary of State for the Environment, Transport and the Regions and Liverpool CC* (2000) 81 P & CR 236 'Parliament has deliberately prescribed a window rather than simply an end date in s 23(4)(b) and in those circumstances … it is not sufficient to show that the application was made before an end date. It must come within the window'.

34   Section 24(1) of the Acquisition of Land Act 1981.

35   Section 24(2) of the Acquisition of Land Act 1981.

Declaration and, presumably, other subsequent steps to the confirmation of the compulsory purchase order which can then be challenged on conventional public law principles.[36]

JUDICIAL REVIEW PROCEEDINGS

Sufficient interest

5.32 A claimant for judicial review must have a 'sufficient interest' in the subject matter to which the application relates.[37] The approach to standing has become increasingly liberal over the years such that provided a genuine interest in the litigation can be shown the requirement is likely to be satisfied.

5.33 Under s 31 of the Senior Courts Act 1981 a 'sufficient interest' is seen as a precondition to the grant of permission: 'a discrete issue which could be decided irrespective of the merits of the claim'.[38] It has been used in the past as a threshold test to filter out busybodies so as to prevent abuse of the process.[39] But the decision may be affected by all of the circumstances in the claim so as to influence whether the claimant is entitled to the remedy claimed.[40]

5.34 In *R v Secretary of State for the Environment, ex p Rose Theatre Trust* [1990] 1 QB 504 the applicants were a company formed by archaeologists to preserve the site of Shakespeare's Rose Theatre. They had written to the Secretary of State asking that the remains of the theatre be listed as a scheduled monument but despite that Scheimann J expressed the view that they had no locus to bring proceedings.

5.35 In contrast, in *R v Somerset County Council, ex p Dixon* [1998] Env LR 111 Sedley J said: 'Public law is not at base about rights, even though abuses of power may and often do invade private rights; it is about wrongs – that is to say misuses of public power: and the courts have always been alive to the fact that a person or organisation with no particular stake in the issue or outcome may, without in any sense being a mere meddler, wish and be well placed to call the attention of the court to an apparent misuse of public power.'[41]

5.36 In *R (Kides) v South Cambridgeshire DC* [2002] EWCA Civ 1370[42] the Court of Appeal could not see 'how it can be just to debar a litigant who has a real and genuine interest in obtaining the relief which he seeks from relying, in support of his claim for that relief, on grounds (which may be good grounds) in which he has no personal interest'. The words 'real and genuine interest' were adopted in *R (Hammerton) v London Underground Ltd* [2002] EWHC 2307 to apply also to a public interest litigant with no property or other interest in the site.[43]

---

[36] *Belfields v Sefton Metropolitan Borough Council* [2008] EWHC 1975.
[37] Section 31(3) of the Senior Courts Act 1981.
[38] *R (Edwards) v Environment Agency* [2004] EWHC 746 Admin.
[39] *R v Somerset County Council v Dixon* [1998] Env LR 111 – 'a busybody being someone with no legitimate concern at all' per Sedley J.
[40] *R v Somerset CC, ex p Dixon* (supra).
[41] At para 121.
[42] Parker LJ at para 133.
[43] Ouseley J at para 209.

5.37   A company formed by residents who wish to oppose the grant of planning permission has sufficient standing with which to bring proceedings: see *R v Leicester City Council, ex p Blackferry and Boothsthorpe Action Group* Limited [2001] Env LR 35,[44] *Hereford Waste Watchers v Hereford Council* [2005] EWHC 191. 'Sufficient interest' is a different test to that of a 'person aggrieved' which needs to be shown to raise a challenge under s 288 of the Town and Country Planning Act 1990. In *Residents Against Waste v Lancashire County Council* [2007] EWHC 2558 the issue arose where the residents had formed a company limited by guarantee and the defendant sought to argue that the test was the same as that under s 288. That was rejected. 'The "persons aggrieved" test is designed precisely to afford rights of challenge to individuals whose private interests are affected and which very often do not turn on any suggested illegality or "public wrong" by a public body. The situations are not the same.'[45]

5.38   In *R (Edwards) v Environment Agency* [2004] EWHC 736 Admin it was not abuse to bring a challenge to a process in which claimant had not participated even if the claimant was put up[46] to front the claim to secure public funding.

5.39   Whilst a financial or legal interest is not required[47] to establish a 'sufficient interest', commercial challenges in planning cases are often the motivating force behind the challenge: *R v Canterbury City Council, ex p Springimage Ltd* [1993] 3 PLR 58 – 'sufficient that a person's commercial interest was realistically affected by the decision', *R v (Mount Cook Land Ltd) v Westminster City Council* [2003] EWCA Civ 1346 'judicial review applications by would be developers or objectors to development in planning cases are by their nature driven primarily by commercial or private motive rather than a high minded concern for the public weal'. The recent case of *R (on the application of Sainsburys Supermarkets) v Wolverhampton City Council* [2010] UKSC 20 illustrates that point. That was the culmination of a ten year battle between Sainsburys Supermarkets Ltd and Tesco Stores for the re-development of a site in Wolverhampton in which each had an interest. Tesco also controlled another site nearby which the council wanted to redevelop.

5.40   The issue of costs, in particular, in relation to claimants has become increasingly important where the claimant is dependent on public funding or with slender resources of their own. Protective costs orders are dealt with in another chapter (see Practice and Procedure) but such orders are of considerable importance both for claimants and defendants in planning and environmental cases. Third party costs are recoverable only in restricted circumstances where the third party raises issues which have not been raised by the defendant and where those arguments have been successful.

---

[44]   'Technically, it may be said, the company does not have a relevant interest of its own; but in substance it represents the interests of local residents, many of whom do have a relevant interest. Incorporation has a number of advantages, some of which motivated the incorporation of the action group in this case. It is true that another advantage is the avoidance of substantial personal liability of members for the costs of unsuccessful legal proceedings. But that should not preclude the use of a corporate vehicle, at least where incorporation is not for the sole purpose of escaping the direct impact of an adverse costs order (and possibly even where it is for that purpose). The costs position can be dealt with adequately by requiring the provision of security for costs' Richards J.

[45]   Irwin J at para 17.

[46]   See para 21.

[47]   *R v Secretary of State for the Environment v Rose Theatre Trust Co* [1990] 1 QB 504 at 520D.

The need to be prompt and avoid undue delay

5.41   The issue of delay has a particular resonance in the planning context where the pressure is to complete the financing and delivery of the project in question. The approach of the courts has varied. Whilst matters seemed to be settled after *R (Burkett) v London Borough of Hammersmith and Fulham* [2002] UKHL 23 there are signs of the judicial pendulum swinging back towards a shorter time period than three months by emphasising the importance of promptness in challenging planning decisions.

5.42   Under CPR 54.5 a claim for judicial review must be filed promptly; and in any event not later than three months after the grounds to make the claim first arose. If there is delay which the High Court considers is undue by virtue of s 31(6) of the Senior Courts Act 1981

> 'the Court may refuse to grant
>
> (a)   leave for the making of the application; or
> (b)   any relief sought on the application, if it considers that the granting of relief sought would be likely to cause substantial hardship to, or substantially prejudice the rights of, any person or would be detrimental to good administration.'

5.43   The time limit cannot be extended by agreement between the parties and it does not apply if some other statutory provision applies a shorter time within which to bring a claim for judicial review.

5.44   Prior to the decision in *Burkett* the trend of judicial decisions was to emphasise the importance of a challenge to a planning decision within a comparable period to the six week period allowed for a statutory challenge[48] under the Town and Country Planning Act. There was also conflicting dicta as to whether it was the planning permission itself or the resolution to grant planning permission that had to be challenged. The House of Lords in *Burkett*, led by Lord Steyn, made it clear that time for commencement of a judicial review application ran from the grant of planning permission and that the time period allowed was of three months.

5.45   There appeared to be a position of clarity. However, since then judicial decisions have begun to indicate a movement back from that clear position. In *R (on the application of Candlish) v Hastings* [2005] EWHC 1539 it was said 'in the field of planning it seems to me to be of the greatest importance that challenges should be notified at the earliest practicable moment. It is not necessarily sufficient or appropriate to defer the intimation or issue of a claim to the end of the three-month period mention in the Rule. As often as not, perhaps more often than not, developers wish, for commercial and financial reasons, to press on with a development as soon as planning permission has been obtained'.[49] In the factual context there the claimant was entitled to take time to consider her position and as the interested party's claim for prejudice rested on a financial basis only no lack of promptness was found on the part of the claimant.

5.46   The issue of promptly or within three months developed further in the case of *R on the application of Hardy v Pembrokeshire CC* [2005] EWHC 1872 where Sullivan J followed the three tests set out in *R v Secretary of State for Trade and Industry ex p Greenpeace Ltd* [2000] Env LR 221 which were:

---

[48]   See *R v Ceredigion CC, ex p McKeown* [1998] 2 PLR 1 and *R v Camden LBC, ex p Williams* [2000] 2 PLR 93.
[49]   Para 20, Davis J.

'(i)   Is there a reasonable objective excuse for applying late?

(ii)   What, if any, is the damage, in terms of hardship or prejudice to third party rights and detriment to good administration, which could be occasioned if permission were now granted?

(iii)   In any event, does the public interest require that the application should be permitted to proceed?'

5.47   The decisions that were sought to be impugned were all outside the three month time limit except one in respect of which the challenge was lodged in the last day of the three month period. Sullivan J rejected arguments that the Court was under a duty to secure compliance with an EC Directive relying on a decision of the Court of Appeal in *R (on the application of the Noble Organisation Ltd) v Thanet DC* [2005] EWCA Civ 782 and said 'There is no suggestion in *Wells* that individuals wishing to challenge a failure to require an EIA should not be governed by the procedural rules of each Member State, provided that those rules must not render such a challenge impossible in practice or excessively difficult.' He found also that it would be highly detrimental to good public administration to allow such challenges out of time and that the public interest did not demand that permission be granted out of time as the claimant's concerns were not representative of the views expressed by other consultees.

5.48   The Court of Appeal[50] upheld the approach of Sullivan J. It rejected any contention that CPR 54.5 offended against the European principle of legal certainty and was unlawful observing that the leading case of *Lam v United Kingdom* had dealt with and rejected the same point. It had not been cited in *Burkett*. Keene LJ made the point that 'It is important that those parties, and indeed the public generally, should be able to proceed on the basis that the decision is valid and can be relied on, and that they can plan their lives and make personal and business decisions accordingly'.[51]

5.49   In the case of *R (on the application of Catt) v Brighton and Hove City Council* [2007] EWCA Civ 298 Pill LJ identified two important factors[52] when dealing with delay:

'where there is a challenge to that permission based on the alleged unlawfulness of the screening opinion, the party challenging the planning permission will normally have had notice of that opinion. In considering delay, the court would be entitled to take into account that prior knowledge when considering the time by which proceedings should have been instituted following the grant. The second point is that, even when a decision to proceed with a development has been taken at a time when challenge is possible, and work has proceeded, subsequent delay remains capable of causing prejudice to the developer and detriment to good administration'.

5.50   *Finn Kelcey v Milton Keynes District Council* [2008] EWCA Civ 1067 re-stated the importance of acting promptly in planning cases. The pre *Burkett* cases with their reference to a six week period within which a challenge is to be brought were set out again. 'While there is no "six weeks rule" in judicial review challenges to planning permissions, the existence of that statutory limit is not to be seen as necessarily wholly irrelevant to the decision as to what is "prompt" in an individual case. It emphasises the need for swiftness of action.' The case of *Uniplex UK Ltd v NHS Business Services Authority* (C-406/08) 28 January 2010 may threaten the jurisprudential trend. The ECJ held that in the context of the Public Contracts Regulations 2006 which are worded in

---

50   *Hardy & Others v Pembrokeshire CC* [2006] EWCA Civ 240.
51   Para 10.
52   Para 52.

an identical way to the judicial review requirements that the requirement for 'promptness' infringed the Community requirements of legal certainty and effectiveness. It was unlawful. Further, the three month time limit ran from when the prospective claimant knew of the potential cause of action. The question is then whether the judgment in a procurement case is of application to planning and environmental cases? The case of *Carroll v Westminster City Council and TfL* [2010] EWHC 2019 which was a renewed application for permission on the grounds of an alleged breach of the Environmental Impact Assessment Regulations held that *Uniplex* was confined to its own facts and the Procurement Directive. The remarks are obiter and so the final decision may not rest there.

5.51   As ever there have been exceptions to a tight application of the time limits. In the case of *R v Bassetlaw District Council, ex p Oxby* [1998] PLCR 283 the Leader of the Council applied to judicially review a decision on the part of his own council some two years after the grant of planning permission. The Court of Appeal held that the legitimate interests of the landowners with the benefit of planning permission were not prejudiced by delay in mounting the application. 'If anything in the extraordinary circumstances of the case the proceedings had been brought in the name of good administration.' The case of *Usk Valley Conservation Group v Brecon Beacons National Park Authority* [2010] EWHC 71 quashed a planning permission granted on 21 of June 2005 when proceedings were not commenced until 5 February 2009 where the fact that the permission was invalid and should in principle be quashed, absent strong contrary reasons which did not exist, was decisive. That is to be contrasted with the case of *Gavin v Haringey LBC* [2003] EWHC 2591 where a claim to quash a planning permission granted some two and a half years earlier was dismissed due to the very harsh effect that would have on the developers.

5.52   The general position on delay is that if it has been raised at the permission stage and permission granted the issue does not fall to be re-opened again: *R v Criminal Injuries Compensation Board, ex p A* [1999] 2 AC 330 but 'what the Court can do under s 31(6) is to refuse to grant a remedy'.[53] *R v Lichfield Securities Ltd v Lichfield District Council* [2001] EWCA Civ 304 dealt with when the respondent should be permitted to re-canvass, by way of undue delay, an issue of promptness which has been decided at the permission stage in the applicant's favour. That was 'only (i) if the judge hearing the initial application has expressly so indicated, (ii) if new and relevant material is introduced on the substantive hearing, (iii) if, exceptionally, the issues as they have developed at the full hearing put a different aspect on the question of promptness, or (iv) if the first judge has plainly overlooked some relevant matter or otherwise reached a decision per in curiam'.[54]

5.53   Examples of where a remedy sought has been refused due to delay are found in *R v Swale Borough Council v Medway Ports Authority, ex p RSPB* (1991) Admin LR 790 where there had been a breach of a legitimate expectation but the remedy was refused for delay on the basis that third parties had relied on the decision; in *R v North West Leicestershire District Council, ex p Moses* [2000] Env LR 443 where third parties had spent money substantially in reliance on planning permission for a runway. But equally, there are decisions where a remedy has been refused as part of the court's discretion having regard to hardship, prejudice and detriment to good administration even where

---

[53]   See page 341B.
[54]   Para 34.

there has been no undue delay in bringing proceedings: *R v Secretary of State for the Environment, ex p Walters* (1997) 30 HLR 328.

Grounds of review

5.54   The basic grounds of challenge for a judicial review are illegality (error of law), irrationality (unreasonableness) and procedural impropriety (unfairness). There is often an overlap between the grounds which are not mutually exclusive.

Illegality

The influence of EC law

5.55   The influence of EC law in the field of planning and environmental law is extensive. Coupled with heightened awareness of environmental issues the allegation that there is some breach of an EC Directive or national regulations that transpose the Directive so that the grant of planning permission is unlawful is not an uncommon ground of challenge.

5.56   Through the European Communities Act 1972 all the rights and obligations that EU law creates are incorporated into domestic law. Anything in domestic law inconsistent with EU rights or obligations is abrogated or must be modified to avoid inconsistency. Basic EU rights, obligations and principles including principles of direct effect, effective protection of rights and compatible interpretation are incorporated into domestic law and are capable of informing all grounds of judicial review.

5.57   Another strand that is important is the ability of the European Parliament to made regulations and issue directives, take decisions, make recommendations or deliver opinions.[55] Directives are binding on Member States as to the result to be achieved and require national measures to be adopted to give effect to them. How the result is to be achieved is left to the Member State. All regulations are directly applicable so that they become part of the national law without any need for member States to transpose them into national law.

5.58   Decisions of the ECJ are thus binding on the High Court in the same way as decisions of the higher courts are here. The application of compatible interpretation was illustrated in *Wells v Secretary of State for Transport, Local Government and the Regions* (Case C-201/02) [2004] ECR 1-273 where an old planning permission which was being reviewed under the Planning and Compensation Act 1992 was held to be subject to the requirements of environmental impact assessment as a result of Article 4 of Directive 85/337/EEC read in conjunction with Annexes I and II. Consent had been granted for mining operations at Conygar Quarry without an EIA having first been carried out. The old permission was registered and, as a result, no development could be carried out unless there was an approval of a new scheme of planning conditions. No consideration was given to the need for an EIA. The court held that where there was a consent procedure involving two stages, one a principal decision and the other an implementing decision, which cannot extend beyond the parameters set by the principal decision the effects of the project on the environment must be identified and assessed at the time of the procedure relating to the principal decision. It is only if the effects were not identifiable until the time of the procedure relating to the implementing decision that the

---

[55]   Art 249 EC.

EIA should be carried out during the course of that procedure. The decision means that all such projects must be made subject to an assessment with regard to their effects before (multi-stage) development consent is given.

5.59   That decision was taken further in the case of *R (Barker) v Bromley London Borough Council* [2006] UKHL 52 when the House of Lords held that the Town and Country Planning (Environmental Impact Assessment) Regulations 1988 failed to adequately implement Directive 85/337/EEC. That was because the then current Regulations precluded any consideration of the need for an EIA at the reserved matters stage. The Regulations overlooked the fact that the relevant development consent may be a multi stage process.[56]

5.60   If there has been a misdirection as to EC Law then the decision, save in very limited circumstances, will be quashed: *R v Secretary of State for the Environment, ex p Royal Society for the Protection of Birds* [1997] QB 206 when it was held that the Secretary of State was not allowed to take into account economic considerations when classifying a Special Protection Area or designating its boundaries applying Directive 79/409/EEC but economic considerations may constitute imperative reasons of over-riding public interest of the kind referred to in Art 6(4) of Directive 92/43/EEC.

5.61   Further, the need to interpret, as far as possible, national legislation in the light of the wording and purpose of directives has been a common theme. In *Marleasing SA v La Comercial Internacional de Alimentación SA* (Case C-106/89) [1990] ECR I-4135, 1439 the European Court of Justice defined this obligation as follows: 'It follows that, in applying national law, whether the provisions in question were adopted before or after the directive, the national court called upon to interpret it is required to do so, as far as possible, in light of the wording and the purpose of the directive in order to achieve the result pursued by the latter and thereby comply with the third paragraph of Article 189 of the Treaty.'

5.62   The *Marleasing* approach has been followed by the courts on many occasions.[57] The courts do recognise that the obligation to interpret legislation is not without boundaries. The case of *Ghaidan v Godin Mendoza* [2004] UKHL 30 made it clear that the obligation imposed by the ECJ is only to interpret national law in conformity with a Directive as far as possible. Lord Rodgers defined the position as follows, 'When the court spells out the words that are to be implied, it may look as if it is amending the legislation, but that it not the case. If the court implies words that are consistent with the scheme of the legislation but necessary to make it compatible with Convention rights, it is simply performing the duty which Parliament imposed on it and others. It is reading the legislation in a way that draws out the full implications of its terms and of the Convention rights. And, by its very nature, an implication will go with the grain of the legislation or with its essential principles as disclosed by its provisions does not involve any form of interpretation, by implication or otherwise. It falls on the wrong side of the boundary between interpretation and amendment of the statute.' The phrase 'as far as possible' provides certain parameters and the court must 'go with the grain of the legislation'.[58]

---

[56]   *Commission v United Kingdom.*
[57]   *Horner v Lancashire County Council* [2007] EWCA Civ 784 as one example.
[58]   *Ghaidan v Godin- Mendoza* [2004] UKHL 30.

5.63   The case of *R v Durham County Council, ex p Huddleston* [1999] EWCA Civ 792 illustrates a further example of where a direct effect solution adopted as primary legislation was incompatible with an EC Directive and convergent construction was not possible.[59] The Court decided that Mr Huddleston was entitled to insist that the State should act as Durham could not act (as an emanation of the State when there was failure by the State to transpose a Directive), in conformity with the Directive. An individual's rights which arose from his interest in the legal protection of the environment were such as to prevent the state from 'taking refuge in its own neglect to transpose them into national law'.

5.64   *R v Rochdale Borough Council, ex p Tew* [1999] EWHC Admin 409 brought about a change in approach to assessment of large development projects. A large business park proposal was approved by Rochdale Borough Council on the basis of an illustrative master plan submitted with the application and subject to conditions attached to the planning permission. As a matter of practice at the time the procedure followed was not unusual. Under Directive 85/377 there was a requirement to take into account effects on the environment at the earliest possible stage. The amending Directive 97/11, as part of its Recitals, set out that it 'aims at providing the competent authorities with relevant information to enable them to take a decision on a specific project in full knowledge of the project's likely significant effects on the environment … the assessment procedure is a fundamental instrument of environmental policy as defined by Article 130 of the Treaty …'. Having regard to the purpose of the Directive the Court held that the procedure that had been followed was defective, that the purpose of the Directive as transposed into national legislation was to secure at the outset of the assessment process sufficient information to be able to assess the likely significant environmental effect of the development proposed and quashed the decision.

5.65   *Berkeley* (see later) is one of a wealth of Environmental Impact Assessment cases that have come before the courts in challenges that have been described as 'unduly legalistic'. The courts have been clear that EIA processes are 'not an obstacle course'[60] for applicants for planning permission to follow slavishly. Sullivan J set out the position clearly in *Blewett v Derbyshire County Council* [2003] EWHC 2775 when he said:[61]

> 'There will be cases where the document purporting to be an environmental statement is so deficient that it could not reasonably be described as an environmental statement as defined in the Regulations (*Tew* was an example of such a case), but they are likely to be few and far between. It would be no advantage to anyone concerned with the development process – applicants, objectors or local authorities – if environmental statements were drafted on a purely "defensive basis", mentioning every possible scrap of environmental information just in case someone might consider it significant at a later stage. Such documents would be a hindrance, not an aid to sound decision making by the local planning authority, since they would obscure the principal issues in a welter of detail.'

5.66   The preceding question of whether the development is EIA development at all has been the subject of considerable litigation. Whether development is EIA development is a decision for the local planning authority which provided they ask the right question and arrive at an answer within the bounds of reason and the four corners

---

[59]   Per Sedley LJ at para 10 'to construe the statutory provisions so as to converge with the Directive by "writing in" further words would set off a chain reaction likely to disrupt the whole planning regime for mineral extraction'.

[60]   *R (Jones) v Mansfield District Council* [2003] EWCA Civ 1408, *Younger Homes (Northern) Limited v FSS and Calderdale MBC* [2004] EWCA Civ 1060 at paras 46–47.

[61]   At para 41.

of the evidence before them cannot be categorised as unlawful. The question of whether an EIA is needed can be reviewed by the courts on the basis of irrationality only: *R (Vivienne Morge) v Hampshire County Council* [2010] EWCA Civ 608. Although now the subject of a decision of the Supreme Court at [2011] UKSC 2 that is on two grounds which do not affect the basis of challenge to an EIA. The Supreme Court took the view that it was not necessary to refer the interpretation of Article 12(1)(b) of the Habitat's Directive 92/43/EEC to the ECJ as it was unrealistic to suppose that the ECJ would feel able to provide any greater assistance. The court then proceeded to give detailed guidance on the interpretation of the article. Lord Brown held that certain broad considerations governed the approach to the article which were fourfold, namely, that the article afforded protection to species and not to habitats, that the protection extended to species and not to the protection of 'specimens of the species', an assessment of the nature and extent of the negative impact of the activity in question on the species was not precluded and was required for a judgment as to whether that was sufficient to a 'disturbance' to the species, it was implicit that activity at breeding, rearing, hibernation and migration periods was more likely to have a sufficient negative impact on the species to constitute prohibited 'disturbance' than activity at other times.

5.67   In addition, the Human Rights Act 1998[62] enacted into domestic law protection for the European Convention of Human Rights (ECHR). Compulsory purchase cases subsequent to that enactment, in particular, show considerable reliance upon Convention Rights as part of any challenge to a decision.[63] Often the issue of proportionality is raised against a Compulsory Purchase Order. It is regarded as a test of substance: *R (Hart District Council) v Secretary of State for Communities and Local Government* [2008] 2 P & CR 16. Provided the intensity of review is greater in the courts than it would be in a domestic judicial review then that will satisfy the Convention requirements.[64]

5.68   *R (Alconbury Developments Ltd) v Secretary of State for the Environment, Transport and the Regions* [2001] UKHL 23 raised the fundamental issue about whether the decision-making processes on the part of the Secretary of State for the Environment, Transport and the Regions in a planning context where the Secretary of State is the decision-maker were compatible with Article 6 of the ECHR. The basis of challenge was that the Secretary of State was not an independent and impartial tribunal as he would take account of his own policies that he had formulated. The Divisional Court held that the Secretary of State was not independent and impartial and granted declarations of incompatibility in relation to the call in and appeal sections of the Town and Country Planning Act.[65] The House of Lords unanimously rejected that position and held that the part of the planning system under challenge was compatible.

5.69   In *R (on the application of Baker) v North East Somerset District Council* [2009] EWHC 595 Admin[66] a challenge was brought to planning permissions that had been granted for modifications/extensions to existing green waste composting facilities. No environmental impact assessment (EIA) was sought as the proposed modifications were

---

[62]   The long title of which reads: 'An Act to give further effect to rights and freedoms guaranteed under the European Convention of Human Rights.'

[63]   *R (Pascoe) v First Secretary of State* [2006] EWHC 2356 – challenges brought under Arts 1 and 8 – no requirement under CPO to use the least intrusive means, *Smith & others v Secretary of State for Trade and Industry & London Development Agency* [2007] EWHC 1013 Admin – a decision to confirm a CPO may be proportionate even though not the least intrusive interference with Art 8 rights.

[64]   *R (SD) v Governors of Denbigh High School* [2006] UKHL 15 at para 30.

[65]   Sections 77 and 78 together with various sections under the Transport and Works Act.

[66]   Under appeal at the time of writing.

under the threshold set out in the Town and Country Planning Environmental Impact Assessment Regulations 1999 which triggered the requirement for such a statement. A challenge was brought which considered whether Directive 85/337/EC (as amended) was properly transposed. Having regard to EC jurisprudence and the Directive the court found that it was wrong to have regard only to the modification itself. There should be regard to the cumulative effect on the whole development as a result of the modifications to it. A case by case appraisal of the modifications, which was provided for in the Regulations, was no answer as that excluded the public and part of the purpose of the Directive was to secure public involvement in EIA development. As a result the permissions were quashed.

5.70 Whilst not an EC based challenge the decision in the case of *R (Mellor) v Secretary of State for Communities and Local Government* Case C-75/08 provides that a competent authority does not have to make available to the public reasons for a negative screening opinion. However, if a member of the public asks for such a document the competent authority is under an obligation to supply it. The reasons stated can be short but one can see future litigation about the extent of the duty. It is another illustration of the role of EC jurisprudence.

5.71 Allegations of unlawfulness through breach of an EC Directive were made as part of the case in *Ardagh Glass v Chester City Council* [2009] EWHC 745 Admin. This was another chapter in a long running saga about Europe's largest glass making factory built entirely without planning permission. Judicial review was sought of: (i) the Council's failure to take enforcement action within the four year period after which the development would become immune from enforcement (and the expiry of which was looming), and (ii) that the EIA Directive prohibited the grant of retrospective development consent. The Court ordered service of enforcement notices and held that Article 2(1) of Directive 85/337 did not appear to rule out the possibility of retrospective development consent provided that it was preceded by a full and proper EIA with a full and genuine opportunity for the public to understand the proposals, express their views and for those views to be taken into account. Such an approach complied with the objectives of the Directive. The Court of Appeal[67] upheld the judge saying that his decision accorded with: (a) common sense, (b) the need to ensure that measures to ensure compliance with the directive are proportionate in accordance with community law, and (c) the ECJ's judgement in the *Ireland* case which recognised that, subject to certain conditions, national law may permit regularisation of unauthorised EIA development.

5.72 Breaches of an EC Directive and Regulations were used as a basis for a challenge under s 113 of the Planning and Compulsory Purchase Act 2004 in respect of planning policies contained in the East of England plan relating housing development around certain towns in the London Arch.[68] It was held that contrary to Directive 2001/42 and the Environmental Assessment of Plans and Programmes Regulations 2004, no proper environmental assessments had been performed before the policies were adopted. Article 5 of the Directive and Regulation 12 of the Regulations required that reasonable alternatives to the proposals should be described and evaluated before a choice was made as to how a plan should be modified. The information that accompanied the policies meant that in exceptional circumstances, such as sustainable development including housing, encroachment into the Green Belt would probably be necessary.

---

[67] [2010] EWCA Civ 172.
[68] *Hertfordshire CC, City and District of St Albans v SSCLG* May 2009.

Within Hatfield, Welwyn Garden City and Hemel Hempstead no reasonable alternatives that might affect development in the Green Belt had been identified and examined. Part of the South East England Plan was quashed.

5.73   If there is a breach of European Law then the discretion on the part of the Court to quash the decision is limited. The case of *Berkeley v Secretary of State for the Environment* [2000] UKHL 36 made it clear that Article 10 of the EC Treaty obliged the national court to ensure that Community rights are fully and effectively enforced. It was only if there was substantial compliance with the Directive and domestic regulations that the impugned decision could be saved. As there had not been substantial compliance in *Berkeley* in that there was no Environmental Statement at all but reliance had to be placed on the environmental information being available in a series of documents, the planning authority's statement of case, officer reports and proofs of evidence at the public inquiry that required what Lord Hoffman referred to as a paper chase as opposed to a single and accessible compilation produced by the applicant at the start of the application, the decision could not be saved.[69]

5.74   Since that decision the courts have expressed some unease at an over reliance on the House of Lords' rejection in *Berkeley* of the use of discretionary refusal of relief as impermissible 'retrospective dispensation' of the requirements of the an EIA or similar EU 'pre-condition' of grants of permission under other domestic planning or regulatory regimes. In *Bown v Secretary of State* [2003] EWCA Civ 1790 Carnwath LJ said, 'The speeches need to be read in context. Lord Bingham emphasised the very narrow basis on which the case was argued in the House (pp 607F–608A). 'The developer was not represented in the House, and there was no reference to any evidence of actual prejudice to his or any other interests. Care is needed in applying the principles there decided to other circumstances, such as cases where, as here, there is clear evidence of a pressing public need for the scheme which is under attack.'

5.75   In *R (on the application of Edwards and Anor) v Environment Agency and others* [2008] UKHL 22 at paragraph 63 Lord Hoffman agreed with the remarks of Carnwath LJ when he emphasised 'that the speeches in *Berkeley* need to be read in context. Both the nature of the flaw in the decision and the ground for exercise of discretion has to be considered. In *Berkeley*, the flaw was the complete absence of an EIA and the sole ground for the exercise of discretion was that the result was bound to be the same'. In *Edwards* the House of Lords approved the approach of the Court of Appeal and the judge below in refusing to quash the IPPC permit on the basis that it would be pointless to enable the public to be consulted on out of date data. To that pointlessness Lord Hoffman added waste of time and resources both for the company and the Environment Agency. There appears, therefore, to have been some judicial rowing back from the high water mark of the speeches in *Berkeley*.

Duty to give reasons for the grant of planning permission

5.76   Whilst reasons for refusing an application for planning permission have always had to be given, reasons for the grant of planning permission have not. It was frustrating for a developer or a third party not to know the basis for a grant of planning permission when that decision was taken contrary to officer advice as set out in the

---

[69]   See also *Downs v Secretary of State for the Environment, Food and Rural Affairs* [2008] EWHC 2666 when the failure to apply the relevant Directive correctly resulted in an order that the Secretary of State rectify his policy.

report to Committee. That changed with Article 22 of the Town and Country Planning (General Development Procedure) Order 1995 (brought into effect in December 2003) which reads:

> '(a)   When a local planning authority give notice of a decision or determination on an application for planning permission or for approval of reserved matters and –
> (b)   planning permission is granted subject to conditions, the notice shall:
> (c)   include a summary of their reasons for the grant together with a summary of the policies and proposals in the development plan which are relevant to the decision to grant permission:'

5.77   Three issues arise. First, what is the extent of the duty to give reasons? Second, what is the duty to provide a summary of the policies in the Development Plan and third, what are the principles to be applied in the exercise of discretion when the court considers whether to quash the decision notice?

5.78   The background to the introduction of the requirement was set out in *R (Wall) v Brighton & Hove City Council* [2004] EWHC 2582:

> 'Over the years the public was first enabled and then encouraged to participate in the decision making process. The fact that, having participated, the public was not entitled to be told what the local planning authority's reasons were was increasingly perceived as a justifiable source of grievance, which undermined the confidence in the planning system. The requirement to give summary reason for the grant of planning permission will principally be for the benefit of interested members of the public .... Parliament decided that this extension of the public's rights under the Planning Code was necessary even though in many cases it could reasonably be inferred that members would have granted planning permission because they agreed with the planning officer's report ...'.

5.79   The requirement to give reasons was said to be particularly valuable in cases where members have not accepted officer advice, where the officer has not felt able to make a recommendation, where the officer's report fails to take into account a material consideration, but that omission is said to be remedied by members in the course of their discussions or where an irrelevant factor has been relied upon by some members during the course of their discussions and it is important to ascertain whether it was one of the reasons for granting planning permission. In short, it enables a third party to consider whether there is a possible basis for a challenge to the decision.

5.80   Subsequent cases[70] set out factors that the court thought relevant in setting out reasons that were adequate. Whilst the judges are not totally of the same view it seems to be that reasons can be stated very shortly but that they should deal with important issues which were raised in connection with the planning permission in question.[71]

---

[70]   *R (Ling) (Bridlington) Limited and others v East Riding of Yorkshire Council* [2006] EWHC 1604. *R (Jacqueline Tratt) v Horsham District Council* [2007] EWHC 1485 Admin 'summary reasons must deal in summary form, with the substantial issues which have formed part of the consideration of the planning application and that they are likely to be used by objectors to see whether there may be some reasons to seek judicial review', at para 42.

[71]   *R (on the application of Aldergate Projects Limited) v Nottinghamshire County Council* [2008] EWHC 2881 at para 50. Although note in Ling at para 48 'it does not require a summary of the reasons for objecting to the grant of planning permission'. See also *R (Siraj) v Kirklees MDC* EWCA Civ 1286 where the members agreed with the officer recommendation they were not required to give anything other than summary reasons.

5.81 As to the duty to set out a summary of the relevant planning policies 'what was thought to be needed was an indication for the reader of what were the relevant policies. All that was needed was to indicate what the policies went to.'[72] There is a distinction between providing a summary and providing a list of policies, although the Court of Appeal in *R (on the application of Roudham and Larling Parish Council) v Breckland Council* [2008] EWCA Civ 714 found adequate a decision notice which set out the policy in the Development Plan only with which it was said that the decision had been taken in accord. They were satisfied that that, together with the conditions imposed on the planning permission with the reasons for their imposition, meant that there was an implicit explanation that the concerns of those who objected had been dealt with.

5.82 On discretion, the courts have said:

'A failure to include the summary reasons in a decision notice will not render the grant of planning permission null and void (see Brayhead ...). On the other hand, such a failure could not be described as "so nugatory or trivial that the authority can safely proceed without remedial action" (see *London & Clydeside* ...). If the defective decision notice is challenged in an application for judicial review the court will have a discretion to quash the notice. How it exercises that discretion will depend upon the particular facts of the case, where it fits within the "spectrum of possibilities" referred to by Lord Hailsham in *London & Clydeside*.'[73]

5.83 The approach of the 'spectrum of possibilities' was approved by the Court of Appeal. It was applied in the case of *Loader v Poole District Council* [2009] EWHC 1288 where a breach of the duty under Article 22 was found but because the failure was trivial and no one was left in any real doubt as to the defendant's reasons for granting the planning permission the challenge failed.

The interpretation of planning policy

5.84 What a planning policy means is an old chestnut in challenges to planning decisions. In *R v Derbyshire County Council, ex p Woods* [1997] JPL 958 the Court of Appeal held that it was for the court to determine as a matter of law what the words are capable of meaning:

(a)   if in all the circumstances the words are capable of bearing more than one meaning and the LPA adopts and applies a meaning which it is capable as a matter of law as bearing then they will not have gone wrong;

(b)   if a decision maker attaches a meaning to the words that they are not properly capable of meaning he will have made an error of law.

5.85 Such an approach was consistent with *Northavon District Council v Secretary of State for the Environment* [1993] JPL 761 where it was observed that 'the words spoke for themselves and were not readily susceptible to precise legal definition. Whether a proposed development was within the description was in most cases likely to be a matter of fact and degree and planning judgement.' The same approach was also taken in *Virgin Cinema Properties Ltd v Secretary of State for the Environment* [1998] 2 PLR 24.

5.86 Later cases have sought to provide limits to the approach. 'The courts must be wary of an approach whereby decision makers can live in the planning world of

---

[72]   *Aldergate Projects* (supra) para 54.
[73]   *R (Wall) v Brighton and Hove City Council* [2004] EWHC 2582.

Humpty Dumpty, making a particular planning policy mean whatever the decision maker decides that it should mean.'[74] Some constraint was sought to be provided in the four tests laid down in *Cranage Parish Council v First Secretary of State* [2004] EWHC 2949 Admin:

1.   the interpretation propounded by a decision maker is one that the words are properly capable of bearing;

2.   there may be instances on a point of interpretation in a relevant planning context where the ambit of reasonableness is narrow or even nil;

3.   there may be cases where even if the words taken on their own prima facie support the interpretation of the decision maker, consideration of the purpose and underlying objective of the policy in question may show that such linguistic interpretation will not accurately represent the true policy;

4.   decision makers will need to bear in mind that the adoption of a particular interpretation of a policy in a development plan in a particular case will make it difficult, at all events in the absence of a convincing explanation, for them to adopt a different interpretation in another case without attracting a challenge on the ground of arbitrariness or collateral purpose or the like.

5.87   Nevertheless, the Court of Appeal has retained the view that a planning decision maker's approach to policy will only be interfered with by the court if it goes beyond the range of reasonable meanings that can be given to the language used: *R (on the application of Springhall) v Richmond upon Thames LBC* [2006] EWCA Civ 19. Unless the decision maker attaches a meaning to the words of a planning policy that they cannot reasonably bear, it is not for the court to substitute its own interpretation of policy. Further, the application of such policy to the facts of any particular case is a matter of planning judgement for the decision maker, subject only to considerations of *Wednesbury* irrationality.

5.88   There was some move to introduce a different approach in the case of *Raissi* [2008] EWCA Civ 72, a non planning case but in which the Court of Appeal discussed planning cases and remarked that even within the reasonable range of meanings approach there was not unanimity. The Court concluded that the test was to ask what a reasonable and literate person would make of the policy.

5.89   Subsequent cases in the Court of Appeal have not adopted that approach in planning cases and have sided with that set out in *Woods:* see *S Cambridgeshire DC v Secretary of State for Communities and Local Government* [2008] EWCA Civ 1010; *R (on the application of Heath and Hampstead Society) v Camden LBC* [2008] EWCA Civ 193 which emphasised also the importance of context of the policy under challenge.

5.90   For the time being, therefore, the reasonable range of meanings approach covers the interpretation to planning policy subject only to a challenge on *Wednesbury* grounds.

---

[74]   *Cranage Parish Council v First Secretary of State* [2004] EWHC 2949 Admin at para 50.

Other areas of illegality

Omission of a material consideration / statutory duty

5.91   Failure to discharge the duty under the Race Relations Act 1976, s 71 resulted in planning permission for a mixed use development being quashed in *R (on the application of Janet Harris) v Haringey London Borough Council & Grainger Seven Sisters Ltd, Northumberland & Durham Property Trust Limited and the Equality and Human Rights Commissions* [2010] EWCA Civ 703. The planning authority had granted planning permission for the redevelopment of an indoor market comprising various business units and residential properties. Some 64 per cent of the market traders were of Latin American origin or Spanish speaking. Section 71 was found to be integral to the decision-making process. The duty under s 71 (1) was to have 'due regard' to the need to 'promote equality of opportunity and good relations between persons of different racial groups' and was not demonstrated in the decision-making process. The duty to have due regard need not require the promotion of the equality of opportunity but 'it did require an analysis of that material with the specific statutory considerations in mind'. There was no reference to the s 71 duty in the report to committee or in the deliberations of the Committee resulting in the decision being quashed.

Legitimate expectations / estoppel

5.92   Legitimate expectations can be another facet of illegality. Although the principles involved and the nature of the evolving concept has been reviewed in *Bhatt Murphy v The Independent Assessor* [2008] EWCA Civ 755[75] the concept of legitimate expectations in planning is limited. Planning law provides a comprehensive code imposed in the public interest (see the House of Lords decision in *Pioneer Aggregates (UK) Ltd v Secretary of State for the Environment* [1985] 1 AC 132). As such, the concept of legitimate expectation in planning operates only in exceptional circumstances. This was made clear in the case of *Henry Boot v Bassetlaw* [2002] EWCA Civ 983. 'It is possible that circumstances might arise where it was clear that there was no third party or public interest in the matter and a court might take the view that a legitimate expectation could then arise from the local planning authority's conduct or representations. But, ... one suspects that such cases will be very rare'. 'Even more than many areas of public law which concern an individual and a public body, planning law is likely to have to reflect the fact that third parties and the public generally may have interests in any decision'.[76]

5.93   The public nature of, and public involvement in, the planning processes was emphasised in *R v East Sussex CC, ex p Reprotech (Pebsham) and Another* [2002] UKHL 8 'a determination is not simply a matter between the applicant and the planning authority in which they are free to agree on whatever procedure they please. It is also a matter which concerns the general public interest and which requires other planning authorities, the Secretary of State on behalf of the national interest and the

---

[75] See review by Laws LJ from para 26 et seq 'Legitimate expectation is now a well-known public law headline. But its reach in practice is still being explored. In one of the leading cases, *Ex p Coughlan* [2001] QB 213, Lord Woolf MR as he then was, giving the judgment of the court, described it as 'still a developing field of law' (para 59). The cases show that put broadly (there are refinements) it encompasses two kinds. There is procedural legitimate expectation, and there is substantive legitimate expectation. But in certain types of case these terms are more elusive than they appear. These appeals therefore call for some account of the material principles, however well trodden the ground. I acknowledge that much of the ground is at the foothills. But the path falters a little further up'.

[76] At para 52.

public itself to be able to participate'.[77] That was said as part of the rationale as to why the private law concept of estoppel had no role to play in planning law. The rationale applies to the concept of legitimate expectations equally as was recognised in the case of *R (Wandsworth BC) v SSTLGR* [2003] EWHC 622 Admin.[78]

Conditions

5.94   Another frequent area of dispute is the lawfulness of conditions attached to a planning permission. To be lawful a condition must pass the tests set down in Circular 11/95. In summary, conditions must be necessary, relevant to planning and reasonable in all respects. They need to be read benevolently in the context of the planning permission granted or the decision letter that preceded the grant of planning permission on appeal. A planning permission is 'to be given the meaning that a reasonable reader would give to it', having regard to the terms of the permission itself together with any further admissible documentary evidence: see Arden LJ at page 1054 of *Carter Commercial Developments Limited (in Administration) v Secretary of State for Transport, Local Government and the Regions and Mendip District Council* [2002] EWCA Civ 1914. However, there is a limit to what conditions can do. For example, they cannot rectify a flawed screening opinion: *R (on the application of Birch) v Barnsley Metropolitan Borough Council* [2010] EWCA Civ 1180.

5.95   As any planning permission is a public document there is no scope for implied conditions. In *Green v Secretary of State for the Communities and Local Government* [2010] EWCA Civ 64, Pill LJ expressed discomfort at having to construe a condition creatively but adopted the words of Lord Denning in *Fawcett Properties Ltd v Buckinghamshire CC* [1961] AC 636 'I am of opinion that a planning condition is only void for uncertainty if it can be given no meaning or no sensible or ascertainable meaning, and not merely because it is ambiguous or leads to absurd results. It is the daily task of the courts to resolve ambiguities of language and to choose between them; and to construe words so as to avoid absurdities or to put up with them. And this applies to conditions in planning permissions as well as to other documents.' The Court was prepared to consider the Inspector's decision in the context of planning guidance and model conditions to ascertain what the Inspector had intended in the imposition of the disputed condition.

Relationship with other controls

5.96   The interrelationship between planning and other areas, in particular pollution control, has been a source of review by the courts. In *Gateshead MBC v Secretary of State for the Environment* [1994] 1 PLR 85 the court expressed the view that the existence of another regime of control, in this case pollution control, dealing with issues that would be considered also as part of the planning process could not be ignored and was a highly material consideration. It is a point re-iterated in planning guidance in PPS 23.

Use of a statutory power for an improper purpose

5.97   In *Cala Homes (South) Ltd v Secretary of State for Communities and Local Government* [2010] EWHC 2866 the court held that the Secretary of State had acted unlawfully by using s 79(6) of the Local Democracy Economic Development and

---

[77]   Lord Hoffman at para 29.

[78]   'The circumstances in which it will be appropriate to find a legitimate expectation in the planning field are limited, and the decision taker is engaged in a task that is very different from an attempt to decide whether or not there is an estoppel in private law' at para 22.

Construction Act 2009 to revoke all Regional Strategies as a result of using the power for an improper purpose, namely, in a way not intended by Parliament since to proceed in the way that the Secretary of State had was to denude primary legislation of any practical effect, without having to seek the approval of Parliament for such a course by passing further legislation to achieve that effect. Had Parliament intended to create such a power it would 'have used clearer language to achieve that effect and would have given the provision far greater prominence than section 79(6) has, tucked away as a final subsection in a provision otherwise dealing with revision of Regional Strategies'.[79] The challenge was successful also on the second ground of challenge which was that there had been no screening assessment nor a more detailed strategic environmental assessment in relation to the decision on the part of the Secretary of State to revoke the South East Plan.

Consideration of officer reports

5.98 Frequently challenges are brought on the basis that the officer report is incomplete or inadequate in that it has not identified all relevant material considerations or misdirected or misled the committee in a material particular. The oft cited words of Judge LJ in *Oxton Farms v Selby District Council* [1997] EGCS 60 are to be borne in mind. 'The report by a planning officer to his committee is not and is not intended to provide a learned disquisition of relevant legal principles or to repeat each and every detail of the relevant facts to members of the committee who are responsible for the decision and who are entitled to use their local knowledge to reach it. The report is therefore not susceptible to textual analysis appropriate to the construction of a statute or the directions provided by a judge when summing a case up to the jury.'[80] Those remarks were drawn upon in the case of *Siraj v Kirklees MBC* [2010] EWCA Civ 1286 when Sullivan LJ said 'It has been repeatedly emphasised that officers' reports such as this should not be construed as though they were enactments. They should be read as a whole and in a commonsense manner, bearing in mind the fact that they are addressed to an informed readership, in this case the respondent's planning subcommittee.' That approach was followed and said to be appropriate also when considering the oral contributions made by members of the committee when debating a particular development proposal which had been reported to them particularly bearing in mind that 'the words will not have been formulated in the quiet of an officer's room with all relevant documentary material to hand'. Further, opinions and views can change as a result of debate: see *Oadby Hilltop and others v Oadby and Wigston Borough Council* [2011] EWHC 60.

5.99 It is beyond the scope of this chapter to go through all possible areas of illegality that can be the source of a challenge to a planning decision. What it has sought to do is to distil certain themes that emerge from frequent areas of challenge.

Irrationality

5.100 Irrationality is a ground often relied upon but for reasons set out with great clarity in R *(Newsmith) v Secretary of State for the Environment, Transport and the Regions* [2001] EWHC 74 one that is difficult to succeed upon in planning challenges

---

[79] Sales J at para 52(i).
[80] And see Pill LJ 'that is not to say that a report is to be construed as if it were a statute or that defects of presentation can often render a decision made following its submission to the council liable to be quashed. The overall fairness of the report, in the context of the statutory test, must be considered'.

(where the claimant was described as facing a 'particularly daunting task'[81] given that the decision was one of planning judgement reached on the evidence and having seen the site). Although the decision itself related to a challenge under s 288 the observations apply equally to a planning decision taken by a Committee. The traditional test set out in *R v Monopolies and Mergers Commission, ex p South Yorkshire Transport Limited* [1993] 1 WLR 23 as to whether 'the decision is so aberrant that it cannot be classed as rational' still applies. A recent illustration of the difficulty in running an irrationality challenge is seen in *R (Griffin) v London City Airport* [2011] EWHC 53 where a ground of challenge that the failure to consult with the nearby planning authorities of Waltham Forest and Redbridge was irrational failed as the local planning authority had made a judgment not to do so on the basis of noise contours which showed the level of noise taken as representing the onset of noise annoyance not to affect those authorities which was held to be a rational basis upon which to take the decision not to consult. Conversely, in *Technoprint and another v Leeds City Council* [2010] EWHC 581 the irrationality challenge succeeded where no reasonable planning authority would have granted planning permission with conditions given that there were so many outstanding matters which were unresolved relating to contaminated land and open space.

5.101   The role of the Court is supervisory only. It has repeatedly made it clear that it is no part of its role to substitute its own decision on the merits given that there will always be a broad range of planning judgements that the decision maker could arrive at: *R v Leominster District Council, ex p Pothecary* (1998) P & CR 346. Inconsistency in decision making can be a basis for a challenge to a planning decision. Both the planning history of the site and a decision of a planning inspector on appeal on the same site can be material.[82] Where a planning authority departs from its previous decision on the same site it may need to be prepared to give an explanation for that change of course.[83] But if the background is well known to members there is no duty on the part of the reporting officer to set out every fact to the members: *R v Mendip District Council, ex p Fabre* (2000) 80 P & CR 500.

Procedural impropriety (unfairness)

5.102   Planning procedures set out in the Town and Country Planning General Procedure Development Order 1995 seek to encapsulate principles of fairness in the processing of a planning application in setting out who to consult and procedures to be followed. Approaching an appeal, the rules of natural justice provide for procedural fairness in the Town and Country Planning (Inquiries Procedure) Rules 2000.[84] As a result it is rare that there are challenges brought which allege impropriety based on a breach of the rules.

5.103   Most of the judicial review challenges which use this ground of challenge have been brought on the basis of bias or apparent bias and apparent pre-determination. The test applied has been that set out in *Porter v Magill* [2001] UKHL 67, namely, what a fair minded and informed observer would have made of proceedings.[85]

---

[81]   At para 8.
[82]   *North Wiltshire District Council v Secretary of State for the Environment* [1993] 3 PLR 113 at 112 F to H, *R (Chisnell) & another v Richmond on Thames LBC* [2005] EWHC 134.
[83]   *R v Aylesbury Vale District Council, ex p Chaplin* [1997] 3 PLR 55.
[84]   See also equivalent provisions for written representation appeals, enforcement appeals and CPO Inquiries.
[85]   *R v Secretary for State for the Environment & Anr, ex p Kirkstall Valley Campaign Ltd* [1996] 3 All ER 304;

5.104 The case of *Persimmon Homes Teesside Ltd v R (on the application of Lewis)* [2008] EWCA Civ 746 re-iterated the importance of understanding the local government context in which planning decisions are taken. 'Councillors are not in a judicial or quasi-judicial position but are elected to provide and pursue policies. Members of a Planning Committee would be entitled, and indeed expected, to have and to have expressed views on planning issues.'[86] The Court of Appeal upheld an appeal against a decision which had quashed a planning permission on the basis of apparent bias given that the decision to grant permission had been taken during a period leading up to a local election and various members of the Liberal Democratic party had expressed very positive and supportive views about the application which subsequently they had to determine. The Court held that it was for the court to assess whether Committee members made the decision with closed minds or that the circumstances gave rise to such a real risk of closed minds that the decision ought not in the public interest be upheld. The importance of appearances was more limited in the local government context than in a judicial context.

5.105 It was thought that that decision would slow the challenges by third parties on the basis of apparent predetermination. The case of *R (on the application of Gardner) v Harrogate BC (Mr and Mrs Atkinson)* [2008] EWHC 2942 Admin showed that not to be the case. The Local Government Ombudsman had reported that the grant of permission was procedurally flawed because there was apparent bias on the part of the chair of the Council's Area Planning Development Control Committee on whose casting vote the planning permission was granted. The court applied the fair minded and informed observer test but again emphasised the surrounding context. In that case the context was that the applicant for planning permission was a fellow councillor who was regarded by the chair with 'liking, affection and loyalty'. The Ombudsman's report was one from which the court should be slow to depart and the fact that the council acknowledged that the grant of planning permission was improper and that other councillors expressed concerns were factors that did not give the court good reason to do so.

5.106 Most local planning authorities now have well established procedures to be followed in making planning determinations so that those, together with a full understanding of the local government context, will make it difficult for the claimant to succeed under this head.

5.107 Other areas where the issue of procedural unfairness has been raised are when an Inspector failed to address the conclusion of a noise expert's report. The Court found that he was not bound to do so. From a reading of the decision letter as a whole it was clear that he had taken the report into account and understood it. The Inspector had visited the site, made his own inspection and was entitled to rely upon his experience, expertise and common sense: *Georgiou v Secretary of State for Communities and Local Government* [2010].[87] In the case of *R (on the application of the Friends of Hethel Ltd) v South Norfolk District Council and another* [2010] EWCA Civ 894 the court quashed a planning permission on the basis that the delegation arrangements put in place by the local planning authority to decide whether to grant or refuse an application for planning permission were unlawful as they overrode a statutory provision in the Local Government Act 1972.

Georgiou v Enfield London Borough Council [2004] LGR 497; *Condron v National Assembly for Wales & Anr* [2006] EWCA Civ 1543, *R (on the Application of Island Farm Development Ltd & Anr) v Bridgend County Borough Council* [2006] EWHC Admin 2189.

[86] At para 69.
[87] Extempore judgment on 2 July 2010.

LOOKING AHEAD: THE COALITION GOVERNMENT PROPOSALS

5.108 The Planning Act 2008 came into effect on 26 of November 2008. Its proposals had barely had an opportunity to take effect when there was a change of government. Section 118(1) and 118(2) provide that legal challenges to an order granting or refusing development consent granted under the provisions under the Act must be brought by judicial review but within six weeks of grant of consent or the date of the issue of the statement of reasons if later. It, therefore, puts into statutory form the trend observed earlier in *Finn Kelcey* with the courts emphasising the need to bring challenges promptly. That procedure though is restricted to the consents for major infrastructure projects and the like which receive consent under the 2008 Act. It does not apply to the normal grant of planning permission given under 1990 Act. Those parts of the 2008 Act relating to regional planning will not have effect with the abolition of the Regional Planning Boards and Regional Spatial Strategies[88] by the Coalition government. Similarly, the provisions relating to the Infrastructure Planning Commission (IPC) will be ineffective upon its abolition.

5.109 There are various other detailed provisions as to how to challenge other decisions under the Act within s 118 including the suspension of a National Policy Statement. The same procedure and timescale is to be followed if there is to a challenge to a National Policy Statement under s 13.

5.110 That means that summary grounds of resistance will be required from the Secretary of State and any Interested Party. If permission is granted full evidence will need to be filed and detailed grounds of resistance lodged with the court.

5.111 National Planning Statements (NPS) on airports and nuclear power stations will be site specific as the Act curtails the right to challenge the NPS at the later consent stage.

5.112 The consultation requirements are set out in s 8 of the Act. To decide what publicity is appropriate the Secretary of State must consult the Local Authority in which the land is located and the adjoining authority. Challenges to the extent of consultation or how it is proposed to be carried out may well be evident as was the case in *R (on the application of Medway Council) v Secretary of State for Transport* [2002] EWHC 2516.

5.113 A National Policy Statement needs to be subject to Strategic Environmental Assessment. The interaction of SEA with procedures for adoption of NPS under the Planning Act may well be a source of challenge.

The Localism Bill

5.114 The Infrastructure Planning Commission (IPC) would have faced many difficult procedural decisions such as whether a matter required cross examination, when a challenge should be brought ie at the procedural stage or when a substantive decision is made. However, the Localism Bill provides for the abolition and the transfer of the functions of the IPC to the Secretary of State. The provisions provide that the Secretary of State may appoint an inspector or a panel of up to five inspectors who will examine the application and make a recommendation on the application as to the decision to be

---

[88]   See earlier reference to *Cala Homes (South) Ltd* [2010] EWHC 2866.

made to the Secretary of State. Existing proposals with the IPC will continue to be processed and it is said that there will be a seamless transition to the new arrangements. The expertise, processes and special character of the IPC are to be retained by creating a Major Infrastructure Unit as part of a revised Communities and Local Government Structure.

5.115 It is the announced intention of the Coalition Government that the Localism Bill will become law in 2011.

5.116 The explanatory notes to the Bill set out that reform of the Planning system is another key element of the Bill. It includes provision to abolish regional strategies, provision for neighbourhood plans, provision to make pre-application consultation compulsory, provision for changes to planning enforcement and provisions relating to nationally significant infrastructure.

5.117 What is clear is that if the Bill is passed in its current form there will be considerable reforms to the current planning system as part of the rolling back of the state that the Coalition government wishes to deliver as evidenced through amendments to the TCPA to introduce neighbourhood development orders, neighbourhood development plans and community rights to build orders. It will not, however, change the approach to judicial review in relation to planning and environmental decisions as set out in this chapter. The role of judicial review in challenging planning and environmental decisions is thus likely to remain active and may continue to increase.

Chapter 6

COMMUNITY CARE

PREFACE

6.1   This area of the law does not benefit from a single source of legislation. It is founded upon various statutory provisions and guidance resulting in a complicated mirage of laws. This is despite the general importance of this area of law: it does not seek to govern or regulate particular forms of behaviour, rather it implements societal responsibilities for the benefit of those who are disabled or those who require assistance. This complexity has been caused by the implementation of various legislations that reflected (at the relevant time) the constantly evolving relationship between the state and the citizen. Lord Justice May expressed his consternation when considering community care law in *Crofton v NHS Litigation Authority* [2007] EWCA Civ 71 at paragraph 111:

> 'We cannot conclude this judgment without expressing our dismay at the complexity and labyrinthine nature of the relevant legislation and guidance, as well as (in some respects) its obscurity. Social security law should be clear and accessible. The tortuous analysis in the earlier part of this judgment shows that it is neither.'

6.2   Fortunately, in 2008 the Law Commission announced a long awaited review of adult social care. The ultimate aim is to provide a coherent legal structure for social care services,[1] preferably in the form of a single statue. Areas under review include statutory principles, community care assessment (amalgamation of existing duties, focus of the assessment and self assessment), carers assessments (assessment trigger and direct payments), eligibility of services (defining in a single statute), ordinary residence, scope of adult social care, delivery of adult social care, joint working and safeguarding. It is anticipated that a final report will be published in May 2011. A draft Bill is expected in the Second Parliamentary session in 2012.

6.3   Support for the review has been far reaching. Mr Justice McCombe in *R v Wirral Borough Council, ex p F, J, S, R & Others* [2009] EWHC 1626 (Admin) stated that:

> 'The law in this field is exceptionally tortuous. It is encouraging to note, from the Law Commission's spring 2009 newsletter, that it is in the process of reviewing the law relating to the provision of adult social care in order to "modernise and consolidate this outdated area of the law". This would be very welcome.'

6.4   Whatever the outcome of the review, it is clear that the number of individuals seeking recourse to a wide ambit of community care services is increasing. The ageing population is the likely cause. As such, this area of law is likely to be at the forefront of judicial review litigation for some time.

---

[1]   www.lawcom.gov.uk/adult_social_care.htm.

6.5　　In terms of the future, paragraph 28 of the Coalition Agreement[2] contains the Government's commitment on social care and disability. It states that, 'The Government believes that people needing care deserve to be treated with dignity and respect. We understand the urgency of reforming the system of social care to provide much more control to individuals and their carers, and to ease the cost burden that they and their families face.'

6.6　　In respect of the present law, however, the Administrative Court has battled and succeeded in attempting to simplify this unduly complex area. As such, the Court has played an important role in providing redress and holding public bodies to account in respect of community care provisions. This is despite the common perception that society has become far too litigious and overly preoccupied with asserting rights rather than accepting individual responsibilities.

6.7　　Such an argument may have some merit in other areas of litigation, however, it is the author's view that community care law has been greatly assisted by the Court's intervention. The recent paper prepared by Platt, Sunkin and Calvo, titled 'Judicial Review Litigation as a Incentive Change in Local Authority Public Services in England & Wales'[3] considered this very issue. The paper analysed the relationship between judicial review litigation and the quality of local authorities as indicated by the government's performance measures. In their conclusions the authors provided that:

> '... Far from being a negative irritant, our research indicated that judicial review may actually help authorities to improve. The findings also have important implications in relation to the funding of legal services. They highlight the extent to which judicial review is used to help meet the needs of the most vulnerable people who depend on having access to high quality and properly funded expert services. In short, they underscore the link, rather the tension, between access to justice and improvements in the quality of local government.'

6.8　　The above findings are difficult to dispute.

INTRODUCTION

6.9　　There is no definition of what is meant by 'community care law', however, it embraces the loose interpretations of social and health care. In a broad sense, community care services can include support at home, access to respite care and day care, family placements, the provision of sheltered housing and placement in residential or nursing homes. In most cases, the responsibility of such services fall to the local authority, but are increasingly provided by the NHS.

6.10　　The most common community care services that local authorities provide, or arrange services for, are those provided under:

- The Mental Health Act 1983, s 117 ('MHA 1983');

- The National Assistance Act 1948, ss 21 and 29 ('NAA 1948'); and

- The Chronically Sick and Disabled Persons Act 1970, s 2(1) ('CSDPA 1970').

---

[2]　　http://www.cabinetoffice.gov.uk/media/409088/pfg_coalition.pdf.
[3]　　ESRC research paper February 2009, http://www.iser.essex.ac.uk/files/iser_working_papers/2009-05.pdf.

6.11   When a local authority carries out its obligations under one or various statutory regimes, it is prerequisite that it follows good and reasonable decision making processes, thereby complying with public law principles. In order for any decision to be deemed lawful the decision maker must observe the requirements of (see Chapter 1):

- rationality;

- legality;

- procedural propriety (including compliance of policy, guidance and directions and proper consultation); and

- compatibility with rights under the European Convention of Humans Rights ('ECHR') as enshrined by the Human Rights Act 1998 ('HRA').

6.12   With the above in mind, this chapter will provide an overview of community care law, consider specific significant areas, and finally analyse relevant cases that seek to exemplify how community care decisions are challenged by way of judicial review.

6.13   Part 1 provides an overview of community care law with references to challenges by way of judicial review in the Administrative Court. Part 2 considers specific areas of community care law, and more importantly disputes, which seek resolution by the Administrative Court. Finally, Part 3 analyses how judicial review, as a remedy, has been utilised as a means of challenging decisions. In particular, Part 3 seeks to exemplify how *specific* grounds of judicial review are used to challenge community care decisions.

PART 1 – AN OVERVIEW OF COMMUNITY CARE LAW

The community care decision making process

6.14   The process of decision-making relating to community care can be divided up into basic stages. The flowchart best illustrates the steps.

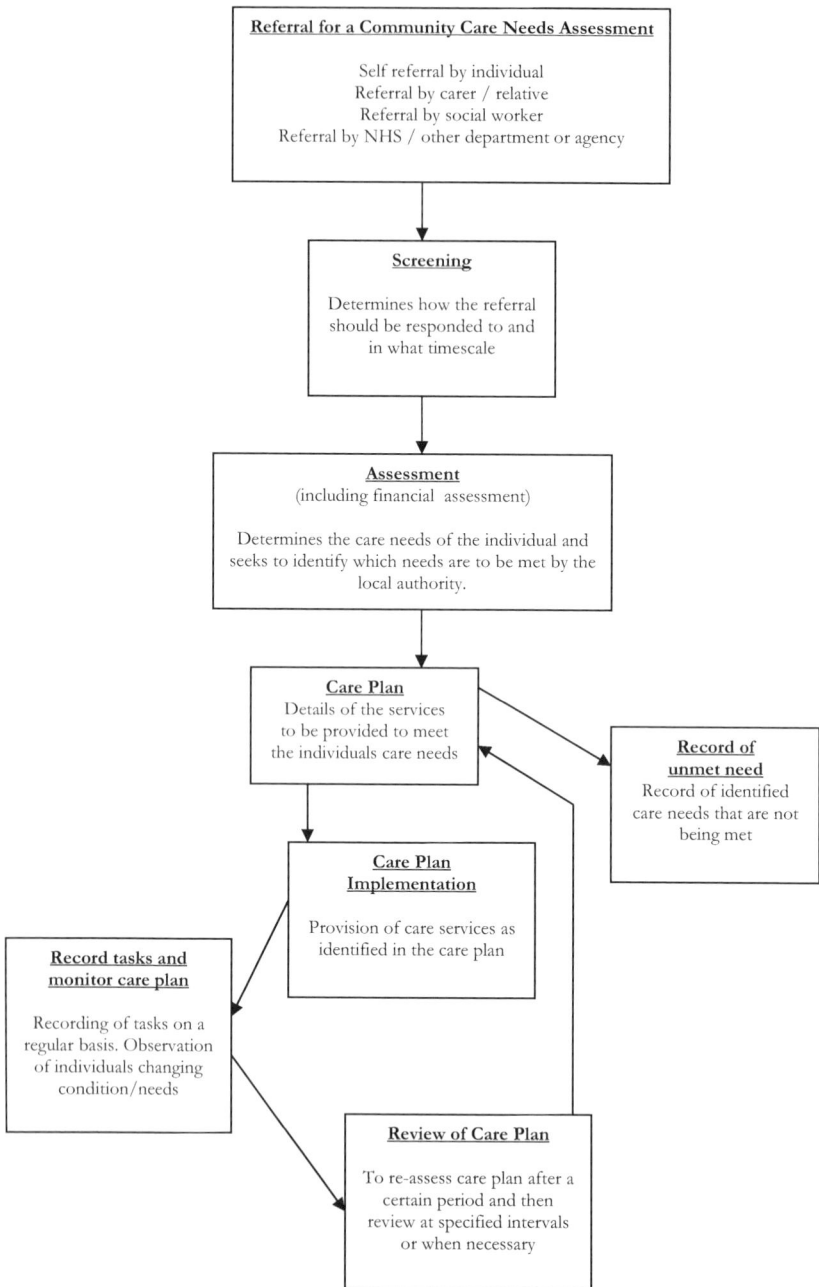

Referral for a Community Care Needs Assessment

Self referral by individual
Referral by carer / relative
Referral by social worker
Referral by NHS / other department or agency

Screening

Determines how the referral
should be responded to and
in what timescale

Assessment
(including financial assessment)

Determines the care needs of the individual and
seeks to identify which needs are to be met by the
local authority.

Care Plan
Details of the services
to be provided to meet
the individuals care needs

**Record of
unmet need**
Record of identified
care needs that are not
being met

**Care Plan
Implementation**

Provision of care services as
identified in the care plan

**Record tasks and
monitor care plan**

Recording of tasks on a
regular basis. Observation
of individuals changing
condition/needs

Review of Care Plan

To re-assess care plan after a
certain period and then
review at specified intervals
or when necessary

6.15   The important stages can be described as:

- **Community care assessment of needs** – the obligation is upon the local authority but often in practice cooperation between health and social services is required.
  A local authority is required to assess the community care needs of any person in respect of whom it has a power to provide community care services – *R v Berkshire CC, ex p P* 1 CCLR 143. By virtue of section 22 of the National Health Service Act 1977 ('NHSA 1977'), Primary Care Trusts ('PCT') and local authorities must cooperate in exercising their respective functions.

- A decision as to whether or not the individual's needs require provision of community care services (ie the **eligibility** stage).

- A **service provision decision**, ie a decision as to what services are going to be provided. Once a decision has been made that it is necessary to provide services to meet the individual's needs. The local authority is then under an individual duty to make those arrangements as soon as is reasonably practicable – *R v Kirkham MBC, ex p Daykin and Daykin* (1997–8) 1 CCLR 512, 527B.

- The **care planning** stage. When care plan(s) are created for the implementation of a provision of services to meet the identified and eligible needs highlighted in the service provision decision.

6.16   Professor Luke Clements and Pauline Thompson[4] have argued that there are five key 'underpinning principles' of community care law which ought to apply throughout the above process, ie the decision making process, namely that of non-discrimination, dignity, independent living, choice and cost effectiveness.

The statutory framework

6.17   Section 47(1) of the National Health Service and Community Care Act 1990 ('NHSCCA 1990') provides:

> '(1)   Subject to subsections (5) and (6) below, where it appears to a local authority that any person for whom they may provide or arrange for the provision of community care services may be in need of any such services, the authority –
>   (a)   shall carry out an assessment of his needs for those services; and
>   (b)   having regard to the results of that assessment, shall then decide whether his needs call for the provision by them of any such services.'

The assessment

6.18   The duty to assess a person's needs for community care services arises *where it appears* that the person *may be in need of such services*.[5] The elementary aspects of this duty are as follows:

(a)   the identification of a need is matter of judgment for the social worker who carries out the assessment. In *R (B) v Cornwall CC & The Brandon Trust* [2009] EWHC 491 (Admin) the Court emphasised the importance that a local authority cannot

---

4   Community Care and the Law (4th edn), Legal Action Group, para 4.42.
5   See SAP (single assessment process) policy guidance, annex f.

avoid its obligation to assess needs by failing to make an appropriate assessment itself, for example by relying on a 'self assessment';

(b)   it is trite that the duty to assess is *not* dependent on a request by any individual;

(c)   the duty is activated upon the 'possibility of need'. In *R v Bristol CC, ex p Penfold* [1998] 1 CCLR 315 the Court of Appeal reinforced the notion that the threshold for entitlement to an assessment was very low and that the duty to undertake an assessment is a strong obligation, rather than an absolute/mandatory duty;

(d)   the duty is a social services function and cannot be delegated to another body, see *Daykin*;[6]

(e)   the duty has been deemed to apply even when the disabled person is not ordinarily resident in a local authority's area, see *R v Berkshire County Council, ex p Parker* (1996) 95 LGR 449;

(f)   if, during the assessment of needs, it seems that the person is disabled, there is a specific duty to ensure that a decision is made as to the services without the need for a request, section 4 of the Disabled Persons (Services, Consultation and Representation) Act 1986;

(g)   there is a duty to inform a relevant PCT, health authority or local housing authority to invite them to assist in the assessment if there is need for services provided by those bodies, section 47(3) of the NHSCCA 1990;

(h)   there is no prescribed timetable to complete an assessment. The Local Government Ombudsman ('LGO') considered that an adaptation assessment that took three months was 'simply unacceptable'.[7] Policy guidance and Department of Health indicators do assist certain groups of individuals, namely: (i) disabled children whose initial assessment should be concluded within 7 working days and core assessment within 35 working days; and (ii) older people in relation to whom a single assessment process ('SAP') should commence within 48 hours of initial contact with conclusion within a month;

(i)   if an individual's needs are considered to be urgent, a local authority may use its power under section 47(5) of the NHSCCA 1990[8] to provide services on a temporary basis until the completion of the assessment, see *R (AA) v Lambeth LBC* [2001] EWCA Admin 741;

---

6   Formal partnership agreements are permitted with a NHS body.
7   Complaint number 05/c/07195 – Northumberland CC, 18 April 2006, paras 7, 29 and 30. See also complaint number 07A11108 – Surrey County Council, November 2008 where the Council agreed to pay the complainant £5,000 in respect of delays in assessment that would have allowed her to leave residential care and return to her family home. Finally, complaint number 06A08746 – LB of Ealing, May 2008, where the Council agreed to pay the complaint £16,700 which was the value of the direct payments she had missed during a period in which the Council had delayed in reassessing her needs. The LGO stated that the reassessment could have been achieved in six months.
8   Section 47(5) provides, 'Nothing in this section shall prevent a local authority from temporarily providing or arranging for the provision of community care services for any person without carrying out a prior assessment of his needs in accordance with the preceding provisions of this section if, in the opinion of the authority, the condition of that person is such that he requires those services as a matter of urgency'.

(j)   resources of a person in need of community care services are not relevant to their needs as such, save that if services and/or accommodation are actually being provided. Resources become relevant at the stage of charging for community care services;

(k)   similarly, in *Penfold* at paragraph 322G of the judgment, it was made clear that it is unlawful for a local authority to take resources into account when deciding whether or not to carry out a community care assessment. In *R v Birmingham CC, ex p Taj Mohammed* (1998) 1 CCLR 441 it was explicitly held that resources could not be taken into account when deciding whether or not to approve a disabled facilities grant; and

(l)   a local authority's resources are relevant to its thresholds for assessment of need and whether or not it is necessary to meet the need, ie when framing the eligibility criteria (*R v Gloucestershire CC, ex p Barry* [1997] AC 584). Once, however, it has been determined that it is necessary to provide services to meet a need, a local authority cannot rely upon its own limited resources as a justification for failing to meet the need (see eg *Batantu v Islington Borough Council* LTL 9/11/2000).

6.19 In respect of what an assessment should address, the Community Care Assessment Directions 2004 require a local authority to consult with the person being assessed; consider whether consultation with a carer is appropriate; take reasonable steps to reach agreement with the person (and carer) in terms of services to be provided to meet their needs; and to provide information about the amount of charge that the person may be required to make in respect of any services that may be provided.

6.20 Within the context of community care assessments, the case of *Lambeth LBC v Irenenschild* [2007] EWCA Civ 234 must be borne in mind. The Court of Appeal made forceful comments regarding challenges to community care assessments under section 47 of the NHSCCA 1990. The judge at first instance had found that an assessment had been unlawful for a number of reasons, in particular because the assessor had failed to obtain, and to take into account, an Occupational Therapist ('OT') report and because she had failed to take into account the statutory Fair Access to Care Guidance 2002 ('FAC'). The Court of Appeal allowed the appeal, but the decision is important for the views expressed as to the circumstances under which such challenges should be brought. Lady Justice Hallett emphasised that assessments cannot be the subject of:

> '... over zealous textual analysis. Courts must be wary, in my view, of expecting so much of hard pressed social workers that we risk taking them, unnecessarily, from their front line duties ... a community care assessment ... is operational and inevitably judgmental. It must be carried out quickly. I accept the Appellants' argument that a social worker preparing such an assessment cannot be expected to engage in a detailed analysis of the material obtained (often from many sources), decide what particular points have and have not been specifically addressed by the "service user" thus far, and then take steps to ensure that any points which have been missed or not sufficiently addressed are drawn to the attention of the "service user" for his or her response'.[9]

---

[9]   Paras 57 and 71. See also *R (on the application of L) v Barking and Dagenham LBC* [2001] EWCA Civ 533 in which Schiemann LJ said at para 27 in these terms, 'It seems to us however that, leaving aside for the moment any undertakings to the Court, the Court is not the appropriate organ to be prescriptive as to the degree of detail which should go into a care plan or as to the amount of consultation to be carried out with Ms L's advisers. In practice these are matters for the Council, and if necessary its complaints procedure. If the Council has failed to follow the Secretary of State's guidance and is arguably in breach of its statutory

6.21   More recently in *R v Wirral BC, ex p F & Others* [2009] EWHC 1626,[10] Mr Justice McCombe at paragraphs 76 to 80 criticised further and said:

> 'While the Administrative Court is astute to correct any illegality of approach on a public authority's part, it is not the proper forum in which to probe into the adequacy of community care assessments in the manner which Mr Prescott belatedly sought to do in this case .... If any of these individual caimants truly have a grievance in respect of their community care provision it has not been identified here. None of them, for example, says, "I need help in getting myself a hot meal" or "I cannot get out to do my shopping" and "the Council should be providing this". All has been fought out amongst the abstraction of form filling and the contents of official documents. The process was initiated by an entirely unjustified global complaint that no assessments had been carried out at all. If a claimant has a true claim that his or her eligible needs are not being met by the Council, there is a full and adequate complaints procedure in which that can be resolved .... Even in cases in which such a proper claim exists the courts have pointed out on many occasions that the remedy of judicial review will not be granted where there is an alternative remedy: see especially *Pulhofer v Hillingdon LBC* [1996] AC 484 , *R (on the application of L) v Barking & Dagenham LBC* [2001] EWCA Civ 533 and *Lambeth LBC v Ireneschild* [2007] EWCA Civ 234 .... If any of the assessments or care plans is truly inadequate in these cases and such inadequacy is giving rise to a true failure on the part of the Council to meet an eligible need, then the relevant claimant has a proper remedy through the statutory complaints procedure.'

6.22   This decision makes it extremely difficult to challenge community care assessments by way of judicial review without having recourse the complaint procedure as the alternative remedy. It is questionable, however, whether the Court would criticise the instigation of proceedings where a failure to meet eligible needs is placing the service user within the realms of real and tangible physical and/or mental harm.

Eligibility

6.23   The Department of Health has issued policy guidance with a view to standardising individual local authority eligibility criteria for community care services, namely FACS.

---

duties in relation to the way it carries out its assessment and what it puts into its care plans then aggrieved persons should in appropriate cases turn first to the Secretary of State. Where there is room for differences of judgment the Secretary of State and his advisers may have a useful input. The Court is here as a last resort where there is illegality. Here there is not ...'.

[10]   F & Others were adults who suffered from various disabilities. They lived in accommodation, within the local authority's area, let to them by a company (S). S considered that the local authority had improperly failed to meet its legal obligations to F in the social services field and as a result had deprived them of funds which would in turn reimburse S for the assistance provided by it to them. F, via S and their litigation friends, wrote to the local authority alleging that it was in breach of its duty under the National Health Service and Community Care Act 1990, s 47 in that it had failed to comply with its legal duty by carrying out an assessment of each of their needs. F asked that the matter be referred immediately to the second stage of the statutory complaints procedure, that of 'investigation', under the Local Authority Social Services Complaints (England) Regulations 2006, reg 9, and that within 14 days the local authority would carry out a multi-disciplinary assessment of each of them in accordance with its legal obligations under s 47. The local authority responded by stating that it was felt that the first stage of the complaints procedure, that of 'local resolution' under reg 7, was more appropriate and it proceeded to set out the current position in respect of each of F, indicating that, contrary to the allegation made in the complaint letters, in the cases of all but one of them (who was unknown to the local authority as a welfare claimant at all), assessments had been completed or reviewed or that current social work was being carried out. Two days later, without any further request for engagement of the complaints procedure, F sent judicial review pre-action protocol letters to the local authority alleging again that it had failed to carry out any assessment of F's needs under s 47 and making no reference to the local authority's letter stating that assessments had indeed been carried out, and F subsequently issued their judicial review claim. The local authority submitted that complaints as to the details of individual assessments or care plans or both were not appropriate for judicial review.

6.24 The eligibility framework is graded into four bands:[11]

(a) Critical – when

- life is, or will be, threatened; and/or
- significant health problems have developed or will develop; and/or
- there is, or will be, little or no choice and control over vital aspects of the immediate environment; and/or
- serious abuse or neglect has occurred or will occur; and/or
- there is, or will be, an inability to carry out vital personal care or domestic routines; and/or
- vital involvement in work, education or learning cannot or will not be sustained; and/or
- vital social support systems and relationships cannot or will not be sustained; and/or
- vital family and other social roles and responsibilities cannot or will not be undertaken.

(b) Substantial – when

- there is, or will be, only partial choice and control over the immediate environment; and/or
- abuse or neglect has occurred or will occur; and/or
- there is, or will be, an inability to carry out the majority of personal care or domestic routines; and/or
- involvement in many aspects of work, education or learning cannot or will not be sustained; and/or
- the majority of social support systems and relationships cannot or will not be sustained; and/or
- the majority of family and other social roles and responsibilities cannot or will not be undertaken.

(c) Moderate – when

- there is, or will be, an inability to carry out several personal care or domestic routines; and/or
- involvement in several aspects of work, education or learning cannot or will not be sustained; and/or
- several social support systems and relationships cannot or will not be sustained; and/or
- several family and other social roles and responsibilities cannot or will not be undertaken.

(d) Low – when

- there is, or will be, an inability to carry out one or two personal care or domestic routines; and/or
- involvement in one or two aspects of work, education or learning cannot or will not be sustained; and/or

---

[11] http://www.dh.gov.uk/en/Publicationsandstatistics/Publications/PublicationsPolicyAndGuidance/DH_ 4009653.

- one or two social support systems and relationships cannot or will not be sustained; and/or
- one or two family and other social roles and responsibilities cannot or will not be undertaken.

6.25 In *Barry* the Court concluded that the threshold of eligibility can lawfully differ between local authorities, and that resources can be a relevant factor in its determination. A variation of the threshold must be done at the social services committee level. For an example of this, see the case of *R v Wigan MBC, ex p Tammadge* (1998) 1 CCLR 581.

6.26 Based on the demand of services, it is becoming growing practice for local authorities to shift the threshold to 'critical needs' only. The case of *R v Harrow London Borough Council, ex p Chavad* [2007] EWHC 3064, however, deemed that the local authority's decision to *only* provide services for 'critical' needs was held to be unlawful as the decision-maker had failed to consider, with any particular weight, the duties under the Disability Discrimination Act 1995 ('DDA 1995').[12]

6.27 The recent case of *R (JL a child, by his mother and litigation friend LL(1), LL(2)) v Islington LBC and Others* [2009] EWHC 458 ('JL') is of particular relevance as it considered the question of the lawfulness of the eligibility criteria for children services. JL was a 14-year-old autistic child who lived with his mother who also had health problems. The claimant challenged the eligibility criteria that reduced his number of hours from 1, 248 to 624 hours per year. Mrs Justice Black held that the criteria was unlawful because: (i) the local authority was operating a banding system which (indirectly) imposed a maximum ceiling of 12 hours irrespective of need under section 2 of the CSDPA 1970; (ii) the decision to reduce the number of hours was made by a eligibility assessment tool rather an a core assessment; and (iii) the local authority used one criteria without distinguishing between the different services and their statutory source.

6.28 Note, however, that it has been deemed to be lawful to reduce and/or withdraw services following a reassessment of an individual's needs if the local authority's threshold of eligibility has changed, *Barry*. This is to be balanced against the Department of Health's guidance[13] that refers to caution in withdrawing services to which service users have become dependent and would not be able to cope without its availability.

The decision and care planning

6.29 Once a local authority has made a decision under section 47(1)(b) of the NHSCCA 1990 that an individual's needs are such that community care services are required, then the local authority must make arrangements for those identified services

---

[12] Section 49A of the DDA 1995 places a duty on all public bodies to have due regard to the need to promote equality of opportunity between disabled persons and other people. As a result, public bodies must acquire a Disability Equality Scheme pursuant to Regulation (Disability Discrimination (Public Authorities) (Statutory Duties) Regulations 2005 (SI 2005/2966), that promotes involvement in public life (see also the Social Care Sector and the Disability Equality Duty: A guide to the Disability Equality and Disability Discrimination Act 2005 for social care organisations). It also worth noting that Article 19 of the UN Convention on the Rights of Persons with Disabilities contains a declaration regarding the right of disabled individuals to live independently in the community. Article 14 of the ECHR can be deployed to build arguments.

[13] LAC (2002) 13, paras 47 and 60.

to be provided. Those identified needs require also to be 'eligible needs', based on a local authority's individual eligibility criteria outlined above.

6.30 Once the needs have been assessed and deemed to be eligible, the local authority is under an *absolute/mandatory duty* to provide those services, *Barry*. Failure to comply with this duty can be remedied by seeking an interim relief order in the form a mandatory order, see case of *Tammadge*. There are, however, particular circumstances when an 'assessed need' will not require a local authority to provide services: when those needs do not achieve the threshold of eligibility as discussed above or, when those needs can be and are to be, provided by other statutory organisations, eg a housing authority/association or the NHS.

6.31 There is no formal statutory requirement to prepare a care plan. However, it has been considered to be at the very heart of the community care process. Bear in mind that the FACS guidance provides that:[14]

> '... If an individual is eligible for help then, together with the individual, councils should develop a care plan. The written record of the care plan should include as a minimum:
>
> – A note of the eligible needs and associated risks.
> – The preferred outcomes of service provision.
> – Contingency plans to manage emergency changes.
> – Details of services to be provided, and any charges the individual is assessed to pay, or if direct payments have been agreed.
> – Contributions which carers and others are willing and able to make.
> – A review date.
>
> There should be an initial review within three months of help first being provided or major changes made to current services. Thereafter, reviews should be scheduled at least annually or more often if individuals' circumstances appear to warrant it. Reviews may be considered on request from services users, providers of services and other appropriate individuals or agencies'.

6.32 The practice guidance also illustrates the necessity of a written care plan:[15]

> 'Care plans should be set out in concise written form, linked with the assessment of need. The document should be accessible to the user, for example, in Braille translated into the user's own language. A copy should be given to the user but it should also, subject to constraints of confidentiality, be shared with other contributors to the plan ....'

Services

6.33 'Community care services' are defined in section 46 of the NHSCCA as services which the local authority may provide or arrange to be provided under:

(a) Part III of the National Assistance Act 1948 – accommodation and welfare services for persons in need of care and attention and/or who are 'blind, deaf or dumb, suffer from mental disorder, or over 18 and substantially and permanently handicapped by illness, injury or congenital deformity';

---

[14] Para 60 of the FACS policy guidance.
[15] Care Management & Assessment – A Practitioner's Guide, HMSO, 1991, para 4.37.

A local authority is empowered to provide 'normal' housing under section 21 of the NAA 1948 – see *Penfold* and *Tammadge* [1998];[16]

(b)   section 45 of the Health Services and Public Health Act 1968 – promotion of welfare of elderly people;

(c)   section 21 and Schedule 8 to the National Health Service Act 1977 ('NHSA 1977') – services in relation to the care of expectant or nursing mothers, prevention, provision of centres for training and occupation of persons whose care is preventative, who are ill, or who have been ill, and home help and laundry facilities for those who are ill, or handicapped; and

(d)   section 117 of the MHA 1982 – after care services for those who have been discharged from compulsory detention under this Act.

6.34   Beyond the above, there are various services that can be provided. What is set out below seeks to summarise the extent of those services:

(a)   As regards accommodation, section 21 of the NAA 1948, which falls within Part III of that Act, provides that 'local authorities may, with the approval of the Secretary of State, and to such extent as he directs must, make arrangements for providing residential accommodation for persons aged 18 or over who by reason of age, illness, disability or any other circumstances are in need of care and attention which is not otherwise available to them'. By virtue of Appendix 1 to LAC (93) 10 the Secretary of State directs local authorities to make arrangements under section 21 in relation to persons ordinarily resident in their area. Under section 22 of the NAA 1948, the local authority can charge for such accommodation.

Whether a potential service user is ordinarily resident in a particular local authority's catchments area is a recurring problem. *R (Greenwich LBC) v SS Health* [2006] All ER (D) 178 concerned an individual, D, who had lived in Bexley in a residential home as a self-funder. In 2006 due to problems at the home she had to move as a matter of urgency. The only suitable placement put forward by Bexley was a home in Greenwich, to which she moved. Four and a half weeks later she became entitled to funding under section 21 of the NAA 1948. The ordinary residence dispute was referred to the Secretary of State who accepted that D had not chosen the new home but nevertheless held that D had ceased to be ordinarily resident in Bexley. Her house had been sold and she was no longer living in the area, and therefore, her ties were severed. Greenwich challenged the decision on the basis that they were not responsible for monies in relation to the same. The Court rejected Greenwich's challenge, holding that the question was *fact dependant* and since the Secretary of State had applied the correct criteria, and given adequate reasons, the decision could not be quashed.

More recently in *R (Buckinghamshire CC) v Kingston upon Thames Royal London Borough Council and SL & others* [2010] EWHC 1703 (Admin), the claimant local authority sought to judicially review a decision of the defendant local authority to move the service user into its area. SL had been placed by Kingston in a school for children with learning difficulties, however, she was then placed in a National Society for Epilepsy Centre after which she moved into supported living in a privately rented bungalow in the Buckinghamshire area.

---

[16]   See Chapter 26 for further details.

Kingston initially funded the care, but sought that Buckinghamshire take over the funding, asserting that SL had become ordinarily resident in its area. Buckinghamshire refused, and sought a declaration that the decision to move SL was unlawful and that Kingston should indemnify it for any expense it had incurred or would incur in consequence of that decision.

The Court held that Kingston did not owe any duties of fairness to Buckinghamshire to notify it of SL's proposed move, to consult with it, or give it an opportunity to participate in the decision. Kingston was under no duty to act fairly towards Buckinghamshire when carrying out the community care assessment or before making any decision consequent to it. Its duties towards other persons or bodies were limited to those stated expressly in section 47 of the 1990 Act, in the Community Care Assessment Directions 2004 and sections 21 and 26 of the 1948 Act. While the fact that a decision might impact adversely upon an individual or body was a factor in deciding whether there was a duty to act fairly towards that person, its significance depended on the factual circumstances. In the instant case, it was neither important nor determinative.

Note that commencing 19 April 2010, new statutory guidance came into place on the identification of the ordinary residence of people in need of community care services.[17] Other directions that also took effect on that date included: (1) Ordinary Residence Disputes (National Assistance Act 1948) Directions 2010; (2) Ordinary Residence Disputes (Community Care (Delayed Discharges etc) Act 2003 Directions 2010; and (3) Ordinary Residence Disputes (Mental Capacity Act 2005) Directions 2010.

The guidance can be summarised as providing some key principles when two or more local authorities fall into dispute over a person's ordinary residence, namely:

(1) the fundamental main concern of local authorities should be the well-being of the service user;
(2) the services (including accommodation) must not be delayed or adversely affected as a result of uncertainty over which local authority is responsible; and
(3) one local authority must accept responsibility for the provision of services while the dispute is being resolved in accordance with the directions issued by the Secretary of State.

The Ordinary Residence Disputes (National Assistance Act 1948) Directions 2010 is relevant insofar as it sets out which one of the local authorities is to provide services:

(a) if the person is already in receipt of services, the local authority providing them should continue to do so;
(b) if the person is not in receipt of services, the local authorities in dispute may agree which of them will provide services pending the resolution of the dispute;
(c) if the local authorities in dispute cannot agree, the local authority in which the person is living must provide the services; and
(d) if the person is not living anywhere, the local authority in whose area the person is physically present (the 'local authority of the moment') must do so.

(b) With respect to more general welfare services, section 29 of the NAA 1948, which falls within Part III of that Act, provides that 'local authorities may with the

---

[17] http://www.dh.gov.uk/en/SocialCare/Deliveringadultsocialcare/Ordinaryresidence/index.

approval of the Secretary of State, and to such extent as he directs must, make arrangements for promoting the welfare of persons aged 18 or over who are blind, deaf, dumb, suffer from mental disorder or are substantially and permanently handicapped by illness, injury, or congenital deformity or such other disabilities as may be prescribed by the Minister'.

(c) Section 29 services include a range of services, and can include workshops, hostel accommodation, and recreational facilities. Similarly, by virtue of Appendix 2 to LAC (93) 10 the Secretary of State directs local authorities to make arrangements under section 29 in relation to persons ordinarily resident in their area for the purposes of providing facilities for occupational, social, cultural and recreational activities and facilities for social rehabilitation and adjustment to disability including assistance in overcoming limitations of mobility or communication.

(d) Section 2 of the Chronically Sick and Disabled Persons Act 1970 ("CSDPA") provides that:

> 'Where a local authority having functions under section 29 of the National Assistance Act 1948 are satisfied in the case of any person to whom that section applies who is ordinarily resident in their area that it is necessary in order to meet the needs of that person for that authority to make arrangements for all or any of the following matters, namely –
> (a) the provision of practical assistance for that person in his home;
> (b) the provision for that person of, or assistance to that person in obtaining, wireless, television, library or similar recreational activities;
> (c) the provision for that person of lectures, games, outings or other recreational facilities outside his home or assistance to that person in taking advantage of educational facilities available to him;
> (d) the provision for that person of facilities for, or assistance in, travelling to and from his home for the purpose of participating in any services provided under arrangements made by the local authority under ... section 29 or, with the approval of the local authority, in any services provided otherwise than as aforesaid which are similar to services which could be provided under such arrangements;
> (e) the provision of assistance for that person in arranging for the carrying out of any works of adaptation in his home or the provision of any additional facilities designed to secure his greater safety, comfort or convenience ... then ... It shall be the duty of that authority to make those arrangements in exercise of their functions under the said section 29'; and

(e) Section 4 of the Disabled Persons (Services, Consultation and Representation) Act 1986 provides that:

> 'When requested to do so by –
> (a) a disabled person
> (b) his authorised representative; or
> (c) any person who provides care for him in the circumstances mentioned in section 8, a local authority shall decide whether the needs of the disabled person call for the provision by the authority of any services in accordance with section 2(1) of the 1970 Act (provision of welfare services).'

6.35 In performing its functions under the above legislation, local authorities are required by virtue of section 7(1) of the Local Authorities Social Services Act 1970 ('LASSA') to act under the guidance of the Secretary of State. The Secretary of State has issued policy guidance pursuant to LASSA, which local authorities are effectively required to follow.[18] The Secretary of State has also issued other guidance (not pursuant to LASSA) to which local authorities must have regard and deviation from which, may be deemed to be unlawful: see *Rixon*.[19]

6.36 As outlined above, section 2(1)(e) of CSDPA 1970 incorporates obligations pertaining to adaptations and additional facilities to a service user's property. The duty, however, is a specific one which arises when an assessment has deemed it necessary for this service to be provided. The ambit of this obligation and its interface with the Disability Facilities Grant is considered in detail in Chapter 26.

6.37 Finally, it has been found to be lawful for a local authority to implement the cheapest option to meet an individual's need when there are two or more alternatives. In *R (on the application of McDonald) v Kensington & Chelsea LBC* [2009] EWHC 1582 (Admin), the local authority had reduced a care package from £703 to £450 per week. The basis of the reduction was that during the night she required assistance to use a commode, as she needed to urinate frequently due to a bladder condition. It was argued that the needs of the service user could be met by the use of incontinence pads, which were cheaper. The services user argued a breach of her Article 8 right. The Court held that the local authority was entitled to take the cheaper option so long as it met her needs and that there was no breach of Article 8. On appeal [2010] EWCA Civ 1109 the Court of Appeal held that the authority was 'responsible also for acting on behalf of the interests of all clients whose welfare it supports with limited resources and that its decision to meet the claimant's reassessed need was a reasonable decision'. The claim under Article 8 was dismissed also. A converse approach, however, was applied in the case of *R v Birmingham City Council & Birmingham University* [2009] EWHC 688 which also surrounded the issue of incontinence pads. In this matter the Court held that the defendants had failed to have due regard to the duty under section 49(a)(1) of the DDA 1995.

Direct payments

6.38 The power under the Community Care (Direct Payment) Act 1996 has since been superseded by the provisions of section 57 and 58 of the Health and Social Care Act 2001. The Community Care, Services for Carers and Children's Services (Direct

---

[18] As per Sedley J in *R v Islington LBC, ex p Rixon* [1998] 1 CCLR 119: 'Parliament by section 7(1) has required local authorities to follow the path chartered by the Secretary of State's guidance, with liberty to deviate from it where the local authority judges on admissible grounds that there is good reason to do so but without the freedom to take a substantially different course.'

[19] In the *Rixon* case Sedley J (as he then was) said, 'What is the meaning and effect of the obligation to "act under the general guidance of the Secretary of State"? clearly guidance is less than direction, and the word "general" emphasises the non-prescriptive nature of what is envisaged. Mr McCarthy, for the local authority, submits that such guidance is no more than one of the many factors to which the local authority is to have regard. Miss Richards submits that, in order to give effect the words "shall ... act", a local authority must follow such guidance unless it has and can articulate a good reason for departing from it. In my judgment Parliament in enacting section 7(1) did not intend local authorities to whom ministerial guidance was given to be free, having considered it, to take it or leave it. Such a construction would put this kind of statutory guidance on a par with the many forms of non-statutory guidance issued by departments of state. While guidance and direction are semantically and legally different things, and while "guidance does not compel any particular decision" (*Laker Airways v Department of Trade* [1977] QB 643, 714 per Roskill LJ), especially when prefaced by the word "general", in my view Parliament by section 7(1) has required local authorities to follow the path charted by the Secretary of State's guidance, with liberty to deviate from it where the local authority judges on admissible grounds that there is good reason to do so, but without freedom to take a substantially different course.'

Payments) (England) Regulations 2003[20] essentially provides that direct payments can only be made to those service users who appear to be capable of managing the payments alone or with assistance. In addition, the local authority must be satisfied that the person's needs for the relevant service can be met by securing the provision of direct payments.

6.39   The recent case of *R v Secretary of State for Health & Others, ex p Harrison* [2009] EWHC 574 confirmed that the NHS had no power to make direct payments under the statutory provisions that govern it. At the time of publication, a further application in this case has been sought to clarify whether the NHS can make indirect payments by transferring funds to social services pursuant to section 256 of the National Health Service Act 2006 ('NHSA 2006').

Personalisation and independent living

6.40   The personalisation agenda is a radical re-engineering of the provision of care services. It signals a major change in the paradigm of the relationship between the citizen and the state. At the heart of the model are three concepts, namely: (i) control; (ii) choice of service; and (iii) flexibility of support.

6.41   The above terms have become a catchall phrase, which began its existence as a result of the Green Paper 'Independence, Well-Being and Choice' and the White Paper 'Our Health, Our Care, Our Say'. Further reports crystallised this school of thought in 'Putting People First: a shared commitment to the transformation of adult social care'[21] (2007) and the Local Government Circular (2008) 'Transforming Social Care'.[22] Paragraphs 21 and 26 of the Circular provide:

> 'Reforming social care to achieve personalisation for all will require a huge cultural, transformational and transactional change in all parts of the system, not just in social care, but also for services across the whole of local government and the wider public sector. The scale and purpose of this ambition should not be underestimated. The experience with direct payments makes this clear. For the past ten years, direct payments have successfully given some people the ability to design the services they want but their impact has been very limited. The latest figures show that about 54,000 people out of a potential million recipients receive support through a direct payment. Evidence shows major variations in take up across the country, with success determined less by the characteristics of people who use services or the features of direct payments themselves, than by local leadership, professional culture and the availability of support ....
>
> The purpose of this reform is to ensure people have choice and control over the support they need to live the lives they want. It is necessary to tackle all four together to deliver the Government's aims of better health and better care for people who need treatment and support, as well as better value for taxpayers.'

---

[20]   SI 2003/762.
[21]   Produced by six government departments, namely the local government association, the association of adult social services, the NHS, the representatives of independent sector providers and the commission of social care inspections.
See   http://www.dh.gov.uk/en/Publicationsandstatistics/Publications/PublicationsPolicyAndguidance/DH_081118.
[22]   http://www.dh.gov.uk/en/publicationsandstatistics/lettersandcirculars/localauthoritycirculars/dh_081934.

6.42 The essential principles include:

(a) that service users should have choice and control over the support delivered in a manner that promotes independence, well-being and dignity;

(b) the emphasis of self assessment with social workers acting as 'brokers' and 'advocates' rather than 'gate keepers' of social services;

(c) to promote self-directed support to enable individual arrangements to be designed by the service user; and

(d) that the above transformations are to be implemented by the continuation of direct payments, individual budgets and personal budgets.

6.43 There are some fundamental foundations to the concept of 'personalisation' and 'independent living', namely:

(a) The UN Convention on the Rights of Persons with Disabilities,[23] in particular, see Article 19: Living independently and being included in the community which provides that:

> '(a) Persons with disabilities have the opportunity to choose their place of residence and where and with whom they live on an equal basis with others and are not obliged to live in a particular living arrangement;
>
> (b) Persons with disabilities have access to a range of in-home, residential and other community support services, including personal assistance necessary to support living and inclusion in the community, and to prevent isolation or segregation from the community;
>
> (c) Community services and facilities for the general population are available on an equal basis to persons with disabilities and are responsive to their needs.'

(b) Section 49A of the DDA 1995 – Public Equality Duty:

> '49A General duty
> (1) Every public authority shall in carrying out its functions have due regard to—
> (a) the need to eliminate discrimination that is unlawful under this Act;
> (b) the need to eliminate harassment of disabled persons that is related to their disabilities;
> (c) the need to promote equality of opportunity between disabled persons and other persons;
> (d) the need to take steps to take account of disabled persons' disabilities, even where that involves treating disabled persons more favourably than other persons;
> (e) the need to promote positive attitudes towards disabled persons; and
> (f) the need to encourage participation by disabled persons in public life.'

(c) Article 8 of the ECHR considerations, in particular the case of *R (A & B) v East Sussex County Council No 2* (2003) 6 CCLR 194 in which Munby J reinforced the right of a disabled individual to participate in the life of the community and to have what he described as 'access to essential economic and social activities and to an appropriate range of recreational and cultural activities', thereby prevented isolation and being deprived of the possibility of developing a personality.

---

[23] See http://www.un.org/disabilities. Ratified by the UK in 2009.

6.44   The parameters of the personalisation agenda are yet to be known. However, the Government has made it clear in 'A Vision for Adult Social Care' that it is one of seven principles on which its vision for a modern system of social care is based. The Law Commission has highlighted personalisation as being part of its reform agenda although it states that its approach is to create, as far as possible, a neutral legal framework that is not wedded to any particular policy and that is capable of accommodating different policies and practices in the future.

6.45   In *R (S) v Royal Borough of Kensington & Chelsea* [2010] EWHC 414 (Admin) the elderly claimant was in receipt of £170.45 per week for her care (assessed in July 2009). In November 2009 she was admitted to hospital and discharged which resulted in a further assessment in December 2009. Despite the assessment noting the claimant's decline in skills the local authority left the payment unchanged. The clamant challenged the methodology for calculating the payments using a formula called 'Resource Allocation System' and that the local authority had failed to give adequate reasons for its decision. The Court concluded at paragraph 48 that, '... without being able to properly understand the use made of the RAS, the service user and anyone acting on her behalf, is left totally in the dark as to whether the monetary value of £170.45 is adequate to meet the assessed need of a 28 point score. The process of conversion made by the Panel is not explained to the service user. It should have been underpinned by an evidential base, and it was not.'

6.46   Interestingly, the Court rejected the argument that the system failed to discharge the local authority's statutory duty to meet assessed need because it imposed an unlawful cap on the budget. The Court stated at paragraph 51 that, 'Personal budgets are new and in many ways represent a fundamental shift in community care. It must be incumbent on those responsible for this provision, to be transparent, and to explain individual decisions in a precise and clear manner. I fail to see how such an obligation would be unduly burdensome.' That decision was upheld by the Court of Appeal in [2010] EWCA Civ 1209 which said that the figure generated by the RAS was a start rather than an end of the process and that 'when a local authority converts an established right – the provision of services to meet an assessed need – into a sum of money, the recipient is entitled to be told how the sum has been calculated.' It also worthy of note that the Audit Commission produced a report in October 2010 'Financial management of personal budgets: challenges and opportunities for councils'.[24] The report provides that personal budgets can promote health and wellbeing, user satisfaction and opportunities for costs saving (see page 3). The report also observes that only six per cent of the social care budget (nationally) is currently being spent through personal budgets and recommends that details of the resource allocation scheme processes are published by local authorities and they should increase provision of information and support for those utilising the scheme.

PART 2 – SPECIFIC AND SIGNIFICANT AREAS OF COMMUNITY CARE LAW

6.47   Having considered the overview of the community care decision-making process, the following will set out specific areas, which require a detailed analysis in view of their prevalence in community care disputes.

---

[24]   See www.aduit-commission.gov.uk/SiteCollectionDocuments/20101028
        financialimplicationsof
        personalbudgets.pdf.

Children

6.48   The community care structure regarding children, to some degree, is very separate from the adult community care system. This is best seen by reference to section 47 of the NHSCCA 1990[25] and sections 21 and 29 of the NAA 1948, both of which only apply to adults.

6.49   The main remit of services pertaining to disabled children is found within Part III of the Children Act 1989[26] ('CA 1989') and Schedule 2 of the CA 1989. Note, however, that in some instances there are community care provisions that apply both to children and adults.[27]

Statutory framework

Section 17 of the Children Act 1989

6.50   Section 17(1) of the CA 1989 imposes on a local authority a broad duty to safeguard and promote the welfare of children in need. It provides that:

'It shall be the general duty of every local authority (in addition to other duties imposed on them by this Part) –

(a)   to safeguard and promote the welfare of children within their area who are in need; and

(b)   so far as consistent with that duty, to promote the upbringing of such children by their families, by providing a range of level of services appropriate to those children's needs.'

6.51   Section 17(10) defines a child 'in need' in the following manner:[28]

'For the purposes of this Part a child shall be taken to be in need if—

(a)   he is unlikely to achieve or maintain, or to have the opportunity of achieving or maintaining, a reasonable standard of health or development without the provision for him of services by a local authority under this Part;

(b)   his health or development is likely to be significantly impaired, or further impaired, without the provision for him of such services; or

(c)   he is disabled.'

6.52   Section 17(11) defines 'disabled child' as:

'... a child is disabled if he is blind, deaf or dumb or suffers from mental disorder of any kind or is substantially and permanently handicapped by illness, injury or congenital deformity or such other disability as may be prescribed; and in this Part—

---

[25]   With reference to the duty to assess.

[26]   Sections 17 to 30.

[27]   Section 2 of the CSPA 1970, read with s 28A, concerns to the system of services to disabled children.

[28]   See para 24.7, p 677 of Clements & Thompson, *Community Care & the Law*, LAG, 4th edn, for a detailed analysis of a child in need. They opine that children with Aspergers's Syndrome who have above average IQs could still be defined as disabled children for the purposes of CA 1989 and entitled to services under CSDPA 1970 if an assessment bears out an eligible need. As would children with Attention Deficit Hyperactivity Disorder (ADHD) and Attention Deficit Disorder (ADD).

"development" means physical, intellectual, emotional, social or behavioural development; and

"health" means physical or mental health.'

6.53   Section 17 was considered in detail by the House of Lords in *R (G) v Barnet LBC* [2004] 2 AC 208 which confirmed that there is a general duty to provide an appropriate range and level of services.[29] As aptly stated by Mrs Justice Black in *JL* at paragraph 58, the duty, '... does not itself impose a mandatory duty on a local authority to take specific steps to satisfy the assessed needs of a particular individual child in need, regardless of the local authority's resources. A child in need is eligible for the provision of services but has no absolute right to them'. The duty can be described as a 'target duty' rather than a specific law duty.[30]

6.54   Local authorities have a power to provide accommodation to children and their families pursuant to section 17(6) of the CA 1989.[31]

Section 20 of the Children Act 1989

6.55   Section 20 of the Children Act 1989 is entitled 'Provision of accommodation for children: general' and provides:

> "(1)   Every local authority shall provide accommodation for any child in need within their area who appears to them to require accommodation as a result of—[32]
>   (a)   there being no person who has parental responsibility for him;
>   (b)   his being lost or having been abandoned; or
>   (c)   the person who has been caring for him being prevented (whether or not permanently, and for whatever reason) from providing him with suitable accommodation or care.[33]
> (3)   Every local authority shall provide accommodation for any child in need within their area who has reached the age of sixteen and whose welfare the authority consider is likely to be seriously prejudiced if they do not provide him with accommodation.
> (4)   A local authority may provide accommodation for any child within their area (even though a person who has parental responsibility for him is able to provide him with accomodation) if they consider that do so would safeguard or promote the child's welfare.

---

[29]   This was applied in *R (T, D and B) v. Haringey LBC* [2005] EWHC 2235 (Admin) and *Blackburn-Smith v Lambeth LBC* [2007] EWHC 767 (Admin).

[30]   However, s 17 (2) and Sch 2 set out specific duties and powers although these duties gave the local authorities a degree of discretion as to provision. See also on this Ouseley J in *R (T) v LB Haringey* [2005] EWHC 223 at para 73.

[31]   See also the Department of Health, 'The Children Act 1989, Guidance and Regulations, Volume 6, Children with Disabilities', HMSO, 1991, para 3.3.

[32]   See *H and others v LB Wandsworth* [2007] EWHC 1082 (Admin) where the Court observed that a factual spectrum exists which begins with the undoubted provision of accommodation and ends with matters which are not the provision of accommodation, such as the provision of practical assistance with accommodation. In *JL* the Court considered that overnight stays does not fall within the remit of s 20(1). However Black J did say at para 97 that, 'I do not have to go so far as to say that short breaks can never come within that section. That issue would have to be determined if it arose in a particular case'.

[33]   In *Barnet* Lord Nicholls said that 'prevented ... for whatever reason' is to be interpreted widely stating 'it includes a case where the person caring for the child is intentionally homeless. A child is not to be visited with the shortcomings of his parents'. In *R (L) v Nottinghamshire CC* [2007] EWHC 2364 Burton J made it clear that he would be inclined to the view that serious ill health on the part of the mother and her inability to control her child would also be sufficient to prevent the mother from providing accommodation. This view was adopted by Baroness Hale in *R (M) v Hammersmith & Fulham LBC* [2008] UKHL 14 when she took the view that the mother may not have been prevented from providing her daughter with any accommodation or care but she was from providing her daughter with 'any suitable' accommodation or care.

(6)   Before providing accommodation under this section, a local authority shall, so far as is reasonably practicable and consistent with the child's welfare—
  (a)   ascertain the child's wishes [and feelings] regarding the provision of accommodation; and
  (b)   give due consideration (having regard to his age and understanding) to such wishes [and feelings] of the child as they have been able to ascertain.
(7)   A local authority may not provide accommodation under this section for any child if any person who—
  (a)   has parental responsibility for him; and
  (b)   is willing and able to—
    (i)   provide accommodation for him; or
    (ii)   arrange for accommodation to be provided for him,
  objects ....'

6.56   In *R (FL) v Lambeth LBC* [2010] EWHC 49 (Admin) the Court helpfully summarised section 20 as follows:

'94. ... Ward L.J. in *R(A) v Croydon London Borough Council* [2009] LGR 113 at paragraph 75 set out a series of judgments that arise under section 20. These were adopted by Baroness Hale in *R(G) v Southwark LBC* [2009] 1 WLR 1299 at paragraph 28. Those judgements are:

(i)   Is the applicant a child? There is no dispute that she is in this case.
(ii)   Is the applicant a child in need? Again no issue in this case, she is.
(iii)   Is she within the local authority's area? Again no dispute in this case, she is.
(iv)   Does she appear to the local authority to require accommodation? That is in issue.
(v)   Is that need the result of: ... (c) the person caring for them being prevented from providing her with suitable accommodation or care? That is in issue.
(vi)   What are the child's wishes and feelings regarding the provision of accommodation for her? There is little if any dispute the claimant wants to be accommodated independently from her mother in semi-independent accommodation or similar and does not want to be placed in foster care.
(vii) What consideration (having regard to her age and understanding) is duly to be given to those wishes? That is in issue.
(viii) Does any person with parental responsibility who is willing to provide accommodation for her object to the local authority intervention? Her mother does not object while being content to have her home.
(ix)   If there is objection does the person in whose favour a residence order is in force agree to the child being looked after by the local authority? This is not applicable.'

6.57   The distinct terminology between section 20(1) and 20(4) is clear. Section 20(1) provides that a local authority 'shall' provide for accommodation compared to 'may' under section 20(4). As such, the cases of *A v Croydon* [2008] EWCA Civ 1445 and *R (M) v Gateshead MBC* [2006] QB 650 have established that section 20(1) gives rise to an absolute duty which applies if a child is ordinarily resident in the area and requires accommodation for the reasons set out in the subsection. In *JL* the Court concluded at paragraph 71 that section 20(1) did impose an absolute duty on a local authority, and as such, an eligibility criterion could not be used to determine whether it had a duty to act under that section.

6.58   There are, however, a number of conditions that need to be fulfilled before the section 193 duty is triggered. One such provision is that the housing authority is satisfied that the applicant has a priority need. By virtue of Articles 2 and 3 of the Homelessness (Priority Need for Accommodation) England Order 2002 (made under section 189 HA 1996), a person to whom a local authority owes a duty to provide accommodation under section 20 CA 1989 is deemed not to have a priority need. In short, therefore, this means that where section 20 CA 1989 applies, the housing authority does not have a duty to secure accommodation for the child in question.

6.59 It is important to bear in mind the importance of the first two considerations under section 20(1), namely whether any of the three criteria are met under section 20(1) are met,[34] and whether, the child 'appears to' the local authority 'to require accommodation' by reason of satisfying one of the three criteria. A local authority is able to conclude that a child does not require accommodation when he or she is sufficiently resourceful to be able to obtain accommodation via support under section 17 of the CA 1989 despite them having no accommodation.[35]

6.60 Distinct to the above community care duties, a housing authority has obligations and power under the Housing Act 1996 ('HA 1996'). Under section 193 a housing authority has a duty to 'secure that accommodation is available for occupation' where it is 'satisfied that an applicant is homeless, eligible for assistance and has a priority need, and are not satisfied that he became homeless intentionally'. There can be considerable confusion when both a local authority and a hosing association/authority provide concurrent services.

6.61 In *R (S) v LB Sutton* [2007] EWCA Civ 790 S lived in a hostel for homeless women and was re-housed (following eviction) by the local authority as a homeless person. It was not disputed that the local authority had failed to assess her needs under CA 1989 and as an alternative to have directed her to contact the housing authority. The local authority accepted that if it had carried out an assessment it would have placed S in the hostel for homeless women under CA 1989. In view of the same, the Court of Appeal deemed that she had in fact been placed at the hostel, '... in fulfillment of the respondent's obligations under section 20(1)' CA 1989 and had been a 'looked after child'.

6.62 In *R (M) v Hammersmith and Fulham LBC* [2008] UKHL 14 Baroness Hale stated that the social services authorities owed CA 1989 duties, whilst HA 1996 duties were owed by a housing authority. Thereby, neither department had the power to carry out the other's function. The Court equally stressed that the Homelessness Code of Guidance for Local Authorities provided that there was need for joint protocols between a housing authority and social services.

6.63 Finally in the recent decision in *R (MM) v LB Lewisham* [2009] EWHC 416 (Admin), the Court considered the local authority's decision that MM did not meet the criteria in section 20 of the CA 1989 because she was housed at a woman's refuge. The refuge referred her to social services, describing her as vulnerable. Social services recommended that MM be referred to a support scheme, however no further action was taken. The Court was critical of how social services had handled the referral. It provided that any reasonable local authority acting lawfully would have been bound to conclude that MM required accommodation under section 20 of the CA 1989, given her urgent need for accommodation, health and vulnerability. The Court urged local authorities to ensure that '(a) Child in need assessments are not carried out in a summary manner as occurred in this case; (b) that its Housing Department do not simply fail to respond to

---

[34] If no criteria is met then there is no duty under s 20(1) as per *R (M) v LB Barnet* [2008] EWHC 2354 (Admin) where the Court held that the criteria was not met as her parents were able and willing to provide her with suitable accommodation and care but M did not wish to live with them.

[35] See cases of *R (G) v Southwark LBC* [2008] EWCA Civ 877; *R (A) v Coventry CC* [2009] EWHC 34 (Admin); and [2009] 1 WLR 1299 (appeal of *G*).

applications in respect of children; (c) that steps are taken to ensure that the immanence of a child attaining 18 years is not taken as a basis for failing to take any action; and (d) that there is due and proper contact between its housing authority and its Social Services authority.'

Section 2 of the Chronically Sick and Disabled Persons Act 1970[36]

6.64 Section 2 of the CSDPA 1970 creates specific duties to provide certain services to persons who are 'ordinarily resident in the local authorities' area' in order to meet the needs of that person. Section 28A provides that the Act applies with respect to disabled children in relation to whom a local authority has functions under Part III of the CA 1989. As considered above it includes practical assistance in the home and provision of recreational and educational facilities. In *Bexley* the Court held that if there was a option of providing services under the CSDPA 1970 or under section 17 of the CA 1989, then the duty under the 1970 Act goes beyond the duty in the 1989 Act because it is a specific duty rather than a target duty. As stated above, once it is deemed that it is necessary to provide services under the CSDPA 1970 the local authority is under an enforceable duty to provide those services.

6.65 Other relevant duties include those under:

(i)   Section 23 of the Children Act 1989 (provision of accommodation and maintenance by local authorities for children whom they are looking after).

(ii)   Section 22 of the Children Act 1989 (general duty to children looked after by the local authority).

(iii) Section 21 of the Children Act 1989 (provision of accommodation for children in police protection or detention or on remand).

(iv)   Section 17A of the Children Act 1989 (as amended by the Health & Social Care Act 2001) (direct payments).

The assessment process

6.66 There is no specific or explicit duty on a local authority to assess under the CA 1989 equivalent to that found in section 47 of the NHSCCA 1990.[37] In *Barnet*, however, the House of Lords has made clear that there is a obligation to assess under the CA 1989, as per Lord Hope at paragraph 77:[38]

---

[36] See para 32(d) above for a general and detailed analysis.
[37] See Sch 2 of the CA 1989, however, which does state that an assessment under s 17 may take place at the same time as an assessment under other legislation such as the CSDPA 1980.
[38] Lord Nicholls also stated at para 32 that, 'The first step towards safeguarding and promoting the welfare of a child in need by providing services for him and his family is to identify the child's need for those services. It is implicit in s 17(1) that a local authority will take reasonable steps to assess, for the purposes of the Act, the needs of any child in its area who appears to be in need. Failure to carry out this duty may attract a mandatory order in an appropriate case, as occurred in *R (AB and SB) v Nottinghamshire County Council* (2001) 4 CCLR 295. Richards J ordered a local authority to carry out a full assessment of a child's needs in accordance with the guidance given by the Secretary of State in Framework for the Assessment of Children in Need and their Families (March 2000).'

'... The duty of the local authority to take reasonable steps to identify the extent to which there are children in need in their area is to be found in paragraph 1 of the Schedule. That will involve assessing the needs of each child who is found to be in need in their area as paragraph 3 makes clear.'

6.67   The obligation is heavily supported by policy guidance under the 'Framework for the Assessment of Children in Need'[39] ('assessment guidance'). As discussed above, section 7 of the Local Authority Social Services Act 1970 requires local authorities in their social services functions to act under the general guidance of the Secretary of State. See the case of *Rixon* which reinforced that local authorities are bound to follow the guidance unless there is good reason not to.[40]

6.68   The assessment guidance is clearly an important document, of which the following are relevant parts, namely:

(a)   social services departments have the lead responsibility for undertaking assessments of children in need [paragraph 4.18];

(b)   an 'initial assessment' should be undertaken within a maximum of seven working days of a child being referred to social services [paragraph 3.9] and a 'core assessment' (if necessary after initial assessment) should be undertaking within a maximum of 35 working days [paragraph 3.11];

(c)   the direct involvement of the child is fundamental to the process [paragraph 3.4]. It must include 'seeing, observing, talking, doing and engaging' [paragraph 3.42]. 'As part of an initial assessment, the child should be seen. This includes observation and talking with the child in an age appropriate manner' [paragraph 3.10];

(d)   exclusive requirements for assessment of groups of vulnerable individuals, i e those who 'require particular care and attention during assessment' [paragraphs 3.58–3. 60];[41]

(e)   the conclusion of the assessment must result in [paragraph 4.1]:

   (i)   analysis of needs and parenting capacity to respond to those needs;
   (ii)   identification of and whether intervention is required to secure well being of child; and
   (iii) a plan of action (outlining what services are to be provided) detailing who is responsible, a timetable and process of review; and

(f)   continuing and review assessment are required under paragraph 1.53, 'assessment should continue throughout a period of intervention'.

---

[39]   Department of Health, Department for Education and Employment and Home Office, TSO, 2000.
[40]   Para 123 J to K.
[41]   They include children whose families 'have a long history of contact with social services'; children in transition; children 'about whom there are concerns that they are becoming or might become involved in prostitution'; and children who are drug users and whose level of use is unknown to family and teachers. Such groups of children require, 'a high degree of cooperation and coordination ... in planning and preparing for assessments, in undertaking and completing them' and 'responsibility for action and providing services must be clearly identified and recorded, with specific timescales'.

6.69   The weight of the guidance has been heavily emphasised by the Court. In *R (AB and SB) v Nottingham City Council* (2001) 4 CCLR 294 Mr Justice Richards stated that:

'... it is important, moreover, to be clear about the three-stage process: identification of needs, production of care plan, and provision of identified services. It seems to me that where an authority follows a path that does not involve the preparation of a core assessment as such, it must nevertheless adopt a similarly systematic approach with a view to achievement of the same objectives. Failures to do so without good cause will constitute an impermissible departure from the guidance ....'[42]

6.70   Similarly, in *R (J) v Newham LBC* [2001] EWHC 992 (Admin) the Court ordered a mandatory order for the local authority to undertake a section 17 assessment within 35 days. Also in *R (LH and MH) v Lambeth* [2006] EWHC 1190 (Admin)[43] the Court concluded that the completed care plan failed to accord with the relevant statutory obligations because it failed to specify adequate support to meet LH's identified needs. The Council's decision that the 'package of support' offered, much of which remains to be identified, was to be preferred to the residential placement was seriously flawed and irrational. Mr Justice Crane granted a declaration that the defendant was in breach of the Children Act 1989 as supplemented by the Children Act 2004 and the Carers (Recognition of Services) Act 1995.

Leaving care

6.71   The relevant 'leaving care' provisions in the Children Act 1989 were incorporated by the Children (Leaving Care) Act 2000. The rationale behind the implementation derived from a consultation paper produced in 1999.[44] As succinctly put by Clements and Thompson, the main purpose of the Act:

'... is to help young people who have been looked after by a local authority moved from care into living independently in a stable a fashion as possible. It seeks to promote this aim by amending key provisions of the CA 1989 to place specific duties on social services authorities in respect of "eligible" and "relevant" children.'[45]

6.72   Leaving care encompasses three differing circumstances, namely:

(i)   the 'relevant child' – an individual who is aged 16 or 17 (a child), but who is no longer being looked after by the local authority;

(ii)   the 'former relevant child' – an individual who has reached the age of 18 and who, before that date, was either a relevant child, or a 'looked after' child who was also an 'eligible child' immediately before ceasing to be 'looked after'; and

(iii)   the 'qualifying child or young person over 16' – an individual who is under 21 and who, when aged 16 or 17, was, but is no longer, looked after, accommodated or fostered.

---

[42]   Para 306G–I.
[43]   The local authority produced a core assessment and carer's assessment. The social worker recommended that LH should attend a residential school but the placement was not arranged. LH's judicial review application was adjourned pending a further assessment. In the new assessment the social worker concluded that a residential placement was no longer appropriate. Instead, the social worker thought that a 'parenting skills programme' and an adjustment to the respite arrangements would suffice.
[44]   'Me, Survive, Out There? – New Arrangements for Young People Living in and Leaving Care'.
[45]   Para 24.23, page 683, *Community Care and the Law,* LAG, 4th edn.

Eligible and relevant child

6.73 Section 23A of the CA 1989 stipulates that the responsible local authority shall have duties (set out in section 23B) in respect of a relevant child who is aged 16 or 17 and who would have been 'eligible'[46] before last ceasing to be looked after by a local authority.[47]

6.74 A relevant child is a 'looked after child' by virtue of section 22 if:

(a) the child is in the care of the relevant local authorities; or

(b) has been provided with accommodation by the relevant local authority in the exercise of any social service functions excluding those functions under sections 17, 23B and 24B.

6.75 The duties owed to a relevant child are as follows:

(i) section 23B provides that an assessment of needs and pathway plan should be undertaken by a responsible local authority ('RLA') to safeguard and promote the child's welfare within three months of their 16th birthday. The local authority must support him or her by maintaining him, provide suitable accommodation or by other means unless is it satisfied that his welfare does not require it; and

(ii) Regulation 11 also provides that the RLA 'must provide' assistance to meet the relevant child's needs with regards to education, training or employment as outlined in the pathway plan.

Former relevant child

6.76 A 'former relevant child' is by virtue of section 23C a young person aged 18–21 who has been an eligible child and/or a relevant child. The same section of the Act outlines the duties which exist until the relevant child is 21:

(i) a RLA 'must take reasonable steps' to keep in touch and re-establish contact if it is lost, to continue the appointment of a personal adviser and to continue to keep the young person's pathway plan under regular review; and

(ii) under section 23C(4)(c) to provide 'other assistance to the extent that his welfare requires it' which can be in kind or, in exceptional circumstances, in cash.[48]

6.77 Under section 23D all eligible, relevant and former relevant children must be provided with a personal advisor who will provide advice, information and support to young persons and keep them informed of their progress and well being. They must also be involved in the assessment of needs and the production of a pathway plan.

---

[46] A is a child aged 16 or 17 who has been looked after by a local authority for a period or periods totalling at least 13 weeks beginning after the age of 14 and continuing after he reached the age of 16.

[47] A further class of relevant children includes those who do not fall within this definition but did not for the sole reason that, on their 16th birthday, they were in penal or hospital detention.

[48] Section 23C(5).

Young people over 16 and qualifying children

6.78   Under section 24, advice and assistance is to be provided by a RLA to those who are 'qualifying', namely those who include an individual aged 16 to 20, for whom a special guardianship order was in place or in force when he reached the age of 18 and was looked after until that order was made. Alternatively, it includes a person aged 16 to 20 and whilst aged 16 to 17 was looked after by accommodation[49] or fostering.[50]

6.79   The duties outlined below include a general obligation to keep in touch with care leavers to the extent that is appropriate for the discharge for their functions under sections 24A and 24B. In practice, this duty to 'keep in touch' can last for some time, if not extended over many years.

6.80   Section 24 provides duties of advice and assistance[51] to such individuals and those relating to employment, education and training as outlined above. Specifically, under section 24B there is a duty to contribute to the expenses incurred by him in living near a place of education, training or employment, or to make a grant to enable him to meet expenses connected with his education or training.[52]

Guidance

6.81   Guidance has been provided by the Department of Health[53] to which appropriate weight must be given. Paragraph 11 of Chapter 1 provides:[54]

> 'The culmination of young people's experience of being looked after by a local authority, private foster carers, a voluntary organisation or in a children's home is a successful return to their family or the establishment of a stable and positive relationship with another responsible person. Alternatively, where this is necessary, they should be enabled to become as self-supporting as possible.'

6.82   Important aspects of the guidance are as follows:

(i)   that young people who qualify for leaving care provision should already have a care plan, which will have been reviewed regularly and updated as part of the process for children who are looked after [chapter 5, paragraph 13];

---

[49]   Subsection 24(2) defines 'accommodated' as accommodated by a voluntary organisation or in a private children's home or, for at least three months, by any health authority or LEA or care home or similar.

[50]   'Fostered' means 'privately fostered'. Those who are fostered by the local authority meet the separate definition of being looked after.

[51]   Note that under s 24B, a person who qualifies for advice and assistance also qualifies for help with accommodation during a vacation where he is in full-time further or higher education and his term-time accommodation is not available to him. That duty subsists until the person turns 24 years of age.

[52]   Obviously only if his needs require it.

[53]   Department of Education and Skills, *Children (Leaving Care) Act 2000 Regulations and Guidance*, 2001.

[54]   See guidance for further details. There are also frequent reminders that although a social services department will take the lead, it will need to liaise with other agencies internally and externally: housing and education departments, health authorities, Connexions and the Careers service, Benefits Agency, the Employment Service, Job Centre Plus, Youth Offending Teams and the voluntary sector. Note s 27 of the Children Act 1989, which empowers a local authority to request help in its discharge of these functions from any other local authority and other agencies – such requests must be complied with if they are compatible with the other agency's own duties. There is considerable emphasis on the need for preparation for leaving care, starting well in advance. This is dealt with in Chapter 4 of the guidance. Preparation for leaving care should be incorporated in the care plan for young people as soon as they start to be looked after, accommodated or privately fostered.

(ii)   the assessment of needs is subject to the detailed requirements of the Regulations;

(iii)   regulation 5 provides that the authority is to prepare a written statement in which the needs of each eligible and relevant child will be assessed, including details of those involved, the timetable, how the outcome is to be recorded and the procedure if there is a disagreement;

(iv)   regulation 6 states that the RLA is to seek and have regard to the views of the child or young person and to take all reasonable steps to enable him to attend and participate in any meetings;

(v)   regulation 7 provides some timescales, namely eligible children must be assessed within three months of turning 16 or otherwise becoming eligible;

(vi)   regulation 7 also prescribes a list of matters to be considered;[55]

(vii)   that any multi-agency assessment will follow the spirit of the Framework for the Assessment of Children in Need and their Families; and

(viii) insofar as lack of engagement is concerned, the RLA should give clear and specific details of the steps, which it has taken to try to engage with the child and explain why it has not been reasonably practicable to do everything contemplated by the Regulations.

Leaving care decisions and judicial review

6.83   The starting point for any practitioner must be the case of *H v LB of Wandsworth and others* [2007] EWHC 1082 Admin. As fittingly stated by the Court at paragraphs 64 and 103:

> '... in certain circumstances, the local authority may consider that what the child requires is not "accommodation" (which would give rise to the duty under s 20(1)), but "help with accommodation", which would not. If they then provide no more than help (e g some limited funding) then neither a duty under s 20(1), nor the statutory consequence of the child becoming a looked after child under s 22(1) arise ... there is clearly a factual spectrum between undoubted provision of accommodation at one end, to mere or incidental help with accommodation at the other. At the first end of the spectrum, a social services department may actually house a person rent-free in accommodation which they actually own. At the other end of the spectrum, they may merely provide practical assistance by introducing a person to a private landlord and perhaps help with completing the necessary documents.'

6.84   The majority of reported cases converge on the actual assessment and pathway plan, and whether the necessary statutory and/or guidance requirements have been satisfied. An example of such a case was *R (P) v Newham LBC* [2004] EWHC 2210 (Admin) where the Court held that a RLA had acted unlawfully by failing to provide a personal pathway plan before the severely disabled in care turned 19 years of age.

---

[55]   These include health and development; support available from family or other relationships; financial needs; practical and other skills; need for education, training or employment; and the needs for care and support and accommodation. Regulation 7 also provides that the RLA must seek and take into account the views of parents and those with PR and carers; school, college or LEA; any independent visitor; healthcare providers; personal adviser; and anyone else with relevant views.

6.85   In *R (J) v Caerphilly County Borough Council* [2005] EWHC 586 (Admin) a 17 year old had been in care for four years. He was unwilling to engage with the RLA. His pathway plan ought to have been put into place by September 2003 but not produced until November 2004. The Court reinforced the importance of involving the child in the assessment and planning process.[56] Mr Justice Munby considered it 'wholly unsatisfactory' for the RLA to have produced the plan before discussing or engaging the child. He also fond that the assessment and plans were inadequate.

6.86   At paragraph 43 the Court said:

'The deficiencies in this are all too apparent. Where are the details of the "nature and level of personal support" to be provided to J? Where is the "detailed plan" for J's education and training? Where are the details of the "programme to develop the practical and other skills necessary for [J] to live independently"? Where are the details of the "financial support" to be provided to him? How are his "mental health needs" to be met? Too often, as can be seen, the answer is that the plan is to arrange an appointment with someone else, or to "explore options", or to "develop" a programme. In no case is the "date by which" any of these actions will be carried out specified. Everything is either to be done "ASAP" or is "On going". There seems in some instances to be a lack of clarity in distinguishing between the plan and the contingency plan. What are identified in Parts 1, 3 and 5 as aspects of the contingency plan would seem more appropriately to be required as part of the main plan.'

6.87   The Court also referred to the case of *R (AB and SB) v Nottingham CC* [2001] EWHC Admin 235, (2001) in which Mr Justice Richards emphasised the rigour and detail required of a local authority embarking upon an assessment such as this. At the end of the process, what is needed is a document, as the Court put it at paragraphs 20 and 43:

'it should be possible to see what help and support the child and family need and which agencies might be best placed to give that help ... it was essentially a descriptive document rather than an assessment, and in any event sufficient detail was still lacking both as regards the assessment itself and as regards the care plan and service provision. There was no clear identification of needs, or what was to be done about them, by whom and by when.'

6.88   In concluding, the Court outlined at paragraph 45:

'To repeat, because the point is so important, and a clear statement of what is required may assist not merely this but other local authorities: *A pathway plan must clearly identify the child's needs, and what is to be done about them, by whom and by when.* Or, if another aphorism would help, *A pathway plan must spell out who does what, where and when.* As the *Children Leaving Care Act Guidance* makes clear in paragraph 7.7: "The Pathway Plan should be explicit in setting out the objectives and actions needed to achieve these; this should include who is responsible for achieving each action and time–scale for achieving it." I draw attention to and wish to emphasise the word "explicit". At the risk of stating the obvious, the pathway plan here was very far indeed from being explicit.'

6.89   In *R (C) v LB Lambeth* [2008] EWHC 1230 (Admin) the Court was similarly asked to find that the RLA had failed to discharge their duties in respect of pathway plans. In particular, two criticisms were made without prejudice to the generality: namely (a) there was no timescale provided for addressing her needs and her training and educational needs; and (b) that there was a failure to connect the absence of

---

[56]   See above stated guidance, particularly para 4 of Chapter 4.

educational progress with the housing difficulties; and that in itself reflected the associated difficulties, mental health, behavioural and otherwise that this young person had.

6.90   The Court (allowing the declarations that the pathway plans failed to comply with the Regulations and mandatory orders requiring the local authority to produce a lawful assessment and pathway plan) concluded that the deficiencies in the process were obvious. In particular, the RLA had embarked on the process too late; the pathway plan should have been completed by September 2003; the steps taken to involve the child in the process were also inadequate; the pathway plans were hopelessly inadequate and contained little more than aspirations; and the RLA used standard pro forma pathway plans which failed to address financial support and would have been better advised to have used the Department of Health's pro forma prepared in 2002; a pathway plan had to clearly identify the child's needs, and what was to be done about them, by whom and by when.

6.91   Finally in *R (O) v Barking and Dagenham London Borough Council* [2010] EWHC 634 (Admin) the Court considered the question of whether the local authority or NASS was responsible for accommodating an adult who was a 'former relevant child' within the meaning of section 23C of the Children Act 1989 ('the 1989 Act'). The claimant was a 19-year-old failed asylum seeker who had made fresh representations to the Secretary of State. No decision had been made in respect of this application, ie whether it amounted to a fresh claim. The local authority had accommodated and supported him as a child under the Children Act 1989 until he reached 18, after which his support was terminated. The local authority accepted that the claimant was a 'former relevant child' within the meaning of section 23C of the 1989 Act, however, the main issue of contention was whether the local authority or NASS was primarily or solely responsible for providing him with accommodation, either until he was removed from the country or until the Secretary of State had reached a conclusion. The local authority argued that: (i) it was prevented by Schedule 3 of the Nationality Immigration and Asylum Act 2002 from providing the claimant with leaving care services under the 1989 Act; and (ii) as the claimant would be entitled to hard cases support from NASS under section 4 of the Immigration and Asylum Act 1999, he would not be destitute so as to require support to avoid a breach of his human rights.

6.92   The Court held that section 23C(4)(c) of the 1989 Act was not concerned with the provision of accommodation, and a local authority could not use this section to provide accommodation to former relevant children. The only respect in which accommodation may be provided and paid for by a local authority under section 23C for former relevant children is in connection with work or educational needs under section 23C(4)(a) and (b). Accordingly, the claim failed, as the local authority had no duty to provide accommodation to the claimant.

6.93   The Court of Appeal completely disagreed, [2010] EWCA Civ 1101, and concluded that: (i) the Judge had erred in holding that the above sub-section did not afford the local authority the power to provide accommodation to a former relevant child (see paragraph 28 of Tomlinson LJ's judgment); and (ii) the local authority is not entitled, when considering whether a formal relevant child's welfare requires that he be accommodated by it, to take into account the possibility of support from NASS.

6.94 This decision impacts on care leavers where young people, for example those seeking asylum or those coming out of custody, are unable to access suitable accommodation through the normal housing routes.

Carers

6.95 Section 8 of the Disabled Persons (Services, Consultation and Representation) Act 1986 provides that: 'Where (a) a disabled person is living at home and receiving a substantial amount of care on a regular basis from another person (who is not a person employed to provide such care by anybody in the exercise of its functions under any enactment), and (b) it falls to the local authority to decide whether the disabled person's needs call for the provision by them of any services for him under any welfare enactment, the local authority shall, in deciding that question, have regard to the ability of that person to continue to provide such care on a regular basis'.

6.96 The Carers (Recognition & Services) Act 1995 provides recognition for carers by requiring the social services authority (if so requested) to carry out a separate assessment of the carer at the same time as it assesses the person for whom the care is provided. The carer can be of any age. As aptly stated by relevant policy guidance:

> '... many young people carry out a level of caring responsibilities which prevents them from enjoying normal social opportunities and from achieving full school attendance. Many young carers with significant caring responsibilities should therefore be seen as children in need ....'[57]

6.97 In order to qualify for an assessment under the Act, a carer must satisfy the following criteria:

- a community care assessment (or reassessment) of the person for who he or she cares must be in the process of being carried out (ie a side by side assessment);

- the carer must be providing (or intending to provide) a substantial amount of care on a regular basis. People who provide care as a result of a contract of employment or as a volunteer placed by a voluntary organisation are excluded; and

- the carer must request a carers assessment. The guidance, however, requires social workers to 'inform any carer who appears eligible under this Act of their right to request an assessment'.

6.98 The Act entitles qualifying carers to an assessment of their ability to provide and continue to provide care. If, as a result of such an assessment, it transpires that the carer is no longer able (or willing) to provide the same level of care, then the authority will have to decide whether to change the service user's care plan by increasing the level of services provided. Note that practice guidance accompanying the Act states that social workers should not 'assume a willingness by the carer to continue, or to continue to provide the same level of support'.

6.99 Free standing carer's assessments are available under the Carers and Disabled Children's Act 2000, which enables carers of adults in need of community care services,

---

[57] Policy Guidance Letter CI (95), Annex X, para 1.1, adopted under Carers Act 1995.

and carers of disabled children (irrespective of whether community care assessment of person cared for is being carried out), to request a carer's assessment which must then be provided.

6.100 Section 1 provides for free standing carers assessments; that is a carer can be assessed even if the person who s/he cares refuses a community care assessment. The requirements are that the carer is over 15 years of age, is carrying for someone aged 18 or over and the carer requests an assessment. The assessment enables the local authority to decide whether to provide services to the carer under section 2.

6.101 Section 2 enables the local authority to provide services to carers following a carer's assessment. Potentially there is little restriction upon the services that can be made available, provided the service helps 'the carer care for the person cared for'. The explanatory notes to the Act indicate that the services may take the form of physical help, for example assistance around the house, or other forms of support such as training or counselling for the carer.

6.102 Respite/short break care is not, however, a carers service. This has been explained by the DOH in the following way, '... people who care may be assessed as needing a break from their caring role. This need will be clearly recorded on their own assessment documentation ... [and imperatively] ... *the additional service remains a community care service delivered to the cared for person, not the carer service under the [2000] Act ...* [emphasis added]'

6.103 Section 1 of the Carers (Equal Opportunities) Act 2004 places an obligation on social services authorities to inform carers of the rights to be assessed under the Carers (Recognition & Services) Act 1995 or the Carers & Disabled Children Act 2000. Section 2 requires that in any assessment under either the above stated Acts that consideration be given as to whether the carer: (i) works or wishes to work; and (ii) is undertaking, or wishes to undertake, education, training or any leisure activity.

6.104 Section 3 aims to facilitate co-operation between local (social services) authorities and other bodies in connection with the authorities' provision of service for carers and the provision by those other bodies of services that may benefit carers. It provides:

- that a local authority may request another authority or health body (PCT etc) to assist it in planning the provision of services to carers and persons being cared for. These other bodies are required to give 'due consideration' to such a request; and

- that where a local authority forms the view that a carer's ability to provide care might be enhanced by the provision of services by another authority or health body it may request that the other body is to provide the service, to which request the other body must give due consideration.

The social care and healthcare overlap

Cooperation

6.105 Unfortunately, given the overlap of statutory provisions, there is an area of confusion that relates to the interplay of services provided by a local authority and the NHS.

6.106 Despite this, however, there are specific obligations upon both the NHS and local authorities to cooperate with each other. Some have already been considered above, others include:

(i) Section 46 of the NHSCCA 1990 which imposes a requirement on local authorities to prepare and keep under review a plan for the provision of community care services in their area. Section 46(2) states that in performing these duties, including the duty to review, the local authority must consult, inter alia, with any Health Authority and Local Health Board.

(ii) Part 3 of the NHSA 2006 combines a number of provisions governing the relationship between local authorities and the NHS. Section 82 states that NHS bodies and local authorities must cooperate with one another in order to secure and advance the health and welfare of the people of England and Wales.

(iii) Section 74 of the NHSA 2006 incorporates Health Authorities, Special Health Authorities and Primary Care Trusts under the Local Authorities (Goods and Services) Act 1970. Section 74(3) provides that each local authority must make services available to each NHS body acting in its area, so far as is reasonably necessary and practicable to enable the NHS body to discharge its functions under this Act.

(iv) Section 75 and the NHS Bodies and Local Authority Partnership Arrangements Regulations 2000 empowers NHS bodies and local authorities to engage into a partnership arrangements including pooled fund arrangements and the delegation of functions by local authorities to NHS bodies and vice versa.

Division between social care and medical care services

6.107 In *R v North and East Devon Health Authority, ex p Coughlan* [1999] All ER (D) 801, the Court of Appeal acceded to the argument that there are circumstances in which a local authority may have the responsibility for providing nursing care for a chronically sick patient as part of its role as a social service provider. A local authority has no responsibility to provide medical care.

6.108 In *R (on the application of D and another) v Haringey London Borough Council* [2005] EWHC 2235 the Court considered the scope of section 17 and Schedule 2 of the Children Act 1989 and of section 2 and 28A of the CSDPA 1970. The Court accepted and highlighted the distinction between health and social care provisions and concluded that whilst section 2 of the CSDPA makes a provision for a local authority to provide 'practical assistance' in the home, it could not extend to the provision of day or night respite care provided by a nurse.

6.109 In establishing the same the Court identified a number of relevant factors, namely:

(a) the question whether the care is incidental or ancillary to the provision of some other service which a social services authority is lawfully providing the scale and type of care;

(b) whether or not the service is of a nature which such authority can be expected to provide;

(c)   the gravity of the consequences of a failure in care; the duration of the care need; whether the care is incidental to or arises out of other medical treatment; and

(d)   the nature of the training an individual needs to provide the care.

6.110 This approach may be contrasted, however, with the Court of Appeal's broader interpretation of section 21(5) of the NAA 1948 at paragraph 27 of *Coughlan*.

Can a local authority provide healthcare provision?

6.111 There are some statutory bars to the provision of care services by local authorities.

6.112 Section 21(8) of the NAA 1948 applies to the provision of accommodation under section 21(1). Services in connection with accommodation can include nursing services, *Coughlan*.[58] A local authority cannot provide services, which are authorised or required to be provided under the NHS Act 2006.

6.113 Section 29(6) of the NAA 1948 applies to the making of arrangements under section 29(1) for promoting the welfare of adults who are blind, deaf, dumb, or suffer from mental disorder or are substantially and permanently handicapped by illness, injury or congenital deformity or other prescribed disabilities. Section 29(6) makes it unlawful for a local authority to provide accommodation or services pursuant to such arrangements where that accommodation or services is required to be provided under the NHS Act 2006 or to be provided by or under any other enactment; it is not sufficient that provision of the accommodation or services is merely authorised under the NHS Act 2006.

6.114 Finally, section 49(1) of the Health and Social Care Act 2001 makes it unlawful for a local authority to provide or arrange for any person to be provided with nursing care by a registered nurse in connection with the provision of community care services. Interestingly, section 49(2) defines nursing care by a registered nurse so as to exclude services which, although provided by a registered nurse, do not need to be provided by a registered nurse, having regard to their nature and the circumstances in which they are provided.

6.115 However, although these statutory bars are potentially far-reaching, it is important to recognise their limits. Thus, where section 21(8) of the NAA 1948 applies it only applies to bar a local authority from providing accommodation and services in connection with accommodation under section 21(1) and 21(5) of the NAA 1948. Likewise section 29(6) only bars a local authority from providing accommodation and services under section 29(1). These provisions do not prevent the local authority from providing other care to an individual under other community care powers such as section 254 and Schedule 20 of the NHSA 2006; nor do they exclude the local authority's duties to do so. The fact that an individual is receiving some types of care from an NHS body does not mean that the local authority can assume that all types of care that are needed by that individual are being met or should be met by that NHS body.

---

[58]   Para 27(c).

Section 117 after care service

6.116 Duties under the MHA 1983 are a perfect example of the joint working cooperation between the NHS and a local authority. Section 117 of the Act places a duty jointly on Primary Care Trusts and social services authorities, in co-operation with relevant voluntary agencies, to provide after-care services for patients who have been detained in hospital for treatment under section 3, under a section 37 hospital order, under a section 45A hospital direction or after transfer from a prison under sections 47 or 48 of the MHA 1983.

6.117 The duty is triggered when the patient comes to an end of the detention and leaves hospital and continues until the health and local social services authorities are content that the patient is no longer in need of those services.[59] The House of Lords in the case of *R v Secretary of State for the Home Department, ex p H* [2003] UKHL 59 held that:

'The duty of the health authority, was not absolute, whether it arose under s 117 of the 1983 Act or in response to the tribunal's order. The authorities had to use their best endeavours to procure compliance with the conditions laid down by the tribunal.'

6.118 Section 117 after care services are community care services as outlined at section 46 of the NHSCCA 1990. The assessment obligations under section 47 apply, and the services can include home care, residential care, social work support in helping patients with employment, relationships, accommodation provision of domiciliary services, use of day centres and residential facilities. With regards to which authorities are responsible, in *R v Mental Health Review Tribunal, ex p Hall* Scoot Baker LJ held that:

'For the purposes of s 117 of the 1983 Act, the relevant health and social services authorities were those for this area where the patient was ordinarily resident at the time of his detention, unless he had no place of residence. In the latter case, the relevant authorities would be those of the area where the patient was sent on discharge, but the placing authority where the patient resided did not cease to be the appropriate local social services authority by virtue of the fact that he was sent to a different authority on discharge.'

6.119 In *R (MM) v Greenwich LBC & Bromley LBC* [2010] EWHC 1462 (Admin) the Court clarified the extent of this duty in the following manner:

'61. Section 117 requires the relevant authorities to provide a patient on discharge from section 3 with "after-care services". "After-care services" are not defined in the statute ....

63. In relation to the scope of section 117 services, the respected commentary on the 1983 Act by Richard Jones says (Mental Health Act Manual, 12th Edition, at paragraph 1-1053)

"It is suggested that an after-care service is a service which is (1) provided in order to meet an assessed need that arises from a person's mental disorder; and (2) aimed at reducing that person's chance of being re-admitted to hospital for treatment for that disorder."

64. ... The duty derives from a provision in mental health legislation; and it is described as a duty to provide "after-care services". As Ms Richards submitted, section 117 is not

---

[59] Section 117(2) of the MHA 1983 provides that the relevant bodies will not be satisfied in the case of a community patient while he remains a patient.

concerned with the provision of support and accommodation at large, but rather with the provision, to the specified category of patients who have been detained on account of their mental disorder, of services tailored to meet needs arising from that disorder. An after-care service must, in my judgment, be a service that is necessary to meet a need arising from a person's mental disorder.

...

66. That, it seems to me, is the principle. In practice, the assessment of needs that do arise from a mental disorder may of course give rise to difficult issues. It is for the relevant authorities – the local authority and the health authority – to reach their own view as to what need the person has, and, in making an assessment under section 47 of the 1990 Act, they enjoy a discretion as to what if any services are required to meet such needs. As Lord Phillips MR said in *R (K) v Camden and Islington Health Authority* [2001] EWCA Civ 240 at [29]:

> "The nature and extent of those [after-care] facilities must, to a degree, fall within the discretion of the [authorities] which must have regard to other demands in [their] budget."

The reference to "nature", as well as "extent", of the services in my view emphasises both the potential broad scope of section 117 and the wide discretion of the authorities within that scope. The recognition of this discretion, given to the authorities by Parliament, appears to me to be vital.

...

68. I consider that my construction of the section 117 – restricting its scope to services necessary to meet a need arising from a person's mental disorder – is generally supported by those authorities. In *Clunis v Camden and Islington Health Authority* [1998] 3 All ER 180, Beldam LJ, after noting that the term is not defined in the 1983 Act, said of "after-care services" (at page 191E–F):

> "They would normally include social work, support in helping the ex-patient with problems of employment, accommodation or family relationships, the provision of domiciliary services and the use of day centre and residential facilities. No doubt some assessment of the patient's needs would in the first instance be made by the hospital that discharged him."

69. In *Richmond Borough Council v Watson* [2000] EWCA Civ 239, Otton LJ (quoting Beldam LJ from that earlier case) said:

> "[T]he words 'after-care services' in [the 1983 Act] can include residential accommodation which is specifically designed to care for the needs of persons who have been detained under section 3 and who have left hospital."

...

70. When that case proceeded to the House of Lords (as *R (Stennett) v Manchester City Council* [2002] UKHL 34), Lord Steyn, again having quoted Beldam LJ in *Clunis*, commented that "caring residential accommodation ... (ensuring, for example, that prescribed medication is taken)" fell within the scope of after-care services, and indeed that appears to have been common ground by then (see [9] and [15]). He too referred to residential accommodation being available under section 21 (at [7]).

71. These authorities do not directly deal with bare accommodation – but they are at least consistent with the construction I consider correct. Indeed, although on their facts they all concern "accommodation plus", they appear particularly careful not to include mere accommodation in their comments; and there are several references to the residual power to accommodate in section 21.

…

75. In addition to authority, I consider that the construction of section 117 I favour is supported by the following.

76. First, relevant government guidance indicates that, in the view of the respective departments, services under section 117 are designed to meet needs that are related to the former patient's mental disorder. In relation to England, the Department of Health's guidance, The National Framework for NHS Continuing Healthcare and NHS-funded Nursing Care (July 2009) states, at paragraph 116, that:

> "… [A] person in receipt of after-care services under section 117 may also have needs for continuing care that are not related to their mental disorder and that may, therefore, not fall within the scope of section 117."

So far as Wales is concerned, there is in substance the adoption of Mr Jones' suggested construction of section 117. The Welsh Assembly Government's Code of Practice for Wales, at paragraph 3.12, provides:

> "After-care services are provided to meet an assessed need arising from the patient's mental disorder and are aimed at reducing the likelihood of the patient being readmitted to hospital for treatment for that disorder."

77. Second, local authorities cannot charge for services provided under section 117 (*Stennett*). That is a reflection of the nature of the services that are required to be provided under that provision, ie services provided to particularly vulnerable people particularly to cover the aspired transition from section 3 detention to living in the community by providing services to satisfy needs deriving from the mental disorder in respect of which they had been detained. Of course, in some cases, that might be a long-term requirement. However, it simply cannot have been the intention of Parliament to have required local authorities (let alone health authorities), free of charge, to provide a roof over the head of former section 3 patients so long as they simply required housing.

78. Third, as the legal authorities remark, even if mere housing is not available under section 117, there is provision for former patients to obtain ordinary housing, under section 21. Although a residual duty, section 21 seems to me a far more appropriate vehicle for requiring authorities to provide mere housing, than the provisions relating to mental health.

79. For all of those reasons, I consider that an authority's responsibility to provide services under section 117 is restricted to those services necessary to meet a need arising from a person's mental disorder.'

6.120 Note the recent case of *R (JM) v London Borough of Hammersmith & Fulham; and R (Hertfordshire CC) v London Borough of Hammersmith & Fulham* [2010] EWHC 562 (Admin). There the Court considered the question of which local authority was responsible for meeting the accommodation costs of an individual detained under section 3 of the Mental Health Act 1983 who is then discharged back into the community. The issue focused on the apparent difference between the use of the word 'resident' in section 117(3) as compared to the words 'ordinarily resident' in sections 21 and 24 of the National Assistance 1948 Act. Mitting J concluded that there was no perceptible difference between the three phrases, 'resident', 'ordinarily resident' and 'normally resident'. All three connoted settled presence in a particular place other than under compulsion.

Analysis

6.121 This is a heavily commented area. Of particular interest, Clements and Bowen[60] have argued that where a person's needs as assessed by the social services authority are not being met fully by the NHS, either in terms of the nature or the quantity of the service provided, the social services authority may then be under a duty to address this deficit. They identify three situations in which this problem might arise: where an NHS body refuses to provide the relevant service because of a lack of financial resources; because of a lack of physical or human resources; or where the NHS body assesses the person's needs differently. The third possibility is when the local authority identified a need for more extensive respite care than the Primary Care Trust believed to be necessary or was willing to provide.

6.122 Commonly, however, it is believed that it is in the service users' best interest to be found eligible for NHS support provisions given that it is free at the point of source. Nevertheless, it is important to bear in mind that those found eligible for residential services under NAA 1948 or for residential home based care under CSDPA 1970 are entitled to enforce those duties in judicial review proceedings. This is significant when compared to the duty to provide NHS services under the NHSA 2006, which is a target duty which a Court will not enforce compared to the individually enforceable duties under the NAA or CSDPA.

Community care support for asylum seekers and migrants

6.123 Recently a number of reports have highlighted that certain improvements are required in the legislative framework relating to asylum seekers and their recourse to community care and housing services. The report entitled 'Deserving Dignity' prepared by the Independent Asylum Commission (2008) criticised the policy of destitution as a lever to encourage return and sought the end of detention of child and age-disputed young persons. 'Improving the care of unaccompanied asylum seeking children' (January 2008) investigated alternatives to the detention of children and presented a code of practice. In June 2008 the report prepared by the UK Commissioners to the UN Committee on the Rights of the Child (report on UK children's rights record) stressed the poor treatment of some of the UK's most vulnerable children, which it concluded was in clear breach of the UN Convention on the Rights of the Child.

6.124 It is quite understandable, therefore, that this specific area has been at the forefront of socio-political and legal debate.

---

[60]   NHS continuing care and independent living: the law reviewed, *Legal Action*, June 2007, pp 39–42.

Statutory framework

6.125 The basic provisions are as follows:

(i) to recap, under section 21 of the NAA 1948 a local authority is to make arrangements for providing residential accommodation for reasons of age, illness, disability or any other reason which may them a person in need of care and attention. SubSection 1A specifically provides that:

> '(1A) A person to whom s.115 of the Immigration and Asylum Act 1999 (exclusion from benefits) applies may not be provided with residential accommodation under subsection (1)(a) if his need for care and attention has arisen solely—
> (a) because he is destitute; or
> (b) because of the physical effects, or anticipated physical effects, of his being destitute.'

(ii) section 95 of the Immigration and Asylum Act 1999 ('IAA 1999') transfers responsibility for providing support to asylum seekers from local authorities to the Secretary of State for the Home Department ('SSHD'). By s 94(3), a claim for asylum shall be treated for the purposes of s 94(1) as having been determined at the end of such period as may be prescribed, beginning with the date on which the SSHD notifies the claimant of her decision on the claim, or, if the claimant appeals against the SSHD's decision, the date on which the appeal if disposed of. By s 95(1)(a), the SSHD may provide, or arrange for the provision of, support for asylum seekers who appear to the SSHD to be destitute. A person is 'destitute' for the purposes of s 95(1)(a) if he does not have, and cannot obtain, both adequate accommodation and food and other essential items. By s 98, the SSHD may provide or arrange for the provision of support for asylum seekers who it appears to the SSHD may be destitute. Support under this section may only be provided until the Secretary of State is able to determine whether support may be provided under s 95; and

(iii) Schedule 3, paragraph 1(1) of the Nationality, Immigration and Asylum Act 2002 ('NIAA 2002') states:

> 'The person to whom this paragraph applies shall <u>not</u> be eligible for support or assistance under ...
> (a) section 21 or 29 of the National Assistance Act 1948 ...,
> (g) section 17, 23C, 24A or 24B of the Children Act 1989 ...,
> (j) section 188(3) or 204(4) of the Housing Act 1996 ...,
> (k) section 2 of the Local Government Act 2000,
> (l) a provision of the Immigration and Asylum Act 1999.'

Paragraph 3 provides for an exception where support is necessary to prevent a breach of the individual's Convention rights. Paragraph 6 is headed 'Third class of ineligible person: failed asylum-seeker' and provides that a person is not eligible for support or assistance if: '(a) he was (but is no longer) an asylum seeker, and (b) he fails to co-operate with the removal directions issued in respect of him'. Paragraph 7 is headed 'Fourth class of ineligible person: person unlawfully in UK' and provides that a person is within paragraph 1 if: (a) he is in the UK in breach of the immigration laws within the meaning of s 11, and (b) he is not an asylum-seeker. By s 11 of the same Act a person is in the UK in breach of the immigration laws if (and only if) he: (a) is in the UK, and (b) does not have the right of abode, (c) nor have leave to enter or remain, nor benefit from any of the specific listed exemptions.

Section 21 support

6.126 The best starting point is the case of *R (M) v Slough BC* [2008] UKHL 52 which related to a Zimbabwean national who was HIV positive. He had overstayed on his visa and alleged that in view of his medical condition, and the lack of treatment in Zimbabwe, to return him would infringe his rights under Article 3 of the ECHR. He also sought accommodation from the local authority and argued that there was no immediate risk to him provided that he complied with his healthcare regime and that his accommodation needed refrigeration for his medication. The House of Lords held that his needs did not bring him within the scope of s 21(1)(a) 'as a person who is in need of care and attention not otherwise available to him'. In doing so, the Court emphasised that a natural and ordinary meaning of 'care and attention' was required, which meant doing something which the person could not, or should not, be expected to do for himself. The need, therefore, for a refrigerator for the keeping of medication was not a need for 'care and attention' in that sense.

6.127 Baroness Hale stated[61] that:

'Although the respondent is HIV positive, his medical needs are being catered for by the National Health Service. So even if they did amount to a "need for care and attention" within the meaning of s 21(1)(a) he would not qualify. But for the reasons given above, I do not think that they do amount to such a need. There may of course come a time when they do, but people with the virus can now live normal lives for many years and we must hope that the respondent is able to do so. As he does not fall within s 21(1)(a) it is unnecessary to decide whether he would be excluded by s 21(1A). Unless and until one knows what care and attention a claimant needs, one cannot sensibly ask whether his need for it arises solely from destitution or its actual or anticipated effects.'

6.128 Post *M*, in *R (N) v Coventry City Council* [2008] EWHC 2786 (Admin)[62] the Court refused his application for judicial review and rejected the claimant's argument that the local authority should carry out an assessment under section 47 of the services which *would be* available in South Africa. The Court clearly held that the authority was only required to assess what services it might provide,[63] As such, the local authority's assessments were deemed to be lawful in the light of the approach in *M*. At paragraph 51 the Court emphasised that even if the assessments had been wrong, in the light of the failure of the asylum claim, and the possibility of a return to South Africa, support would not have been necessary to avoid a breach of Convention rights, in the light of the defendant's undertaking to assist him in obtaining a free flight there, and to accommodate him for 21 days while arrangements for his return were made.

---

[61] Para 36.
[62] The claimant was a South African who was HIV positive and suffered from cognitive disturbance. He claimed asylum and while waiting for his claim to be decided, he applied to a local authority for support under s 21 assistance. His medical condition was stable and had family help. The authority assessed his needs under s 47 of the NHSCA 1990, and decided that he was not in need of care and attention. His asylum claim was then refused. The authority then decided that, in accordance with para 3 of Sch 3 to the NIAA 2002 it was not necessary to provide him with assistance in order to avoid a breach of his Convention rights since he could return to South Africa.
[63] Para 39 of the judgment.

6.129 *R v Lewisham LBC, ex p Pajaziti* [2007] EWCA Civ 1351 involved an asylum seeker who was in receipt of support from the National Asylum Support Service ('NASS') (on the condition of dispersal). He requested that he remain in London on health grounds. NASS declined to support him. He then sought NAA 1948, s 21 support from the local authority and relied upon medical evidence stating that both he and his wife suffered major depressive episodes and that the most powerful intervention would be to accommodate them in London. The Court of Appeal provided that the essential question was whether need for care and attention by the provision of residential accommodation was made more acute by virtue of the psychiatric disorder. As the claimants were ill, the crucial question was whether their need for that separate head of care and attention was made more acute by the depressive disorder and the fact that, absent any NAA 1948, s 21 assistance, they would have had to cope with that disorder on the streets. The authority had not answered that question, and it followed that its decision was materially flawed.

6.130 In *R v Leeds CC, ex p Gnezele; R (Dayina) v Leeds CC* [2007] EWHC 3275 (Admin) both individuals who were refused asylum were pregnant and nursing mothers. They sought NAA 1948, s 21 support. The Court concluded that they were not entitled to such support and were only permitted to care and attention due to destitution, not due to being expectant or nursing mothers.

Unaccompanied asylum-seeking children

6.131 Unaccompanied asylum seeking children ('UASCs') present a real and practical problem to local authorities. Of paramount obvious importance is the age of a person who claims to be a UASC. If under the age of 18, the local authority will potentially owe him or her a range of obligations under the Children Act 1989 ('CA 1989'). Otherwise (if over the age of 18) the responsibility falls to the Home Office ('HO'). The United Kingdom Border Agency and the Association of Directors of Social Services have developed an 'Age Assessment Joint Protocol' in which it is explicit that local authorities (rather than the HO) will make age assessment decisions.

6.132 As one can imagine, age assessment decisions are extremely difficult. Relevant decisions include:

(i) *R (A) v Croydon London Borough Council* [2008] EWCA Civ 1445.

Claimants were young individuals who claimed to be children from abroad. The local authority rejected those claims. On an application for judicial review the Court upheld the local authorities' decisions. The Court of Appeal also upheld the decision.

The Court of Appeal concluded that the age of a young person is a question for the local authority within the parameters of review on *Wednesbury* unreasonable grounds, it is not for the Court to make a decision upon. The Court held that it was necessary to read the following words (in italics) into section 20, namely that '*Every local authority shall provide accommodation for any person whom the local authority have reasonable grounds for believing to be a* child in need'.[64] It was for the local authority to make that decision as stated above. Finally, the Court concluded that if section 20 of CA 1989 provided a right to accommodation, which was a civil right (for the purposes of Article 6 of the ECHR), supervision by the Court on judicial review grounds complied with Article 6.

---

[64] Para 30 of the judgment.

(ii) *R (A (by his litigation friend Valbona Mejzninin)) v Croydon London Borough Council* [2008] EWHC 2921 (Admin).

This case related to a dispute relating to the significance of a report by an expert consultant pediatrician. The local authority rejected the report for reasons, which the Court concluded, lacked cogency and were unsound. The local authority put forward the contention that such reports were not helpful as they *could only* indicate the general range of age. The Court emphasised the fact that the defendant was required to individual consideration to the report and clearly explain (based on its contents) the reasons for the rejection.

(iii) *R (Liverpool City Council) v Hillingdon London Borough Council* [2009] EWCA Civ 31.

This case surrounded a dispute between two local authorities as to which authority was responsible for a failed asylum seeker who claimed to be a child. The claimant was assessed as being an adult, however, in the course of an asylum appeal the AIT assessed his age as 15 years. He moved between two detention centres. There was an agreement that there would be a re-assessment of the failed asylum seeker's age, pursuant to the Joint Protocol, however, neither could agree who ought to be responsible for carrying it out. The claimant applied for judicial review, and at first instance, the Court held that the claimant was responsible for the individual. The claimant appealed. The Court outlined a number of issues pertaining to the character of such an assessment to be carried out by a local authority under section 20. Lord Justice Dyson, considered that in some situations (although not on this appeal) it is possible for two authorities to owe concurrent duties to a child.[65]

(iv) *R(A) v Croydon LBC & R(WK) v SSHD & Kent CC* [2009] EWHC 939 (Admin).

The conjoined applications sought to judicially review the decision of the local authority that they were over the age of 18. Both had been examined by medical experts who considered them to be under 18. Despite the same, the local authority did not change its initial decision. The key points in the judgment were:

- the decision on age is one for the local authority's age assessors;[66]
- paediatric reports are not trump cards and that Paediatricians are no better placed than social workers to assess age;[67]
- the decision of Stephen Morris QC to that effect in *R(A) v Croydon LBC* [2008] EWHC 2921 (Admin) last December was wrong;[68] and

---

[65] Paras 44 and 45 of the judgment.

[66] See para 21 'The evidence from Croydon and Kent and … Cambridgeshire show that … those responsible can be trusted to carry out their tasks properly so that the authorities and the Home Office can rely on their conclusions'.

[67] See para 47, 'No paediatrician other than the very few prepared to produce reports for claimants will agree to become involved and … a medical view is not likely to be any more reliable or helpful than that formed by a properly trained and experienced social worker. Nor is it the case that opinions obtained from Drs Michie and Birch can be regarded as reliable'; paras 34 and 35, 'It is for them [LAs & SSHD] to decide how much weight to attach to such a report and it is in a given case open to the decision maker to attach no weight. I would expect that only in rare cases would such a report persuade the decision maker to reach a different view'; para 75, 'Thus Kent and so the Secretary of State are entitled to attach little if any weight to reports which make assessments based to a significant degree on a contradictory [to their own] findings'; and para 25, 'It is Dr Stern's view that a paediatrician is unlikely to be able to reach a conclusion which is superior to that reached by an experienced social worker, provided, of course, that the social worker is properly trained and experienced and conducted the necessary interview in an appropriate fashion'.

[68] See para 47, 'I do not accept that the approach adopted by Mr Morris was correct (para 6). There is no obligation on the authority to obtain medical advice [in order to disagree with a medical report on age]'.

- all other cases should now proceed. Mr Justice Collins made an express order that all age dispute claims should progress on the law as it currently stands (ie applying his judgment and the Court of Appeal's judgment in *A v Croydon; M v Lambeth* [2008] EWCA Civ 1445). The Court also made an order that claimants in such cases should not be removed from the UK pending the outcome of the Supreme Court appeal in *A v Croydon; M v Lambeth* (considered below). He also observed that a similar order or undertaking should be made in relation to the age dispute cases which have been issued.

(v)   *R (A) v Croydon LBC & one other action; R(M) v Lambeth LBC & one other action* [2009] UKSC 8.

As above, A and M were both unaccompanied asylum seeking children who disputed their respective local authorities' decision that they were 18 or over. The claimants were unsuccessful at the Administrative Court and the Court of Appeal.

The Supreme Court held unanimously that where there is a dispute about a young person's age between a local social services authority and a young person seeking assistance under the Children Act 1989 (as is common with unaccompanied young asylum seekers) the Administrative Court should decide the case on the balance of probabilities. This means the Administrative Court will no longer ask 'was the local authority's decision reasonable?' but 'was the local authority's decision correct?'

The Court accepted the argument of M (in the case of *M v Lambeth*) that, as a matter of construction of s 20 of the Children Act 1989, whether a person is a child is a question which must be objectively decided. In addition, the Court found it unnecessary to decide, A's contention (in *A v Croydon*), that traditional judicial review was inadequate for the purposes of Article 6 of the ECHR on the grounds that accommodation under s 20 was a civil right and social workers were not independent and impartial.

In practice, the judgment means that age dispute cases will become trials of fact with witness examination. This is a distinct digression from the usual position that the Administrative Court is the not suitable arena to resolve factual disputes.[69] As stated by Lady Hale at paragraph 33:

> 'The final arguments raised against such a conclusion are of a practical kind. The only remedy available is judicial review and this is not well suited to the determination of disputed questions of fact. This is true but it can be so adapted if the needs arises: see *R (Wilkinson) v Broadmoor Special Hospital Authority* [2004] EWCA Civ 1545, [2002] 1 WLR 419. That the remedy is judicial review does not dictate the issue for the court to decide or the way in which it should do so, as the cases on jurisdictional fact illustrate. Clearly, as those cases also illustrate, the public authority, whether the children's services authority or the UK Border Agency, has to make its own determination in the first instance and it is only if this remains disputed that the court may have to intervene. But the better the quality of the initial decision-making, the less likely it is that the court will come to any different decision upon the evidence.'

---

[69]   This proposition has been made plain in case-law, namely in *R v Horsham DC, ex p Wenman* [1995] 1 WLR 680 at 709G, '... judicial review proceedings are wholly inappropriate as the forum for the resolution of issues of disputed facts ...' and *R v West Sussex County Council, ex p Wenman* (1993) 5 Admin LR 145 at 154BA–B, '... [judicial review] is not appropriate for he kind of fact finding exercise on disputed facts that a court at first instance, or a statutory body with statutory responsibilities to investigate facts, is equipped to perform ...' It is equally trite that the Court has (on some occasions) acceded to resolve factual disputes when it inhibits a correct legal conclusion, *R (Corner House Research) v Director of Serious Fraud* [2008] EWHC 714 (Admin) at [8] or when the resolution is crucial to the case, *R v SOSDE, ex p LBI* [1997] JR 21 at 127.

(vi) Post *Croydon*, in *R (PM) v Hertfordshire CC* [2010] EWHC 2056 (Admin), the claimant who was a asylum seeker applied for judicial review of a decision of the defendant local authority to withdraw accommodation and support that it had provided under s 20 of the Children Act 1989. The claimant asserted that he was 14 years of age and the local authority had initially considered that it was more likely than not that PM was a child, and accordingly provided him with accommodation and support. The Secretary of State refused PM's asylum claim, finding that he had fabricated his age to strengthen his claim. PM appealed to the First-tier Tribunal Immigration and Asylum Chamber, which rejected his appeal, holding that he was over 18. The local authority considered that it had to respect the tribunal's decision and so withdrew its support for M on the basis that he was over 18.

Higginbottom J concluded that:

(1)   The tribunal's conclusion that PM was an adult was not binding on all, and that under Part 5 of the Nationality, Immigration and Asylum Act 2002, the tribunal had no primary jurisdiction to determine age;

(2)   The local authority could not simply adopt the tribunal's finding as to age. The 1989 Act places a burden upon local authorities to assess the age of young people who may be under 18 years old, and who may therefore be entitled to s 20 support. The local authority was not bound by the tribunal's finding. Before ceasing support under the 1989 Act, they were obliged to review their earlier age assessment, taking account of:

(a)   Any evidence as to age that may have been put before the tribunal that was not previously put before the local authority; and

(b)   The tribunal judge's reasoning and process by which he came to the conclusion that the claimant was an adult.

(3)   Under the 1989 Act, the local authority had been bound substantively to review its earlier age assessment, taking account of the tribunal's determination in a limited manner, before ceasing support.

This case is interesting. Whilst the Secretary of State treated the claimant as an adult, the tribunal agreed with that conclusion, he was appeal rights exhausted and his removal was imminent, the local authority still had to conduct an age assessment to determine whether he is a child. It is believed that the local authority is seeking permission to appeal!

(vii) *FZ v London Borough of Croydon* [2011] EWCA Civ 59 where Sir Anthony May, President of the Queen's Bench Division, said that at the permission stage in an age assessment the court should ask whether the material before the court raises a factual case which, taken at its highest, could not properly succeed in a contested factual hearing. If so, permission should be refused. The Court stated if the decision-maker formed the provisional view that the applicant was lying as to his age, the applicant must be given the opportunity to address matters that led to that view. In the absence of formal central government guidance, the court should not be prescriptive of the way in which that might be done.

Further representations by failed asylum seekers

6.133 This situation arises when a failed asylum seeker submits further representations under Immigration Rule 353.[70] If the SSHD decides to treat those further representations as a fresh claim, the person becomes an asylum seeker (again) and, therefore, entitled to the provision of support and to a right of appeal against a refusal of the fresh claim for asylum. Naturally, if the SSHD refuses to accept the further representations as constituting a fresh claim, then no right of support or appeal arises.

6.134 In *R v Croydon, ex p AW* [2005] EWHC 2950 (Admin) a failed asylum seeker attempted to argue that it should not have been open to a local authority to decline to provide support on the basis of any inadequacy in a purported fresh claim. The local authority argued that they were entitled to consider the adequacy of the contents of the further submissions alleging amounting to a fresh claim. In such circumstances, the local authority could legitimately withhold support if the representations were not adequate. The Court agreed and reinforced this approach. Mr Justice Lloyd Jones concluded at paragraphs 73 and 74 that:

> '... local authorities now are required to take decisions relating to the immigration status of individuals as a matter of course. ... in considering whether the provision of support to failed asylum-seekers is necessary in order to prevent a breach of Convention rights it will be necessary for the public body concerned to have regard to all relevant circumstances including, where appropriate, the matters which are alleged to constitute a fresh claim for asylum. In many cases – possibly the great majority – it may well be inappropriate for a public body to embark on any consideration of the purported fresh grounds. However, there may well be cases in which the purported fresh grounds are manifestly nothing of the sort and where it would be appropriate for the public body to take account of that fact in arriving at its decision in relation to asylum support ....'

6.135 Subsequent cases have largely followed this approach. In *R (B) v Southwark LBC* [2006] EWHC 2254 (Admin) the Court reinforced *AW* and concluded that the issue for a local authority was whether the outstanding human rights application pending was 'manifestly unfounded', however, it was not to assess the general merits of the application, which was a matter for immigration authorities. On a similar vein, but in a more narrow approach, in *R (N) v Lambeth LBC* [2006] EWHC 3427 (Admin) the Court reaffirmed *AW* and clarified that 'only in the clearest cases

---

[70]   Please see the Immigration Chapter for further details of this provision. In short, Immigration Rule 353 provides, 'When a human rights or asylum claim has been refused or withdrawn or treated as withdrawn under paragraph 333C of these Rules and any appeal relating to that claim is no longer pending, the decision maker will consider any further submissions and, if rejected, will then determine whether they amount to a fresh claim. The submissions will amount to a fresh claim if they are significantly different from the material that has previously been considered. The submissions will only be significantly different if the content: (i) had not already been considered; and (ii) taken together with the previously considered material, creates a realistic prospect of success, notwithstanding its rejection. This paragraph does not apply to claims made overseas.' Rule 353A should be read alongside rule 353, 'Consideration of further submissions shall be subject to the procedures set out in these Rules. An applicant who has made further submissions shall not be removed before the Secretary of State has considered the submissions under paragraph 353 or otherwise. This paragraph does not apply to submissions made overseas.' Further submissions by a person seeking asylum can be met by the Secretary of State in one of three ways: (i) they are accepted: the person is granted leave to enter or remain; (ii) they are rejected, but they are recognised as constituting a fresh claim for asylum. As a result the person has a right of appeal from the refusal under s 83 of the Nationality, Immigration and Asylum Act 2002 ('the 2002 Act') in the ordinary way; or (iii) they are rejected, and the SoS refuses to recognise them as a fresh claim. There is no appeal from the Secretary of State's decision that they do not amount to a fresh claim – but that decision is subject to judicial review in the Administrative Court.

would it be appropriate for the public body concerned to refuse relief on the basis of the manifest inadequacy of the purported fresh grounds'.

6.136 An amendment to the Immigration Rule 353 now means that an individual who makes further submissions shall not be removed from the country. In *Gnezele*, Mr Justice Mitting made the following obiter observations:[71]

> 'To the extent that that falls on local authorities it may be that the effect of r 353A will be to impose upon them the burden of providing accommodation to those who have made representations, until they have been determined by the Secretary of State, whether or not the representations are well founded or even abusive. Those are matters for another day. They do not arise for decision directly in this case in the light of my finding that it is upon the Secretary of State that the power and, in so far as it exists, the duty to provide accommodation for these claimants existed or continues to exist.'

6.137 Outside the ambit of 'further submissions' in *Birmingham CC v (1) Clue; (2) SSHD; & (3) Shelter* [2010] EWCA Civ 460 the Jamaican national claimant entered the UK with her daughter with a visitor visa. The claimants applied for further leave (before the expiry the visitor visa) to remain as a student. This was dismissed, however, the claimant remained in the UK for some time and subsequently applied to remain on the basis that her eldest daughter had been in the UK for more than seven years pursuant to the Secretary of State's policy DP 5/06. She applied for assistance but was refused under Schedule 3 of the 2002 Act, save to enable the family to return to Jamaica. The Court granted the application on the basis that the local authority did not have regard to the underlying reasons of policy DP 5/96, namely that when applying Schedule 3, the local authority should not consider the merits of an outstanding application for leave to remain. It is required to be satisfied that the application is not 'obviously hopeless or abusive'.

PART 3 – COMMON EXAMPLES OF JUDICIAL REVIEW CHALLENGES OF COMMUNITY CARE DECISIONS

6.138 Having undertaken a broad overview of community care law and considered some specific significant areas, it is now imperative to gauge how judicial review, as a remedy, has been utilised as a means of challenging decisions. The below, therefore, seeks to exemplify how community care decisions are challenged by specific grounds of judicial review.

6.139 A major percentage of community care decisions, which are subject to judicial review proceedings have one common feature, namely that during the lifetime of judicial review proceedings, the care plan or pathway plan will be substantially modified and possibly improved. In some cases the improvements are insufficient to persuade the claimant to dispose of their legal challenge, and as such, the hearing proceeds as a challenge to the latest plan, and not to the plan, which originally was the subject of judicial review proceedings.

6.140 In many cases, however, proceedings bring about a satisfactory level of improvement, which then leads to settlement, and in that way they can serve a useful

---

[71]   Para 31.

purpose to both sides. This process of negotiation and evolution is a reminder of the very purpose of community care provisions, ie to assist and facilitate help to disabled individuals.

6.141 It is important to bear in mind that judicial review must be used as a remedy of last resort after local resolution procedures have been exhausted, or alternatively when a substitute remedy is not available. Common examples include the local authority complaints process and the LGO. Note the existence of the new Social Services and NHS Complaints Procedure Regulations 2009, which applies to complaints against either the NHS or local authority. The aim is to provide a simpler, quicker and more efficient complaint handling and resolution, with proper investigation and timely response and action. Consider the recent case of *R v Wirral BC, ex p F & Others* [2009] EWHC 1626 stated above.

6.142 In usual circumstances, judicial review (within the context of social welfare law) ought to be confined to cases of: (i) genuine urgency, for example when interim relief is sought; (ii) involving human rights arguments; (iii) when alternative remedy is not equally convenient, expeditious or effect, see *R v Devon County Council, ex p Baker* [1995] and *R(JL)* [2009]; and/or cases (iv) that require clarification of statutory instruments or provisions.

Grounds of Judicial Review	Case Name	Details
Illegality Assessing need – general principles	*R v Berkshire CC, Ex p P* Judges Laws, J. (1997–98) 1 CCL Rep 141	The local authority ('LA') refused to undertake s 47 assessment because he was in a care home funded by the PCT. LA said that s 47(1) presupposed the physical availability of services to the applicant for the duty to assess to be invoked. Held, allowing the application and declaring that LA should make the appropriate assessment, that on a proper construction of s 47(1) of the 1990 Act there is no condition that the duty to assessment is dependent upon the physical availability of services. The duty to assess arises where the local authority has the legal power to make provision or provide community care to an individual.
	R v Islington LBC, Ex p Rixon Judge Sedley, J. (1997–98) 1 CCL Rep 119	R contended that LA had failed to comply with guidance by DOH under CSDA 1970 and acted unlawfully by deviating. Held, allowing the application, that under the NHSCCA 1990, s 47 a local authority was subject to a duty to assess based on need. The LA was required to follow DOH guidance. If LA wishes to depart clear reasons must be given.

Grounds of Judicial Review	Case Name	Details
	R v Sefton MBC, Ex p Help the Aged Jowitt, J. (1997) 36 BMLR 110	LA argued that entitled to have regard to its resources when assessing a person's need for accommodation under the NAA 1948. Held, dismissing the applications, that S was entitled to have regard to its resources when deciding whether a person was in need under s 21(1)(a) following the House of Lords ruling in *R v Gloucestershire CC Ex p Barry* [1997] AC 584. Any policy framework for prioritising need cannot fetter the discretion of the authority.
	R v North Yorkshire CC, Ex p William Hargreaves Judge Dyson, J. (1997–98) 1 CCL Rep 104	H applied for judicial review of the decision to offer his sister a place for respite care, as part of the council's community care service, which was not the placement of her choice. Held: Application allowed. Provided that a care user was capable of making her preference known as regards respite care, a council was under an obligation to take account of that preference.
Procedural Impropriety	*R (on the application of Ireneschild) v Lambeth LBC* [2007] EWCA Civ 234	The LA appealed against the decision assessment of X was unlawful. X was severely disabled and required ground floor access. LA disagreed because this did not comply with the housing allocation policy. The Court quashed the decision and ordered to carry out the assessment again. The local authority submitted that the judge had erred on various findings. Appeal allowed as had not shown that there was a failure to take into account relevant consideration or guidance.
	R (on the application of Goldsmith) v Wandsworth LBC Judges Brooke, LJ.; Chadwick, LJ.; Wall, LJ. [2004] EWCA Civ 1170	G was an elderly woman in residential care accommodation who the local authority decided should be moved to a nursing home. Decision made after a fall at the care home. Panel recommended move. An assessment was undertaken which conversely concluded that she was safe at home. LA instructed doctor who confirmed, without seeing her, that she needed nursing care. G contended that LA's decision-making process was defective and they had failed to apply their own policy. Appealed allowed. LA was under a duty to take a rounded decision, which took into account all relevant factors, rather than treat a doctor's views on the resident's nursing needs as determinative. In the instant case, the local authority's decision-making process was sufficiently defective to vitiate its decision. It had based its decision that G should be put in a nursing home on the assessment of a panel to which it had referred the case and the apparent confirmation of that assessment by a doctor which it had later instructed. It made its decision without having before it the community care assessment, which was carried out afterwards and contradicted its view.

Grounds of Judicial Review	Case Name	Details
Irrationality	*R v Staffordshire CC Ex p Farley*, April 8, 1997 Judge Forbes, J.	F, aged 86, applied for an interim injunction, pending the full hearing of her application for judicial review, to reinstate a community care package that had been provided by LA in accordance with its duties under the NHSCCA 1990 and the CSDPA 1970. She was assessed in S's original care plan as requiring a night sitter as she needed regular toileting throughout the night. In November 1996, however, that care plan was changed and the night sitting provision was withdrawn. Instead F was supplied with an attendant between 10pm and 10.30pm to help prepare for bed and ensure she was comfortable for the night. Held, granting the application, that it was appropriate in judicial review proceedings to grant an interim injunction. There was no evidence that F's circumstances or needs had changed and the decision to withdraw the night care services was *Wednesbury* unreasonable.
	R v Sutton LBC, ex p Tucker (1998) 1 CCLR 251	The care plan was held to be woefully inadequate. There was a failure to arrange supported accommodation to allow discharge from hospital to take place. There was no statement of the overall objectives in the care plan or the obligations of the service providers or carers and the lack of objectives meant there was a lack of criteria to assess if they objectives had been met. Key matters such as costing or possible alternative provision had not been recorded. The procuring of short term and interim outcomes instead of long-term objectives meant that there had been such a departure from the guidance of the Secretary of State that the actions of the authority had been *Wednesbury* unreasonable or irrational.
	R v Secretary of State for the Home Department Ex p Zakrocki Judge Carnwath, J. (1997–98) 1 CCL Rep 374	H applied for judicial review of the Secretary of State's refusal to extend their leave to remain in the UK to enable them to care for an elderly relative, a British citizen, who was entitled to care under the care in the community policy and for whom social services could make no suitable alternative arrangements. Held, allowing the application, that the objective of the care in the community policy was to promote domiciliary care, and that in the absence of suitable alternative arrangements it was unreasonable, in the *Wednesbury* sense, for the Secretary of State to refuse Z leave to remain in the UK to care for their relative.

Grounds of Judicial Review	Case Name	Details
	R (on the application of Khana) v Southwark LBC Judges Henry, LJ.; Mance, LJ.; McKinnon, J. [2001] EWCA Civ 999	J, a 91 year old Iraqi Kurd suffering from paranoid schizophrenia and severely impaired mobility, appealed against the refusal of her application for judicial review of LA's decision to make her an offer of full time residential care. J and her husband had been granted permission to enter the United Kingdom on condition that they did not have recourse to public funds; hence they were entitled to community care services pursuant to the NAA 1948 and the NHSCCA 1990. J, her husband and daughter lived in a one bedroom second floor flat. Following an assessment of J's needs, S offered a joint placement in a residential home for J and her husband, the primary carer. It was J's contention that her needs would be best met by the provision of a two bedroom ground floor flat so that her daughter could continue to live with them. First instance the application was refused. J appealed alleging that LA had acted in a way that no reasonable local authority could and had behaved unlawfully in failing to take her wishes into account. Held, dismissing the appeal, that whilst LA was under a duty to consider J's preferences and beliefs, the assessment of J's accommodation needs and how those needs were best met were ultimately matters for LA who had made an offer of accommodation of the only type which it considered would meet J's assessed needs. LA was required to take J's wishes into account but was under no obligation pursuant to s 21 of the 1948 Act to provide an alternative that would satisfy J's preference if that alternative would not meet all of the assessed needs, *R v Kensington and Chelsea RLBC Ex p Kujtim* [1999] 4 All ER 161.

Grounds of Judicial Review	Case Name	Details
	R (On the application Collins) v Lincolnshire HA Judge David Pannick Q.C. [2001] EWHC Admin 685	H suffered from a severe learning disability caused by cerebral palsy. She sought judicial review of a decision of the health authority to cease providing long-term care for her. The health authority planned to transfer H and other long-term residents from NHS care into the community. H maintained that: (a) the health authority had misunderstood and misapplied government policy, and (b) by reneging on a promise that H's present home was for life the authority had abused its power and had breached C's human rights. Held, dismissing the application, that: (1) the general aim of government policy was to remove people with learning disabilities from long term institutional care in order to promote their independence. In applying this policy all cases had to be individually assessed. The authority's policy documents and reports demonstrated that it had not simply proposed that all persons with learning disabilities should be discharged into the community from NHS care but that such a move should be made where there were no individual health reasons for keeping a person in NHS care. In H's case there were no such reasons and it could not be said that the health authority had misunderstood and misapplied government policy, and (2) the authority was acting in what it regarded to be H's best interests and upon its belief that C would benefit substantially from the move rather than from any financial motive Furthermore, the promise made to H in the present case was to a degree uncertain and lacking in clarity. Accordingly, there had been no abuse of the authority's power and no breach of H's human rights.
	R (On the application of Tucker) v Sutton LBC Hidden J (1998) 1 CCLR 251.	The Court granted JR where the Defendant had unlawfully and/or irrationally failed: (i) to provide a Care Plan (contrary to statutory policy guidance issued by the Secretary of State, which was binding on it), and (ii) to make a service provision decision (pursuant to its statutory duty).

Chapter 7

HOUSING

INTRODUCTION

7.1   This Chapter on housing focuses necessarily on those circumstances in which the Administrative Court is called upon to adjudicate on public law matters in this frequently changing area of law.

7.2   Preference will be given to practical and procedural questions rather than to a detailed exposition of the substantive legislative codes which underpin all aspects of the provision, management and condition of social housing.

7.3   This chapter adopts the meaning of 'social housing' provided by the Housing and Regeneration Act 2008, s 68: namely, low cost rental or low cost ownership accommodation. 'Low cost', for the purposes of the Housing and Regeneration Act 2008 means accommodation available at below market rates for those people whose needs are not met adequately by the commercial housing market.[1]

7.4   By concentrating on the work of the Administrative Court, it is not to be forgotten that a substantial body of public law has developed since the transfer to the County Court of the lion's share of homelessness cases as a consequence of the Housing Act 1996, Part VII. Indeed, by the mid-1990s one third of all judicial review applications to the High Court concerned homelessness decisions.[2] Whilst many of the seminal homelessness cases were decided before this transfer of jurisdiction took place, their full import is outside the terms of reference of this work.

7.5   Similarly, save to acknowledge its impact on the judicial review of social housing decisions, this Chapter does not address in separate detail the Human Rights Act 1998.

THE ROLE OF PUBLIC LAW IN SOCIAL HOUSING

7.6   Public law is at the heart of and permeates nearly every aspect of the provision and management of social housing. Historically, social housing has been provided by local housing authorities, who are creatures of statute. However, the increasing decentralisation of the provision and management of social housing has led to a wider range of social housing providers exercising public functions and accordingly susceptible potentially to judicial review.

---

[1]   Housing and Regeneration Act 2008, ss 69 and 70.
[2]   De Smith's *Judicial Review* (6th edn), 17-045.

7.7   Presently, local housing authorities,[3] Registered Social Landlords ('RSLs'),[4] charities and private commercial organisations all play a role in the provision and management of social housing (although please note the Housing and Regeneration Act 2008, which brings all social housing providers under a unified regulatory scheme).

7.8   Despite operating within a legislative framework, the relationship between social housing providers and occupiers (both current and prospective) is underpinned by conventional public law principles. Although there are various ways of classifying the grounds on which administrative decisions can be challenged before the Administrative Court, it is convenient to adopt the 'triumvirate' set out by Lord Diplock in the *Council of Civil Service Unions v Minister for the Civil Service*:[5]

(1)   illegality;

(2)   irrationality;

(3)   procedural impropriety.

7.9   Indeed, some of the statutory provisions represent an attempt to codify these principles. For example, the Allocation of Housing and Homelessness (Review Procedures) Regulations 1999, Reg 8[6] provides for a right to make oral or written representations where a reviewing officer considers that there is a deficiency or irregularity in the original decision,[7] but he is minded nonetheless to reach a decision contrary to the interests of the applicant. A small but important body of jurisprudence has built up around the proper ambit of this right to be heard,[8] with each case emphasising that procedural fairness lies at the heart of the 1999 Regulations.[9]

7.10   Various complex and evolving statutory codes regulate social housing, but whilst public law principles underpin the rights and duties of providers and users alike, the use of judicial review as a means of challenging decisions about social housing has become increasingly curtailed. The legislative tendency is now to draft self-contained statutory codes which have their own internal review and appeal mechanisms, the most obvious example of which is the transfer of the vast majority of homelessness cases from the Administrative Court to the County Court by virtue of Part VII of the Housing Act 1996. Similarly, the Housing Act 2004 was enacted in order to improve housing standards and to assist urban renewal. Whilst the powers and duties exercised by local authorities under the Housing Act 2004 involve issues of public law, there is a comprehensive statutory code that provides for the consideration of representations and the right of appeal to the Residential Property Tribunal.

---

3   Within the meaning of the Housing Act 1985, s 1.
4   Within the meaning of the Housing Act 1996, ss 1 and 2.
5   [1985] AC 374, 410.
6   SI 1999/71.
7   Made under the Housing Act 1996, s 184.
8   *Hall v Wandsworth LBC* [2004] EWCA Civ 1740; [2005] 2 All ER 192; *Lambeth LBC v Johnston* [2008] EWCA Civ 690; *Banks v Kingston-Upon-Thames RLBC* [2008] EWCA Civ 1443.
9   eg *Banks v Kingston-Upon-Thames RLBC* [2008] EWCA Civ 1443 at [65].

7.11 Similarly, the failure to request a review[10] of a decision to seek possession of premises held under an Introductory Tenancy[11] is likely to preclude a judicial review of the decision by the local housing authority to commence possession proceedings.[12]

7.12 In each of these circumstances, the Administrative Court is highly unlikely to entertain judicial review proceedings given the existence of an alternative remedy in the form of the schemes established by statute. Judicial review is, after all, the remedy of last resort.[13]

7.13 Nevertheless, judicial review continues to play an important role in the supervision of social housing providers and the enforcement of rights of both actual and prospective occupiers of social housing.

7.14 The specific areas most frequently encountered are homelessness, the allocation of social housing and challenges to decisions in relation to introductory tenancies under the Housing Act 1996. It is on these three substantive areas that this Chapter focuses.

7.15 The judicial review of social housing decisions also raises its own peculiar procedural and costs issues, which will also be examined.

JURISDICTION

7.16 It is always necessary as a first step to determine whether the decision is one that is amenable to judicial review. It is not the status of the body in question, but the function being exercised which is crucial.

7.17 In the vast majority of housing cases, it should be apparent whether the decision-maker is a body who carries out public functions. For example, a local housing authority (for the purposes of the Housing Act 1996) which make decisions as to the allocation of social housing or the duties owed to persons claiming under the Housing Act 1996, Part VII (homelessness) are, quite obviously, susceptible to judicial review of acts or omissions taken within the context of that legislation.[14]

7.18 However, the advent of the Human Rights Act 1998 and the decentralisation of social housing provision (less than half of all social housing is now managed by local authorities) have led to some 'blurring at the edges'.

7.19 Until recently, there has been a conflicting and confusing line of authority on the test of a public authority within the meaning of the Human Rights Act 1998, and also which bodies fall within the jurisdiction of the Administrative Court.

---

10 Under the Housing Act 1996, s 129.
11 A probationary tenancy governed by Chapter 1 of Part V of the Housing Act 1996.
12 *R (on the application of Chelfat) v Tower Hamlets LBC* [2006] EWHC 313 (Admin); [2006] ACD 61.
13 See for example *R v Hammersmith and Fulham LBC, ex p Burkett* [2002] UKHL 23; [2002] 1 WLR 1593.
14 Although note the availability of alternative remedies.

7.20   However, the question of the extent to which public law and the provisions of the Human Rights Act 1998 govern the actions of social housing providers has been considered comprehensively in *R (Weaver) v London and Quadrant Housing Trust*.[15]

7.21   Mrs. Weaver was an assured tenant of the Trust[16] and alleged that its decision to terminate her tenancy was amenable to judicial review and that it engaged her right to a home under Article 8 of the European Convention on Human Rights. The success of these arguments depended upon Mrs Weaver establishing that the Trust was a public body attracting the operation of public law principles and that it was a public authority for the purposes of the Human Rights Act 1998, s 6(3)(b). Equally importantly, the Court had to determine whether the termination of the tenancy was a private act within the meaning of the Human Rights Act 1998, s 6(5), even if the Trust was a public authority.

7.22   The Court of Appeal considered that the starting point was to analyse the housing association's function of allocating and managing housing. Particular regard was to be had to the extent to which in carrying out the relevant function the body was publicly funded, or was exercising statutory powers, or was taking the place of central government or local authorities or was providing a public service.[17]

7.23   The Court appeared to be particularly persuaded by the following factors:

(a)   It was Government policy to provide affordable housing to those who cannot secure their housing needs in the market.

(b)   Registered Social Landlords were subject to regulation by the Housing Corporation, an executive non-departmental public body responsible to the Secretary of State.[18]

(c)   Housing management guidance was subject to consultation with and approval by the Secretary of State.

(d)   There was statutory regulation of Registered Social Landlords, particularly as to the disposal of land or housing.[19]

(e)   Registered Social Landlords received grants from the Housing Corporation, the source of which were public funds.

(f)   There was a statutory obligation for Registered Social Landlords to cooperate with housing authorities. For example under the Housing Act 1996, s 170, a Registered Social Landlord is required to cooperate 'to such extent as is reasonable in the circumstances' with a local housing authority where the latter seeks to allocate housing under Part VI of that Act.

---

[15]   [2010] 1 WLR 363; [2009] EWCA Civ 587, CA. Note that permission to appeal to the Supreme Court was refused. Whilst the Supreme Court considered that the point was appropriate for it to consider, it was not a 'suitable case on its facts'.

[16]   Which was a Registered Social Landlord under the Housing Act 1996.

[17]   *Aston Cantlow and Wilmcote with Billesley Parochial Church Council v Wallbank* [2003] UKHL 37, [2004] 1 AC 546.

[18]   Although note that the mere fact of regulation tells us nothing about whether the body is a public one. *YL v Birmingham City Council* [2007] UKHL 27; [2008] 1 AC 95 per Lord Neuberger [135].

[19]   See the Housing Act 1996, ss 8–10.

(g) Virtually all provision of new social housing is delivered by Registered Social Landlords, and increasingly they are becoming responsible for the management of former housing authority stock by voluntary transfer.

7.24 It was further concluded that:

(a) the provision of subsidised housing was a governmental function;

(b) the housing association was acting in the public interest; and

(c) it had charitable objectives which placed it outside the traditional area of private commercial activity.

7.25 Ultimately, it would appear that the question of reviewability of decision-making in the sphere of social housing depends upon an overall assessment of the functions of the body in question, and the legislative framework within which it operates.[20] Nevertheless, it is suggested that the factors which are set out in the preceding paragraphs provide a good general guide to follow in the event that there is any dispute as to whether the acts or omissions of social housing providers are amenable to judicial review.

7.26 The Weaver case was decided on a set of facts prior to the enactment of the Housing and Regeneration Act 2008. Since then, the question of whether social housing providers are amenable to judicial review should be easier to resolve. The 2008 Act creates the Tenants Services Authority ('TSA'), which is the operating name for the Office for Tenants and Social Landlords. The TSA has taken over the regulatory powers of the Housing Corporation and will be responsible for the regulation of all affordable housing providers including local authorities and Registered Social Landlords.[21] However, following a review of social housing regulation,[22] it is likely that the regulatory functions of the TSA will be transferred to the Homes and Communities Agency ('HCA') under the provisions of the Localism Bill.

7.27 Given that all social housing providers are currently required to be registered with the TSA, and may be subject to enforcement action in the event that standards are not met, it is difficult to envisage circumstances in which social housing providers registered with the TSA will not be amenable to judicial review. Whilst the Government's review[23] envisaged less regulatory intervention, it is unlikely that this will affect fundamentally their susceptibility to judicial review.

7.28 It should be noted, however, that the immediate practical effect of Weaver is likely to be limited in scope. Whilst it establishes that the decisions of Registered Social Landlords to seek possession orders against assured tenants are likely to be amenable to judicial review, the number of people affected by this apparent broadening of the ambit of judicial review, is likely to be small. Indeed, even if a Registered Social Landlord is

---

[20] Although note that in refusing permission to appeal the Supreme Court considered that the point of law was suitable for the Supreme Court, it was not suitable for determination on the facts of the case: [2009] 5 November, UKSC.

[21] See generally Part 2 of the Housing and Regeneration Act 2008.

[22] http://www.communities.gov.uk/documents/housing/pdf/1742903.pdf.

[23] Ibid.

seen acting in a public law sphere, the Administrative Court will not ordinarily be the forum in which arguments about the legality of possession proceedings will be fought out; it will be the County Court.[24]

JUDICIAL ATTITUDE

7.29   In order properly to set the context for the remainder of this Chapter, it is worth considering whether there is a prevailing attitude amongst the judiciary towards cases which involve issues of social housing. In so far as it is possible to identify any general trend in relation to social housing, the courts have inclined towards an attitude of judicial deference to the decision-maker, recognising that Parliament has entrusted the distribution of limited social resources to local authorities and central government.[25]

7.30   Whilst the jurisprudence abounds with examples of judges expressing a desire not to interfere with the exercise of powers by local housing authorities to manage or allocate social housing save in the most obvious cases, this judicial deference is perhaps best illustrated by the oft-quoted speech of Lord Brightman in the homelessness case of *R v LB Hillingdon, ex p Puhlhofer*:[26]

> 'My Lords, I am troubled at the prolific use of judicial review for the purpose of challenging the performance by local authorities of their functions under the Act of 1977. Parliament intended the local authority to be the judge of fact. The Act abounds with the formula when, or if the housing authority is satisfied as to this, or that, or has reason to believe this, or that. Although the action or inaction of a local authority is clearly susceptible to judicial review where they have misconstrued the Act, or abused their powers or otherwise acted perversely, I think that great restraint should be exercised in giving leave to proceed by judicial review. The plight of the homeless is a desperate one, and the plight of the applicants in the present case commands the deepest sympathy. But it is not, in my opinion, appropriate that the remedy of judicial review, which is a discretionary remedy, should be made use of to monitor the actions of local authorities under the Act save in the exceptional case.'

7.31   More recently, in *R (Ahmad) v Newham LBC*,[27] a case concerning the legality of an allocation scheme under the Housing Act 1996, Part VI, the House of Lords reinforced this mind-set through Lord Neuberger:

> 'However, it seems unlikely that the legislature can have intended that Judges should embark on the exercise of telling authorities how to decide on priorities as between applicants in need of rehousing, save in relatively rare and extreme circumstances. Housing allocation policy is a difficult exercise which requires not only social and political sensitivity and judgment, but also local expertise and knowledge.'

7.32   Judicial deference is not necessarily an entirely negative concept. It occurs when judges assign varying degrees of weight to the judgment of the elected branches of

---

[24]   *Kay v Lambeth LBC* [2006] UKHL 10, [2006] 2 AC 465; and *Doherty v Birmingham City Council* [2008] UKHL 57, [2009] 1 AC 367.See also *R (McIntyre) v Gentoo Group Ltd* [2010] EWHC 5 (Admin); (2010) 154(2) SJLB 29; [2010] 2 P & CR DG6, a post Weaver decision in which the claimant sought to challenge a RSL's decision to impose conditions on an exchange of tenancy. Whilst judicial review was not ruled out entirely as a means of challenging such a decision, it should normally be brought by private action.

[25]   Although note that the use of the expression 'judicial deference' has recently been deprecated by the House of Lords: *Huang v Secretary of State for the Home Department* [2007] UKHL 11, [2007] 2 AC 167, per Lord Bingham at [16].

[26]   [1986] 1 AC 484 HL per Lord Brightman at p 518.

[27]   [2009] UKHL 14.

central and local government, out of respect for their superior expertise, competence or democratic legitimacy. Nevertheless, it is relevant for the practitioner to note that whilst the Court will not hesitate to intervene in the appropriate case, it can often appear that the claimant has a particularly high hurdle to overcome before obtaining the relief he seeks.[28]

HOMELESSNESS

7.33   Following the enactment of the Housing Act 1996, homeless applicants were given a right of appeal on a point of law to the County Court where an applicant has requested a review under the Housing Act 1996, s 202, of a homelessness decision. This is an essential pre-requisite of an appeal to the County Court. The right to appeal arises in two circumstances: (i) where the applicant is dissatisfied with the decision on review; or (ii) where the review decision itself is not communicated to the applicant within any time prescribed by the Secretary of State.[29]

7.34   An applicant has the right to request a review of the following decisions:

(a)   a decision by the local housing authority under the Housing Act 1996, s 184 following enquiries into whether the applicant is eligible for assistance under the Housing Act 1996, Part VII;

(b)   any decision as to what duty (if any) is owed to the applicant under the Housing Act 1996, ss 190 to 193;

(c)   any decision relating to or arising out of the referral of the application to another authority;[30]

(d)   any decision as to the suitability of accommodation offered to the applicant in the discharge of its duties under any of the aforementioned provisions or under the Housing Act 1996, s 193(7).

7.35   The reason for setting out these classes of decision is as follows: for the applicant who is dissatisfied or who has not been notified of a relevant decision, the first – and usually the only – port of call will be the County Court.

7.36   Nevertheless, there are two circumstances in which the Administrative Court is likely to become involved in homelessness cases: (i) where exceptional circumstances pertain such that the Court is prepared to exercise its residual discretion; and (ii) where the Housing Act 1996 does not provide a right of review and subsequent appeal to the County Court.

---

[28]   For a more detailed examination of judicial attitudes, see Jeff A King *Institutional approaches to judicial restraint*, (2009) Oxford Journal of Legal Studies, p 409. See also *R (Adow) v LB Newham* [2010] EWHC 951 (Admin): the Court held that the practical difficulties of public authorities had to be recognised, particularly in the area of housing where, with limited resources and high demands, they had to make decisions quickly, humanely and in accordance with the law that was not always clear. However, where the law was clear and the authority realised that its procedures required amendment, the Court was prepared to express its displeasure and would have been prepared to award costs on an indemnity basis.

[29]   Housing Act 1996, s 204(1).

[30]   See Housing Act 1996, ss 198 and 200.

Exceptional circumstances

7.37   The exercise of the Administrative Court's jurisdiction to intervene in the context of homelessness decisions has not been taken away by the Housing Act 1996, but will only be exercised in exceptional circumstances.[31] For example: in *R (Lynch) v Lambeth LBC*,[32] Ms Lynch sought to challenge a decision under the Housing Act 1996, s 184 by the housing authority that she and her family were not homeless. Whilst she requested a review of the decision and sought to appeal to the County Court, she launched judicial review proceedings in the Administrative Court principally on the basis that the original decision was so defective (particularly in its lack of reasoning) that it was incapable of being reviewed.[33] The statutory review process, Ms Lynch reasoned, was therefore ineffective.

7.38   The Court held that whilst the original decision under s 184 of the Housing Act 1996 was inadequate, that meant that it was defective rather than a nullity.[34] These defects were capable of being remedied by the statutory review procedure.[35] Importantly, the Court confirmed the general proposition that whilst there is a residual remedy available in the Administrative Court in relation to Housing Act cases, it will only be exercised in exceptional circumstances.[36]

7.39   This approach is consistent not only with the practical considerations of avoiding the Administrative Court from being overburdened with cases which could otherwise have been dealt with by the County Court, but also with the principle that all alternative remedies should be exhausted before judicial review proceedings are commenced: it is the remedy of last resort.[37] It is also relevant to note that the prospects of persuading the Administrative Court to intervene are further reduced by virtue of the fact that appeals to the County Court under Part VII of the Housing Act 1996 are on a point of law,[38] with the grounds of appeal being essentially the same as judicial review.[39]

7.40   Despite the narrow construction of the residual jurisdiction of the Administrative Court, there may occasionally be circumstances in which a point of law is of such wider significance that the Administrative Court will permit a claim by way of judicial review rather than under the statutory scheme. In *R v Brent LBC, ex p Sadiq*,[40] the Court granted relief on a judicial review claim notwithstanding the availability of an alternative remedy in the County Court. Moses J was particularly influenced by the fact that it was likely that the point raised by the challenge would probably have been considered by the Court of Appeal in any event.[41]

---

[31]   *R (Lynch) v Lambeth LBC* [2006] EWHC 2737 (Admin); [2007] HLR 15. See also *Nipa Begum v Tower Hamlets LBC* [2000] 1 WLR 306; (2002) 32 HLR 445, CA; *R v Merton LBC, ex p Sembi* (2000) 32 HLR 439, QBD; *R v Brent LBC, ex p O'Connor* (1998) 31 HLR 923, QBD, *R v Brent LBC, ex p Sadiq* (2001) 33 HLR 47, QBD and *R (on the application of Ahmed (Ashfaq)) v Waltham Forest LBC* [2001] EWHC Admin 540.

[32]   [2006] EWHC 2737 (Admin); [2007] HLR 15.

[33]   Although see *R v Camden LBC, ex p Mohammed* (1998) 30 HLR 315, QBD, at 323 in which it was held that judicial review might be available if the original decision was so defective that any internal review under the Housing Act 1996, s 202 would be unfair.

[34]   [2006] EWHC 2737 (Admin); [2007] HLR 15 at [26].

[35]   Ibid.

[36]   Supra at [27].

[37]   See in a different context *R v Hammersmith and Fulham LBC, ex p Burkett* [2002] UKHL 23; [2002] 1 WLR 1593. See also the homelessness case of *R v Brent LBC, ex p O'Connor* (1999) 31 HLR 923, QBD, at p 924.

[38]   See the Housing Act 1996, s 204.

[39]   *Tower Hamlets LBC v Begum (Runa)* [2003] UKHL 5; [2003] 2 AC 430 at [17].

[40]   (2001) 33 HLR 47, QBD.

[41]   Ibid at [42].

7.41   A further example of the exceptional circumstances in which the Administrative Court will entertain a judicial review claim is provided by *R (Van der Stolk) v Camden LBC*,[42] the claimant was a single man with significant and worsening mental health problems. He approached the local authority for assistance, but was found to have made himself intentionally homeless from tied accommodation. The claimant sought a review under the Housing Act 1996, s 202 and did not appeal to the County Court within 21 days of being notified that the original decision had been upheld.[43] Whilst the Court recognised that the statutory code provided for a right to appeal to the County Court, the severe and deteriorating nature of the claimant's mental health established that there were exceptional circumstances which permitted the Administrative Court to intervene.[44]

7.42   In *R (W) v Sheffield City Council*,[45] the claimant was the victim of a dispute between two housing authorities, neither of which would accept responsibility for housing him pending the resolution of the disagreement. He had sought a review and was prosecuting an appeal in the County Court against one of the local authorities, against which the claimant could have sought an interim injunction under the Housing Act 1996, s 204A. However, notwithstanding the existence of this alternative remedy, the Court was prepared to entertain the judicial review claim, particularly in the light of unnecessary hurdles put in the way of the claimant and the failure of the competing housing authorities to accept responsibility for accommodating him.[46]

Decisions outside the statutory code

7.43   Apart from the extremely limited circumstances in which the Administrative Court will intervene by way of exercise of its residual jurisdiction, there are a number of discrete areas of homelessness law in which the Court regularly does become involved. These decisions raise issues which lie – strictly speaking – outside the statutory code laid down by Part VII of the Housing Act 1996.

Interim accommodation

7.44   The most important use of judicial review in this arena is the challenge to decisions about the provision (or refusal) of temporary accommodation pending the making of a review decision under the Housing Act 1996, s 202.[47] Prior to 30 September 2002, when the jurisdiction to consider issues of temporary accommodation pending an appeal to the County Court was transferred to the County Court,[48] the Administrative Court would have been the jurisdiction of choice for all questions of interim accommodation.

7.45   Pending the outcome of enquiries as to whether an applicant is eligible for assistance under Part VII of the Housing Act 1996, a housing authority is under a duty

---

[42]   [2002] EWHC 1261 (Admin).
[43]   Housing Act 1996, s 204(2). Note that the County Court is now able to extend time for appealing where there is a good reason for doing so: s 204(2A), inserted by Sch 1, para 17 of the Homelessness Act 2002.
[44]   Ibid at [46] and [47].
[45]   [2005] EWHC 720 (Admin).
[46]   Ibid at [34].
[47]   M Sunkin et al, 'Mapping the Use of Judicial Review to Challenge Local Authorities in England and Wales' [2007] PL 545 at 555.
[48]   See Housing Act 1996, s 204A, inserted by the Homelessness Act 2002, s 11.

to ensure that accommodation is available to the applicant.[49] This duty ceases on notification of the decision, even if the applicant requests a review, although the authority has a discretion to continue to secure that accommodation remains available pending a decision on the review.[50] There is no right of review of the decision as to whether to continue to provide accommodation under the Housing Act 1996, s 188; any challenge must be made by way of judicial review.[51]

7.46   The housing authority is not obliged of its own motion to consider whether to accommodate pending a review, but may wait to see whether the applicant requests that it exercise the power.[52]

7.47   Given that there is an unfettered right to request a review under the Housing Act 1996, s 202, a council may decide to exercise its discretion to accommodate under section 188(3) only in exceptional circumstances.[53] However, in each case the authority must apply the following tests, as laid down in *R V Camden LBC, ex p Mohammed* and must do so in a way that demonstrates that more than mere lip service has been paid to them:[54]

(a)   the merits of the applicant's case (that the original decision was flawed)[55] and the extent to which it can be said that the decision was either contrary to the merits or one which involved a fine balance of judgment;

(b)   whether consideration is required of new material or argument which alters the original decision; and

(c)   the personal circumstances of the applicant.

7.48   The overarching test is to ensure that the right balance is struck between the rights of other homeless persons and a proper consideration of the possibility that the applicant's challenge to the original decision is well founded.

Challenge to policy

7.49   Given the wide variety of circumstances in which people present themselves as homeless to local housing authorities and the significant resource implications of processing such applications, it makes practical sense for authorities to adopt and apply policies in relation to homelessness. In most cases, a claim by way of judicial review rather than a statutory review and appeal under Part VII of the Housing Act 1996 will be the appropriate vehicle by which to challenge the legality of a policy.[56] However,

---

[49]   Section 188(1) of the Housing Act 1996.

[50]   Section 188(3) of the Housing Act 1996.

[51]   *R v Camden LBC, ex p Mohammed* (1998) 30 HLR 315, QBD.

[52]   *R (Ahmed) v Waltham Forest LBC* [2001] EWHC Admin 540, at [16].

[53]   *R v Camden LBC, ex p Mohammed* (1998) 30 HLR 315, QBD; *R v Hammersmith & Fulham LBC, ex p Fleck* (1997) 30 HLR 679, QBD, at p 683; *R (on the application of Spencer) v Lambeth LBC* [2006] EWHC 3611 (Admin).

[54]   *R (Paul-Coker) v Southwark LBC* [2006] EWHC 497; [2006] HLR 32, QBD, at [49]; and see *R (Kelly and Mehari) v Birmingham City Council* [2009] EWHC 3240 (Admin), in which there had been a systematic failure of the housing authority to mention, let alone apply, the statutory tests under the Housing Act 1996, s 188.

[55]   The bracketed words were added in *R v Newham LBC, ex p Lumley* (2001) 33 HLR 11, QBD, at [54].

[56]   See *Kensington and Chelsea RLBC, ex p Byfield* (1997) 31 HLR 913, QBD, at p 922.

practitioners should be wary of cloaking what is in essence a challenge to a particular homelessness decision in the guise of an attack on the underlying policy which informed it.[57]

7.50   In practice, the level of scrutiny applied to homelessness policies can appear to be slight. However, the courts are ever mindful of the observations of Lord Brightman in *R v Hillingdon LBC, ex p Puhlhofer*,[58] that, whilst recognising the plight of the homeless, the remedy of judicial review should only be available in exceptional circumstances.

7.51   Importantly, whilst the rights to request a review and to appeal under Part VII of the Housing Act 1996 are available only to the applicant himself, judicial review as a remedy is available to third parties, provided that they establish sufficient interest in the subject matter. In *R (on the application of Hammia) v Wandsworth LBC*,[59] the local authority had a policy of requiring homeless applicants to relinquish their tenancy before accepting the 'full' homeless duty under the Housing Act 1996, s 193. The claimant was the husband of a woman (with whom he held a joint tenancy) who applied as homeless following allegations of domestic violence. In line with the council's policy, the homeless applicant served a Notice to Quit on the claimant, against whom possession proceedings were eventually brought by the local authority. The possession proceedings were adjourned pending the outcome of judicial review proceedings, which challenged the legality of the authority's policy. The Court held that the council's policy introduced an additional and unlawful pre-condition for accepting that a homeless applicant should be accommodated pursuant to the Housing Act 1996, s 193; in short, it placed an additional hurdle to an applicant which did not arise out of the statutory scheme.[60]

7.52   This decision is important not only as to the extent to which local housing authorities are entitled to give effect to the statutory homelessness code by the adoption of policies, but also as to the right of third parties to challenge such policies. Indeed, it is entirely possible that judicial review provides an avenue by which interest groups acting on behalf of homeless persons can take on policies which they consider to be unlawful.[61]

Statutory appeal ineffective

7.53   The County Court's powers under the Housing Act 1996, s 204(3) are limited to confirming, quashing or varying the housing authority's review decision or – if a review decision is not made – the original decision under the Housing Act 1996, s 184. The County Court has no inherent jurisdiction to order a local authority to carry out a statutory review. Consequently, where a housing authority has failed or refused to carry out any review, judicial review remains the appropriate method of securing a mandatory order that they do so.[62]

---

[57]   See *Kensington and Chelsea RLBC, ex p Byfield* (1997) 31 HLR 913, QBD, at p 922.
[58]   [1986] AC 484, HL at 518.
[59]   [2005] EWHC 1127 (Admin); [2005] HLR 45. See also *Savage v Hillingdon LBC* [2010] EWHC 88 (Admin).
[60]   Ibid at [24].
[61]   Cf: *R v Secretary of State for the Environment, ex p Shelter and the Refugee Council* [1997] COD 49, a challenge to the lawfulness of the removal of rights of persons subject to immigration control under the homelessness legislation.
[62]   *R (Aguiar) v Newham LBC* [2003] EWHC 1325 (Admin).

Refusal to extend time to review

7.54   A request for a review under the Housing Act 1996, s 202 must be made within 21 days of the date on which the applicant is notified of the authority's decision 'or such longer period as the authority may in writing allow'.[63] The discretion to extend time is wide and the authority may (but are not obliged to) balance the length of delay and reasons for it against the prospects of success. They are entitled to reach a decision without forming a provisional view of the underlying merits of the case if, in all the circumstances, they consider it reasonable not to do so.[64] The decision to refuse to extend time for requesting a review is only challengeable by way of judicial review.

Local connection

7.55   As part of their enquiries as to a person's eligibility for assistance under Part VII of the Housing Act 1996 and any duty owed to him, housing authorities may enquire whether the applicant has a local connection with another authority with a view to referring the person to that other local authority.[65]

7.56   A person has a local connection with an area if he has a connection:

(a)   because he is, or in the past was, normally resident there, and that residence is or was of his own choice;

(b)   because he is employed there;

(c)   because of family associations; or

(d)   because of special circumstances.[66]

7.57   If a housing authority decides that the applicant has a local connection and refers him to another authority, the applicant has a right of review of this decision.[67] However, there is no right of review where an authority refuses to make a local connection referral. Any such challenge should be made by way of judicial review.[68]

7.58   The referral of a homeless applicant to another authority can and does lead to disputes between housing authorities as to the basis on which the referral is made. Additionally, it is open to the referee authority to challenge the substantive decision of the referring authority as to whether any duty is owed to the homeless applicant. This can only be done by judicial review.[69]

---

[63]   Section 202(3) of the Housing Act 1996.
[64]   *R (on the application of C) v Lewisham LBC* [2003] EWCA Civ 927; [2004] HLR 4 at [49]; see also *R (on the application of Slaiman) v Richmond-Upon-Thames LBC* [2006] EWHC 329 (Admin); [2006] HLR 20 at [22] to [24].
[65]   Section 184(2) of the Housing Act 1996.
[66]   Section 199(1) of the Housing Act 1996.
[67]   Section 202(1)(c),(d) and (e) of the Housing Act 1996.
[68]   *Hackney London Borough Council v Sareen* [2003] EWCA Civ 351; [2003] HLR 54, CA at [36].
[69]   e g *R (on the application of Bantamagbari) v Westminster City Council* [2003] EWHC 1350 (Admin).

Refusal to entertain a homelessness application

7.59   On occasions, a housing authority may refuse even to entertain an application under Part VII of the Housing Act 1996 on the basis that it is made on the same facts as a previously rejected application. In such circumstances, judicial review is the appropriate legal route of challenge.

7.60   The circumstances in which a housing authority may reject an application as incompetent were considered in *Rikha Begum v London Borough of Tower Hamlets*:[70]

(a)   it is for an applicant to identify, in the subsequent application, the facts which are said to render that application different from the earlier application;

(b)   if no new facts are revealed in the application document, the authority may, indeed at least normally should, reject it as incompetent;

(c)   if the subsequent application document purports to reveal new facts which are, to the authority's knowledge and without further investigation, not new, fanciful or trivial, the same conclusion applies;

(d)   where the subsequent application document appears to reveal new facts which are, in light of the information then available to the authority, neither trivial or fanciful, the authority must treat the application as a valid application. In such a case the authority would not be entitled to investigate the accuracy of the alleged new facts before deciding whether to treat the application as valid, even where there may be reason to suspect the accuracy of the allegations.

Pre-emptive strikes

7.61   The question of intentional homelessness is a complex area of law and one which has given rise to a fairly substantial body of case law. Consequently, for those persons who are at risk of losing their homes or who feel that they must soon leave accommodation, there is a temptation to obtain some assurance that if they apply to the local housing authority as homeless, they will not be found to be intentionally homeless.

7.62   The most obvious means of pre-empting a decision as to intentionality is to seek a declaration in judicial review proceedings that the prospective applicant will not be found intentionally homeless if he applies to the local authority. However, it is extremely unlikely that any such attempts to obtain a guarantee will be successful. To do so would be to take away from the housing authority the power entrusted to them by Parliament to make decisions as to whether a person is entitled to assistance under Part VII of the Housing Act 1996.[71]

---

[70]   [2005] 1 WLR 2103. See also *R (Gardiner) v Haringey LBC* [2009] EWHC 2699 (Admin).
[71]   See *R v Hillingdon LBC, ex p Tinn* (1988) 20 HLR 305, QBD, at 312.

ALLOCATION

7.63   The allocation of social housing is governed principally by Part VI of the Housing Act 1996. Its purpose is to provide a 'single route into social housing'[72] whatever the starting point of the applicant: homeless applicants, transfer applicants or waiting list applicants.

7.64   A local authority allocates housing accommodation for the purposes of Part VI of the Housing Act 1996 if it:[73]

(a)   selects a person to be a secure or introductory tenant[74] of accommodation held by them; or

(b)   nominates a person to become a secure or introductory tenant (or licensee) of accommodation held by another person, such as a housing action trust; or

(c)   nominates a person to be an assured tenant of accommodation held by a Registered Social Landlord.

7.65   The allocating authority must only allocate housing to eligible persons.[75]

7.66   The allocation of housing accommodation by local authorities must be carried out in accordance with the provisions of Part VI of the Housing Act 1996, particularly those sections relating to the establishment and operation of an allocation scheme.[76] An authority must have a scheme for determining priorities and procedures in the allocation of their housing.[77] It is in relation to the drafting and operation of allocation schemes that most jurisprudence has developed.

7.67   On the face of it, local housing authorities have a very broad discretion as to the allocation of social housing.[78] However, an allocation which is made other than in accordance with the adopted allocation scheme will be unlawful.[79] For example, in *Begum (Amirun) v Tower Hamlets LBC*,[80] the housing authority sought to earmark a property for a particular applicant before applying the provisions of the allocation scheme. The Court held that a housing authority must apply its policy, and exercise any residual discretion, when it allocates the accommodation in question, not before.[81] Thus, the decision to allocate 'in advance' fell foul of the Housing Act 1996, s 166(8).

7.68   However, one should compare the *Begum* decision with the more recent judgment in *Birmingham City Council v Qasim*[82] in which the Court of Appeal held that tenancies granted in breach of the housing authority's allocation scheme were not

---

[72]   *Hansard* (HC), Standing Committee G, 16th sitting, 12 March 1996, col 614.
[73]   Section 159 of the Housing Act 1996.
[74]   Tenancy includes licence: see the Housing Act 1996, s 126.
[75]   Section 160A of the Housing Act 1996; Allocation of Housing and Homelessness (Eligibility) (England) Regulations 2006 (SI 2006/1294); Allocation of Housing and Homelessness (Miscellaneous Provisions) (England) Regulations 2006 (SI 2006/2527).
[76]   Sections 167 and 168 of the Housing Act 1996.
[77]   Section 167 of the Housing Act 1996.
[78]   See section 159(7) of the Housing Act 1996.
[79]   Section 166(8) of the Housing Act 1996.
[80]   [2002] EWHC 633 (Admin); [2003] HLR 8.
[81]   Ibid at [29].
[82]   [2010] HLR 19; [2009] EWCA Civ 1080, CA.

invalid. In *Qasim*, an officer of the council was granting secure tenancies to persons of his choosing, without authority and in contravention of the statutory allocation scheme. The Court of Appeal held that power to grant a tenancy was conferred by Part 2 of the Housing Act 1985 and was separate from the allocation of housing, which was governed by Part VI of the Housing Act 1996. Whilst the two activities would often be closely connected, and the distinction between allocation and disposal was rather technical, allocation was simply a preliminary step to disposal. It was possible to have a lawful allocation without a subsequent disposal if, for example, an applicant decided not to accept the property.

7.69 Similarly, if an authority makes a decision to refuse accommodation to an applicant, they must apply the allocation scheme. In *Sahardid v Camden LBC*,[83] the allocating authority's scheme provided that a homeless applicant with a child under five years old was only entitled to one-bedroom accommodation, whereas this entitlement was enlarged to a two-bedroom property when the child reached the age of five. The authority offered the appellant one-bedroom accommodation, but failed to consider the age of her son, who was five years and three days old when the offer was made. This failure was found to be a clear error of law in that the authority had not applied the terms of its own allocation scheme.[84]

7.70 The authority's allocation scheme must be framed so as to give reasonable preference to the following groups:[85]

(a)   homeless persons (within the meaning of Part VII of the Housing Act 1996);

(b)   people to whom a duty is owed under Part VII of the Housing Act 1996;[86]

(c)   occupants of unsanitary or overcrowded or otherwise unsatisfactory housing;

(d)   people who need to move on medical or welfare grounds (including grounds relating to a disability);

(e)   people who need to move to a particular locality where, if that need were not met, they would suffer hardship.[87]

7.71 The question of reasonable preference was considered in *R (on the application of Mei Ling Lin) v. Barnet LBC*.[88] The local housing authority had established a points-based allocation scheme which awarded applicants a certain number of points depending upon a number of criteria, based generally on the statutory preference categories under the Housing Act 1996, s 167(2). applicants were requested to bid for accommodation as and when it became available, with the accommodation being allocated to the applicant with the highest number of points. Homeless families were housed under assured shorthold tenancies controlled by Registered Social Landlords and were given 10 'homeless family points' for as long as they occupied it, save where the RSL's lease expired, in which case they were awarded 300 'lease end points' for a limited

---

[83]   [2005] HLR 11.
[84]   Ibid at [29].
[85]   Section 167(2) of the Housing Act 1996.
[86]   Sections 190(2), 193(2) or 195(2), together with people occupying accommodation provided under section 192(3) of the Housing Act 1996.
[87]   e g the need may arise from a requirement to give or receive care or to receive specialised medical treatment.
[88]   [2007] EWCA Civ 132; [2007] HLR 30.

period of time. However, existing tenants who requested a transfer and who were not expressly included in any of the categories of statutory preference were able to accumulate up to 350 points (including 100 points for merely requesting the transfer), the effect of which was to defeat most homeless applicants. The claimant asserted that the scheme did not afford her 'reasonable preference'.

7.72 The case went up to the Court of Appeal. The salient points are as follows:

(a) the test is not whether the homeless are *excluded* from accommodation under Part VI of the Housing Act 1996, but whether they were given reasonable preference relative to people who did not fall within the section 167(2) categories;[89]

(b) 'reasonable preference' is not about prospects of success or outcomes but about giving the applicant a reasonable head start in his search for social housing;[90]

(c) whether a preference is 'reasonable' is a matter for the local housing authority;[91]

(d) having regard to the above, the award of 10 points to homeless families did constitute a reasonable preference because it placed such a person in a better position than somebody who did not qualify for these points.[92]

7.73 A scheme fails to comply with the requirements of the Housing Act 1996, s 167 if it does not explain what criteria apply for awarding reasonable preference or indicate when they will be applied.[93]

7.74 Nevertheless, the scope for challenge has been curtailed considerably by the House of Lords in the recent case of *R (on the application of Ahmad) v Newham LBC*.[94] The London Borough of Newham operated a two-part allocation scheme which involved either Choice Based Lettings[95] or a direct offer. The House of Lords was required to determine the following issues:

(a) whether the Housing Act 1996, s 167 required a local housing authority to accord priority as between 'reasonable preference' applicants by reference to the relative gravity of their needs;

(b) whether Newham's scheme was unlawful because the Choice Based Lettings involved allocating a significant proportion of housing to a class of applicants who did not satisfy any of the requirements in paras (a) to (e) of the Housing Act 1996, s 167(2).

---

[89] Ibid at [25].
[90] Ibid at [25], [50]; see also *R v Wolverhampton MBC, ex p Watters* (1997) 29 HLR 931 at 938.
[91] Ibid at [28], [50], [51].
[92] Ibid at [28]–[30].
[93] *R (on the application of Cali, Abdi and Hassan) v Waltham Forest LBC* [2006] EWHC 302 (Admin); [2007] HLR 1.
[94] [2009] UKHL 14.
[95] Introduced by the Homelessness Act 2002; see the Housing Act 1996, s 167(1A) in particular.

7.75   Their Lordships answered the questions as follows:

(a)   Section 167 of the Housing Act 1996 does not impose any requirement for an authority to rank reasonable preference applicants depending upon the weight of their need.[96]

(b)   In the case of transfer applicants (who did not fall within the reasonable preference categories under section 167(2)(a)–(e)), it was entirely legitimate to operate an allocation scheme which, in some circumstances, meant that they were given preference over reasonable preference candidates. Section 167(2) of the Housing Act 1996 only required that those groups be given a 'reasonable preference'. It did not require that they should be given absolute priority over everyone else. Still less did it require that an individual household in one of those groups should be given absolute priority over an individual household which wished to transfer.[97]

7.76   The important point for judicial review practitioners to note is that the House of Lords made it very clear that matters of housing allocation require difficult judgments to be made, which depend upon juggling different social, political and economic priorities. It seemed very unlikely that Parliament would have intended that the courts should embark on an assessment of how priorities were to be accorded, save in the rarest and most exceptional circumstances.[98]

7.77   Thus, it would appear that the circumstances in which an allocation scheme (or a decision made under it) will be quashed or even scrutinised closely by the Court will now be few and far between. It is only where a scheme is patently irrational that the courts are likely to intervene.[99]

7.78   However, practitioners should be aware that whatever the latitude enjoyed by allocating authorities, allocation decisions should still be made in accordance with the adopted scheme.

INTRODUCTORY TENANCIES

7.79   Introductory tenancies (introduced by Part V of the Housing Act 1996) provide a good example of the important, yet increasingly circumscribed role played by housing judicial review proceedings before the Administrative Court.

7.80   An introductory tenancy is, in essence, a probationary tenancy (Our Future Homes, White Paper) offered by a local housing authority or housing action trust in order that they can monitor the actions and behaviour of their tenants for a period of one year (although this may be extended by the landlord by a maximum of six months: Housing Act 1996, s 125A).

7.81   The landlord may bring the introductory tenancy to an end relatively efficiently and speedily by serving a notice seeking possession which complies with the

---

[96]   Ibid at [39].
[97]   Ibid at [18]–[20], *per Baroness Hale*.
[98]   See generally the speech of Lord Neuberger, especially at [46] and [62].
[99]   *R (on the application of Ariemuguvbe) v Islington LBC* [2009] EWCA Civ 1308, which re-iterated the broad discretion that is available to housing authorities in the allocation of housing.

requirements of the Housing Act 1996, s 128. The requirements of the Housing Act 1996, s 128 may be summarised as follows:

(a)   that the notice states that an order for possession of the dwellinghouse will be sought;

(b)   the reasons for the landlord's decision to apply for such an order;

(c)   the notice shall specify a date after which possession proceedings may be commenced; this may not be earlier than the date on which the tenancy could, apart from Chapter I of Part V of the Housing Act 1996, have been brought to an end by the service of a notice to quit given by the landlord on the same date as the notice of proceedings;

(d)   the notice must inform the tenant of the right to request a review of the decision to commence possession proceedings and that such a request must be made within 14 days of service of the notice seeking possession;

(e)   the tenant must also be told that he can obtain legal assistance from a solicitor, the Citizens Advice Bureau or a housing aid or law centre.

7.82   Provided that these requirements have been met, and possession proceedings are commenced, the court must grant possession of the dwellinghouse (Housing Act 1996, s 127(2)).

7.83   It is the penultimate requirement of s 128 (s 128(6)) that is of most relevance because it refers expressly to the right of an introductory tenant to request a review of the decision to commence possession proceedings, in much the same way as the dissatisfied homeless applicant may do under s 202 of the same Act. Indeed, similar issues are likely to arise as to the lawfulness of the decision on review. In brief, the principal questions that are likely to surface are as follows:

(a)   the adequacy of reasons (Housing Act 1996, s 129(5)): however, it should be noted that the reasons given for confirming the decision to commence proceedings need not be the same as those contained in the notice seeking possession, provided that the tenant is given the proper opportunity to respond to any new allegations upon which the landlord proposes to rely;[100]

(b)   the procedural fairness of the review: the tenant has a right to make oral or written representations and to be legally represented throughout the review process (Housing Act 1996, s 129(4)(b));

(c)   the rationality of the decision: in practice, it will be only in the most obvious and exceptional case that it will be established that no reasonable landlord would have upheld the decision to seek possession (eg in *R (on the application of Chowdhury) v Newham LBC*,[101] the tenant blamed his rent arrears on a failure of the housing authority to pay housing benefit. The Court upheld the authority's view that the tenant had a responsibility properly to inform himself as to the requirement of the

---

[100]   *R (on the application of Laporte) v Newham LBC* [2004] EWHC 227.
[101]   [2003] EWHC 2837 (Admin).

housing benefit system and to ensure that any application was complete. Consequently, the landlord's decision that the tenant was unsuitable to remain in social housing was not irrational).

7.84 Questions arising out of possession proceedings for dwellings held under introductory tenancies can be dealt with either in the County Court or the Administrative Court. However, the clear legislative and jurisprudential steer is that challenges are principally to be considered in the County Court. For example, the Housing Act 1996, s 138(3) provides that if a person takes proceedings in the High Court which he could have commenced in the county court, he is not entitled to any costs.

7.85 Similarly, it would appear that where a tenant fails to take issue with lawfulness of a decision to commence proceedings (either by failing to request a review or by failing to commence proceedings after an unsuccessful review) it will subsequently be too late to challenge the lawfulness of the review or the substantive decision to start possession proceedings (*R (Chelfat) v Tower Hamlets LBC*).[102]

7.86 A clear exception to this general proposition is the case where a tenant seeks to raise public law arguments as a defence to possession proceedings in the county court. Whilst as a general proposition it is open to a defendant to run a public law defence to possession proceedings (*Wandsworth LBC v Winder*)[103] it has been decided in the context of introductory tenancies that any challenge to the conduct of an internal review must be done by way of judicial review (*Manchester CC v Cochrane*).[104] In the event that a public law defence is raised in the county court, the appropriate course is to adjourn the possession proceedings pending the determination of a claim before the Administrative Court. However, in these circumstances the county court acts as a filter in that it must be satisfied that there is a real chance of the defendant obtaining permission to apply for judicial review.

7.87 In practice, most deficiencies in an internal review can be rectified if the landlord carries out a second review.[105] In such circumstances, whilst the question of costs may still be 'live', any judicial review claim challenging the original decision is likely to be wholly academic.

PROCEDURE

7.88 The judicial review of housing decisions presents some particular procedural issues, if only by virtue of the urgency of many of the claims and the precarious position in which claimants sometimes find themselves.

7.89 The two main areas of procedural relevance are urgent applications and interim relief and costs.

---

[102] [2006] EWHC 313.
[103] [1985] AC 461; 17 HLR 196, HL.
[104] (1999) 31 HLR 810, CA.
[105] *R (McDonagh) v Salisbury DC* [2001] EWHC Admin 567.

Interim relief

7.90 Given that housing judicial review claims often (but not exclusively) concern issues as fundamental as the roof over a person's head, the question of interim relief is particularly relevant to a full understanding of this area of law. Practitioners will most regularly encounter the need to apply for or to resist an application for interim relief in the context of homelessness.

7.91 It is possible to combine a claim for judicial review with an application for interim injunctive relief.[106] In urgent cases, Form N463 (Request for Urgent Consideration) must be completed together with the draft claim form and a copy of a draft order. Justification for the urgency of the case must also given.[107]

7.92 In practice, it is not at all unusual for such interim applications to be determinative of the claim. In many cases, the claimant will simply be seeking somewhere to stay for a limited period of time and by the time the substantive judicial review claim is to be heard, the issues between the parties may have been resolved or may no longer be relevant.[108]

7.93 In practice, it has appeared that the Court is willing to grant interim relief fairly readily, especially in relation to claims by homeless persons. This willingness is likely to have been borne out of a desire to preserve the *status quo* pending the resolution of the substantive claim and the, perhaps understandable, wish to provide a claimant with somewhere to live so that he is better able to prosecute the claim.

7.94 Practitioners should nevertheless be wary of the temptation to commence proceedings which have dubious merit in order simply (or primarily) to secure a short lived benefit for their clients. The Court has deprecated such practices and in recent years has appeared more willing to investigate the substantive merits before granting interim relief. Alternatively, claimants who launch a poorly founded claim may ultimately be penalised in costs. The practice of applying for interim relief as a matter of course even where the substantive merits are weak has been subject to criticism. In *R (Lawer) v Restormel Borough Council*,[109] an interim injunction made without notice was set aside where there had been material non-disclosure by the claimant and where the substance of the claim was hopeless.

7.95 Occasionally, the responsibility for prolonging the *status quo* for perhaps too long may lie with the Administrative Court itself. For example, in *R (Casey) v Restormel Borough Council*.[110] Munby J (citing the Magna Carta) expressed concern at the length of time which the defendant local authority had to wait before its application to discharge the interim injunction was heard. The judge also referred to *R (Lawer) v Restormel Borough Council*[111] in which there was a similarly unacceptable delay.[112]

---

[106] Section 31(1)(b) of the Senior Courts Act 1981; CPR 54.3.
[107] See Practice Statement (Administrative Court: annual statement) [2002] 1 All ER 633 at 635.
[108] M Sunkin et al, 'Mapping the Use of Judicial Review to Challenge Local Authorities in England and Wales' [2007] PL 545 at 556: housing and homelessness cases are much more likely to drop from the judicial review process than planning, childcare and education cases.
[109] [2007] EWHC 2299 (Admin) at [70]–[77].
[110] [2007] EWHC Admin 2554 at [28].
[111] [2007] EWHC 2299 (Admin).
[112] *R (Casey) v Restormel Borough Council* [2007] EWHC Admin 2554 at [31].

7.96 It is to be hoped that the delays to which to the parties were subjected in the Casey and Lawer cases will be reduced, if not eliminated as a consequence of the regionalisation of the Administrative Court.

7.97 In an application for interim relief, the Court will have regard to a number of principles which can be extracted from the authorities:

(a) There must be a strong prima facie case demonstrating a breach of the authority's statutory obligations before the Court will grant an injunction.[113] In De Falco, the court expressly disapproved of the application of the American Cyanamid[114] balance of convenience test in such cases on the basis that it was not appropriate to apply such private law concepts to the field of administrative law.[115]

(b) An injunction will usually follow if permission is granted to move for judicial review. See *R v Cardiff City Council, ex p Barry*.[116] Thus, if there is an arguable case at the permission stage of judicial review proceedings, there is a strong chance of obtaining interim relief pending the substantive hearing.

Costs

7.98 Public money is almost invariably in play in housing judicial review claims. Moreover, decisions are often (but by no means always) reviewed by the decision-maker due to changing circumstances or in the light of the strength of the claimant's challenge. So it is that proceedings do not always run their full course.

7.99 As we have already seen, in the field of housing judicial review claims, the granting of interim relief or permission to move to a substantive hearing will often be determinative of both the legal and practical issues between the parties. Consequently, a body of case law has developed to deal with the situation in which costs are incurred but where the claim does not proceed to a full hearing.

7.100 One should be ever mindful of avoiding protracted satellite litigation when the substantive claim has been resolved. It is unlikely to promote the overriding objective of the Civil Procedure Rules[117] or be a proportionate course of action if the parties engage in what for all intents and purposes is a fully contested substantive hearing merely to seek a ruling as to who would have been successful when the only 'live' issue is one of costs.

7.101 In *R v Waltham Forest DC, ex p Boxall*,[118] a number of principles were laid down as to the payment of costs in such circumstances:[119]

(a) the court has power to make a costs order when the substantive proceedings have been resolved without a trial but the parties have not agreed about costs;

(b) it will ordinarily be irrelevant that the claimant is in receipt of public funding;

---

[113] *De Falco v Crawley BC* [1980] QB 460 at 467.
[114] *American Cyanamid Co v Ethicon Ltd* [1975] AC 396 HL.
[115] Ibid.
[116] (1990) 22 HLR 261 at 263.
[117] CPR 1.1.
[118] (2001) 4 CCL Rep 258.
[119] Ibid at [22].

(c)   the overriding objective is to do justice between the parties without incurring unnecessary court time;

(d)   there will be cases where it is obvious that the claim would have been successful and where it is clear that it is without merit. In between, the position will be less clear. How far the court will look into previously unresolved substantive issues will depend upon the circumstances of the case and in particular the amount of costs involved and the conduct of the parties;

(e)   in the absence of a good reason to make any other order, the fallback is to make no order as to costs;

(f)   the Court should be mindful of not discouraging parties from settling proceedings at any early stage: e g where a local authority makes a concession at an early stage.

7.102 However, the hard pressed Administrative Court judge should make a reasonable and proportionate attempt to analyse the situation and not be overly tempted to adopt the fallback position of no order for costs.[120]

7.103 By way of a more recent example, just such an issue arose in *Mendes v London Borough of Southwark*.[121] This was a homelessness case in which the housing authority came to the erroneous decision that Mr Mendes was not a worker within the meaning of the Immigration (European Economic Area) Regulations 2006 (and therefore not entitled to assistance with housing under Part VII of the Housing Act 1996) because he was not working due to an injury. They duly proposed to evict him and his family from temporary accommodation provided under the Housing Act 1996, s 188(3). Mr Mendes' solicitors, anxious to prevent the eviction, issued judicial review proceedings coupled with an application for an interim injunction. At 4.30 pm on the day of issue, the council agreed to continue to provide accommodation pending a review of its decision under the Housing Act 1996, s 184, that Mr Mendes was not eligible for assistance with his homelessness. The following day, interim relief was granted by the Administrative Court with an indication that the claimant had a strong *prima facie* case. In the light of the authority's concession, the claimant withdrew the claim and the question of costs was considered on the basis of written submissions. At first instance, the Court determined to make no order for costs. The claimant appealed.

7.104 The Court of Appeal held that it was plain at the time that the Administrative Court made no order for costs that Mr Mendes would have won: there was an obvious error in the decision letter and the local authority conceded as much. There was no sufficient reason for the Court to have resorted to the default position of no order for costs.[122]

7.105 There is also an obligation in certain circumstances to put forward a more cost effective means of resolving the litigation prior to proceedings being commenced.[123] The defendant local authority was liable for the costs unnecessarily incurred, where they refused to consider an alternative resolution of the dispute. This requirement is likely to be given greater weight in the light to the duty to consider Alternative Dispute

---

[120]   *R (Scott) v London Borough of Hackney* [2009] EWCA Civ 217, CA at [51].
[121]   [2009] EWCA Civ 594.
[122]   *Mendes v London Borough of Southwark* [2009] EWCA Civ 594, [2010] 20 HLR 3, CA at [24] and [25].
[123]   *R (H) v Kingston-Upon-Thames RLBC* [2002] EWHC 3158.

Resolution. However, the time for negotiating a mutually acceptable outcome without resorting to litigation is unlikely to be available where, for example, a prospective claimant is about to become street homeless.

Chapter 8

MENTAL HEALTH

INTRODUCTION

8.1   Until relatively recently, judicial review or challenge by way of case stated was the only procedure by which there could be challenges to the Mental Health Review Tribunal, that being the only court or tribunal designed specifically for the purpose of deciding applications under the Mental Health Act (MHA). Cases concerning the other side of mental health law, involving those who lack the capacity to make certain decisions, if they reached a court at all, were decided under the inherent jurisdiction of the High Court; the Family Division in cases concerning treatment and welfare issues, and by the Chancery Division where the issues concerned property related matters, including wills.

8.2   However, with recent legislation the entire landscape of mental health law has changed. First, the Mental Capacity Act 2005 (MCA) has not only placed the common law relating to those lacking capacity on a statutory footing but has also created a new superior court of record, the Court of Protection to deal with the interpretation of the new statutory code as well as resolving disputes that arise, and making declaratory decisions to enable those dealing with the mentally incapable to act on their behalf. The mental capacity landscape has been further clouded by the amendments made to the Act by the Mental Health Act 2007 which introduced a new administrative procedure to enable those lacking capacity to be deprived of their liberty in a manner which is consistent with Article 5 of the European Convention of Human Rights (ECHR) the procedure under Schedule A1 of the MCA, the Deprivation of Liberty Safeguards (universally referred to as DOLS), under which an appeal lies to the Court of Protection.

8.3   The Mental Health Act 2007 also brought about the end of the Mental Health Review Tribunal. Instead a virtually identical jurisdiction was passed onto the new Tribunal system which was created by the Tribunals, Courts and Enforcement Act 2007 (TCEA). The critical change is the two-tier system. At first instance the cases that were heard by the MHRT are now heard by a similarly constituted First-tier Tribunal (FTT) which is part of the Health, Education and Social Care Chamber (HESC). However, appeals from the FTT now lie to the Administrative Appeals Chamber of the Upper Tribunal (UT). This is a statutory appeal on a point of law. There is still the option of judicial review which can be brought in the UT or, in appropriate cases, in the High Court. In addition, the new system enables each Tribunal to review its own decisions thereby creating a 'mezzanine level' between the FTT's first instance decision and an appeal to the UT.

8.4   As a result, the place of public law in the mental health sphere is somewhat more complicated than in many of the other areas of law dealt with in this book. Most of the bodies involved in cases under the MHA will be public bodies. So, too, will be many of those involved in MCA cases. Judicial review to the Administrative Court will only be appropriate in certain limited and selected instances. What I aim to do is to indicate to the puzzled practitioner which types of challenge arise in the mental health sphere and which judicial route needs to be taken to resolve them.

8.5   This chapter is not intended to explain in great detail the vast area of mental health and mental capacity law. What it is intended to do is to explain how the various judicial bodies discharge their functions within the area and where judicial review now stands.

8.6   As part of this introduction it is important to set out the most significant provision within the ECHR that concerns mental health law:

'Article 5 Right to Liberty and Security

(1)   Everyone has the right to liberty and security of person. No one shall be deprived of his liberty save in the following cases and in accordance with a procedure prescribed by law ... (e) the lawful detention of ... persons of unsound mind ... (4) Everyone who is deprived of his liberty by arrest or detention shall be entitled to take proceedings by which the lawfulness of his detention shall be decided speedily by a court and his release ordered if the detention is not lawful.'

8.7   The term 'unsound mind' is nowhere defined in the Convention. It is, however, consistent with both 'mental disorder' and 'mental incapacity'.[1] In the case of mental disorder, the fact of a disorder itself does not justify deprivation of liberty. In *Winterwerp v The Netherlands*[2] the European Court of Human Rights (ECtHR) ruled that mental disorder from which the patient suffered had to be of a kind or degree which warranted detention. As we shall see that is reflected in the provisions of the MHA. There is some doubt as to whether *Winterwerp* applies to cases involving mental incapacity following the case of *G v E*, which is the subject of comment later in this chapter.

PUBLIC LAW AND THE MENTAL HEALTH ACT

8.8   The purpose of the Mental Health Act is to create an essentially administrative procedure for the admission into detention and other forms of restriction of those who suffer from mental disorder, as well as having in place a proper procedure for regulating and regularising their treatment whilst in Hospital or in the community. The Act ensures that there are safeguards to ensure that those detained or subject to orders have their detention reviewed and are discharged when the criteria for admission is no longer satisfied. The purpose of the Act, in other words, is to satisfy Article 5 of the ECHR. Indeed, in the landmark case of *HL v UK*[3] the ECtHR held up the MHA in order to criticise the pre-MCA regime for the treatment of the mentally incapacitated. At [120], the Court said:

'In particular, and most obviously, the Court notes the lack of any formalised admission procedures which indicate who can propose admission, for what reasons and on the basis of what kind of medical and other assessments and conclusions. There is [in HL's case] no requirement to fix the exact purpose of admission (for example for assessment or for

---

[1]   This has been confirmed recently by the Court of Appeal in *G v E* [2010] EWCA Civ 822.
[2]   (1979) 2 EHRR 387.
[3]   (2004) 40 EHRR 761.

treatment) and, consistently, no limits in terms of time, treatment or care attach to that admission. Nor is there any specific provision requiring a continuing clinical assessment of the persistence of the disorder warranting detention. The appointment of a representative of a patient who could make certain objections and applications on his or her behalf is a procedural protection to those committed involuntarily under the 1983 Act would be of equal importance for patients who are legally incapacitated and have, as in the present case, extremely limited communication abilities.'

8.9   In other words, the ECtHR was delivering a critique of the treatment of the 'Bournewood patient' by holding up the MHA as a paradigm against which Article 5 compliant procedures ought to be judged.[4] The MHA is divided into parts, each of which fulfils a particular role in ensuring that the orders made under the Act are lawful. So the first 'gateway' to an order for detention under the Act is 'mental disorder' which is expressly defined in Part I of the Act, which contains only one section. That definition (given in section 1(2)) is sufficiently wide to keep abreast with psychiatric diagnosis, but specific enough to satisfy the need for certainty and predictability under Article 5.

8.10   The second section of the Act fixes formalised admission procedures for compulsory admission to hospital and into guardianship. For instance, sections 2 and 3 of the Act are specifically designed to adhere to Article 5 as interpreted by the ECtHR in *Winterwerp v The Netherlands*,[5] by requiring that the mental disorder must be of a 'nature or degree' that would warrant or make it appropriate for the person to be detained in a Hospital, and that it is necessary for him to be so detained for his own health and safety or for that of others. A legally sound reason for admission is thus created. Furthermore, the requirement of necessity means that the admission must be proportionate. Finally, there is a need for appropriate medical treatment to be available – therefore ensuring that the purpose for admission can be met. The sections each have time limits attached to them, ensuring their compliance with the Convention. Section 37 of the Act provides powers to the crown court or the magistrates court after conviction to order admission to and detention at hospital or to order guardianship in appropriate cases. The power is similar to section 3 but one imposed by the criminal courts.

8.11   What the Act also does is to ensure that there are functions to be discharged by certain actors within the statutory framework. In summary, the procedures for admission under sections 2, 3 and 7 of the MHA are governed by section 11. This places the obligation to carry out the procedure on the approved mental health professional (AMHP). The Act requires the AMHP to consult with another specific actor, the nearest relative (NR), who is intended to represent the patient's family or partner, with input into the decision-making process informed by the patient's social circumstances. The process may only proceed on the basis of the recommendations of two registered medical practitioners – thus ensuring that the procedure is based on a proper medical diagnosis or suspicion of a mental disorder (as the case may be). The NR can derail the admission process by his objection to it. If the objection is unreasonable, the AMHP may apply to displace the NR and replace him with another.[6] Once the application for admission is complete, and in the proper form, the documentation must be delivered to the Hospital Managers (HM). It is the HM 'who have the authority to detain patients under the Act'.[7] They have the primary duty to ensure that the provisions of the Act are

---

4   So called because of the name of the NHS Trust in the HL case, and the domestic name of the case: *R v Bournewood Community and Mental Health NHS Trust, ex p L* [1999] 1 AC 458. The 'Bournewood patient' will be defined in the section of this chapter concerned with mental capacity.

5   (1979–80) 2 EHRR 387.

6   Under s 29 of the MHA.

7   See Chapter 30 of the MHA Code of Practice for full details.

followed, that patients are detained only as the Act allows, and that they are treated only in accordance with the provisions of the Act.

8.12   What is clear from these procedures is that the legality of the section is determined by whether the application procedure has been properly followed. At this stage in the proceedings procedural flaws may be challenged in the High Court. Some examples may assist in illustrating this point. Under section 11(3) of the MHA, the AMHP is obliged 'before or within a reasonable time after an application for admission of a patient for assessment is made ...' to 'take such steps as are practicable to inform the person (if any) appearing to be the nearest relative of the patient that the application is to be or has been made and of the power off the nearest relative under section 23(2)(a)'.[8] When the AMHP fails to do this in good faith the application is not invalidated, but if done in bad faith it may be.[9]

8.13   Another example concerns section 11(4) of the MHA where the AMHP may not make an application for admission for treatment or guardianship in either of the two following cases: first, where the NR has notified the AMHP (or the case of guardianship the Local Social Services Authority) that he objects to the admission; or, secondly, where the AMHP had not consulted a person (if any) appearing to be the NR (although the requirement does not apply if it appears to the AMHP that in the circumstances such a consultation would not have been reasonably practicable or would involve unnecessary delay). The Courts have been willing to investigate factual issues that arise out of applications that may flout the requirements of these provisions. In one case the Court made a decision as to how long a couple had lived together (thus determining status as NR).[10] In another, whether the consultation had been effective.[11]

8.14   Challenging the diagnostic requirements for admission through the High Court is problematic and is best left to an application to the Managers or to the Tribunal, where a full consideration of the medical opinion, with cross-examination and the use of an independent expert can take place.

8.15   The medical evidence in support of admission will usually be a diagnosis of a recognised mental disorder and will be supported by a reference to one of the recognised diagnostic criteria.[12] The nature and degree of the disorder is disjunctive. Either may justify the order that follows, including detention.[13] There will often be a need for a high level of clinical judgment in determining nature and degree. The nature of the disorder is not simply which ICD-10 or DSM-IV category it falls into (if any). It is the history of the disorder over the patient's life, how chronic it has been, the patient's response to treatment, whether the patient's condition has deteriorated rapidly in the absence of treatment, the chronicity of the condition and possibly other factors that determine the nature of the disorder.[14] The degree of the disorder is the current manifestation of his

---

8   The right of the NR to apply to the HM for discharge.
9   See *R v Birmingham Mental Health Trust, ex p Phillips* (C/O/1501/95).
10   *R v Hospital managers of the Park Royal Hospital, ex p Robinson* (QBD Admin 26 November 2007).
11   *BB v Cygnet Health Care & Lewisham LBC* [2008] EWHC 1259 (Admin) and *GD v Manager of the Dennis Scott Unit* (QBD Admin, 27 June 2008). I am grateful for the details of the unreported cases here, as well as the commentary from Laura Davidson's article 'Nearest Relative Consultation and the Avoidant AMHP' [2009] JMHL 70.
12   More usual in the UK is reference to the ICD-10 Classification of Mental and Behavioural Disorders (WHO) or, sometimes, to the Diagnostic and Statistical manual of Mental Disorders (or DSM-IV), presently in its Fourth Edition.
13   See *R v MHRT for South Thames Region, ex p Smith* [1998] EWHC 832 (Admin) Popplewell, J.
14   See *ex p Smith* (above) and *Smirek v Williams* [2000] EWCA Civ 3025.

disorder. Therefore, a patient with no history of a mental disorder may be detained under the MHA if he presently exhibits serious enough symptoms of such a disorder. Equally, and more controversially, a person who suffers from a disorder which is of a serious enough nature may be detained even if asymptomatic, in certain circumstances. For instance, a person who suffers from chronic and enduring paranoid schizophrenia and who is maintained in good health by medication, may be detained under the MHA if he were to discontinue his medication where a period of non-medication is likely to result in rapid deterioration into serious illness.[15]

8.16   Many of these decisions will be based almost entirely on the professional judgment of those deciding. Consequently, they are difficult in the extreme to challenge on the usual judicial review bases. Only in extreme cases will the decision to detain a person with a mental disorder be *Wednesbury* unreasonable. However, challenges can be made by way of JR in the event of non-compliance with the rules laid down by the MHA, as we shall see below. Equally, the Code of Practice to the MHA must be adhered to unless there are very good reasons for not so doing so. Although it falls short of having statutory effect, a breach of the code may assist in a challenge to the decision made in breach.[16]

8.17   Appropriate medical treatment must be available. Therefore, the availability of 'appropriate medical treatment' is another prerequisite for detention. The MHA does not define what 'appropriate' means in this context. The definition of medical treatment is given in the interpretation section, section 145. At section 145(1) medical treatment 'includes nursing, psychological intervention and specialist mental health habilitation, rehabilitation and care ...'. To this a caveat is added at section 145(4), namely: 'Any reference in this Act to medical treatment, in relation to mental disorder, shall be construed as a reference to medical treatment the purpose of which is to alleviate, or prevent the worsening of, the disorder or one of more of its symptoms or manifestations'. This definition is elaborated upon in the Code of Practice to the MHA at Chapter 6, which casts some additional light on the issue of appropriateness. At paragraph 6.6 the Code states:

> 'Even if particular mental disorders are likely to persist or get worse despite treatment, there may well be a range of interventions which would represent appropriate medical treatment. It should never be assumed that any disorders, or any patients, are inherently or inevitably untreatable. Nor should it be assumed that likely difficulties in achieving long-term and sustainable change in a person's underlying disorder make medical treatment to help manage their condition and the behaviours arising from it either inappropriate or unnecessary.'

8.18   This passage was concerned with the argument that those with treatment resistant conditions, including some personality disorders, could not be detained under Hospital orders because no appropriate treatment could ever be available. However, it also illuminates another issue. The available treatment does not need to be the best treatment possible, or even, by the same measure, the best treatment available. At paragraph 6.12 of the Code this is made clear, the medical treatment available at the time need only be 'an appropriate response to the patient's condition and situation'.[17] Once again, the appropriateness test is dependent on the professional judgment of those supporting the order under the MHA. As the Code makes clear at paragraph 6.14 what is appropriate '... will depend, in part, on what might reasonably be expected to be

---

[15]   See *Smirek* (above) (per Hale, LJ) and *R(H) v MHRT* [2001] EWCA Civ 415 (per Lord Phillips, MR).

[16]   *R (Munjaz) v Mersey Care NHS Trust* [2005] UKHL 58.

[17]   My emphasis.

achieved given the nature and degree of the patient's disorder'. That treatment may not include any active therapeutic input in the form of medication or a psychological programme. It may consist 'only of nursing and specialist day-to-day care under the clinical supervision of an approved clinician, in a safe and secure therapeutic environment with a structured regime' (Code, paragraph 6.16).

8.19 Consequently, detention in a Hospital without active treatment may satisfy the appropriate treatment condition. Although (Code, paragraph 6.17) 'simply detaining someone – even in a Hospital – does not constitute medical treatment' paragraph 6.16 does not require that treatment to be any more than nursing support in a safe environment. This is particularly important in the case of those with personality disorders[18] who may require 'relatively intense and long term, structured and coherent' treatment (Code, paragraph 35.10). Any challenge by way of JR to an order made under the MHA on the basis of the 'availability of appropriate medical treatment', where the Responsible Clinician (RC)[19] is able to satisfy the tests outlined in the Code will be very difficult. The better mode of challenge is through the FTT, where the evidential basis and professional opinions of those supporting detention maybe challenged in an adversarial way in front of an expert Tribunal and with independent experts who contradict that view may be instructed.[20]

8.20 The appropriateness of medical treatment has also been considered in relation to whether a patient is eligible to be detained under the MCA/DOLS because he is detainable under the MHA. This issue will be revisited below in the MCA section of this chapter.[21] It is important, however, that the treatment must be for a mental disorder. This raises difficult questions as to the predominant purpose of the treatment proposed. Admission to Hospital under the MHA can only be lawful if the core treatment proposed is for a mental disorder. This, however, can include the consequences of that disorder, such as the treatment of wounds inflicted by a mentally disordered person,[22] or the force-feeding of an anorexic patient.[23] However, it does not stretch to a case where a diabetic person, suffering from Korsakoff's syndrome and who is unable to manage his blood-sugar levels is detained in Hospital so that that management can take place.[24] Whilst judicial review proceedings are not unknown to challenge the diagnostic element for detention under MHA, or the clinical decision as to what the primary purpose of the treatment is, in the absence of clear error the Court will be slow to interfere with a competent professional's exercise of clinical judgment.

8.21 One of the RC's duties is to review the detention criteria (the *Winterwerp* conditions) on a continuous basis. Once he or she is of the view that those conditions are not met (for whatever reason) the RC has must discharge the patient from section.[25] A failure to do so will render the detention unlawful. The decision can be challenged by way of JR or by a writ of habeas corpus. The Hospital Managers can also discharge. If the matter comes before a Tribunal and the RC does not support further detention on

---

18   ICD-10, F-60. Also listed in DSM-IV in chapter on personality disorders.
19   Defined in s 34.
20   For a recent consideration of this issue as well as an example of how the matter may be challenged in the FTT, see *MD v Nottinghamshire Health Care NHS Trust* [2010] UKUT 59 (ACC) – Judge Jacobs sitting alone.
21   *GJ v The Foundation Trust, A PCT and The Department of Health* [2009] EWHC 2972.
22   See *B v Croydon HA* [1995] 2 WLR 294.
23   *C (A minor: Medical Treatment: Court's Jurisdiction)* [1997] 2 FLR 180.
24   *GJ v The Foundation Trust, A PCT and the DOH* [2009] EWHC 2972 (Fam).
25   *R v Drew* [2003] UKHL 25 and the Code of Practice (MHA) 29.16 and s 23 MHA.

the grounds that the criteria are not met, the Tribunal should discharge, and a failure to do so ought to be challenged by appeal to the Upper Tribunal.

LEGAL REVIEW OF THE LAWFULNESS OF DETENTION

8.22   As we have seen, the admission of a person into detention is an administrative process governed by detailed rules, and conducted by actors with particular designated roles and duties. These include the Hospital Managers, who have a duty to ensure that admission is legally correct, and to review continued detention. These procedures are subject to the jurisdiction of the High Court by way of JR and habeas corpus.

8.23   The writ of habeas corpus requires the detaining authority to show lawful justification for a person's detention, in default of which the person must be freed. As we know, JR is a procedure that does not challenge the merits of a decision but rather its lawfulness. A decision can be challenged on the grounds that it is illegal (ie there was an error of law), that there is procedural impropriety, that it is irrational (or *Wednesbury* unreasonable), that there has been an abuse of power, or that there has been a breach of breach of the ECHR.

8.24   Section 139 of the MHA(1) provides:

> 'No person shall be liable, whether on the ground of want of jurisdiction or any other ground to any civil or criminal proceedings to which he would have been liable apart from this section in respect of any act purporting to be done in pursuance of this Act or any rules or regulations made under this Act unless the Act was done in bad faith or without reasonable care.'

8.25   Under section 139(2) no proceedings shall be brought against any person in any Court in respect of such an act without the leave of the High Court (in civil proceedings) or the DPP (in criminal proceedings). That is, however, subject to section 139(4), namely that the section does not apply to the Secretary of State or NHS Trusts.[26] Whether an act (or omission) was done in bad faith or without reasonable care, does not preclude public law applications for judicial review or habeas corpus.[27] That being said, in *R (Wilkinson) v RMO Broadmoor Hospital*[28] the Court of Appeal suggested that a claim for damages under section 7 of the Human Rights Act 1998 would probably require leave. If leave is not obtained then no claim can proceed and any proceedings that have started without leave are a nullity.[29]

8.26   Section 139 does not breach Article 6(1) of the ECHR according to *Seal v Chief Constable of South Wales*[30] although the dissenting speech of Baroness Hale considered it to be a disproportionate interference with a right of access to the Court in the absence of evidence that the person was vexatious.[31] It is probable that the limits imposed by section 139 are based on an outdated and discriminatory view of those who are subject to the MHA. It is likely that a challenge on those grounds in the ECtHR (or possibly domestically) may succeed.

---

[26]   See the list in full at s 139(4).
[27]   See *R(W) v Doncaster MBC* [2003] EWHC 192 (Admin) Stanley Burnton, J.
[28]   [2001] EWCA Civ 1545.
[29]   See *Seal v Chief Constable of South Wales* [2007] UKHL 31.
[30]   *Seal* at [20].
[31]   See also *Salontaji-Drobnjak v Serbia* (ECtHR) 36500/05.

The hospital managers and nearest relatives

8.27   The hospital managers have the central role in reviewing the admission and continued detention of a patient under the MHA and have the power to discharge a patient. The hospital managers exercise a public function and their decisions are amenable to judicial review.

8.28   The duties of the hospital managers in relation to the admission of patients under section are best outlined in the Code of Practice at Chapter 13.[32] The admission documents must be delivered to a person who is authorised by the hospital managers to receive them (13.4), those completing the documents (the AMHP) must take care to comply with the requirements of the Act and those acting on the authority of the documents (the Hospital Managers and those detaining the patient) should make sure they are in proper form. There is a distinction between receipt and scrutiny (13.6), the latter 'involves more detailed checking for omissions, errors and other defects and, where permitted, taking action to have the documents rectified after they have already been acted upon'.[33] There is an obligation on the person receiving the documents to go through the documents with the AMHP to check their accuracy (13.9). Also at 13.12 is a requirement that: 'Documents should be scrutinised for accuracy and completeness and to check whether they do not reveal any failure to comply with the procedural requirements of the Act in respect of applications for detention. Medical recommendations should also be scrutinised by someone with appropriate clinical expertise to check that the reasons given appear sufficient to support the conclusions stated in them.'

8.29   The Managers are entitled to detain a patient once the admission documents appear to be in order or, to use the words of section 6(3) of the MHA the application 'appears to be duly made'. The MHT does not adjudicate on the validity of admission. The only way to challenge the validity of admission is by way of JR or by an application for habeas corpus. The status of a flawed admission under section from the date of admission until a Court adjudicates that it was flawed is still uncertain. In *R v Managers of South Western Hospital, ex p M*[34] the Court ruled that the admission was lawful unless and until overturned by the Court.

8.30   The Court reached the opposite conclusion in *Re S-C (Mental Patient: Habeas Corpus)*.[35] There the Court of Appeal made it clear that from the date of admission to the finding that the admission (and continued detention was unlawful) the detention was unlawful. What section 6(3) (particularly when read in conjunction with section 139) appears to do is provide a defence to those who detain a patient wrongly but in good faith.[36]

8.31   This issue has recently been considered by the High Court in *TTM v Hackney LBC*.[37] The AMHP who made the application for admission failed to notify the hospital managers that the patient's NR had objected to his admission. This was an innocent mistake. She honestly believed that the NR's objection had been lifted, but it had not. This rendered the admission unlawful under section 11(4) of the MHA. The

---

[32]   Entitled 'Receipt and Scrutiny Of Documents'.
[33]   Section 15 of the MHA allows rectification in certain circumstances.
[34]   [1993] QB 683.
[35]   [1996] QB 599 (CA).
[36]   See *Principles of Mental Health Law and Policy* – Gostin etc (Oxford 2010) at 12.136.
[37]   [2010] EWHC 1349 (Admin) Andrew Collins, J at first instance.

brother applied for a writ of habeas corpus, which he obtained and the patient was released. The issue before Collins, J[38] was whether TTM could pursue a claim for damages for breaches of his Article 5(5) and 8 rights? He also claimed that the Court should declare section 139(2)[39] and section 6(3) incompatible with the ECHR. The claimant argued that the hospital managers had a duty to scrutinise the AMHP's application and they failed to do so. At the earlier hearing Burton, J had concluded that the AMHP had made an 'honest mistake' and that the NR's objection had been withdrawn. Collins, J went on:

> 'Lawfulness of detention, as it seems to me, does not depend on whether the AMHP reasonably believes that there is no objection but on whether in fact there was no objection. That is what has to be decided if there is an issue raised. Compensation should only follow (subject to the ECHR claim …) if there is negligence or bad faith.'[40]

8.32   The Judge concluded that on the findings made by Burton J, there was no evidence of negligence or bad faith. Since there was no reasonable prospect of success the Judge declined to give leave for the claim, under section 139(2) (considered above).The Judge then went on to consider whether there was a claim for damages for breach of Articles 5 and 8 of the ECHR?[41] The Judge thought that the critical question was whether detention is regarded in domestic law as lawful until the decision granting habeas corpus is made and the patient is discharged from the section 3 order? This raises the issue whether an administrative decision which was found to have been unlawful is to be regarded as void ab initio or voidable so that it has effect until set-aside? The Judge rejected Lord Irvine, LC's view[42] that when delegated legislation or administrative action is pronounced unlawful it must be recognised as never having had any effect at all. In *S-C* the Court of Appeal concluded that the detention was to be regarded as unlawful. However, Collins, J then considered what that finding actually meant. He relied on *R v Central London County Court, ex P London*,[43] a case about displacement of the nearest relative in which the Court of Appeal was concerned with whether unlawfulness of the administrative act should be regarded as prospective or retrospective. In *ex P London* the Court of Appeal concluded that detention was lawful (until found to be otherwise) but invalid. Collins, J in TTM reached the same conclusion.

8.33   TTM has now been considered by the Court of Appeal. The Court re-iterated that SC was authority for three propositions: (1) that the Hospital acted lawfully by reason of s 6(3) (because the application appeared to be properly made); (2) this, however, did not 'clothe the conduct of the AMHP in lawfulness'; and (3) the patient's detention was unlawful throughout.[44] Furthermore, the patient was deprived of his liberty as a direct consequence of AMHP's unlawful act in breach of s 11(4) of the MHA. Section 139(1) does not prevent the AMHP's conduct from being unlawful. What it does is to limit the civil liability of the AMHP (and the local authority) to cases where the act was done in bad faith or without reasonable care. The Court of Appeal read down s 139 to permit a claim for compensation in TTM. Although TTM was decided on the basis of a breach of s 11(4), the application went ahead where there was a known objection from the NR, the Court also considered the provisions of s 12(2) of the MHA.

---

[38]   The patient's release had been granted at an earlier hearing by Burton, J.
[39]   Considered above.
[40]   TTM [37].
[41]   A claim brought under s 7 of the Human Rights Act 1998.
[42]   *Boddington v British Transport Police* [1998] 2 All ER 203–2210G.
[43]   [1999] QB 1260.
[44]   *TTM v Hackney LBC, East London NHS Foundation Trust and Secretary of State for Health* [2011] EWCA Civ. 4 at [56] per Toulson LJ.

The word 'practicable' should be construed with sufficient elasticity to account for situations where a s 3 application is made as a matter of urgency.[45] Furthermore, the Court considered the two different types of breaches of procedural requirements in the case. First, there are breaches of procedural requirements which go to jurisdiction. In TTM the s 11(4) breach went to jurisdiction. The objection of the NR meant that the AMHP had no jurisdiction to make the application. Secondly, the breach of procedural requirements in the exercise of a jurisdiction. The breach of s 12(2) (if there was one) came under this category, because it went to the form of evidence needed to support an application.[46] Although the Court did not wish to give a firm decision on the point (in the absence of detailed argument), it made it clear that a breach of the latter type of procedural requirement (ie in exercising of a jurisdiction) would not make the outcome unlawful provided 'there was no breach of the underlying purpose behind' in this case s 12(2) of the MHA.

8.34   Since the legality of a patient's status under the MHA depends on his satisfying the criteria for admission, one of the RC's duties is to review that status on a continuous basis. Once he or she is of the view that those conditions are not met (for whatever reason) the RC has must discharge the patient from section: see *R v Drew*[47] and the Code of Practice[48] and section 23 of the MHA. If the RC reaches the conclusion that the patient no longer qualifies for detention (or guardianship or CTO) but does not discharge him, it is unlawful for that patient to remain under that status. If the RC offers such an opinion to the FTT on review, it is submitted the FTT is obliged to ensure that the patient is discharged, either by informing the RC that continued detention is unlawful, or by ordering discharge under section 72. Any Hospital policy that fetters the RC's ability to discharge a patient is also unlawful. These cases should be challenged by judicial review or habeas corpus.

8.35   A patient may apply to the hospital managers for discharge from detention or CTO (also under section 23(2) of the MHA). That power may be exercised by 'three or more members of that authority, trust, board or body authorised by them' or 'by three or more members of a committee or sub-committee which has been authorised by them' (section 23(4) and (5)). The managers' duties are listed in the Code of Practice at Chapter 30. The managers may review the detention of a detained patient at any time. They must review when the RC seeks to renew detention under section 20. They should review when a request is made by a patient or when the RC makes a report to them under section 25 barring discharge by the NR. The reviews must be conducted in a fair and reasonable manner. The Code requires them (at 31.23–31.32) to adopt a fair procedure, not make irrational decisions and to adhere to the MHA and Human Rights Act. The panel must have before it sufficient information to be able to make a decision including past history and future care plans. The patient must be provided with disclosure of evidence in advance, his NR informed, and to be legally represented. The managers are subject to judicial review where there is a breach of procedural or natural justice, or where there is a clear breach of the law.

---

[45]   *TTM* at [81].
[46]   [84] and [85].
[47]   [2003] UKHL 25.
[48]   Para 29.16.

TREATMENT AND THE CONTINUING DUTY TO REVIEW

8.36   The MHA also codifies compulsory treatment. Part 4 of the MHA and Chapters 23 and 24 of the Code of Practice are where that code is found. Compulsory treatment engages a number of Convention rights and the statutory code, notably Article 3 (the prohibition of torture and inhuman and degrading treatment) and Article 8 (privacy and family life). Article 8(2) prohibits public authorities interfering with family rights except in accordance with the law and as is necessary in a democratic society, the protection of health or for the protection of the rights and freedom of others. In order to be in accordance with the law there must not only be a relevant domestic law but it must be accessible and its consequences and effects foreseeable (with legal advice if necessary). In order to fulfil that role the MHA specifies rules and procedures that must be followed. The limited scope of this chapter means that these rules shall not be gone through in detail here. However, if the rules are not followed then the treatment is likely to be unlawful and challengeable by way of judicial review and/or actions for damages.

8.37   It is important to remember that where detention is under the treatment sections of the MHA those detaining must provide a therapeutic environment. An anti-therapeutic environment may amount to arbitrary detention. In the Code of Practice at 3.130 this point is made: since detention is grounded in the patient's unsoundness of mind, its therapeutic purpose can only be achieved in 'a place equipped to provide minimally adequate care and treatment'. This must be born in mind by anyone whose role is to review detention – the RC, the Hospital Managers, the Tribunal or the High Court.

8.38   The provision of 'urgent treatment' is the subject of section 62 of the MHA.[49] This provides that the patient's consent shall not be required for any treatment given to him for the mental disorder from which he is suffering if giving by or under the direction of the approved clinician in charge of his treatment unless sections 57, 58 or 58A apply. Sections 57 and 58 outline the second opinion procedure. The first category (section 57) concerns psychosurgery and the surgical implantation of hormones to reduce sex drive. In the case of any patient for whom this treatment is contemplated there must be valid consent (certified by a panel of three appointed by the Mental Health Act Commission – now Care Quality Commission) and it must be approved by a member of the second opinion panel (known as Second Opinion Appointed Doctor – or SOAD).[50] A decision not to authorise treatment is susceptible to judicial review.[51]

8.39   Sections 58 and 58A concern the administration of medicines for mental disorder and electro-convulsive therapy (ECT) respectively. Section 58 only applies to patients who are detained. It is only required once a period of three months has passed from the first day on which any form of medication for mental disorder has passed. Here treatment may be administered with the patient's consent, or without his consent, provided it is authorised by a Second Opinion Appointed Doctor (SOAD). A RC must always seek the patient's consent, however, even if he is entitled to treat the patient without consent with a SOAD's authorisation. Section 58A outlines the role of the SOAD, and there is no three month period during which the treatment can be administered without the use of section 58A.

---

[49]   The definition of 'urgent' is encapsulated in s 62(1)(a) to (d).
[50]   Section 58(3).
[51]   *R v Mental health Act Commission, ex p W* (1988) 9 BMLR 77.

8.40   To what extent can treatment plans for those detained under the MHA, including those certified by SOADs be challenged? A challenge to the treatment given under section 62 (or the other sections) may be challenged on the grounds that it was not for the patient's mental disorder – ie the core purpose of the treatment is not concerned with the mental disorder.[52] Judicial review proceedings are not ideally suited to deal with cases in which there are genuine disputes over diagnosis and treatment and where oral evidence is required. However, following *R (Wilkinson) v Responsible Medical Officer for Broadmoor Hospital*,[53] it is recognised that the Court on a judicial review may go beyond a *Wednesbury* exercise and decide the matter itself having heard all the evidence. However, the Court of Appeal has sounded a note of caution here, and many of the issues that will come before the High Court on treatment challenges can be considered without the need for live evidence,[54] and the High Court has gone further in suggesting that live evidence will only be required in a 'rare case'.[55] If one is seeking to challenge the decision to administer treatment without consent to a detained patient, those seeking to administer the treatment have to 'convincingly show' the Court that the treatment is both medically necessary and in the patient's best interests.[56] With such a high standard it is submitted that it is usual for this to be satisfied (or not) on paper. The whole purpose of the SOAD procedure is to ensure that compulsory treatment is only administered if there is a convincing case of medical necessity, and that it is in the patient's best interests. The SOAD's decision, therefore can be reviewed, but the reviewing Court's primary function is not to put itself in the shoes of the SOAD.

8.41   If the subject of the challenge is, in fact, the patient's detention in a hospital, rather than the proposed treatment regime then the Court of Appeal has stated that such a challenge is one that ought to be referred to the FTT in the first instance.[57]

8.42   In the case of patients subject to restrictions the Ministry of Justice has to consent to decisions that the RC would make in relation to patients not subject to such restrictions, such as leave and discharge. The Secretary of State's decisions in this area are susceptible to JR and challenge in the FTT.

TREATMENT IN THE COMMUNITY

8.43   When the MHA 1983 was amended by the MHA 2007 a new form of community treatment was introduced. Sections 17A–G now contain the regime for supervised community treatment (SCT) or community treatment orders (CTO). These join the other two orders available for non-restricted mental health patients, namely guardianship (section 7) and leave of absence (section 17).

8.44   Prior to November 2008, it was common for RCs to allow detained patients ever increasing periods of section 17 leave.[58] The alternative under the old section 25A was discharge under supervision. The new provisions under section 17A–G create an

---

[52]   See *B v Croydon HA* [1995] 2 WLR 294, and *GJ v The Foundation Trust (etc)* [2009] EWHC 2972 (Fam) [2010] 3 WLR 840.

[53]   [2001] EWCA Civ 1545.

[54]   See *R (N) v M* [2002] EWCA Civ 1789.

[55]   *R (Taylor) v Haydn-Smith etc* [2005] EWHC 1668 (Admin) Andrew Collins, J. See also *M v South West Hospital & St Georges Mental Health Trust* [2008] EWCA Civ 1112.

[56]   See *R (n) v M*, applying the ECtHR decision in *Herczegfalvy v Austria* (1992) 15 EHRR 437.

[57]   *R (B) v Dr SS (RMO) SOAD & SSH* [2006] EWCA Civ 28.

[58]   See *B v Barking, Havering and Brentwood Community Healthcare NHS Trust* [1999] 1 FLR 106, CA and *R (CS) v MHRT* [2004] EWHC 2958 (Pitchford, J).

alternative whereby the patient is discharged from liability to be detained, with conditions attached, and with the power of recall without the need to go through the admission process under section 11 first. In order for a patient to be subject to a CTO he must already be detained under either section 3 (including where he is on section 17 leave), section 37, section 47 or section 48. The RC has a discretion whether to grant section 17 leave or a CTO, provided the relevant criteria under section 17A(5) are met. If the RC considers it appropriate to grant ever increasing periods of leave he may do so. If he wishes to extend the period of leave beyond one week the only requirement that the Act imposes on the RC is to consider whether the patient should be dealt with by way of a CTO.[59] Provided he has considered the option, the granting of longer term leave is lawful.

8.45 The available statistics suggest that CTOs are more popular than was envisaged. The number of CTOs in the year 2009/10 was 4,107. In the 17 months from the date section 17A came into force (November 2008) there were 6,241 CTOs created, which is 367 per month.[60] The benefits of the CTO over leave are fairly clear. In order for the CTO to be granted there are rigorous criteria to be applied. The patient on a CTO is entitled to section 117 funding. He is no longer liable to be detained, which means that unlike the case of section 17 leave, the patient cannot be deprived of his liberty. Under section 17E(2) he may only be recalled if he breaches the mandatory conditions and requires medical treatment in Hospital for his mental condition, failing which there would be a risk to his health or safety or another person. Such a recall must be based on objective medical evidence.

8.46 Challenges to a CTO may be made through the Managers or the Tribunal. The Tribunal's powers are limited to discharging the CTO or making non-statutory recommendations to vary or add conditions.[61] Likewise the Tribunal may not discharge a patient onto a CTO, but may make a recommendation for the RC to do so.[62] Legal challenge to conditions attached to a CTO where the existence of the CTO itself is not challenged, must be by way of judicial review. The two mandatory conditions are that the patient must make himself available for examination when it is time to renew the CTO (under section 20A), and when it is proposed that a certificate under Part 4A of the MHA is to be given (in respect of treatment – see below).[63] Those conditions cannot be challenged. Other conditions maybe specified by the RC only with agreement from the AMHP and only then if those conditions are 'necessary or appropriate for one or more of the following purposes: (a) ensuring that the patient receives medical treatment; (b) preventing risk of harm to the patient's health or safety; (c) protecting other persons'.[64] Unless the conditions can be justified by the RC on those grounds, they can be challenged. Note, however, the threshold is low: the condition need only be necessary *or* appropriate.

8.47 One issue that has arisen at first instance in the FTT is where the actual working of the CTO involves a deprivation of the patient's liberty. The FTT has no jurisdiction to vary the conditions of the CTO, so it cannot remove the condition that amounts to a deprivation of liberty. It could discharge the CTO if it considers that section 72(1)(c) is

---

[59] Section 17(2A) and (2B).
[60] These figures as well as commentary on the operation of the MHA are printed in the Care Quality Commission's Monitoring the Use of the MHA in 2009/10 (2010).
[61] MHA, s 72(1)(c).
[62] MHA, s 72(3A).
[63] MHA, s 17B(3)(a) and (b).
[64] MHA, s 17B(2).

not satisfied – because the power of recall is unnecessary (as the patient is already detained), but that may place the patient and the public at risk. It would seem appropriate in such circumstances for the RC and the responsible local authority to seek to formalise the deprivation of liberty through the Mental Capacity Act (assuming the patient lacks capacity) either by way of a welfare order of the Court of Protection or, if appropriate, using the DOLS. Other conditions the author has encountered have included 'not to drink excessive amounts of alcohol', which the FTT cannot strike down, but which was removed when its uncertainty was pointed out. Other conditions may be challenged on human rights grounds. For instance, a CTO that prevents a patient from entering certain geographical areas, or have contact with certain people may be challenged on conventions grounds, notably Articles 8, 11, and generally 14.

8.48   Guardianship under sections 7 and 8 of the MHA is another option for community care. There is no right to community care services under the National Health Service and Community Care Act 1990. The important issue concerning guardianship now is the extent to which it should be chosen instead of the orders that can be used under the Mental Capacity Act 2005 and the DOLS. Obviously, for a patient to be entered into guardianship he does not have to lack capacity, although many do. However, guardianship does not expressly authorise that a patient may be deprived of his liberty, whereas the MCA/DOLS can. This issue is considered in the section on the MCA.

THE TRIBUNAL

8.49   Before the MHA 2007 amendments the Mental Health Review Tribunal (MHRT) dealt with applications and references by and in respect of patients under the provisions of the Act.[65] The MHRT could be challenged either by JR or by way of case stated under the old section 78(8).[66] Now the role of the MHRT falls within the new Tribunal system. First instance applications[67] are now made to the FTT (Mental Health) which is part of the Health, Education and Social Care Chamber (HESC).

8.50   The FTT has almost entirely the same constitution and function as the old MHRT and there has been continuity of membership. The procedure in the FTT is governed by the Tribunal Procedure Rules.[68] Appeals are now made to the Upper Tribunal (Administrative Appeals Chamber) (UT) on a point of law other than in the case of an 'excluded decision'.[69] The UT also has a statutory power to JR cases from the FTT.[70] The rules also provide for the FTT and UT to review their own decisions.[71] In the HESC Tribunal Rules the FTT has a number of powers which are designed to prevent unnecessary appeals. Clerical mistakes, accidental slips or omissions may at any time be corrected under rule 44. If it is in the interests of justice to do so and there have been the irregularities listed in rule 45(2)(a) to (c), the FTT may set-aside a decision which disposes of the proceedings. When an application is made to appeal a decision of the FTT under rule 46, rule 47 provides that the FTT 'must first consider' whether 'taking into account the overriding objective ... whether to review the decision in

---

[65]   The old s 65(1) and (1A).
[66]   Now repealed.
[67]   Under s 66 MHA.
[68]   Full title: Tribunal Procedure (First-tier Tribunal) (Health, Education and Social Care Chamber) 2008 (SI 2008/2699). These are printed in Jones.
[69]   Section 11 of the Tribunals Courts and Enforcement Act 2007.
[70]   Section 15 of the TCEA.
[71]   Sections 9 and 10 of the TCEA respectively.

accordance with rule 49'. Rule 49 provides that the Tribunal may only undertake a review of a decision in a mental health case if 'it is satisfied that there was an error of law in the decision'. Section 11(5) TCEA defines 'excluded decisions' that are relevant to the mental health jurisdiction as:

'(d) a decision of the First-tier Tribunal under section 9 – (i) to review or not to review, an earlier decision of the tribunal, (ii) to take no action, or not to take any particular action, in the light of a review of an earlier decision of the tribunal, (iii) to set aside an earlier decision of the tribunal or (iv) to refer, or not to refer, a matter to the Upper Tribunal.'

8.51 Since the UT cannot hear an appeal against an excluded decision, an application may be made to JR such a decision to the UT (or the High Court). In *R(RB) v The First-tier Tribunal*[72] the decision of the FTT (in the form of one of its senior judges) to set aside a decision of the FTT on review, and to remit it to a freshly constituted FTT, was an excluded decision. It was challenged by way of judicial review to the UT. The UT quashed the judge's decision on review, and set out some guidance as to how and when the power of review can properly be used. At paragraph 31 the UT said:

'In the present case the question we ask ourselves is whether the reviewing judge properly directed himself as to the law governing the power of review. In particular, did he focus upon the need to make sure that the review did not usurp the Upper Tribunal's function in determining appeals on contentious points of law? This was a case where law had to be particularly clear if the review was to be justified.'

8.52 It is clear that in mental health cases where the liberty of the individual is at stake on the one hand, and there is a need to protect the individual and the wider public on the other, that to review a decision unless it is clearly wrong is a serious move. Furthermore, the FTT is an expert tribunal including not only a legally qualified judge, but also a Consultant Psychiatrist and a third member who will usually have expertise in the mental health field (often a nurse, a social worker/AMHP, or psychologist) to set aside any decision which turns on an assessment of facts, technical evidence or an evaluation of risk is likely to be justified only when clearly wrong.

8.53 The *RB* case concerned a restricted patient detained under sections 37/41 in a secure psychiatric hospital. He suffered from 'a mental illness in the form of a persistent delusional disorder, which has caused him to be a life-long paedophile attracted to boys aged between approximately 9 and 13 years'. After 13 years of detention those treating him wanted him to be transferred to a care home with a restrictive regime so that he would only be able to leave if escorted. He could not be transferred because the care home was not a hospital in which patients under section could be placed. The MOJ declined to permit him to stay there on extended leave. The only option was a conditional discharge. The MOJ refused to consent to that option, so the matter came before the FTT. The issue the FTT had to decide was whether the restrictions placed upon RB would amount to him being detained/deprived of his liberty and, if so, whether such a 'discharge' was lawful. There were a number of authorities on or around the point which the FTT considered before granting a conditional discharge. The reviewing judge drafted a lengthy written decision in which he reviewed the authorities and found that: (a) the conditions imposed under the proposed conditional discharge would inevitably deprive the patient of his liberty, and the FTT had erred in finding

---

[72]   [2010] UKUT 160 (AAC).

otherwise, and (b) on the authorities his conditional discharge amounted to a transfer between one state of detention and another and was an order the Tribunal could not make.[73]

8.54 Review, other than for obvious errors, is likely to prove difficult in mental health cases. The large majority of cases are essentially matters of fact or a judgment of risk. It is likely that reviews should be granted only where there has been a plain mistake as to the law – such as making an unlawful order, or applying the wrong legal test, or where the written reasons are plainly inadequate, that a review ought to be granted.

The Upper Tribunal

8.55 The Tribunals Courts and Enforcement Act 2007 (TCEA) establishes the new Tribunal system (see Chapter 2, section 3), with the Upper Tribunal being 'a superior Court of record' (section 3(5)). It has the powers to hear appeals from the FTT, and, in doing so, fulfils the function previously carried out by the High Court. Under section 12 of the TCEA if the UT finds that the making of the decision under appeal involved the making of an error on a point of law it 'may' set aside the FTT's decision, in which case it must then either remit the decision to the FTT with directions for its consideration (for instance whether there should be a newly constituted Tribunal, or re-make the decision.[74] If it decides to re-make the decision then, under section 12(4)(a) and (b) the UT may make any decision the FTT could have made and 'make any such findings of fact as it considers appropriate'.

8.56 As we have seen, the UT also has the power to JR decisions of the FTT. When doing so it acts, for all intents and purposes as the High Court, granting such relief as that Court may grant, applying the same principles in both granting relief and permission for relief as the Court would.[75]

8.57 Recently, the status of the UT was considered by the Court of Appeal in *R (Cart) v UT, SSJ and others*,[76] in particular, what was meant by the term 'superior Court of record' and whether the UT was itself amenable to judicial review. What Cart has established is that the UT is part of 'a new Tribunal structure' which (paragraph [42]):

> 'while not an analogue of the High Court, is something greater than the sum of its parts. It represents a newly coherent and comprehensive edifice designed, among other things, to complete the long process of divorcing administrative justice from departmental policy, to ensure the application across the board of proper standards of adjudication, and to provide for the correction of legal error within rather than outside that system.'

8.58 The High Court retains its supervisory jurisdiction but, in view of the new statutory based appeals powers of the UT, that jurisdiction is *pre-Anisminic*.[77] At [36] the Court of Appeal stated:

> 'It seems to us that there is a true jurisprudential difference between an error of law made in the course of an adjudication which a tribunal is authorised to conduct and the conducting

---

[73] As this text is written the UT's decision in the substantive appeal is awaited.
[74] Section 12(2)(a) & (b)(i) and (ii).
[75] Section 15(3), (4) and (5) and s 16.
[76] [2010] EWCA Civ 859.
[77] *Anisminic Ltd v Foreign Compensation Commission* [1969] 2 AC 147.

of an adjudication without lawful authority. Both are justiciable before the UT if committed by the FTT, but if committed by the UT will go uncorrected unless judicial review lies. The same of course is true of errors of law within jurisdiction; but these, in our judgment, reside within the principle that a system of law, which it can guarantee to be fair, cannot guarantee to be infallible. Outright excess of jurisdiction by the UT and denial by it of fundamental justice, should they ever occur, are in a different class: they represent the doing by the UT of something that Parliament cannot possibly have authorised it to do.'

8.59   Interestingly, the position is different in Scotland. In *Eba v Advocate General for Scotland*[78] the Inner House of the Court of Session decided that the UT is susceptible to judicial review in general and not just in a limited, pre-Anisminic sense – although this may have something to do with the different way in which Anisminic has been interpreted and applied by the Scottish courts.[79]

8.60   The status of the UT is relevant where the UT decides not to exercise its own judicial review powers, particularly where a party wishes to challenge an excluded decision. It is also relevant when considering whether the UT is bound by decisions of the High Court, and in particular those from the all but identical pre-TCEA decisions. This has not yet been authoritatively decided.[80] However, there are two lines of argument. The first is that the UT is not of equal status to the High Court.[81] Decisions of the higher courts remain binding on lower courts even where those lower courts are then granted equivalent jurisdiction by statute.[82] Hence, decisions of the High Court on JR and appeals by way of case stated from the MHRT are binding on the UT when exercising identical jurisdiction. The contrary argument is that the UT is now part of a whole new system of administrative justice and it cannot have been the intention of Parliament that the UT is strictly bound by the decisions of the High Court exercising a JR jurisdiction under the old system. In *The Secretary of State for Justice v RB* the UT (with Lord Justice Carnwath, SPT presiding) concluded that the latter was the right approach. The UT is not strictly bound by the decisions made by the High Court when supervising the inferior Tribunals that the UT now supervises.[83]

The First-tier Tribunal

8.61   Since November 2008 applications and references concerning patients subject to the provisions of the MHA have been heard by the FTT, which is part of the Health, Education and Social Care Chamber (HESC). Since the FTT is part of the Tribunal system appeals against its decisions are made to the Upper Tribunal. The constitution of the membership of the FTT is specified in Schedule 2 of the MHA. It is the same as with the old MHRT, namely a legal member (Tribunal Judge), a medically qualified member and another member (previously called a 'lay' member). All are appointed by the Lord Chancellor on the recommendation of the Judicial Appointments Commission.[84] Section 78 MHA enables the Lord Chancellor to make rules in relation

---

[78]   [2010] CSIH 78.

[79]   See para 43 in *Eba*.

[80]   The decision is awaited in *SSJ v RB & Lancashire Care NHS Trust* (the latest incarnation of *R(RB) v FTT*), where this is one of the issues the UT is to decide.

[81]   This is made clear in *Cart*.

[82]   See *Howard de Walden Estates Limited v Aggio* – in particular the Court of Appeal at [2007] EWCA Civ 499 – the Note on Precedent from paragraph [86] onwards – the comments of precedent were not overturned by the House of Lords [2008] UKHL 44.

[83]   [2010] UKUT 454 (AAC), at [40] to [46].

[84]   Schedule 2, para 1 and 1A.

to applications to the FTT, procedure within the FTT and to restrict membership of the FTT in certain cases to appropriately qualified.[85]

8.62   Section 78 must be read in conjunction with the relevant provisions of the TCEA, the Tribunal Rules,[86] and the Code of Practice.[87] The rules introduce into the FTT a more flexible procedure than under the previous MHRT Rules. As with the Civil Procedure Rules, the Tribunal is required to ensure that it complies with the overriding objective,[88] as well as requiring parties to co-operate with the Tribunal to achieve the same end.[89] To this end the FTT has significant case management powers under rule 4 designed to ensure the efficient running of cases, to minimise delays and to ensure that adjournments are made only where it is appropriate to do so. At the beginning of 2009, a number of full-time, salaried Tribunal Judges were appointed. Previously, the MHRT Judiciary had been almost entirely made up of part-time legal members. The FTT judiciary is still predominantly part-time (or fee paid) deputy Tribunal Judges. The salaried (full-time) Tribunal Judges are now given a case management role and are usually called upon to make decisions over disclosure of documentation, vacating hearings, and convening hearings to determine pre-hearing issues. The Tribunal Judges also tend to consider whether FTT decisions should be reviewed and whether permission ought to be given for an appeal to the UT.

8.63   This is a publication on the subject of judicial review and since the FTT has been integrated into the Tribunal system, judicial review is no longer the automatic route to appeal. Of course, the mental health cases prior to 2008 all started as High Court challenges to MHRT decisions. In the future similar issues will be determined by the UT as appeals or, sometimes, under its JR jurisdiction. It is yet to be seen the extent to which the UT considers itself bound by pre-2008 High Court decisions. It is not within the subject matter of this publication to outline the FTT procedures and case law save where JR is relevant.

8.64   One of the Article 5 requirements that was made clear by litigation in the early 2000s was the need for timely hearings of applications under the MHA. In *R(C) v MHRT*[90] the MHRT's policy to list cases eight weeks from the date of the application was held to be a breach of Article 5(4). In *R (K) v MHRT*[91] a delay in the hearing of a patient's case was found to be the responsibility of the Government (due to the inadequate funding of staff) and damages were awarded. This delay has been held to include the appellate process.[92] Such delays would still come within the jurisdiction of the High Court and would be subject to JR in that Administrative Court.

8.65   The FTT decisions that are subject to JR are the 'excluded decisions'. These are defined above. The first case that came before the UT from the mental health jurisdiction considered whether the decision it was asked to consider was an excluded decision, or not? The case, *Dorset Healthcare NHS Foundation Trust v MH*[93] concerned

---

[85]   Most notably this applies to the consideration of restricted cases in which the Tribunal Judge is usually a serving or retired Circuit Judge or a Recorder with considerable criminal experience and usually a QC.
[86]   The Tribunal Procedure (First-tier Tribunal) (Health, Education and Social Care Chamber) Rules 2008 (SI 2008/2699).
[87]   Published pursuant to s 118 MHA. The relevant chapter being 32.
[88]   Outlined in detail in r 2.
[89]   Rule 2(4).
[90]   [2002] 1 WLR 176 (CA).
[91]   [2002] EWHC 639 (Admin) Stanley Burnton, J.
[92]   See *Reid v UK* (2003) 37 EHRR 9.
[93]   [2009] UKUT 4 (AAC).

a common problem for Tribunals, namely the disclosure of information to patients, and their representatives. The Trust agreed to disclose all the patient's records to the patient's solicitor save for a small number of documents which were withheld. The patient's solicitor made an application to the FTT for disclosure of all the material. The application was heard by Deputy Regional Tribunal Judge (sitting on his own) and granted the patient access to her own records, including any third party material, subject to the Trust opposing disclosure on the grounds outlined in rule 14 of the Tribunal Rules.[94] The decision was made without the DTJ seeking representations from the Trust. The Trust did not avail itself of the mechanism provided in the rules to challenge such a direction.[95] The Trust, instead, applied for a review under section 9 of the TCEA. The matter had already been set down before a fully constituted FTT for a hearing of the patient's application. The FTT considered reviewing the DTJ's decision but, instead, decided not to do so because '… the direction was made competently and by the Tribunal at a level of authority equivalent to (or greater than) that which we enjoy today'.[96] The FTT decided that the matter ought to be referred to the UT for guidance on disclosure. The UT raised the issue as to whether it had jurisdiction (qua appeal court) to hear the case. The UT decided that section 11 of the TCEA is not to be construed as excluding an interlocutory decision to grant (or not grant) disclosure. In any event, the UT also stated that if a decision of the FTT is not within the scope of section 11, either because it is not a decision or it is an excluded decision, the UT is able to hear a challenge to that decision through its judicial review powers. This is what it did in *R (RB) v The First-tier Tribunal*[97] as discussed above. As outlined above, the decision to review a case and to set it aside is not appealable but can be challenged on public law grounds in the UT by way of judicial review. The question that then arises is what happens if the UT decides it will not grant permission for JR or, in the case of an appeal, it will not grant permission to appeal. These are both excluded decisions under section 13(1) and (8) of the TCEA. On the basis of the decision in *R (Cart)*[98] these cannot be challenged by way of judicial review in the High Court (unless the cases is a Scottish case, when it appears it can).

8.66 Judicial review is still relevant to the FTT process. In the case of CTO, the FTT has no power to vary the conditions attached. Under section 17B of the MHA conditions may be attached by the RC (with the agreement of the AMHP) if he thinks them 'necessary *or* appropriate' either to ensure that the patient receives treatment (my emphasis), to prevent the risk of harm to the patient's health or safety, or for the protection of other persons.[99] The FTT has the power to discharge a patient from a CTO under section 72(1)(c). Under section 72(3A) the FTT is not required to discharge a patient detained under an assessment or treatment order if it considers that the patient could or should be the subject to a CTO, but it may recommend that the RC consider making a CTO and can reconvene at a later date to consider the patient's case further if no CTO has been made. What the FTT cannot do is to make a CTO. It is also not able to vary conditions attached to CTO, whether by revoking or adding conditions. Ultimately, a patient may challenge the conditions attached to his CTO by way of judicial review. It is submitted that it will be difficult to overcome the statutory language outlined above – 'necessary *or* appropriate' – unless the condition is plainly unnecessary

---

94   Under r 14(2) the FTT may prohibit disclosure of documents or information to a person: (a) such disclosure is likely to cause that person or some other person serious harm, and (b) having regard to the interests of justice the FTT thinks it is proportionate to do so.

95   Under r 6(5) the Trust may have challenged that decision before the hearing.

96   This the UT described (rather charitably) as 'timid' see [19].

97   Ibid [2010] UKUT 160 (AAC).

98   [2010] EWCA Civ 859.

99   Section 17B(2)(a) to (c).

and inappropriate. From the author's experience a condition 'not to drink excessive amounts of alcohol' appears impossible to uphold due to its uncertainty. However, faced with such a condition the FTT can do nothing other than discharge the patient (which is likely to be contrary to the patient's best interests) or include a strong comment in the written reasons as to why the condition should be removed or modified ('not to consume alcohol' would be certain, if difficult to police). It is also clear that a CTO does not provide lawful authority to deprive a patient of his liberty. It is submitted that conditions purporting to do so can be challenged by judicial review. In the case of a patient who lacks capacity issues concerning deprivation of liberty could be dealt with in conjunction with a CTO either in the Court of Protection by way of a welfare order, or, where the patient resides at a care home by way of the DOLS.[100]

8.67   The other area in which judicial review still plays an important part in mental health law, and, in particular, in relation to Tribunal proceedings is in the area of aftercare. The subject of the provision of community care and services, as well as their funding, is dealt with elsewhere in this publication. The following is a summary of the relevance of that subject to mental health law. The Code of Practice[101] outlines the purpose of aftercare:

> '[27.5] After-care is a vital component in patients' overall treatment and care. As well as meeting their immediate needs for health and social care, after-care should aim to support them in regaining or enhancing their skills, or learning new skills in order to cope with life outside hospital.'

8.68   Section 117 of the MHA imposes a duty on certain bodies to provide after-care services free of charge to certain categories of mentally disordered persons who have been detained under the Act. Those bodies are the PCT or Local Health Board and LSSA in conjunction with any relevant voluntary agencies. The persons to whom the section applies are:

> 'those who are detained under section 3 ... or admitted to hospital in pursuance of a hospital order made under section 37 ... or transferred to a hospital in pursuance of a hospital direction made under section 45A above or a transfer direction made under section 47 or 48 ... and then cease to be detained and (whether or not immediately after so ceasing) leave hospital.'

8.69   The duty falls upon the Local Social Services Authority (LSSA)/health body responsible for the area in which the person concerned is resident or to which he is sent on discharge by the hospital in which he is detained.[102] The duty only crystallises when the patient ceases to be detained. Consequently, a patient subject to section 3 is entitled to section 117 aftercare if he is no longer actually detained but only liable to be detained. If the patient is granted extensive leave of absence under section 17, the duties to provide aftercare services under section 117 arises. Long term leave is less likely now that the CTO regime is in force. Those subject to CTO are entitled to section 117 aftercare. Case law has confirmed that although the NHS body has the power to take preparatory steps in anticipation of discharge from detention[103] there is no duty to do so.[104]

---

[100]   If the patient resides in a hospital he is likely not to be eligible for DOLS or the MCA: see *GJ (or J) v Foundation Trust*.
[101]   Chapter 27.
[102]   Section 117(3).
[103]   *R(K) v Camden & Islington HA* [2001] EWCA Civ 240.
[104]   *R(B) v Camden LBC* [2005] EWHC 1366 (Admin) Stanley Burnton, J.

8.70 However, in *W v Doncaster MBC*[105] the Court of Appeal recognised that although the duty did not arise until discharge from detention in reality it was 'reasonable to suppose' that the relevant authorities had in place procedures to help cope with situations where they become responsible upon a patient's discharge. In *R v MHRT, ex p Hall*[106] the Court of Appeal considered the Code of Practice and stated that it suggested that at 'at least in embryo, plans should be available before a Tribunal takes place'.

8.71 In the present Code under the section After-care Planning (at 27.7) it states:

> 'When considering relevant patients' case, the Tribunal and hospital managers will expect to be provided with information from the professionals concerned on what after-care arrangements might be made for them under section 117 if they were to be discharged. Some discussion of after-care needs, involving LSSAs and other relevant agencies, should take place in advance of the hearing.'

8.72 If, at the time of a Tribunal hearing, there is insufficient information before it for the Tribunal to consider the issue of aftercare, then the Tribunal ought to adjourn and make directions for such information to be provided at the adjourned hearing.[107] This must not be done where the issue of aftercare is academic – ie where a discharge is unlikely whatever package maybe in place. A failure on the part of a Health Authority to use 'reasonable endeavours' to fulfil conditions imposed by the MHRT would probably be regarded as an unlawful use of its discretion; but a discretion it is nevertheless. The services provided under section 117 are community care services. If a person is in need of such services then an obligation falls on a LSSA to assess that person's needs.[108] Following the result of the assessments the LSSA must under section 47(1)(b) consider whether the person's needs call for the provision of community care services. It would seem that in the case of a patient discharged under section 117, and who has a right to be provided with services, the outcome of the section 47 assessment must always be that he needs to be provided with such services. However, the LSSA retains discretion to decide the level of those services[109]. Consequently, although there is an absolute duty under s.117 to fund aftercare there is no absolute duty to fund any and all conditions that the Tribunal may impose[110]. Note also that patients discharged into aftercare, including those subject to CTOs, will be subject to the Care Programme Approach.

8.73 There are practical problems for Tribunals associated with a failure of those providing and/or funding aftercare services and which frustrate a patient's discharge. In *R(H) v Home Secretary*[111] an MHRT granted a conditional discharge to a patient detained under section 37, with restrictions under section 41, having concluded that he was no longer suffering from a mental illness. The hearing was adjourned so that the health authority could arrange services under section 117. This it was unable to do. When it reconvened, the Tribunal made the same order but deferred the discharge until the package was in place. Much later the Home Secretary referred the patient (who was still detained) to the MHRT (under section 71). The MHRT found that the patient did suffer from a mental illness which required his detention. The patient brought JR

---

[105] [2004] EWCA Civ 378.
[106] (1999) 2 CCLR 383 and [1999] MHLR 63 (CA).
[107] *R (Ashworth Hospital) v MHRT and R(H) v Ashworth Hospital* [2002] EWCA Civ 923.
[108] This arises under ss 46 and 47 of the National Health Service and Community Care Act 1990.
[109] See the discussion on this subject in Jones Mental Health Act Manual (11th edn) at 1-1074.
[110] *R v Camden and Islington Health Authority, ex p K* [2001] EWCA Civ 240, per Lord Phillips, MR.
[111] [2003] UKHL 59 and [2004] 2 AC 253.

proceedings. The House of Lords found that the lack of power of the MHRT to require a package to be put in place did not invalidate its coercive powers and was not a breach of Article 5(4). The proper approach where it decided to discharge if, and only if certain measures were in place, was to defer discharge and if, when it reconvened, those conditions had not been put in place, the MHRT should reconsider its decision and treat the original decision as provisional.

THE MENTAL CAPACITY ACT AND THE COURT OF PROTECTION

8.74   The Mental Capacity Act 2005 which came into force on 1 October 2007 was the culmination of a long period of discussion and debate about the reform of the law relating to those unable to make decisions. The detail of that discussion is beyond the scope of this publication. The purpose of the Act is to empower people who lack mental capacity to 'make decisions for themselves wherever possible' and to protect them 'by providing a flexible framework that places individuals at the very heart of the decision making process'. The intention is to 'ensure that they participate as much as possible in any decision made on their behalf, and that they are made in their best interests'. Also it 'allows people to plan ahead for a time in the future when they might lack the capacity' to make those decisions.[112] The main planks of the new code are: (1) a statutory presumption of capacity which must be rebutted on the balance of probabilities by those challenging capacity: section 1(2); (2) placing on a statutory footing the time and issue specific nature of capacity: section 2(1); (3) placing the functional test for capacity and the need to assist the person to make the decision so far as practicable before deciding that he lacks capacity (providing information, explaining, deferring the decision until the person is likely to be able to make the decision): section 3; (4) any decision made on behalf of a person lacking capacity must be in his best interests: section 1(5) and section 4; (5) providing a defence for those who act in connection with care or treatment and who otherwise would commit an assault or other tort on a person, if they have acted in accordance with the Act: sections 5 and 6.

8.75   The Act also places the 'advance decision' (AD) on a statutory footing. Section 24 defines the AD as 'a decision made by a person, after he has reached 18 and when he has capacity to do so, that if: (a) at a later time and in such circumstances as he may specify, a specified treatment is proposed to be carried out or continued by a person providing health care for him, and (b) at that time he lacks capacity to consent to the carrying out or continuation of the treatment, the specified treatment is not to be carried out or continued'. New methods for delegated decision-making are also created by the Act. The lasting power of attorney (LPA) replaces the enduring power or attorney (EPA):[113] sections 9 to 13. LPAs have a greater scope than their predecessor, whereas the EPA was limited to property and affairs, the LPA also includes issues concerning welfare, care and treatment. The Act also creates the Court of Protection (section 45) which is a superior Court of record, and which has the jurisdiction to determine issues that arise in respect of those mentally incapable (or reasonably suspected of being so until the issue is determined), as well as making declarations in relation to those issues. The Court may make decisions on behalf of the person. Equally, the Court may appoint deputies to make decisions on behalf of the person: see sections 19 and 20.

---

[112]   These quotations are taken from the Foreword to the Code of Practice to the Act, by Lord Falconer, LC.
[113]   A creation of the Enduring Powers of Attorney Act 1985.

8.76 The Court of Protection deals with the overwhelming majority of cases that arise under the MCA. These are therefore not subject to judicial review and beyond the scope of this publication.[114] Two issues that are relevant to this publication concern the interface between the Mental Health Act and the MCA, and the challenging of the decisions of public bodies when they conflict with best interest decisions under the MCA.

8.77 Section 28 of the MCA states:

'(1) Nothing in this Act authorises anyone –
  (a) to give a patient medical treatment for mental disorder, or
  (b) to consent to a patient's being given medical treatment for mental disorder if, at the time when it is proposed to treat the patient, his treatment is regulated by Part 4 of the Mental Health Act.'

8.78 In other words the MHA treatment 'code' discussed above has primacy over the MCA if a patient is a detained patient under MHA. However, this straightforward rule is complicated by the effects of amendment made to the MCA by the MHA 2007, when the deprivation of liberty safeguards (DOLS) were introduced.

8.79 The DOLS were intended to ensure that the criticisms made of the domestic law of England and Wales in the *Bournewood* case were answered. The *Bournewood* patient was a person deprived of his liberty in a hospital, incapable of consenting to being there, but not trying to leave so as to prompt detention under the MHA. Such persons were not protected by a regime that was compliant with Article 5(1) and (4) of the ECHR. The DOLS introduced a complicated administrative admissions regime, similar to the MHA, under Schedule A1 of the MCA. In brief, these provisions enabled residents in hospitals and care homes to be deprived of their liberty provided standard authorisations were obtained by the managing authority of the hospital or care home from the supervisory authority (the PCT in the case of a hospital, local social services in the case of a care home). Urgent authorisations were also possible in emergency situations. The procedure requires a number of 'qualifying requirements' to be satisfied (under Part 3, Schedule A1). The satisfaction of these requirements make a decision Article 5 compliant. The authorisations are for a limited time, and they must be reviewed. There is a right of challenge to the Court of Protection under section 21A. The court has the power to make orders depriving a person of his liberty under section 16A(2), but in doing so the court must also ensure that it considers the requirements necessary to make the order Article 5 compliant.[115]

8.80 With the MCA allowing persons to be deprived of their liberty the question arises as to when it is appropriate to exercise powers under the MCA and when to use the MHA? The MHA may only be used where the patient suffers from a mental disorder as defined by the Act. The MCA may only be used where the person lacks capacity to

---

[114] See Court of Protection Practice 2010 (Jordans 2010) for the relevant primary and delegated legislation, COP Rules, and extremely valuable and authoritative commentary and case studies.

[115] It is submitted that the Court ought to ensure that a welfare order that will deprive a person of his liberty is only made when the requirements in part 3 of the DOLS are satisfied. The only authority on this issue from the higher courts so far is *G v E and others* [2010] EWCA Civ 822. The Court of Appeal rejected the submission that there was a threshold in DOL cases, such as in care proceedings under the Children Act 1989. Rather, the Court must decide what was in the incapacitate person's best interests whilst ensuring that the decision was Article 5 compliant. It would seem that since the MCA itself has a test (ie Part 3 of Schedule 1A) that is designed to ensure that a DOL decision is Article 5 compliant, the Court ought to apply that test in the same was as a supervisory body must apply it.

make decisions as to the relevant care or treatment. Not all those with mental disorder lack capacity. Not all those who lack capacity will suffer from a mental disorder, and even if they do, often the treatment they require will not be treatment for a mental disorder. The problem arises where these clear boundaries are blurred. And this is particularly relevant when a decision has to be made whether a patient is to be subject to the MHA or the MCA/DOLS in hospital.

8.81   In *GJ v The Foundation Trust*,[116] the Court of Protection had to consider whether a patient subject to a standard authorisation in a psychiatric Hospital was eligible to be detained under DOLS or whether, as his legal representatives argued, he ought to be under the MHA regime. Under paragraph 12 of Part 3 of Schedule A1 of the MCA the patient must satisfy the eligibility requirement in order to be deprived of his liberty under MCA. Whether a patient is eligible or not depends on Part 2 of Schedule 1A and, in case of *GJ* the issue was whether he came within Case E – namely that he was 'within the scope of the Mental Health Act but not subject to any mental health regime' and whether he objected to being a mental health patient. The MHA has primacy over the MCA when they overlap. However, in determining whether they overlap it is important to establish the core or primary purpose of the treatment that has led to the decision-maker requesting a DOLS authorisation (whether under the DOLS or through the Court of Protection).[117]

8.82   Then the Court went on to consider what the expression 'within the scope of the Mental Health Act' meant. Schedule 1A, Part 2 paragraph 12 states that 'P is within the scope of the Mental Health Act if: (a) an application in respect of P could be made under section 2 or 3 of the Mental Health Act, and (b) P could be detained in a hospital in pursuance of such an application, were one made'. For the purposes of this provision it is to be assumed that the recommendations necessary to trigger the civil admission process under the MHA had been given. The Court had to decide what 'could be detained' meant. The PCT and Hospital (as supervisory body and managing authority respectively) argued that in order to overturn the authorisation the Court had to find that no reasonable decision-maker could have concluded that GJ could not be detained under the MHA ('the high probability or effective certainty test'). GJ argued that the decision-maker ought to have asked himself whether it was possible that the patient could be detained under the MHA ('the possibility test'). Finally, the Secretary of State argued that the provision ought to be read as devolving the decision entirely to the decision-maker: that is to say, what does the decision maker think? The Court decided the 'what the decision-maker thinks test' was the correct one. This meant that the Court had to decide and decided that GJ was rightly detained under the DOLS because the primary purpose of the detention was for the treatment of his diabetes.[118]

8.83   What if the Court of Protection makes a decision that a certain care plan is in the best interests of a person but the services necessary for that plan to be enacted are not made available by the public authorities that could provide them? It is possible for the

---

[116]   [2009] EWHC 2972, reported as *J v The Foundation Trust* at [2010] 3 WLR 840.
[117]   GJ at [57].
[118]   It is beyond the scope of this book to consider the ramifications of this decision. On the one hand, by devolving the decision to the clinician deciding whether the MCA of MHA should apply the Court has given the clinician the right to exercise clinician judgment taking into account the circumstances of the case. However, another consequence is that the s 21A appeal means that the Court of Protection has to make a *de novo* decision, rather than reviewing the decision of the original decision-maker. This is more in keeping with the role of the Tribunal in the MHA, and consequently it is probable that Mr Justice Charles' decision in GJ was in keeping with the intention behind the DOLS.

public law issue arising out of the COP case to be decided simultaneously, and, if the case is heard by a High Court Judge by the same Judge sitting in the Family Division.

CONCLUSION

8.84 Something of a revolution took place in mental health law in 2008. The effects of the Mental Health Act 2007 which both amended the MHA 1983 and completed the MCA 2005 have brought into place two regimes which are intended to work in parallel but which perversely may overlap. These two regimes largely exclude the need judicial review. The MHA brings the Tribunal within the new Tribunal system, which is intended to create a new administrative justice system with its own statutory appeal Court, the UT. This is intended to be the new face of public law. The MCA has its own court, the Court of Protection which determines the issues that arise under the MCA regime. The primacy of the MHA over the MCA is intended to solve problems that arise where there is an overlap. However, the two regimes necessarily involve public authorities and their decision-making processes may at some stage be amenable to public law challenge by way of judicial review. Those involved in litigation in this field, lawyers in particular, will be aware that when a case comes before a Court or Tribunal those proceedings will represent the tip of a large iceberg. An individual application to the Court of Protection concerning the placement of, for instance, a person suffering from autism may well be preceded by a long struggle between parents or carers to obtain services at home. The proceedings in the Court of Protection are likely to be tainted by the hostility those parents or carers will feel towards the local authority that has in the past frustrated their access to suitable services, as they see it. That frustration will become anger when the same authority takes proceedings in the Court of Protection to move that person to a placement where the services can be provided. The use of judicial review at an earlier stage is likely to reduce the need for Court of Protection proceedings by bringing the issue concerning the provision of services to the surface before the care of the person breaks down to the point where the use of the MCA is needed. The role of the Tribunals will also be interesting to watch in the years to come. The author's hunch is that the Upper Tribunal will wish to assert its status at the apex of a new administrative justice system by developing the law in a way that serves the purpose of the Tribunals – by making it better suited to the needs of those who use the system. The Tribunal should keep up with the trends in clinical practice – that is part of the expert function of a Tribunal. In doing so the Upper Tribunal should shape the substantive law so that it has regard to the realities of those who use the Tribunal, whether they be patients, clinicians, NHS Trusts, PCTS or the Ministry of Justice. The fact that so many people are now treated in the community through independent living means that many of the old precepts upon which mental health law has been based are outdated.

Chapter 9

CRIMINAL LAW

INTRODUCTION

9.1   Judicial reviews in a criminal context raise a number of issues that do not arise in other areas. The procedure can be different. There are specific statutory provisions that have an impact upon the jurisdiction of the court. This chapter seeks to identify the specific issues that arise in a criminal context.

WHETHER THE MATTER IS A CRIMINAL CAUSE OR MATTER

The importance of knowing whether a matter is a criminal cause or matter

9.2   The distinction between a criminal cause or matter and other cases is significant, as the procedure adopted when bringing proceedings in the Administrative Court depends on whether a matter is a criminal cause. In particular, there is no right of appeal to the Court of Appeal from any judgment of the Administrative Court in any criminal cause or matter, except in very limited circumstances.[1] In addition, although in principle it is possible for a single High Court judge to consider a criminal judicial review, the practice is that a criminal judicial review will normally be heard by a Divisional Court.[2]

9.3   The procedural distinctions that arise mean that practitioners will need to ensure that they know whether a case relates to a criminal cause or matter, so that they follow the correct procedure.

The decision that determines whether a matter is a criminal cause or matter

9.4   The court will not be concerned with the nature of the order made by the Administrative Court. Indeed, the orders that might be sought, when applying for a judicial review in a criminal cause or matter, are broadly the same as those that are sought in other matters. Instead, the court will consider whether the decision that was being challenged in the Administrative Court was a criminal cause or matter.[3]

---

[1]   Senior Courts Act 1981, s 18(1)(a).
[2]   In addition, matters relating to criminal justice that are not technically criminal will often be heard by a Divisional Court (e g *R (McFetrich) v Secretary of State for the Home Department* (2003) *The Times*, 28 July).
[3]   *Carr v Atkins* [1987] QB 963 at 967B.

Determining whether a matter is a criminal cause or matter

9.5   The appeal courts have given a wide definition to the phrase 'criminal cause or matter'. For example, Lord Esher has held that the phrase:

> '[A]pplies to a decision by way of judicial determination of any question raised in or with regard to proceedings, the subject-matter of which is criminal, at whatever stage of the proceedings the question arises.'[4]

9.6   Similarly, Lord Wright held that:

> '[I]f the cause or matter is one which, if carried to its conclusion, might result in the conviction of the person charged and in a sentence of some punishment, such as imprisonment or fine, it is a "criminal cause or matter".... Every order made in such a cause or matter by an English court, is an order in a criminal cause or matter, even though the order, taken by itself, is neutral in character and might equally have been made in a cause or matter which is not criminal. The order may not involve punishment by the law of this country, but if the effect of the order is to subject by means of the operation of English law the persons charged to the criminal jurisdiction of a foreign country, the order is, in the eyes of English law for the purposes being considered, an order in a criminal cause or matter.'[5]

9.7   Although these judgments appear to suggest that the phrase 'criminal cause or matter' relates to a decision of a court, other authorities show that there is no need for the decision-maker to be a court. A decision to refer or to refuse to refer a matter to the criminal courts can be a criminal cause or matter. For example, under the legislative scheme that existed before the establishment of the Criminal Cases Review Commission, a refusal by the Secretary of State to refer a matter to the Court of Appeal was a criminal matter.[6] A decision of the Criminal Cases Review Commission is also a criminal matter.[7]

9.8   A decision to caution an offender is treated as a criminal cause or matter.[8] This conclusion was reached in the past because the Court of Appeal concluded that a caution was one manner of disposing of a criminal matter.[9]

9.9   The decision need not be a final decision of a criminal court for it to be a criminal cause or matter. For example, a decision relating to evidence that may be used in criminal proceedings is a criminal cause or matter even if the proceedings have not commenced. Thus, an order of a Crown Court judge in relation to the production of special procedure material under Sch 1 to the Police and Criminal Evidence Act 1984 is a criminal cause or matter, even if proceedings have not commenced.[10]

9.10   At one stage it appears to have been thought that once the criminal courts have imposed a sentence, a decision about the effect of the penalty imposed by the criminal court should also be treated as a criminal cause or matter. Thus, a case considering the calculation of the number of days to be served as a result of the imposition of a

---

4   *Ex p Alice Woodhall* (1888) 20 QBD 832 at 836.
5   *Amand v Home Secretary* [1943] AC 147 at 162.
6   *R v Secretary of State, ex p Garner* [1990] COD 457.
7   *R (Saxon) v Criminal Cases Review Commission* [2001] EWCA Civ 1384.
8   *R (Aru) v Chief Constable of Merseyside* [2004] 1 WLR 1697.
9   *Ibid* at [10].
10   *Carr v Atkins* [1987] QB 963.

sentence of imprisonment was treated as a criminal cause or matter.[11] More recent case law suggests that this is wrong. For example, cases about the correct application of licence provisions have not been treated as criminal causes.[12] Similarly, a case about the compatibility of the sex offender registration scheme with the European Convention on Human Rights was not treated as a criminal cause.[13] As a consequence, current practice appears to be that decisions about the effect of a penalty are not treated as a criminal cause or matter.

9.11   It may be difficult to draw any firm conclusions from the case law summarised in the paragraph above because it appears that there was little argument regarding the principles to be applied. However, the recent tendency to treat challenges to decisions regarding the effect of a sentence as not being criminal causes does better accord with the dicta of Lord Esher and Lord Wright set out above. That is because that dicta suggests that decisions of the executive are not criminal causes. Clearly challenges to decisions such as the calculation of a prisoner's release date are essentially challenges to an executive decision as to the effect of a sentence. The judicial determination of the sentence is not in issue.

9.12   The practice of treating the effect of a sentence as not being a criminal cause is consistent with the case law considering challenges to the exercise of a discretionary power regarding the effect of a sentence. A challenge to the exercise of such an executive discretion is not treated as a criminal cause or matter. Thus, a challenge to a deportation order made following a recommendation by a criminal court is not a criminal cause or matter, although the actual recommendation is a criminal cause or matter.[14] Similarly, a challenge to a decision to decline to release a prisoner who has been recommended for early release by the Parole Board is not a criminal cause or matter.[15]

9.13   Although the decision that is being challenged need not be a decision of a criminal court if the case is to be a criminal cause or matter, it must however relate in some way to a possible trial by a criminal court.[16] Thus, a general challenge to a police policy is clearly not a criminal cause or matter.[17] In addition, the proceedings must relate in some way to the 'enforcement and preservation of public law and order' rather than being merely domestic disciplinary proceedings.[18] Thus, as already noted, proceedings relating to an alleged breach of prison rules are not a criminal cause or matter.[19] Similarly, disciplinary proceedings against a solicitor are not a criminal cause or matter.[20]

9.14   Not every decision by a criminal court in relation to criminal proceedings is a criminal cause or matter. This is because some decisions of the criminal courts are so collateral to the criminal proceedings that gave rise to the decision that the decision cannot be regarded as a criminal cause or matter.[21] The Court of Appeal has held that a decision to enforce a recognizance is not a criminal cause or matter as '[a] recognizance

---

[11]   *R v Secretary of State for the Home Department, ex p Francois* [1999] 1 AC 43.
[12]   *R (Stellato) v Secretary of State for Justice* [2007] 2 AC 70.
[13]   *R (F) v Secretary of State* [2010] 2 WLR 992.
[14]   *R v Secretary of State for the Home Department, ex p Dannenberg* [1984] QB 766.
[15]   *R (Black) v Secretary of State for Justice* [2009] 1 AC 949.
[16]   Per Lord Justice Shaw, *R v Board of Visitors of Hull Prison, ex p St Germain* [1979] QB 425 at 453C.
[17]   e g *R v Chief Constable of North Wales and Others, ex p Thorpe* [1999] QB 396.
[18]   Per Lord Justice Shaw, *R v Board of Visitors of Hull Prison, ex p St Germain* [1979] QB 425 at 452B.
[19]   *R v Board of Visitors of Hull Prison, ex p St Germain* [1979] QB 425.
[20]   In *Re EF Hardwick* (1883) 12 QBD 148.
[21]   Per Sir John Donaldson MR, *Carr v Atkins* [1987] 1 QB 963 at 970F.

is in the nature of a bond. A failure to fulfil it gives rise to a civil debt'.[22] The issue of a witness summons is, however, not so collateral that it is not a criminal cause or matter.[23]

9.15   Challenges to the decisions of criminal courts may also not be a criminal cause or matter if the decision challenged relates to civil proceedings. For example, there are forms of civil proceedings that are brought in the magistrates' court. Thus, a decision to commit a person to jail for non-payment of non-domestic rates is not a criminal cause or matter.[24]

9.16   The definition of a criminal charge for the purposes of the European Convention on Human Rights is different to the domestic law definition. It would appear that a finding that proceedings are criminal for the purposes of article 6 makes no difference to the determination to whether a judicial review is a criminal cause or matter for procedural purposes.[25] That is perhaps not surprising as article 6 does not entitle a person any particular form of appeal proceedings (which is essentially what judicial review often is in a criminal context).

DECISIONS THAT CANNOT BE CHALLENGED

Interim decisions

9.17   The High Court is very reluctant to allow judicial reviews of decisions of criminal courts where there has been no final decision in the proceedings. Judicial review is a discretionary remedy. That means that the High Court will not necessarily intervene to quash every decision where there are grounds for intervening. When deciding whether to quash a decision taken by a court during criminal proceedings, the High Court will take account of the stage that those proceedings have reached. Applicants for judicial review will normally be expected to wait for a final decision before bringing an application for judicial review. Lord Justice May has held that because nothing will be lost if parties wait until the final determination of the matter, interim rulings should only be challenged before a final determination 'in a very special instance'.[26]

9.18   The authorities in this area were reviewed by the Divisional Court in *R (K) v Bow Street Magistrates Court* (2005) *The Times*, 27 July. The Court noted that it was argued that it had no jurisdiction to consider challenges to interim decisions.

9.19   It declined, however, to rule on these arguments. It concluded that the judicial review was premature because it was impossible to know how the legal issues raised would arise until the evidence was heard and findings of fact made. It does appear to be difficult to see why there should not be jurisdiction given that, in general, there is jurisdiction to challenge decisions of magistrates.

---

22   Per Lord Denning MR, *R v Southampton Justices, ex p Green* [1976] QB 11 at 15H. Care must be taken when considering this case as it is clear that the full scope of the judgment of the Court of Appeal is regarded as unreliable. See, eg, Sir John Donaldson MR, *Carr v Atkins* [1987] 1 QB 963 at 969E onwards.
23   *Day v Grant* [1987] QB 972.
24   *R v Thanet Justices, ex p Dass* [1996] COD 77.
25   *R (International Transport Roth Gmbh) v Secretary of State for the Home Department* [2003] QB 728 in which the Court of Appeal concluded that the decisions challenged were criminal for the purposes of article 6.
26   *Streames v Copping* [1985] QB 920 at 929.

9.20   Jurisdiction was accepted in *R (CPS) v Sedgmoor Magistrates' Court* [2007] EWHC Admin 1803 in which an interim decision to refuse to admit evidence was challenged. The Administrative Court held that judicial review proceedings should not have been brought and that the prosecution should have waited until proceedings were concluded before commencing an appeal by way of case stated. The Court was, however, willing to consider the claim for judicial review because: (i) dismissing it would have resulted in further delay, (ii) there was no need for facts to be found by the magistrates to enable the judicial review to be determined, and (iii) the ruling challenged had the effect of determining the proceedings before the magistrates' court.

9.21   There are, however, some circumstances where it will be appropriate to challenge an interim decision. It is probably not possible to identify all the circumstances in which it will be appropriate to bring a judicial review of an interim decision in criminal proceedings. There are, however, some principles that can be seen in the decided cases. In particular the precedents set out in the paragraph below show that the High Court is likely to be concerned about the reason why the applicant cannot wait for a final determination of the criminal proceedings. It is less concerned about the type of decision being challenged. As a result, applicants for judicial review should always explain in their pleadings why they have not waited for a final decision of the court before bringing a judicial review application.

9.22   The High Court has held that a decision that has resulted in a person being detained may be challenged by judicial review even where there is no final conviction.[27] In addition, the High Court is more likely to exercise its discretion to quash an interim decision where quashing that decision is likely to result in the final determination of the matter.[28] This is particularly likely to be true in the context of proceedings against juveniles. This is because the courts are keen to avoid putting juveniles through criminal trials if there is no need for that trial.[29] The same considerations may also apply in cases where there are juvenile witnesses where there will be a desire to avoid these witnesses giving evidence unnecessarily.

9.23   It does appear to be accepted that a challenge may be brought before a final conviction where a mode of trial has been determined wrongly. Thus a decision to decline jurisdiction where the matter could only be tried summarily could be challenged by judicial review before there had been a final conclusion of the matter.[30] Similarly an unreasonable decision to accept jurisdiction could be challenged by way of judicial review before there had been a final conviction.[31] This is presumably because it is not in the interests of justice for a court to waste court time on a matter that it should not be considering.

---

[27]   Eg *R v Maidstone Crown Court, ex p Clark* [1995] 1 WLR 831.
[28]   Eg *R v Horseferry Road Magistrates' Court, ex p Bennett* [1994] 1 AC 42 in which the House of Lords held that in certain circumstances judicial review proceedings should be brought in the High Court where it was said that a matter should be stayed as an abuse of process. See also *R v Horseferry Road Justices, ex p Independent Broadcasting Authority* [1987] QB 54 in which the High Court held that it should decide whether a criminal offence existed and *R (Latham) v Northampton Magistrates' Court* [2008] EWHC Admin 245 in which the issue of a summons was quashed as being unreasonable.
[29]   *R v Chief Constable of Kent ex p L; R v DPP, ex p B* 93 CrAppR 416, DC. In this case the High Court considered an application for judicial review of a decision to prosecute juveniles. The court held that it would be more willing to quash a decision to prosecute in a case involving juveniles than it would be in a case involving adults. The same principles are likely to apply to judicial reviews of interim decisions taken during criminal proceedings.
[30]   *R v Hatfield Justices, ex p Castle* [1981] 1 WLR 217.
[31]   *R v Northampton Magistrates, ex p Commissioners for Customs and Excise* [1994] COD 382.

Decisions of the Crown Court

9.24　The jurisdiction of the Administrative Court to consider applications for judicial review from decisions of the Crown Court is governed by section 29(3) of the Senior Courts Act 1981. It provides that judicial review can be used to challenge all decisions of the Crown Court other than 'matters relating to trial on indictment'. The Administrative Court has rejected arguments that it has an inherent jurisdiction to consider judicial reviews of decisions of the Crown Court that would otherwise be excluded from the scope of judicial review by section 29(3) of the Senior Courts Act 1981.[32]

9.25　Clearly, there are some matters that do not relate to a trial on indictment, because no indictment is involved in the proceedings. For example, judicial review may be used to challenge the decisions of the Crown Court while exercising its jurisdiction to consider appeals from the magistrates' court.[33] Similarly, a decision to refuse legal aid in an application to remove a disqualification from driving is also subject to challenge in the Administrative Court.[34] There are also other matters that clearly cannot be challenged in the Administrative Court, such as conviction and sentence on a matter committed to the Crown Court for trial on indictment. In this context, the term 'trial' includes proceedings where a defendant pleads guilty to an indictment.[35] It also covers pre-trial hearings where no jury is sworn.[36]

9.26　When the Crown Court makes a decision that is ancillary to proceedings on indictment, it can be difficult to determine whether the Administrative Court has jurisdiction to consider the matter. For example, is it possible to challenge decisions made by the Crown Court that relate to legal aid in a case being tried on indictment?

9.27　The House of Lords has considered the scope of the Administrative Court's jurisdiction on at least four occasions.[37] Their Lordships have declined to define the statutory phrases used to limit the jurisdiction of the Administrative Court.[38] They have, however, stated that if the decision of the Crown Court was one affecting the conduct of a trial on indictment given in the course of the trial or by way of pre-trial directions, it cannot be challenged by judicial review.[39] If the decision was such a decision, an aggrieved defendant normally has the opportunity to appeal to the Court of Appeal under the Criminal Appeal Act 1968. For example, a decision to refuse to grant legal aid has been held to be a matter that relates to a trial on indictment.[40] This is not surprising, because the Court of Appeal has held that it is entitled to quash a defendant's conviction where it is rendered unsafe by a trial judge's decision regarding legal aid.[41]

9.28　The absence of a right of appeal to the Court of Appeal does not necessarily mean that the Administrative Court will accept jurisdiction. For example, the Court has

---

[32]　*R v Chelmsford Crown Court, ex p Chief Constable of the Essex Police* [1994] 1 WLR 359 but cf *R v Maidstone Crown Court, ex p Harrow London Borough Council* [2000] QB 719 holding that there might be a judicial review challenging a lack of jurisdiction in circumstances where the challenge might be said to relate to trial on indictment.

[33]　*R v Bournemouth Crown Court, ex p Weight* [1984] 1 WLR 980.

[34]　*R v Recorder of Liverpool, ex p McCann* (1994) *The Times*, 4 May.

[35]　*Re Smalley* [1985] AC 622.

[36]　*R v Harrow Crown Court, ex p Perkins* (1998) *The Times*, 28 April.

[37]　*Re Smalley* [1985] AC 622, *Re Sampson* [1987] 1 WLR 194, *R v Manchester Crown Court, ex p DPP* [1993] 1 WLR 1524, *Re Ashton* [1994] 1 AC 9.

[38]　*Re Smalley* [1985] AC 622.

[39]　*Ibid.*

[40]　*R v Chichester Crown Court, ex p Abodunrin* (1984) 79 Cr App R 293.

[41]　*R v Kirk* (1983) 76 Cr App R 194.

no jurisdiction to consider a challenge to a decision to refuse to order costs after acquittal.[42] This is because the statutory limit on the jurisdiction of the Court means that matters relating to a trial on indictment include orders made at the conclusion of a trial on indictment, if these orders are an integral part of the trial process.[43] Orders are an integral part of the trial process if they are based on what is learnt during the trial process.[44] Clearly costs orders are based on what is learnt during the trial process.

9.29 The absence of a right of appeal does not even necessarily result in the Administrative Court accepting jurisdiction if a person can claim to be a victim of a violation of the European Convention on Human Rights as a consequence of a Crown Court decision.[45] That is because there is no right under the rights incorporated into domestic law by the Human Rights Act 1998 to challenge the decision that is said to violate European Convention rights.[46]

9.30 If a claimant wrongly challenges a decision of the Crown Court by bringing judicial review proceedings when they are able to appeal, it is possible for the court to correct the problem by re-constituting itself as the Court of Appeal.[47]

9.31 Further assistance on the scope of the Administrative Court's jurisdiction is provided by Lord Browne-Wilkinson, who noted that decisions held to be open to challenge in the Administrative Court are those in which the order was made in a wholly different jurisdiction or where the order has been made against someone other than the accused.[48] The only possible exception to this is serious fraud cases, where the Administrative Court may be able to consider decisions to dismiss a case that has been transferred to the Crown Court under the special procedure provided by the Criminal Justice Act 1987.[49] Lord Browne-Wilkinson formulated the following guidance:

> "'Is the decision sought to be reviewed one arising in the issue between the Crown and the defendant formulated by the indictment (including the costs of such issue)?" If the answer is "Yes", then to permit the decision to be challenged by judicial review may lead to delay in the trial: the matter is therefore probably excluded from review by the section. If the answer is "No", the decision of the Crown Court is truly collateral to the indictment of the defendent and judicial review of that decision will not delay his trial: therefore it may well not be excluded by the section.'[50]

9.32 The decisions of the House of Lords have not prevented a degree of uncertainty about whether a matter is something that relates to a trial on indictment. Indeed, the lack of certainty has prompted Lord Justice Rose to call for legislation to clarify the

---

[42] *Re Meredith* (1973) 57 Cr App R 451, DC; *R v Harrow Crown Court, ex p Perkins* (1998) *The Times*, 28 April.

[43] Per Lord Bridge in *Re Sampson* [1987] 1 WLR 194 at 198G.

[44] Ibid at 197E.

[45] *R (Regentford) Ltd v Canterbury Crown Court* [2001] HRLR 18.

[46] *R (Shields) v Crown Court at Liverpool and the Lord Chancellor* [2001] UKHRR 610 at [58].

[47] *R (Lichniak) v Secretary of State for the Home Department* [2002] QB 296.

[48] *R v Manchester Crown Court, ex p DPP* [1993] 1 WLR 1524 at 1530C.

[49] In *R v Manchester Crown Court, ex p DPP* [1993] 1 WLR 1524 at 1530G, Lord Browne-Wilkinson declined an opportunity to express a view on the correctness of *R v Central Criminal Court and Nadir, ex p Director of the Serious Fraud Office* [1993] 1 WLR 949. Although his Lordship noted that the decision in *ex p Director of the Serious Fraud Office* relied on cases that he held had been wrongly decided, he went on to say that the wording of the Criminal Justice Act 1987 might give rise to special considerations. Since the decision in *ex p DPP*, the Administrative Court has continued to consider judicial reviews of decisions to dismiss proceedings following a transfer under the provisions of the Criminal Justice Act 1987. See eg *R v Snaresbrook Crown Court, ex p Director of the Serious Fraud Office* (1998) *The Times*, 26 October.

[50] *R v Manchester Crown Court, ex p DPP* [1993] 1 WLR 1524 at 1530F.

scope of judicial review of Crown Court decisions[51] and there has been consultation about such legislation. There are, however, a number of precedents that give examples of matters that have been held to relate to a trial on indictment or matters that do not relate to a trial on indictment. These precedents can, on a cursory reading, appear to be slightly arbitrary. For example, although a decision to remit a legal aid contribution at the end of a trial is not subject to judicial review,[52] a decision to make a contribution order is subject to review.[53] These precedents, however, are a useful guide to whether the Court will accept that it has jurisdiction to consider a challenge to a particular decision.

9.33　Matters held to be matters relating to a trial on indictment and therefore excluded from judicial review and appeal by way of case stated include the following:

(a)　an order discharging a jury;[54]

(b)　an order that an indictment lie on the file marked 'not to be proceeded with without leave of the court';[55]

(c)　the decision of a judge to order a defence solicitor to pay the costs occasioned by the granting of a defence application for an adjournment;[56]

(d)　a decision as to whether the trial of one indictment should proceed before the trial of another indictment faced by the same defendant;[57]

(e)　a refusal to stay an indictment as an abuse of process;[58]

(f)　an order quashing an indictment because the Crown Court lacks jurisdiction;[59]

(g)　an order that matters should be stayed as an abuse of process;[60]

(h)　an order regarding costs after the prosecution announce their intent to offer no evidence at a pre-trial hearing;[61]

(i)　an order preventing the naming of a witness under section 11 of the Contempt of Court Act 1981;[62]

(j)　a decision to refuse to dismiss a charge sent for trial under section 51 of the Crime and Disorder Act 1998;[63] and

---

[51]　*R v Manchester Crown Court, ex p H* [2000] 1 WLR 760.
[52]　*R v Cardiff Crown Court, ex p Jones* [1974] QB 113.
[53]　Per Lord Bridge, in *Re Sampson* [1987] 1 WLR 194 at 199F.
[54]　*Ex p Marlowe* [1973] Crim LR 294.
[55]　*R v Central Criminal Court, ex p Raymond* (1986) 83 Cr App R 94.
[56]　*R v Smith (M)*, [1975] QB 531, but note doubts expressed by Lord Bridge in *Re Smalley* [1985] AC 622 at 644F.
[57]　*R v Southwark Crown Court, ex p Ward* [1996] Crim LR 123.
[58]　*R v Maidstone Crown Court, ex p Shanks & McEwan (Southern) Ltd* [1993] Env LR 340.
[59]　*R v Manchester Crown Court, ex p DPP* [1993] 1 WLR 1524.
[60]　*Re Ashton and Others; R v Manchester Crown Court, ex p DPP* [1994] 1 AC 9.
[61]　*R v Harrow Crown Court, ex p Perkins* (1998) *The Times*, 28 April.
[62]　*R v Central Criminal Court, ex p Crook* (1984) *The Times*, 8 November.
[63]　*R (Snelgrove) v Woolwich Crown Court* [2005] 1 WLR 3223.

(k)   a decision to decline to make a compensation order.[64]

9.34   Matters that have been held to be matters that do not relate to a trial on indictment and therefore may be challenged by judicial review or appeal by way of case stated include the following:

(a)   forfeiture orders made against a person who was not a defendant in the trial;[65]

(b)   an order committing an acquitted defendant to prison unless he agrees to be bound over;[66]

(c)   a decision to extend a custody time-limit;[67]

(d)   an order enforcing the recognizance of a surety;[68] and

(e)   an order lifting restrictions on the naming of juvenile defendants made under section 39(1) of the Children and Young Persons Act 1933.[69]

9.35   Ingenious arguments seeking to extend the Administrative Court's jurisdiction to consider decisions of the Crown Court have found little favour. For example, the Administrative Court has no jurisdiction to consider a challenge to a warrant of committal to prison, if that challenge is in reality a challenge to sentence.[70]

9.36   The one argument that has succeeded is that the Administrative Court can exceptionally quash a decision that was by the Crown Court in circumstances in which it lacked jurisdiction if no alternative remedy is available.[71] The Administrative Court has, however, sought to limit the scope of this jurisdiction. In particular, it is clear that an unlawful decision is not sufficient to enable the Administrative Court to intervene.[72] This is despite the fact that it might be thought that there is no jurisdiction to make an unlawful decision.

9.37   It used to be thought that one decision of the Crown Court that cannot be challenged by judicial review, though it might not relate to a trial on indictment, is a decision by a Crown Court judge in Chambers to refuse bail.[73] This is because there was an alternative remedy as the High Court had jurisdiction to grant bail.[74] There is now a clear jurisdiction to consider judicial reviews of bail decisions because the High Court no longer has jurisdiction to grant bail.[75] This is true even when proceedings on indictment are pending.[76] That jurisdiction will, however, be exercised sparingly.[77] In

---

[64]   *R (Faithfull) v Ipswich Crown Court* [2008] 1 WLR 1636.
[65]   *R v Maidstone Crown Court, ex p Gill* (1987) 84 Cr App R 96.
[66]   *R v Inner London Crown Court, ex p Benjamin* (1987) 85 Cr App R 267.
[67]   *R v Norwich Crown Court, ex p Cox* (1993) 5 Admin LR 689.
[68]   *Re Smalley* [1985] AC 622.
[69]   *R v Manchester Crown Court, ex p H* [2000] 1 WLR 760.
[70]   *R v Lewes Crown Court, ex p Sinclair* (1993) 5 Admin LR 1.
[71]   *R v Maidstone Crown Court, ex p Harrow LBC* [2000] QB 719.
[72]   *R (Faithfull) v Ipswich Crown Court* [2008] 1 WLR 1636.
[73]   *Re Herbage* (1985) *The Times*, 25 October.
[74]   Criminal Justice Act 1967, s 22(1).
[75]   *R (M) v Isleworth Crown Court* [2005] EWHC Admin 363.
[76]   *R (Mongan) v Isleworth Crown Court* [2007] EWHC Admin 1087.
[77]   Ibid.

addition, there are suggestions that decisions on bail during the course of a trial cannot be challenged as they are matters relating to trial on indictment.[78]

GROUNDS FOR APPLYING FOR JUDICIAL REVIEW

9.38   The grounds for applying for judicial review are essentially the same as those that apply in other contexts. There are, however, some differences in the approach to those grounds when claims for judicial review are brought in a criminal context.

Decisions of prosecutors

9.39   Elsewhere in this book it will be noticed that the intensity of review when the Administrative Court considers a claim for judicial review depends upon the subject matter of the claim. This flexibility is perhaps clearest when the Court considers challenges to decisions to bring a prosecution.

9.40   The decision of a public authority as to whether to prosecute a person is subject to judicial review.[79] Similarly it is possible to bring a judicial review of a decision to reinstate proceedings.[80] In practice, however, the High Court is unlikely to exercise its discretion to quash a decision to prosecute. For example, the High Court has held that it will only quash a decision to prosecute in the most extreme circumstances such as where the decision to prosecute was the result of fraud, corruption or mala fides.[81] The only exception to this general reluctance to quash decisions to prosecute may arise when the High Court considers prosecutions brought against juveniles. The High Court has held that it would be willing to quash a decision to prosecute a juvenile if that decision was clearly contrary to the policy of the prosecuting authority that was designed to protect the public interest.[82] The general reluctance to consider challenges to decisions to prosecute arises because it is in the public interest to discourage satellite litigation in a criminal context.

9.41   It is not only as a result of the High Court's reluctance to quash a decision to prosecute that a defendant is unlikely to seek a judicial review of a decision to prosecute. A defendant is also unlikely to seek judicial review as they will almost certainly be able to challenge the decision to prosecute during the criminal proceedings. Firstly, the defendant will be able to argue that the prosecution should be stayed as an abuse of process. Criminal proceedings that are 'oppressive and vexatious' should be stayed as an abuse of process.[83] As a result it is very difficult to conceive of circumstances where the High Court could quash a decision to prosecute during judicial review proceedings but the criminal courts could not stay proceedings as an abuse of process. If such circumstances did arise, it is now clear that criminal courts have jurisdiction to consider public law defences. In particular, it is able to consider arguments about 'the invalidity of subordinate legislation *or an administrative act under it*'[84] (emphasis added) unless the

---

[78]   *R (KSS) v Northampton Crown Court* [2010] EWHC Admin 723.
[79]   Eg *R v Elmbridge Borough Council, ex p Activeoffice Ltd, The Times,* 29 December 1997 in which the applicant unsuccessfully tried to challenge a decision of a local authority to prosecute in a planning matter.
[80]   Eg *R v DPP, ex p Burke* [1997] 2 CL 184 holding that there was no need for special circumstances before the CPS decide to reinstate proceedings. It was enough that the decision to discontinue was clearly wrong.
[81]   Per Steyn LJ *R v Panel on Takeovers and Mergers, ex p Fayed, The Times,* 15 April 1992.
[82]   *R v Chief Constable of Kent, ex p L* [1993] 1 All ER 756.
[83]   Per Lord Salmon *R v Humphries* [1977] AC 1 at 46D.
[84]   Per Lord Irvine *Boddington v British Transport Police* [1998] 2 WLR 639 at 651 G.

statute excludes this jurisdiction. The use of the phrase 'administrative act' clearly implies that a public law challenge to the decision to prosecute might be raised as a defence.

9.42   The availability of public law defences in the criminal courts is a matter that the High Court is likely to take account of when it considers whether to exercise its discretion to quash a decision to prosecute. As a result practitioners representing prosecuting authorities should normally raise the availability of an alternative remedy in opposition to a defendant's application for judicial review of a decision to prosecute.

9.43   Although the House of Lords has held that judicial reviews of decisions not to prosecute will only succeed in exceptional circumstances,[85] the High Court may be slightly more willing to entertain judicial review applications challenging a failure to prosecute.[86] As a result there have been a number of judicial reviews of decisions of the Crown Prosecution Service not to prosecute.[87] For example, the High Court quashed a decision not to prosecute where the Crown Prosecution Service had failed to take account of a reasoned judgment of a civil court that suggested that the evidence that would have been relied on during any criminal prosecution had merit.[88] The High Court quashed the decision not to prosecute because it was irrational in all the circumstances. In reaching its decision, the High Court took account of the Code for Crown Prosecutors. The High Court did, however, indicate that usually it would be reluctant to intervene to quash a decision not to prosecute. In part that is because there is a presumption that civil courts should not determine whether behaviour is criminal.[89]

9.44   When the High Court considers a judicial review of a decision to refuse to prosecute, it will take account of the availability of an alternative remedy when it decides whether to exercise its discretion to allow the judicial review. In particular, the possibility of a private prosecution will be considered in cases where it is as effective a remedy as judicial review. In determining the effectiveness the High Court will take account of the resources of the applicant.[90]

9.45   Historically it has been held that the High Court will not consider judicial reviews of decisions of the Attorney General regarding the entry of a nolle prosequi.[91] This is because the High Court has been reluctant to consider judicial reviews of the exercise of prerogative powers. There is, however, some indication that the High Court is showing a greater willingness to consider judicial reviews of the prerogative powers.

Legitimate expectation

9.46   It does appear easier to establish a legitimate expectation when challenging decisions of criminal courts regarding sentencing than it appears to be in some other contexts.

---

[85]   *R (Corner House Research) v DPP* [2008] 3 WLR 568.

[86]   Eg *R v Commr of the police for the Metropolis, ex p Blackburn* [1968] 2 QB 118 CA in which the applicant successfully challenged a police policy against prosecuting certain illegal gambling.

[87]   Eg *R v CPS, ex p Waterworth* unreported, 1 December 1995, DC, *R v DPP, ex p Panayiotu* [1997] COD 83 and *R v DPP, ex p M and R v CPS, ex p Hitchins*, unreported, 13 June 1997, DC.

[88]   *R v DPP, ex p Treadway*, *The Times*, 31 October 1997.

[89]   *R v DPP, ex p Camelot Croup plc* (1998) 10 Admin LR 93 at 104D.

[90]   *R v DPP, ex p Camelot Croup plc* (1998) 10 Admin LR 93 at 105B.

[91]   *R v Comptroller of Patents* [1899] 1 QB 909.

9.47   In *R v Nottingham Magistrates' Court, ex p Davidson*[92] Lord Bingham CJ held that:

> 'If a court at a preliminary stage of the sentencing process gives to a defendant any indication as to the sentence which will or will not be thereafter passed upon him, in terms sufficiently unqualified to found a legitimate expectation in the mind of the defendant that any court which later passes sentence upon him will act in accordance with the indication given, and if on a later occasion a court, without reasons which justify departure from the earlier indication, and whether or not it is aware of that indication, passes a sentence inconsistent with, and more severe than, the sentence indicated, the court will ordinarily feel obliged, however reluctantly, to adjust the sentence passed so as to bring it into line with that indicated.'[93]

9.48   The important point about this dicta is that it does not require reliance upon a statement for a legitimate expectation to arise. That contrasts with the approach to legitimate expectation in some other contexts.

9.49   The dicta does state that the court must give an indication as to the sentence that it will impose for a legitimate expectation to arise. However, the facts of *R v Feltham Justices, ex p Rees*[94] demonstrate that the indication need not be the sort of firm promise required in other areas. In that case the magistrates heard submissions about the adequacy of their powers. They then invited mitigation before stating that 'they' required more information. As a consequence, they adjourned stating that 'all options' were open. It might be thought that saying 'all options' are open is sufficient to prevent a legitimate expectation arising. However, the Court held that the approach of the magistrates' court implied that they would not commit the defendant to the Crown Court.

9.50   Another difference that arises when the courts consider claims relying on a legitimate expectation in a criminal context is that the conduct of one court can bind another court. As a consequence, a statement by a magistrates' court that a defendant will not be imprisoned can bind the Crown Court.[95] That contrasts with the normal reluctance to find that a promise by one public body binds another.

ALTERNATIVE REMEDIES

Appeal to the Crown Court

9.51   An appeal to the Crown Court does not prevent an application for judicial review of a conviction in the magistrates' court.[96] Essentially it was held that the standards of procedural fairness are higher in criminal proceedings. Parliament has decided that a person is entitled to a fair trial in the magistrates court and that will potentially be denied if a person cannot apply for a judicial review of a decision of a magistrates' court merely because they can appeal to the Crown Court.[97] An appeal to the Crown Court will only ensure one fair hearing.

---

[92]   [2000] 1 Cr App R (S) 167.
[93]   Ibid at 169.
[94]   [2001] 2 Cr App R (S) 1.
[95]   *R v Isleworth Crown Court, ex p Irwin, The Times*, 5 December 1991.
[96]   *R v Hereford Magistrates' Court, ex p Rowlands and Ingram; R v Harrow Youth Court, ex p Prussia* [1998] QB 110.
[97]   Ibid.

9.52 The High Court must be informed of any appeal that is pending in the Crown Court.[98] As judicial review is a discretionary remedy, the possibility of an appeal to the Crown Court and the status of the appeal in the Crown Court is a matter that can be taken into account when the High Court considers whether it should intervene to quash a conviction. Thus a judicial review that was intended to procure delay of an appeal in the Crown Court in an attempt to secure the dropping of charges was rejected.[99] The High Court will also wish to ensure at the permission stage in an application for judicial review that there are good grounds for bringing an application for judicial review.[100]

Appeal by way of case stated

9.53 The courts have held that judicial review is only the appropriate method for applying to quash a conviction imposed by the Magistrates' Court or the Crown Court where an appeal by case stated was in apposite or inappropriate. For example, Mr Justice Brooke criticised applicants for judicial review of a conviction in a magistrates' court when he stated:

> 'Our task in this case was made unnecessarily difficult because the applicants did not adopt the procedure prescribed by Parliament for referring a point of law which has arisen in the magistrates' court to the High Court for decision. If the justices had stated a case for our opinion, we would have known what their findings of fact had been and their reasons for the decisions they took and they would have identified the relevant points of law for our decision in the familiar way.'[101]

9.54 This approach has been endorsed in a judicial review of a conviction that was upheld by the Crown Court following an appeal.[102] The court did, however, go on to say that where a judicial review was brought, the court that had made the original decision that was subject to challenge should at least write a letter stating whether they intended to resist the challenge.

9.55 As a result any challenge to a conviction should be by way of case stated where the High Court needs a full record of the findings of fact and law before the magistrates' court or the Crown Court. For example, this means that it is normal to challenge a conviction based on a misconstruction of the statute that gives rise to the offence by an appeal by way of case stated.[103]

9.56 An appeal by way of case stated is also normally the correct procedure where a person seeks to challenge an acquittal as there are limits to the scope of judicial reviews of acquittals.

---

[98] *R v Mid-Worcester JJJ, ex p Hart* [1989] COD 397, DC. In this case the High Court endorsed the comments of Alverstone LCJ in *R v Barnes* (1910) 102 LT 860 stating that the court considering a judicial review should be told of any pending appeal. The same comments suggested that in many cases the High Court will not wish to determine a judicial review until the appeal has been concluded.

[99] *R v Hereford Magistrates' Court, ex p Rowlands and Ingram; R v Harrow Youth Court, ex p Prussia* [1998] QB110, DC considering and explaining *R v Peterborough Magistrates' Court, ex p Dowler* [1997] QB 911, DC.

[100] Per Lord Bingham CJ *R v Hereford Magistrates' Court, ex p Rowlands and Ingram; R v Harrow Youth Court, ex p Prussia* [1997] 2 WLR 854 at 866C.

[101] *R v Morpeth Ward JJ, ex p Ward* 95 CrAppR 215. It is significant to note, however, that despite these comments the High Court did consider the substantive merits of the judicial review application.

[102] *R v Gloucester Crown Court, ex p Chester*, The Independent, 6 July 1998, QBD.

[103] Eg *Vigon v DPP* [1998] Crim LR 289, DC.

9.57   In practice the availability of an appeal by way of case stated does not prevent a significant number of judicial reviews of convictions in the magistrates' courts or the Crown Court. This is because the High Court often does not need a record of the findings of fact and findings of law when it considers a challenge to the conviction. Instead it needs evidence about things that happened during the trial of the matter and this evidence cannot normally be presented during an appeal by way of case stated. The procedure that the court adopts when considering applications for judicial review is usually the only appropriate way of presenting the High Court with the evidence that it needs in these circumstances.

9.58   For example, complaints about matters such as bias, a failure to adopt a procedure that satisfies the requirements of natural justice or a decision that is contrary to the applicant's legitimate expectation do not require a record of the court's findings of fact or law. Instead they require written evidence from persons present in court explaining the procedure adopted by the court. Judicial review is the procedure that allows a party to present this evidence.[104]

9.59   In addition to cases where the procedure in judicial review is preferable to that in appeal by way of case stated, there is one circumstance where a judicial review is the appropriate method of challenging a conviction. The justices or the Crown Court have a discretion to refuse to state a case. In these circumstances it is possible to bring a judicial review of the failure to state a case. Where it is necessary to apply for a judicial review of the failure to state a case, the judicial review should also challenge the conviction. That enables the High Court to consider whether it is in a position to consider quashing the conviction on the basis of the information available to it.[105] The High Court will wish to avoid the unnecessary waste of time associated with ordering the justices or the Crown Court judge to state a case before being able to consider the merits of the conviction.

9.60   If a person wrongly applies for judicial review when they should have appealed by way of case stated or vice versa, the High Court can sometimes act in way that avoids that person being prejudiced. For example, in one case where a party wrongly proceeded by way of judicial review, the High Court extended the time allowed for lodging an appeal by way of case stated. That then enabled the High Court to consider the case as if it was an appeal by case stated.[106]

PROCEDURE

Bail as a form of interim relief

9.61   The first matter that needs to be considered when a claimant is detained is whether they wish to apply for bail. This may not be as straightforward an issue as it might appear to be. If a claimant is serving a criminal sentence applying for bail in the course of an unsuccessful judicial review claim may require them to return to prison without any reduction in the time that they serve.[107] They will be released from prison

---

[104]   Although judicial review is normally the correct form of proceedings, it may be possible to bring an appeal by way of case stated if the justices were asked to rule on an issue such as bias. See *Johnson v Leicestershire Constabulary*, *The Times*, 7 October 1998.
[105]   *R v Southwark Crown Court, ex p Brooke* [1997] COD 81.
[106]   *R v Clerkenwell Stipendiary Magistrate, ex p DPP* [1984] QB 821 at 836D.
[107]   *R (Akhtar) v Governor of Newhall Prison* [2001] ACD 69 and Civil Procedure Rules 1998 (SI 1998/3132) ('the CPR 1998'), Part 25.3.

later than they would have been had bail not been granted. That may mean that in practice it is in the interest of the claimant to seek an expedited hearing of the claim for judicial review rather than bail.

9.62   When a person has sought permission to bring judicial review proceedings for a quashing order challenging proceedings in the Crown Court, that person is entitled to apply to the Crown Court for bail.[108] There is no equivalent power allowing the magistrates' court to grant bail.[109] The application to the Crown Court must be on at least 24 hours notice.[110] The procedure for making an application is the same as when a defendant in proceedings in the magistrates' court seeks bail in the Crown Court.[111] If the Crown Court does grant bail, and an application of judicial review is determined or withdrawn, magistrates may issue a process enforcing the decision that is the subject of the judicial review.[112]

9.63   The power of an inferior court or tribunal to consider a bail application does not necessarily mean that the Administrative Court cannot also consider an application. Where a defendant applies for permission to seek an order quashing a conviction or sentence in the magistrates' court or challenging proceedings in the Crown Court, there is a statutory right to apply to the Administrative Court for bail.[113] The Administrative Court also has an inherent power to grant bail in the course of applications for judicial review.[114] It has become accepted that this is true whether the case is a criminal cause or matter or some other form of proceedings.[115]

9.64   There is some suggestion that a judicial review claimant should only apply for bail to the Administrative Court after they have tried to apply for bail by taking advantage of any alternative jurisdiction that permits an application for bail to an inferior court or tribunal.[116] In practice the Administrative Court is generally willing to hear bail applications despite the existence of an alternative right of application. That is perhaps not surprising as the Administrative Court will be best able to judge the merits of the judicial review, which is clearly a factor that will be relevant to the grant of bail.

9.65   The procedure rules provide that bail applications should be made by claim form using Form 97.[117] However, in practice an application for bail is normally made by indicating that an application is being made for bail on the claim form or alternatively filing an application notice seeking bail.

9.66   In a criminal case the bail application must be served on the prosecutor and on the Director of Public Prosecutions, if the prosecution is being carried on by him.[118]

---

[108]   Senior Courts Act 1981, section 81(1)(e).

[109]   *Ex p Blyth* [1944] 1 KB 532; holding that an express statutory provision is required if a person is to be bailed after conviction. This, however, contrasts with decisions of the High Court that it has an inherent power to grant bail during a judicial review.

[110]   Criminal Procedure Rules (SI 2010/60), part 19.18(2).

[111]   Criminal Procedure Rules (SI 2010/60), part 19.18.

[112]   CPR 1998, Sch 1, RSC Ord 79, r 9(11).

[113]   Criminal Justice Act 1948, section 37(1)(b)(ii) and (d).

[114]   *R v Secretary of State for the Home Department, ex p Turkoglu* [1988] QB 398.

[115]   See e g *Armand v Home Secretary* [1943] AC 147 for a case where in the context of a criminal habeas corpus application, it was assumed that there was an inherent power to grant bail. That inherent power may be limited following conviction: *ex p Blyth* [1944] 1 KB 532.

[116]   *R v Secretary of State for the Home Department, ex p Kelso* [1998] INLR 603.

[117]   CPR 1998, Sch 1, RSC Ord 79, rule 9 (2). Form 97 is not a standard court form which supports the practice of not submitting it.

[118]   CPR 1998, Sch 1, RSC Ord 79, rule 9 (2)(a).

9.67   Service must take place at least 24 hours before the date set for the hearing.[119] The rules state that the application must be supported by a witness statement or affidavit.[120] In practice, this is usually unnecessary in the context of a claim for judicial review as the evidence in support of the judicial review claim can normally stand as the evidence in support of the bail application. Clearly, if this is to happen, the evidence in support of the judicial review claim must include matters relevant to the grant of bail.

9.68   In principle, there is no reason why bail should not be granted before permission to apply for judicial review has been ordered, as the inherent and statutory jurisdiction to grant bail extends to applications for permission.[121] In practice, however, the application for bail is normally considered at the same hearing as the application for permission, partly because a High Court judge is unlikely to be willing to grant bail unless they are satisfied that the application for judicial review is arguable.

9.69   In principle bail can be considered by the High Court judge who considers the paper application for permission. If bail and permission are refused it will be possible to make a renewed application for permission in the Administrative Court. It would appear, however, that in a criminal cause or matter bail cannot be sought from a High Court judge when an application for bail has previously been refused.[122] That means that it may be worth asking the judge not to rule on bail when he considers a paper application if he is minded to refuse permission.

9.70   Clearly, if a High Court judge refuses permission to apply for judicial review following an oral hearing, the Administrative Court is functus officio and so is unable to consider a bail application.

9.71   The fact that there is a need for bail is highly likely to justify a request for the judicial review claim to be given urgent consideration.

9.72   The right to bail under s 4 of the Bail Act 1976 does not apply to bail applications during judicial review proceedings in the Administrative Court.[123] That does not, however, mean that the Administrative Court will not grant bail. It merely means that there is no presumption that bail should be granted.

9.73   Prosecutors or others can make an application to the Administrative Court for an order varying the conditions imposed on bail by the High Court. At least 24 hours notice of the application should be given to the person who has been granted bail.[124] This application should be supported by an affidavit or witness statement.[125]

Role of the defendant

9.74   In judicial review proceedings, magistrates whose decision is challenged will often not be represented at any hearing. Indeed, it has been held that justices should not be represented by counsel unless there is some special factor such as an allegation of

---

[119]   Ibid rule 9(2).
[120]   Ibid rule 9(3).
[121]   *R v Secretary of State for the Home Department, ex p Turkoglu* [1988] QB 398.
[122]   CPR 1998, Sch 1, RSC Ord 79, rule 9(12).
[123]   Bail Act 1976, s 4(2).
[124]   CPR 1998, Sch 1, RSC Ord 79, rule 9(2)(b).
[125]   Ibid, rule 9(3).

misconduct on the part of the justices.[126] However, the High Court will be very keen to have the views of the respondent when it determines the application.[127] As a result in most cases respondents should serve written evidence commenting on the application. In particular the written evidence should highlight any factual matters in the applicant's written evidence and grounds that are not agreed or any other matters that the court will find relevant.

9.75   The purpose of the written evidence described above should not be to advocate for any particular outcome. It is intended merely to assist the court. The effective defendant in any judicial review claim should be the opposing party in the magistrates' court. Hence, if a judicial review claim is brought by a defendant to a criminal prosecution, the effective defendant to a judicial review claim will be the prosecutor. They will have standing as an interested party.

Relief at the conclusion of proceedings

9.76   All of the normal remedies that are available in judicial review proceedings are also available in a criminal matter. However, in addition, section 43(1) of the Senior Courts Act 1981 provides the Administrative Court with a specific statutory power to vary a sentence imposed by a magistrates' court or the Crown Court following a committal for sentence or an appeal against a sentence if there has been a successful application for a quashing order. Before exercising the power, the Administrative Court must be satisfied that the sentence was one that the magistrates' court or Crown Court had no power to impose. When the Administrative Court exercises the power, it can impose any sentence that the court that passed sentence could have imposed.

9.77   Although s 43(1) requires the High Court to be satisfied that the sentence was not one that the magistrates' court or Crown Court had the power to impose, that does not mean that the power can only be exercised where the sentence imposed was in excess of the maximum prescribed by law. For example, a sentence imposed in breach of natural justice can be quashed and a fresh sentence imposed after the Administrative Court has heard the representations that magistrates would have heard had they not acted in breach of natural justice.[128]

COSTS AGAINST MAGISTRATES' COURTS

9.78   When magistrates are involved in proceedings in the High Court as the respondent or as the decision-maker in an appeal by way of case stated, the High Court will be reluctant to order costs against the magistrates.

9.79   Mr Justice Cazalet has stated that the principles that should be applied when determining whether costs should be awarded against magistrates are:

---

[126]   *R v Cambourne Justices, ex p Pearce* [1954] 2 All ER 850 at 856E. But note the remarks of Lord Justice Simon Brown asking Treasury Solicitors to instruct counsel to review the merits of a large number of judicial reviews of warrants of commitment in the light of his judgment in *R v Oldham Justices, ex p Cawley* [1996] 1 All ER 464 at 481G which suggests that the court increasingly finds that it is assisted by respondents being represented.

[127]   For example in *R v Gloucester Crown Court, ex p Chester, The Independent*, 6 July 1998, QBD it was held that even where an applicant erred by bringing judicial review proceedings instead of an appeal by case stated the respondent should at least write a letter stating whether they opposed the application.

[128]   *R v Pateley Bridge Justices, ex p Percy* [1994] COD 453.

(i)   that costs would only be awarded against justices in the rarest of circumstances when they have done something which calls for strong disapproval; and

(ii)   that it was the practice not to grant costs against justices merely because they have made a mistake in law, but only if they have acted perversely or with some disregard for the elementary principles which every court ought to obey, and even then only if it was a particularly bad case.[129]

9.80   Thus, applying these principles, the High Court has awarded costs against magistrates in a case where they took a perverse decision in flagrant disregard of elementary principles.[130]

9.81   In general, magistrates should not be represented in cases where their decision is being challenged. If magistrates do attend at a hearing when they should not have attended the High Court will be required to take account of the reasonableness of their conduct before ordering costs.[131] In practice this means that the High Court will consider whether their decision to attend was a reasonable decision. This means that if the magistrates attend and are unsuccessful, they increase the risk that costs will be awarded against them. If they are successful, the High Court will be unwilling to order costs in their favour unless they can show that there were particularly good reasons why they should attend.

9.82   The High Court will be particularly reluctant to award costs against magistrates in cases when they have not appeared.[132] That does not mean, however, that there can never be a costs order against magistrates. For example, costs have been awarded in cases where the magistrates have caused an unnecessary substantive hearing by failing to sign a consent order[133] and where they failed to take a grant of permission sufficiently seriously in a case challenging a refusal to state a case.[134]

Costs from central funds

9.83   The Divisional Court has the power to award costs to a defendant from central funds in any criminal cause or matter that it determines.[135] Similarly the House of Lords may make such an order in an appeal from the Divisional Court.[136] A similar power exists to award costs to a prosecutor who is not a public authority or a person acting on their behalf.[137]

---

[129]   *R v Bristol Magistrates Court, ex p Hodge* [1997] QB 974 at 982C applying the test in *R v York City Justices, ex p Farmery* (1988) 153 JP 257.

[130]   *R v Lincoln Justices, ex p Count* (1996) 8 Admin LR 233 in which magistrates refused to adjourn a case as there was no specific statutory power enabling them to adjourn.

[131]   CPR 44.3(4).

[132]   *R v Newcastle under Lyme Justices, ex p Massey* [1994] 1 WLR 1684 at 1692A.

[133]   *R v Newcastle under Lyme Justices, ex p Massey* [1994] 1 WLR 1684.

[134]   *R v Huntingdon Magistrates' Court, ex p Percy* [1994] COD 323; See also *R v Metropolitan Stipendiary Magistrate, ex p Ali, The Independent,* 12 May 1997 where costs were awarded against a magistrate for continuing to refuse to state a case when the judge who had granted permission had said that it would be impossible to know if the magistrate had erred if they did not state a case.

[135]   Prosecution of Offences Act 1985, s 16(5)(a); see para 9.5 onwards for a definition of the scope of a 'criminal cause or matter'.

[136]   Prosecution of Offences Act 1985, s 16(5)(b).

[137]   Prosecution of Offences Act 1985, s 17.

9.84   The power to make an order for costs from central funds can be important in legally aided cases where the defendant is a magistrates' court. From a claimant's point of view a failure to obtain a costs order may result in their lawyers receiving a lower rate of remuneration. It may also result in less funds being available for other claims. These matters have persuaded courts to make orders for costs from central funds despite the fact that the claimant is in receipt of public funding.[138]

Appeal to the Supreme Court

9.85   A party to a judicial review in a criminal cause or matter can only appeal to the Supreme Court.[139] The Administrative Court can grant permission to appeal.[140] However, that is extremely unlikely. In practice it is likely to be necessary to obtain permission to appeal from the Supreme Court.[141] However, for reasons that are expanded upon below, the Supreme Court may lack jurisdiction to consider an application for permission to appeal.

9.86   An application for permission to appeal should be made to the Administrative Court within 28 days of the date that the Court dismisses the claim for judicial review.[142] The Supreme Court should then be petitioned within 28 days of the decision of the Administrative Court refusing permission.[143] These time limits can only be extended where the party seeking permission to appeal was a defendant in the criminal proceedings.[144] Time can be extended when the delay is the result of delay in determining an application for public funding. Where the Registrar is informed that an application is being made for public funding, time is extended so that it runs until 28 days from the final decision on that application.[145]

9.87   Before the Supreme Court can be petitioned for permission to appeal the Administrative Court must issue a certificate that there is a point of law of general public importance.[146]

9.88   Technically it would appear that an application for a certificate of public importance is not subject to the same time limits as an application for permission to appeal.[147] In practice, however, the application to the Administrative Court for it to certify a point of law of general public importance is made at the same time as the application for permission to appeal. That is primarily because the Administrative Court must certify a point of law of general public importance at the same time as they grant permission to appeal if they grant permission to appeal.

9.89   Great care must be taken to draft a question that both reflects the issues raised in the case and raises a point that is of significant general importance. The Administrative Court is unlikely to permit a prospective appellant to have more than one attempt to formulate a question and so it is important that the question is formulated the first time.

---

[138]   Eg *R v Sheffield Magistrates' Court, ex p Ojo* (2000) 164 JP 659.
[139]   Administration of Justice Act 1960, s 1.
[140]   Ibid.
[141]   Ibid.
[142]   Administration of Justice Act 1960, s 2.
[143]   Ibid.
[144]   Ibid and *R v Weir* [2001] 1 WLR 421 holding that time could not be extended for a prosecutor to appeal.
[145]   Supreme Court Rules 2009 (SI 2009/1603), rule 5(5).
[146]   Administration of Justice Act 1960, s 1.
[147]   *Westley v Hertfordshire County Council*, unreported, 22 October 1998.

CONCLUDING REMARKS

9.90   Judicial review in crime has always been and remains a specialist area of judicial review governed by distinct rules. In addition, as the recent House of Lords decision in *R (Corner House Research) v DPP* [2008] 3 WLR 568 demonstrates by limiting the scope of challenges to decisions of prosecutors, the higher courts are determined to limit satellite litigation in crime. These matters may explain why there is surprisingly little judicial review in crime. The volume of work undertaken by the magistrates court and the relative lack of legal training of many lay magistrates all suggest that there could be far more claims for judicial review brought. However, it may well be that many criminal practitioners feel uncomfortable in the unfamiliar environs of the Administrative Court.

9.91   The apparent unwillingness of parties to criminal proceedings to bring proceedings in the Administrative Court means that it is welcome that the Law Commission is reviewing this area. It may well be that a more accessible procedure for challenging errors of the inferior courts can be devised.

Chapter 10

EDUCATION

INTRODUCTION

10.1   In family life and for society, relatively few issues attract greater importance than the provision of education. The law of education is highly complex and closely entwined with political policy. Where competing public, private and commercial interests converge and conflict, judicial review has become a prevalent means of challenge. In this chapter, we start by providing a brief overview of the education system, followed by a more detailed consideration of the areas in which public law challenges are common, including relevant practice issues, before concluding with a brief examination of the impact of Human Rights law in this area.[1]

OVERVIEW

The legislative framework

10.2   In England and Wales, the main principles and framework of the schools system are set out in the Education Act 1996 (EA 1996), the School Inspections Act 1996 (SIA), the School Standards and Framework Act 1998 (SSFA) and the Education Act 2002 (EA 2002).

10.3   These Acts consolidated the principles of the Education Act 1944 (EA 1944) and successive statutes such as the Education Reform Act 1988 (ERA). Since 1996, several major pieces of education legislation have been introduced, including the following:

- Teaching and Higher Education Act 1998

- Learning and Skills Act 2000

- Special Educational Needs and Disability Act 2001

- Higher Education Act 2004

- Children Act 2004

- Education Act 2005

- Education and Inspections Act 2006

---

[1]   For more detailed consideration of the law of education see *Education Law and Practice* (3rd edn: Jordans 2010), *The Law of Education* (2nd edn: Jordans 2004) and *The Law of Education* (Butterworths: looseleaf).

- Childcare Act 2006

- Further Education and Training Act 2007

- Education and Skills Act 2008

- Children and Young Persons Act 2008

- Apprenticeships, Skills, Children and Learning Act 2009

- Children, Schools and Families Act 2010

- Academies Act 2010

10.4 Section 7 of the EA 1996 confirms the principles of education as being those of providing free, efficient full-time education, suitable to the age, ability and aptitude, and any special educational needs that the child may have, for all children during defined, compulsory stages of education.

10.5 The EA 1996 continues to provide the basis for the management of schools in England and Wales, whilst the SSFA introduced a new framework for the legal status of schools.

10.6 The EA 2002 restated the division of compulsory education into four key stages,[2] whilst at the same time creating a legislative distinction between key stages 1 to 3 and key stage 4 of compulsory education (5–7, 7–11, 11–14 and 14–16 years respectively). The EA 2002 also consolidated earlier legislation, altered the basis on which teachers and support staff could be employed and introduced changes regarding admissions to and exclusions from maintained schools.

10.7 The Government of Wales Act 1998 began a series of radical changes to education law in Wales, with transfer of functions from Westminster to Cardiff on an ongoing basis. The National Assembly for Wales (and now the Welsh Assembly Government) can make its own Measures, Orders and Regulations, many of which operate in parallel to statutory provisions in England. The Education and Skills Act 2008 (ESA) further enhanced Welsh independence from Westminster on matters of education. Where appropriate, the applicable legislation or guidance for Wales is noted below.

Categorisation of schools and colleges

State schools

10.8 State schools in England and Wales are categorised by ownership, funding, pupil age and intake. Section 20(1) of the SSFA provides that schools maintained by local education authorities (LEAs) shall be divided into the following categories:

---

[2] Key stages were first introduced by the Education Reform Act 1988 upon the introduction of the National Curriculum and the delegation of budgets to schools. The ERA also made important reforms to higher education, taking polytechnics and higher education colleges out of local authority control.

(a)   community schools;[3]

(b)   foundation schools;[4]

(c)   voluntary schools,[5] comprising:

    (i)   voluntary aided schools;[6] and
    (ii)   voluntary controlled schools;[7]

(d)   community special schools;[8] and

(e)   foundation special schools.[9]

10.9   Within the above categorises, schools are also defined by their pupils' age range namely as either:

(a)   a nursery school;[10]

(b)   a primary school;[11]

(c)   a middle school;[12]

(d)   a secondary school (or high school);[13]

(e)   a sixth-form.[14]

10.10 Schools defined by their selective pupil intake fall into two main groups; grammar schools and those which otherwise select on the basis of aptitude. Grammar

---

[3]   A 'community school' is a mainstream (as opposed to special) school belonging to the LEA, including those formerly described as 'county schools'.

[4]   A 'foundation school' is a category of maintained school, as defined by the SSFA, s 21(1), and is owned by a trust, foundation body or statutory corporation.

[5]   A 'voluntary school' was historically one provided by a church or philanthropist.

[6]   A 'voluntary aided school' is a maintained school owned and run by a voluntary organisation.

[7]   A 'voluntary controlled school' is a maintained school, the original buildings of which are owned by a voluntary organization.

[8]   A 'special school' is one specifically organised to make educational provision for pupils with special educational needs. LEA provision for special educational needs is made either through a community special school or a foundation special school.

[9]   See note 8 above, SFFA, s 21(1), and the School Organisation (Foundation Special Schools) (Application of Provisions Relating to Foundations) (England) Regulations 2007 (SI 2007/1329).

[10]   A 'nursery school' is a school used wholly or mainly for providing education for children who have attained the age of two, but are under compulsory school age, as provided by the EA 1996, s 6.

[11]   A 'primary school' is a school providing primary education; ie education suitable to the requirements of children between two and compulsory school age, children above compulsory school age who are under ten and a half years and older children whom it is expedient to educate with the latter group, as provided by the EA 1996, s 2(1).

[12]   A 'middle school' teaches children from about age 8–9 to age 12–13 and is likely to straddle one or more Key Stage boundaries. See EA 1996, s 5(3).

[13]   A 'secondary school' is a school providing secondary education; ie education suitable to the requirements of children above compulsory school age who are over ten and a half years and older or whom it is expedient to educate with children over that age), as provided by EA 1996, s 5(2).

[14]   A 'sixth-form' denotes education of those over compulsory school age. A 'sixth form' may be part of a secondary school or a separate 'sixth-form college', the latter representing a further education establishment, as opposed to a school.

schools select pupils of high ability by examination, usually at 11+, and are designated as such by the SSFA.[15] Some maintained schools select pupils for admission on the basis of aptitude. This is permitted where, at the beginning of the 1997–1998 school year, the school made provision for selection of its pupils by ability or aptitude (the so called 'pre-existing arrangements' exemption). These arrangements must have operated continuously and without significant change to the basis of selection.[16]

10.11 Specialist schools are funded, both by the DfE and sponsorship, with a view to developing talent within PE, sport, performing arts, visual arts, modern foreign languages, design technology, engineering or information technology. A specialist school may select up to 10 per cent of its intake by means of carefully-set aptitude tests in one or more specialism.[17]

Independent schools

10.12 Independent schools, as defined,[18] are typically financed by means of fees payable by parents and, in some cases, donations and grants from benefactors. The EA 2002 requires providers to register with the DfE and the Welsh Assembly Government respectively.[19] Schools must meet standards covering the quality of education; spiritual, moral, social and cultural development of pupils; welfare, health and safety of pupils; suitability of the people running the school; standards of premises; provision of information and handling of complaints. The authorities are empowered to require an independent school to be inspected by Ofsted in England or Estyn in Wales.[20]

10.13 The curriculum and governance of an independent school is the responsibility of the proprietor and typically administered under the auspices of a board of governors. The curriculum is one of the major aspects considered in a school inspection and both the range and the depth of the curriculum offered must be appropriate for the age, aptitude, ability and any special educational needs of the pupils in the school. A school which fails to meet the required standards may be deleted from the register.[21]

10.14 The relationship between the parent of a pupil registered at an independent school and the body responsible for administering the school is usually contractual. On this basis, independent schools are not generally amenable to judicial review by parents, although it is an implied term that decisions, where appropriate, will be reached in accordance with the principles of natural justice.[22]

---

[15] Section 104, SSFA.
[16] SSFA as amended, s 100.
[17] SSFA as amended, s 102.
[18] EA 1996, s 463.
[19] Section 158, EA 2002.
[20] For England, see EA 2002, s 162A, (details at www.ofsted.gov.uk) For Wales, see EA 2002, s 163 (details at www.estyn.gov.uk).
[21] It is an offence to conduct an independent school which is not registered: EA 2002, s 159.
[22] See *R(B) v Fernhill Manor School* [1994] ELR 67; *R(T) v Governors of Haberdashers' Aske's Hatcham College Trust* [1995] ELR 350 (city technology college amenable to review); *R(S) v Cobham Hall School* [1998] ELR 389 (decision to withdraw an assisted place amenable to review); *R(R) v Muntham House School* [2000] ELR 287 (non-maintainable fee-paying school not amenable to review, although it fell outside the definition of an 'independent school' under EA 1996, s 463).

Further education

10.15 Under the Further and Higher Education Act 1992 ('FHEA'), most 'further education' institutions became independent of home LEAs as 'further education corporations' and 'designated institutions'. These institutions included FE colleges (both general and specialist) and sixth-form colleges. Under the Learning and Skills Act 2000 (LSA), former voluntary aided schools which had joined the further education sector in 1992 as 'designated institutions' also became incorporated. As public corporations, FE institutions are subject to company law and are typically administered under the direction of a governing body (with a role similar to the board of directors of a company). The governing body will be responsible, within the limits imposed by its statutory obligations, for all decisions affecting the institution.

10.16 Under the FHEA, adult education centres which provided largely part-time further education courses for adults continued to be maintained by home LEAs. Under the LSA, any provision made by an LEA is now funded by the Learning and Skills Council (LSC) in England, and the Department for Children, Education, Lifelong Learning and Skills (DCELLS) in Wales.[23]

10.17 Legal challenges by way of judicial review against FE institutions are unlikely to prove common. Whilst being statutory bodies and amenable to public law challenge in principle, FE institutions are likely to employ appropriate multi-layered appeal and complaints procedures, which need to be exhausted.[24] In *R (Griffiths) v Lewisham College*,[25] Collins J allowed an application for judicial review where the defendant college had failed to adhere to its own disciplinary procedures in connection with a permanent exclusion. The claimant had not, amongst other matters, been given the stipulated notice period, a clear, advance statement of the nature of the conduct complained of or a proper opportunity to dispute the facts relied upon. A subsequent appeal hearing did not cure these defects, as its scope of review was unduly limited.

Higher education

10.18 Higher education in England and Wales is provided by a single, unified sector of institutions which are independent, self-governing bodies constituted by Royal Charter or by statute to develop their own programmes of study and award individual degrees.

10.19 A programme of 'higher education' is defined as any course fulfilling one of the following descriptions:[26]

(a)   a course for the further training of teachers or youth and community workers;

(b)   a post-graduate course (including a higher degree course);

(c)   a first degree course;

(d)   a course for the Diploma of Higher Education;

---

[23]   For further information visit http://www.dcsf.gov.uk/furthereducation. For Wales, visit http://new.wales.gov.uk/topics/educationandskills/.

[24]   For example, see *R (Carnell) v Regent's Park College and other* [2008] ELR 268 (permission refused in claim against Higher Education body, where claimant had failed to exhaust alternate remedies).

[25]   [2007] EWHC 809 (Admin).

[26]   Sections 120(1), 235(2)(e) and Sch 6 of the ERA 1988.

(e)   a course for the Higher National Diploma or Higher National Certificate of the Business & Technician Education Council, or the Diploma in Management Studies;

(f)   a course for the Certificate in Education;

(g)   a course in preparation for a professional examination at higher level;

(h)   a course providing education at a higher level (whether or not in preparation for an examination).

10.20 The governance of a HE establishment is amenable to judicial review, subject to an aggrieved party exhausting alternative means of redress.[27] In particular, universities and other HE institutions must participate in the scheme for dealing with student complaints set up under Part 2 of the Higher Education Act 2004 (HEA).[28] The operator of the student complaints scheme under section 13 of the HEA is the 'Office of the Independent Adjudicator for Higher Education' (OIA).

10.21 Anyone who was or is registered as a student at a participating HE institution can complain to the OIA about the following matters; a programme of study or research for which he or she is or was registered; a service provided to him or her by a HE institution; a final decision by a HE institution's disciplinary or appeal body. There is, however, no general obligation on the OIA to express an opinion on the strength of a particular allegation, for example a complaint of disability discrimination, although it is possible for it to do so in the exercise of its discretion.[29]

10.22 An aggrieved student must exhaust any internal complaints procedure before approaching the OIA. The OIA will not investigate a complaint if it relates to a matter of academic judgement[30] or if the matter is or has been the subject of court proceedings. A claim for judicial review, in the event of dissatisfaction, will lie against the HE institution and/or OIA on conventional public law grounds.[31]

SUBSTANTIVE AREAS OF CHALLENGE

School organisation

10.23 Detailed consideration of the law relating to school organisation, including establishment of new or alteration of existing state schools, is beyond the scope of this

---

[27]   *R (Shi) v King's College London* [2008] ELR 414; *R (Carnell) v Regent's Park College and other* [2008] ELR 268; *R (Clarke) v Cardiff University* [2009] NPC 105 (successful challenge against BVC provider upon grounds of substantive unfairness).

[28]   The traditional role of the 'Visitor', who used to investigate student and staff complaints, was abolished in the HEA, s 20.

[29]   *R (Maxwell) v Office of the Independent Adjudicator & University of Salford* [2010] EWHC 1889 (Admin).

[30]   It is extremely difficult, in any event, to challenge an exercise of academic judgement: see *R (Vijayatunga) v Her Majesty the Queen in Council* [1989] 3 WLR 13; *R (Bashir) v Cranfield University* [1999] ELR 317; *R (Persaud) v Cambridge University* [2001] ELR 480.

[31]   *R (Siborurema) v Office of the Independent Adjudicator* [2008] ELR 209; *R (Arratoon) v Office of the Independent Adjudicator* [2009] ELR 186; *R (Budd) v Office of the Independent Adjudicator* [2010] EWHC 1056 (Admin).

work.[32] For the most part, the threatened closure of a school is the most likely subject matter of a public law challenge in this context.[33]

10.24 Parents reasonably expect schools to remain open and, accordingly, Part 2, sections 15–17 of the Education and Inspection Act 2006 (EIA) requires LEAs and governors to publicise proposed closures (or discontinuances as they are described within the EIA). Detailed requirements for the publishing of proposals are provided at Sch 2 and in the regulations made under section 15 of the EIA.[34] Every closure proposal must begin with consultation under section 16 of the EIA. Schedule 2 of the EIA provides for the detailed consideration of such proposals by the home LEA and the procedure for independent review by the adjudicator.[35]

10.25 Rural primary schools and special schools have added protection from closure,[36] although the latter are subject to a fast-track closure scheme where the pupils are thought by the Secretary of State to be at risk to their health, safety or welfare.[37]

10.26 It remains to be seen whether, as intended, improved consultation and closer independent scrutiny, as provided under Part 2 of the EIA, bolsters public assurance and reduces the number of judicial review applications in this context.[38]

School admissions

Introduction

10.27 School admission arrangements remain one of the most contentious and extensively litigated areas within the education sphere. For many parents, especially in rural areas, there is only one school that is both suitable for their child's education and within an appropriate travelling distance. For others, particularly those living in urban areas, there are often several suitable, accessible schools and a real element of choice exists. The school admissions process attempts to resolve the inherent conflicts within an

---

[32] See the *Law of Education* (Butterworths: looseleaf), Division A, Chapter 3 for further detail.

[33] Although the establishment of institutions can also form the subject matter of challenge: *R (Chandler) v Camden LBC and others* [2009] BLGR 4127, approved [2010] ELR 192 (failed challenge to the proposed establishment of a city academy).

[34] School Organisation (Establishment and Discontinuance of Schools) (England) Regulations 2007 (SI 2007/1288).

[35] Appointed under SSFA 1998, s 25(3).

[36] EIA, ss 15(4) and 16.

[37] EIA, s 17.

[38] Examples of cases decided before and following the above legislative changes include: *R (N) v Leeds CC* [1999] ELR 324 (claim dismissed where consultation effective); *R (T) v Secretary of State for Education* [2000] Ed CR 652 (use of wrong language in decision letter implied application of wrong test by minister upon approval of reorganisation plan); *R (Beaumont) v Kirklees MBC* [2001] ELR 204 (council resolution to close school quashed owing to substantial risk of bias); *R (B and C) v Lambeth LBC* [2001] HWHC 515 (Admin) (unsuccessful claim based upon alleged failure to have appropriate regard to SEN requirements of pupils); *R (WB) v School Organisation Committee for Leeds* [2003] ELR 67 (unsuccessful challenge based upon inadequate notice of consultation meeting); *R (Louden) v School Organisation Committee for Bury* [2002] EWHC 2749 (Admin) (claim on various grounds dismissed on merits and by reference to delay); *R (P) v Schools Adjudicator* [2007] BLGR 346 (unsuccessful challenge of decision to approve the discontinuance of a maintained primary school); *R (Elphinstone) v Westminster CC and others* [2009] ELR 24 (unsuccessful challenge based upon allegedly defective consultation); *R (Parr) v Hertfordshire CC* [2008] EWHC 3379 (Admin) (successful challenge to primary school closure decision where proposal failed to adequately address SEN provision); *R (McDougal) v Liverpool CC* [2009] ELR 510 (unsuccessful challenge to comprehensive school closure).

administrative system based on parental preference, but where places at preferred establishments are limited and often oversubscribed.

10.28 Judicial review has played a significant role in shaping the law and practice relating to school admissions and continues to offer an appropriate means of challenge in some cases. This section provides an overview of the legal framework and its guiding principles, highlighting reported cases of continuing relevance.

The legal framework

10.29 The principle legislation is Part III of the SSFA, sections 84–98 as amended, which is supplemented by comprehensive statutory guidance, namely the School Admissions Code and the School Admission Appeals Code.[39]

10.30 The school admissions system in England[40] applies to community, foundation and voluntary schools and to academies, whilst nursery school admissions are handled separately.[41] The application of the system to academies derives contractually from the institution's public funding agreement, whilst other 'state' schools are included in the system by statute.

Co-ordination of school admissions

10.31 Each school is served by an 'admission authority' which has initial responsibility for allocating places. The admission authority must know how many children it can and will admit in each relevant year and, in the event of oversubscription, it must have a transparent policy by which it will accord precedence to applications. To enable multiple and/or out-of-area applications, each admission authority must also co-ordinate its annual admissions process with those of its neighbouring admission authorities.

10.32 The admission authority for each of the five main school categories is summarised below:

School	Admission authority
Academies	Governing body
Community schools	Local authority
Foundation schools	Governing body
Voluntary-aided schools	Governing body
Voluntary-controlled schools	Local authority

10.33 In recognition of the need among parents for certainty and clarity, admission authorities are required to work closely together. To facilitate such co-operation, section 85A of the SSFA requires each LEA to establish an 'admission forum'. The role

---

[39]   The Codes came into force on 10 February 2009 and, save where indicted, these apply with immediate effect – See *R (Buckinghamshire CC) v School Admissions IAP for Buckinghamshire* [2010] ELR 172.

[40]   In Wales, see the School Admissions Code and the School Admission Appeals Code for Wales (July 2009).

[41]   See SSFA as amended, s 98.

of an admission forum, as prescribed, is 'to provide a vehicle for admission authorities and other key interested parties to discuss the effectiveness of local admission arrangements, consider how to deal with difficult admission issues and advise admission authorities on ways in which their arrangements can be improved'.[42] Admission forums examine whether arrangements serve the interests of children and parents within the relevant area and promote fair allocation of places, according to preference, by seeking agreement on key issues.

10.34 Responsibility for the admission arrangements of an academy fall to its governing body, though it must have regard to any advice received from the local admission forum.[43]

10.35 Each admission authority must, before the beginning of each year, determine the admission arrangements which are to apply for that academic period having consulted with the LEA (if the governing body is the admission authority). It must also consult with the admission authorities for all other maintained schools in the LEA area and other parties as prescribed.[44] Where the admission authority for a community or voluntary controlled school is the LEA, it must also consult the governing body of the school in question.

10.36 Each LEA must organise a 'qualifying primary scheme' and a 'qualifying secondary scheme', to co-ordinate arrangements for pupil admissions to primary and secondary schools in its area. These must provide a common application form for all relevant schools, with common deadline dates for every stage of the application and decision-making process. Under a 'qualifying scheme', the individual applications are handled centrally and the LEA (or other central organising body) will allocate places for all applicants at the included schools, making each admission or refusal decision according to the individual admissions priority list (or 'oversubscription criteria') supplied by each admission authority.

10.37 Co-ordination arrangements must provide for admission and refusal decisions to be announced on the same day. This 'announcement day' is chosen at local level for primary school admissions, but is designated the 1 March (or the next working day) for all secondary school admissions.[45] Otherwise, the main requirements for such arrangements are as follows:

- A common application form must be circulated allowing parents to express at least three preferences in rank order and to provide reasons (as considered below). This may be for schools within or outside the home LEA. The common application form must allow parents to provide their name, their address (including documentary evidence in support), and the name, address and date of birth of the child.

---

42   See Education (Admission Forums) (England) Regulations 2002 (SI 2002/2900), as amended, and the School Admissions Code at Paragraphs [4.28]–[4.33]. For Wales, see the Education (Admission Forums) (Wales) Regulations 2003 (SI 2003/2962) and the School Admissions Code, Paragraph [1.9] and Annex B.
43   See SSFA, s 85B.
44   See SSFA, s 88C and the School Admissions (Admissions Arrangements) (England) Regulations 2008 (SI 2008/389), Parts 2 and 4–6. For Wales, see SSFA, s 89.
45   School Admissions (Co-ordination of Admission Arrangements) (England) Regulations 2007 (SI 2007/194), Regs 8 and 9.

- LEAs and admission authorities in the area must exchange information on applications made and potential offers by the dates specified in the scheme.

- The home LEA must pass information on applications to other LEAs ('maintaining authorities') about applications to schools in their area. The maintaining authority must determine the application in the normal way, and inform the home LEA if a place is available by the dates specified in the scheme.

- In the event of multiple school places being available, the home LEA must ensure, so far as is reasonably practicable, that a parent is offered a place at whichever of these schools was the highest ranked preference.

- Offers of primary and secondary places must be sent by the home LEA. Schools must not contact parents about the outcome of applications until after these offers have been received. Only the home LEA can make an official offer.

- Parents who cannot be offered one of their preferred schools must be offered a place at another school, if there are places available.

10.38 In relation to sixth form admissions,[46] each LEA is required to make provision for children over compulsory school age and parents in its area to express a preference as to the school at which sixth form education (or any level of education) is to be provided. In contrast to the general admissions procedure, a child may independently express a preference as to the school at which his or her sixth form education is to be provided, make an application for admission and pursue a right of appeal.

10.39 Admission arrangements may not permit or require any interview with a child or parent for the purpose of determining whether the child is to be admitted to a school, save as permitted for the purposes of assessing suitability for a boarding place and where selection by aptitude is permitted.[47]

The schools adjudicator

10.40 The schools adjudicator[48] has a key role in ensuring a fair admissions system by enforcing statutory requirements and the mandatory provisions of the School Admissions Code. An objection to an admission arrangement may be referred to the adjudicator by any interested party.[49]

10.41 Section 151 of the ESA places a new duty on the adjudicator to consider the legality of admission arrangements referred to him via the LEA report or the Secretary of State. The adjudicator may also consider any admission arrangements that come to his attention by other means, if he considers they may not be compliant.

---

[46] See generally SSFA, ss 86A, 86B and 94, and the School Admissions (Admissions Arrangements) (England) Regulations 2008 (SI 2008/389).

[47] See SSFA, s 88A. For Wales, SSFA, s 88R.

[48] The Adjudicator is appointed under SSFA, s 25. In Wales, the role of the Adjudicator is undertaken by the National Assembly.

[49] School Admissions (Alteration and Variation of, and Objections to, Arrangements) (England) Regulations 2007 (SI 2007/496), as amended. For Wales, see Education (Determination of Admission Arrangements) (Wales) Regulations 2006 (SI 2006/174).

10.42 For obvious reasons, it is desirable that admission arrangements are consistent from one year to the next and the circumstances in which these can be altered or varied are closely circumscribed.[50] An admission authority must implement any direct decision and may revise its admission arrangements in light of a decision by the adjudicator upholding, or partially upholding, an objection to the admission arrangements of another school.

10.43 A decision by the adjudicator must be upheld in the admission arrangements for two subsequent school years, promoting continuity and preventing a school from being required to meet the same objection in successive years.[51]

10.44 In *R (Governing Body of London Oratory School) v Schools Adjudicator*,[52] the claimant challenged the decision of the adjudicator that he had jurisdiction to determine an objection, concerning interview arrangements, from the governors of a local primary school. The adjudicator had upheld a similar objection made in the previous year. On judicial review, the Court had quashed this decision on a number of grounds, but declined substantive relief on the basis that it was too late for the claimant to be reasonably required to change its admission process by omitting interviews. In the circumstances, the Court had not remitted the matter back to the adjudicator as there was only one decision that the adjudicator could lawfully take at that point, irrespective of the merits, namely to dismiss the primary school's objection for reasons of practicability.

10.45 Dismissing the claimant's application for judicial review, Crane J held that there had been no earlier decision by the adjudicator for the purposes of regulations,[53] the original adjudication having been quashed. The underlying purpose of the statutory framework was to ensure that parties, if practicable, were able to obtain an adjudicator's decision on the merits of their objections and the adjudicator has not, in these circumstances, erred in accepting jurisdiction to consider the matter afresh.

10.46 If the adjudicator receives an objection, he may consider admission arrangements for the school as a whole, not simply the specific complaint raised, and also their effect upon other admission arrangements in the relevant area. The adjudicator may also consider admission arrangements that he considers to be complex, including those using convoluted points systems, and amend or replace the same.

10.47 However, the latitude afforded to the adjudicator is not boundless. In *R (Wandsworth LBC) v Schools Adjudicator*,[54] the claimant acted as admission authority for a college (EBC) that operated a selective admissions policy under which it could choose up to 33 per cent of its pupils on the basis of aptitude. Objections were made to the adjudicator on the basis that the policy resulted in an unequal spread of ability across the area and, in particular, produced a damaging effect upon a local secondary school. The claimant demonstrated by intake analysis that the policy caused no distorting effect on local admissions and that the respective intakes of the two

---

[50] See School Admissions (Alteration and Variation of, and Objections to, Arrangements) (England) Regulations 2007, Reg 4.
[51] See School Admissions (Alteration and Variation of, and Objections to, Arrangements) (England) Regulations 2007, Reg 14.
[52] [2005] ELR 484.
[53] In this case, the Education (Objections to Admission Arrangements) Regulations 1999, which were replaced by the School Admissions (Alteration and Variation of, and Objections to, Arrangements) (England) Regulations 2007.
[54] [2004] ELR 274.

establishments were broadly comparable. Notwithstanding, the adjudicator decided to require EBC to reduce its proportion of selective places to 30 per cent in light of the objections. Allowing the claimant's application for judicial review, Goldring J held that the adjudicator had acted unlawfully:[55]

> 'Once the defendant decided that the objectors were wrong in their fundamental complaint regarding an imbalance in intake, it seems to me it made it difficult rationally to justify any interference with it …. The objective of creating a more balanced intake by reference to the intake into other schools in Wandsworth became by definition impossible to achieve as far as EBC was concerned for it was balanced already ….'

10.48 Other challenges have succeeded on conventional public law grounds. In *R (Watford GS for Girls & another) v Schools Adjudicator*,[56] the adjudicator had reduced the permitted percentage of pupils that could be selected on the basis of aptitude by the claimant school from 35 per cent to 25 per cent following objections by some local schools. Allowing the claimant's application, Collins J held that the adjudicator had failed to take into account all relevant considerations. Following earlier parental objection, the school had been forced to reduce its selection on the basis of aptitude from 50 per cent to 35 per cent. No further objections had been received by parents and, otherwise, the aim of having more pupils accepted on the basis of proximity to the school might be achieved in other ways. Accordingly, the adjudicator's decision was quashed.

10.49 In *R (Governing Body of Drayton Manor High School) v Schools Adjudicator*,[57] the claimant school applied for judicial review of the adjudicator's decision to change one of the criteria it applied in the event of over-subscription. Whilst the adjudicator had been entitled on the evidence to find that the criterion indirectly discriminated against poorer families, it was unable to ascertain whether he had addressed the school's counter submission that the substituted criterion would disadvantage other groups. Accordingly, the decision was quashed on the basis that the adjudicator had failed to provide adequate reasons and/or take account of a fundamental part of the school's case. It was not possible to demonstrate on the evidence that its scheme was inequitable and thus in need of rectification.

Parental preference, admission numbers and oversubscription

10.50 At the heart of the admissions system are three key considerations: parental preference, admission numbers and oversubscription. In terms of individual participation, the admissions system must provide parents with an opportunity to make informed decisions about school places and to fully communicate their preferences. In terms of administration, the number of available school places must be ascertained and a fair and transparent allocation method adopted where the number of places exceeds demand.

Parental preference

10.51 The underlying aim of legislative developments in this area, in particular since the 1980s, has been to actively promote choice and involvement by parents in the

---

[55] [2004] ELR 274 at [72].

[56] [2004] ELR 40. See also *R (Governing Body of London Oratory School) v Schools Adjudicator* [2005] ELR 162 (a case concerning selection by a faith school on the basis of interview; a practice now outlawed under SSFA, s 88A).

[57] [2009] ELR 127.

education of their children within the state sector. Due regard to parental wishes is an overriding obligation in public education provision, as provided by section 9 of the EA 1996:

> 'In exercising or performing all their respective powers and duties under the Education Acts, the Secretary of State and local education authorities shall have regard to the general principle that pupils are to be educated in accordance with the wishes of their parents, so far as that is compatible with the provision of efficient instruction and training and the avoidance of unreasonable public expenditure.'

10.52 In the context of school admissions, this guiding principle of 'parental preference' is enshrined in section 86(1) of the SSFA which provides that every LEA must enable the parent of a child in its area to 'express a preference as to the school at which he wishes education to be provided for his child ... and to give reasons for his preference'. The right to express a 'preference' in respect of nursery, primary and secondary school provision is vested in the parent, not the child.[58]

10.53 However, an LEA is not under an absolute obligation to educate a pupil in accordance with parental preference. An LEA must do no more than have regard to this guiding principle, weighing parental preference in the balance together with and against other relevant considerations. The obligation is no more than a 'target' duty, as confirmed in the case of *R (Watt) v Kesteven CC*.[59]

10.54 A Roman Catholic parent sought a declaration that the defendant LEA was liable to pay school fees in respect of Catholic boarding school places for his sons, having declined to send his children to a local independent secondary school on religious grounds. The LEA was in fact willing to fully fund the places at an independent school, with which arrangements had been agreed, or otherwise to make a contribution to the fees payable at the boarding school, as there was no grammar school provision within the area in which the family resided. Dismissing the parent's appeal, Lord Denning MR stated:[60]

> '[The section] does not say that pupils must in all cases be educated in accordance with the wishes of their parents. It only lays down a general principle to which the county council must have regard. This leaves it open to the county council to have regard to other things as

58 See SSFA, s 94.2A (the wider implications of which are considered at **10.148** below).

59 [1955] 1 QB 408; See also *R (W) v Gwynedd CC* (1993) *The Times*, June 25, 1993 (failed challenge against school's refusal to confirm to a parent that his daughter would not be placed against her will into classes that were taught in Welsh); *R (Ali) v Inner London Education Authority* [1990] 2 Admin LR 822 (an alleged failure to provide sufficient places for primary school children in the Tower Hamlets area was not amenable to review because, in the circumstances, there was no prospect of the court exercising its discretion to grant relief); *R (O) v Hackney LBC* [2007] ELR 405 (LEA had not acted unlawfully in rejecting a parent's wishes, having provided a place at a suitable school which it was reasonably practicable for the pupil to attend). For examples of challenges in the context of the 'suitability' of education provided see: *R (G) v Westminster City Council* [2004] ELR 135 (whether the duty arising under section 19 of the EA 1996 to make arrangements for the provision of suitable education had been triggered); *R (Southern) v Oxfordshire CC* [2004] ELR 489 (unsuccessful challenge of LEA refusal to make a discretionary grant to assist a child of exceptional intelligence); *R (Jones and others) v Ceredigion CC* [2004] ELR 506 (successful challenge to transport funding refusal where no suitable arrangements existed for pupils to be registered locally); *R (R and other) v Leeds CC* [2006] ELR 25 (conversely, LEA entitled to withdraw free school transport for out-of-area school where suitable local provision existed); *R (C) v Brent LBC* [2006] ELR 435 (unsuccessful challenge to LEA decision as to suitability of pupil referral unit placement); *R (R) v Kent CC* [2007] ELR 648 (unsuccessful challenge to the suitability of provision for a pupil who had been subject to bullying at the school named by the defendant LEA).

60 [1955] 1 QB 408 at p 424.

well, and also to make exceptions to the general principle if it thinks fit to do so. It cannot, therefore, be said that a county council is at fault simply because it does not see fit to comply with the parent's wishes ....'

10.55 Once ascertained, the LEA and the governing body of a maintained school are obliged to comply with the expressed preference of a parent regarding school admission, unless a lawful exception applies.[61] The circumstances under which parental preference can be overridden are limited as follows:

- if compliance with the preference would prejudice the provision of efficient education or the efficient use of resources;

- the school is a grammar school or otherwise selects some pupils on ability or aptitude as permitted; or

- the child has within the previous two years been excluded from two or more schools.

Prejudice to the provision of efficient education or the efficient use of resources

10.56 Under section 86(3)(a) of the SSFA the duty to make educational provision in accordance with parental preference will not apply 'if compliance with the preference would prejudice the provision of efficient education of the efficient use of resources'. For the most part, this qualification on parental choice is only a relevant issue where an application is made in respect of a school that is oversubscribed, as considered below. In the context of infant school admissions, specific regard must be had to the statutory restriction of class sizes.[62]

10.57 Such prejudice may, however, arise in other more specific circumstances. In *R (N and E) v Governors of the Hasmonean High School*,[63] the Court of Appeal considered the position of two prospective pupils whose admission had been refused by the defendant's appeal committee taking into account their respective special educational needs and the existing demands on the school's resources. The parents alleged that allocation on this basis amounted to selection by ability and was thus unlawful. The defendant considered that the prejudicial effect likely upon admission of either pupil outweighed parental preference. Dismissing the parents' application for judicial review, the Court of Appeal held that whilst academic ability was clearly a factor in the decision not to admit, there was compelling evidence that the difficulty in providing a suitable, appropriately supported education for each pupil had been a significant factor. The admission of either pupil to the school, which was already oversubscribed, was also likely to be detrimental to the education of the other children and the appeal committee had not erred in these circumstances.

Selection

10.58 Parental choice is qualified where compliance with any preference would be incompatible with permissible selective admission arrangements. Save as provided below, any admissions policy based on selection is prohibited:

---

[61]   See SSFA, s 86(2).
[62]   See SSFA, s 1.
[63]   [1994] ELR 343.

- grammar school arrangements;[64]

- any arrangements for selection based upon aptitude which were in place for the school year 1997–98 and which have not changed;[65]

- where the arrangements are designed to secure that in any year the pupils admitted to the school in any relevant age group are representative of all levels of ability among applicants for admission and no level of ability is substantially over or under represented (so called 'banding' arrangements);[66] or

- where the school has one or more specialism (music, sport, art etc) and selective admissions by ability or aptitude do not exceed 10 per cent in any relevant age group.[67]

Exclusion

10.59 Where a child has been permanently excluded from two or more schools, a parent can still express a preference regarding admission, but the requirement to comply with that preference is removed for a period of two years from the date on which the latest exclusion took place. This exception does not apply to the following:

- children with statements of special educational needs;[68]

- children who were below compulsory school age when excluded;[69]

- children who were reinstated following a permanent exclusion;[70] or

- children who would have been reinstated if it had been practicable to do so.[71]

Informing and ascertaining parental preference

10.60 To properly give effect to parental preference, parents must be placed in a position to make informed decisions when applying for places. Each LEA must annually issue a composite prospectus for the maintained schools in its area with prescribed content.[72] The prospectus must include information on arrangements regarding school transport or other support, religious educational provision, curriculum and subject choice etc and, importantly, the criteria to be applied in the event of oversubscription for each school. Where catchment areas or distances are used as oversubscription criteria, the admission authorities must now provide a map of the areas.[73]

---

[64] See SSFA, s 104.
[65] See SSFA, s 100.
[66] See SSFA, s 101.
[67] See SSFA, s 102.
[68] See SSFA, s 98(7).
[69] See SSFA, s 87(4)(c).
[70] See SSFA, s 87(4)(a).
[71] See SSFA, s 87(4)(b).
[72] See the Education (School Information) (England) Regulations 2002 (SI 2002/2897) as amended. For Wales, see the Education (School Information) (Wales) Regulations 1999 (SI 1999/1812).
[73] See Schools Admissions Code, para 2.45. Contrast the position in *R (W) v Stockton on Tees BC* [2000] ELR 93, where a challenge involving, among other matters, failure to supply a map was dismissed upon consideration of earlier, permissive guidance.

10.61 As part of the co-ordination role described above, each LEA will ascertain parental preference by sending out a form which allows parents to rank choices of schools. Forms must afford parents the opportunity to positively express reasons for their preference, without making assumptions.

10.62 In *R (Clark & others) v Rotherham BC*,[74] the Court of Appeal upheld a public law challenge to the defendant's allocation of secondary school places. The LEA provisionally allocated places to children by home catchment area. Parents were advised that if they were happy with allocation on this basis, no further action was required. If a different school was preferred, parents were advised to complete and return a specified form. A number of parents, whose expressed preferences had been declined, claimed that the authority's policy and the individual decisions refusing to admit the children to their preferred school were unlawful on the ground that the statutory requirements had not been met. Upholding the parents' objection, Lord Bingham LCJ rejected the legality of a system based upon inference or acquiescence:[75]

> 'Because parents who were happy with the provisionally-allocated school (in whose catchment area they lived) were not invited to express a preference, it followed that they were not invited to give reasons. On no reasonable reading of the language used could it be said that the authority made arrangements which enabled parents happy to accept their provisional allocation to give reasons. The system which the authority established was not in any meaningful sense such as to give them that opportunity. That was, in truth, because they were not invited to express a preference either.'

10.63 Similarly, in *R (K) v Newham LBC*,[76] a devout Muslim, whose daughter was about to commence her secondary school education, successfully applied for judicial review of the authority's decision not to allocate a place at a single sex school in accordance with his religious beliefs. Whilst the authority had issued a leaflet to parents outlining its school selection policy and confirming that preference for same sex education was one of its criteria for selection, the authority had simply inferred such a preference where parents indicated a same sex school as their first choice. Moreover, there had been no indication whether the claimant's religious beliefs had been considered in reaching the decision. Collins J held that there ought to be a means of separately identifying religious preference and that attention ought to be drawn to that in guidance literature provided by the authority. Moreover, where applications were made to a single sex school, there ought to be some means of ensuring that the authority knew who deliberately made the choice to apply for single sex education. It was clear that neither the authority nor the appeal panel appreciated the importance of the claimant's religious convictions and the decision was remitted.

10.64 Accordingly, there is a need for a positive expression of parental preference where stipulated; arrangements based upon silence or acquiescence will not suffice.

Admission numbers

10.65 If a school has an available place for a prospective pupil, expressed parental preference must be given effect to. Accordingly, the starting point for each admissions authority is to determine the number of pupils in each relevant age group that it proposes to admit to the school in that academic year.[77] The authority must also

---

74 [1998] ELR 152.
75 [1998] ELR 152 at 183.
76 [2002] ELR 390.
77 See SSFA, s 88D(1). For Wales, see SSFA, s 89A(1).

establish the number of boarding school and day places as appropriate.[78] For some
schools, more than one admission number may be necessary for discrete entry points,[79]
eg the number of places that are available to pupils from local primary and middle
schools and where secondary schools have different admission numbers for sixth-form
places. The admission number does not include pupils already of compulsory school age
and already within the school, ie those simply moving up a year within the same
establishment.

10.66 Some exceptions apply. Admission arrangements for nursery places are dealt with
separately.[80] A child with a statement of special educational needs will be allocated a
school place in accordance with his or her assessment.[81]

Oversubscription

10.67 Many challenges have arisen out of the selection criteria applied by admission
authorities in the event of oversubscription. Necessarily, when a school has more
applications than the number of places that have been determined in accordance
section 88D of the SSFA, some scheme or policy must be applied to determine which
applications should be successful.[82]

10.68 In *Choudhury v Governors of Bishop Challoner RC Comprehensive School*, the
House of Lords recognised the inevitability of making choices that were popular with
some parents, but not with others:[83]

> '... when a school is over-subscribed ... [and] ... "compliance with the preference" of all
> applicants would prejudice proper education at the school through overcrowding ... it is
> absolutely necessary that the school should have an admissions policy of some kind in order
> to select from all those who have expressed such preference which of them are to be accepted
> and which rejected. Since whatever admissions criteria are adopted the selection of some
> only of the applicants will necessarily result in defeating the parental preference of those
> who are rejected, what reason is there for Parliament to object to any given set of criteria
> being adopted? ... if the school is over-subscribed, the parental wishes of some parents must
> be defeated whatever criteria are adopted ....'

10.69 Provided that the various statutory requirements and mandatory aspects of the
School Admissions Code are observed, admissions authorities retain considerable
latitude when determining admission criteria, as confirmed by Lloyd LJ in *R (Governors
of John Ball Primary School) v Greenwich LBC*:[84]

> '... I do not regard efficient education or the efficient use of resources as being the sole
> source of lawful policy. Local education authorities were always entitled to have an
> admission policy ... see *Cumings v Birkenhead Corporation* [1972] 1 Ch 12, per Lord Denning
> at p 37C. In my judgment a local education authority can have any reasonable policy they
> think fit, provided it does not conflict with their duties under [section 86 of the SSFA], or
> any other enactment ....'

---

78 See SSFA, s 88D(2). For Wales, see SSFA, s 89A(2).
79 See Schools Admissions Code, para [1.16]. For Wales, see Schools Admissions Code, paras [2.7]–[2.8].
80 See SSFA, s 98(4) and the Schools Admissions Code, para [2.65].
81 See SSFA, s 98(7).
82 Extensive guidance on the setting of fair oversubscription is contained in the respective Schools Admissions
    Codes, Chapter 2.
83 [1992] 2 AC 182 per Lord Browne-Wilkinson at 193D–G.
84 (1990) 88 LGR 589 at 599.

10.70 *R (Governors of John Ball Primary School) v Greenwich LBC* concerned the prohibition on discrimination against pupils from other LEAs, so called out-of-area applications, as provided by section 86(8) of the SSFA. Discrimination may be alleged to arise directly, as in the case of John Ball Primary School, or indirectly, for example, where a geographical restriction is placed on the grant of scholarships or other awards provided under section 518 of the EA 1996.[85]

10.71 The prohibition on out-of-area discrimination is strict and cannot be justified with reference to any other educational duty.[86] Whilst catchment areas may lawfully follow part of a LEA boundary,[87] those which do so closely may be susceptible to challenge.[88]

10.72 It is unlawful for a school to discriminate against a child on the grounds of his or her religion or belief.[89] However, in the event of oversubscription, faith schools are permitted to use faith-based oversubscription criteria in order to give a higher priority to children who are members of, or who practise, their faith or denomination.[90] Such criteria must be framed so as not to conflict with other legislation, such as equality and race relations legislation, and the mandatory provisions of the School Admissions Code. Such criteria are liable to be strictly construed.[91]

10.73 Admissions may be determined by faith, but not by ethnicity. In *R (E) v Governing Body of JFS and others*,[92] a child whose father was Jewish by birth, but whose mother was Jewish by conversion, applied for a place at a publicly maintained Jewish school. The school was oversubscribed and its policy was to give priority to children who were recognised as Jewish by the Office of the Chief Rabbi. The Office of the Chief Rabbi did not recognise the validity of the mother's conversion to Judaism because it had not been conducted by an Orthodox synagogue. It only regarded a child as Jewish if his or her mother was Jewish and the child was thus refused admission to the school. On appeal, the Court of Appeal held that requirement imposed by the school was a test of ethnicity which contravened the Race Relations Act 1976. The matter ultimately concluded on further appeal to the Supreme Court.[93] By a majority, the Court rejected the school's argument that the matrilineal test derived from religious law, and what had motivated the school was compliance with that law. The Court confirmed that the motive of a discriminator for applying the discriminatory criteria was irrelevant. A person, who discriminated on the ground of race, as defined by the Act, could not rely on the fact that the ground of discrimination was one mandated by religion. The Court also concluded that, had the school's policy not amounted to directed discrimination, it would otherwise have amounted to unlawful indirect discrimination, as it could not be regarded as a proportionate means of achieving a legitimate aim.

---

[85] See *R (G) v Lambeth LBC* [1994] ELR 207.

[86] See *R (C and others) v Bromley LBC* [1992] 1 FLR 174 and *R (Kingwell) v Royal Borough of Kingston-upon-Thames* [1992] 1 FLR 182. (In each case, reliance was unsuccessfully placed on target duties to make sufficient educational provision within the LEA area.)

[87] See *R (Razazan) v Wiltshire CC* [1997] ELR 370 and *R (LT) v Rotherham MBC* [2000] LGR 338.

[88] See *R (LT) v Rotherham MBC* [2000] LGR 338 per Lord Justice Stuart-Smith at 344–345.

[89] See Equality Act 2006, s 49.

[90] See *Choudhury v Governors of Bishop Challoner RC Comprehensive School* [1992] 2 AC 182 and the Schools Admission Code at paras [2.46]–[2.58]. For Wales, see Schools Admissions Code, paras [2.39]–[2.41].

[91] *R (T) v Governors of La Sainte Union Convent School* [1996] ELR 98 per Sedley J at 101D.

[92] [2009] 4 All ER 375.

[93] [2010] 2 WLR 153.

10.74 Typically, in the context of prejudice for the purposes of section 86 of the SSFA and faith school admissions, the authority's focus will be on the likely effect upon an over-subscribed establishment. The 'efficient use of resources' within an admission area may, however, entail consideration of problems at other schools, eg where numbers would be short or distorted.[94]

10.75 For example, in *R (F) Lancashire CC*,[95] the parents of a Roman Catholic child had expressed a preference for their son to attend a non-denominational secondary school. Almost a quarter of the schools in the LEA area were Roman Catholic voluntary aided schools, a particularly high percentage. Faced with the prospect of a shortage of places for non-Roman Catholic children, the LEA introduced an admissions policy giving priority to non-Roman Catholic children over Roman Catholic children for places at non-denominational secondary schools in the event of oversubscription. The school was oversubscribed and the parents challenged the arrangement by judicial review. The Court upheld the authority's policy on the grounds that unless such an arrangement existed, it would not be possible to offer places to a number of children in the area in which they lived.

10.76 If a maintained faith-school is under-subscribed, the school must admit a child of another faith or of no faith by virtue of section 86 of the SSFA unless to do so would otherwise prejudice the provision of efficient education or the efficient use of resources.[96]

10.77 Children in care are recognised to be among the most vulnerable in society and all admission authorities must give highest priority within their oversubscription criteria to such pupils.[97] This obligation also applies, with certain modifications, to faith schools and those operating selective admission arrangements.

School admission appeals

10.78 Under section 94 of the SSFA an appeal lies to an Independent Appeal Panel (IAP) for parents aggrieved by a refusal to comply with an expressed preference.[98] The appeal must be organised by the admission authority and constituted and conducted in accordance with the Education (Admissions Appeals Arrangements) Regulations 2002, as amended.[99] As indicated above, the legislative framework is supplement by a detailed Admission Appeals Code.

10.79 An IAP must consist of three to five members appointed by the admission authority at least one of whom must be a lay member and one a person who has experience in education, is acquainted with educational conditions in the area of the authority or is a parent of a pupil registered at the school.[100] In the event of

---

[94] For example, the provisional view of Kay J in *R (Taylor) v Blackpool BC* [1999] ELR 237 (application was dismissed with reference to delay).

[95] [1995] ELR 33.

[96] As in the case of *R (N and E) v Governors of the Hasmonean High School* [1994] ELR 343 above.

[97] In England, see the Education (Admission of Looked After Children) (England) Regulations 2006 (SI 2006/128) and the Schools Admission Code at paras [2.9]–[2.10]. For Wales, see the Education (Admission of Looked After Children) (Wales) Regulations 2009 (SI 2009/821) and For Wales, see Schools Admissions Code, para [2.28].

[98] Save in respect of a 'twice excluded child' – SSFA, s 95(1).

[99] (SI 2002/2899). For Wales, see the Education (Admission Appeals Arrangements) (Wales) Regulations 2005 (SI 2005/1398), as amended.

[100] See Sch 1 of the applicable Regulations.

disagreement between the IAP members, an appeal will be decided by a simple majority vote.[101] There must be continuity of membership and a quorate decision or the appeal must be reheard.[102]

10.80 The decision of an IAP is susceptible to judicial review and the admission authority must provide an indemnity to the members in respect of any legal costs.[103]

10.81 The overwhelming majority of all school admission appeals are in practice about section 86(3)(a) of the SSFA, ie the competing contentions of admission authorities, schools and parents regarding the pervasive issue of 'prejudice'. An IAP must adopt a two-stage process in respect of appeals,[104] save in respect of decisions based upon infant class size prejudice and multiple appeals, as considered below.

10.82 The first stage involves establishment of the relevant facts, namely:

- whether the school's admission arrangements comply with the Part III of the SSFA and the mandatory aspects of the School Admissions Code;

- whether the admission arrangements were correctly applied in the individual's case; and

- whether 'prejudice' would arise were the child to be admitted.

10.83 Relevant considerations include any preferences expressed by the parent, the published admission arrangements and the reasons expressed in favour or against admission.

10.84 The IAP is entitled, in its consideration of all relevant circumstances, to consider the lawfulness of the published admissions arrangements,[105] though it will rarely be necessary for these to be subject to public law scrutiny:[106]

> '... Appeal panels are obliged to take appropriate account of procedural or substantive errors, if they are relevant to the question they have to determine. This may readily apply to relevant errors which are established or self-evident. By contrast, although general admission arrangements are not, as I have said, immune from examination, it will scarcely ever be necessary to go further than to consider whether their application to the particular child was perverse ....'

10.85 Examples of an incorrect application of individual criteria include *R (S) v Governors of Dame Alice Owens School*.[107] The relevant admission policy provided for

---

[101] Sch 2 of the applicable Regulations at paras 1(7) and 2(9).

[102] See *R (S) v Camden LBC* (1990) *The Times*, 7 November and the Admission Appeals Code at paras [1.8]–[1.9]. For Wales, see the School Admission Appeals Code at para [2.18].

[103] Education (Admissions Appeals Arrangements) Regulations 2002, Reg 8. For Wales, see the Education (Admission Appeals Arrangements) (Wales) Regulations 2005, Reg 8.

[104] See *R (Croydon LBC) v Commissioner for Local Administration* [1989] 1 All ER 1033 (as approved in *R (W (A Minor)) v Education Appeal Committee of Lancashire CC* [1994] ELR 530); see also *R (M) v IAP of Haringey* [2010] ELR 823.

[105] See *R (Hounslow LBC) v Schools Admissions Panel for Hounslow* [2002] 1 WLR 3147 per May LJ at [22] where the Court of Appeal considered its earlier decision in *R (H) v Sheffield CC* [1999] ELR 511.

[106] R (Hounslow LBC) per May LJ at [61].

[107] [1998] Ed. CR 101; [1998] COD 108; for an example of a failed challenge on the basis of the application of individual criteria see *R (S) v IAP of St Thomas Catholic Primary School* [2010] EWHC 3785 (Admin).

specified numbers of pupils to be admitted from three alternate categories; those who passed an entrance exam, those who demonstrated specified connections with the school and those who demonstrated aptitude for either music or sport. Whilst fulfilling the third criteria, the pupil was refused a place when the school chose to admit more pupils from the second category. McCullough J held, allowing the application for judicial review, that the merits of applications satisfying the third criteria fell to be considered before any unfulfilled places might be offered to applicants from other groups in accordance with the published policy.

10.86 Whilst it will primarily be for the admission authority to address the issue of prejudice by way of evidence, there is no strict onus or burden of proof in this context.[108] The IAP must consider all of the material placed before it and unless it is satisfied that giving effect to the expressed preference would result in prejudice, it must uphold the appeal.[109]

10.87 If prejudice has been established, the IAP must move on to the second stage of balancing the arguments. This represents an independent, discretionary exercise, weighing the degree of prejudice to the school against the appellant's case for the child being admitted to the preferred school before arriving at a reasoned decision based upon all relevant factors.[110]

Infant admissions

10.88 The size of an infant class is limited to 30 with a single school teacher by virtue of section 1 of the SSFA. An IAP can only uphold an appeal where the admission decision was made on the ground of prejudice in this context if either of the following requirements can be established by the parent:[111]

(a) that the decision was not one which a reasonable admission authority would make in the circumstances of the case ('ground (a)'); or

(b) that the child would have been offered a place if the admission arrangements (as published in accordance with regulations made under section 92) had been properly implemented ('ground (b)').

10.89 In *R (LBC) v Schools Admissions Panel for Hounslow*, May LJ described the appropriate process for such appeals as follows:[112]

---

[108] See *R (Croydon LBC) v Commissioner for Local Administration* [1989] 1 All ER 1033 per Woolf LJ at 1041a–c and *R (G and B) v Brighouse School Appeal Committee* [1997] ELR 39 per Sedley J at 44f–h.

[109] See the Admission Appeals Code at paras [3.2]–[3.5]. For Wales, Admission Appeals Code at para [5.16].

[110] See the Admission Appeal Code at paras [3.6]–[3.7]. For Wales, see Admission Appeals Code at paras [5.19]–[5.20] For example, see *R (Jacobs) v Essex CC* [1997] ELR 190 (successful challenge of decision failing to have regard to separate living arrangements of estranged parents with reference to catchment criteria). Relevant factors may include legitimate expectation: *R (K) v Beatrix Potter School* [1997] ELR 468 (dismissal of challenge to IAP decision following the making of a offer to pupil in error, which was promptly withdrawn).

[111] See the Education (Admissions Appeals Arrangements) Regulations 2002 (SI 2002/2899), Reg 6(2) and the Admission Appeal Code at paras 3.17–3.31. For Wales, see the Education (Admission Appeals Arrangements) (Wales) Regulations 2005 (SI 2005/1398), Reg 6(2) and the Admission Appeals Code at paras [5.10]–[5.12].

[112] [2002] 1 WLR 3147 at [63]. See also *R (Hampshire CC) v IAP for Hampshire* [2007] ELR 266 (successful challenge by LEA of IAP decision on the grounds of failure to have regard to its primary contentions and in taking into account irrelevant considerations).

'... parents need to make a particular case which is so compelling that the decision not to admit the child is shown to be perverse. A local education authority opposing an appeal will need to explain their admission arrangements, explain their particular problems in relation to the school in question, and show that, unfortunate though it may be, it was objectively fair not to admit the child in question. They may wish to show that they had to refuse admission to several children with good cases, but that admitting one or more of those children would have entailed refusing one or more of those who were admitted because of the class size limit. As to the Panel, their task is not simply to rubber stamp the local education authority's decision, but they can only uphold the appeal if they conclude that it was perverse in the light of the admission arrangements to refuse to admit the particular child. Their task is not to take again the original decision ....'

10.90 When considering ground (a), the IAP can properly have regard to additional evidence in certain circumstances, including but not limited to information that the admissions authority ought reasonably to have been aware of, but it cannot conduct a rehearing.[113] By contrast, ground (b) is in effect a 'slip clause' which empowers the IAP to put right any error made by the admissions authority on the information that had been available to it.[114]

Multiple appeals

10.91 The Admissions Code provides comprehensive guidance regarding the conduct of multiple appeals, ie where there are two or more appeals by children against admission decisions in respect of the same school.[115] In *R (Tarmohamed) v Education Committee of Leicester CC*,[116] the Court recognised that if more than one parent's preference outweighed the relevant prejudice, but the cumulative admission of all such children could not be coped with by the school, there was no alternative but to rank the children in order of priority. That entailed a third stage at which the individual applicants were compared. The decision ensures that multiple appeals are conducted simultaneously, consistently and in accordance with the principles of natural justice.

Reasons

10.92 The IAP must communicate its decision, including the grounds upon which it was made, in writing to the appellant and the admission authority ('the decision letter').[117] The decision letter must be expressed clearly and enable parties to see what matters were taken into consideration, to understand what view the IAP took on questions of fact or law which it had to resolve and to understand, in broad terms, the basis on which the IAP reached its decision.[118]

10.93 The decision letter must reflect the type of appeal that being was considered, ie be appropriately tailored in the case of infant admissions and/or multiple appeals, and make reference to the two-stage process as appropriate. It must contain a summary of the relevant factors raised and considered by the IAP,[119] details of how these were

---

[113] *R (JC) v Richmond LBC* [2001] ELR 21 per Kennedy LJ at [50]–[53].

[114] *R (JC) v Richmond LBC* [2001] ELR 21 per Kennedy LJ at [41].

[115] See paras [3.8]–[3.16]. For Wales, see Admission Appeals Code at paras [5.21]–[5.25].

[116] [1997] ELR 48 per Sedley J at 59b–e.

[117] Sch 2 of the application Regulations at paras 1(8) and 2(10).

[118] *R (T) v Hackney LBC* [1991] COD 454; *R (M) v Lancashire CC* [1995] ELR 136 ('broad grounds must be set out rather than what may be termed detailed reasons'); *R (B) v Birmingham CC Education Appeals Committee* [1999] ELR 305 (standard letter an appropriate staring point, to be modified as required); *R (L) v IAP of St Edward's College* [2001] ELR 542.

[119] *R (K and S) v Admissions Appeal Panel of Cardiff CC and other* [2003] EWHC 436 (Admin).

resolved[120] and a summary of any legal advice received.[121] The level of detail required will depend on the nature of the issues that have been raised.[122]

10.94 If the letter does not explain the decision or otherwise satisfy the Court that the IAP conducted the appeal in a procedurally and substantively lawful manner, the decision is liable to be quashed. In some cases, however, the Court may decline relief where the complaint is one of form rather than substance.[123]

Special educational needs and learning disability

Introduction

10.95 The role of judicial review in the context of special educational needs and learning disability has been significantly curtailed over recent years.[124]

10.96 In 1993, the Special Educational Needs Tribunal (SENT) was introduced. In the first instance, appeals were heard by an Appeal Committee of the relevant Local Education Authority (LEA) or by the Secretary of State. In September 2002, SENT became the Special Educational Needs and Disability Tribunal (SENDIST) and latterly SENDIST became part of the First-tier Tribunal (Special Educational Needs and Disability Discrimination) on 3 November 2008 ('the Tribunal').

10.97 In common with other public law areas, the existence of the Tribunal, which offers a specialist appeals process, precludes many prospective applications for judicial review particularly those cases involving the assessment, provision, review or maintenance of statements identifying special educational needs provision.

10.98 However, the overwhelming majority of children with special educational needs do not have a statement based upon the degree of their learning difficulties. In January 2010, some 220,890 (or 2.7 per cent of) pupils across all schools in England had statements, whilst there were 1,470,900 pupils (18.2 per cent of pupils across all schools in England) with special educational needs in respect of which a statement had not been made.[125]

10.99 In this section, consideration is given to the jurisdiction of the Tribunal in the context of special educational needs and learning disability and to those areas in which judicial review still has a residual role to play.

---

[120] *R (L) v IAP of St Edward's College* [2001] ELR 542; *R(C) v the Admission Panel of Nottinghamshire CC and other* [2004] EWHC 2988 (Admin).

[121] *R (I) v IAP for G Technology College* [2005] EWHC 558 (Admin).

[122] *R (C) v South Gloucestershire Appeals Committee* [2000] ELR 220. See also *R (E) v Education Appeal Committee of Lancashire CC* [1994] ELR 530; *R (Taylor) v Education Committee of Blackpool BC* [1999] ELR 237; *R (M) v Lancashire CC* [1994] ELR 478; *R (D) v Northamptonshire CC* [1998] ELR 291; *R (C) v Admission Panel of Nottinghamshire CC and another* [2005] ELR 182; *R (T) v IAP for Devon CC and Governing Body of X College* [2007] ELR 499; *R (Reading BC) v IAP for Reading BC and others* [2006] ELR 186; *R (S and B) v IAP of Birmingham CC* [2007] ELR 57.

[123] *R (L) v IAP of St Edward's College* [2001] ELR 542; *R (L) v Governors of the Buss Foundation Camden School for Girls* [1991] COD 98.

[124] For more detailed consideration of law relating to special educational needs and its development, please see *Special Educational Needs and the Law* (2nd edn: Jordans 2007).

[125] SFR19/2010, 23 June 2010 (DfE).

The Tribunal

10.100   Forming part of the Health, Education and Social Care Chamber (HESC), the Tribunal is wholly independent. The Government cannot influence the Tribunal's decision and the Panel will have no connection with any LEA.

10.101   The Tribunal considers parental appeals against a decision by a LEA about a child's special educational needs or learning disability provision where agreement cannot be reached.[126]

10.102   Individual appeals are heard by a panel of three appointed people. The panel is chaired by a tribunal judge (who is a lawyer), and the other two members are non-legal (specialist) members who have knowledge and experience of special educational needs and disability.

10.103   The Tribunal also considers some claims regarding alleged disability discrimination in schools, nursery schools and nursery classes in schools, as well as some functions of the LEA in providing education for children. In the case of admissions and permanent exclusions from LEA maintained schools, appeals are instead dealt with by independent appeal panels. Accordingly, a second appeal route is available (to the Upper Tribunal) in respect of some school admission and permanent exclusion decisions, whereas judicial review may be appropriate in other cases.

10.104   The position at first instance is summarised below:

	Independent (private) and non maintained schools	**Maintained (LEA) schools including voluntary schools and city technology colleges**
Admissions	Tribunal	LEA admissions appeal panel
Permanent exclusions	Tribunal	LEA exclusions appeal panel
Fixed-term exclusions	Tribunal	Tribunal
Education and associated services	Tribunal	Tribunal

10.105   Academies make individual arrangements for admission appeals and appeals against permanent exclusions and these must be investigated locally by parents or advisers on a case by case basis.

10.106   The primary legislative sources are Part IV of the EA 1996 and the Special Educational Needs and Disability Act 2001 (the latter making important changes to the EA 1996).

10.107   Practice and procedure in the Tribunal is governed by the Special Educational Needs and Disability Tribunal (General Provisions and Disability Claims Procedure)

---

[126]   Each LEA must make arrangements for avoiding or resolving disagreements between parents and schools about special educational needs provision: EA 1996, s 332B. These arrangements apply to all schools, including an independent school named in the statement of child maintained by the LEA.

Regulations 2002 and by the Tribunal Procedure (First–tier Tribunal) (Health, Education and Social Care Chambers) Rules 2008.

10.108 At first instance, a parent (but not a child)[127] is able to appeal about the following decisions made by the LEA concerning special educational needs provision:

- Failure or refusal by a LEA to carry out a statutory assessment of child's SEN following a parental and/or school request.

- Refusal by a LEA to make a statement of SEN after a statutory assessment.

- Failure or refusal by a LA to reassess a child's SEN after a period of six or more months following a parental and/or school request.

- A LEA decision not to maintain (to cancel) a statement of SEN.

- A LEA decision not to change a statement of SEN following reassessment.

- Refusal by a LEA to change the school named in a child's statement of SEN (if the statement is one year or more old).

10.109 If the LEA has made a statement, or has changed a previous statement, a right of appeal also lies against any or all of following:

- The description of the child's SEN (part 2).

- The detail of special educational provision (help) necessary to meet the child's SEN (part 3).

- The school or type of school named in part 4 of the statement.

- The LEA not naming a school in part 4.

10.110 The following matters do not fall within the jurisdiction of the Tribunal:

- The way the LEA carried out the assessment or the length of time that it took.

- How the LEA or the school arranges to provide the help set out in the child's statement.

- The way the school is meeting the child's needs at School Action or School Action Plus (SEN provision in 'early years' schooling).

- The description in parts 5 and 6 of the statement of a child's non-educational needs or how the LEA plans to meet those needs.

- The LA refusal to amend the statement following an annual review.

---

[127] *(R) S v SENT & City of Westminster* [1996] ELR 102.

• The LA refusal to name an independent school, a non-maintained school or a different type of school (where the LEA has been asked to make a change to part 4 and the statement is at least one year old).

10.111 In relation to the last two complaints, the Tribunal offers the following advice to parents: '... you would need to ask your LA to reassess your child and appeal to us if they refused that reassessment or if you remained dissatisfied at some later point in the process of amending your child's statement ...'.[128]

10.112 The force of this guidance is illustrated by *R (W) v Kent County Council*.[129] The parents of a child with special educational needs challenged the refusal of the LEA to amend their son's statement to name the residential school at which he had been enrolled or, alternatively, to meet the fees payable. The school named as being suitable within part 4 of the child's statement attracted substantially higher fees, but the LEA considered (as observed by an earlier SENDIST panel) that the preferred option of the parents did not offer an environment apposite for the child's assessed needs. Rejecting the application on this and other grounds, Silber J observed as follows:

> '... The Council contend that the claimant's parents had an alternative remedy as they could have sought a statutory assessment pursuant to the 1996 Act. So it would have been open to the claimant's parents to obtain redress by requesting reassessment in accordance with the statutory procedure set out in section 328(2) of the 1996 Act, which enables a parent to request the local education authority to make a re-assessment of the SSEN.
>
> Further, any parent dissatisfied with any such re-assessment decision could appeal to what is now the First-Tier Tribunal (Health, Education and Social Care Chamber) and what was previously SENDIST. On such an appeal, the Tribunal would be obliged to carry out a merits review which, of course, is of much wider scope than that which is permitted on the present application or on any judicial review application. In addition, there is a right of appeal to SENDIST against a refusal of re-assessment. These statutory remedies constitute suitable alternative remedies especially as they permit a merits review followed by an opportunity to appeal any subsequent decision of this tribunal ....
>
> ... I came across the apposite comment that "where Parliament has introduced a new procedure to deal with a particular problem which it perceives to exist, the court should hesitate long before considering that procedure to be less satisfactory" (per Collins J in *R (G) v Immigration Appeal Tribunal* [2004] 3 All ER 286 [11]). The alternative procedure falls exactly into that category and that fortifies my conclusion that as there was an appropriate alternative remedy for the claimant, I must reject the claim ....'

10.113 The right of appeal to Upper Tribunal will generally preclude the judicial review of a first instance decision within the HESC, as with the statutory appeal route from a SENDIST decision that was available before reform of the Tribunals Service,[130] particularly as the power to grant interim relief in such cases exists, where exceptional circumstances can be demonstrated.[131]

---

[128] How to Appeal a SEN decision: A Guide for Parents (SENDIST 2008) at p 4.
[129] [2009] ELR 536.
[130] *R (South Glamorgan CC) v SENT* [1996] ELR 326.
[131] *R (JW) v The Learning Trust* [2010] ELR 115.

10.114 It remains the position that careful consideration will need to be given to the very small number of cases in which, by reason of the need for interim relief, judicial review may remain appropriate.[132]

10.115 For example, in *R (G) v Barnet LBC*[133] the Administrative Court was concerned with an application for permission for judicial review in respect of the LEA's handling of the renewal of a child's statement. Ouseley J addressed the question of whether judicial review was appropriate in a case where a statutory appeal to the SENDIST was available. Whilst having regard to earlier authorities, he found that the particular case was 'exceptional' as the LEA proposed significant changes, on short notice, in respect of the provision for a child with severe physical and mental disabilities:

> '... The substantive remedy before SENDIST does not mean that there are no circumstances, however exceptional, in which this court on the grant of permission to apply for judicial review should not require that some of interim relief be provided.
>
> ... I regard this as one such exceptional case. I bear in mind that the availability of the substantive remedy means that the power is to be exercised sparingly, and the fact that there is no statutory provision for a stay by SENDIST means that it should be exercised even more sparingly. However that may be, this is an exceptional and unusual special educational needs case, where the educational needs are provided for 52 weeks of the year exclusively at a residential school. The care is not provided at the child's family home in the evenings, or at weekends or during any school holidays. The severity of the child's needs mean that it would be very difficult for any provision to be made at home, and although [counsel for the respondent] dangles the prospect of social services' assistance as a means of making good some of the problems, I consider that that does not by itself assuage the severity and urgency of the situation which the parents face here. The position, so far as they are concerned, is that in a very short space of time, by the end of July, this severely disabled child whose most recent statement of education needs required 52 weeks a year of residential care, would be at home with them where they could not cope ....'

Residual jurisdiction of the High Court

10.116 In cases concerning special educational needs and learning disability that fall outside of the jurisdiction of the Tribunal, individual consideration will need to be given as to both the appropriateness and merits of pursuing judicial review on a conventional basis. Reported examples include:

- Failure by the LEA to appropriately consider and consult upon a revised funding allocation for a grant-maintained school, which left the school unable to provide for the identified needs of pupils with statements.[134]

- Failure by the Secretary of State to consult effectively over the withdrawal of a school's approved status, so as to preclude its continued acceptance of pupils with statements.[135]

---

[132] In contrast to the powers of the Upper Tribunal, the First-tier Tribunal has no power to grant interim relief pending a final determination: see *MH v Nottinghamshire CC* [2009] UKUT 178 (ACC) (following *R (White) v Ealing LBC* [1998] ELR 203 per Dyson J at 220 E–F).

[133] [2006] ELR 4; see also *R (HR) v Medway Council* [2010] ELR 513 (unsuccessful attempt to obtain interim relief in connection with naming of a school within a SEN Statement).

[134] *R (Governing Body of Queensmead School) v Hillingdon LBC* [1997] ELR 331.

[135] *R (McCarthy) v SoS for Education and Employment* [1996] *The Times*, July 24.

- Failure to fund out-of-area transport costs having named the school to which the child travelled within his statement.[136]

- Failure to have proper regard to the individual needs of a child with SEN when refusing to provide free transport to a preferred further education placement.[137]

- Declaration granted as to which LEA had responsibility for maintaining a child's SEN statement following an out-of-area residential placement.[138]

- Failure to appropriately implement statement of SEN.[139]

- Failure to conclude an assessment and report to the Learning and Skills Council to enable consideration of educational funding support.[140]

- Failure, when making a report to the Learning and Skills Council, to recommend placement with a particular provider of education or otherwise suggest which providers could reasonably meet a child's needs.[141]

- Declaration as to whether a local authority had been correct to end a child's status as being 'looked after' under the Children Act 1989 when placing him in a full-time residential school in accordance with his SEN Statement.[142]

10.117 Consideration will need to be given, as usual, to the exhaustion of LEA complaints and procedures and, thereafter, a request for intervention by the Secretary of State as appropriate. A careful balancing exercise needs to be conducted with reference to the issues of delay and whether other routes provide appropriate and sufficiently timely redress. Where an extension of time is required, due weight is likely to be given to time spent exploring alternative resolution and generic difficulties such as obtaining public funding.[143]

Pupil discipline and exclusion

Introduction

10.118 Pupil discipline and, in particular, exclusion decisions are amongst the most important yet highly contentious matters in education. Historically, the latter sanction has proved a particularly prevalent source of public law challenges, as considered below.

10.119 In such a highly legislated area, it is perhaps surprising that this aspect of school governance remains rooted in the common law, as clarified and supplemented in Part VII of the EIA. The EIA replicates the common law position that teachers (and duly authorised staff) exercise parental responsibility and may discipline their pupils in

---

[136] *R (H) v Brent LBC* [2002] ELR 509.
[137] *R (A) v North Somerset Council* [2010] ELR 139.
[138] *R (L) v Waltham Forest LBC* [2008] LGR 495; followed in *R (JK) v Haringey LBC* [2009] ELR 412 (permission to appeal declined [2010] EWCA Civ 495).
[139] *R (N) v North Tyneside BC* [2010] ELR 312 (allowing the claimant's appeal against [2010] ELR 130).
[140] *R (A) v Bromley LBC* [2008] EWHC 2449 (Admin).
[141] *R (P) v Windsor & Maidenhead RBC and the Learning & Skills Council* [2010] EWHC 1408 (Admin).
[142] *R (O) v East Riding of Yorkshire CC* [2010] ELR 318 (proceeding by way of appeal).
[143] *R (H) v Brent LBC* [2002] ELR 509 above, per Michael Supperstone QC at [15].

any reasonable way.[144] Maintained schools, but not academies, must set out their 'behaviour and discipline policy' and periodically review the same.[145]

10.120 There are a number of ways in which schools seek to maintain discipline and safety. The common methods include confiscation of personal property,[146] detention[147] and, in appropriate cases, physical restraint.[148] Those which most commonly come to the attention of the administrative court are exclusion decisions, including those associated with school uniform policy.

Exclusion

10.121 Pupil exclusions are a serious matter and, hence, the relevant decision-making and appeal processes are closely regulated by statute. Exclusion of pupils for a fixed period or permanently is permitted under section 52 of the EA 2002. Under section 52, a number of regulations have been issued ('the Regulations').[149] These must be observed by head teachers, governing bodies, LEAs and Independent Appeal Panels (IAPs) as appropriate. These parties must also have regard to government guidance issued under section 52.[150]

10.122 It is not possible to exhaustively describe the exclusion and appeals processes for these purposes, but the main features can be summarised as follows:

- the power to exclude a pupil may only be exercised by the head teacher of a maintained schools (or acting head teacher) or teacher in charge of a pupil referral unit;[151]

- exclusion should be used only as a last resort, when all other methods have failed;[152]

- a pupil should only be excluded when he or she has committed a serious breach of the school's behaviour policy or when allowing the pupil to remain in school would seriously harm the education and welfare of other pupils at the school;[153]

---

[144] For example, see *Fitzgerald v Northcote* (1865) 4 F&F 856 and *Gateshead Union Guardians v Durham CC* [1918] 1 Ch 146.

[145] See EIA, s 89.

[146] See EIA, s 94.

[147] See EIA, s 92.

[148] See EIA, s 93.

[149] See the Education (Pupil Exclusions and Appeals) (Maintained Schools) (England) Regulations 2002 (SI 2002/3178) and the Education (Pupil Exclusions and Appeals) (Pupil Referral Units) (England) Regulations 2008 (SI 2008/532) revoking and replacing the Education (Pupil Exclusions and Appeals) (Pupil Referral Units) (England) Regulations 2002 (SI 2002/3179) For Wales, see the Education (Pupil Exclusions and Appeals) (Maintained Schools) (Wales) Regulations 2003 (SI 2003/3227) and the Education (Pupil Exclusions and Appeals) (Pupil Referral Units) (Wales) Regulations 2003 (SI 2003/3246).

[150] See EA 2002, s 52(4)(b). The relevant guidance in England is the DfE publication 'Improving Behaviour and Attendance: Guidance on Exclusion from Schools and Pupil Referral Units' ('the DfE Guidance'). The DfE Guidance is revised and updated regularly, most recently in September 2008. For Wales, see 'Exclusion from schools and pupil referral units' NAFW Circular No 1/2004, as amended (January 2004) ('the NAFW Guidance').

[151] See EA 2002, s 52(1)–(2), and DfE Guidance [15] For Wales, see NAFW Guidance Part 1[1.2].

[152] See DfE Guidance [16] For Wales, see NAFW Guidance Part 1 [1.3].

[153] See DfE Guidance [13] For Wales, see NAFW Guidance Part 1 [1.1].

- before excluding a pupil, the head teacher must be satisfied 'on the balance of probabilities' that the incident has been fully investigated (or more commonly incidents), that all of the evidence has been considered and that the pupil has been given a chance to explain his or her version of the allegations;[154]

- a pupil cannot be excluded based upon, in whole or in part, the behaviour of his or her parent(s);[155]

- whilst fixed term exclusions are permissible, a pupil may not be excluded for longer than 45 days in one academic year;[156]

- a pupil may not be 'unofficially excluded';[157]

- particular caution must be exercised when considering the position of pupils with statements of SEN or other relevant disability;[158]

- similar considerations pertain to 'looked after' children;[159]

- a head teacher must inform 'the relevant person' (a parent of the child, or the pupil if he or she is over 18) about any exclusion and the reasons for it. In certain situations, the head teacher must also notify the governors and the LEA;[160]

- a 'relevant person' who is unhappy with the decision to exclude the pupil may make representations on the matter to the school's governing body;[161]

- in the case of a permanent exclusion, the 'relevant person' may appeal from the governors' decision to an IAP.[162]

Challenging IAP decisions

10.123　Since the statutory appeal route must generally be exhausted before judicial review proceedings can be contemplated,[163] it is appropriate to consider the IAP process in detail.

---

[154] See DfE Guidance [16], [20] and [23] and *R (H) v Camden LBC and the Governors of the Hampstead School* [1996] ELR 360 and *R (W) v Solihull BC* [1997] ELR 489 For Wales, see NAFW Guidance Part 1 [3.1]–[3.2].

[155] See DfE Guidance [26f] For Wales, see NAFW Guidance [4.1f]. The cases of *R (Whippe) v Board of Governors and Appeal committee of Bryn Elian High School* [1999] ELR 380 and *R (S) v Neale* [1995] ELR 198 should be considered doubtful authority in this context, though parental behaviour is arguably a relevant consideration when considering the separate issue of reinstatement.

[156] See DfE Guidance [35]. For Wales, see NAFW Guidance Part 1 [6.1].

[157] See DfE Guidance [27]–[29].

[158] See DfE Guidance [63]–[72]. For Wales, see NAFW Guidance Part 1 [13]–[14]. Exclusion of a pupil on the grounds of behaviour affected by his or her disability is liable to constitute discrimination under the DDA 1995: see *Governing Body of X School v (1) SP and (2) SENDIST* [2008] ELR 243; *R (RW) v IAP of Harrow LBC* [2008] EWHC 2433 (Admin); *R (T) v IAP for Devon CC and Governing Body of X College* [2007] ELR 499.

[159] See DfE Guidance [77]–[83]. For Wales, see NAFW Guidance Part 1 [16].

[160] SI 2002/3178, Reg 4 and SI 2008/532, Reg 5. For Wales, see SI 2003/3227, Reg 4 and SI 2003/3246, Reg 5.

[161] SI 2002/3178, Reg 5; SI 2008/532, Reg 6 and *R (X) v Newham LBC* [1995] ELR 303. For Wales, see SI 2003/3227, Reg 6 and SI 2003/3246, Reg 7.

[162] SI 2002/3178, Reg 6 and SI 2008/532, Reg 7. For Wales, see SI 2003/3227, Reg 7 and SI 2003/3246, Reg 8.

[163] See *R (DR) v Head Teacher of St George's Catholic School and other*; *R (AM) v Governing Body of Kingsmead School and others* [2003] LGR 371 and *R (A) v Fernhill Manor School* [1994] ELR 67 (a fair hearing before an IAP may be sufficient to cure irregularities below). In exceptional cases, recourse might

10.124 An IAP must be constituted and conducted in accordance with the requirements set out in the Schedule to the Regulations. An IAP must consist of three or five members appointed by the LEA and drawn from three categories: lay members, persons who are (or have been) a head teacher of a maintained school in the past five years and persons who are (or have been) a governor of a maintained school in the past six years (for a period of at least twelve months). Where the IAP has three members, each category must be represented. Where the IAP has five members, there must be one lay member and two people from each of the other two categories.

10.125 An appeal to an IAP must be made in writing, within 15 'school days' and set out the grounds of appeal.[164] At the appeal hearing, the 'relevant person', the head teacher, the governing body and the LEA shall be given the opportunity to make representations to the panel. Additional guidance is provided regarding the conduct of combined appeals, e g where the position of two or more pupils are related or connected.[165] The relevant parties must be notified of the appeal decision in writing, no later than the end of the second working day after the appeal hearing.

Procedural fairness

10.126 Hearings are subject to and must be conducted in accordance with the principles of natural justice and this is where most public law challenges will lie. In *R (S) v Brent LBC*,[166] the Court of Appeal considered three consolidated judicial review appeals arising from exclusion decisions. Although the appeals principally related to the lawfulness of the prevailing government guidance issued under the precursor to section 52 of the EIA, the Court proceeded to make a number of useful statements regarding the appropriate conduct of IAP hearings:

- the LEA must maintain an objective stance; it is not part of its function to press for a particular finding or outcome in respect of A pupil;[167]

- the IAP must avoid permitting the LEA or any other party to unduly influence or monopolise the hearing through its representations;[168]

- the IAP must entertain any credible material, written or oral, which is reasonably and fairly capable of affecting what it has to decide;[169]

---

properly be had to judicial review without exhausting the IAP process: see *R (M) v Governors of St Gregory's RC Aided High School* [1995] ELR 290 (appeal before Governors not properly constituted), *R (K) v Governors of the W School and West Sussex CC* [2001] ELR 311 (family health considerations were relevant).

[164] Notification will be valid if provided before midnight on the last day: see *R (P) v Haringey LBC* [2009] ELR 49.

[165] See DfE Guidance [121]–[122] and *R (S and B) V IAP of Birmingham CC* [2007] ELR 57; *R (on the application of O) v The IAP for Tower Hamlets LBC* [2007] ELR 468 (appeal based on failure to advise that there could be a joint appeal failed in the absence of apparent unfairness to the appellant); *R (W) v Governors of Bacon's City Technology College* [1998] ELR 488 (need for consistency of penalty). For Wales, see NAFW Guidance Part 4[3].

[166] [2002] ELR 556.

[167] [2002] ELR 556 at [22]–[24].

[168] [2002] ELR 556 at [25] approving the observations of Newman J in *R (T) v Head Teacher of Wembley High School and Others* [2001] ELR 359. See also *R (W) v Governors of Bacon's City Technology College* [1998] ELR 488 (failure of the chair to indicate the panel's need to hear from a pupil directly, as opposed to his loquacious representative, gave rise to unfairness).

[169] [2002] ELR 556 at [27]. See also *R (W) v Governors of Bacon's City Technology College* [1998] ELR 488 (allowing a limited period of time for appeals was a dangerous policy as it would serve to unduly restrict the scope of inquiry and representations in some cases).

- if there is a material conflict of evidence involving an adult witness, there is no reason why the witness cannot be invited to attend and be questioned. If a witness declines to come for no reason, or for an unacceptable one, the IAP will be entitled to draw whatever inferences seem appropriate in the circumstances;[170]

- the IAP is entitled to restrict confrontational cross-examination of witnesses and to require questions to be put through or by the chair;[171]

- whilst there may be good reasons for seeking to preserve the anonymity of witnesses, for example in the context of bullying allegations, use by the IAP of anonymised statements has the potential to cause injustice. Use of such statements may be unfair; in particular, if they are damaging to the pupil in ways that he or she cannot be expected to address without knowing the maker.[172]

10.127 In *R (B) v Head Teacher of Dunraven School*,[173] the Court of Appeal had earlier given guidance on disclosure in the context of IAP hearings:

- if there are discrepancies within the material relied upon in support of the allegations made against the pupil, fairness will ordinarily dictate making sufficient disclosure to reveal such inconsistency;[174]

- it is unfair for the IAP to have access to damaging material to which the pupil has no access;[175]

- disclosure of such material is not dependent upon a request by the pupil; the duty to ensure fairness is not conditional upon applications or demands more appropriate to adversarial litigation.[176]

10.128 Far and above the most contentious issues before the Courts have been the degree to which the matters complained of should be investigated and the proper application of the burden of proof to those facts ascertained. It has been held that an IAP is not determining a pupil's civil rights and obligations so as to engage art 6 of the ECHR and it is not determining a criminal charge so as to import the criminal burden of proof, even where the conduct giving rise to the exclusion is of a criminal character.[177]

---

[170] [2002] ELR 556 at [28].

[171] [2002] ELR 556 at [28]. See also *R (W) v IAP for Bexley* [2008] ELR 301 per Burton J at [20]–[29] (it is for the IAP to hear all the evidence and consider any challenge to its reliability and weight).

[172] 2002] ELR 556 at [27]. See also *R (B) v Head Teacher of Dunraven School* [2000] ELR 156 (a governing body may, in some cases, be forced to elect to proceed in the absence of a statement or otherwise reinstate a pupil); *R (K) v Governors of the W School and West Sussex CC* [2001] ELR 311 (failure to provide witness evidence on which the decision was based to the applicant handicapped his defence) and *R (T) v Head Teacher of Elliott School* [2002] ELR 160 (decisions on admission are fact sensitive and the IAP, in each case, must be conscious of any possible unfairness).

[173] [2000] ELR 156.

[174] [2000] ELR 156 per Sedley LJ at 190. Similarly, a head teacher with reason to doubt the reliability or impartially of a statement must draw such concerns to the attention of the IAP: *R (T) v Head Teacher of Elliott School* [2002] ELR 160 per Schiemann LJ at [37].

[175] [2000] ELR 156 per Sedley LJ at 190.

[176] [2000] ELR 156 per Sedley LJ at 193.

[177] *R v (LG) v IAP Tom Hood School* [2010] ELR 291 (affirming [2009] ELR 248).

10.129 The Regulations expressly provide that all factual determinations are to be made on the 'balance of probability', but the more serious the nature of the allegation and thus the possible sanction, the more compelling the evidence necessary to support it will need to be.[178]

10.130 The nature and extent of the investigation required will depend on the facts of the case. In *R (S) v Roman Catholic Schools*, Moses J accepted the following principles as being of general application (whilst cautioning specifically about the evaluation of identification evidence):[179]

- the overriding principle is that a pupil must have a fair opportunity to exculpate him or herself;

- whether such an opportunity has been afforded will depend upon the issues raised in the inquiry;

- those conducting an inquiry must decide what critical issues of fact they should resolve and what inquiries could reasonably be made to resolve those issues;

- they must give careful and even-handed consideration to all the available evidence in relation to those issues; and

- those conducting an inquiry do not need, on every occasion, to carry out searching inquiries involving the calling of bodies of oral evidence.

10.131 The statutory constitution of appeals panels is in conformity with the impartial tribunal provisions of art 6(1) of the ECHR.[180] Whilst no mention is made of a clerk to the IAP in the Regulations, it is a long-established and lawful practice for IAP to have a clerk.[181] There is no real danger of bias where, as is ordinarily the case, the clerk is employed by the LEA.[182] A clerk may advise the IAP during its deliberations, but if this is done in private, the clerk should repeat the advice in open session thereby affording the interested parties with an opportunity to make representations.[183]

10.132 Concerns regarding impartiality may arise from an IAP member having worked closely with the head teacher or Governing Body of the excluding school, or from being a teacher or governor of a school (or PRU), to which the pupil might be admitted if the

---

[178] See *R (S) v Governing Body of YP School* [2004] ELR 37; *R (H) v IAP for Y College* [2005] ELR 25; *R (Culkin) v Wirral IAP* [2009] ELR 287 (investigation sufficient to identify serious and persistent conduct); *R (A) v IAP for Sutton LBC* [2009] ELR 321 (error in not making finding as to the true nature of the conduct complained of rendering assessment of proportionality of sanction impossible); *R (G) v IAP of Bexley LBC* [2009] ELR 100 (IAP had made sufficient findings of fact to justify exclusion for one-off serious act of violence against a member of staff).

[179] [1998] ELR 304. See also *R (C) v IAP of Sefton MBC and Governors of Hillside High School* [2001] ELR 393 (unnecessary to carry out searching inquiries where assault substantially admitted) and *R (A) v Head Teacher of North Westminster Community School and others* [2003] ELR 378 (clear opportunity afforded by IAP, but no issued raised by pupil or representative at hearing).

[180] *R (B) v Head Teacher of Alperton Community School* [2001] ELR 359, affirmed in *R (S, T and P) v Brent LBC, Oxfordshire CC, Head Teacher of Elliott School and the Secretary of State for Education and Skills* [2002] ELR 556.

[181] See DfE Guidance [132]–[133]. For Wales, see NAFW Guidance, Part 4[5].

[182] *R (S) v Head Teacher of C High School* [2002] ELR 73.

[183] See *R (I) v IAP for G* [2005] ELR 490.

exclusion is confirmed. Familiarity or past teaching involvement is liable to give to concern.[184] The test to be applied is that set out by Lord Phillips MR in *Re Medicaments and Related Classes of Goods (No 2)*:[185]

> '... When the Strasbourg jurisprudence is taken into account, we believe that a modest adjustment of the test in *R v Gough* is called for, which makes it plain that it is, in effect, no different from the test applied in most of the Commonwealth and in Scotland. The court must first ascertain all the circumstances which have a bearing on the suggestion that the judge was biased. It must then ask whether those circumstances would lead a fair-minded and informed observer to conclude that there was a real possibility, or a real danger, the two being the same, that the tribunal was biased .... The material circumstances will include any explanation given by the judge under review as to his knowledge or appreciation of those circumstances. Where that explanation is accepted by the applicant for review it can be treated as accurate. Where it is not accepted, it becomes one further matter to be considered from the viewpoint of the fair-minded observer. The court does not have to rule whether the explanation should be accepted or rejected. Rather it has to decide whether or not the fair-minded observer would consider that there was a real danger of bias notwithstanding the explanation advanced. Thus in *R v Gough*, had the truth of the juror's explanation not been accepted by the defendant, the Court of Appeal would correctly have approached the question of bias on the premise that the fair-minded onlooker would not necessarily find the juror's explanation credible ....'

Reasons

10.133 Decision letters have proved a contentious area, as poorly drafted documents cause confusion and undermine the perceived reliability of the IAP process. Whilst a decision letter must give the panel's reasons for its decision in as much detail as possible,[186] including clear information about the offences or behaviour for which the pupil has been excluded, the Courts have shown considerable reluctance to accept challenges on this basis alone. For example, it has been held unnecessary for the IAP to set out each and every option short of exclusion and give reasons for its rejection of the same.[187] The key consideration is whether the parties can understand why the decision has been made.[188]

10.134 If an internal exclusion policy was at variance with the statutory guidance, and the IAP considers it appropriate to give the local policy additional weight, it must explain why this is so in the decision letter.[189] Similarly, where the IAP overturns the exclusion but does not direct reinstatement of the pupil, its reasoning must be explained.[190]

10.135 Where the adequacy of the reasons given by an IAP is challenged within judicial review proceedings, the Court may exceptionally receive further evidence giving

---

[184] See *R (M) v Board of Governors of Stoke Newington School* [1994] ELR 131 (decision of IAP quashed where panel included a teacher-governor who had been the head of year for the pupil in the academic year which formed a relevant part of the pupil's record) and *R (T) v Head Teacher of Elliott School* [2002] ELR 160 per Sedley LJ at [46].

[185] [2001] 1 WLR 700 at [85]–[86] applied in *R (Culkin) v Wirral IAP* [2009] ELR 287 per Nicol J at [40]–[43].

[186] See DfE Guidance [170]. Contrast the position in Wales, where the guidance simply states that 'The decision letter should give the panel's reasons for its decision in sufficient detail for the parties to understand why the decision was made'. NAFW Guidance, Part 4 [12.2].

[187] *R (H) v Camden LBC and the Governors of Hampstead School* [1996] ELR 360 and *R (W) v Solihull BC* [1997] ELR 489.

[188] *R (W) v Northamptonshire CC* [1998] ELR 291.

[189] *R (S and B) v IAP of Birmingham CC* [2007] ELR 57; *R (Culkin) v Wirral IAP* [2009] ELR 287 (absence of evidence as to existence or consideration of school behavioural policy was not a fatal flaw).

[190] See DfE Guidance [170] For Wales, see NAFW Guidance, Part 4 [10.5].

a fuller explanation of the decision. Even where the Court is satisfied, as it must be, that such evidence represents the actual reasons operative in the minds of IAP members at the relevant time, it will not automatically receive such material, but rather it will always be a matter of discretion.[191]

10.136 The degree of scrutiny and caution to be applied by the Court when considering additional material depends on the subject matter of the administrative decision in question. Where important human rights are concerned anxious scrutiny is required. Where the subject matter is less important, the Court may be less demanding and readier to accept subsequent reasons.[192] The Court must, however, bear in mind the qualifications and experience of the persons involved:[193]

'It is one thing to require comprehensiveness and clarity from lawyers and those who regularly sit on administrative tribunals; it is another to require those qualities of occasional non-lawyer tribunal chairmen and members.'

Reinstatement

10.137 Following its deliberations, an IAP panel may make one of three determinations:

- it may uphold the decision to exclude;

- it may direct immediate reinstatement or reinstatement at some future date; or

- it may decide that because of exceptional circumstances or other reasons it is not practical to give a direction requiring reinstatement, but that it would otherwise have been appropriate to give such a direction.

10.138 If the panel directs reinstatement, the date specified must be reasonable in the circumstances. Whilst the IAP may not attach conditions, reinstatement does not necessarily mean a return to the position that existed immediately prior to the exclusion. If it is acting in good faith, the adoption by the school of a special regime for the reinstated pupil in the exercise of education and management duties is within its direction.[194] The maintenance of such a regime will have to be regularly reviewed and its reasonableness and the reasonableness of its continuation will depend on the facts.[195]

10.139 When considering exclusions arising out of oppressive behaviour towards pupils or staff, the IAP must have regard to the effect of reinstatement on the victims of

---

[191] *R (W) v Northamptonshire CC* [1998] ELR 291; *R (AF) v Brent and Vassie LBC* [2000] ELR 550 (admission of fuller and more accurate statement of reasons which IAP considered); *R (H) v IAP for Y College* [2005] ELR 25 (clerk's notes providing a permission degree of clarification, thus negating the need for supplementary witness evidence); *R (T) v IAP for Devon CC and Governing Body of X College* [2007] ELR 499 (inappropriate to admit evidence where there was a substantial risk that the additional material did not represent the actual reasons of the decision maker); *R (Culkin) v Wirral IAP* [2009] ELR 287 (clerk's notes and decision letter collectively explaining the sanction of exclusion); *R (W) v IAP of Bexley LBC* [2008] ELR 301 (clerk's notes simply a clarification or supplementation of the decision letter on the facts).

[192] *R (Nash) v Chelsea College of Art and Design* [2001] EWHC 538 (Admin) per Stanley Burnton J at [35]; extracted in the asylum case, *R (B) v Merton LBC* [2003] 4 All ER 280.

[193] *R (Nash) v Chelsea College of Art and Design* [2001] EWHC 538 (Admin) per Stanley Burnton J at [36].

[194] *R (L) v Governors of J School* [2003] UKHL 9; see also *R (C) v Governors of B School* [2001] ELR 285 (affirmed in *R (W) v Governors of B School* [2002] ELR 105).

[195] *R (O) v Park View* [2007] ELR 388 (affirmed [2007] ELR 454).

such behaviour.[196] Similarly, there may be a difficult balancing exercise when, for example, attempting to keep a child with special educational needs in mainstream schooling.[197]

School uniform

10.140 The adoption of uniforms by schools is normal, lawful and, indeed, positively endorsed within official guidance. As stated within the School Admissions Code for England,[198] 'School uniform plays a valuable role in contributing to the ethos and setting the tone of a school, and the Government strongly encourages schools to consider the introduction of uniforms where they do not already have them'. It is a mandatory requirement that admission authorities include information regarding school uniform policies within composite prospectuses, including information about schemes to defray the costs of purchase for eligible families.[199]

10.141 Conflict may arise where it is alleged that a uniform policy conflicts with anti-discrimination legislation and disciplinary sanctions, including exclusion, are imposed. Save where discrimination is established, it is permissible to exclude a pupil for infringements of uniform policy 'where these are persistent and in open defiance of such rules'.[200] This will always be a course of last resort.

10.142 The leading case is *R (Begum) v Headteacher and Governors of Denbigh High School*,[201] in which the House of Lords considered whether, in refusing to allow a Muslim girl to wear the jilbab instead of the permitted shalwar kameeze, the school and its governors had, among other matters interfered with the claimant's right to manifest her religion under article 9 of the ECHR and whether the interference, if any, was justified. The claimant, an existing pupil of the school, had adhered to its uniform code for two years. She later came to believe that the shalwar kameeze was not an appropriate form of dress for herself as a Muslim girl upon reaching puberty. She, therefore, attended the school dressed in a jilbab, a form of dress which concealed the shape of her arms and legs. She refused to attend school unless permitted to wear a jilbab, whilst the school refused to allow her to attend unless she complied with the uniform code.

10.143 The claimant contended that the defendant had unjustifiably limited her right under article 9 to manifest her religion or beliefs and violated her right not to be denied education under article 2 of Protocol 1 of the ECHR. The claim was dismissed by Bennett J at first instance, accepted by the Court of Appeal, before being ultimately rejected by the House of Lords.

10.144 By a majority, the House of Lords the held that the claimant's article 9 rights had not been infringed, whilst they were unanimous in stating that any interference was justified. The Court confirmed that article 9 did not entail freedom to manifest one's religion at any time and place of one's own choosing. The right to manifest one's belief

---

[196] See SI 2002/3178, Reg 6(3)(4) and *R (H) v Camden LBC and the Governors of Hampstead School* [1996] ELR 360.

[197] *R (S) v Headteacher and Governing Body of Almondbury Junior School and Kirkless MBC* [2004] ELR 612 (decision of school not to admit child with behavioural difficulties during lunch period where the available level of supervision reduced).

[198] (2008) at [1.90]–[1.91]. For Wales, Schools Admissions Code (Wales) at [3.71]–[3.72].

[199] School Information (England) Regulations 2008 (SI 2008/3093) Sch 2, para 17 and Sch 3, para 4. For Wales, see the Education (School Information) (Wales) Regulations 1999 (SI 1999/1812), Sch 1, para 10.

[200] DfE Guidance [26f]. For Wales, see NAFW Guidance Part 1 [4.1e].

[201] [2007] 1 AC 100. See also *R (X) v Y School* [2007] ELR 278.

was qualified and what constituted interference would depend on all the circumstances of the case, including the extent to which an individual could reasonably expect to be at liberty to manifest her beliefs in practice. The Court placed particular reliance on the fact that the claimant's family had chosen the school for her with knowledge of its uniform requirements and that she could have sought the help of the school and the LEA in solving the problem, if necessary, by changing schools.

10.145 In *R (Playfoot) v Governing Body of Millais School*,[202] the High Court considered whether wearing a 'purity' ring at school was a manifestation of the claimant's belief in pre-marriage celibacy, whether the school's refusal to permit the wearing of the ring constituted interference with her right to manifest her belief, and if so, whether it was justified. Whilst extending time to pursue the challenge, the Court rejected the claim relying, among other considerations, on findings that the wearing of a ring was not 'intimately linked' to the belief in chastity before marriage. There were also other means open to her to practise her belief, such as attaching the ring to a chain or to a bag, as the school had suggested. Otherwise, the school's policy was plainly prescribed by law, the rules were made for the legitimate purpose of protecting the rights and freedoms of others and this had been clearly communicated to the claimant. In the particular circumstances, the school was fully justified in acting as it did.

10.146 In *R (Watkins-Singh) v Governing Body of Aberdare Girls' High School*,[203] the High Court considered whether the exclusion of a Sikh pupil from school for wearing a religious bangle (a Kara) was unlawful. The pupil believed that, as supported by objective evidence, the wearing of the Kara bangle was of exceptional importance as an expression of her race and culture. The Court held that the defendant had clearly failed to comply with its obligations under 71 of the Race Relations Act 1976 and that race equality played no part, as it should have done, in its decision-making process. As wearing the Kara was unobtrusive and was unlikely to make inroads into the school uniform policy, the discriminatory effect far outweighed any justification for the school's treatment of the claimant.

10.147 Uniform cases are, as they have been expressly described by the Courts, likely to be fact-sensitive. Schools have considerable freedom in determining their ethos and character. If the relevant issues have been identified and considered by policy makers, the Courts are highly unlikely to interfere.

PARTICULAR CONSIDERATIONS

Standing and funding

10.148 In judicial review proceedings arising from educational provision, the appropriate claimant will invariably be the parent, save where a pupil is provided a direct right of appeal.[204] If a pupil is named with the intention of manipulating public funding, where otherwise this would be restricted on the grounds of financial eligibility, parties and their advisers can expect robust censure.[205]

---

[202] [2007] ELR 484.
[203] [2008] ELR 561.
[204] For example, the co-extensive right of appeal to a child who expresses a preference for a sixth-form school place, as created by recent amendment to SSFA, s 94.
[205] *R (B) v Head Teacher of Alperton Community School* [2001] ELR 359 (exclusion); *R (T) Hackney LBC*

Delay

10.149   It is well established that delay in the context of applications for judicial review of an education decision is highly unlikely to be excused. In most, if not each case there is liable to be an effect on other pupils or otherwise prejudice to efficient administration of relevant establishment. Undue delay has precluded the grant of permission or relief across the education spectrum, for example:

- School reorganisation and closure.[206]

- Higher education determinations.[207]

- Admission arrangements.[208]

- Registration issues.[209]

- Exclusion appeals.[210]

10.150   If funding difficulties are experienced, these must be evidenced.[211] Failure to do so is likely to result in refusal of an extension.[212]

HUMAN RIGHTS

10.151   Human rights jurisprudence has, to date, had a muted influence on education law. The ECHR which guarantees basic rights and freedoms is given effect in the United Kingdom by the Human Rights Act 1998 (HRA). Article 2 of First Protocol to the ECHR provides that:

> 'No person shall be denied the right to education. In the exercise of any functions which it assumes in relation to education and to teaching, the State shall respect the right of parents to ensure such education and teaching in conformity with their own religious and philosophical convictions.'

10.152   The principle, as stated by the European Court of Human Rights in the Belgian Linguistic Case[213] (No 2), is that art 2 of the First Protocol does not confer a right to an education which the domestic system does not provide:

[1991] COD 454 (admissions); *R (JC) Richmond LBC* [2001] ELR 13 (admissions); *R (Bandtock) v Secretary of State for Education* [2001] ELR 333 (school closure); *R (S) v SENT & City of Westminster* [1996] ELR 102 (special educational needs).

206   *R (N) v Leeds CC* [1999] ELR 324; *R (Melton and others) v Oxford CC* [2001] EWHC Admin 245.

207   *R (Lakareber) v University of Portsmouth* [1999] ELR 135; *R (K) v University of Nottingham* [1998] ELR 184.

208   *R (Ali) v Bradford MBC* [1994] ELR 299; *R (B) v Rochdale MBC* [2000] Ed. CR 117; *R (Taylor) v Blackpool BC* [1999] ELR 237.

209   *R (X) v Governing Body of Gateway Primary School* [2001] ELR 321; *R (M) v Barking and Dagenham LBC* [2003] ELR 144.

210   *R (M) v Secretary of State for Home Department* [1999] Ed. CR 656.

211   *R (T) v Governors of La Sainte Union Convent School* [1996] ELR 98.

212   *R (Lakareber) v University of Portsmouth* [1999] ELR 135 (distinguishing *R (Jackson) v Stratford-on-Avon DC and others* [1985] 3 All ER 769 on the basis of failure to provide information regarding funding enquiries).

213   (1968) 1 EHRR 252 at 281.

'all member States of the Council of Europe possessed, at the time of the opening of the Protocol to their signature, and still do possess, a general and official educational system. There neither was, nor is now, therefore, any question of requiring each State to establish such a system, but merely of guaranteeing to persons subject to the jurisdiction of the Contracting Parties the right, in principle, to avail themselves of the means of instruction existing at a given time.'

10.153 It was authoritatively stated in *R (Begum) v Headmaster and Governors of Denbigh High School*,[214] that regard should be had, in the first instance, to domestic provision:

'The Strasbourg jurisprudence ... makes clear how art 2 should be interpreted. The underlying premise of the article was that all existing member states of the Council of Europe had, and all future member states would have, an established system of state education. It was intended to guarantee fair and non-discriminatory access to that system by those within the jurisdiction of the respective states. The fundamental importance of education in a modern democratic state was recognised to require no less. But the guarantee is, in comparison with most other convention guarantees, a weak one, and deliberately so. There is no right to education of a particular kind or quality, other than that prevailing in the state. There is no convention guarantee of compliance with domestic law. There is no convention guarantee of education at or by a particular institution. There is no convention objection to the expulsion of a pupil from an educational institution on disciplinary grounds, unless (in the ordinary way) there is no alternative source of state education open to the pupil (as in *Eren v Turkey* [2006] ECHR 60856/00). The test, as always under the convention, is a highly pragmatic one, to be applied to the specific facts of the case: have the authorities of the state acted so as to deny to a pupil effective access to such educational facilities as the state provides for such pupils?'

10.154 Similarly, in *A v Essex County Council*,[215] the Supreme Court considered the position of a severely disabled child with SEN who was left without schooling for an 18-month period while the LEA secured a place at one of the few specialist schools which could cope with his behaviour. A complicated assessment of A's medical and psychiatric problems was necessary before any long-term plans could be made for his continuing education. This took eight months to undertake and it was a further ten months before A could be placed in a special residential school where he was able to receive the 24-hour supervision that he needed.

10.155 Dismissing A's appeal against the striking-out of his claim at first instance, the Court held (by a majority) that whilst, during the 18-month period, there had been a failure to comply with the requirements of the EA 1996 and a failure to provide any significant education to A, that did not mean that there had been an infringement of his rights under art 2 of the First Protocol.

10.156 In such a case, it was hardly surprising that a LEA might be unable, through lack of resources, to immediately satisfy the obligations imposed by the EA 1996. In so far as a state's system of education made provision for children with SEN, art 2 guaranteed fair and non-discriminatory access for those children to the special facilities that were available. But if the facilities were limited, so that immediate access could not be provided, regard must be had to that limitation.

---

[214] [2006] 2 AC 363 per Lord Bingham of Cornhill at [24].
[215] [2010] 3 WLR 509.

10.157 Accordingly, whilst it is accepted that everyone is entitled to be educated to a minimum standard,[216] the right under art 2 extends no further.

CONCLUSIONS

10.158 In the exercise of any functions which it assumes in relation to education and to teaching, the state must respect the right of parents to ensure that such education and teaching conforms to their religious and philosophical convictions.[217] A conviction is only liable to be respected in so far as it is compatible with the provision of efficient instruction and training and the avoidance of unreasonable expenditure. It would appear that Convention rights are unlikely to be a more effective basis of challenge, procedurally or substantively, in the context admission or with regard to exclusion appeals.[218]

---

[216]   *R (Holub) v Secretary of State for the Home Dept* [2001] ELR 401.

[217]   *R (Watkins-Singh) v Governing Body of Aberdare Girls' High School* [2008] ELR 561 (failure to respect religious conviction); *R (K) v Newham LBC* [2002] ELR 390 (failure to ascertain parental conviction); *R (Begbie) v Secretary of State for Education and Employment* [2000] ELR 445 (right to education did not guarantee the right to an assisted place at an independent school); *L (Hughes) v Hereford and Worcester CC* [2000] ELR 375 (no requirement to provide special facilities to accommodate a particular conviction).

[218]   *R (JC) v Richmond LBC* [2001] ELR 21 (admissions); *R (B) v Head Teacher of Alperton Community School* [2001] ELR 359 (exclusions).

Chapter 11

CONSUMER PROTECTION

INTRODUCTION

11.1   Consumer protection involves various forms of policing and enforcement including the service of statutory notices, criminal prosecutions and adjudication proceedings before specialist bodies. It is regulated both at a local and national level. A regulator often derives the power to police the provisions of the regulatory codes from the respective statute itself. For example, under the Food Safety Act 1990 a 'food authority' (for the purpose of that Act, a local Council) has a statutory duty to enforce the provisions of that Act in its geographic area. Similarly, there are instances where the duty is placed on the Food Standards Agency usually to enforce the legislative provisions nationally. Likewise, under the Consumer Protection Act 1987 a weights and measures authority (in other words, a Council) also has a statutory duty to enforce the safety provisions of that Act in its area. Many more similar statutory schemes impose obligations on public authorities to enforce particular Codes. In certain circumstances the statutory code may provide a choice as to whether enforcement should take place at national or local level. For example, statutory notices under the Consumer Protection Act 1987 may be issued by a local authority or by the Secretary of State (see, for example, the Consumer Protection Act 1987, s 14). Some areas of consumer protection such as advertisements are regulated nationally by specialist bodies such as the Committee of Advertising Practice and the Advertising Standards Authority. All these bodies are public bodies which carry out public functions and are therefore potentially susceptible to judicial review.

11.2   Other areas of consumer protection are enforced through the High Court or County Court. For example, enforcing authorities (which may include local trading standards departments and the Office of Fair Trading) may apply to the Court for an enforcement order pursuant to the Enterprise Act 2002; in effect, an order prohibiting a person from engaging in conduct which would constitute an infringement of specified legislative provisions. This, however, is outside the scope of this Chapter since the civil procedure which pertains to proceedings before those courts should be followed, as opposed to the principles and procedure of judicial review.

11.3   This chapter will address the policing and enforcement of consumer protection both at a local and national level which is carried out by central or local government and by specialist bodies. It will also consider the identity and responsibilities of enforcing bodies and the role of the Crown Court and Magistrates' Court in the process. The areas that inform the enforcement process, such as policies and codes of practice, are also explored together with the use of publicity.

THE POLICING OF CONSUMER PROTECTION

National level policing

11.4   National policing of consumer protection is carried out by a variety of different regulatory bodies such as Ministerial Departments and bodies such as Ofcom and the Office of Fair Trading. As explained below, there are also other specialist bodies that carry out such public functions.

Local level policing

11.5   In practice, a large part of the policing of consumer protection issues is carried out at a local level. Indeed, local level policing appears to have been the intention of Parliament when it enacted a number of the regulatory codes. Indeed, to achieve that end Parliament has vested responsibilities for enforcement (for example, the issuing of enforcement notices and bringing of prosecutions) in the hands of local authorities. Although it should be recognised that enforcement powers under the regimes also rest with a number of national bodies.

11.6   Whilst much depends on the statutory scheme, local level policing is generally unobjectionable. This was explained in *R (on the application of Alba Radio Ltd & Others) v Department of Trade and Industry*[1] where the claimants to judicial review proceedings were importers and distributors of electrical goods. After receiving a complaint, the local trading standards department investigated a particular item and found it to be unsafe under the Electrical Equipment (Safety) Regulations 1994. A suspension notice under the Consumer Protection Act 1987 was issued prohibiting the sale of the item. The 1994 Regulations were intended to implement European law; the Low Voltage Directive 73/23/EEC. Article 9 of that Directive provided, amongst other things, that if a Member State prohibited the sale of an item on safety grounds it should immediately inform other Member States and the European Commission. In accordance with that provision, the local trading standards department informed the Department of Trade and Industry which then made a notification to Member States and the Commission under the process set out in Article 9 of the Directive.

11.7   The issue in the judicial review proceedings was whether this notification process could be commenced at a local level, perhaps even by a junior trading standards officer, or whether it could only be commenced at national level by the Secretary of State. The claimant argued that the Directive only permitted such notification to take place at a national level (in that case, by the Department of Trade and Industry). This was said to be so because the Department of Trade and Industry had a 'higher level of discretion' to exercise before it took the step of prohibiting a product or interfering with the free movement of goods in the market. It was said that a local complaint could only be a trigger to a broader and more informed investigation by a national authority. As such, it was argued that it was only if the Secretary of State had used the powers to issue such notices could it then move on to act internationally.

11.8   The judicial review claim was dismissed. It was held that on its true construction, Article 9 of the Directive did not prevent a local trading standards department from making a triggering decision to remove a product, which had been deemed unsafe. The Court explained that Article 9 of the Directive did not prevent a triggering decision

---

[1]   (unreported) 30 November 2000.

being made at a local level by a trading standards department. The judgment explains that the European legislator must have appreciated that consumer protection was likely to operate within Member States at a localised level. Nigel Pleming QC (sitting as a Deputy High Court Judge) explained that 'it was almost inconceivable that the "policing" of product safety would not be carried out a local level'. That said, the Administrative Court also observed that one would expect a standardisation of approach so as to ensure that there is uniformity in the application of the rules within States.

The geographic impact of local policing

11.9   Whilst consumer protection is usually policed at a local level, the enforcement action taken by local agencies may still nonetheless have a national impact. As considered below, however, much will depend on the statutory powers which enable the enforcement action to be taken.

11.10   The issue of whether a statutory suspension notice served by a local trading standards department had effect nationwide, or just within the area which it had responsibility for policing was touched on in the decision in *Alba Radio*. The Administrative Court did not resolve the issue and explained that a decision on the geographic reach of a notice would have to wait.

11.11   This was eventually decided in *Brighton & Hove City Council v Woolworths PLC*.[2] In this case, a trading standards department of a local Council issued a notice under the Consumer Protection Act 1987, s 14 suspending the sale of a children's toy on the grounds of safety. An issue arose as to whether a trading standards department could issue a notice which had national impact or whether it could only have effect for the area of the local Council. It was held that the local trading standards department was empowered to issue a suspension notice with countrywide effect. Field J explained that the terms of that legislation did not limit the power of an enforcement authority to issue a notice only in respect of its area. It was observed that the statutory power to issue a notice was conferred on an 'enforcement authority' which could be the Secretary of State, any other Minister of the Crown or a local Council. Furthermore, it was common ground that the Secretary of State and any other Minster of the Crown were empowered to issue a notice with countrywide effect. Field J held therefore that if this was so, then the 'same must be true' as concerns a local authority.

The restrictions on legal proceedings

11.12   However, the *Woolworths* litigation also decided that if the person the subject of the notice acted in contravention of a notice then a trading standards department could only prosecute for breaches which occurred in its area (the 1987 Act includes criminal prohibitions against contravention of a notice) since *ex-hypothesi* prosecuting for offences occurring outside its area could not be expedient for the promotion or protection of the interests of the inhabitants in its area. Thus, it was held in the *Woolworths* case that the trading standards department could only prosecute for breaches which occurred in the Brighton & Hove area. This reasoning was based on the terms of the Local Government Act 1972, s 222 which explains that a local authority may prosecute, defend or appear in any legal proceedings if it considers it expedient for the promotion of the protection of the interests of the inhabitants of their particular

---

[2]   [2002] EWHC 2565 (Admin).

area. It should be recognised that the terms of the Local Government Act 1972, s 222 are not just applicable to criminal proceedings. The provision is very wide and encompasses 'any legal proceedings'. It explains that a local authority 'may prosecute or defend or appear in any legal proceedings and, in the case of civil proceedings, may institute them in their own name'.

11.13 The approach in Woolworths, however, should be contrasted with the approach in *R (on the application of Donnachie) v Cardiff Magistrates' Court & Others*.[3] This case concerned criminal proceedings under the Trade Descriptions Act 1968 in respect of the application of false odometer readings to cars (it was in fact the second time that the same proceedings had been before the Administrative Court. The previous appearance of the case before the Administrative Court is considered below). The alleged offences were said to have been actually committed outside the area of Cardiff and in the areas of Gloucester and Newport. Sweeney J, applying the observations of Rose LJ in *R v Jarret & Steward*[4] to the effect that the terms of s 222 are 'extremely wide', held that the local authority could prosecute for offences in Gloucester and Newport. The Administrative Court found that given the nature of the business (of which the defendant was the company secretary) and the closeness of its connection with Cardiff, it was self evidently in the interests of the inhabitants of Cardiff for the defendant to be prosecuted for alleged offences in Gloucester and Newport. Sweeney J explained that 'the 1972 Act is extremely widely worded, there is no warrant for limiting its terms, thus the Council may prosecute any legal proceedings, provided that on proper grounds they "consider it expedient for the promotion or protection of the interests of the inhabitants of their area"'. The decision in *Woolworths* was distinguished on the basis that 'in that case, the level of risk, and hence the need for protection from it, was negligible'. In those circumstances, Sweeney J explained that it was 'hardly surprising' that the court concluded that the Local Government Act 1972, s 222 was of no application. It was held that the facts between the two cases were very different.

11.14 In any event, it is also apparent from the decision in *Woolworths* that a local authority may prosecute on behalf of a different Council if the power to prosecute the proceedings has been properly delegated to it by the other local authority. In this regard, Field J accepted the submissions on behalf of Woolworths that the other local authorities had the power to delegate to another authority the prosecution of breaches of the suspension notice which occurred in their area provided that they considered the prosecution for the breaches expedient for the promotion of the protection of the interests of the inhabitants in their particular areas. Similarly, in *Donnachie* it was held that 'if only to avoid prolonged debate as to whether section 222(1) was properly engaged in a particular case, it would be wiser for local authorities to enter into section 101 agreements before laying informations alleging offences outside their area'. By section 101 agreements the Administrative Court were referring to the Local Government Act 1972, s 101 which enables a local authority to arrange for the discharge of its functions by another local authority.

THE IDENTITY AND ROLE OF THE ENFORCING BODY

11.15 A body may act as an enforcing body if it is lawful for it to do so. Such a body carries out its responsibilities in the interest of the public (whether that is the local public or the national public). An enforcing body is obliged to discharge its

3   [2009] EWHC 489 (Admin) per Sweeney J.
4   (unreported) 30 January 1997.

responsibilities lawfully. Discretion must be exercised rationally. In carrying out its enforcement role, it is also required to act fairly and proportionately. This includes retaining independent control over the enforcement action and ensuring that such enforcement action is brought without any unjustifiable delay.

Exercising discretion and discharging duties lawfully

11.16 In many cases, enforcement bodies are subject to statutory duties which oblige them to enforce the statutory codes. In carrying out this duty, regulators are often given a wide range of enforcement options including the issuing of statutory notices and warnings etc. Some statutory schemes give the body a general duty to enforce the provisions but discretion as to when and how this is done. Other schemes may be more prescriptive and oblige the body to take enforcement action when specified factors are fulfilled. For example, in the environmental context, a judicial review claim succeeded where an enforcement authority was in breach of a mandatory statutory duty to serve an abatement notice if it was satisfied of a statutory nuisance.[5] Some statutory provisions expressly specify that enforcement authorities shall act proportionately when enforcing the respective legislation.[6] The scope of the duties placed on an enforcing authority therefore is an important factor in a challenge to their enforcement decisions.

11.17 Any challenge to a decision of whether or not to take enforcement action will be influenced by the scope of the statutory duty imposed on the enforcing body. As a general rule, the Administrative Court is reluctant to interfere with discretionary decisions of enforcement bodies as to whether or not to take enforcement action. In *R v Commissioners of Customs & Excise, ex p International Federation for Animal Welfare*[7] the Court of Appeal considered a renewed application for permission to bring judicial review proceedings challenging the decision of Customs & Excise. Customs had decided not to implement a ban in respect of animal pelts (a ban which appeared to have been anticipated by European regulations). In giving judgment, Henry LJ explained that the case illustrated the particular difficulty that arises when an enforcement authority or a prosecuting authority's failure to act is challenged by way of judicial review proceedings. Indeed, it was pointed out by the Court of Appeal that had Customs implemented such a ban then it is likely that it would have been judicially reviewed by the other parties, for instance, the importers whose products had been turned away by Customs. Henry LJ provided some general guidance on this issue explaining that 'such a failure to act is theoretically justiciable' but that as other decisions in the area reveal 'it is a jurisdiction very sparingly exercised, only in what would have to be a truly exceptional situation. While those rules have been developed in relation to individual cases, it seems to me that they can be read across when the circumstances are right'.

11.18 This approach is apposite in respect of challenges to decisions whether or not to prosecute criminal proceedings. A number of decisions in the non-consumer law context illustrate this. It has been held that challenges to decisions to prosecute by way of judicial review proceedings should be very rare indeed (see, for example, a review of the principles by the Privy Council in *Sharma v Antoine* [2006] UKPC 57 per Lord Bingham of Cornhill). In such circumstances, a defendant to criminal proceedings has recourse through the procedures of the criminal court.[8] However, issues may arise in practice as

---

5   See *R v Carrick District Council, ex p Shelley* (1996) Env LR 273.
6   See, for example, General Product Safety Regulations 2005, SI 2005/1803, reg 10(5).
7   (unreported) 8 July 1996.
8   See the observations in the cases of *R (on the application of Kebilene) v DPP* [2000] 2 AC 326 as applied in *R (on the application of Pepushi) v Crown Prosecution Service* [2004] EWHC 798 (Admin).

to whether the arguments, for example abuse of process arguments, are more appropriately pursued before the Administrative Court as opposed to the criminal courts. Indeed, there are decisions which identify the restricted scope of the jurisdiction of the Magistrates' Court to hear such applications.[9] The route taken will depend on the circumstances of the case.

11.19 It is right to recognise, however, that that there is a distinction between challenging: (1) a decision not to prosecute, and (2) a decision to prosecute. In respect of the former then judicial review is the only remedy available to challenge the decision. However, that is not so with regards to the latter type of decision. Nonetheless, in general, the Administrative Court is reluctant to interfere with prosecutorial decisions and will only do so sparingly and with caution.

11.20 However, whilst such guidance remains sound as a general principle, it has to be considered in the context of the grounds of challenge. This was explained by Buxton LJ in *R (on the application of Jones) v Director of Public Prosecutions*,[10] a case which considered whether a decision of the DPP not to prosecute health and safety based proceedings was unlawful. In this case, the Court of Appeal explained that the duty of the Court was not to do the prosecution's work for it and that there were significant limits on the extent to which the Court could intervene. Furthermore, Buxton LJ had in mind the decisions which identified that intervention should be sparing. However, it was observed that such guidance was mainly directed to issues of weight given to the evidence by the prosecution and matters of professional judgment. It was further held that 'none of the statements in earlier authorities can have been intended to exclude from this court's consideration other fundamental aspects of the judicial review jurisdiction, for instance, as at least potentially relevant to our present case: (1) Has the decision–maker properly understood and applied the law? (2) Has he explained the reasons for his conclusions in terms that the court can understand and act upon? (3) Has he taken into an irrelevant matter or is there a danger that he may have done'.[11] Therefore, all the usual grounds of challenge are potentially available.

11.21 Moreover, in *R (on the application of Donnachie) v Cardiff Magistrates' Court & Others*[12] the Administrative Court was considering criminal proceedings under the Trade Descriptions Act 1968. Sweeney J explained that 'a decision whether or not to issue a summons following the laying of an information involves the exercise of a judicial discretion, and is subject to potential judicial review'. Whilst these theoretically are challenges to the judicial decisions of the Magistrates' Court they are also, in effect, challenges to the prosecutorial decisions themselves. As will be considered later in this Chapter, there are examples of judicial review challenges in respect of the decisions of Magistrates' Courts during criminal proceedings. Enforcement action under the consumer protection statutory codes is broader than just prosecutions; for example, it may also include warnings, cautioning, and the issuing of statutory notices. Potentially, all the usual grounds of judicial review are available to challenge enforcement action. That said, the appropriateness of a judicial review claim will depend on the circumstances of the case (not least whether there is an alternative appropriate remedy).

---

9   See in this regard, for example, *R v Horseferry Road Magistrates' Court, ex p Bennet* [1994] 1 AC 42.
10   (unreported) 23 March 2000.
11   See also the similar observations on the scope of the review available in the following health and safety related decisions: *R (on the application of Pullen) v Health and Safety Executive* [2003] EWHC 2934 (QB) and *R (on the application of Dennis) v DPP* [2006] EWHC 3211 (Admin).
12   [2009] EWHC 489 (Admin).

It should also be recognised that, depending on the circumstances, a claimant may face some reluctance on the part of the Administrative Court to intervene.

Ensuring that proceedings are lawfully brought by the correct body

11.22 Issues may arise as to whether a body has lawful power to bring enforcement action. The issue will depend on the terms of the statutory scheme in question. The following decisions reveal that if Parliament has specifically provided that a particular person must institute the criminal proceedings then that statutory power cannot be delegated by that person to another person. Indeed, in *R v Croydon Justices, ex p WH Smith Ltd*[13] the Administrative Court considered a challenge by WH Smith Ltd, by way of judicial review proceedings, to a decision of a Magistrates' Court that it had jurisdiction to hear a prosecution under the Health and Safety at Work etc Act 1974. Section 38 of the 1974 Act explained that 'proceedings for an offence under any of the relevant statutory provisions shall not, in England and Wales, be instituted except by an inspector or ... by or with the consent of the Director of Public Prosecutions'. The proceedings were not instituted by an Inspector but rather a solicitor of the prosecuting local authority. The Administrative Court decided that the prosecution had been unlawfully commenced. It held that proceedings were instituted when the information was laid before the Magistrates' Court and that this role could not be delegated by an Inspector to another person such as the Council's solicitor. Elias J explained:

> 'Section 38 does not in terms say that there is no power to delegate, and nor is there any express restriction elsewhere in the Health and Safety at Work etc Act. However, where the power to take certain steps is given to an officer appointed pursuant to statute then it is only going to be in a very exceptional case that the courts will imply a power to delegate in the absence of any express provision .... In my view there is nothing in the circumstances here which would justify the inference that there should be a power to delegate because of any overwhelming administrative convenience or anything of that kind. Indeed, on the contrary, where one is dealing with the institution of criminal proceedings then, in my judgment, if delegation is ever permissible, it would need a very strong administrative inconvenience indeed to infer that there was a power to delegate authority which Parliament had laid specifically on a named individual'.

11.23 The outcome of issues such as the above depends upon the construction of the statutory provisions. This is particularly illustrated by the decision in *MFI v Hibbert*.[14] In this case, MFI was prosecuted for offences of giving misleading price indications contrary to the Consumer Protection Act 1987, s 20. The proceedings were instituted by Mr Hibbert, the Assistant Director (Consumer and Environmental Protection) at Newcastle Upon Tyne City Council. MFI argued that there had been no effective delegation of power to Mr Hibbert which would allow him to prosecute and lay the charges before the Magistrates' Court. The Court decided that the minutes of the City Council, whilst not a model of clarity and precision, had effectively delegated power to Mr Hibbert to institute the proceedings. However, the Court also went on to explain that, if it was wrong about that, then Mr Hibbert still had the power to prosecute and institute the proceedings. Balcombe LJ explained section 27(1)(a) of the 1987 Act imposed a duty upon a weights and measures authority (such as the Council in that case) to enforce the provisions of the Act. However, the Court explained that the Act did not limit the power of others to prosecute for such offences. Therefore, Mr Hibbert, like any other person, had the power to prosecute the proceedings. Consistently with the

---

[13]   (2000) *The Times*, 22 November.
[14]   (1995) *The Times*, 21 July.

reasoning in the *WH Smith Ltd* case, Collins J also explained that it was 'not a case where the right to prosecute is limited to the local authority. If it were, any lack of delegation could indeed be fatal because Mr Hibbert could not himself be entitled to prosecute'.

11.24 It should also be recognised that a local authority does have the power to institute proceedings in its own name; as opposed to instituting them through an officer with delegated power to do so. This was the issue considered by the Administrative Court in the criminal context in *Monks v East Northamptonshire District Council*.[15] In this case it was held that a local authority was entitled to issue summonses and prosecute in its own name in respect of offences under the Food Safety Act 1990. It was said that the summonses could be issued in the name of the authority; they did not have to be issued in the name of an identified individual, for example, an officer of the authority with delegated power to institute such proceedings. The Administrative Court's reasoning was based upon the fact that the local authority was the body that had a statutory duty to enforce the provisions of the 1990 Act and, as the enforcing authority, was entitled under the 1990 Act to institute proceedings under that Act. The reasoning of Silber J was also based on the terms of the Local Government Act 1972, s 222. The Administrative Court explained that the terms of this statutory provision entitled a local authority to institute both civil and criminal proceedings in its own name.

11.25 A similar statutory duty to that in the Food Safety Act 1990 was considered in *Donnachie*. In this case, the Administrative Court considered the source of a local authority's power to enforce the provisions of the Trade Descriptions Act 1968. The Administrative Court considered, specifically, the source of a Council's power to prosecute criminal proceedings under the 1968 Act. Sweeney J explained that it was common ground in that case that a power could arise from sources including: (1) necessary implication from the statutory duty to enforce the provisions of the 1968 Act within its area, and (2) the terms of the Local Government Act 1972, s 222.

11.26 Where criminal proceedings are instituted by an officer of a local authority who has delegated power to do so, the 'prosecutor' for the purposes of the proceedings is still the local authority. This was explained in the earlier *Donnachie* decision of *R (on the application of Donnachie) v Cardiff Magistrates' Court & Others*.[16] In this case, Nelson J considered who the 'prosecutor' for the purposes of offences under the Trade Descriptions Act 1968 was. Nelson J observed that the local authority was the relevant enforcing authority for the purpose of the Act and held that they were the 'prosecutor' and not the officer who had delegated power to institute proceedings and lay informations before the Magistrates' Court.

Exercising independent control over the enforcement action

11.27 Consumer protection matters may give rise to issues which require expertise and resources outside the scope of the enforcing authority. By way of illustration, an enforcing authority could be a small trading standards department within a local Council with minimal resources. It may therefore be appropriate for the enforcing authority to enlist the assistance of other bodies such as the Police, the industry to which the issues pertain and even those directly affected by the offending behaviour. In

---

[15] [2002] EHC 473 (Admin) per Silber J.
[16] [2007] EWHC 1846 (Admin).

R v Milton Keynes Magistrates' Court, ex p Roberts[17] the Court considered that 'hands on' assistance in that case from a third party who was affected by the offending behaviour was 'not only sensible but also necessary'. However, whilst the assistance of others may be engaged, the enforcing authority should always remain the true enforcing body and exercise its duties in this regard independently.

11.28 In *ex p Roberts* a defendant to a trading standards prosecution applied by judicial review proceedings for an order prohibiting the Magistrates' Court from committing the defendant to the Crown Court for trial. The case concerned counterfeit Ford motor parts and offences under the Trade Marks Act 1938, s 58A and the Trade Descriptions Act 1968. It was argued that the proceedings were an abuse of process of the Court since the proceedings were not being brought by the trading standards department but rather by the Ford Motor Company.

11.29 In support of that argument the claimant referred to a number of matters said to show that the trading standards department had failed to exercise control, care and independence over the prosecution. These included the extent of Ford's part in the investigation and the fact that Ford had agreed to indemnify the trading standards department against liabilities that they might incur in respect of compensation claims under the 1968 Act. The proceedings were dismissed. Beldam LJ explained that the jurisdiction of the Court to restrain a prosecution was one to be exercised sparingly. It was held that the evidence did not show that the trading standards department had failed to exercise independent judgment and, in particular, there was no evidence that the indemnity influenced the decisions of the trading standards department. Buxton J explained that such cases may give rise to issues of a technical nature and 'hands on assistance from third parties is therefore not only sensible but also necessary'.

11.30 The judgment of Buxton J also sets out some general guidance to issues of this kind. It was explained that: 'we can readily accept that if a prosecutor did indeed make himself the creature of a private interest in exercising his powers, then that conduct would at least prima facie be abusive .... The important question, however, in assessing such an investigation from the point of view of abuse of process is whether the role of the third parties has been allowed to grow to such an extent that they have caused the prosecutor to abdicate his responsibility'.

11.31 In *R v Leominster Magistrates' Court & Others, ex p Aston Manor Brewery*,[18] McCowan LJ considered similar issues. In this case, the defendant was prosecuted for offences under the Food Safety Act 1990. The bringing of the criminal proceedings had resulted from a complaint by Schweppes who were involved in parallel civil proceedings against the defendant relating to passing off and breach of statutory duty. The judicial review complaint considered the issue of disclosure. McCowan LJ held that the prosecuting authority had been put into a position where they had been in close alliance with Schweppes, to the extent that Schweppes had controlled the issue of disclosure. It was explained that this put the prosecuting authority in a position where they were unable to exercise independently their duties as the prosecutor. It was said that the control was in the hands of a trade body which was most likely to be the only person who benefited from the prosecution. The integrity of the proceedings had been compromised to the extent that a fair trial was no longer possible.

---

[17] [1995] Crim LR 224.
[18] (1997) *The Times*, 8 January.

11.32 The issue of Police assistance was considered in *R v Croydon Justices, ex p Holmberg*[19] where a defendant challenged by judicial review proceedings a Magistrates' Court's decision to commit the defendant for trial at the Crown Court. The case concerned allegations in respect of counterfeit video recordings. It was argued that the local authority was not an appropriate prosecutor given the Police's involvement with the proceedings. The proceedings were dismissed. Watkins LJ explained that merely seeking Police assistance in performing their duties did not turn proceedings brought by a local authority into proceedings brought on behalf of the Police. The local authority was thus not an inappropriate prosecutor.

Bringing enforcement action without unjustifiable delay

11.33 There is a plain public interest in the enforcement of consumer protection being timely and undertaken without delay. Furthermore, it is part of domestic and European law that such enforcement should be carried out without unreasonable delay. Indeed, an undue delay may give rise to arguments that the action is unlawful and an abuse of power or the Court's process.

11.34 A number of the consumer protection statutory codes set time limits within which enforcement action has to be brought. This is particularly so in respect of criminal prosecutions. A common provision in such legislation is one which states that no proceedings shall be commenced after a specified period; usually three years beginning with the date of the offence or the end of the period of one year beginning with the date of discovery of the offence by the prosecutor, whichever is the earlier.[20]

11.35 The reasons for such statutory time limits were considered in *Tesco Stores Limited v Harrow London Borough Council*.[21] In this case, Newman J explained the legislative policy underpinning the time period provisions. It was held that the setting of time limits for the prosecution of offences is designed to achieve two important consequences. The first is to provide protection to the citizen(s) who may have committed the criminal offence and the second is to bring about a timely and efficient investigation of the alleged offence.

11.36 Much litigation has turned on the approach to the issue of 'discovery'. The principal test is that laid down by McNeil J in *John Charles Brooks v Club Continental Ltd*.[22] This case was concerned with a misleading holiday brochure. A complaint was made by a holiday-maker to the trading standards department in July 1979. Witness statements were made by the complainant in July and September 1979. The criminal charges were not brought until November 1980. The prosecution said that they had been delayed because they had had difficulty in discovering the proper name of the tour operator. However, it was found as a fact that they discovered the name in October 1979. The Court upheld the decision of the Magistrates' Court that the charges had been brought out of time. McNeil J explained that:

> 'I think it is sufficient, for the purposes of this case, to say that the word "discovery" means no more in this context than that all the facts material to found the relevant charge under the Act were disclosed to the appropriate officer. The word "discovery" here does not import any

---

[19]   [1992] Crim LR 892.
[20]   See, for example in this regard, the Food Safety Act 1990, s 34 and the Consumer Protection from Unfair Trading Regulations 2008, SI 2008/1277, reg 14.
[21]   [2003] EWHC 2919 (Admin).
[22]   [1981] TrL 126 (DC).

investigation by the officer. It is simply his knowledge, from disclosure to him in some way, of the material facts which would found the offence.'

11.37 See also *R v Beaconsfield Justices, ex p Johnston and Sons Ltd* (1985) 149 JP 535 and *R v Stoke on Trent Magistrates' Court, ex p Leaf United Kingdom Ltd* (unreported) 6 November 1997 both of which are decisions that applied the approach of McNeil J in the *John Charles Brook* case.

11.38 The issue of 'discovery' was considered again in the case of *Tesco Stores Limited v Harrow London Borough Council*[23] in which the Administrative Court again applied the approach set out in *John Charles Brook*. Newman J re-shaped the questions that should be asked in any such case. It was explained that it was material to ask what Parliament would have intended as being the appropriate time when the prosecuting authority should assume a duty to investigate. It was said that this question could be answered by reference to the approach of McNeill J in *John Charles Brooks*. Newman J explained that the Magistrates may have been assisted by asking the question 'whether the facts disclosed, objectively considered, would have led a prosecuting authority to have reasonable grounds to believe that an offence may have been committed by some person who has been identified to it?'. It was further said that discovering the offence should be taken as meaning discovering grounds sufficient to found a reasonable belief that an offence has been committed. Newman J explained that this approach accorded with the statutory purpose of such time limit provisions.

11.39 The fact that enforcement action has been commenced within the statutory time limit does not of itself, however, preclude a defendant from still arguing that a delay in taking enforcement action renders it an abuse of process or power.[24] In *Olins*, criminal proceedings were stayed since the delay had caused serious prejudice to the defendant. Generally, such applications involve showing that it is unfair to take the action or that the person can no longer have a fair hearing.

POLICIES, ADVICE AND CODES OF PRACTICE

11.40 Guidance provided by the regulator may range from policies explaining how the regulator's enforcement responsibilities will be exercised to advice on the regulatory framework. Codes of practice which supplement the statutory code may also inform the decision-making process and provide guidance to those who operate their undertakings within the relevant regulated field.

The role of enforcement policies

11.41 Policies play an important role in the enforcement obligation. They guide those charged with the duty of deciding whether enforcement should be taken and they assist the public in understanding the basis on which those decisions as to enforcement action will be made.

11.42 Generally these policies should be followed and only departed from if there is good reason to do so. An unjustified departure could render any subsequent enforcement action unlawful.

---

[23] [2003] EWHC 2919 (Admin).
[24] See, for example, *Daventry District Council v Olins* (1990) 154 JP 478 per Nolan J.

Failure to follow enforcement policies

11.43 Such complaints do, however, involve a high threshold and the Administrative Court is usually reluctant to interfere with the enforcement discretion of regulators, particularly when it involves decisions in the criminal jurisdiction. The power to do so is exercised sparingly.

11.44 Moreover, as with judicial review proceedings generally, all appropriate alternative remedies should be exhausted prior to any claim for judicial review being issued. Much will depend on the enforcement action being brought and whether there is an appropriate alternative remedy which could properly address and resolve the grievance. For example, the usual recourse for a prosecution brought in breach of an enforcement policy would be before the criminal courts with an application to stay proceedings as an abuse of process of the Court.[25] If such an argument is pursued in the Magistrates' Court then the decision of that Court may, in appropriate cases, be susceptible to challenges by way of judicial review. As explained earlier, claims relating to matters on indictment cannot be brought before the Administrative Court by way of judicial review proceedings. However, recourse may be available to the Court of Appeal in such circumstances. In *Adaway*, the Court of Appeal acted on principles akin to public law grounds in staying the criminal proceedings.

11.45 In *Adaway* the prosecuting local authority had an enforcement policy in respect of consumer protection matters which explained that in order to institute a prosecution the individual or organisation must have either been engaged in fraudulent activity or have deliberately or persistently breached their legal obligations. A prosecution was commenced, in breach of this policy, alleging offences under the Trade Descriptions Act 1968. The Court of Appeal decided that the proceedings should have been stayed as an abuse of process of the Court. The criterion set out in the enforcement policy had not been satisfied and the prosecution was therefore oppressive. In the course of giving judgment Rose LJ strongly emphasised that before criminal proceedings are instituted by a local authority acting in relation to strict liability offences, the authority must 'consider with care the terms of their own prosecuting policy'. It was further explained by Rose LJ that if a local authority failed to do so or if they reached a conclusion to prosecute which is wholly unsupported by material establishing the criteria for prosecution, the Courts will be unsympathetic to attempts to justify prosecutions.

11.46 The Court of Appeal in *Adaway* made reference to the decision of Phillips LJ in *Walker v Simon Dudley Ltd*[26] in which Phillips LJ considered the 1968 Act and explained that the construction of the 1968 Act may mean that 'technical offences' will be committed in circumstances where a civil law claim is the only remedy that the facts of the case require. Phillips LJ explained that trading standards officers must exercise discretion when deciding whether or not a particular case warrants the intervention of the criminal law.

11.47 Following the decision in *Adaway*, the Administrative Court has reviewed the principles and the authorities in respect of enforcement policies in a non consumer protection case: see *R (on the application of Mondelly) v Commissioner of Police of the Metropolis.*[27] The claimant in this case applied for judicial review of the Police's decision to caution him for possession of cannabis. It was alleged that the decision was in breach

---

[25]   See *R v Adaway* [2004] EWCA Crim 2831.

[26]   (1997) *The Times*, 3 January.

[27]   [2006] EWHC 2370 (Admin).

of the police's policy. Moses LJ explained that the effect of the claimant's interpretation of the policy was that a person could not be cautioned unless aggravating factors applied. The Administrative Court reviewed the authorities relating to such challenges and explained:

(1)   Generally there is a reluctance of the courts to intervene in relation to decisions to prosecute and the administration of cautions.

(2)   A refusal to intervene save where the policy which it is suggested has been breached is clear and settled and the breach is itself established.

11.48 In *Mondelly* Moses LJ and Ouseley J held that on a proper construction of the policy in question it did not preclude the Police from administering the caution for the offence. In a dissenting judgment Walker J held that the decision to caution did contravene the Police's policy and applied similar reasoning which had been applied by the Court of Appeal in the *Adaway* case.

11.49 The majority of the Administrative Court in Mondelly also explained that: 'were there to be a police/CPS policy that no one should be prosecuted for simple possession of cannabis unless it fell within the aggravating circumstances specified, and if that were said to make a decision to prosecute unlawful in such circumstances, it would be an unlawful policy itself. Parliament did not enact those aggravating factors into the offence of simple possession, and it is not for executive prosecution policy to change it'. It was said that such an enforcement policy 'would be akin to a policy not to prosecute for theft, and merely to retrieve stolen goods, unless their value exceeded £100, not far distant from the example of an unlawful policy given by Denning MR in *R v Commissioner of Police of the Metropolis, ex p Blackburn* [1968] QB 118'.

11.50 Interestingly, the policy in *Adaway* would appear to be the type of policy which the majority of the Administrative Court in *Mondelly* considered to be an unlawful one. Of course, as explained by Walker J in *Mondelly*, a regulatory body would hardly seek to defeat such a challenge by arguing that the policy was unlawful (it would 'hardly lie in his mouth to do so', per Walker J).

11.51 However, it is not just those who are the subject of the enforcement action who would be able to challenge decisions as to whether or not to take enforcement action. Others may also be affected by decisions as to whether or not to take such action, for example, a complainant. Indeed, they could be justifiably aggrieved by the application of such an enforcement policy as considered in *Mondelly* which seeks to restrict what Parliament had otherwise implemented. In *R v DPP, ex p C*[28] Kennedy LJ, after reviewing the authorities, explained that the Court could interfere by way of judicial review proceedings if it is was persuaded that the decision not to take action was arrived at because of some unlawful policy.

Assurances and advice given by regulators

11.52 Decisions such as that in *Adaway* may, on one view, be explained as involving a breach of a clear assurance that a person would not be prosecuted for offences unless specified factors were present. The clear assurance being set out in the policy which informs those affected.

---

[28]   [1995] 1 Cr App R 136.

11.53 Indeed, issues may arise as to whether enforcement action is an abuse of power in that it contradicts assurances or advice which had been previously given by the regulator. Such an issue arose in *R (on the application of Sovio Wines Limited) v Food Standards Agency (Wine Standards Branch) & Others.*[29] In this case, the claimant applied for relief by way of judicial review proceedings in respect of a statutory notice issued by the Food Standards Agency prohibiting the movement of its low alcohol wine based product. The case concerned labels which were said to be misleading. The background to the case was that the Wine Standards Board had informed the claimant that the product in question did not come within their jurisdiction and that it was regulated by the trading standards department. The claimant was further told that the trading standards department should check the labeling of the product. Thereafter, the trading standards department approved certain labeling. However, the labeling offended the relevant Regulations and a statutory notice was issued by the Food Standards Agency who, contrary to its earlier representations, did have jurisdiction for the regulation of the product and the issues relevant to that case. The claimant argued that: (1) the Board did not have jurisdiction over the product and the issues in the case, and (2) the enforcement action was an abuse of power since it breached its legitimate expectation arising from representations by the Board. The latter argument was advanced on the basis of three alleged representations. First, that the Board did not have jurisdiction in respect of the product, secondly, that the Board would not take action in respect of the product and, thirdly, that the jurisdiction rested with the trading standards authority and not the Wine Standards Board.

11.54 Dobbs J rejected the arguments. In relation to the second ground of challenge (namely, the breach of a legitimate expectation) the Administrative Court decided that, on the facts of the case, the claimant did not enjoy the legitimate expectation they had argued that they possessed.

11.55 The judgment of Dobbs J is of wider interest for the application of general principles which also formed the basis for, and were part of, the decision. In particular, it was also explained that:

(1)   Even if a legitimate expectation had been created, the expectation would have to yield to the Food Standards Agency's duty to enforce the law. In this case, there was a statutory duty to enforce the provisions of the Regulations (applying the approach in *R v Secretary of State for Education & Employment), ex p Begbie*).[30]

(2)   Even if the Administrative Court had accepted the claimant's argument as to jurisdiction, in its discretion, it would have refused to grant relief. This was on the basis that the claimant had breached the Regulations. Dobbs J explained that to grant the relief in such a case would have been to condone a breach of the Regulations.

11.56 This approach may be contrasted with the approach in the criminal jurisdiction, see *Postermobile v London Borough of Brent*[31] (a non-consumer law case). In *Postermobile*, a local authority officer had informed a party that planning consent was not required for temporary advertisements. The party thereafter erected the advertisement hoardings and was subsequently prosecuted for failing to obtain the

---

[29]   [2009] EWHC 382 (Admin).
[30]   (2000) 1 WLR 1115.
[31]   (1997) *The Times*, 8 December.

necessary consent. It was held that the prosecution should have been stayed by the Magistrates' Court as an abuse of the Court's process. Schiemann LJ explained that: 'I see no substantial public purpose being served in continuing to prosecute an individual who has come to the Council for advice as to whether something which he proposes to do is lawful, is advised that it is and in reliance on that representation does that very thing'. Schiemann LJ was referred to the planning decision in *Western Fish Products Limited v Penwith District Council & Others*[32] and the reasoning in that case that an estoppel cannot be raised to prevent the exercise of a statutory discretion or the performance of a duty. Schiemann LJ recognised that administrative law may give rise to conflicting factors but held that where all that is at stake is whether a person should be prosecuted for what they did in good faith, greater weight should be given to the fact that a citizen should be able to rely on what a public official tells him.

The role of Codes of Practice

11.57 Codes of Practice also play an integral part in the policing and enforcement of consumer law. Some statutes place a duty on the enforcing authority to have regard to a Code of Practice in the carrying out of its functions.[33] As such, these Codes may inform the regulator's decision-making process and enforcement procedures.

Application of Codes of Practice

11.58 It is important to appreciate, however, that such Codes cannot replace or usurp the relevant statute. Moreover, the scope of the particular statutory duty should also be recognised; typically it is merely to have 'regard' to the Code of Practice. That said, such Codes (whether statutory or non-statutory) provide important guidance for the regulator and for those affected by the regulation. In general, any departure from a Code should be justified and reasoned.

11.59 In *AG Stanley Limited (t/a FADS) v Surrey County Council*[34] the Court was concerned with a Code of Practice issued under the Consumer Protection Act 1987, s 25, part of which was to give guidance as to the requirements of section 20 of the Act (that is the prohibition against giving misleading indications as to price). The Act explained that compliance or non-compliance with the Code may be relied on to show whether or not there had been a breach of the section 20 prohibition. Proceedings in the Magistrates' Court had focused on whether there had been a breach of the Code. The Magistrates' Court found there was, as did Scott Baker J, who held that there was a clear breach of the Code in that case.

11.60 Some general guidance as to how Codes of Practice should be interpreted may be taken from the judgment of Scott Baker J. It was explained that, when applying a Code, it must be construed in the context of the legislation under which it is made. The judgment of the Court also explains that the fundamental question to be decided is whether there is a breach of the Act, not the Code. This illustrates the earlier point that the focus should be on the legislation.

---

[32] [1981] 2 ALL ER 204.
[33] See, for example, the Food Safety Act 1990, s 40.
[34] (1994) 159 JP 691.

THE ROLE OF THE CROWN AND MAGISTRATES' COURT

11.61 Enforcement proceedings under the consumer protection legislation appear in various guises including prosecutions before the criminal Courts, appeals against statutory notices and civil proceedings before the Magistrates' Court and Crown Court. As can be seen, both the civil and criminal jurisdiction of these Courts play an integral part in regulating the consumer law.

Criminal jurisdiction – overview

11.62 The criminal courts are also public bodies that carry out public functions. As such, in appropriate cases, their actions may be susceptible to judicial review challenges. A potential claimant, however, should always bear in mind that the Senior Courts Act 1981, s 29(3) excludes matters relating to trial on indictment from the remit of judicial review proceedings. This is a principle that has received judicial consideration in the context of judicial review proceedings.[35]

Civil jurisdiction – overview

11.63 In addition to its criminal jurisdiction, the Magistrates' Court and the Crown Court also determine appeals against the service of statutory notices and other statutory applications. An example of the latter is applications for forfeiture of counterfeit goods pursuant to the provisions of the Trade Mark Act 1994, s 97. A judicial review in respect of such an application came before the Administrative Court in *R v Crown Court at Harrow & Others, ex p UNIC Centre SARL*[36] in which Newman J considered whether such proceedings were criminal or civil in nature. The Administrative Court explained that the proceedings were civil in nature. The judgment is also instructive as to the scope of forfeiture applications and who has the right to bring them before the Court. Newman J explained that whilst the right to commence such proceedings was of particular value to local trading standards departments, the power to bring such matters could be exercised by any person, for example, a trademark proprietor. Therefore, whilst it assists local authorities in the discharge of their functions, it also allows a person to protect their private interests. Depending on the statutory scheme, therefore, consumer protection laws may provide powers not just to the relevant regulator, but also to those individuals who have been affected by relevant alleged offending behaviour.

Appeals – alternative remedies

11.64 It is important to ensure that a person wishing to challenge enforcement action chooses the appropriate forum to do so. Judicial review may not always be the appropriate forum. It is often said that judicial review is a remedy of last resort which should only be embarked on once all another remedies have been exhausted. The issue of alternative remedies and judicial review has spawned much jurisprudence over the years and continues to do so. Choosing the incorrect route may lead to permission for judicial review, or the relief sought, being refused.

11.65 The issue of whether it was more appropriate to pursue a statutory appeal rather than judicial review was considered in the consumer safety context in *R v Birmingham*

---

[35] See the non consumer law case of *R (on the application of Kebilene) v DPP* [2000] 2 AC 326.
[36] [2000] 1 WLR 2112.

City Council, ex p Ferrero Ltd.[37] In this case a suspension notice had been issued pursuant to the Consumer Protection Act 1987, s 14. The particular statutory code provided for a right of appeal to the Magistrates' Court. Rather than pursuing the statutory appeal route the recipient of the notice challenged it by way of judicial review. The Court of Appeal considered whether it was appropriate to do so. Taylor LJ identified the relevant factors to be considered and explained that the question to be asked when considering such an issue was as follows:

'..what, in the context of the statutory provisions, was the real issue to be determined and whether a s 15 appeal was suitable to determine it. The real issue was whether the goods contravened a safety provision and the s 15 appeal was geared exactly to deciding that issue. If the goods did contravene the safety provision and were dangerous to children then, surely, procedural impropriety or unfairness in the decision-making process should not persuade a court to quash the order. The determining factors are the paramount need to safeguard consumers and the emergency nature of the s 14 powers. Suppose that judicial review of a s 14 notice were entertained where the enforcement authority suspected certain goods to be poisonous. Suppose further the affidavit evidence raised a strong presumption that the goods were poisonous, but it was clear the authority had taken into consideration irrelevant factors or had omitted to consider relevant ones. The court would clearly decline to quash the notice'.

Case stated or judicial review?

11.66 Similarly, when challenging the decision of the Magistrates' Court or the Crown Court it may be more appropriate to pursue an appeal to the Administrative Court by way of case stated. Some guidance in terms of deciding upon the appropriate route was provided (in a non consumer law case) by Collins J in *R (on the application of P) v Liverpool City Magistrates' Court.*[38] It was explained that the normal (and more appropriate) route for challenging an alleged error of law against the decision of the Magistrates' Court was by an appeal by way of case stated. In general, a failure to go by way of case stated in such a situation is 'likely to result in a refusal of permission for judicial review on the basis that it is the wrong way'.

11.67 However, Collins J also recognised that there were conflicting authorities which did not always make it easy to decide whether judicial review or an appeal by way of case stated was the appropriate route. As such, further guidance was provided by Collins J to the effect that judicial review is more appropriate where, for instance, there is an issue of fact which may have to be raised and which the Magistrates' Court could not have decided for itself. An example would be where it is alleged that there was unfairness in the Court proceedings.

11.68 All may not be lost, however, should a person choose the wrong route. In *R (on the application of Brighton & Hove City Council) v Brighton & Hove Justices,*[39] Stanley Burnton J explained that the Administrative Court may refuse relief in a claim for judicial review if the case stated procedure was appropriate but that such refusal was discretionary and not mandatory. In that case it was said that the decision should have been challenged by way of the case stated procedure, but the Administrative Court decided in the exercise of its discretion to allow it to proceed by way of judicial review. Stanley Burnton J explained that unless prejudice has been caused to a party or there is

---

[37]   [1993] 1 All ER 530.
[38]   [2006] EWHC 887.
[39]   [2004] EWHC 1800 (Admin).

some other good reason to refuse the judicial review claim to proceed then the Administrative Court 'should be reluctant to cause a good claim to be defeated by an error as to the form of proceedings'.

11.69 Moreover, should adequate reasons have already been provided by the Magistrates' Court then judicial review may not be an inappropriate route (see, for example, *R (on the application of Stace) v Milton Keynes Magistrates' Court*).[40] Such an approach, however, depends to a large extent on the content and detail provided in the reasoning.

11.70 The restrictions on the case stated procedure at the interlocutory stages should also be recognised. In *R v Greater Manchester Justices, ex p Aldi Gmbh and Co KG*[41] Butler Sloss LJ considered criminal proceedings under the Consumer Protection Act 1987. It was explained that the Magistrates' Court had no power to state a case in criminal proceedings unless and until the Magistrates had reached a final determination on the matter before them. See also the approach in *Durham County Council v North Durham Justices*.[42] However, in civil proceedings, the Magistrates' Court does have discretion to state a case at an interlocutory stage but it is a discretion to be exercised sparingly (see, for example, *R v Chesterfield Justices, ex p Kovacs*).[43] Judicial review is potentially available at interlocutory stages. However, see the cautionary words of Moses J in the *Durham County Council* case and Butler Sloss LJ in the *Greater Manchester Justices* decision. A review of the principles is set out by Hughes LJ in *R (on the application of Singh) v Stratford Magistrates' Court*[44] and *Crown Prosecution Service v Sedgemoor Justices*.[45] In *Sedgemoor*, it was explained that 'in general terms, this Court will not entertain, whether by application for judicial review or by way of appeal by case stated, an interlocutory challenge'. It was however recognised that the Court is sometimes persuaded to hear a case at an interlocutory stage but there has to be good reason to do so. In *Gillan v DPP*[46] the Administrative Court allowed an appeal by case stated to proceed by way of judicial review adopting the *Sunworld* procedure below.

11.71 A situation may occur, however, in practice where the Magistrates' Court or the Crown Court refuses to state a case. This in itself is a decision which may be challenged by way of a claim for judicial review. In *Sunworld Ltd v London Borough of Hammersmith and Fulham*[47] a defendant to a trading standards prosecution appealed to the Crown Court against convictions imposed by a Magistrates' Court. This appeal was dismissed and the defendant requested the Crown Court to state a case for the opinion of the High Court on three particular questions. The Court agreed to state a case in respect of one of the questions but refused as regards the other two questions. Simon Brown LJ set out a general procedure to be followed in cases of this kind whilst recognising that such a procedure may not apply in every case:

---

[40]   [2006] EWHC 1049 (Admin) per Keith J.
[41]   (1994) 159 JP 717.
[42]   [2004] EWHC 1073 (Admin).
[43]   [1992] 2 ALL ER 325.
[44]   [2007] EWHC 1582 (Admin).
[45]   [2007] EWHC 1803 (Admin).
[46]   [2007] EWHC 380.
[47]   (2000) 1 WLR 2102.

(1)   Where a Court, be it a Magistrates' Court or a Crown Court, refuses to state a case then the party aggrieved should without delay apply for permission to bring judicial review either: (a) to direct it to state a case, and/or (b) to quash the order sought to be appealed.

(2)   If the Court below has already given a reasoned judgment containing all the necessary findings of fact and/or explained its refusal to state a case in terms which clearly raise the true point of law in issue, then the correct course would be for the single Judge, assuming that the Judge thinks the point to be properly arguable, to grant permission for judicial review which directly challenges the order complained of, thereby avoiding the need for the case to be stated at all.

(3)   If the Court below has stated a case but in respect of some questions only, as in the *Sunworld* case, the better course may be to apply for the case stated to be amended unless again, as in *Sunworld*, there already existed sufficient material to enable the Administrative Court to deal with all the properly arguable issues in the case.

(4)   The Administrative Court will adopt whatever course involves the fewest additional steps and the least expense, delay and duplication of proceedings. Whether it is possible to proceed at once to the substantive determination of the issues must inevitably depend in part upon whether all the interested parties are represented and prepared, and in part upon the availability of court time.

THE ROLE AND FUNCTIONS OF SPECIALIST BODIES

Is the body susceptible to judicial review?

11.72 It will be readily appreciated that the bodies referred to above are public bodies carrying out public functions. They are, therefore, susceptible, in appropriate cases, to claims for judicial review. However, issues may arise in respect of some of the specialist bodies which carry out functions and specifically as to whether their actions may be subject to judicial review claims. There is no single test for determining whether a body is susceptible to judicial review proceedings. The issue of whether the decision of a body may be the subject of judicial review proceedings depends largely on the functions that the body is performing and whether they involve a public element. A body carrying out a function which is derived from statute would generally point to a body susceptible to challenges by way of judicial review proceedings.

11.73 Examples of such specialist bodies with a consumer protection role include those responsible for the regulation of advertisements. Such policing is carried out by the Committee of Advertising Practice and the Advertising Standards Authority. The former is responsible for writing the codes of advertising practice and the latter is responsible for the handling and resolution of complaints made in respect of the advertisements. An integral part of their functions is consumer protection and to ensure that consumers are not mislead by advertising.

11.74 These bodies are responsible for regulating both advertisements which are broadcast on television and radio and those advertisements which are not. The responsibilities in respect of broadcast advertising have been contracted out to these bodies by Ofcom pursuant to a statutory order. Under the Communications Act 2003

Ofcom has responsibility in respect of setting standards to protect against misleading advertisements on television and radio. The bodies' responsibilities in respect of advertisements which are not broadcast on television or radio derive from the advertising industry. In effect these bodies fulfil roles within a self regulating system set up by the advertising industry to regulate standards within the industry.

11.75 In *R v Advertising Standards Authority Ltd, ex p Insurance Service PLC*,[48] the Insurance Service PLC sought judicial review and the quashing of a decision of the Advertising Standards Authority that advertising literature distributed by it was in breach of the Code of Advertising Practice. Glidewell LJ referred to the decision in *R v Panel on Take-overs and Mergers, ex p Datafin PLC*[49] and explained that the Advertising Standards Authority could be supervised by the Courts by way of judicial review proceedings. It was explained that whilst the authority had no powers granted to it by statute or common law, it was nevertheless 'clearly exercising a public law function which if the ASA had not existed would no doubt have been exercised by the Director of Fair Trading'.

11.76 Similarly the Committee of Advertising Practice is also, in appropriate cases, susceptible to judicial review. In *R v Committee of Advertising Practice, ex p Bradford Exchange*[50] Bradford Exchange Ltd sought judicial review of a decision by the Committee not to approve an advertisement. In this case it was accepted that the Committee was a body amenable to judicial review. Now, pursuant to the responsibilities under the Communications Act 2003 which have been contracted out by Ofcom to both the Advertising Standards Authority and the Committee of Advertising Practice, both these bodies fulfill statutory objectives.

The parameters of challenge

11.77 Given that such bodies are reviewable, the usual principles pertaining to judicial review proceedings apply to the decision-making processes and roles undertaken by these bodies. In *Insurance Service plc* (1989) Glidewell LJ applied the normal principles of judicial review and granted relief since the facts had not been accurately presented to the decision-making body.

11.78 In *R v Advertising Standards Authority, ex p DSG Retail Ltd*,[51] it was identified that the Court would interfere with decisions of the Authority on classic administrative law grounds. In other words, where there is irrationality, illegality or procedural impropriety.

The width of discretion

11.79 However, as a general principle the Administrative Court usually shows restraint before interfering with the decisions of bodies which comprise expertise and specialism. Such bodies are usually afforded a significant width of discretion in their decision-making processes.

---

[48]   (1989) *The Times*, 14 July.
[49]   [1987] QB 815.
[50]   [1991] COD 43.
[51]   [1997] COD 232.

11.80 In *R v Radio Authority, ex p Bull* [1995] All ER 481 the Radio Authority (now Ofcom) was challenged by way of judicial review proceedings. The Authority refused to allow an advertisement to be broadcast since it was said to be 'political' and therefore contravened the Broadcasting Act 1990, s 92. In considering the issue the Court held that the Authority had a large measure of discretion when determining whether or not an advertisement was 'mainly of a political nature' (the relevant statutory term in issue). The Court declined to interfere with the Radio Authority's decision. Kennedy LJ explained that a large measure of discretion must be left to a regulatory authority which has particular expertise in the relevant area.

11.81 The matter was appealed to the Court of Appeal (see *R v Radio Authority, ex p Bull*).[52] In dismissing the appeal Lord Woolf MR, in contrast to the approach taken by Kennedy LJ, concentrated instead on the fact that the Radio Authority was a 'regulatory body consisting of lay members which is intended to take a broad brush approach to its task'. It was also explained that because of its lay nature the Court hearing the judicial review should allow the Authority a 'margin of appreciation and only interfere with its decision when there is a manifest breach of the principles' relied on in the proceedings to support the judicial review claim.

11.82 It thus appears that bodies such as this enjoy a significant width of discretion in their decision-making functions. See also the observations of Lord Woolf MR in *R v Broadcasting Standards Commission, ex p BBC*[53] and Balcombe LJ *R v Broadcasting Complaints Commission, ex p Granada Television Limited*.[54] This principle was applied by Newman J in *R (on the application of Boyd Hunt) v Independent Television Commission & Others*[55] when considering a claim against the Independent Television Commission. A similar approach was taken in *R v Advertising Standards Authority Ltd, ex p Charles Robertson (Development) Ltd*.[56] The issue was whether or not a column in the style of an editorial, which was printed alongside an advertisement for a company (and paid for by that company), fell within the jurisdiction of the Advertising Standards Authority. In other words, whether it was an advertisement. Moses J decided that the question of whether material is part of an advertisement was a paradigm of an issue to which there is no clear cut answer and to which decision-makers may reach different conclusions. It was held that such an issue was therefore a matter which should be left to the judgment of the decision-maker. It should only be interfered with if the only true and reasonable conclusion contradicted that judgment.

11.83 The above being said, the Administrative Court will not abdicate its supervisory responsibilities and will interfere if appropriate grounds for judicial review are made out by a claimant.

Alternative remedies

11.84 In general, it is important to ensure that all other appropriate remedies have been pursued before a claimant embarks on proceedings by way of judicial review. The general principles and law which pertain to issues of this kind apply equally to the challenges of specialist bodies.

---

[52]   [1997] 2 ALL ER 561.
[53]   [2000] 3 WLR 1327.
[54]   (1994) *The Times*, 16 December.
[55]   [2002] EWHC 2296 (Admin).
[56]   (1999) *The Times*, 26 November.

11.85 This is illustrated in *R (on the application of Debt Free Direct Ltd) v Advertising Standards Authority*.[57] These proceedings involved a challenge to the Advertising Standards Authority. In this case, the complaints about the Authority's adjudication process were within the ambit of an independent review procedure carried out by an 'Independent Reviewer'. It was held that there was nothing about the complaints to suggest that judicial review was a more appropriate remedy than an independent review.

PUBLICITY OF CONSUMER PROTECTION

Importance of publicity

11.86 Publicity plays a key part in the regulation of consumer protection and there is a strong public interest in such matters being made public. Amongst other things, such publicity promotes the protection of the public (by, for example, raising awareness), provides transparency to the regulatory process, deters those who may deliberately seek to breach regulations and works to improve the diligence of those who are involved with businesses which impact on consumers.

Restraining publicity

11.87 There is also a plain public interest in matters such as convictions and other adjudications or findings being made public. A line of authorities in respect of the Advertising Standards Authority has recognised the appropriateness of publishing such adjudications and decisions.

11.88 In *R (on the application of Vernons Organisations Ltd) v Advertising Standards Authority*,[58] Laws J considered an application for an injunction restraining the Authority from publishing an adjudication in respect of an advertisement relating to a pools competition being run by the claimant. The Administrative Court's reasoning explained that 'if a private individual will not be restrained from expressing his opinion save on pressing grounds I see no reason why a public body having a duty, other things being equal, to express its opinion should be subject to any less rigid rules. It seems to me that the case is, if anything, analogous to one where an administrative body has an adjudicative function and in the course of its duties publishes a ruling criticising some affected person and the ruling is later disturbed'.

11.89 In *R v Advertising Standards Authority, ex p Direct Line Financial Services Ltd*[59] Popplewell J considered the reasoning of Laws J and explained that he did not find the analogy used by Laws J helpful. He granted a restraining injunction.

11.90 The approach of Popplewell J, however, has not been followed. The Administrative Court has consistently followed the approach taken by Laws J. In both *R v Advertising Standards Authority & Independent Reviewer of the Advertising Standards Authority, ex p Matthias Rath BV & Others*[60] and *R (on the application of J) v A*[61] the Administrative Court expressly indicated its preference for the Laws J approach. In the latter case, David Lloyd Jones QC (sitting as a Deputy High Court Judge) explained that

---

[57]   [2007] EWHC 1337 (Admin) per Sullivan J.
[58]   [1992] 1 WLR 1289.
[59]   [1998] COD 20.
[60]   (2000) *The Times*, January 10 per Turner J.
[61]   [2005] EWHC 2609 (Admin) per David Lloyd Jones QC (sitting as a Deputy High Court Judge).

the correct approach was that adopted by Laws J. The Administrative Court further explained that this was a matter of public law and should be addressed in public law terms. It explained that:

'... the general principle is that the courts will not restrain the expression of an opinion or the conveyance of information whether by private individual or a public body, save on exceptional grounds, and that principle is not disengaged because an intended publication contains material which is subject to legal challenge. A public body would not normally be restrained from discharging its ordinary duties on that ground. That is particularly so where, as in the present case, the public body has a duty to protect the public. The judgment of Laws J was delivered in 1992, and his reasoning is all the more compelling today in the light of the effect of the Human Rights Act 1998'.

11.91 More recently, in *R (on the application of Debt Free Direct Ltd) v Advertising Standards Authority*[62] Sullivan J appears to have put the issue beyond any further debate. In this case, the claimant to judicial review proceedings applied for an injunction to restrain the Authority from publishing an adjudication in respect of a television advertisement. Sullivan J stated that he 'unhesitatingly' preferred the reasoning of Laws J. The Administrative Court further explained that compelling reasons would have to be shown to restrain publication of an adjudication by a public body exercising a quasi-judicial function.

11.92 It was said that the claimant would suffer financial damage by reason of the effect on its commercial reputation. Sullivan J held, however, that it was difficult to see how the case differed, save in terms of degree, from the ordinary case where a regulator publishes an adverse report in respect of the person or body who is subject to the regulator's jurisdiction. A similar argument as to the effect on the businesses' commercial reputation was advanced in a different forum in *R v Dover Justices, ex p Dover District Council and Wells*.[63] In this case, the defendant carried on a restaurant business and was being prosecuted for food hygiene offences. An application was made by the defendant for an order under section 11 of the Contempt of Court Act 1981 to prevent the publication of the proceedings. This was principally on the alleged ground that publicity would be highly prejudicial to the business. The Magistrates' Court granted the application and made an order preventing publication of the criminal proceedings. The issue became the subject of judicial review proceedings and the decision of the Magistrates' Court was quashed. In giving judgment, Neill LJ explained that the power to prevent or restrict the publication of court proceedings was a jurisdiction which is only to be exercised very sparingly in exceptional circumstances where it is shown necessary. In this case, it was held that although the publicity of the proceedings might cause great prejudice and result in severe economic damage to the defendant, that did not allow the Magistrates' Court to make the orders preventing the publication of the Court proceedings.

Prejudicing justice or fairness

11.93 Publicity should not, however, operate so as to prejudice the administration of justice or impede on the fairness of legal proceedings. *R v Marylebone Magistrates' Court, ex p Amdrell Ltd (t/a Get Stuffed)*[64] concerned an investigation in respect of the trade in endangered species. A search warrant was granted by the Magistrates' Court.

---

[62]   [2007] EWHC 1337 (Admin).
[63]   (1991) 156 JP 433.
[64]   (1998) 162 JP 719.

Prior to the application, the media had been briefed and a television crew had been invited to attend whilst the warrant was executed. The decision to apply for the warrant was the subject of judicial review proceedings. The claim was dismissed. However, in doing so, Rose LJ explained that the fundamental principle in respect of such issues was that nothing should be done to prejudice the proper course of justice or the fairness of a trial, by whatever tribunal.

Circumventing legal process

11.94 Furthermore, such publicity should not operate in a way which would circumvent express statutory codes. In *R v Liverpool City Council, ex p Baby Products Association & Others*[65] the Council issued a press release in respect of a baby walker product. The press release announced that samples of ten models had been tested and found not to comply with the British Standard Safety specification. The issue in the case was whether the issuing of such a press release was unlawful and beyond the powers of the City Council. The legal background to the case involved the Consumer Protection Act 1987 and the General Product Safety Regulations 1994. Lord Bingham CJ explained that the statutory provisions comprised a detailed and carefully crafted code designed to promote the protection of the public against unsafe products but also to give fair protection to the interests of manufacturers and suppliers.

11.95 The statutory code included powers which would have, amongst other things, allowed the Council and the Secretary of State to issue a suspension notice in respect of the products and which would have allowed the Secretary of State to issue a prohibition notice or warning notice in respect of the product (in other words, a notice warning against the safety of goods). The recipient of such notices has the right to statutory remedies. For example, suspension notices may be the subject of an appeal to the Magistrates' Court and thereafter the Crown Court. In respect of a prohibition notice or a warning notice, the recipient may ask for the matter to be re-considered at an oral hearing by a person appointed by the Secretary of State.

11.96 It was held that the Council had acted unlawfully by circumventing the statutory code. The submissions, which found favour with the Court, were explained by Lord Bingham CJ as follows:

> '(1) the press release ... was the clearest possible warning to the public that the identified models of babywalker were said to be unsafe. The council had no statutory power to issue such a warning. The Secretary of State could have required the companies involved themselves to publish a warning about the specified goods, but only if he considered that they were unsafe and complied with the statutory conditions regulating the exercise of this power. Had he taken this course the company would have enjoyed the rights and safeguards already listed. By acting as it did the council purported to exercise a power it did not have and in so doing deprived the companies of rights and safeguards which Parliament had enacted that they should enjoy. (2) One inevitable and intended object of the press release was to cause a suspension of supply of the identified products by the companies named. Under the Act the council did have power to give notice suspending supply for a limited period. But this power was one which the council could only exercise subject to conditions specified in the Act, which gave recipients of the notice important rights and safeguards, and it was a power which the council did not exercise because no suspension notice was ever served. By acting as it did, the council again purported to exercise a power it did not have and in so doing deprived the companies of rights and safeguards which Parliament had enacted'.

---

[65]   [2000] LGR 171.

11.97 The Court distinguished a previous authority in which the issuing by the Director General of Fair Trading of a press release which recorded the conviction of a company for contravening safety regulations was upheld (see *R v Director General of Fair Trading, ex p F H Taylor & Co Ltd*).[66] The distinction relied on by the Court in this instance was that the issuing of the press release in those circumstances did not in any way circumvent the statutory codes.

THE FUTURE

11.98 In recent years we have seen the introduction of further legislative regulation designed to ensure that consumers are protected and the continued commitment to enforce those provisions. For example, the Consumer Protection from Unfair Trading Regulations 2008 came into force in May 2008. The explanatory memorandum explains that the Regulations put in place a comprehensive framework for dealing with sharp practices and rogue traders and creating a modern simplified consumer protection framework. To ensure that those Regulations are being properly enforced, the Department for Business, Innovation and Skills has set up a 'fighting fund' to tackle rogue traders and consumer targeted scams. The purpose of the fund is to support 'enforcement activity such as investigations, prosecutions or civil proceedings of national or regional importance or for innovative enforcement activity'.[67] These developments lend support to the view that there will be more consumer protection based litigation coming before the Courts and therefore coming before the Administrative Court.

---

[66]   [1981] ICR 292.
[67]   See BIS Fighting Fund, Guidance for Local Authority Trading Standards Services, dated February 2010.

Chapter 12

LICENSING

INTRODUCTION

Local decision-making

12.1   Many functions under the various licensing regimes are carried out by local authorities. These licensing functions range from hackney carriages, street traders to sex establishments. The scope of the licensing responsibilities vested in local authorities has also increased significantly following the implementation of the Licensing Act 2003. This places the responsibility for the licensing of alcohol sales, regulated entertainment and the provision of late night refreshment in the hands of local Councils. Local Councils discharge their licensing responsibilities through committees and sub committees comprising Councillors and/or through Council officials who have delegated powers. The statutory schemes usually involve rights of appeal from the decisions of Councils to the Magistrates' Court (and in some instances the Crown Court). All these bodies are of course public bodies carrying out public functions and as such their actions may, in appropriate cases, be susceptible to challenges by way of claims for judicial review.

Specialist tribunals

12.2   Some of the other licensing functions are carried out by specialist tribunals. Examples of these include the Gambling Commission (who deal with certain licences in respect of gambling) and the Office of the Traffic Commissioner (who deal with, for example, the licensing of the road haulage industry). The applicability of judicial review claims to such bodies is not as prevalent as it is in respect of the licensing functions carried out by local Councils. These bodies operate within tribunal systems which involve statutory rights of appeal to specialist tribunals.

Chapter outline

12.3   This Chapter will consider, in the context of judicial review and Administrative Court proceedings, the status of a licence, those responsible for regulating them and some of the key areas that inform the decision-making process within the licensing sphere.

STATUS OF A LICENCE

Permission/authorisation

12.4   A licence is a permission or authorisation allowing the licence holder to carry on a particular activity. In effect, it sets out the scope of that which has been authorised by the regulator. Depending on the circumstances, a person seeking to carry on an activity may need multiple authorisations, ie, permissions under different regulatory regimes if the activity crosses different regulatory contexts.[1] Sometimes the scope of an activity is restricted by reference to conditions, which are imposed on the licence. Breach of an authorisation often engages significant criminal sanctions under the respective statutory codes. In the light of that, both domestic and European jurisprudence require that the licence must be sufficiently certain.[2] In the latter case Mitting J referred to the observations of Scott Baker LJ in *Crawley Borough Council v Attenborough*.[3] In *Attenborough*, the Administrative Court was considering the clarity of conditions which had been attached to a premises licence under the Licensing Act 2003. Scott Baker LJ explained that it must be apparent from reading the licence what the licence and its conditions mean. The licence and the conditions must be clear, not just to those having specialist knowledge of licensing but to those who have no knowledge of licensing at all. Indeed, breach of a condition carries criminal sanction and a vague and unclear licence could render the terms of it unenforceable.

Possession or property?

12.5   As explained, a licence is an authorisation or permission. In other words, it is a regulatory approval. Ordinarily understood, therefore, a licence in itself would not appear to be the 'possession' or 'property' of a licence holder. Notwithstanding this, the issue has generated not insubstantial litigation before the Administrative Court and higher appellate jurisdiction.

12.6   A question that often arises is whether a licence is the possession or property of the licence holder and whether, therefore, it engages the protection afforded by Article 1 of the First Protocol of the European Convention of Human Rights. Article 1 of the First Protocol explains:

> 'Every natural or legal person is entitled to the peaceful enjoyment of his possessions. No one shall be deprived of his possessions except in the public interest and subject to the conditions provided for by law and by the general principles of international law.
>
> The preceding provisions shall not, however, in any way impair the right of a State to enforce such laws as it deems necessary to control the use of property in accordance with the general interest or to secure the payment of taxes or other contributions or penalties'.

12.7   It was explained by the European Court of Human Rights in *Sporrong v Sweden*[4] that the Article comprises three rules.[5] Those three rules are as follows. The first rule states the principle of peaceful enjoyment of property. The second rule deals with deprivation of possessions. The third rule recognises that Member States are entitled to control the use of property in accordance with the general interest by enforcing such law as they deem necessary for that purpose. It should be recognised that merely because the Article is engaged this does not necessarily mean that there has been a violation of the right. The importance of the Article becoming engaged is that the burden thereafter

---

[1]   See, for example, *R (on the application of Kelly) v Liverpool City Council* before the Administrative Court on 5 September 2008 (unreported) per HHJ Langan QC and the Court of Appeal (permission hearing) at [2009] EWCA Civ 191 per Dyson LJ.

[2]   See, for example, *R (on the application of the Mayor and Citizens of Westminster City Council) v Metropolitan Stipendary Magistrate* [2008] EWHC 1202 (Admin).

[3]   [2006] EWHC 1278 (Admin).

[4]   [1982] 5 EHRR 35.

[5]   See also *Fredin v Sweden* [1991] ECHR 12033/86 in this regard.

shifts to the public authority as the State to justify any interference in accordance with the Convention so as to show there has been no violation of the Article.

12.8 The issue was considered by the Administrative Court *in R (on the application of Royden) v Wirral Metropolitan Borough Council.*[6] This case concerned the decision of a Council to remove the limit on the number of vehicles licensed as hackney carriage vehicles within its area. The claimant was a proprietor of a hackney carriage vehicle licensed by the Council and he argued, amongst other things, that a hackney carriage vehicle licence was a 'possession' and that the Council's decision constituted an interference with the peaceful enjoyment of that possession. The case was argued specifically on the basis that the result of the Council's decision would be to eliminate the value of the claimant's licence. Christopher Bellamy QC (sitting as a Deputy High Court Judge) reviewed a number of decisions of the European Court of Human Rights and the European Commission. It was explained that he had 'some difficulty accepting that an authorisation granted by the State under public law to carry out a particular activity' could itself be property or a possession under the Convention.

12.9 The Deputy Judge adopted the reasoning from the European Court of Human Rights decision in *Tre Trakoter Aktiebolag v Sweden.*[7] In this case, a company (TTA) had a licence to sell alcoholic beverages at a restaurant, Le Cardinal. The licence was withdrawn by the relevant authorities in Sweden. The European Court found that Article 1 of the First Protocol was engaged. This was not because the licence itself constituted a 'possession' or 'property' but rather because the economic interests connected to the running of the restaurant were 'possessions' for the purpose of the Article. It was decided that:

> 'the Court takes the view that the economic interests connected with the running of Le Cardinal were "possessions" for the purposes of Article 1 of the Protocol. Indeed, the Court has already found that maintenance of the applicant company's business and that its withdrawal had adverse effects on the goodwill and value of the restaurants. Such withdrawal thus constitutes, in the circumstances of this case, an interference with TTA's right to the "peaceful enjoyment of [its] possessions".'

12.10 The interference in this case, however, was held to be justified in accordance with the Convention. It was held to be in compliance with Swedish law and proportionately undertaken in the pursuit of the general interest, namely the control of the sale of alcoholic beverages.

12.11 It therefore appears that a licence in itself does not constitute a possession or property for the purposes of the Convention. However, as in the *Tre Trakoter* case, economic interests connected to the running of a business or the underlying assets may well do so.

12.12 There is, however, domestic authority from the Court of Appeal which approached the issue on the basis that a licence did constitute a 'possession' or 'property' for the purposes of Article 1 of the First Protocol (see *Crompton v Department of Transport,*[8] a case concerning the revocation of a road haulage operators' licence). It is right to recognise that the issue of whether the licence was a 'possession' was not actually argued in *Crompton*. The Court of Appeal proceeded on the agreed

---

[6]   [2002] EWHC 2484 Admin.
[7]   [1991] EHRR 309.
[8]   [2003] EWCA Civ 64.

basis that the licence did constitute a possession for the purposes of Article 1 of the First Protocol. Indeed, the approach by the Court of Appeal in *Crompton* is difficult to reconcile with the European jurisprudence (see, for example, the reasoning in *Tre Trakoter*) and the approach taken in the other domestic authorities. The erroneous approach in *Crompton*, namely, that a licence was a possession for the purposes of Article 1 of the First Protocol, has now been recognised by the Court of Appeal in *Waltham Forest NHS Primary Care Trust & Others v Malik*[9] (however, on its facts, the decision in *Crompton* was justified since the underlying economic interests were affected).

12.13 *Malik* was a case which considered whether the inclusion of a doctor on a NHS Primary Care Trust's approved list of medical practitioners was a possessory right for the purpose of Article 1 of the First Protocol. The Court of Appeal in *Malik* held that it was not a 'possession' for the purposes of Article 1. The Court rejected the argument that a licence to practise a profession could be a 'possession' and also rejected the argument that future loss of income was a loss of a 'possession'. *Malik* has also been considered in different licensing contexts (see, for example, *Security Industry Authority v Stewart & Others*).[10]

12.14 In *Stewart & Others* the Administrative Court considered whether people who had licences to work as door supervisors under the regime in place before the Private Security Industry Act 2001, but who were disqualified under the 2001 Act by reason of the statutory criteria in that Act, were thereby unlawfully deprived of their 'possessions' for the purposes of Article 1 of the First Protocol. The Court said that in the light of *Malik* the contention that earlier permissions were 'possessions' for the purposes of the Convention involved '*mountainous*' difficulties.

12.15 *Stewart & Others* illustrates a departure from the previous authority on the point, *Nicholds & Others v Security Industry Authority*:[11] a case which considered the same issue and legislation as in *Stewart & Others*. In *Nicholds & Others*, Kenneth Parker QC sitting as a Deputy High Court Judge held that, despite his reservations, he had to proceed on the basis that the permissions previously enjoyed by the claimants did constitute 'possessions'. This was in the light of decisions such as *Crompton* and *Malik* at first instance but it was, however, recognised in *Nicholds & Others* that an expectation of future income is not a 'possession' and would not engage the protection afforded by Article 1 of the First Protocol.

12.16 The issues have so far been considered from the perspective of a licence being withdrawn. However, a decision to refuse to grant a licence may also engage Article 1 of the First Protocol. This occurred in the *Miss Behavin'* litigation.[12] In this case, it was argued that a decision of Belfast City Council to refuse to grant a licence for a sex establishment under the Local Government (Miscellaneous Provisions) (Northern Ireland) Order 1985 (the equivalent to the 1982 Act in England and Wales) engaged Article 1 of the First Protocol. Lord Kerr CJ in the Northern Irish Court of Appeal held that the refusal of the Council to allow the appellant to use its premises in a way that would permit their commercial exploitation engaged Article 1 of the First Protocol. In the House of Lords it was acknowledged that the Article may have been engaged.

---

9   [2007] EWCA Civ 265.
10   [2007] EWHC 2338 (Admin).
11   [2006] EWHC 1792 (Admin).
12   See Northern Irish Court of Appeal [2006] NI 181 and House of Lords [2007] UKHL 19.

However, given the circumstances being considered in that case (namely, the right to sell pornography), the House Lords considered the argument that there was a violation of the Article to be weak.

Summary of the principles

12.17 The following summary appears to follow from the above review of authorities:

(1)   a licence is a regulatory approval. The scope of the authorisation must be sufficiently certain and clear from the licence;

(2)   a licence is not a 'possession' or 'property' for the purposes of Article 1 of the First Protocol;

(3)   however, connected economic interests may well be (see for example, *Tre Traktoer* where goodwill and the value of the restaurant were said to be such); but

(4)   the economic interest must be existing or vested. By way of example, a mere right or expectation to future income will not engage Article 1 of the First Protocol.

ROLE OF LOCAL LICENSING BODIES

12.18 As explained earlier, a number of the licensing regimes specify that the functions are carried out by local Councils. The responsibilities are often carried out through committees, sub committees or officers of the Council. To lawfully carry out the licensing functions, the responsibilities must be properly delegated (note, the Local Government Act 1972, s 101 allows a Council to delegate its responsibilities to committees, sub committees and individual Officers of the Council). The identity of the body within the Council responsible for the function will depend on how matters have been delegated within the particular Council. However, some statutes, see for example the Licensing Act 2003, also include specific provisions relating to the delegation of licensing responsibilities and who may carry out the particular functions.

Quasi-judicial function?

12.19 The local Council committees comprise democratically elected local Councillors. It has been generally accepted that proceedings before such committees are by their nature quasi-judicial. A clear statement of this proposition is found in *R v London Borough of Wandsworth, ex p Darker Enterprises Limited*,[13] a case which concerned an application for the renewal of a sex establishment licence under the Local Government (Miscellaneous Provisions) Act 1982, Sch 3. Turner J recognised that it is generally accepted that proceedings before such a sub-committee are quasi-judicial in their nature.

12.20 Similar observations were made by the Court of Appeal in *R v Preston Borough Council, ex p Quietlynn Ltd*,[14] a case concerning the licensing of sex establishments. In that case Simon Brown LJ explained that a local Council was exercising an administrative function involving an element of judicial process when it considered applications for licences. However, more recently, the Court of Appeal in *R (on the*

---

[13]   (unreported) 15 January 1999.
[14]   (1984) 83 LGR 308.

application of Hope & Glory Public House Ltd) v Westminster Magistrates' Court & Others[15] has explained that whilst a local Council has a duty to carry out its decision-making process fairly under the Licensing Act 2003, the decision itself is not a judicial or quasi-judicial act. Rather, it is an adminstrative function and 'the exercise of a power delegated by the people as a whole to decide what the public interest requires'.

Local decision-making

12.21 One of the objects of the licensing regimes is to promote local decision-making by local people based on local knowledge. This is why Parliament vests the responsibilities for such issues in the hands of local Councils. As such, the fact that a local Council in a different part of the Country has granted a similar, perhaps even identical, application would not generally oblige a local Council in an another part of the Country to do the same. By way of example, this has been specifically recognised in respect of the licensing of private hire vehicles: see *Chauffeur Bikes Limited v Leeds City Council*.[16] In this case, Poole J explained that the legislation, namely, the Local Government (Miscellaneous Provisions) Act 1976, permitted local Councils to individually consider the issues. Poole J illustrated this point by explaining that the fact that a local Council in Kent may have come to one conclusion on whether a particular vehicle should be licensed did not oblige one in Yorkshire to do the same. That said, depending on the context, it may be that the experience and practice of other local authorities cannot properly be ignored and would be a relevant consideration.[17]

12.22 It should always be borne in mind that licensing decisions are being taken by democratically elected Councillors and not lawyers. In *R v Reading Borough Council, ex parte Johnson*[18] Goldring J considered the decision of a licensing committee to issue further hackney carriage licences in its district. It was explained that:

> 'Real deference should be paid to the decision of decision takers who are democratically elected and who take their decision following at least adequate consultation (as in my view this undoubtedly was) with interested parties. That decision should not be judged in an over refined and over legalistic way'.

Local knowledge

12.23 Local knowledge plays a key part in the decision-making processes undertaken by local Councils. In *ex p Johnson* the Administrative Court explained that local Councillors would be failing in their duty as Councillors if they ignored their local knowledge when making licensing decisions. Goldring J explained that:

> 'I see nothing objectionable in local councillors, plainly familiar with [the area], using their local knowledge of how the taxi system operates in practice. Indeed, they would be failing in their duty as councillors if they ignored their local knowledge'.

12.24 The Administrative Court is often more reluctant to interfere with decisions that are highly dependent on local knowledge. In *R (on the application of 4 Wins Leisure*

---

15 [2011] EWCA Civ 31.
16 [2005] EWHC 2369 (Admin).
17 See *R (on the application of Lunt & Others) v Liverpool City Council* [2009] EWHC 2356 (Admin) per Blake J.
18 [2004] EWHC 765 (Admin).

Limited) v *Blackpool Licensing Committee & Others*,[19] proceedings in respect of the Licensing Act 2003, the issue was whether a trade competitor was a person with a business within the vicinity of the applicant's premises and whether, therefore, it was entitled to make representations in respect of the application for a licence. Sullivan J decided that:

> 'Whether or not premises can sensibly be said to be in the vicinity of another must be very much a question of fact and degree. Moreover, it is a question that is highly dependent upon local knowledge. That, no doubt, is why the question was left for local licensing committees to determine. It would only be in very unusual circumstances that this court, never having seen the site and being wholly unfamiliar with the area in question, would be able to say that such a judgmental conclusion of a local committee was unlawful on the ground of being irrational.'

12.25 However, a decision-maker must measure their own local knowledge and views against the evidence presented to them. In *R (on the application of Daniel Thwaites PLC) v Wirral Magistrates' Court & Others*[20] the decision of a Magistrates' Court hearing an appeal under the Licensing Act 2003 to refuse to grant extended hours of operation to a licensed premise was judicially reviewed. In that case, importantly, the Police had no objection to the application. Black J explained that:

> 'It is clear from the Guidance that drawing on local knowledge, at least the local knowledge of local licensing authorities, is an important feature of the Act's approach. There can be little doubt that local Magistrates are also entitled to take into account their own knowledge but, in my judgment, they must measure their own views against the evidence presented to them. In some cases, the evidence presented will require them to adjust their own impression. This is particularly likely to be so where it is given by a responsible authority such as the Police'.

12.26 Indeed, the limits of acting on local knowledge should be appreciated. Local knowledge should not be equated with expertise in a specialist area of assessment (*R (on the application of Lunt & Others) v Liverpool City Council*).[21]

ROLE OF LOCAL COUNCILLORS

Strong and robust opinions

12.27 Local Councillors are also politicians. In their roles as local politicians, Councillors are likely to have views (perhaps strong views) about issues of local public interest and to have expressed them publicly. In general, such should not disqualify them from hearing and determining licensing matters.

12.28 This is supported by a number of decisions concerning the licensing of sex establishments. In *R v Reading Borough Council, ex p Quietlynn*,[22] the case concerned an application for a sex establishment licence. Members of a sub-committee who determined the application had previously decided it was opposed to sex establishments and some opposition had been expressed publicly. The issue in the case was whether the decision to refuse the licence was objectionable on the grounds of bias. Kennedy J

19   [2007] EWHC 2213 (Admin).
20   [2008] EWHC 838 (Admin).
21   [2009] EWHC 2356 (Admin) per Blake J.
22   [1986] 85 LGR 387.

explained that a Councillor's role was to formulate and express views on subjects of local interest (such as the licensing of sex establishments) and that they should not be disqualified from deciding something, which Parliament has expressly decided to vest in local Councillors, by merely carrying out this role. See also the approach in *R v Chesterfield Borough Council, ex p Darker Enterprises Ltd*.[23] The key point is that the Councillors should be prepared to fairly consider the issues.

12.29 Notwithstanding the above as a matter of law, the Court did explain in *ex p Quietlynn* that as a matter of practice it would be better if Councillors who have been particularly vocal in respect of the relevant issues are not appointed to the committees deciding the applications. It is also important to recognise that the outcome of complaints of bias or predetermination largely depend on the facts of the individual case. This is an area of law that is highly fact sensitive.

A closed mind approach?

12.30 The authorities referred to earlier pre-date what is presently the leading case on issues of bias, namely, the House of Lords decision in *Porter v Magill*.[24] In this case, the House of Lords set out the general test to be applied when considering complaints of apparent bias; namely, whether the circumstances were such that it would lead a fair minded and informed observer to conclude that there was a real possibility that the decision-maker was biased.

12.31 This test was applied by Richards J in *Georgiou v Enfield Borough Council & Others*[25] to the decisions of local Councillors comprising planning committees. The test applied was whether the circumstances would lead a fair minded and informed observer to conclude that the members of the planning committee were biased in the sense of approaching the decision with a closed mind and without impartial consideration of the planning issues.

12.32 This approach was applied in the licensing context in *R (on the application of Aujla & Others) v Slough Borough Council*.[26] These proceedings were concerned with a decision of the Council to de-limit the number of hackney carriage vehicle licences issued in its district. It was unsuccessfully alleged that this decision was tainted by bias since two of the Councillors had a past and present connection with the private hire trade.

12.33 In *Aujla & Others* the Court considered whether the Council had approached the matter with a closed mind, or predetermined it. It concluded that the ground had not been made out. Whilst not relevant to the issues in that case, Goldring J observed *obiter* that 'councillors are entitled to have robust views without the decision in which they participate being defective'. This observation provides some support post decisions such as *Porter* and *Georgiou* for the approach that was taken in the *Quietlynn Ltd* and *Darker Enterprises Ltd* line of authorities.

---

23   [1992] COD 466.
24   [2001] UKHL 67.
25   [2004] EWHC 799 (Admin).
26   [2005] EWHC 1866 (Admin) per Goldring J.

A less strict approach?

12.34 The decision of Collins J in *R (on the application of Island Farm Development) v Bridgend County Borough Council*[27] appeared to signal a departure from the stricter application of the *Porter* test as modified in *Georgiou*. Collins J acknowledged that Councillors would have views on issues of public interest and are likely to have expressed them publicly. This has also been recognised more recently, again in the planning field, by the Court of Appeal in *R (on the application of Lewis) v Persimmon Homes Teesside Ltd.*[28] It was held that there was an important difference between predisposition (which was legitimate) and predetermination (which was illegitimate). In considering complaints that a decision-maker had predetermined the outcome or approached the matter with a closed mind the Court explained that the context of the case, in particular the role of elected Councillors, should always be borne in mind. This means acknowledging, and bearing in mind, that local Councillors do, and are entitled to, express their views publicly on issues of public interest.

Summary of the general principles

12.35 The key point appears to be that Councillors should act fairly when considering matters and be willing to listen. The present position of the authorities might be summarised as follows:

(1)   Local Councilors are of course also politicians. In this role, they are likely to have views (perhaps strong views) about issues of local public interest and to have expressed them publicly. In general, the expression of strong views should not, without more, disqualify them from carrying out licensing functions in which the issues they have previously spoken about are relevant (see, for example, *R v Amber Valley District Council, ex p Jackson*;[29] *R v Reading Borough Council, ex p Quietlynn*;[30] *R (on the application of Aujla) v Slough Borough Council*[31] and *R (on the application of Island Farm Development) v Bridgend County Borough Council*).[32] It is important to recognise however that this is an area of the law which is highly fact sensitive and therefore largely dependant on its specific facts.

(2)   In considering a complaint that the decision-maker had a closed mind then the role and responsibilities of local Councillors and the context of the case are important and have to be borne in mind (see eg, *R (on the application of Lewis) v Redcar & Cleveland Borough Council & Others*).[33]

(3)   The responsibility of local Councillors when acting as decision-makers is to approach the issues fairly and on their merits, even though they may approach those issues with a predisposition to an outcome. They are obliged to fairly consider the issues and to be prepared to change their views if so persuaded (see, for example, *R v Amber Valley District Council, ex p Jackson*;[34] *R (on the*

---

[27]   [2006] EWHC 2189 (Admin).
[28]   [2008] EWCA Civ 746.
[29]   [1985] 1 WLR 298 per Woolf J.
[30]   [1986] 85 LGR 387 per Kennedy J.
[31]   [2005] EWHC 1866 (Admin) per Goldring J.
[32]   [2006] EWHC 2189 (Admin) per Collins J.
[33]   [2008] EWCA Civ 746 per Pill LJ, Rix LJ & Longmore LJ.
[34]   [1985] 1 WLR 298 per Woolf J.

application of Island Farm Development) v Bridgend County Borough Council[35] and
R (on the application of Lewis) v Redcar & Cleveland Borough Council & Others).[36]

(4) There is an important distinction between predisposition to an outcome (which is
legitimate) and to predetermination of an outcome (which is illegitimate). The
latter test of predetermination is a difficult test to satisfy (see, for example, *R (on
the application of Lewis) v Redcar & Cleveland Borough Council & Others*[37] and see
also *R (on the application of Chandler) v London Borough of Camden & Others*).[38]

12.36 The more recent authorities have considered the role of local Councillors in the
planning context and have approached the issues in the context that planning
committees do not sit in a judicial or quasi-judicial capacity. It has been said that
licensing committees do sit in a quasi-judicial capacity. There may, therefore, be some
argument as to the differing status between a planning committee and a licensing
committee and thus the context within which a complaint has to be considered and
whether a licensing committee could seek support from the more recent legal decisions
concerning planning authorities. That said, the point remains that Councillors exercise a
constitutional role and are likely to be vocal in their area on issues of public interest.
This context is important when considering arguments relating to predetermination.

ROLE OF THE APPEAL COURTS

12.37 It should be recognised that claims for judicial review are not appeals. A judicial
review is a supervisory review of the decision-making process. Some of the licensing
regimes do, however, provide for statutory rights of appeal to the Magistrates' Court
and the Crown Court. The legislation itself usually provides for how and when an
appeal should be made. The particular legislation should be carefully considered to
ascertain whether it provides for such a right of appeal.

Time periods for appealing

12.38 The statutes often set out a fixed time period within which an appeal must be
brought. It is usual for such provisions not to include a power to extend that time
period. If that is so, then such a power cannot usually be implied into the legislation.
Moreover, the Court does not possess any inherent jurisdiction or discretion to extend
time. As such, a Court would not have jurisdiction to hear an appeal brought out of
time. This was the situation in *Stockton on Tees Borough Council v Latif*[39] where an
appeal was brought in respect of a hackney carriage and private hire licensing matter
under the Local Government (Miscellaneous Provisions) Act 1976 which incorporated
the Public Health Act 1936. A fixed period of 21 days was provided in which an appeal
could be brought to the Magistrates' Court from the decision of a local Council. The
Administrative Court held that there was no power to extend the time limit. Christopher
Symons QC (sitting as a Deputy High Court Judge) explained that Parliament had not
provided for an extension of time and could have done so if that had been the
intention.[40]

---

35 [2006] EWHC 2189 (Admin) per Collins J.
36 [2008] EWCA Civ 746 per Pill LJ, Rix LJ & Longmore LJ.
37 [2008] EWCA Civ 746 per Longmore LJ at para 109.
38 [2009] EWHC 219 (Admin) per Forbes J.
39 [2009] EWHC 228 (Admin).
40 See also the approach in *R v Pembrokeshire Justices, ex p Bennell* [1968] 2 WLR 858.

The nature of the appeal

12.39 Statutory appeals are unrestricted. Permission, therefore, is not usually required. The appeal involves a rehearing of the applications on its merits. In effect, the appeal Court when hearing such an appeal stands in the shoes of the licensing committee or sub committee who determined the matter. This is a well-established practice and has been explained in many cases. The leading case is *Sagnata Investments Ltd v Norwich Corporation*.[41] This case concerned an application for a permit to provide amusements with prizes under the now repealed Betting, Gaming & Lotteries Act 1963. The principle is, however, applicable to all forms of licensing which involve unrestricted statutory appeals from the decision of Councils.

12.40 It has been applied in a variety of other licensing contexts. Other examples include *Darlington Borough Council v Paul Wakefield*[42] (a case involving the licensing of hackney carriage drivers) and *R (on the Application of Blackwood) v Birmingham Magistrates Court & Others*[43] (a case concerning an application for a premises licence under the Licensing Act 2003). In *Rushmoor Borough Council v Richards*[44] (a case involving an appeal against the decision of a Council to vary an entertainment licence) Tuckey J confirmed that the appeal was a rehearing. The reasoning in this case is instructive as to the general approach to be taken to cases involving similar statutory appeals. Tuckey J explained that there was nothing in the particular legislation itself to suggest that the procedure was to be any different to the procedure that would usually be found in other situations where this type of process is in place; that is, a rehearing of the case on the appeal.

12.41 The rehearing, however, should be confined to the issues raised in the notice of appeal and effective case management by the appeal courts should identify the live issues in any event.

Admissibility of fresh evidence

12.42 Since the appeal is by way of re-hearing then fresh evidence is admissible. In *Rushmoor Borough Council v Richards*[45] Tuckey J explained that the appeal court is not restricted to hearing evidence about events before the Council's decision. It must consider all the relevant evidence, whether it relates to events before or after that decision.

The appeal – a true rehearing?

12.43 An issue often arises in practice as to the extent to which the appeal Court should have regard to the decision of the local Council. This approach stems from the reasoning in *Stepney Borough Council v Joffe*[46] (a case involving the revocation by a local Council of a street traders licence) in which Lord Goddard CJ held that:

> 'if there is an unrestricted right of appeal, it is for the court of appeal, in this case the metropolitan magistrate, to substitute its opinion for the opinion of the borough council.

---

[41]   [1971] 2 QB 614.
[42]   [1989] 153 JP 481.
[43]   [2006] EWHC 1800 (Admin).
[44]   [1996] *The Times*, 5 February.
[45]   [1996] *The Times*, 5 February.
[46]   [1949] 1 KB 599.

That does not mean to say that the court of appeal ought not to pay great attention to the fact that the duly constituted and elected local authority have come to an opinion on the matter and ought not lightly to reverse their opinion'.

12.44 The above observation was expressly endorsed by the Court of Appeal in the leading case of *Sagnata* as being the correct approach to the hearing of such appeals. Furthermore, in *R v Essex Quarter Sessions, ex p Thomas*[47] (a case which involved an appeal from a betting licensing committee to the quarter sessions), Lord Parker CJ stated that:

> 'Speaking for myself, I would hesitate, and I would expect any chairman of quarter sessions to hesitate, long before he differed from the local justices who had dealt with the matter in their locality with the greatest care'.

12.45 The appeal court will of course need to be aware of the decision and the reasons which have led it to hear the case in the first place. It is often said, however, that the above observations are difficult to reconcile with the practice that such appeals are by way of a rehearing in which the appeal court should substitute its own opinion on the merits for that of the Council.

12.46 In *R v Preston Crown Court, ex p Chief Constable of Lancashire & Others*[48] the Administrative Court touched on a similar issue. This case was concerned with the composition of a Crown Court when hearing appeals from licensing justices. It principally held that the Crown Court should not comprise Magistrates from the same area as those comprising the bench whose decision was under challenge. However, when considering the nature of the hearing before the Crown Court, Laws LJ also observed that:

> 'An appeal against a decision of licensing justices to the Crown Court is, as I have indicated, by way of rehearing. There is some contest on the skeleton arguments as to the extent to which, in reality, a rehearing is conducted. A dictum of Lord Parker advanced by Mr Saunders displays, or did in its time display, a certain reluctance on the part of the Crown Court (or Quarter Sessions) to part company from decisions reached by licensing justices. It seems to me plainly right, however, to proceed on the basis that the Crown Court conducts a rehearing in the full and proper sense ....'

12.47 This tension as to the correct approach has been considered in a number of recent decisions. A direct challenge to the *Stepney/Sagnata* approach was mounted in *R (on the application of Hope and Glory Public House Limited) v City of Westminster Magistrates' Court & Others*.[49] In this case, Burton J refused permission to bring a claim for judicial review after hearing detailed argument on the point. In his judgment Burton J confirmed that the correct approach to such appeals was set out in *Sagnata* and *Stepney*. It was explained that the appeal is by way of a re-hearing – a fresh appeal with fresh evidence – but after hearing all the evidence the appellate decision-maker will have to be satisfied that the decision below was 'wrong'. The decision of Burton J has been upheld by the Court of Appeal (*R (on the application of Hope and Glory Pubic House Limited) v City of Westminster Magistrates' Court & Others*).[50] The Court of Appeal explained that: 'in all cases, magistrates should pay careful attention to the reasons given by the licensing authority for arriving at the decision under appeal, bearing in mind that

---

[47]   [1966] 1 All ER 353.
[48]   [2001] EWHC Admin 928.
[49]   [2009] EWHC 1996 (Admin).
[50]   [2011] EWCA Civ 31.

Parliament has chosen to place responsibility for making such decisions on local authorities. The weight which the magistrates should ultimately attach to those reasons must be a matter for their judgment in all the circumstances, taking into account the fullness and clarity of the reasons, the nature of the issues and the evidence given on appeal'.

12.48 If, however, the local Council has a policy then the appeal Court must apply that policy when arriving at its decision on appeal. In *R (on the application of Westminster City Council) v Middlesex Crown Court & Chlorion PLC & Fred Proud*[51] Scott Baker J explained:

> 'How should a Crown Court (or a Magistrates Court) approach an appeal where the council has a policy? In my judgment it must accept the policy and apply it as if it was standing in the shoes of the council considering the application. Neither the Magistrates Court nor the Crown Court is the right place to challenge the policy'.

The appeal – an alternative remedy

12.49 It should be borne in mind that the availability of an unrestricted right of appeal to the Magistrates' Court and the Crown Court is not available in respect of all decisions of local Councils. Such rights of appeal must be expressly provided for in the relevant legislation. The availability of a statutory appeal process impacts on the appropriateness of judicial review.

12.50 As a general principle, judicial review is considered an option of last resort and one that should not be embarked upon unless all alternative remedies have been exhausted. Such alternative remedies include appeals to the Magistrates' Court and the Crown Court.

12.51 The availability of an alternative remedy is likely to lead the Administrative Court to refuse permission to proceed with a claim for judicial review or to refuse the relief sought. The issue of alternative remedies in the licensing context has been considered in a number of cases. As these cases illustrates the main consideration is the appropriateness of the alternative remedy:

(1) In *R v Huntingdon District Council, ex p Cowan*[52] (a case involving the licensing of sex establishments) Glidewell J explained that 'the court should always ask itself whether the remedy that is sought in the court, or the alternative remedy which is available to the applicant by way of appeal, is the most effective and convenient, in other words, which of them will prove to be the most effective and convenient in all the circumstances, not merely for the applicant, but in the public interest. In exercising discretion whether or not to grant relief, that is a major factor …'.

(2) In *R v Nottingham City Council, ex p Howitt*[53] (a case concerning taxi licences) Dyson J held that the Court must ask itself what is the real issue to be determined and whether the statutory appeal is suitable to determine that issue.

---

[51] [2002] EWHC 1104.
[52] [1984] 1 ALL ER 58.
[53] [1999] COD 530.

(3)   In *R v Leeds City Council, ex p Hendry*[54] (a case concerning the licensing of the private hire industry) Latham J decided that the question to be asked in cases where there is an alternative statutory procedure is whether the real issues can sensibly be determined by the statutory procedure.

12.52   These authorities, and others, were reviewed by Beatson J in *R (on the application of JD Wetherspoon PLC) v Guildford Borough Council*.[55] This case concerned a challenge to the Council's decision to refuse to grant Wetherspoons' application to extend its permitted hours. On the particular circumstances of the case, the issue raised was one on which, in the Court's judgment, there was a need for uniformity in the understanding of licensing authorities as to the scope of their policies in the light of guidance published by the Secretary of State. Therefore it was appropriate to proceed by way of judicial review.

Case stated or judicial review?

12.53   The Magistrates' Court and Crown Court are carrying out public functions, and similarly to local Councils, are susceptible in appropriate cases to challenges by way of judicial review. It should be borne in mind, however, that the decisions of the Magistrates' Court and the Crown Court may also be appealed to the Administrative Court by way of the case stated procedure.

12.54   In any case, a decision will need to be made as to which route is the most appropriate. This will depend upon the circumstances of the particular case. An often overlooked fact is that an appeal by way of case stated on a non-criminal matter (such as a licensing case) is final. In other words, there is no further right of appeal to the Court of Appeal or House of Lords (see *Westminster City Council v O'Reilly*,[56] a case concerning special hours certificates issued under the previous liquor regime, the Licensing Act 1964).

POLICIES AND GUIDANCE

Licensing policies – an overview

12.55   The starting point is that a licensing authority is entitled to have a policy in respect of its licensing functions. Policies have become a key part of many licensing regimes. They inform those who may be affected by how the authority will exercise its powers and the policies also act as a guide to inform the decision-makers making the decisions. Such policies, therefore, promote consistency. Indeed, an absence of a published policy may leave an authority more open to criticism or challenge on the grounds of inconsistency or a lack of transparency.

12.56   In practice, policies range from the licensing of entertainment venues, sex establishments, the sale of alcohol through to the hackney carriage and private hire industry. The more recent licensing regimes under the Licensing Act 2003 and the Gambling Act 2005 now place a statutory obligation on licensing authorities to formulate and implement polices setting out how they will approach their licensing functions (see, for example, the Licensing Act 2003, s 5).

---

[54]   (1994) *The Times*, 20 January.
[55]   [2006] EWHC 815 (Admin).
[56]   [2003] EWCA Civ 1007 per Auld LJ.

12.57 Policies are not exclusive to the field of licensing law. They play an integral part in other areas of public administration and decision-making and decisions in those areas may be equally applicable to licensing cases. If an authority has a policy then it should be made public. It is contrary to good public administration for an authority to have a policy but not make it public.

Policies – summary of general principles

12.58 A summary of the fundamental principles relating to licensing policies is set out below:

(1)   The starting point is that a licensing policy must have reasonable objectives and not run counter to the policy of the respective legislation. This is the well known *Padfield* principle deriving from the House of Lords in *Padfield v Minister of Agriculture, Fisheries and Food*.[57] This principle was applied in the licensing context by Richards J in *British Beer & Pub Association & Others v Canterbury County Council*.[58] In this case the Council's policy under the Licensing Act 2003 was over prescriptive and ran counter to the objectives of the 2003 Act.

(2)   Licensing policies must be properly formulated after adequate consultation. Some statutes, such as the Licensing Act 2003, set out a statutory code of consultation which must be undertaken before a licensing policy is published including who must be consulted. In general terms, the key principles to consultation are set out in *R v North and East Devon Health Authority, ex p Coughlan*.[59] Those principles are: (1) consultation must be undertaken at a time when proposals are still at a formative stage, (2) it must include sufficient reasons for particular proposals to allow those consulted to give intelligent consideration and an intelligent response, (3) adequate time must be given for this purpose, and (4) the product of consultation must be conscientiously taken into account when the ultimate decision is taken.

   Those principles have been applied to licensing functions. See for example, *Sardar & Others v Watford Borough Council*[60] and *Royden*.[61] These were cases which involved decisions of local Councils as to limitations on the number of hackney carriage licenses issued in its district. In *Royden*, Christopher Bellamy QC (sitting as a Deputy High Court Judge) explained the importance of considering the *Coughlan* principles in the context of the particular case and circumstances under challenge. Adequacy depends very much on its context.

(3)   A challenge to a licensing policy on the basis that it has been unlawfully established is a matter for the Administrative Court to resolve by way of judicial review proceedings. This was made clear in *R (on the application of Westminster City Council) v Middlesex Crown Court & Chlorion PLC & Fred Proud*[62] where Scott Baker J stated that 'neither the Magistrates' Court nor the Crown Court is the right place to challenge the policy. The remedy, if it is alleged that a policy has been unlawfully established, is an application to the Administrative Court for judicial review'.

---

[57]   [1968] AC 997.
[58]   [2005] EWHC 1318 (Admin).
[59]   [2001] QB 213.
[60]   [2006] EWHC 1590 (Admin).
[61]   [2002] EWHC 2484 (Admin).
[62]   [2002] EWHC 1104.

(4) A review of the principles relating to policies is set out in the judgments of Richards J in *R (on the application of British Beer & Pub Association & Others v Canterbury City Council*[63] and Beatson J in *R (on the application of JD Wetherspoon) v Guildford Borough Council*.[64] These refer to the following general principles which govern the interpretation of policies. A legalistic approach to the interpretation of licensing policies is to be avoided. Such policies should not be treated as if they were statutes. A policy should be considered mindful of its underlying purpose and the statutory framework to which it relates. Specific passages within policies should be read in the light of the policy as a whole and not merely considered in isolation. It should be recognised, however, that people reading such policies are going to vary in sophistication and there are limitations as to how far they can be expected to read in qualifications expressed elsewhere in a policy document or to be derived from an understanding of the statutory scheme. The meaning of passages must be judged in a common sense way. A policy must be applied in accordance with its meaning. It cannot fulfill its purpose of providing guidance if its intended meaning is different from the actual meaning of the words used.

(5) It is also a general rule that a licensing policy should not be applied inflexibly or rigidly. There needs to be a willingness on the part of the decision-maker to consider individual applications on their merits. In general, a decision-maker should always be willing to listen to see if the circumstances justify a departure from the policy. The classic statement is set out by Lord Reid in *British Oxygen Ltd v Minister of Technology*:[65]

> 'the general rule is that anyone who has to exercise a statutory discretion must not "shut his ears to the application" .... I do not think there is any great difference between a policy and a rule. There may be cases where an officer or authority ought to listen to a substantial argument reasonably presented urging a change of policy. What the authority must not do is to refuse to listen at all. But a Ministry or large authority may have had to deal already with a multitude of similar applications and then they will almost certainly have evolved a policy so precise that it could be called a rule. There can be no objection to that, provided the authority is always willing to listen to anyone with something new to say.'

However, this approach has been said to represent the general position and much will depend on the statutory context under scrutiny. In *Nicholds & Others v Security Industry Authority*,[66] Kenneth Parker QC explained that:

> 'In most instances where a discretionary power is conferred it would be wrong for the decision-maker to frame a rule in absolute terms because to do so would defeat the statutory purpose. However, it seems to me that there are certain exceptional statutory contexts where a policy may lawfully exclude exceptions to the rule because to allow exceptions would substantially undermine an important legislative aim which underpins the grant of the discretionary power to the authority. There is, for example, a well known line of cases concerning "taxi" licensing where licensing rules, which admitted of no exception for any "special" circumstances, were held lawful: see for example, *R v Manchester City Justices, ex p McHugh* [1989] RTR 285; 88 LGR 180; *R v Wirral MBC, ex p The Wirral Licensed Taxi Owners Association* [1983] 3 CMLR 150.'

63 [2005] EWHC 1318 (Admin).
64 [2006] EWHC 815 (Admin).
65 [1971] AC 610.
66 [2006] EWHC 1792 (Admin).

(6)   Moreover, an inflexibly worded policy does not necessarily lead to the conclusion that the policy is unlawful as long as it is applied flexibly in practice and a licensing authority is prepared to listen to each case on its own particular merits. Similarly, a flexibly worded policy which is applied inflexibly in practice may lead to a successful challenge in judicial review proceedings (see, for example, the approaches in *R v Nottingham City Council, ex p Howitt*[67] and *R v City & County of Swansea, ex p Julie Amanda Jones.*[68] See also the cases of *R v Chester Crown Court, ex p Pascoe & Jones*[69] and *R v Licensing Justices at North Tyneside*[70] in which the reasons of the decision-maker did not show that they had considered an application on its merits).

(7)   The burden rests on the person seeking a departure from a policy to persuade the decision-maker that the circumstance of the individual case justifies such a departure from the policy.[71]

Statutory guidance – an overview

12.59 Statutory guidance has also become an integral part of decision-making under the more modern licensing regimes such as the Licensing Act 2003 and the Gambling Act 2005. The 2003 Act requires the Secretary of State to issue guidance to licensing authorities on the discharge of their licensing functions. This guidance may not be issued unless a draft of it has been laid before, and approved by, each House of Parliament. Once issued, licensing authorities must have regard to it when carrying out its licensing functions under the 2003 Act (see Licensing Act 2003, s 182). The 2005 Act requires the Gambling Commission to issue guidance to local Councils (who have responsibility for the licensing of premises under the 2005 Act). This may only be issued following consultation with specified bodies including the Secretary of State.

Guidance – summary of general principles

12.60 Such guidance is not novel. It plays a key part in other areas of public law. There is an overlap with many of the principles relating to policies particularly in respect of interpretation. Set out below are some of the fundamental principles which relate to statutory guidance:

(1)   The key point is that statutory guidance cannot usurp or replace the statute. The focus should always be on the wording and purpose of the respective legislation. A number of recent cases illustrate this point. In *R (on the application of 4 Wins Leisure Limited) v Blackpool Licensing Committee & Others*[72] Sullivan J explained that: 'it is important to remember that, whilst regard must be had to the guidance, it should not be allowed to usurp the clear language in the statute'.

       Similar approaches have been taken in a number of other (licensing) judicial review proceedings. See, for example, Dobbs J in *R (on the application of South Northamptonshire Council) v Towcester Magistrates' Court*;[73] Andrew Nicol QC (sitting as a Deputy High Court Judge in *R (on the application of Betting Shop*

---

[67]   [1999] COD 530, QBD.
[68]   (1996) CO1996/3187/95 unreported.
[69]   (1987) 151 JP 752.
[70]   (1988) 153 JP 100.
[71]   See a review of the authorities on this issue in the *Chorion* decision, supra.
[72]   [2007] EWHC 2213 (Admin).
[73]   [2008] EWHC 381 (Admin).

Services Ltd) v Southend on Sea Borough Council[74] and Black J in *Daniel Thwaites PLC v Wirral Magistrates' Court & Others*[75] who stated that: 'there is no doubt that regard must be had to the guidance by the magistrates but that its force is less than that of a statute'.

(2)   Whilst the statutory guidance cannot replace the statutory words it may, however, assist with interpreting the legislation. In *R (on the application of Blackpool Council) v Howitt and the Secretary of State for Culture Media and Sport*,[76] HHJ Denyer QC sitting as a Judge of the High Court used the statutory guidance issued under the Licensing Act 2003 to interpret the meaning of the phrase 'crime and disorder' as it related to the 2003 Act. Whilst, statutory guidance may assist with interpretation, interpretation always remains a matter for the Court.

(3)   The regard that is given to the guidance is a matter for the decision-maker. If, however, it departs from the guidance it should give proper reasons for doing so. In the *Daniel Thwaites PLC* case, Black J held that: 'any individual licensing decision may give rise to a need to balance conflicting factors which are included in the Guidance and that in resolving this conflict, a licensing authority or Magistrates' Court may justifiably give less weight to some parts of the Guidance and more to others ... it may also depart from the Guidance if particular features of the individual case require that. What a licensing authority or Magistrates' Court is not entitled to do is simply to ignore the Guidance or fail to give it any weight, whether because it does not agree with the Government's policy or its methods of regulating licensable activities or for any other reason. Furthermore, when a Magistrates' Court is entitled to depart from the Guidance and justifiably does so, it must, in my view, give proper reason'.

(4)   Similary in *R (on the application of Bassetlaw District Council) v Worksop Magistrates' Court*[77] Slade J held that a District Judge had erred in failing to give reasons for departing from the statutory guidance when determining an appeal under the Licensing Act 2003. The decision of the District Judge was also overturned because passages in the guidance had been misconstrued and incorrectly applied.

12.61 Furthermore, many of the principles relating to the interpretation of policies (discussed earlier in this Chapter) may also equally apply to statutory guidance. In particular, such guidance should not be read with the fine analysis with which one would read a statute and a legalistic approach to the guidance is to be avoided. A review of the principles may be found in the judgment of Beatson J in *R (on the application of JD Wetherspoon) v Guildford Borough Council*[78] which considered the guidance issued under the 2003 Act.

---

[74]   [2007] EWHC 105 (Admin).
[75]   [2008] EWHC 838 (Admin).
[76]   [2008] EWHC 3300 (Admin).
[77]   [2008] EWHC 3530 (Admin).
[78]   [2006] EWHC 815 (Admin).

OBJECTORS AND REPRESENTORS

Objections and representations – an overview

12.62 Licensing decisions may affect not just the applicant for the licence (or an existing licence holder) but other interested parties as well (for instance, those who will also be affected by the activities authorised by the licence; examples include the Police and local residents). Representations or objections may, therefore, be submitted by these people and bodies.

12.63 The admissibility of such objections and whether they should be properly taken into account by decision-makers is often a live and contentious consideration at any licensing hearing.

12.64 Some licensing regimes set out a statutory procedure that must be followed in terms of notifying people and bodies of licence applications. The purpose underpinning this is to ensure that the application is brought to the attention of those who may be affected by the application. Under the Licensing Act 2003 and the Gambling Act 2005 the respective statutes require applicants to advertise and provide notice of their applications. In effect, Parliament has legislated specific schemes of consultation under the Acts. The provisions also identify who may make representations in respect of the application and the time limits for such representations. Other licensing regimes contain no such statutory provisions. For example, there is no such consultation or codified representation procedure in respect of applications for street trading licences pursuant to the Local Government (Miscellaneous Provisions) Act 1982.

The *Miss Behavin'* litigation

12.65 Challenges may arise as to whether a decision-maker is entitled to take particular objections or representations into account when arriving at its decisions; in other words, whether it is admissible evidence. Judicial review challenges in respect of such issues may arise as they did in the Northern Irish *Miss Behavin'* litigation. These proceedings concerned an application for a sex establishment licence under the Local Government (Miscellaneous Provisions) (Northern Ireland) Order 1985, the equivalent provisions of the 1982 Act. Article 10 of this legislation specified that representations in respect of an application should be made within 28 days of the date of the application and that the Council when considering that application should have regard to the representations which have been made within that time. A number of objections in the case were late and made outside the 28 day time period. The issue arose as to whether a Council could take those objections, which were made out of time, into account when arriving at its decision in respect of the application. The matter proceeded by way of a claim for judicial review and ultimately came before the House of the Lords. It was held that the Council was not precluded from taking into account objections which were late.

12.66 The following principal points emerge from the decision of the House of Lords and, in particular, the opinions of Lord Hoffman and Lord Neuberger of Abbottsbury:

(1) The relevant statutory provisions under the 1985 Order (and therefore the equivalent 1982 Act) are concerned only with the position of the objector. In other words, if an objector did not comply with the 28 day statutory deadline then they would not be entitled to complain if the Council did not take their objection into account.

(2) The proper effect of the provisions is that late objections could, but need not, be taken into account. A local Council has discretion whether or not to have regard to information which comes from outside the scope of a statutory objection. Much depends on the circumstances of the particular case. In exercising this discretion the Council may have regard to all relevant matters including whether the objection was late for lack of good faith, any prejudice caused to the applicant or other relevant parties and/or disruption to Council business. It may well be correct to disregard a late objection if it was intentionally last minute, or if it was received so late that taking it into account would lead to unfairness to the applicant (because he would not have had the chance to consider it) or to unacceptable disruption to the Council's business.

(3) A local Council should not be prohibited from taking all relevant matters into account, whether those matters have been communicated by an objector or others, whether it was communicated early or late, or in any other way. It would be a strange approach if such a provision, designed to allow the Council to carry on its business in an orderly and expeditious manner, had the effect of requiring the Council to shut its eyes to facts which would be considered relevant to the Council's decision-making process.

(4) It would be unrealistic and unjust if a Council was absolutely precluded from taking into account such objections. If an objection, which revealed to a Council for the first time certain highly relevant information, was received one day late, it would be a little short of absurd if it could not be taken into account. It would be contrary to the purpose of the 1985 Order, and to the public interest generally, if the Council was obliged to ignore relevant information. Moreover, it would be the duty of Council officers to open and read any letter of objection or representation received by the Council. Such an officer would then be placed in an impossible situation if he or she had read a late letter of objection, with new and important information, but was effectively precluded from communicating this information to the Committee.

(5) The issue of late objections is governed by general administrative law principles: it is a matter for the Council whether to take it into account, and the Court will not interfere with its decision in that regard, save on administrative law principles, ie unless the decision took into account irrelevant factors or failed to take into account relevant factors or was a decision which no reasonable council could have made in the case.

(6) There could be circumstances in which a failure on the part of the Council to take relevant information into account could itself be judicially reviewable. It would take clear statutory terms to oblige a Council to ignore relevant information and material.

12.67 This decision was in line with the decision of Webster J in *Quietlyn Ltd v Plymouth City Council*[79] which approved the dictum of Woolf J in the earlier case of *R v Chester City Council, ex p Quietlynn*.[80] In the latter case it was held that:

---

[79] [1988] QB 114.
[80] [1983] *The Times*, 19 October.

'in coming to a determination, the authority must be entitled to take account of information which comes into its possession and which is relevant even though it is not from a statutory objector. It may, for example, be necessary for inquiries to be made of the fire authorities and if an oral objection was made by the fire authorities out of time it could not properly be ignored in reaching a decision. It will be necessary, however, in respect of such non-statutory information to act fairly and, if necessary, give the applicant notice of the material upon which it is proposed to rely'.

12.68 These authorities appear to promote the undesirability of subjecting a statutory scheme to a literal analysis and proceeding on the basis that Parliament has laid down a fixed and rigid procedure.

12.69 The issue, therefore, of whether, and in what circumstances, a licensing authority is entitled to take into account information which comes from outside a statutory scheme would appear now to be governed, in general terms, by the principles set out by the House of Lords in the *Miss Behavin'* litigation and the earlier *Quietlynn* decision. In other words the ability on the part of a licensing authority to take into account extraneous information is governed by the classic administrative law principles. However, regard must be had to the relevant statutory scheme.

Importance of the statutory context

12.70 Indeed, such issues have to be considered against the context and setting of the particular case and legislation in question. In some instances it may be that the clear terms of the legislative provisions preclude a licensing authority from taking into account information which would otherwise have been relevant and would have assisted the decision-making process.

12.71 This is illustrated by the decision in *R (on the application of 4 Wins Leisure Limited) v Blackpool Borough Council & Others.*[81] In that case the Administrative Court considered whether a Council's refusal to allow a nightclub operator in Blackpool to make representations in respect of a trade competitors' application for a premises licence under the Licensing Act 2003 was lawful. To make representations under the 2003 Act the person or body must constitute either a responsible authority or an interested party. A person or body is an 'interested party' only if they are 'in the vicinity' of the applicant's premises. The issue in the case was whether the competitor nightclub was a business in the vicinity of the applicant's premises since if not, then the competitor nightclub would not be entitled to make representations in respect of the application.[82] Sullivan J explained:

'On behalf of the claimants, Mr Walsh submitted that such a "narrow" geographical approach to the meaning of "in the vicinity" would drive a coach and horses through the Act because it would mean that representations from businesses which might have a very real contribution in terms of assisting the licensing authority to see whether or not the licensing objectives would or would not be promoted by the application would not be treated as interested parties. I can well see that there may well be very good arguments for submitting that those who could make a useful contribution to that question should be allowed to be heard by the licensing authority. The difficulty is that it treats an interested party as though that term were not constrained by the further definition in section 13(3) ... one may have a business which has business interests that might indeed be affected, but if that business is not

---

[81] [2007] EWHC 2213 (Admin) per Sullivan J.
[82] Note, the Police Reform and Social Responsibility Bill which is presently progressing through Parliament proposes the removal of the 'vicinity' test.

"in the vicinity" then, regardless of the impact on those business interests, it is not an interested party. Mr Walsh submits that that is an absurd position. He may well be right, but that is the effect of Parliament's definition'.

12.72 The issue of late objections under the 2003 Act also gives rise to a different result than it does under the Local Government (Miscellaneous Provisions) Act 1982. Under the 2003 Act, a licensing authority is not entitled to take into account representations which are made outside the statutory time period. Indeed, the clear terms of the 2003 Act preclude a licensing authority from doing so (see *R (on the application of Albert Court Residents Association & Others) v Westminster City Council & Others*).[83]

The strength of opposition

12.73 The mere fact that a large number of objections have been made in respect of an application should not on its own be a sufficient basis for refusing or determining an application. This is illustrated in the Scottish cases of *The Noble Organisation Limited v City of Glasgow District Council (No 3)*[84] and *The Noble Organisation Limited v Kilmarnock and Loudoun District Council.*[85] Both these cases involved applications for public entertainment licences to operate amusement centres. The applications were rejected essentially on the basis of the strength of local opposition to the amusement centres. In the latter case of *Kilmarnock*, Lord Hope approved the reasoning in the *Glasgow* case and explained that: 'the mere number of objections irrespective of their content can never be a good reason for refusing an application. What matters are the grounds on which the objection is based'. It was further explained that 'the licensing authority is not permitted to attach weight to the objection because of the number of persons associated with it regardless of its content'.

12.74 This Scottish approach was considered in *R v Liverpool City Council, ex p Luxury Leisure Limited.*[86] In that case the Court of Appeal rejected the argument that the decision-maker, in that case the Crown Court, had merely relied on the weight of local opposition. The decision does recognise, however, that the reasoning underlying the opposition is important. As Simon Brown LJ explained that: 'if of course the objections of the public are founded on a demonstrable misunderstanding of the true factual position, or otherwise indicate no more than an uninformed gut reaction to a proposal, then I would accept that they can carry no weight whatever and must be ignored'. Aldous LJ observed that: 'opposition which is misinformed is of no weight, and remains of no weight even if held by many people'.

12.75 In general, objections and representations should only be taken into account if the basis of them relates to the statutory objects underpinning the particular scheme and would, therefore, assist the decision-maker in arriving at an informed decision based on statutory grounds. Indeed, the more recent licensing regimes, see for example the Licensing Act 2003, only allow representations to be admitted if they concern the licensing objectives under that Act.

12.76 In the *Glasgow* case, the Scottish Courts left undecided the issue of whether the number of objections could ever be a relevant consideration. Much will depend on the circumstances. In appropriate cases it may well be right that the number of objections is

---

[83] [2010] EWHC 393 (Admin) per McCombe J.
[84] [1991] SCLR 380.
[85] [1992] SCLR 1006.
[86] [1999] LGR 345.

a relevant factor. For instance, it could be relevant to the credibility of, or the weight to be given to, the objections which have been received. By way of example, it could be relevant if a number of similar objections all about similar issues and experiences have been raised by the objectors.

Fair notice of objection or representation

12.77 Procedural fairness requires the applicant to be given notice of any objections to, or representations in respect of, the application. This was explained by Lord Hoffman in the *Miss Behavin'* litigation: 'fairness obviously requires that the terms of any representations which the Council proposes to consider should be communicated to the applicant so that he may have an opportunity to comment'. There is no proper distinction between an objection and a representation in this regard. Fairness requires proper notice irrespective of the technical classification (see *R v Inner Crown Court, ex p Provis*).[87]

12.78 What is proper notice will depend upon the circumstances of any one case. This has been explained in a number of cases (see, for example, *Quietlyn Ltd v Plymouth City Council*;[88] *R v Huntingdon District Council, ex p Cowan and another*[89] and *R v Inner Crown Court, ex p Provis*).[90] In the *Miss Behavin'* litigation Lord Neuberger of Abbottsbury explained that if: 'a late objection is to be taken into account by the council, then the applicant must be informed as to its contents in good time so as to be able to consider it and deal with it appropriately'.

12.79 These authorities consider the position of the applicant. There is additionally the position of an objector who could be, or is, affected by the activities carried on under the licence and is entitled to make representations and be heard in respect of the issues before the decision-maker. Whilst much will depend on the statutory scheme and the circumstances of any one case, in general, it would appear that fairness requires these people to be aware of the applicant's position on issues. By way of example, there may be licensing proceedings in which the applicant seeks to rely on expert evidence in support of its application. A fair process may require other objectors to be given the opportunity to consider this evidence in advance.

HEARINGS AND EVIDENCE

12.80 The key point is that the decision-maker when determining licensing matters should act in accordance with the relevant statutory scheme and in doing so should adopt and follow a procedure which is fair. What is fair will depend on the circumstances of the particular case.

Being properly heard by the decision-maker

12.81 It is important that the decision-maker is aware of the issues to be determined and the representations which are advanced in respect of it. As such the decision-maker will be able to make a proper and informed decision. It is therefore important that the

---

[87] [2000] *The Times*, 11 July.
[88] [1988] QB 114 per Webster J.
[89] [1984] 1 ALL ER 58 per Glidewell J.
[90] [2000] *The Times*, 11 July per Gibbs J.

issues and the representations are accurately reported to the decision-making committee. In *R v Chester City Council, ex p Quietlynn Ltd*[91] Woolf J considered the provisions in respect of the licensing of sex establishments under Schedule 3 of the Local Government (Miscellaneous Provisions) Act 1982. Those provisions afforded an applicant a statutory right to be heard before the decision. Woolf J explained that when an authority is performing the type of function involved in considering whether to grant a licence, such applications must be considered fairly and in many cases it will be necessary for the decision-making body to have at least a summary of the applicant's representations whether they were made in writing or orally at a hearing before a different committee or sub-committee. In the Court of Appeal (see *R v Preston Borough Council, ex p Quietlynn Ltd*[92]), Simon Brown LJ explained that it was a requisite of the statutory provisions that the applicant's representations should be considered by the committee making the decision. In this case, they were not. No report of any kind was put before the decision-making committee. As such, Simon Brown LJ held that there was a breach of the procedural rules which vitiated the decision of the committee. Furthermore, it was said that this procedural irregularity could not be cured by the fact that members of the committee could probably be expected to have been familiar with the locality and could have asked, if they wished, for details of the applicant's representations from those members of the committee who had actually heard the applicant's representations.

12.82 See also the planning decision of *R v Liverpool City Council, ex p Ramm*[93] in which the decision of Simon Brown LJ in *Quietlynn* was cited to Moses J. It was held that no-one could 'seriously dispute' the accuracy of the proposition that it was essential for the decision-making body to apply its mind to material considerations and that if the decision-making body did not consider directly the source material and the representations then it must at least put its mind to a report as to what the source material and representations concern.

12.83 The contents of a report to the decision-making committee could also be the subject of challenge. The widely accepted approach has been set out by Judge LJ in a planning case (*Oxton Farm & Others v Selby District Council*).[94] Whilst that was a planning case, the principles are equally applicable to licensing proceedings before the Council. Judge LJ explained that:

> 'there will no doubt be cases where judicial review is granted on the basis of what is or is not contained in the planning officer's report. This reflects no more than the court's conclusion in the particular circumstances of the case before it. In my judgment an application for judicial review based on criticisms on the planning officer's report will not normally begin to merit consideration unless the overall effect of the report significantly misleads the committee about material matters which thereafter are left uncorrected at the meeting of the planning committee before the relevant decision'.

12.84 That said, it is important to recognise that the duty of an officer reporting to a committee is broader than merely a duty not to mislead. It includes a positive duty to provide sufficient information and guidance to enable the decision-maker to reach a decision applying the relevant statutory criteria: see *R (on the application of Lowther) v*

---

[91]   [1983] *The Times*, 19 October.
[92]   (1984) 83 LGR 308.
[93]   (unreported) 28 January 1998.
[94]   [1997] EGCS 60.

Durham County Council & Others[95] and a review of the relevant authorities by Hickinbottom J in *R (on the application of Miller) v North Yorkshire County Council & Others*.[96] Indeed, there is an obligation on those who assist the decision-makers such as licensing officers to explore relevant issues properly and fairly and to equip the decision-maker with relevant material so as to enable them to arrive at an informed decision.

12.85 It may be that a right to be heard by the decision-maker does not always necessarily have to include a right to be heard orally. However, this will depend on a number of factors not least the statutory scheme and the particular matters and circumstances in issue. In any event, the modern practice is for Councils to hold committee meetings or hearings so that the applicant and any other relevant person or body can make their representations directly to the decision-maker. This is a sensible approach given the quasi-judicial nature of the licensing process.

The procedure at the meeting or hearing

12.86 The procedure to be followed at committee or sub committee meetings or hearings is usually a matter for each Council. Some Acts, such as the Licensing Act 2003, enable Regulations to be made which set out a core procedure that should be followed at a committee hearing. These Regulations however still allow the licensing committees to regulate their own procedure.[97] Other statutes may be silent altogether as to the procedure that should be followed at hearings or meetings.

12.87 The modern practice of many local Councils is for hearings or meetings to take place before the particular decision-making committee or sub-committee and for those affected by the proceedings to be afforded the opportunity of being heard by the decision-making body.

Matters are generally heard in public

12.88 The meetings of committees or sub-committees are generally held in public. Indeed, this is a requirement under section 100A and 100E of the Local Government Act 1972 (subject to specified exceptions). However, these requirements do not necessarily extend to the committee's or sub-committee's deliberations when considering its decision. This was explained by Turner J in *R v London Borough of Wandsworth, ex p Darker Enterprises Ltd*[98] who explained that it accorded neither with the Court's:

> 'experience nor expectation that deliberations by such a body which take place before a decision is reached would take place, or could reasonably take place, in public. Moreover, it is hard to see how sub-committees could effectively conduct their discussions, in relation to decisions whether to grant or renew licences, if they were required to do so in public. I hold that the applicants have failed to establish that the respondents acted in breach of any relevant requirement of the Act of 1972. Even had I been satisfied that there was a breach, the applicants are unable to point to any particular mischief which they have suffered as the result. Reasons for the decision were given as the Act of 1982 required. They could have asked for no more'.

---

[95]   [2001] EWCA Civ 781 per Pill LJ.
[96]   [2009] EWHC 2172 (Admin).
[97]   See, for example, the Licensing Act 2003 (Hearing) Regulations 2005, SI 2005/44.
[98]   (unreported) 15 January 1999.

12.89 Indeed, as long as reasons are provided it difficult to see what prejudice or unfairness an applicant or other relevant party would suffer from the deliberations taking place in private.

12.90 Some of the modern licensing regimes such as the Licensing Act 2003 explain that hearings should take place in public. This is subject to the proviso that a licensing authority may exclude the public from all or part of the hearing where it considers that the public interest in so doing outweighs the public interest in the hearing, or that part of the hearing taking place in public.[99]

The approach of the decision-maker

12.91 The responsibility of decision-makers in these types of licensing proceedings is to apply the statutory test and considerations and to form a responsible judgment based on the relevant information. This has been explained in two cases by Lord Bingham of Cornhill CJ both of which involved 'fit and proper' tests (see *R v Warrington Crown Court, ex p RBNB (a company)*[100] and *McCool v Rushcliffe Borough Council*[101]). The latter was a case which concerned the licensing of a private hire driver. It was explained that:

> 'the borough council and the justices were entitled to rely on any evidential material which might reasonably and properly influence the making of a responsible judgment in good faith on the question in issue. Some evidence such as gossip, speculation and unsubstantiated innuendo would be rightly disregarded. Other evidence, even if hearsay, might by its source, nature and inherent probability carry a greater degree of credibility. All would depend on the particular facts and circumstances'.

12.92 The decision in *McCool* also confirms the widely understood principle that the strict rules of evidence as usually found in the criminal and civil jurisdictions do not apply to licensing proceedings. Licensing proceedings involve the exercise of an administrative function. The leading case on this is the Court of Appeal decision in *Kavanagh v Chief Constable of Devon*.[102] This was a case which concerned the licensing of firearms and, in particular, the principles on which a Crown Court should act when determining an appeal against the decision of the Chief Constable. Lord Denning MR explained as follows:

> 'It seems to me that the Crown Court is in the same position as the court of quarter sessions. The Crown Court is to try cases according to the same rules as the court of quarter sessions used to do. The court of quarter sessions, when trying criminal cases, applied the rules of evidence applicable to criminal cases. But from time immemorial the court of quarter sessions exercised administrative jurisdiction. When so doing, the justices never held themselves bound by the strict rules of evidence. They acted on any material that appeared to be useful in coming to a decision, including their own knowledge. No doubt they admitted hearsay, though there is nothing to be found in the books about it. To bring the procedure up to modern requirements, I think they should act on the same lines as any administrative body which is charged with an enquiry. They may receive any material which is logically probative even though it is not evidence in a court of law. Hearsay can be permitted where it can fairly be regarded as reliable'.

---

99   See in this regard, Licensing Act 2003 (Hearings) Regulations 2005, SI 2005/44, reg 14.
100   [2002] UKHL 24.
101   [1998] 3 ALL ER 889.
102   [1974] QB 624.

12.93 In *R v Licensing Justices of East Gwent, ex p Chief Constable of Gwent*[103] (a case which concerned the previous alcohol licensing regime in the Licensing Act 1964 Act) the Administrative Court applied the *Kavanagh* approach and explained that it equally applied to other forms of licensing functions. In his judgment, Dyson J referring to *Kavanagh* also stated that the weight to be given to the evidence is a matter for the decision-maker (specifically, in this case, the weight which was to be given to the statements of people who had not attended to give oral evidence and as such had not had their evidence tested under questioning).

Judgment and the decision-maker's discretion

12.94 Challenges to the judgmental conclusions of licensing bodies involve a high threshold. This is well illustrated by a case under the previous liquor licensing regime set out in the Licensing Act 1964. In *R v Doncaster Justices, ex p Langfield*[104] an application was made for special orders of exemption (extensions to the permitted hours) to cover half time and immediate post match periods in respect of matches at Doncaster Rovers Football Club. The Police had not objected and had in fact given evidence which positively supported the application. In particular, the Police stated that there had been no serious public order problem at the Club in the previous two seasons and that there was no evidence to show that the availability of alcohol at the ground had contributed to any unruly behaviour in the past. Despite that, the Justices refused to grant the application. The Justices' reasoning was founded principally on their own knowledge and experience as magistrates on the Doncaster bench that offences of a public disorder nature were committed during and after Doncaster Rovers football matches. They further took notice of their own experience that those who are arrested and subsequently appeared before the Court would invariably plead as mitigation some intake of alcohol. The decision was subject to an application for judicial review which was dismissed. Nolan J recognised that the application before the Justices was a strong one. Nonetheless, he held that the Justices had not exceeded their jurisdiction or improperly exercised their discretion.

12.95 More recently in *Mark Carter-Pascoe v Birmingham Magistrates' Court & Others*[105] Lightman J held, on similar relevant facts to those in *Langfield*, that:

> 'In my view the Justices are perfectly entitled to form their own view on whether there was a significant risk of a public order problem. They are not bound by any view taken either way by the Police, though they must plainly take that view into account and give it proper weight. But, if they were minded to disagree with the view of the Police, they were bound to intimate to the Appellant that they were considering acting in this way and put the Appellant on notice that this was a possible outcome of the proceedings in order to obviate the risk that he might be taken by surprise'.

12.96 These authorities appear to reveal that a challenge to the judgmental conclusion of a licensing authority involves a 'high hurdle'. This is also identified in the approach of Sullivan J in the *4 Wins* litigation. In this case, the Administrative Court set out the *Wednesbury*/irrationality test as it related to the decisions of local licensing bodies. In that case it was said that a claimant had to persuade the Administrative Court that no reasonable licensing panel with the local knowledge that the licensing panel had could have come to the conclusion that it did.

---

[103]   (2000) 164 JP 339.
[104]   (1984) 149 JP 26.
[105]   [2002] EWHC 1202 (Admin).

12.97 These decisions (particularly those under the previous liquor licensing regime) should however be contrasted with the approach of the Administrative Court in *Daniel Thwaites PLC v Wirral Magistrates' Court & Others*[106] when considering the Licensing Act 2003. This case involved a judicial review claim in relation to an application under the 2003 Act to extend the licensable hours. The application was initially granted by the licensing authority but this was later overturned by the Magistrates' Court following an appeal by a local group of residents. Central to the decision of the Magistrates' Court was their concern that customers would migrate to the premises from other premises. In this case, the Police had withdrawn its concerns and had therefore not opposed the application. The applicant brought judicial review proceedings to challenge the decision of the Magistrates' Court. In a detailed judgment which considered the policy behind the Licensing Act 2003 and the legal framework within which such licensing decisions should be made, Black J explained that:

> 'The fact that the police did not oppose the hours sought on this basis should have weighed very heavily with them whereas, in fact, they appear to have dismissed the police view because it did not agree with their own .... They proceeded without proper evidence and gave their own views excessive weight and their resulting decision limited the hours of operation of the premises without it having been established that it was necessary to do so to promote the licensing objectives'.

12.98 As explained earlier, Black J was of the view that whilst such a decision-maker may take account of its own local knowledge, it must be measured against the evidence presented to it. The decision in *Thwaites* also reinforces the proposition that the decision-maker must direct itself, and act, in accordance with the respective legal framework and the policy behind it. Moreover, it was explained in *R (on the application of Lunt & Others) v Liverpool City Council*[107] that the margin of discretion afforded to decision-makers under the *Wednesbury* test only applies to those decision-makers who have acted fairly and directed themselves properly as to the relevant considerations to be weighed in making the judgment.

THE FUTURE

12.99 What does the future hold for licensing law? In brief, the answer appears to be that there is potential for much litigation before the Administrative Court. Indeed, over recent years there has been an increase in licensing legislation which has completely changed and consolidated the way in which specific sectors are regulated and licensed. Both the Licensing Act 2003 and the Gambling Act 2005 have been notable entrants to the statute books. Both these Acts are far reaching and have overhauled the way in which alcohol, entertainment and gambling is regulated. Surprisingly, against that background, the number of proceedings before the Administrative Court has not been in the numbers that were expected. It is, therefore, likely that there will be more legal challenges to come. So, too, are challenges expected in the context of the recent Policing and Crime Act 2009 which introduces specific regulation for the lap dancing industry, and the proposals in the Police Reform and Social Responsibility Bill should they be enacted. In contrast to the legal developments in terms of the licensing of alcohol, entertainment and gambling – other regulated sectors have been left untouched for many years. Indeed, the starting point for the licensing of the hackney carriage industry remains an Act of Parliament from 1847 (Town Police Clauses Act 1847). This has been

---

[106]   [2008] EWHC 838 (Admin).
[107]   [2009] EWHC 2356 (Admin).

supplemented by a statute from 1976 (Local Government (Miscellaneous Provisions) Act 1976). Many believe that the regulation of the hackney carriage and private hire industry requires modernising and bringing into line with the current commercial times. It remains to be seen, however, whether this area of the law will be developed by reference to modern legislation.

Chapter 13

LOCAL/CENTRAL GOVERNMENT

INTRODUCTION

13.1 Like central government, local government is a public body amenable to judicial review, and the principles explained in the general chapters of this book apply to them both. Indeed, many of the cases and issues dealt with elsewhere in this book relate to actions taken by or against local authorities. Nevertheless, central and local government differ in two important respects from other bodies.

13.2 First, unlike many bodies delivering public services or regulating activity, a local authority is a multifunctional, not a single issue, body. The functions exercised by an authority are diverse, although the precise functions allocated differ between unitary and two-tier authorities. While some of these specific functions are considered in other chapters of this book, this multifunctional nature raises issues relating to the appropriate relationship between the various powers conferred on local authorities and the factors which can be taken into account in exercising them.

13.3 Clearly, this characteristic is also shared by central government, but there is a difference between the legal bases of the two levels of government, affecting the extent of their powers and the ability to deal with 'cross-cutting' issues. This difference, and the nature of the powers of central and local government, is examined in this chapter.

13.4 Secondly, unlike most other public bodies, local government is an elected body and this democratic accountability raises issues relating to the extent to which the democratic imperative should be respected by the court, and the extent to which constraints should be placed on political action. While central government is not directly elected, it possesses the democratic legitimacy conferred by Parliament and similar issues arise, albeit that the response of the courts is not identical to the two levels of government.

THE LEGAL BASIS OF CENTRAL AND LOCAL GOVERNMENT

Residual and prerogative powers for central government

13.5 As explained in previous chapters, central government possesses not only the statutory powers conferred on it by Parliament but also many of the prerogative powers of the Crown, and other non-statutory non-prerogative powers, and the principles of judicial review have continued to develop in relation to these.[1]

---

[1]   See e g *R (on the application of Bancoult) v Secretary of State for Foreign and Commonwealth Affairs (No2)* [2008] UKHL 61. The residual power of central government has been confirmed recently in relation to the reorganisation of local government in *R (on the application of Shrewsbury and Atcham BC) v Secretary of State for Communities and Local Government* [2008] EWCA Civ 148; [2008] 3 All ER 548.

13.6   The prerogative used to be reviewable only to the extent that it was open to the court to determine whether or not the prerogative existed, and not in regard to its exercise. This left wide discretion in respect to the exercise of these powers.

13.7   It is often said that the prerogative cannot be enlarged.[2] However, permitting it to be adapted to meet new situations allows the courts to come close to recognising new prerogatives.[3]

13.8   On the other hand, the courts have applied fairly rigorously the principle that the prerogative is displaced by statute legislating in regard to the same subject matter, thus respecting the right of Parliament to regulate areas previously subject to prerogative powers.[4]

13.9   However, given that the aim of judicial review is to ensure governmental power is exercised lawfully and properly, whilst the previous position could be understood historically a different judicial review regime for statutory and prerogative powers appeared anomalous in the modern democratic age. Pressure for change culminated in *Council of Civil Service Unions v Minister for the Civil Service,*[5] Lord Scarman stated:

> 'the law relating to judicial review has now reached the stage where it can be said with confidence that, if the subject matter in respect of which prerogative power is exercised is justiciable, that is to say if it is a matter on which the court can adjudicate, the exercise of the power is subject to review in accordance with the principles developed in respect of the review of the exercise of statutory power.'

13.10   Indeed, in *M v Home Office,*[6] Lord Woolf stated, albeit *obiter*:

> 'As a result of even more recent developments, illustrated by the decision in [GCHQ], a distinction probably no longer has to be drawn between duties which have a statutory and those which have a prerogative source.'

13.11   That is not to say that all prerogative powers will be subject to the same degree of scrutiny. As Lord Scarman indicated, not all prerogatives are considered to be justiciable. Lord Roskill clarified this in the *Council of Civil Service Unions* case, albeit *obiter*:

> 'Prerogative powers such as those relating to the making of treaties, the defence of the realm, the prerogative of mercy, the grant of honours, the dissolution of Parliament and the appointment of ministers as well as others are not, I think, susceptible to judicial review because their nature and subject matter are such as not to be amenable to the judicial process. The courts are not the place wherein to determine whether a treaty should be concluded or the armed forces disposed in a particular manner or Parliament dissolved on one date rather than another.'

13.12   Lord Diplock confirmed the justiciability point by noting that while judicial review was possible, many decisions would involve the application of government policy,

---

2   *BBC v Johns* [1965] Ch 32 where Diplock LJ said 'It is 350 years and a civil war too late for the Queen's courts to broaden the prerogative.'

3   *R v Secretary of State for the Home Department, ex p Northumbria Police Authority* [1987] 2 All ER 282; [1988] 1 All ER 556.

4   *R v Secretary of State for the Home Department, ex p Fire Brigades Union* [1995] 1 All ER 888.

5   [1985] AC 374.

6   [1993] 3 All ER 537.

and that such questions were not ones to which 'the judicial process is adapted to provide the right answer'. He therefore considered that such matters should be considered on a case to case basis.

13.13 As the law has developed since then, it has become clear that no areas remain immune from review in principle.[7] Indeed, the House of Lords has given very clear guidance on the point in *R (on the application of Bancoult) v Secretary of State for Foreign and Commonwealth Affairs (No2)*.[8]

13.14 The case concerned the validity of section 9 of the British Indian Ocean Territory (Constitution) Order 2004, made by prerogative Order in Council. One issue was whether this was amenable to review at all. The Government claimed that the courts had no power to review the validity of an Order in Council legislating for a colony, one strand of this reasoning being that it was primary legislation having unquestionable validity comparable with that of an Act of Parliament.

13.15 On this point Lord Hoffman stated:[9]

'It is true that a prerogative Order in Council is primary legislation in the sense that the legislative power of the Crown is original and not subordinate. It is classified as primary legislation for the purposes of the Human Rights Act 1998: see paragraph (f)(i) of the definition in section 21(1). That means that it cannot be overridden by Convention rights. The court can only make a declaration of incompatibility under section 4. But the fact that such Orders in Council in certain important respects resemble Acts of Parliament does not mean that they share all their characteristics. The principle of the sovereignty of Parliament, as it has been developed by the courts over the past 350 years, is founded upon the unique authority Parliament derives from its representative character. An exercise of the prerogative lacks this quality; although it may be legislative in character, it is still an exercise of power by the executive alone. Until the decision of this House in *Council of Civil Service Unions v Minister for the Civil Service* [1985] AC 374, it may have been assumed that the exercise of prerogative powers was, as such, immune from judicial review. That objection being removed, I see no reason why prerogative legislation should not be subject to review on ordinary principles of legality, rationality and procedural impropriety in the same way as any other executive action. Mr Crow rightly pointed out that the *Council of Civil Service Unions* case was not concerned with the validity of a prerogative order but with an executive decision made pursuant to powers conferred by such an order. That is a ground upon which, if your Lordships were inclined to distinguish the case, it would be open to you to do so. But I see no reason for making such a distinction. On 21 February 2008 the Foreign Secretary told the House of Commons that, contrary to previous assurances, Diego Garcia had been used as a base for two extraordinary rendition flights in 2002 (Hansard (HC Debates), cols 547–548). There are allegations, which the US authorities have denied, that Diego Garcia or a ship in the waters around it have been used as a prison in which suspects have been tortured. The idea that such conduct on British territory, touching the honour of the United Kingdom, could be legitimated by executive fiat, is not something which I would find acceptable.'

13.16 Lord Bingham found that there was in fact 'no royal prerogative power to make an order in council containing section 9', but he also concluded that 'if (contrary to that conclusion) there was power to make it, I agree with my noble and learned friends that

---

[7]   For example, on the prerogative of mercy see *R v Secretary State for the Home Department, ex p Bentley* [1993] 4 All ER 442.

[8]   [2008] UKHL 61.

[9]   Paras [34] and [35].

the section is susceptible in principle to review by the courts'.[10] He found that it was unlawful on two grounds, namely irrationality and contradicting a clear representation of the Secretary of State in 2000.

13.17 For Lord Rodger, reliance on the historical approach to the prerogative was no longer acceptable and:[11]

> 'Nowadays, a broader form of review of other prerogative acts is established: *Council of Civil Service Unions v Minister for the Civil Service* [1985] AC 374. Therefore, like Lord Hoffmann, I see no reason in principle why, today, prerogative legislation, too, should not be subject to judicial review on ordinary principles of legality, rationality and procedural impropriety. Any challenge of that kind must, of course, be based on a ground that is justiciable.'

13.18 The concept of justiciability for Lord Rodger has moved from the nature of the power to the grounds raised in any challenge. Indeed, any reticence on the part of the courts to interfere with these powers has shifted from a focus on the power itself to recognising simply that due deference must be shown to the democratic role of the decision-maker. This was seen clearly in the view expressed by Lord Mance:[12]

> '... the prerogative power of the Crown to legislate by order in council on the advice of Her Majesty's ministers in relation to a territory such as BIOT is subject to judicial review. ... I see no good reason why they should not be reviewable in the same way as other steps, administrative or legislative, by the executive, and every reason why they should be, on the familiar grounds of legality, rationality and procedural propriety, due weight being of course given to the executive's effective role as primary decision-maker. A recognition that a legislative order in council is invalid by a judgment given in proceedings such as the present directed against the Minister responsible for the making of the order no more involves the making of an impermissible order against the Sovereign than a successful challenge to any other prerogative act undertaken in Her name.'

13.19 Thus, it can now be said that the basis of governmental power no longer provides the key to the extent to which it is susceptible to judicial review.

13.20 At the same time as the courts have been expanding the ability to review the exercise of the prerogative, there has been increasing recognition that central government can exercise other non-statutory powers.

13.21 To some extent this may be a matter of terminology. While some include in the term 'prerogative powers' only those powers which were historically unique to the Crown, others include all residual non-statutory powers. However, beyond both of these are powers for which there are various descriptions. Whether called 'third source', 'de facto', 'common law', or 'residual' powers, or even 'new prerogatives',[13] they all refer to powers which may be thought to operate under a wide approach to incidental powers, or what is termed the 'Ram doctrine', namely that a Minister can do anything a natural person can do provided it is not prohibited.[14] Authority for this is also said to stem from the common law powers which derive from the Crown's status as a corporation.[15] One example of such a wide power was given judicial recognition in *Malone v Metropolitan*

---

[10]   Para [71].
[11]   Para [105].
[12]   Para [141].
[13]   In contradiction to the established approach to prerogative powers where the categories are closed.
[14]   The 'Ram doctrine' is named after the First Parliamentary Counsel who articulated the doctrine in 1945.
[15]   Written Reply in 2003 by Baroness Scotland, House of Lords, *Hansard,* Vol 645, col WA12, cited in De

Police Commissioner,[16] where telephone tapping was permitted on the basis that the Government could do anything 'except what is expressly forbidden'.[17]

13.22 However, the tension inherent in recognising wide powers lies in the fact that the Government is not simply another natural person, and some consider that the exercise of such power should be scrutinised by the courts carefully, to ensure there is no abuse of such powers and that they are exercised in the public as opposed to Government's interest.

13.23 This tension can be seen in the recent case of *R (on the application of Shrewsbury and Atcham BC) v Secretary of State for Communities and Local Government*,[18] which not only clarifies the approach to 'third source' powers but also illustrates the two approaches to how they should be treated by the courts.

13.24 In that case, the council applied for judicial review of the process adopted by the Secretary of State for considering proposals to abolish it by replacing the existing two-tier local government in the area with unitary authorities.

13.25 Following the publication of a White Paper in which it was stated that such reform was desirable, local authorities were invited by the Government to make proposals for future unitary structures. The council strongly opposed unitary structures advanced by other local authorities in the area. The Government stated that proposals which the Government considered met the relevant criteria would continue to a second stage where there would be wide consultation in the areas affected and, following that consultation, it would re-assess proposals to take account of the outcome of consultation and implement any proposals that succeeded.

13.26 It was acknowledged in the White Paper that the proposals could not be implemented unless and until new legislation was passed, since a policy decision had been made not to use the existing legislative machinery under the Local Government Act 1992. However, the exercise was undertaken prior to the enactment of the Local Government and Public Involvement in Health Act 2007. The challenge was made on the basis that the Secretary of State had no power to undertake the exercise.

13.27 The Court of Appeal considered itself obliged to follow a previous decision of the House of Lords which held that the powers of the Secretary of State were not confined to those conferred by statute or prerogative. As Carnwath LJ stated:[19]

> 'the answer seems to me to be dictated by the decision in [*R v Secretary of State for Health, ex p C* [2000] 1 FCR 471] in the judgment of Hale LJ ... . That decision, which is binding also on us, confirms that the powers of the Secretary of State are not confined to those conferred by statute or prerogative, but extend, subject to any relevant statutory or public law constraints, and to the competing rights of other parties, to anything which could be done by a natural person.'

Smiths *Judicial Review*, 6th edn, para 5-023. She also stated that this flexibility was necessary because otherwise it would 'impose upon Parliament an impossible burden or produce legislation in terms that simply reproduced the common law'.

[16]   [1979] Ch 344.

[17]   This was subsequently held to violate Art 8 of the ECHR.

[18]   [2008] EWCA Civ 148; [2008] 3 All ER 548.

[19]   Para [44]. See also *R (on the application of Hillingdon LBC) v Secretary of State for Transport and Transport for London* [2010] EWHC 626 (Admin).

13.28 This confirms in principle the 'third source' approach. However, the Court took the matter further and outlined the principles applicable to such power.

13.29 The majority warned that this residual category of ministerial power was exceptional, and should be strictly confined. As Carnwath LJ stated:[20]

'Unlike a local authority, the Crown is not a creature of statute. As a matter of capacity, no doubt, it has power to do whatever a private person can do. But as an organ of government, it can only exercise those powers for the public benefit, and for identifiably "governmental" purposes within limits set by the law.'

13.30 Nevertheless, on the facts of the case, Carnwath LJ also held that local government re-organisation as such did not fall within any residual non-statutory government power and so legislation was needed to give effect to the proposals. However, the Secretary of State's actions which fell short of the actual re-organisation were 'governmental' and undertaken for what she perceived to be the public benefit. The Court therefore held that the Secretary of State could promote new legislation and lawfully take some preparatory steps in advance of doing so. That extended to the preparation and publication of the White Paper. He concluded:[21]

'I do not see that it is necessary to invoke a "third source" category for that purpose. I see it as simply a necessary and incidental part of the ordinary business of central government, part of which is the promotion of new policies through legislation. The issue is how far such preparatory steps can properly go before crossing into territory reserved to statute. That issue can only sensibly considered in the context of the present statutory scheme. It therefore overlaps with the second ground of appeal, to which I now turn.'

13.31 That second ground of appeal was whether the actions of the Secretary of State were inconsistent with the existing statutory regime under the Local Government Act 1992 and how far preparatory steps could properly go before crossing into territory reserved to statute. Carnwath LJ held that while the inconsistency principle was well developed,[22] how 'far in any case it is necessary or appropriate to review the procedural steps will depend on the facts and circumstances, including the nature of the illegality and the substantive relief sought in respect of it'. On the facts of that case, he concluded that it would not be appropriate to grant relief because the actions had in effect been ratified by Parliament through the enactment of the Local Government and Public Involvement in Health Act 2007.

13.32 Nevertheless, although not upholding the challenge of the council, Carnwath LJ expressed his concern about the use of such powers:[23]

'As I have made clear, I have more concerns … about the extent to which a wholly non-statutory procedure has been used to prepare the way for decisions, in an area which is accepted as the province of the legislature. I have also pointed out the potential risks of such a course. I understand that one purpose was to limit the period of uncertainty accompanying structural change. But it seems to me a constitutional principle of some importance that local authorities should be able to rely on the safeguards of a statutory framework for the processes leading to decisions of this importance. However, in the end, I find it impossible to

---

20   Para [48].
21   Para [49]
22   *R v Secretary of State for the Home Department, ex p Northumbria Police Authority* [1989] QB 26; *De Keyser's Royal Hotel Ltd* (1920) AC 508; and *Laker Airways Ltd v Department of Trade* [1977] QB 643.
23   Para [70].

avoid the conclusion that Parliament has (if only retrospectively) given its stamp of approval to the procedure in this case, and there is no evidence that the authorities have been prejudiced in presenting their opposition.'

13.33 Although agreeing with Carnwath LJ as to the outcome of the case and much of the reasoning, Richards LJ disagreed on two points.

13.34 First, in relation to the extent of the common law powers, he stated:[24]

'As the first instance judge whose decision was upheld by the Court of Appeal in *R v Secretary of State for Health, ex p C* [2000] 1 FLR 627 I took a broad view of those powers, and nothing in the materials deployed before us in the present case has caused me to change my mind. The Court of Appeal's judgment in that case is not only determinative of the issue at this level (see paras 44 and 49 of Carnwath LJ's judgment) but was in my view correct.

The complex process of government includes a vast amount of work in relation to the formulation of policy, drafting new legislation and preparing for its implementation. Carnwath LJ states that it is not necessary to invoke a "third source" of power for such work, which is simply "a necessary and incidental part of the ordinary business of government" (para 49). To my mind, however, it is still necessary to explain the basis on which that ordinary business of government is conducted, and the simple and satisfactory explanation is that it depends heavily on the "third source" of powers, ie powers that have not been conferred by statute and are not prerogative powers in the narrow sense but are the normal powers (or capacities and freedoms) of a corporation with legal personality. The context is a special one, but the powers are the same.

I accept, of course, that such powers cannot override the rights of others and, when exercised by government, are subject to judicial review on ordinary public law grounds. But I think it unnecessary and unwise to introduce qualifications along the lines of those suggested by Carnwath LJ at para 48, to the effect that they can only be exercised "for the public benefit" or for "identifiably 'governmental' purposes". It seems to me that any limiting principle would have to be so wide as to be of no practical utility or would risk imposing an artificial and inappropriate restriction upon the work of government.'

13.35 The third judge, Waller LJ, noted the disagreement between the two and his own contribution was tentatively on the side of Carnwath LJ:[25]

'I doubt whether anything that I can say will influence any future debate, and since *ex p C* is binding, it is not appropriate to say very much. But it seems to me that once one accepts capacity, the limit so far as any challenge before the courts is concerned cannot be other than by reference to "the limits set by the law". The question is thus whether there should be an ability to challenge as unlawful an action taken "not for the public benefit" or which has not been taken for "identifiably governmental purposes".

I instinctively favour some constraint on the powers by reference to the duty to act only for the public benefit but until one has actual facts by reference to which the matter can be fully tested, it is unwise to say more.'

13.36 Thus, given the lack of unanimity and that strictly the views expressed are *obiter* albeit fully reasoned and deliberate, it will be for a future ruling to decide between the two approaches, and determine the flexibility which the courts will grant to central government outside of its statutory and prerogative powers.

---

[24]   Paras [72] to [74].
[25]   Paras [80] and [81].

13.37 The second point on which Richards LJ disagreed was in relation to whether the actions of the Secretary of State were inconsistent with the 1992 Act. As Richards LJ explained his position:[26]

> 'I do not read the 1992 Act as preventing the taking of action by Ministers by way of preparation for the introduction of a different statutory regime. Moreover the work done did not pre-empt Parliament's decision in relation to the proposed new legislation but prepared for it on a contingent basis. The process engaged in was not intended to produce, and was not capable of producing, a result with legal effects unless and until the proposed legislation was enacted and relevant measures were taken under it. It is true that the existing machinery of the 1992 Act was not used and, so far as one can see, was not intended to be used even as a fall-back in the event that Parliament did not enact the proposed legislation. But nothing done was, in my judgment, inconsistent with the 1992 Act. However improbable it was in practice, it would still have been possible in principle to fall back on the machinery of that Act if the new legislation had not been forthcoming and the Secretary of State had wished to pursue the matter.
>
> On these issues, therefore, I would endorse the conclusion reached by Underhill J, even before the 2007 Act was enacted, that the Secretary of State acted lawfully. The Secretary of State's actions did not depend for their lawfulness on the retrospective effect of the Act. But if there were any doubt about that, then I agree with Carnwath LJ that the position was resolved against the Boroughs by the Act and the measures adopted under it.'

13.38 In relation to this point Waller LJ was less equivocal, agreeing firmly with Carnwath LJ:[27]

> 'One reason I have for supporting his view is that it seems to me that the action being taken was in an area which the 1992 Act was designed to cover. The action was not simply preliminary to bringing in an Act to change the 1992 Act with the intention thereafter of acting under a new statutory scheme. The action being taken was to treat the 1992 scheme as having already been repealed.'

13.39 This approach continues the trend seen in relation to the prerogative whereby the courts seek to respect the authority of Parliament when it legislates in the same sphere.

Residual prerogative powers for local government?

13.40 For local government, it is clear that there is no longer any such residual prerogative power, and certainly no judicial recognition of non-statutory powers. Previously, some local authorities were established by Royal Charter, and as such were deemed to have inherited the relevant powers of the Crown.[28] However during the 19th century the influence of centralism was seen, and many local authorities were the creation of statute. Thus in *Att-Gen v Manchester Corporation*,[29] it was held that the prerogative power was in practice suspended.

13.41 The role of the public sector in the depression was subject to much debate and there was a rise of 'municipal socialism'. In *Att-Gen v Leicester Corporation*,[30] following the enactment of the Local Government Act 1933, the local prerogative was reasserted.

---

[26]   Paras [75] and [76].
[27]   Para [82].
[28]   *Case of Sutton's Hospital* (1612) 10 Co Rep 1; *Riche v Ashbury Railway Carriage and Iron Co* (1874) LR 9 Exch 224.
[29]   [1906] 1 Ch 643.
[30]   [1943] 1 Ch 86.

Nevertheless, this does not accord with current judicial approaches to the prerogative and in *Hazell v Hammersmith and Fulham LBC*,[31] the 'loan swaps' case, the House of Lords held that the council was the creature of statute and possessed only those powers granted by statute.

13.42 Nevertheless, just as there are sound arguments why flexibility and discretion beyond specific statutory powers is necessary for central government, in the form of prerogative and other non-statutory powers, so there are sound reasons why local government also needs appropriate flexibility and discretion.

The 'well-being' power

13.43 This is reflected in a debate in relation to local authority powers as to whether the narrow *ultra vires* doctrine, requiring express or implied/incidental statutory authority is unduly constraining on innovative local government activity.

13.44 Under the common law, the courts held that a corporation may do not only those things for which there is express or implied authority, but also whatever is reasonably incidental to the doing of those things.[32]

13.45 For local government this common law principle was incorporated into statute by s 111 of the Local Government Act 1972. It provides that:

'(1) Without prejudice to any powers exercisable apart from this section but subject to the provisions of this Act and any other enactment passed before or after this Act, a local authority shall have power to do anything (whether or not involving the expenditure, borrowing or lending of money or the acquisition or disposal of any property or rights) which is calculated to facilitate, or is conducive or incidental to, the discharge of any of their functions.'

13.46 However, there has been confusion so as to be unclear whether the 'functions' referred to in s 111(1) must be expressly conferred by statute or can be impliedly conferred.

13.47 The broader view, that s 111 can apply not only to express powers but also implied powers, is not only in accord with the trend in most of the 20th century before s 111 was enacted, but accords with there being no indication that the enactment of s 111 was intended to reduce the width of the common law power. This wider view of s 111 is also reflected in a number of cases, as articulated by Woolf LJ in the Court of Appeal in *Hazell v Hammersmith and Fulham LBC*,[33] where he considered that 'functions' meant the 'specific statutory activities the council is expressly or impliedly under a duty to perform', and by the Divisional Court in *Allsop v North Tyneside Metropolitan Borough Council*.[34]

13.48 On the other hand more restrictive interpretations seemed to be adopted in some cases in the 1990s. In *R v Richmond Upon Thames London Borough Council, ex p McCarthy & Stone (Developments) Ltd*,[35] the House of Lords appeared to take a

---

[31]   [1992] 2 AC 1.
[32]   *Att-Gen v Great Eastern Railway* (1880) 5 App Cas 473.
[33]   [1990] 2 QB 697.
[34]   (1992) 90 LGR 462.
[35]   [1992] 2 AC 48

narrow approach and held that the giving of pre-planning application advice was not itself a 'function' of the council and so charging for it could not be justified by reference to s 111 as that would be 'incidental to the incidental'. However, no consideration was given to the possibility that the giving of pre-application advice was an 'implied function' of the local authority.[36]

13.49 Another principle restricting the scope of s 111 is that of the 'comprehensive code'. Where the court considers that Parliament has made sufficiently detailed provision as to a statutory regime, it is considered that it is not possible to justify additional powers by reference to s 111.[37]

13.50 Whatever the position as a matter of strict interpretation of the cases, by the mid-1990s it was perceived that by restrictive judicial interpretation there had been a narrowing of the width of incidental powers under s 111.

13.51 At the same time there was a resurgence of the debate over the desirability of granting local government a power of general competence, as is done in many continental systems. A modification of the narrow doctrine of *ultra vires*, and consideration of a power of general competence had been recommended in number of official reports.[38] While a power of general competence reverses the presumption in favour of an authority having the power to do something, rather than having to find positive statutory authority, its exercise would remain subject to the other wider principles of judicial review and it does not 'allow a council to do anything' as many of its critics suggest.

13.52 However, a power of general competence expressed as such remained politically unacceptable and, instead, the Government introduced the well-being powers under Part 1 of the Local Government Act 2000, intending to reduce and contain the uncertainty arising from the narrow principle of *ultra vires*.

13.53 The underlying aims of this power was to meet the concerns of local government by:

• reassurance that existing activities were legally possible and not constrained by the recent restrictive interpretations of s 111;

• allowing new ways of undertaking existing activity; and

• allowing new activities.

13.54 The general approach to the legislation was to provide a wide power which could be a 'power of first resort' and thus one which was overlapping with, but wider than, the existing statutory powers under the wide variety of Acts. The idea was that it would not be necessary to use the existing statutory powers and reliance would simply be placed on

---

[36] The *Encyclopedia of Local Government Law* submits that the broad approach is to be preferred, and correctly suggests that *McCarthy &Stone* can be justified by reference to the principle that a power for a public authority to charge for its services must be conferred expressly or by necessary implication, see *Att-Gen v Wilts United Dairies Ltd* (1922) 38 TLR 781.

[37] *Hazell v Hammersmith & Fulham LBC* [1992] 2 AC 1; *Credit Suisse v Allerdale BC* (1996) 94 LGR 628; *R v Liverpool City Council, ex p Baby Products Association* [2000] LGR 171.

[38] See eg the Royal Commission on Local Government in England 1966–69, Cmnd 4039 & 4040 (Redcliffe-Maud).

the new power. However, the enactment of such a power clearly had implications for existing statutory restrictions, and it was not intended that these would be swept away by the new power.

13.55 This general approach resulted in a wide power under s 2(1) to promote economic, social or environmental well-being:

> '(1) Every local authority are to have power to do anything which they consider is likely to achieve any one or more of the following objects—

> (a)   the promotion or improvement of the economic well-being of their area;
> (b)   the promotion or improvement of the social well-being of their area; and
> (c)   the promotion or improvement of the environmental well-being of their area.'

13.56 The three objectives are separate but can be related, and are intended to be all-embracing, e g including cultural or health issues.

13.57 The use of the power can in principle be very particular. Under s 2(2) the power may be exercised not only in relation to or for the benefit of the whole or any part of a local authority's area, but also in relation to all or any persons resident or present in a local authority's area.

13.58 In addition, a wider geographical reach is provided by s 2(5) which makes clear that the power 'includes power for a local authority to do anything in relation to, or for the benefit of, any person or area situated outside their area if they consider that it is likely to achieve any one or more of the objects in that subsection'.

13.59 The power is also intended to allow a wide variety of methods to deliver the aims of the power. Section 2(4) makes clear that, while other methods can be adopted:

> '(4) The power under subsection (1) includes power for a local authority to—

> (a)   incur expenditure;
> (b)   give financial assistance to any person;
> (c)   enter into arrangements or agreements with any person;
> (d)   co-operate with, or facilitate or co-ordinate the activities of, any person;
> (e)   exercise on behalf of any person any functions of that person; and
> (f)   provide staff, goods, services or accommodation to any person.'

13.60 The extensive partnership powers are thus not limited to options for mechanisms in s 2(4).

13.61 This wide power was not of course without its limitations and restrictions. The potentially most far-reaching is the power under s 3(3) and (3A) for the Secretary of State by order to restrict the use of the power:

> '(3) The Secretary of State may by order make provision preventing local authorities from doing, by virtue of section 2(1), anything which is specified, or is of a description specified, in the order.

> (3A) The power under subsection (3) may be exercised in relation to—

> (a)   all local authorities,

(b)   particular local authorities, or

(c)   particular descriptions of local authority.'

13.62 The authority is also obliged under s 4 to prepare a sustainable community strategy for promoting or improving the economic, social and environmental well-being of their area and contributing to the achievement of sustainable development in the United Kingdom. By s 2(3), in determining whether or how to exercise the power under subsection (1), a local authority must have regard to their strategy under section 4. However, if the sustainable community strategy is silent on the matter it does not prevent the power being exercised. Equally, provided regard is had to the strategy, and proper reasons for departing from it are given, the authority is not obliged to follow the strategy.

13.63 Similarly, under s 3(5), in exercising the power the authority must have regard to any guidance for the time being issued by the Secretary of State about the exercise of that power. The Guidance issued has proved to be very important in guiding the interpretation placed on the power by the courts.[39]

13.64 A substantive limitation is imposed by s 3(2) which provides that the power 'does not enable a local authority to raise money (whether by precepts, borrowing or otherwise)'. However, this is generally accepted as permitting the making of a charge, up to full cost recovery for the service provided. As the Guidance states:[40]

> 'The Government considers that the effect of the provision in section 3(2) is to prevent local authorities from using the power in section 2(1) *primarily* to raise money. Where authorities use the power for a different purpose, but *incidentally* receive income as a result, that does not, in the Government's view, amount to raising money.'

13.65 However, the most problematic of the limitations is provided by s 3(1) which carried over many of the existing statutory limitations. It provides that:

> '(1) The power under section 2(1) does not enable a local authority to do anything which they are unable to do by virtue of any prohibition, restriction or limitation on their powers which is contained in any enactment (whenever passed or made).'

13.66 To increase flexibility, s 5 gives a residual enabling power to the Secretary of State:

> '(1) If the Secretary of State thinks that an enactment (whenever passed or made) prevents or obstructs local authorities from exercising their power under section 2(1) he may by order amend, repeal, revoke or disapply that enactment.
>
> (2) The power under subsection (1) may be exercised in relation to—
>
> (a)   all local authorities,
> (b)   particular local authorities, or
> (c)   particular descriptions of local authority.
>
> (3) The power under subsection (1) to amend or disapply an enactment includes a power to amend or disapply an enactment for a particular period.'

---

[39]   The guidance was issued in March 2001, and is available on the DCLG web site, and reproduced in the *Encyclopedia of Local Government Law.*

[40]   Para 67.

13.67   The basic issue in relation to s 3(1) is the possible conflict between the Guidance and the statutory wording. The view of the Guidance is clear in stating that:[41]

> 'councils are able to undertake any activity that promotes the well-being of their area, except where they are specifically restricted from doing so by any prohibition, restriction or limitation spelt out in other legislation.'

13.68   The uncertainty was whether the statutory wording 'contained in' justifies in law the interpretation 'specifically restricted … spelt out'. In other words, could 'any prohibition, restriction or limitation on their powers which is contained in any enactment' include an implied prohibition, restriction, or limitation, or must it be expressly stated? In addition, would this statutory formulation overcome any restriction based on the 'comprehensive code' principle?

13.69   The Guidance provides a clear statement:[42]

> '63. "Contained in any enactment" means spelt out explicitly on the face of the legislation. It does not apply to any limits to local authority powers which might be implied or inferred from the way in which those powers have been drafted. So, for instance, section 93 of the Transport Act 1985 (as amended by Schedule 11 of the Transport Act 2000) confers a power on councils to establish public transport travel concession schemes for certain groups of people. If this provision stated on the face of the Act that authorities *could not* establish such schemes for any other group of people, then that prohibition would also constrain the use of the well-being power. However, the 1985 Act contains no such prohibition: so authorities can now use the wellbeing power to establish concessionary fare schemes for *any* person or group of people, if they consider it appropriate after taking their own legal advice.'

13.70   Clarification has been provided by the courts through a succession of cases. In *R (on the application of J) v Enfield LBC and Secretary of State for Health*,[43] Elias J accepted the argument of the Government that there was distinction between, 'on the one hand, a case where a statute merely confers a power in a specific field so that any limitation arises simply because the power cannot be exercised outside the specified field; and, on the other, a case where the legislation in terms imposes an express restriction or limitation on the exercise of the power'.

13.71   Indeed, even in the latter situation, he considered that it will be necessary in each case to scrutinise the legislation carefully to see whether, properly analysed, it is intended to provide a bar to its exercise at all, or whether it is merely intended to prevent the power being exercised under the particular legislation in which the restriction is to be found.

13.72   He also considered that a 'prohibition, restriction or limitation' is one that will almost always be found in an express legislative provision, and that the power:

> 'is drafted in very broad terms which provide a source of power enabling authorities to do many things which they could not hitherto have done. In my view, a "prohibition, restriction or limitation" is one which will almost always be found in an express legislative provision. I do not discount the possibility that such might arise by necessary implication, but I would have thought that would be very rare. (I note that the Guidance to which I have made

---

[41]   Para 62.
[42]   Para 63
[43]   [2002] EWHC 432 (Admin).

reference assumes that any restriction, prohibition or limitation must be expressly spelt out in the legislation: see paras 62 and 63. However, … I doubt whether it must always do so as a matter of construction of section 3.)'

13.73 This wide approach was then followed in subsequent cases.[44]

13.74 Further clarification has come from the Court of Appeal. In *R v Oxfordshire CC, ex p Khan*,[45] it was held that it was not open to the council to provide financial assistance and accommodation under the 2000 Act, since s 21(1A) of the National Assistance Act 1948 was a prohibition within the meaning of s 3 of the 2000 Act. The Court endorsed the view of Elias J in *Enfield*, but noted that 'it is not always easy to distinguish between a provision which defines the scope of a power and a provision which restricts or limits the exercise of a power'. The Court found:

> 'So far as the policy consideration is concerned, I accept that section 2 has a broad purpose. The scope of the powers given by section 2 should not be narrowly construed. The local authority is given a wide discretion to exercise its powers to promote well-being …. But the fact that section 2 should be construed broadly does not help in deciding the meaning and scope of a prohibition, restriction or limitation on the exercise of powers which is contained in *another* enactment whenever passed or made.'

13.75 The Court was also not willing to accept that all express limitations in another enactment will serve to exclude the use of the power under s 2. That leaves the issue of when, if at all, an express limitation in another enactment will not apply to s 2. There are three parts to the answer to this.

(1)   It will turn on an assessment of the legislative intent. In *Khan*, because no other power existed in 1999 when the Immigration and Asylum Act 1999 introduced a new limited power of funding, it was possible to conclude that Parliament did not wish any other power to be available to fund such expenditure.

(2)   That logic is somewhat circular, however, in that it uses that intention to rebut the suggestion that Parliament, by enacting the later 2000 Act, changed that intention. At root, however, the question is a matter of interpretation for the court to determine how fundamental it considers the limitation or restriction to be to the other statutory scheme.

(3)   Nevertheless, the fact that in most cases s 2 will be the only other possible power means that the principle in *Khan*, that 'the very reason why section 3(1) was enacted was to prevent section 2 being used to do that which is prohibited by another statute', is likely to mean that an express restriction in another enactment will equally apply to s 2. That will only be displaced where the court considers that it was not a fundamental limitation or restriction.

13.76 Another case which found a 'comprehensive code' to exist to exclude the possibility of using the wellbeing power to fund education out of school for a child with

---

44   *R (on the application of W) v Lambeth LBC* [2002] EWCA Civ 613; *R (on the application of Theophilus) v Lewisham LBC* [2002] EWHC 1371 (Admin).

45   [2004] EWHC Civ 309; for the High Court decision see [2002] EWHC 2211 (Admin).

special needs, is *TM v Hounslow and Special Educational Needs and Disability Tribunal.*[46] However, that case could have been decided on the less restrictive basis also found in the *Enfield* case that:

'the mere fact that the power exists does not mean that the local authority is obliged to exercise it in any particular case. Indeed, one might have thought that it would be a relatively exceptional case where the power would be exercised purely for the benefit of an individual; and there is not a duty enforceable by an individual.'

13.77 The generally wide approach to s 2 was again reiterated in the High Court in *Risk Management Partners Ltd v Brent LBC and London Authorities Mutual Ltd.*[47] The judge in the High Court, Stanley Burnton LJ, accepted that 'to the extent that one can discern a legislative policy, the enactment of section 2 indicates expressly a Parliamentary intention to extend the powers of local authorities'. However, in this case the council's aim had been to reduce the costs of insurance to the council by its participation in a mutual insurance company. The High Court found that this was not authorised by s 2:[48]

'The financial well-being of a local authority is not the same as the economic, social or environmental well-being of its area. I reject the submission made that on the basis that a local authority is a "person", and is present in its area, it is a legitimate object of the well-being power. The natural reading of section 2 is that a person who is the object of the power is a person other than the local authority. I cannot read section 2 as authorising a local authority to do whatever it considers likely to promote its own economic well-being. When I consider the consequences of this contention, I conclude that they are so unreasonable that Parliament could not have intended them. If well founded, this interpretation would mean that a local authority would have the power to engage in any business (or indeed any speculation) anywhere of any kind alone or with anyone else provided it thought it would be profitable. If Parliament had intended to confer such an unlimited power, it would have done so in very different terms.'

13.78 Nevertheless, in the opinion of Stanley Burnton LJ, it may have been possible to justify the participation on a different basis, as the judge recognised:[49]

'it follows that the fact that Brent expected that its insurance would be less costly if it participated in LAML cannot, without more, justify the power under section 2'.

13.79 Until the Court of Appeal's decision in the *LAML* case, the approach to the issues in relation to the well-being power was relatively uniform and could be summarised as follows:

- The general trend in interpreting the power had been to rely on underlying purpose, as seen from the Explanatory Notes and the Guidance, rather than its precise wording.

- The case law supported the wide approach and the use of the power as one of 'first resort'.

- The case law supported the view that normally a limitation would almost always be found in an express legislative provision.

---

46   [2008] EWHC 2434 (Admin).
47   [2008] EWHC 692 (Admin).
48   Para 113.
49   Para 114.

- Nevertheless, it was important to note the, albeit rare, possibility that a limitation might arise by necessary implication, thus leaving some uncertainty.

- An express limitation or restriction in another enactment may not apply to s 2, depending on whether it is considered to be fundamental to the other scheme, thus again leaving scope for further litigation.

- While the power may, in principle, be invoked for making payments to individuals, and it is, of course, a matter for the council, the starting point of the courts is that it would be a relatively exceptional case where the power would be exercised purely for the benefit of an individual. It follows that there is not a duty enforceable by an individual in the sense of being able to force the authority to make any such payment.

- A local authority is not a 'person' for the purposes of promoting or improving its well-being under s 2, and the financial well-being of a local authority is not the same as the economic, social or environmental well-being of its area.

13.80 However, some uncertainty and confusion has resulted from the Court of Appeal's decision in the *LAML* case.[50] Not only has the Court upheld the decision of the High Court to quash the council's participation in a mutual insurance company, but it has adopted a more restrictive approach to the power in general.

13.81 Significantly, the council had not sought to argue that authority for insuring lay in s 2 and, as the court noted, the only question in relation to s 2 'is whether the power extends to obtaining insurance by the particular means of being involved in the mutual'.[51] Indeed, the Council had been advised positively that s 2 did not authorise the purchase of insurance.[52] Instead, it relied on the approach that the power to insure lay with s 111 of the 1972 Act, and to participate in the mutual under s 2 with the savings which would result from participation in the mutual being an indirect promotion of well-being in the form of additional resources available for existing or new services.

13.82 In relation to the role of the guidance and the explanatory notes, the Court attributed less importance to these than in previous cases. Reiterating the formal position that such guidance 'cannot relieve the court of its duty itself to construe legislation',[53] it was concluded not only that they are not a proper aid to interpretation but also that they did not shed any real light on the question now before the court, containing 'nothing either way which touches on the question of whether embarking on a course of action which is expected to reduce the authority's costs can of itself and, for that reason alone, be regarded as doing something that will promote or improve the well-being of its area'.[54] Indeed, Pill LJ considered that:[55]

> 'Had it been intended to apply to an arrangement such as the disputed arrangement, I would have expected the power now claimed to have been conferred either specifically or by the use of an expression other than and more directed to the subject matter than the expression "promote the well-being".'

---

[50]   [2009] EWCA Civ 490.
[51]   Para 158.
[52]   Para 186.
[53]   Hughes LJ at para 256.
[54]   Moore-Bick LJ at para 181.
[55]   Para 116.

13.83   Thus, the Court of Appeal was not willing to take a purposive approach to either the power, or the guidance, preferring a narrower and more literal approach. The court moved from supporting a wide purposive approach which regards the power as one of first resort, and sought to define the term 'well-being', albeit largely negatively.

13.84   On the positive side, for Moore-Bick LJ the power:[56]

> 'gives a local authority power to take steps that have as their object, direct or indirect, some reasonably well defined outcome which it considers will promote or improve the well-being of its area. In other words, it gives authorities the power to do things themselves, or to procure or enable others to do things, that directly affect the well-being of their areas.'

13.85   Equally, Pill LJ found that the expression is general one and that:[57]

> 'I accept that the words have, and were intended to have, a broad meaning and were intended to prevent an overtechnical approach to the definition of powers. The Government's purpose was stated in the guidance (paragraphs 5 and 6) to be to reverse the "traditionally cautious approach" to "innovation and joint action".'

13.86   Nevertheless, for Pill LJ:[58]

> 'Promotion of well-being is not an expression one would normally associate with a somewhat complex arrangement to save money, such as the LAML arrangement, rather than with action directly to promote or improve a healthy or prosperous condition. The documents specifically contemplate positive action in a variety of areas: community strategies to promote the well-being of the local community (explanatory note paragraph 13), a wide range of activities for the benefit of the local area (explanatory note paragraph 15), promotion of sustainable development by delivering the actions and improvements identified in the community strategy and action, for example, to combat climate change and to contribute to health improvement programmes (paragraph 6 of guidance).'

13.87   Similarly, for Moore-Bick LJ:

> 'In my view action to reduce the costs of goods or services purchased by the authority which does not have as its object the use of the money saved for an identified purpose which the authority considers will promote or improve well-being does not, on a natural reading of the words, fall within the section.'

13.88   Thus, at its narrowest, the case has decided that, without express justification in the section or perhaps in the guidance, schemes for cost reduction and savings will not be acceptable without a specific and identified end use which itself meets the well-being criteria. As Moore-Bick LJ put it:[59]

> 'there must obviously be some degree of connection between the authority's actions and the promotion or improvement of the area's well-being to enable the authority to conclude that the action it proposes to take is likely to have that effect.'

---

[56]   Para 180.
[57]   Para 114.
[58]   Para 115.
[59]   Para 178.

13.89 Both judges gave some further justification for their conclusions and it is those justifications which are both contentious and likely to cause uncertainty as to the future use of the power.

13.90 For Pill LJ, the section does not represent a move away from the technicality in previous decisions in relation to s 111 of the 1972 Act, but is simply an alternative to it. As he stated:[60]

> 'Clearly, section 2 of the 2000 Act was intended to create a general power and thus, in appropriate circumstances, to limit the need to rely on section 111 of the 1972 Act and the somewhat technical arguments which have arisen on that section. However in analysing the breadth of the power conferred the approach adopted to the construction of statutory powers in such cases as *Hazell* and *Waltham Forest* retains in my view a relevance.'

13.91 This lead him to a view on guarantees when he stated that powers 'which have been held not to be incidental to functions of the authority, such as giving guarantees to companies, do not readily obtain sanction by the use of a general expression, the wording of which does not easily bear upon such activities.'[61] This completely ignores the fact that s 2 replaced the previous powers for economic development, and, in particular, s 33 of the Local Government and Housing Act 1989 which expressly authorised the giving of guarantees, and before that the same was done by s 137(2B) of the 1972 Act. The intention behind s 2 was that it would replace these powers. It also ignores the fact that it was by no means clear that there was a prohibition on the giving of guarantees under s 111.[62]

13.92 In the judgment there is some confusion over whether Pill LJ was really making a finding on narrow *vires* or one of abuse of discretion akin to the fiduciary duty. While he stated that:[63]

> 'The guarantees and degree of speculation involved, in my view take the activity proposed beyond what Parliament intended by the well-being clause. It did not require a specific exclusion to place beyond the section 2 power the enterprise proposed.'

13.93 He also emphasised the degree of speculation suggesting that it was a matter of degree rather than of kind:[64]

> 'Of course, the risks involved may be lessened by the employment of professional agents and the reinsurance they may suggest but the substantial speculative element cannot be ignored. Any enterprise by a local authority involves risks but the local authority becoming insurer for itself and other authorities over a wide area of activity is of a different order.'

13.94 Equally, it is unclear whether the objection was the degree of speculation or whether he was finding that the mechanism was simply not insurance at all and so not implementing the power under s 111:[65]

---

[60] Para 117.
[61] Para 117.
[62] See discussion at Ch 9 of *Law relating to Local Government* by Crawford, Sauvain, Coulson and Clarke, DETR 2000.
[63] Para 119.
[64] Para 120.
[65] Para 121.

'The present venture is not, however, merely a different way of obtaining insurance; it is a venture to set up an insurance company of which the local authority is a member and by which insurance is obtained not only for itself but for other local authorities.'

13.95 Moore-Bick LJ was influenced by s 3(2):[66]

'The fact that a local authority cannot use its powers under section 2(1) to raise money suggests two things: first, that any action taken under section 2(1) must be financed out of authority's existing resources; second, that taking steps to improve the authority's general financial position is not to be treated as something that will of itself promote or improve the well-being of its area.'

13.96 However, both of these reasons are by no means clear. In relation to the first, the guidance makes clear that the power was intended to be used together with the power to charge up to full cost recovery. Thus a council can recover the costs and not meet them from its own resources. It may well be argued that reducing costs is similar, ie it generates extra resources to achieve the identified well-being. In relation to the second, it could equally be argued that although taking steps to improve the authority's general financial position would of itself promote or improve the well-being of its area, it was expressly prohibited in order to avoid extra taxation and to encourage the sort of costs savings the council was attempting.

13.97 Thus, while it can be stated with confidence that the use of s 2 must always identify with sufficient precision the well-being to be achieved, and simply making savings is not sufficient to meet that requirement, it is less clear whether later courts will follow the more restrictive dicta and reasoning of the Court of Appeal. An appeal was heard in the Supreme Court in December 2010 and judgment was awaited when this chapter went to press. In the meantime, the substantive issue has been resolved by s 34 of the Local Democracy, Economic Development and Construction Act 2009 which authorises mutual insurance schemes. The Coalition Government has also sought to introduce a general power of competence in the Localism Bill introduced to Parliament in December 2010, although how far that will alter judicial attitudes to a wide discretionary power remains to be seen.

Multifunctional government and judicial review

13.98 As noted above, unlike many bodies delivering public services or regulating activity, local and central government are multifunctional, and not single issue, bodies. It has been a common criticism of local government, and to a lesser extent central government, that it is seen, and has acted, as a series of separate functions or 'silos', rather than taking a coordinated approach to problems and issues, such as in the area of health where medical, social, educational, environmental, financial and other issues impinge.

13.99 Although much of this criticism can be attributed to the culture in public administration and financial structures, the legal framework has sometimes been seen as a problem in local government. While it allowed for consultation and coordination, each action had to be justified in terms of the purposes of, and considerations relevant to, the particular statutory power being exercised. This, it was said, resulted in a situation where a great amount of time and effort went in to trying to finding a range of powers to use to achieve policies which were otherwise sensible and worthwhile. At worst this could

---

[66] Para 179.

result in an inability to undertake the activity, or it would deter more cautious authorities, and even for the more confident authorities it was at the very least considered to be waste of resources. This legal framework was seen as reinforcing the 'silo mentality' and inhibiting proper community leadership and the most effective use of resources.

13.100   This lack of integration and coordination of powers in local government was intended to be addressed by the well-being power. Given that the purposes for which it can be used are so broad, and that a diverse range of considerations may be taken into account, depending on the particular purpose for which it being exercised, much of the perceived legal barrier to effective community leadership has been removed.

13.101   While this is a step in the right direction, as shown above, the power is not without its uncertainties even in terms of narrow *vires*. In addition, it is subject to the wider principles of review.

13.102   In that respect, comparison can be drawn with the prerogative and other non-statutory powers exercised by central government. While these are not, and never were intended to be wide powers akin to general competence, they are wide discretionary powers which operate where there are no specific statutory powers, and give necessary flexibility to government and administration. As seen from *R (on the application of Bancoult) v Secretary of Stare for Foreign and Commonwealth Affairs (No 2),*[67] these are reviewable in the same way as other administrative actions by the executive, on the grounds of legality, rationality and procedural propriety. However, while the courts have made clear that due weight will be given to the Government's role as primary decision-maker, it remains to be seen the extent to which the courts will respect local government's role as community leader.

DEMOCRATIC ISSUES

Political considerations

13.103   The issue of political considerations in decision-making as a general principle has been dealt with elsewhere in this work.[68] The remainder of this section deals with other aspects of the relevant legal principles which impinge on the making of political decisions.

Fiduciary duty

13.104   There are of course a number of principles which the courts apply to the exercise of discretion by public bodies. However, there is one controversial principle which the courts have applied to local authorities, namely the fiduciary duty.

13.105   A 'fiduciary duty' applies to any person acting as trustee for the benefit of another person. However, it is less clear that an analogous principle should be applied to a body which is elected, in order to give priority to the interests of taxpayers over those of electors. Indeed, critics of the principle point to the fact that it has not been applied

---

[67]   [2008] UKHL 61.
[68]   See Chapter 1, paras **1.29–1.38** and Chapter 5, para **5.104** *Persimmon Homes (Teesside) Ltd v R (on the application of Lewis)* 2008 EWCA Civ 746 – for a specific example of the role of political considerations ain the planning context.

to central government where the courts pay more respect to the democratic nature of the institution. It is also pointed out that most of local government funding comes from central taxation and non-domestic rates over which local government has no control.

13.106 Nevertheless, it is clear that the courts do invoke this concept and local authorities are under a special duty to consider the interests of local taxpayers. However the stringency with which the principle is applied remains a matter of debate for two reasons.

13.107 First, the cases in which it has been invoked can be seen as politically controversial. Thus, in *Roberts v Hopwood*,[69] the House of Lords reversed the Court of Appeal, which had deferred to the views of elected representatives, and found unlawful the council's decision, under its power to pay such wages as it 'may think fit', to pay a minimum wage of £4 per week to all employees, both men and women, when this was above market rates for male labourers. The case is often remembered for comments such as those of Lord Atkinson who found that:

> 'The council would, in my view, fail in their duty if, in administering funds which did not belong to their members alone, they put aside all these aids to the ascertainment of what was just and reasonable remuneration to give for the services rendered to them, and allowed themselves to be guided in preference by some eccentric principles of socialistic philanthropy, or by a feminist ambition to secure the equality of the sexes in the matter of wages in the world of labour.'

13.108 Many commentators took the view not only that this case was out of step with legitimate political thinking, but that it also exceeded the proper limits of judicial review.[70] Following the *Wednesbury* case in 1948,[71] many considered that *Roberts v Hopwood* and the fiduciary duty was to be considered an aberration.

13.109 Nevertheless, the duty formed the basis of the decision in *Prescott v Birmingham Corporation*.[72] There, the council had exercised its power to charge 'such fares as they may think fit' to introduce a scheme for free travel for old people on its public transport. Invoking *Roberts v Hopwood*, the Court of Appeal quashed the decision, Jenkins LJ stating:

> 'Local authorities are not, of course, trustees for their ratepayers, but they do, we think, owe an analogous fiduciary duty to their ratepayers in relation to the application of funds contributed by the latter. Thus local authorities running an omnibus undertaking at the risk of their ratepayers, in the sense that any deficiencies must be met by an addition to the rates, are not, in our view, entitled, merely on the strength of a general power, to charge different fares to different passengers or classes of passengers, to make a gift to a particular class of persons of rights of free travel on their vehicles simply because the local authority concerned are of opinion that the favoured class of persons ought, on benevolent or philanthropic grounds, to be accorded that benefit.'

---

69 [1925] AC 578.
70 See SA de Smith, *Judicial Review of Administrative Action,* 3rd edn, 1973 p 309.
71 *Associated Provincial Picture Houses v Wednesbury Corporation* [1948] 1 KB 223.
72 1955] 1 Ch 210.

13.110   However, it may be thought that this was again out of touch with legitimate political thinking, evidenced by the fact that Parliament validated existing concessions by means of a 1955 Act and finally gave general powers to make such concessions in 1964.[73]

13.111   However, that the adoption of the principle was again not a mere aberration is seen from another political controversial case, *Bromley LBC v Greater London Council*.[74] The case concerned a challenge to supplementary rate levied by the GLC to finance its 'Fares Fair' policy whereby there would be a 25 per cent cut in bus and underground fares in order to reverse the decline in use of public transport and reduce the volume of car traffic. The speeches of the House of Lords adopted such different reasoning that it is impossible to discern a *ratio*, but the majority invoked both the *Roberts v Hopwood* and *Prescott* cases, and the fiduciary duty.

13.112   Again, this decision, while very controversial when it was made and alleged to be out of touch with legitimate political thinking in transport policy, did not ultimately result in frustrating that policy with subsequent cases accepting that fares could be subsidised from the rates.[75]

13.113   The three main cases cited as authority for the doctrine are not only concerned with very controversial subject matter, but the application of the principle by the courts can be seen to be too close a judgment on the merits to be acceptable. That in itself indicates that while the fiduciary principle remains relevant, it is likely to be invoked only exceptionally.

13.114   The second reason for doubting the stringency with which the principle will be applied lies in the fact that, from a strict legal perspective, the cases in which it has been invoked can also be classified as the application of other principles. As noted above, in the *Bromley* case various lines of reasoning were put forward in the five speeches, so that it is possible to conclude that the case turned on the interpretation of the precise statutory power, or that it related to the process of decision-making and slavish adherence to a manifesto commitment. That it was not based on absolute inability to lower the fares and subsidise the operation from general taxation is seen from the subsequent case of *R v London Transport Executive, ex p Greater London Council*.[76]

13.115   Similarly, *Roberts v Hopwood* can be interpreted as narrow illegality or a purposes case in that the payments were not wages but included a 'gift' element, and the purpose was not one of proper remuneration for the task undertaken. Indeed, this view was adopted by Forbes J in *Pickwell v Camden London Borough Council*,[77] where he stated that:

> 'The case seems to me to decide no more than this, that where the inevitable inference which must be drawn is that an obviously excessive wage payment was agreed to be paid without any regard to any commercial consideration and solely on some extraneous principle, as, for instance, philanthropy, such a payment can only be regarded as a gift and is not covered by a statutory power to pay reasonable wages. Looking back as we do, over sixty years of

---

[73]   Public Service Vehicles (Travel Concessions) Act 1955; Travel Concessions Act 1964.
[74]   [1982] 1 AC 768.
[75]   *R v Merseyside County Council, ex p Great Universal Stores* (1982) 80 LGR 639; *R v London Transport Executive, ex p Greater London Council* [1983] QB 484.
[76]   [1983] QB 484.
[77]   [1983] QB 962.

progress in the field of social reform and industrial relations some of their Lordships' observations may, with the benefit of this hindsight, appear unsympathetic. But what has changed over those years is our attitudes to what should be regarded as pure philanthropy; the basic legal principle, that a payment is illegal which cannot be justified by reference to the objects for which a statutory power is granted, still remains.'

13.116 Equally, *Prescott* can be interpreted as the making of an unauthorised gift to a specified class of persons.

13.117 On this basis, the fiduciary principle can be interpreted as an aid to construction of any particular power and its particular application to a given situation, rather than as a freestanding principle to allow the courts to quash decisions. This approach was adopted in *Pickwell* where Ormrod LJ stated that the *Bromley* case affirmed that the fiduciary duty was a relevant factor to be taken into account in determining the scope and use of the statutory powers:

'However, it would not be right to regard this case as authority for the general proposition that this fiduciary duty opens up a route by which the courts can investigate, and if thought appropriate, interfere with any exercise of their discretionary powers by local authorities. This would completely undermine the principle of the *Wednesbury* case ....'

13.118 Nevertheless it is clear from the cases that, as was stated in *Taylor v Munrow* by Lord Parker CJ:[78]

'the council must preserve a balance between the duty owed to that general body of ratepayers and the duty owed to [others]'.

13.119 At the very least it must show that this balancing exercise has been carried out when considering the financial implications of any decision. It is also clear that a proper audit trail, showing the balancing exercise, must be provided. In *R v Hackney LBC, ex p Structadene Ltd*,[79] in quashing a decision to dispose of land, Elias J noted:

'As I have already indicated, the council has not provided any proper explanation why it took the decision which it did. Prima facie I consider that the applicant has made out its claim that the council acted in breach of its fiduciary duty and there is no evidence which effectively counters that allegation. I accept that in an appropriate case it is possible for a council successfully to contend that there are social or other benefits to the local community which outweigh the loss resulting from the failure to obtain the best price. The interests of the local taxpayers are not decisive but must be taken into account; see *Bromley London Borough Council v Greater London Council*. However, in the absence of any indication of what these advantages were perceived to be, I cannot speculate whether they existed or not. In general, however, in the absence of some such benefit, it will be a breach of the fiduciary duty if the council fails to obtain the best price for the local taxpayers: see the *Bromley* case per Lord Diplock, at p 829H. I therefore hold that the council is in breach of that duty.

For essentially the same reason I am compelled to find that it acted *Wednesbury* unreasonably. A rational council would not have rejected an offer which was £100,000 more favourable than the offer which it in fact accepted, in the absence at least of cogent countervailing considerations. The evidence does not enable me to say what the relevant factors are which could render the decision a rational one.'

78 [1960] 1 WLR 151.
79 [2001] LGR 204.

13.120　Although couched in terms of the fiduciary duty, the underlying reasoning in that case equates a breach of it with irrationality. Nevertheless, it is not yet the case that the courts fully accept that the principle does not permit a substitution of its view as to the weight to be attached to the financial interests of taxpayers. In *Regina (Molinaro) v Kensington and Chelsea Royal London Borough Council*,[80] Elias J suggested that this was indeed possible:

> '39. There is no doubt that the council does have a fiduciary duty to its ratepayers. There are numerous authorities to that effect, many of which were considered in the case of *Bromley London Borough Council v Greater London Council*.
>
> 40. The imposition of the fiduciary duty does not, however, mean that financial considerations must outweigh all others. It is a matter of balancing competing interests. But the doctrine of fiduciary duties can sometimes be used to enable the court to consider the weight afforded to the relevant factors, and to ensure that the fiduciary obligation is given proper significance.'

13.121　However, the implication of the last sentence is qualified. He went on to state that:

> '43. Where the effect is as limited, as in the decision under consideration, then in my view the doctrine is not in truth engaged in any significant way. Of course, the council must still have regard to the financial consequences of its actions and it must weigh them in the balance with other relevant considerations, but the effect on local taxpayers of this decision, viewed against the council's finances as a whole, is very minimal.'

13.122　Indeed it may be that the *obiter* sentence will be ignored in the future. In that case Elias J also stated that:

> 'I accept Mr Birks' submission that in a case of this kind the fiduciary duty does not really add anything to the doctrine of irrationality. Of course, if there are no countervailing benefits to offset the loss of rent, then it can be said that the decision was a breach of fiduciary duty but, equally, it will be irrational. That will be, however, an exceptional case (see, for an example, *R (Structadene Ltd) v Hackney London Borough Council*). But once it is shown that the financial consequences were drawn directly to the attention of the members, as well as other countervailing considerations, the court can only interfere with the decision if it was one which no reasonable council could make.'

13.123　In short, the fiduciary principle remains an important symbol in the law relating to local government, and also an active part of the language in which challenges can be framed. Local authorities must ensure that due consideration is given to this factor. Nevertheless, in terms of strict legal analysis it is not a factor which should given priority over other relevant considerations and it is for the local authority to determine where the balance lies between these considerations, subject to a residual test of rationality.

Interests and probity

13.124　The principles of natural justice are considered elsewhere in this book,[81] and the issues of bias, predetermination and predilection are clearly relevant to the operation of democracy.

---

[80]　[2002] LGR 336.
[81]　See Chapter 1, paras **1.48**–**1.51**.

13.125 This section does not seek to repeat that material but simply highlights, within local government, that these issues are not only dealt with by the courts but also by the enforcement of a statutory code of conduct. This has proved to be a very controversial area of law, and it is currently the subject of proposed substantial amendment by means of the Localism Bill, introduced to Parliament in December 2010. However, the remainder of this section explains the law and its development, as at January 2011.

13.126 Every councillor must agree to abide by the Code upon taking office. There have been other Codes of Conduct. Conduct generally including non-pecuniary interests, was dealt with under the National Code of Local Government Conduct, first issued on a non-statutory basis following a recommendation of the Redcliffe-Maud Royal Commission.[82] The Widdicombe Committee's recommendation that the Code should be given statutory status,[83] and that new councillors in their declaration of acceptance of office should undertake to be guided by it in the performance of their functions, was implemented by s 31 of the Local Government and Housing Act 1989. Enforcement at that stage was by the Local Government Ombudsman.

13.127 The existing arrangements were strongly criticised by the Nolan Committee on Standards in Public Life,[84] which concluded that a radical change in the ethical framework was needed. It proposed a code of conduct for councillors developed by each individual council within a general framework approved by Parliament; the establishment by each council of a Standards Committee with powers to recommend the discipline of errant members; the creation of new Local Government Tribunals to act as independent arbiters on matters relating to codes of conduct and to hear appeals; and the involvement of the courts in imposing penalties for misconduct to replace surcharge.

13.128 The general principle of reform identified by Nolan was accepted, but the resulting statutory scheme under Part III of the Local Government Act 2000 was more centralised with a prescriptive and detailed code, all elements of which were mandatory for each local authority to adopt. Every authority had also to establish a standards committee to promote and maintain high standards of conduct within the authority and to monitor the operation of the code, but alleged breaches of codes of conduct by members were to be investigated by a newly created Standards Board for England (now Standards for England) or the Commissioner for Local Administration in Wales. Provision was made for appeals to a new body, the Adjudication Panel.

13.129 Members of the Adjudication Panel for Wales are appointed by the National Assembly. In England, from January 2010 the Adjudication Panel for England became the First-tier Tribunal (Local Government Standards in England) as part of the General Regulatory Chamber. A person who is brought before a case tribunal may be represented by counsel, a solicitor, or any other person they would like to represent them.

13.130 While this basic structure remains, there has been a move towards the original intention of Nolan. By the Local Government and Public Involvement in Health Act 2007, provision is made for more local determination of complaints.

---

[82]   Cmnd. 5636, 1974.
[83]   Committee on the Conduct of Local Authority Business, Cmnd. 9797, 1986.
[84]   Third Report on Standards of Conduct in Local Government in England, Scotland and Wales, Cm 2702–I, 1997.

13.131   The precise details of the Codes are beyond the scope of this work, and they include a requirement to comply with principles wider than those applied by the courts, such as treating others with respect, not bullying, and not bringing the office or authority into disrepute.[85] However, some of the principles, particularly those relating to interests overlap with those applied by the courts and are defined in detail in the Codes.

13.132   This system raises two main issues for judicial review. First, whether and to what extent the decisions taken under the Code are amenable to judicial review. Secondly, what relationship the principles under the Code have to those applied by the courts.

13.133   While it is beyond the scope of this work to analyse the judicial interpretations of the Code and the proper approach to the sanctions which can be imposed, it is clear not only that the court will interfere where appropriate,[86] but also that a different approach is taken depending on whether the challenge is by means of judicial review or on appeal from a case tribunal under s 79(15) of the 2000 Act.[87]

13.134   The relationship of the principles under the Code with those applied by the courts was a matter which concerned the Nolan Committee. The Committee recommended that the test which should apply in the Codes should be that of the common law.[88] However, in *R v Local Commissioner for Administration for North and North-East England, ex p Liverpool City Council*,[89] the Court of Appeal took the view that under the old Code the Ombudsman had been perfectly entitled to apply the test laid down in the Code rather than the test laid down in the common law. More recently in *Scrivens v Ethical Standards Officer*,[90] in rejecting one possible interpretation of the Code, Stanley Burnton J noted that it would provide an inconsistency with the law on bias and 'That is a consequence to be avoided'.

Relationship with officers

13.135   Much of public administration is carried on by professional administrators. Policy may of course be set by politicians, whether by Parliament, ministers or councillors, but the detailed administration is left to unelected officials in public bodies of various types. However, central and local government differs in that politicians often take administrative decisions themselves or together with officials.

13.136   The relationship between the elected and non-elected decision-maker raises two particular issues.

13.137   First, the extent to which officers should be perceived as or should operate as a check on elected politicians.

---

[85]   For the current Codes see the Local Authorities (Model Code of Conduct) Order 2007, SI 2007/1159 and Local Authorities (Model Code of Conduct) (Wales) Order 2008, SI 2008/788.
[86]   *Livingstone v Adjudication Panel for England* [2006] EWHC 2533 Admin; *Sanders v Kingston* [2005] EWHC 1145 (Admin).
[87]   *R (on the application of Mullaney) v Adjudication Panel for England* [2009] EWHC 72 (Admin), at 72 and 73.
[88]   Third Report on Standards of Conduct in Local Government in England, Scotland and Wales, Cm 2702–I, 1997, para 111.
[89]   [2001] 1 All ER 462.
[90]   [2005] EWHC 124 (Admin).

13.138　In central government, despite various debates over whether civil servants owe their loyalty to the minister or the wider public or Parliament,[91] the matter is not regulated by statute or the courts but by prerogative powers and codes of practice.

13.139　In local government, while local authority is given power to appoint 'such officers as they think necessary for the proper discharge by the authority of such of their or another authority's functions as fall to be discharged by them',[92] various restrictions and checks are placed on the council and the ability to appoint political or politicised officers. Together with particular rules relating to the appointment and dismissal of chief officers, and limiting political activity by senior officers, the requirement to appoint specified officers seeks to ensure that the administration of local authority functions achieves a balance of political and professional expertise.

13.140　One aspect of this is that certain officers are charged with a duty to raise issues which could form the basis of a challenge by judicial review or other court action. For example, every local authority must appoint a monitoring officer who must, if it at any time appears to him that any proposal, decision or omission by the authority has given rise to or is likely to or would give rise to a contravention of any enactment or rule of law, prepare a report to the authority with respect to that proposal, decision or omission.[93] The authority is under a duty to provide that officer with such staff, accommodation and other resources as are, in his opinion, sufficient to allow those duties to be performed. Similarly, an authority must appoint a chief finance officer who shall make a report if it appears to him that the authority has made or is about to make a decision which involves or would involve the authority incurring expenditure which is unlawful; has taken or is about to take a course of action which, if pursued to its conclusion, would be unlawful and likely to cause a loss or deficiency on the part of the authority; or is about to enter an item of account the entry of which is unlawful.[94]

13.141　The second main issue about the relationship between the elected and non-elected decision-maker, concerns the extent to which it is legitimate for ministers or elected decision-makers in whom powers are formally vested to allow others to take decisions in their name.

13.142　The starting point is the principle that the exercise of discretion cannot be fettered by unauthorised delegation.[95] However, in practice powers are often conferred on ministers or other named office holders and the realities of administration means that decisions are taken by officers within those departments or organisations, and the basic principle must accommodate that reality while seeking to uphold the underlying principle of ensuring that discretionary power is exercised properly.

13.143　In relation to central government, where powers are vested in a minister it is often suggested that exercise by an official is as an alter ego of the department and power is devolved rather than delegated.[96] As Lord Greene MR pointed out in *Carltona Ltd v Commissioner of Works*:[97]

---

[91]　See e g the issues surrounding *R v Ponting* [1985] CLR 318.

[92]　Local Government Act 1972, s 112.

[93]　Local Government and Housing Act 1989, s 5.

[94]　Local Government Finance Act 1988, ss 112–114.

[95]　See Chapter 1, para **1.18**.

[96]　*R v Secretary of State, ex p Oladehinde* [1991] 1 AC 254.

[97]　[1943] 2 All ER 560.

'In the administration of government in this country the functions which are given to ministers ... are functions so multifarious that no minister could ever attend to them. To take the example of the present case no doubt there have been thousands of requisitions in this country by individual ministries. It cannot be supposed that this regulation meant that, in each case, the minister in person should direct his mind to the matter. The duties imposed on ministers and the powers given to ministers are normally exercised under the authority of the ministers by responsible officials of the department. Public business could not be carried on if that were not the case. Constitutionally, a decision of such an official is, of course, the decision of the minister. The minister is responsible. It is he who must answer before Parliament for anything that his officials have done under his authority, and, if for an important matter he selected an official of such junior standing that he could not be expected competently to perform the work, the minister would have to answer to Parliament.'

13.144   Although that approach stressed the role of Parliament in scrutiny of the appropriateness of the official chosen to decide, it is now clear that courts will examine the suitability of the official on the basis of *Wednesbury* unreasonableness.[98]

13.145   It has been less clear that the *Carltona* principle applies to local government or other public bodies.

13.146   In *Nelms v Roe*, the extension of the *Carltona* principle to other bodies appeared to be rejected by Lord Parker CJ:

'I feel grave difficulties in extending that well-known principle to a case such as this, to the Commissioner of the Metropolitan Police. It is not, I think sufficient to say that it is a principle which it applicable when ever it is difficult or impractical for a person to act for himself, in other words when ever he has to act through others the principle applies. I see grave difficulties in going that far, and, as it seems to me, superintendent Williams was, by reason of his position, not the alter ego of the Commissioner but merely had implied[99] delegated authority, by reason of his position, from the Commissioner.'

13.147   However, clarity has been given by Sedley LJ in *R (on the application of Chief Constable of the West Midlands) v Birmingham Justices*, who considered that:[100]

'9. Although the *Carltona* case is frequently cited as a source of the "alter ego" doctrine, it can be seen that Lord Greene's reasoning is not predicated on this. It is predicated on the proposition that the departmental head is responsible for things done under his authority. The relevance of the alter ego doctrine is that Crown servants were at that time taken in law to hold their positions by grace and not by contract, so that the minister was first among equals, not an employer with servants or a principal with agents. His implied power to delegate functions depended, therefore, on two things: the conferment of a power in terms which implicitly permitted their delegation and the existence of persons to whom he could delegate them without parting with ultimate responsibility.'

13.148   He also considered the reasoning in *Nelms v Roe* and concluded:

'12. With all possible respect, I do not consider that we are required to adopt this reasoning. As has been seen, the *Carltona* principle, which binds this court, does not depend upon the peculiar status of civil servants as the alter ego of their minister. It is sufficiently ample to allow a Chief Constable to discharge functions of the kind we are concerned with through

---

[98]   *R (on the application of Chief Constable of the West Midlands) v Birmingham Justices* [2002] EWHC 1087.
[99]   [1970] 1 WLR 4.
[100]   [2002] EWHC 1087.

an officer for whom he or she is answerable. To fall back instead on implied delegation and sub-delegation is capable of appearing to be a ratification by the court of an accomplished fact and to beg the question of power to delegate.'

13.149 However, to meet the criticism that this opened the principle too widely, Sedley LJ pointed out that there are other functions imposed upon individuals by virtue of their office which may not be delegable at all, for example the function of a health and safety inspector and he concluded:

> '14. For my part I can see good reason to differentiate, where Parliament has conferred powers on the holder of a named office, between those offices which are the apex of an organisation itself composed of office-holders or otherwise hierarchically structured, and those offices designated by Parliament because of the personal qualifications of the individual holder. Thus, … one can readily infer that when Parliament confers functions on a chief officer of police, all but the most important are likely to be delegable; whereas the likelihood is that powers conferred on a medical officer of health or on a statutory inspector, each professionally qualified as an individual, are to be exercised by the office-holder alone. This, with respect, seems to me a better legal test than overriding administrative convenience, although it may produce similar outcomes.'

13.150 Thus, provided the power does not require the exercise of a particular professional expertise, it can be delegated, subject to the residual test that the person chosen is not an irrational choice.

Role of standing orders

13.151 As explained previously,[101] all public authorities are required to comply not only with statutory procedural requirements but also with the procedural principles laid down by the common law. As also explained, while a breach of a procedural requirement may make the decision of no legal consequence, it does not always result in the decision being invalid. Much will depend on the importance of the requirement and the context of the breach.

13.152 These principles will apply to any decision-making process. For local authorities, however, there are also rules contained in the standing orders adopted by the authority. Not only does the local authority have power to make, vary and revoke standing orders to regulate its proceedings and business,[102] but power is given to the Secretary of State to require standing orders to contain particular provisions.[103] While a standing order is subordinate to any statutory requirement, the common law rules will apply only where there is no statutory or standing order requirement in relation to the issue.

13.153 A breach of a standing order is generally treated in the same way as any other procedural requirement and it may result in the decision having no legal effect. One exception to this is in relation to contracts. Authorities are required to make standing orders in respect of contractual matters.[104] However, protection is given to those contracting with the authority since breach of the orders does not invalidate any

---

[101] See Chapter 1, para **1.28**.
[102] Local Government Act 1972, Sch12, para 42.
[103] Local Government and Housing Act 1989, s 20, and see Local Authorities (Standing Orders) Regulations 1993, SI 1993/202; Local Authorities (Standing Orders) (England) Regulations 2001, SI 2001/3384; Local Authorities (Standing Orders) (Wales) Regulations 2006, SI 2006/1275 (W 121).
[104] Local Government Act 1972, s 135(1) to (3).

contract, and they are not bound to inquire whether the standing orders have been complied with.[105] However, this provision does not apply to contracts which are otherwise *ultra vires*.[106]

13.154 Since standing orders are not themselves statutory but are made under statutory powers, they can in turn be subject to judicial review and can be quashed by a court. In *R v Flintshire CC, ex p Armstrong-Braun*,[107] a standing order preventing a councillor from placing a matter on the agenda, unless seconded by another council member, was quashed by the Court of Appeal.

13.155 As Schiemann LJ put it, the Court was concerned with:[108]

> 'the legal validity of a Standing Order made by the Flintshire County Council which prevents any councillor from putting a matter on the agenda for discussion unless he has the support of at least one other councillor. There is thus demonstrated in this case a tension between two desirable and understandable aims. It is desirable that a councillor should be able to raise matters of concern to him or his electors, and that he should be able to do so in a public forum which the public can attend, and of whose deliberations there is a public record. On the other hand it is desirable that a council, which has a vast amount of business to transact, should be able to get through its business with reasonable dispatch, otherwise the quality of persons who are prepared to give their time will, quite possibly decline because too much time will in their estimation, be spent on matters of no intrinsic interest.'

13.156 The Court's approach was that this standing order fell within the meaning of regulating the proceedings or business of the council, within the meaning of the Local Government Act 1972, but that it could be quashed if it fell outside the policy and objects of the act or was otherwise legally objectionable. In that regard, it had been argued that the loss to democracy caused by such a Standing Order was inevitably great and disproportionate to any gain in administrative efficiency. For the Council, it was pointed out that there was no right conferred on councillors by statute to have any matter considered. Schiemann LJ refused to conclude that the standing order was or was not contrary to the policy and objects of the 1972 Act construed as a whole. He identified arguments both ways and indicated that had he been required to do so he may have decided it in the claimant's favour. However, he concluded that it was unnecessary to decide whether or not such a standing order can ever be lawfully adopted because the 'same reasons as make it arguable that the adoption of such a Standing Order is, in principle, unlawful, indicate that before adopting such a Standing Order the matter should be given most anxious consideration'.[109] The Council quite simply had not considered where the correct balance lay. The procedure for making the change to the standing order was a procedure which was so imperfect that it ought to be quashed, without prejudice to it being introduced in an identical form in the future.

13.157 For Sedley LJ, the issue that he 'found by far the hardest' was whether the new standing order fell outside what council can lawfully do to regulate its proceedings and business.[110] He noted that Schiemann LJ set out a powerful case for concluding that it does and that the Council had not sufficiently addressed the question of whether this

---

[105] Local Government Act 1972, s 135(4).
[106] *North West Leicestershire DC v East Midlands Housing Association* [1981] 1 WLR 1396, but see also the Local Government Contracts Act 1997.
[107] [2001] EWCA Civ 345; [2001] LGR 344.
[108] Para 4.
[109] Para 37.
[110] Para 55.

hurdle should be placed in the path of a councilor. He noted the series of good reasons why it may unjustifiably silence an elected member. He also noted that 'the lone voice, though necessarily a nuisance to the majority, plays an important part in a democracy'.[111]

13.158 However, 'and not without hesitation', he accepted the Council's submission that there may be grounds on which a rule such as the standing order can be adopted without violating these broader principles. Nevertheless he found that whether reasons are sufficient to justify a change of that kind in the standing order is a question for the members of the council, voting after careful consideration of the full range of relevant issues and of those alone. He concluded:[112]

> 'What seems to me clear beyond a peradventure is that in this case nobody, neither the members nor the officers, even appreciated the potential damage to local democracy, much less weighed it against the reasons, such as they were, for introducing the new Standing Order. ... His own submissions have demonstrated the exact contrary: a failure on the part of his client authority to perceive, much less to evaluate, the democratic damage capable of being done by the rule-change. As the history set out by Schiemann LJ demonstrates, the exercise was apparently treated simply as one administrative tidying up and went through on the nod. The queries about whether it was ultra vires were more or less brushed aside. The answer, had it been seriously looked into, might not have been that the new Standing Order 8 was in itself ultra vires – though as Schiemann LJ's judgment has demonstrated that is an entirely tenable view – but it would certainly have been that there was far more than administrative convenience at issue.'

13.159 In relation to whether it would be possible to come to the same conclusion after proper consideration he stated:[113]

> 'For my part, I would hold that if any proposal to resurrect Standing Order 8 either in its present form or in some related form is placed before the council or its Policy Committee, it cannot lawfully be entertained, much less be adopted, without consideration by members of objective advice on, as a minimum, the following. First, the legal and constitutional purposes of the Local Government Act 1972 and the related legislation. In the light of what has happened so far, there is no reason, in my judgment, to assume that such advice is unnecessary. Second, the difference in substantive effect between the model Standing Orders (or the existing ones) and the proposed Standing Order 8. It is now clear that this cannot possibly be dismissed either as insignificant or as too obvious to require examination. Third, the obligation of members collectively to regulate the proceedings and business of the council without regard to party or other advantage and in the sole interests of an efficient representative local democracy.'

and he added:[114]

> 'Although it does not arise at the moment for decision, it may well be that this needs to be regarded in law as a question of proportionality: is the proposed measure, having regard to its restrictive effect on the functioning of individual elected representatives, one which is necessary, in a democratic society to achieve the efficient functioning of the county council? In answering such a question, it will be appropriate, among many other things, to consider what net gain in council efficiency is likely to be achieved if the Standing Order is changed in this or some similar way. If the answer is little if any, that should be an end of it. If some

---

[111] Para 57.
[112] Para 58.
[113] Para 59.
[114] Para 60.

appreciable administrative or procedural gain is perceived, it must be set with great care against the contra-indicators touched on in the judgments in this court.'

13.160   A clear warning has, therefore, been given to local authorities that standing orders must pay proper regard to the furthering of democracy and not err on the side of administrative efficiency.

THE FUTURE

13.161   It is trite to say that the future is uncertain. Flexible principles of judicial review are inevitably subject to development and, as seen above, judicial interventionism ebbs and flows. In addition, a new Government will be expected to undertake reforms to the decision-making process to further its policy aims. The Coalition Government has already laid down markers for legislative change which will impact on issues covered in this chapter. Indeed, it has said that 'Localism is a key theme that runs through elect*ion* *m*anifestos as well as the recently published coalition agreement'.

13.162   As noted above, the appeal against the decision of the Court of Appeal in the *LAML* case was heard by the Supreme Court in December 2010. The previous Government sought to resolve the substantive issue by s 34 of the Local Democracy, Economic Development and Construction Act 2009, which authorises mutual insurance schemes. While the present Government has welcomed that, it has expressed the view that this has not addressed the underlying issue. To deal with this, the Queen's Speech noted that the forthcoming Decentralisation and Localism Bill includes a commitment to 'give councils a general power of competence'. The Localism Bill introduced in December 2010 seeks to establish this. If it works, it will shift the emphasis from issues of narrow *vires* to the application of the broader principles of review such as the fiduciary duty, but one of the main issues will be the extent to which the granting of such a power will alter judicial attitudes as reflected in the restrictive interpretations of s 111 of the 1972 Act and in the *LAML* case. The Queens Speech also noted that one of the 'main elements' of the Localism Bill would be proposals to 'Abolish the Standards Board regime'. The Bill seeks to leave most standards issues to the individual local authority. The proposal has not met with approval from Standards for England, which expressed disappointment and stated that:

> 'Since 2007, Standards for England has dealt only with those matters which local authorities could not deal with themselves. Our recent review of this devolved local framework found that it is delivering increased confidence in the accountability of local politicians, improved member behaviour and contributing to better governance.'

Any new system must be measured against these aims.

Chapter 14

IMMIGRATION LAW

INTRODUCTION

14.1   Immigration and asylum claims make up a significant proportion of the total claims which come before the Administrative court. Administrative court figures for 2009[1] show that two thirds of applications for permission to apply for judicial review were immigration or asylum cases. By far the majority of decided applications for permission for the above period were rejected – by a ratio of roughly 7 to 1. However, the courts have recognised that judicial review plays an essential supervisory role in seeking to ensure minimum standards of fairness and consistency in what are often highly contentious and politically sensitive decisions.[2]

14.2   Immigration and nationality law moves swiftly and is found in a complex constellation of sources: statutory, rules,[3] published and unpublished policy, case authority, Country Guidance decisions of the Immigration & Asylum Chamber of the Upper Tribunal and its predecessors and an increasingly important European dimension. Asylum lawyers also need to be familiar with a range of source material relating to country conditions. A short list of useful websites is given at the end of this chapter.

14.3   This chapter looks firstly at the scope for judicial review in the immigration, asylum and nationality context, secondly at a number of specific procedural concerns and thirdly summarises the impact of some key authorities on procedure. A final short section reviews the key principles affecting some frequently occurring substantive issues.

WHO IS THE PROPOSED DEFENDANT?

14.4   Immigration practitioners are likely to be concerned with decisions made by the following public authorities:

- the Secretary of State for the Home Department or Home Secretary, the Minister of State responsible for making immigration decisions;

- an Immigration Officer, who may be exercising her own discretion as provided by statute, or acting under the direction of the Secretary of State;

- an Entry Clearance Officer, based in posts outside the United Kingdom;

---

[1]   Judicial and Court Statistics 2009, Ch 7, p 173, available at http://www.justice.gov.uk/publications/docs/judicial-court-statistics-2009.pdf.

[2]   See e g *R (on the application of RLC) v Secretary of State for the Home Department* [2004] EWCA Civ 1481.

[3]   For a clear analysis of the legal status of the immigration rules see *Odelola v Secretary of State for the Home Department* [2009] UKHL 25; [2009] 1 WLR 1230.

- the First-tier Tribunal (Immigration & Asylum Chamber);

- the Upper Tribunal;

- the Special Immigration Appeals Commission (a statutory body which hears immigration cases certified under section 97 of the Nationality, Immigration and Asylum Act 2002 (NIAA)).

14.5   As a general rule, decisions which are taken in-country will be by the Secretary of State and decisions concerning whether leave to enter or remain should be refused or cancelled at the port will be taken by an Immigration Officer.[4] Either may be identified as a defendant in an appropriate case. Similarly an Entry Clearance Officer, identified by the name of the post at which she is engaged in making decisions, will be the appropriate defendant in a challenge to a refusal of entry clearance.

OVERVIEW OF THE IMMIGRATION AND ASYLUM APPELLATE STRUCTURE

14.6   Previously, challenges to first instance decisions in the Asylum & Immigration Tribunal (AIT) were by way of applications for reconsideration[5] to the Tribunal in the first instance with what became known as an 'opt-in' application on paper only to the Administrative court in the event that reconsideration was refused by the AIT. Since February 2010 with the coming into force of the Tribunals Courts and Enforcement Act 2007 (TCEA), the two-tier appeals structure has been re-instituted.[6] First instance appeals are to the First-tier Tribunal (Immigration & Asylum Chamber) (FTT) and appeals from decisions of the FTT, save 'excluded decisions', on a point of law are to the Upper Tribunal (UT).[7] Any party may appeal, not only the losing party.[8] Excluded decisions in respect of which no appeal lies to the UT are as follows:

- decisions taken by the FTT in the exercise of its power to review its own decisions;[9]

- decisions of the FTT set aside on review;[10]

- where the decision carries another right of appeal to a court or tribunal;[11]

- bail decisions, procedural, ancillary or preliminary decisions on appeals under ss 82, 83 or 83A of the Nationality, Immigration and Asylum Act 2002, EEA decisions and deprivation of citizenship decisions (which will include for example decisions to refuse to extend time for appealing[12]).

---

[4]   But see Immigration (Leave to Enter and Remain) Order 2000 which makes provision for the Secretary of State to exercise immigration officer powers.
[5]   Section 103A of the Nationality Immigration and Asylum Act 2002.
[6]   A reference to the pre-2004 Act structure of adjudicators at first instance with the possibility of an appeal with permission, in non-certified cases, to the Immigration Appeal Tribunal.
[7]   Section 11 of the Tribunals, Courts and Enforcement Act 2007 (TCEA).
[8]   Section 11(2) of the TCEA 2007.
[9]   Section 11(5)(d) of the TCEA 2007.
[10]   Section 11(5)(e) of the TCEA 2007.
[11]   Section 11(6)(a) of the TCEA 2007.
[12]   Appeals (Excluded Decisions) Order 2009, SI 2009/275, made under section 11(5)(f) of the TCEA 2007.

14.7   The TCEA also provides for a judicial review type jurisdiction[13] in the Upper Tribunal but at the time of writing the enabling direction required to be made by the Lord Chancellor in order for that function to be in force in respect of decisions under the Immigration Acts has not been made.[14] When the provisions come into force, judicial review claims of decisions under the Immigration Acts will have to be made to the Upper Tribunal where the following conditions are satisfied:

(1)   the remedies sought are not other than public law remedies, damages, interest and costs;[15]

(2)   the application does not call into question anything done in the Crown court;[16]

(3)   the application falls within a class specified by a direction of the Lord Chief Justice;[17]

(4)   the hearing of the application is presided over by a judge of the High Court, Court of Appeal, Court of Session or such other person as agreed between the Lord Chief Justice, the Lord President, the Lord Chief Justice of Northern Ireland and the Senior President of Tribunals.[18]

14.8   The Act also provides (upon those provisions coming into force[19]) for transfer to the UT of claims made in the Administrative Court where the first three conditions are fulfilled and in addition where the decision under challenge is a refusal by the Secretary of State to accept a fresh human rights or asylum claim.[20] Transfer of a claim must take place 'whether or not it calls into question any other decision'[21] with the effect that a claim which sought to challenge a refusal to accept a fresh claim for asylum which also challenged consequential decisions such as removal directions would be for the UT.

14.9   In *R (Cart) v Upper Tribunal* (CA) the Court of Appeal considered the extent to which non-appealable decisions of the UT were subject to the supervisory jurisdiction of the Administrative Court. The court, while recognising the changed characteristic of the Upper Tribunal as provided by the TCEA, in particular its designation as a superior court of record, noted that the TCEA did not in terms oust the supervisory jurisdiction of the High Court but found that the scope of review of the UT was limited to 'outright excess of jurisdiction by the UT and denial by it of fundamental justice'.[22] The

---

13   Section 15 of the TCEA 2007, ie mandatory orders, prohibiting orders, quashing orders, declarations and injunctions.

14   But see fn 19 below.

15   Section 18(4) of the TCEA 2007.

16   Section 18(5) of the TCEA 2007.

17   Section 18(6) of the TCEA 2007.

18   Section 18(8) of the TCEA 2007.

19   By a written statement (Hansard, 3 March 2011, col WS120) the intention was expressed to commence s 53 of the Borders, Citizenship and Immigration Act 2009 with effect from 1 October 2011 enabling judicial review applications concerning fresh asylum and immigration human rights claims (in England & Wales only) to be heard in the Upper Tribunal and that the Lord Chief Justice was 'minded' thereafter to give a direction specifying fresh claims as a class of case to be transferred to the UT as required by s 18(6) TCEA 2007.

20   Section 31A(2A) and (8) of the Senior Courts Act 1981 as inserted by section 53(1)(b) of the Borders, Citizenship and Immigration Act 2009 not in force at time of writing.

21   Section 31A(8) of the Senior Courts Act 1981.

22   [2011] 2 WLR 36 at [36]. For an example, in the asylum context, of a fundamental breach of natural justice justifying exceptional intervention by the High Court see: *R (AM (Cameroon)) v Asylum and Immigration Tribunal* [2008] 1 WLR 2062.

claimant's appeal on the issue of whether, and if so to what extent, decisions of the Upper Tribunal can be subject to judicial review in circumstances where there is no statutory right of appeal to the Court of Appeal was given permission by the Supreme Court who is scheduled to hear the appeal as this work goes to print.

APPEAL OR JUDICIAL REVIEW?

14.10 The powers of the Tribunal to review and correct public-law errors mirror those of the Administrative Court.[23] This means that the Tribunal may consider, on a statutory appeal, errors such as a breach of the rules of natural justice or a material misapprehension of fact. All immigration-related decisions which do not attract a right of appeal are potentially subject to judicial review. These can include for example decisions to certify a country as 'safe' by means of a statutory instrument,[24] prerogative acts such as refusal of a naturalisation or exclusion by the Secretary of State on 'public good' grounds and delays or omissions. The following list, while not exhaustive, gives a broad indication of the common types of decisions where the appropriate remedy is likely to be by way of judicial review:

(1)   immigration decisions which do not attract a right of appeal or attract a non-suspensive appeal where such appeal is not an adequate alternative remedy;

(2)   refusals to extend time for the giving of notice of appeal to the First-tier Tribunal;

(3)   refusals to treat further representations as a 'fresh claim' under rule 353v of HC 395 Immigration Rules;

(4)   decisions to detain;

(5)   decisions by the First-tier Tribunal to refuse bail;

(6)   decisions – such as the decision to set removal directions – which are not 'immigration decisions' under section 82 of the NIAA 2002 and therefore do not trigger any right of appeal;

(7)   decisions to certify claims as 'clearly unfounded';[25]

(8)   policy decisions – which may be a decision to apply or disapply a policy or the terms of the policy itself;

(9)   decisions to refuse naturalisation[26] or to refuse a passport.[27]

---

[23]   *E v Secretary of State for the Home Department, R v Secretary of State for the Home Department* [2004] INLR 264 per Carnwath LJ at [42].

[24]   *R (on the application of Javed) v Secretary of State for the Home Department* [2001] 3 WLR 323.

[25]   Sections 94, 94A and 96 of the Nationality, Immigration and Asylum Act 2002.

[26]   *R (on the application of AHK & others) v Secretary of State for the Home Department* [2009] EWCA Civ 287.

[27]   *R v Secretary of State for the Home Department, ex p Al Fayed* [1997] 1 All ER 228.

14.11 Assertions by the decision-maker that there is no right of appeal or that the right is circumscribed, for instance by requiring the appeal right to be exercised from outside the UK, should be scrutinised against the statutory appeals framework for accuracy.[28]

PROCEDURE

14.12 Whilst CPR 54 governs all judicial review claims, specific provision is made in respect of applications seeking to defer or stay removal directions[29] and careful attention should be paid to those requirements. In addition to the standard requirements for judicial review applications including that an application be brought promptly and in any event within three months,[30] where a person has been served with a copy of directions for his removal from the United Kingdom by the UK Border Agency of the Home Office and notified that section 2 of PD54A applies and that person makes an application for permission to apply for judicial review before his removal takes effect, the applicant must also:

(1)   indicate on the claim form that section II to PD54A applies; and

(2)   include a copy of the removal directions, any document served with the directions AND UKBA's 'immigration factual summary'; and

(3)   include a detailed statement of grounds of claim; or

(4)   in the event of being unable to comply with the foregoing two requirements provide a statement of the reasons why.

14.13 Further, PD54A requires the claimant to send copies of the issued claim immediately to the address supplied by UKBA[31] and to serve the Treasury Solicitor within seven days of issue. In *R (ota Glenford Lewis) v Secretary of State for the Home Department* [2010] EWHC 1749 (Admin) the claimant's solicitors were criticised by the court for failing, in an urgent case, also to make contact with UKBA by telephone and/or fax.

Pre-action protocol letters

14.14 In normal circumstances, ie where there is no urgency and the decision-maker has a power to change its decision in light of any challenge (unlike a court or Tribunal without jurisdiction to review its own decision) the pre-action protocol should be followed.[32] A structured, detailed letter before claim should set out the decision or omission under challenge, the grounds of challenge, any action required to be taken by the decision-maker and in what timescale and the reasons why it is said that the decision is flawed in a public law sense, ideally citing any relevant statute or case authority. A

---

[28]   For an example of the court on judicial review correcting an incorrect assertion by the Secretary of State for the Home Department that a right of appeal is out of country only see: *R (on the application of BA (Nigeria) v Secretary of State for the Home Department* [2010] 1 AC 444 (SC) and more recently *R (on the application of MK (Tunisia) v Secretary of State for the Home Department* [2010] EWHC 2363 (Admin).

[29]   PD54A, Section II on the Ministry of Justice, Civil Procedure Rules website.

[30]   CPR 54.5.

[31]   At the time of writing that address is Judicial Review Unit, UK Border Agency, St Anne's House, 20–26 Wellesley Road, Croydon, CR9 2RL.

[32]   The protocol is set at http://www.justice.gov.uk/civil/procrules_fin/ contents/protocols/prot_jrv.htm.

good pre-action protocol letter should always be written mindful of the prospect that it will be read by a judge who will be considering – possibly in relation to costs – how clearly the letter gives notice of the substance of the complaint. There is no requirement to adhere to the pre-action protocol and normal 14-day timescale for a response in urgent removal cases. It is wise, however, to alert the Secretary of State to proposals to issue judicial review or seek injunctive relief with a timescale proportionate to the timing of removal. See below for further detailed consideration of best practice in removal cases.

Time limits

14.15 As seen above, judicial review claims must be brought promptly and in any event within three months. It cannot be assumed that an application issued at the outer edge of the time limit will not be penalised for delay, depending on the circumstances of the case. Practitioners should always aim to bring proceedings at the earliest point or be in a position to account for actions taken in the intervening period which delayed issue. For example, where further clarification is legitimately sought regarding an unclear decision, the court may extend time.[33] Time limits are unlikely to be imposed where there is an ongoing unlawful act or failure to act (eg an unreasonable delay in reaching a decision or issuing status documents[34] or ongoing detention) rather than a specific decision.

Urgent applications and interim relief[35]

14.16 Urgent applications are made on form N463 including an explanation of the need for urgency and require a draft order to be attached. They may accompany the claim form and bundle, post-date it or be made and granted in advance of the claim[36] accompanied by an undertaking to issue the claim (usually within 24 hours). The draft order should specify what urgent action the court is asked to take, not the substantive remedy sought. For example, if the matter requires an urgent hearing on notice to the defendant or urgent interim relief it should so state. The standard procedure gives the defendant 14 days to respond to a claim by way of an acknowledgment of service and summary grounds of defence. In cases where the substantive issues are urgent (for example where a stay on removal directions has been refused) it may be appropriate to ask for an abridgment of time for the defendant's acknowledgment of service and consideration of the permission application by a particular date. The draft order should contain a practical route with suggested timescales proportionate to the urgency. If injunctive relief is sought urgently, the grounds on which the injunction is sought should be set out in the N463, or attached. The claimant must serve the application for urgent consideration and attachments by fax and post on the defendant and any interested party. It is good practice to obtain prior permission for filing the urgent application with the Administrative Court by fax and to alert the Administrative Court that an urgent application is to be made. The claimant's duty of full and frank disclosure requires that adverse factors of which the representatives are aware (eg Country Guidance decisions, previous unsuccessful applications) are brought to the attention of the judge.

14.17 In considering the application for interim relief the court will be bound by the normal principles including the balance of convenience[37] but adjusted to reflect the fact

---

33   *R v Secretary of State for the Home Department, ex p Noorain (CA) unreported.* C/00/5412 28/07/2000.
34   *R v Secretary of State for the Home Department, ex p Mersin* [2000] INLR 511.
35   Practice Statement (Administrative Court: Listing and Urgent Cases) [2002] 1 WLR 810 at 811–812.
36   *M v Home Office* [1994] 1 AC 377.
37   *American Cyanamid Co v Ethicon Ltd* [1975] AC 396 (HL).

that in judicial review and, particularly, human rights cases it will normally be the case that the prejudice to a claimant that may result from a refusal of interim relief will not sound in damages.[38] A failure to establish with the court a 'high degree of assurance' of ultimate success where a mandatory injunction is sought may not be fatal where the court considers that the risk of injustice if the interim relief is refused outweighs the risk of injustice if it is granted.[39]

14.18 Every attempt should be made to get a paper application before a judge in working hours. Out of hours applications should be made by telephone to the Royal Courts of Justice[40] and may be made by counsel or a solicitor. The person making the application will need to have to hand the name, date of birth, date of arrival in the United Kingdom and Home Office reference number of the applicant together with as much information about the factual background to the application as can be obtained. The gist of the case will normally be communicated to the duty judge's clerk in the first instance who will check that the application is appropriate to be placed before the judge. It is helpful to have access to a computer or fax in order to send the duty judge a draft version of the order sought. In some cases that will not be possible and the order will be given orally to be submitted for approval during working hours.

14.19 Applicants for urgent relief, particularly in telephone applications, must take care to ensure full and frank disclosure of factors militating against both the grant of urgent relief and the merits of the substantive claim for judicial review.[41] In the immigration context this will mean a warts and all disclosure to the judge of any relevant adverse credibility findings, previous refusals, case authority or country guidance cases impacting on the merits of the substantive claim. A note should be taken of the application (including submissions made) which should be produced to the defendant whether requested or not.[42]

Disclosure

14.20 The 'duty of candour'[43] that applies to defendant public authorities has a particular importance in the context of immigration and detention decision making where decisions are not infrequently taken on the basis of unpublished policy.[44] Tracing the immigration or detention history of a proposed claimant will often be essential to ascertain current status and entitlements. In preference to an application for pre-action disclosure, early applications to the UK Border Agency (UKBA) for a 'subject access request' under the Data Protection Act 1998, which are of statutory entitlement (with some public interest exceptions) and not subject to disclosure principles, are often indispensable but may not have been complied with by the time it is necessary to issue judicial review proceedings. In such circumstances it may be necessary to seek disclosure within judicial review proceedings in reliance on the defendant's duty of candour. Documents to look for include computer records, email trails, immigration decisions and documents on which they are based, records of contact with UKBA, detention

---

[38]   *R v Secretary of State for Transport, ex p Factortame Limited (No 2)* [1991] AC 603.

[39]   *Nottingham Building Society v Eurodynamics Systems* [1993] FSR 468.

[40]   020 7947 6000.

[41]   *R (Lawer) v Restormel* [2007] EWHC 2299 (Admin).

[42]   *Interoute Telecommunications (UK) Ltd v Fashion Gossip Ltd, The Times*, November 10, 1999.

[43]   *R v Lancashire CC, ex p Huddlestone* [1986] 2 All ER 941 at 945g 'all the cards face upwards on the table'. See also Laws LJ in *R (Quark Fishing Ltd) v SS Foreign & Commonwealth Affairs* [2002] EWCA 1409 at [50].

[44]   See for example *R (WL(Congo) & others) v Secretary of State for the Home Department* [2010] 1 WLR 2168.

decisions and reviews, internal memos, reviews by senior immigration officers, copies of previous applications and, importantly, missing documents.

Standing

14.21 The test for 'standing' in judicial review of 'sufficient interest' is less restrictive than that taken by for example the European Court of Human Rights which requires claimants to be a 'victim' of the act in question. As a consequence affected family members or interest groups seeking to challenge a policy decision in immigration and asylum cases may be appropriate claimants.

Anonymity

14.22 The Court of Appeal's practice is to anonymise its judgments by use of initials and a country reference where the party concerned is an asylum seeker[45] on the grounds that an asylum-seeker may face additional risks in her country of origin as a consequence of publication of identity.[46] It is reasonable to request that the same practice be followed by the Administrative Court on usual principles, but such orders will not be made as a matter of course in all immigration cases.

Evidence

14.23 The evidence to be included in a claim for judicial review should include everything material to the issue which was before the Secretary of State at the time of the decision and any relevant material adverse to the claim. In appropriate cases the court will not shut out material which post-dates the decision. See the discussion at para **14.30** below.

Alternative remedies

14.24 Judicial review is a remedy of last resort. In the immigration context that will normally mean that as long as there is no route of appeal available, an applicant will not be refused discretionary relief for that reason. However, there may be some circumstances, particularly regarding remedies for maladministration, or some non-urgent challenges when a complaints procedure,[47] if available, should be pursued.[48]

CHALLENGING DETENTION DECISIONS

14.25 There has been some debate as to whether a writ of *habeas corpus ad subjiciendum* or an application for judicial review (urgent procedure) is the appropriate route of remedy in cases where it is alleged that a claimant is detained unlawfully under the Immigration Acts. There are clear procedural advantages to the *habeas* route. The court prioritises such applications as very urgent and will normally list them as soon as is practicable and certainly within a day or so. By contrast, even a claim accompanied by

---

[45]   Practice Note on Anonymisation in Asylum and Immigration Cases in the Court of Appeal [2006] EWCA Civ 1359.

[46]   See also comments of Lord Simon Brown in *Ahmed Mahad v ECO* [2009] UKSC 16 at [42].

[47]   http://www.ukba.homeoffice.gov.uk/contact/makingacomplaint/how-to-complain.

[48]   The claimants were criticised for a failure to do this in *R (on the application of Dong & others) v Secretary of State for the Home Department* CO/1348/2009 in the context of a challenge to unreasonable delay seeking compensation under the HRA.

an application for urgent consideration will require a reasonable amount of time for the defendant Secretary of State to collate and review the often voluminous files of detention reviews and records which are prepared in what are increasingly lengthy periods of immigration detention[49] in order to respond. The writ of *habeas corpus* issues by right whereas remedies in judicial review are discretionary. However, *habeas corpus* will normally only be appropriate in limited circumstances where it is asserted that there is no power in law to detain.[50] It is important to distinguish between whether there is a power in law to detain and whether the discretion to detain under such power has been exercised reasonably, fairly and lawfully. Where an examination of the lawfulness of the detention requires consideration of an underlying administrative decision or a review of the length of the detention on *Hardial Singh*[51] principles (see below), judicial review is the appropriate route.[52] Examples of the former category might include cases where the detainee is not liable to detention (for example because they are demonstrably exempted from deportation by reason of being a British citizen or subject to the provisions of section 7 of the Immigration Act 1971) or where the circumstances of the case give rise to no statutory power to detain or where the authorisation to detain is based on a misdirection in law. Examples of the latter category include detention which has become unlawful by reason of its unreasonable length or where the administrative decision which gave rise to the power in law to detain (eg a notice of intention to deport) is flawed or where there has been a failure to take into account published policy in exercising a discretion to detain.[53]

Bail

14.26 Where there is a power to detain under the Immigration Acts there is a power to release either on temporary admission or under a restriction order.[54] Those detained under the Immigration Acts may apply for bail from the Chief Immigration Officer or the FTT (IAC)[55] as may those awaiting an appeal.[56] Bail is premised on a lawful detention and the FTT may decline jurisdiction where it is asserted that there is no power in law to detain or that the decision to detain was initially or has since become unlawful. Where there is an application pending in the Administrative Court challenging the legality of detention, the court may grant bail under its inherent jurisdiction even where there is also a right to apply for bail in the FTT.[57] Where bail is applied for it should be included as an application for other relief in the Form N461. A bail summons,[58] including the name of the applicant, proposed release address, proposed sureties' names and addresses must be served on the Treasury solicitor with a minimum of three working days' notice that an application for bail is to be heard in order that the Secretary of State have a reasonable opportunity to check the proposed bail address and sureties. A refusal of bail by the Administrative Court may be appealed to the Court of

---

49   It is not unusual for detainees to be in the immigration detention estate for three or four years.
50   *R v Secretary of State for the Home Department, ex p Muboyayi* [1991] 3 WLR 442.
51   *R v Governor of Durham Prison, ex p Hardial Singh* [1984] 1 WLR 704.
52   See the observations of Mitting J in *Ammar (R on the application of) v Secretary of State for the Home Department* [2008] EWHC 142 (Admin).
53   *R v Secretary of State for the Home Department, ex p Mohammed* [2010] EWHC B6.
54   Immigration Act 1971, schedule 3, paras 2(5) and (6); Asylum and Immigration Act 1996, schedule 2, para 13; and UK Borders Act 2007, s 36.
55   Immigration Act 1971, schedule 2, paras 22 and 24.
56   Immigration Act 1971, schedule, 2 para 29.
57   Senior Courts Act 1981, s 15(3), *R (on the application of Sezek) v Secretary of State for the Home Department* [2001] INLR 675.
58   Recommended best practice – the Civil Procedure Rules do not make specific provision for applications for bail under the Administrative Court's inherent jurisdiction.

Appeal.[59] Where permission to apply for judicial review has been refused, the court no longer has power to grant bail. An application for bail under the court's inherent jurisdiction is not a *Wednesbury*-style review of the decision to detain but an application on its merits[60] following incorporation of article 5 of the ECHR which requires the court to scrutinise whether detention is justified and proportionate. A grant of bail is not fatal to an unlawful detention claim which may properly seek a remedy in damages against periods of detention prior to release on bail or in relation to bail conditions imposed premised on a lawful exercise of a power to detain. For persons detained on arrival in the UK for whom seven days must elapse before an application for bail can be made to the FTT,[61] the appropriate remedy is in the Administrative Court.

14.27 The classic statement of the principles governing a lawful exercise of a discretion to detain is contained in the *Hardial Singh*[62] judgment of Woolf J as he then was. ie whether, where a power to detain exists, detention is for a period which is reasonably necessary to achieve the statutory purpose. On a claim of unlawful detention the court will decide for itself whether detention is reasonably necessary and is not restricted to reviewing the Secretary of State's reasons for detaining.[63] The court in considering what is reasonable will take into account personal circumstances including the mental and physical health of the claimant, any criminal offences, immigration history and the likelihood of removal within the foreseeable future.

14.28 Any claim for damages for false imprisonment in judicial review must be set out in the claim form,[64] including, where appropriate, specific claims for exemplary and or aggravated damages. Where an order for release is sought under the Administrative Court's prerogative powers[65] it will be necessary to challenge detention by way of either habeas or judicial review. A remedy sought in respect of a purely historical period of detention may be brought by way of a private law claim in the county court or Queens Bench Division as appropriate, particularly where there is likely to be a complex factual dispute. It is worth noting here that whereas damages are not generally available for maladministration, where an action in private law giving rise to a remedy in damages would have succeeded (ie the tort of false imprisonment), damages may be awarded in judicial review. Compensation may also be awarded under the Human Rights Act 1998 as 'just satisfaction' but these awards are characteristically low. Lastly, where a breach of European law can be established, *Francovich*[66] damages may also be payable. Whereas the Court of Appeal has recently rejected[67] a claim for *Francovich* damages for a breach of the Qualification Directive,[68] it has also observed that following the codification in European law of what were previously viewed as public law discretionary decisions,[69] it may be only a matter of time before the courts accept that the Qualification,

[59]   *R v Secretary of State for the Home Department, ex p Turkoglu* [1988] QB 398.
[60]   *R v Secretary of State for the Home Department, ex p Kelso* [1998] INLR 603.
[61]   Immigration Act 1971, schedule 2, para 22(1B).
[62]   *R v Governor of Durham Prison, ex p Hardial Singh* [1984] 1 WLR 704.
[63]   *Youssef v Home Office* [2004] EWHC 1884 QBD, see also *R (on the application of A(Somalia)) v Secretary of State for the Home Department* [2007] EWCA Civ 204.
[64]   CPR Part 54.6.
[65]   Ie Mandatory, prohibitory or quashing orders which are only available on an application for judicial review.
[66]   *Francovich & Bonifaci v Italy* [1993] 2 CMLR 66.
[67]   *R (on the application of MK(Iran) v Secretary of State for the Home Department* [2010] EWCA Civ 115.
[68]   Council Directive (2004/83/EC) on minimum standards for the qualification and status of third country nationals or stateless persons as refugees or as persons who otherwise need international protection and the content of the protection granted, *Official Journal*, 30 September 2004, p 12.
[69]   See *Maaouia v France* (2000) 33 EHRR 1037.

Procedures[70] and Reception[71] Directives and related European legislation give rise to enforceable private law rights which sound in damages.[72]

CHALLENGING REMOVALS

14.29 In its published policy 'Enforcement Instructions and Guidance'[73] UKBA sets out how it will normally respond to applications for judicial review where removal directions have been set. A minimum period of 72 hours notice of removal directions should be given which extends to five working days' between setting of removal directions and enforcement in the case of third country cases or non-suspensive appeals and five working days' notice in the case of removal by charter flight. In port cases the 72 hour notice period will only apply where removal has not been effected within seven days of any refusal of leave to enter or where a removal has failed and is attempted again within ten days. The normal policy is to defer removal where a claim for judicial review has been issued and the claim, as issued, together with the grounds for judicial review are received by UKBA. Where removal is by charter flight however, or the grounds of challenge repeat issues raised in a judicial review or appeal rejected within the previous three months, it will be necessary to seek an injunction from the Administrative Court as removal will not be deferred. A further exception may be invoked by UKBA where, in its reasonable view, the grounds of challenge are entirely without merit. Where permission has been refused by the Administrative Court and an appeal is made to the Court of Appeal, such appeal will not act automatically to prolong any injunction or stay[74] and an application should be made to the Court of Appeal in the notice seeking permission to appeal.

14.30 Where the Secretary of State agrees to reconsider her decision, is that the end of the application for judicial review? Removal cases, particularly 'anxious scrutiny' cases where reliance is placed on the Refugee or Human Rights Conventions, fall into the category of 'moving train' cases where the courts will not shut out relevant material from either side which post-dates the removal decision.[75] There is an important distinction to be drawn between cases where the remedy sought is an order to quash a decision with the consequence that the decision must be reconsidered and retaken by the decision-maker, and one where, for instance it is alleged that no reasonable Secretary of State would have been entitled to take the decision complained of and therefore the relief sought is a mandatory order or a judgment the terms of which effectively prevent the Secretary of State from reaching an identical conclusion. In the former case, reconsideration may be the best that can be achieved, but in the latter the court is used to seeing further decisions and amended grounds to reflect any further challenge arising. It is appropriate to adjourn for such a decision-making process and response to it to take place.[76] Similarly, any consent order should reflect the distinction made above and need not dispose of the claim while reconsideration takes place.

---

[70] Council Directive (2005/85/EC) on minimum standards on procedures in Member States for granting and withdrawing refugee status OJ L 326/13.

[71] Council Directive (2003/9/EC) laying down minimum standards for the reception of asylum seekers OJ L 31/18.

[72] *MK (Iran)* supra, see in particular observations of Sedley LJ.

[73] Enforcement Guidance and Instructions, Chapter 60 (UKBA website) with effect from 26 July 2010, subject to change, check the website.

[74] *R (on the application of Pharis) v Secretary of State for the Home Department* [2004] EWCA Civ 654.

[75] See comments of Schiemann LJ in *R v Secretary of State for the Home Department, ex p Turgut* [2000] HRLR 337.

[76] *R v Secretary of State for the Home Department, ex p Alabi* [1997] INLR 124, CA.

14.31 The additional Civil Procedure provisions which affect removal applications are set out above at para **14.29**. Failures to provide an adequate opportunity for those served with removal directions to take legal advice have been strongly condemned by the Administrative Court.[77] A policy of removing certain categories of vulnerable person on no or limited notice was struck down as unlawful.[78] Where the Secretary of State removes a claimant notwithstanding an interim stay, the court retains the power to order the Secretary of State to return him in an appropriate case.[79]

NATIONAL SECURITY CASES AND USE OF 'CLOSED PROCEEDINGS'

14.32 Reliance on 'closed' material on national security or other public interest grounds is increasingly a feature of immigration and nationality decision-making. Closed procedures which originated in the Special Immigration Appeals Commission, such as the use of Special Advocates, have migrated into judicial review in non-appealable decisions such as refusals of naturalisation,[80] or exclusion at the personal direction of the Secretary of State.[81] The extent to which the Secretary of State may be entitled to rely on closed material (that is material that the judge, but not the claimant is able to see) in private law proceedings and whether the court, in the absence of any statutory procedure, has jurisdiction to order closed proceedings, is currently under consideration in the Supreme Court in *Al Rawi and others v Security Service and others (Liberty and others intervening)*.[82] The Court of Appeal in *Al Rawi* drew a distinction between the use of closed procedures including Specially Appointed Advocates in interlocutory proceedings such as a hearing of the Secretary of State's application to rely on a PII certificate or other disclosure issues, and reliance on closed material and procedures in the hearing of the substantive issue. It might be thought that in the absence of sufficient reasons for significant decisions such as the refusal of citizenship the closed procedure affords an important opportunity to test the Secretary of State's justification for withholding material on which the decision was based. However, whether the Secretary of State is entitled to rely on closed material in the ultimate issue is a question which will be examined further in the light of the Supreme Court's judgment in *Al Rawi*.

GROUNDS

Illegality, irrationality and procedural unfairness and the impact of human rights

14.33 As a public authority, the Secretary of State for the Home Department and officers operating under her authority are subject to the normal principles of review which are not repeated here. However, it is important to note that the Secretary of State's powers do not derive solely from statute but are the prerogative powers of one of the great offices of state: that of deciding who can and who cannot enter or reside in the

---

[77] See *R (on the application of Karas & Milandinovic) v Secretary of State for the Home Department* (2006) 103(18) LSG 31, *R (on the application of Collaku) v Secretary of State for the Home Department* [2005] EWHC 2855 (Admin).

[78] *R (on the application of Medical Justice) v Secretary of State for the Home Department* [2010] EWHC 1925 (Admin).

[79] *R (on the application of CM (Jamaica) v Secretary of State for the Home Department* [2010] EWCA Civ 160.

[80] *R (on the application of AHK & others) v Secretary of State for the Home Department* [2009] 1 WLR 2049.

[81] A prerogative power.

[82] UKSC 2010/0107. See also Court of Appeal decision at [2010] 3 WLR 1069.

UK or be granted or retain British citizenship. The result is a preponderance of 'hard-edged'[83] issues before the court on judicial review that throw the relationship between the executive and the judiciary into sharp relief.[84] For practitioners that means an astute awareness of the entrenched unwillingness of the court on judicial review to limit the exercise of discretion by the Secretary of State except within traditional limits. The introduction of human rights principles has had a twofold effect. Firstly, the 'heightened degree of scrutiny' which applies to reviews in human rights cases and secondly, following incorporation by the Human Rights Act 1998, the obligation on the courts, as public authorities[85] subject to section 6 of the Act, to avoid a breach.

Abuse of power and improper purpose in the immigration context

14.34 But where the decision-maker has wide powers with potentially draconian effects on fundamental common law rights such as the right of access to a court, the right to procedural fairness, the right to liberty or Convention rights such as the right to freedom from torture or inhuman and degrading treatment the Administrative Court will scrutinise carefully the actions of the executive. This is a primary constitutional function which the Administrative Court takes profoundly seriously. Accordingly the court will in an appropriate case, consider not only whether a decision is in conformity with statutory or other powers and is rational but also whether the decision amounts to an abuse of power or is exercised in pursuit of an improper purpose or constitutes a misfeasance in a public office.

14.35 The court on judicial review has not shied away from finding that the actions of the executive constitute an abuse where the Secretary of State has refused to grant leave to remain consequent on a successful appeal,[86] where a policy of delaying determination of certain categories of asylum claims had led to past injustice,[87] where the Secretary of State had sought to effect the 'spiriting away of the claimants from the jurisdiction'[88] before they could obtain legal advice. But it is not necessary to demonstrate deliberate misconduct by the Secretary of State to substantiate an allegation of abuse of power, 'conspicuous unfairness' will suffice.[89]

SOME FREQUENTLY OCCURRING ISSUES

Fresh claims and certification

14.36 Further submissions and evidence from claimants whose asylum or human rights appeals have been rejected or withdrawn and any appeal rights exhausted are considered by the Secretary of State under paragraph 353 of HC 395 Immigration Rules. Paragraph 353A provides that a person will not be removed from the UK while such representations are being considered. Current procedure requires an appointment to be

---

[83] See Chapter 16, Michael Fordham's *Judicial Review Handbook*, 5th edn, Hart Publishing, for an excellent analysis.

[84] For a recent discussion see *Secretary of State for the Home Department v Pankina* [2010] 3 WLR 1526.

[85] Section 6(3)(a) of the Human Rights Act 1998.

[86] *R (on the application of S & others) v Secretary of State for the Home Department* [2006] EWHC 1111 (Admin) upheld in *Secretary of State for the Home Department v R (on the application of S & others)* [2006] EWCA Civ 1157.

[87] *R (on the application of Rashid) v Secretary of State for the Home Department* [2008] EWCA Civ 744.

[88] Karas & Milandinovic ibid at [84].

[89] *R (on the application of S) v Secretary of State for the Home Department* [2007] EWCA Civ 546 at [70].

made at a named location for such submissions to be made in person.[90] Representations will be treated as a fresh claim (triggering an immigration decision and therefore, unless certified, a right of appeal), if they are:

- significantly different from previously considered material; and

- taken together with previous material (including any unappealed findings in an appeal determination) they create a realistic prospect of success notwithstanding its rejection.

14.37 A number of authorities have established that the threshold to be satisfied by the claimant on the second issue is a low one.[91]

14.38 Certification, whether under section 94 or 96 of the Nationality Immigration and Asylum Act 2002, is the statutory means by which the Secretary of State can, by certifying an asylum or human rights claim as 'clearly unfounded',[92] prevent a claimant from appealing from within the UK against a refusal which would otherwise attract an in-country appeal by operation of section 92 of the Act. In such circumstances a claimant would have to leave the UK before such appeal could be exercised thereby depriving the claimant of the suspensory protection of section 78 of the Act. The court on judicial review will consider for itself whether a claim is 'clearly unfounded'.[93]

14.39 There has been considerable judicial attention given to whether the test to be applied by the court on judicial review of refusals to treat further representations as 'fresh claims' differs from decisions to certify claims as 'clearly unfounded'. Lord Brown in *ZT (Kosovo) v SSHD*[94] described the distinction to be drawn between the tests applicable under the 'fresh claims' and 'certification' regimes as 'dancing on the head of a pin'. Judicial opinion diverged as to whether the court should apply the standard *Wednesbury* test, including, for example, whether everything material had been taken into account, whether the Secretary of State had asked herself the correct question, whether there were any material misapprehensions of demonstrable fact etc[95] or, alternatively, decide the ultimate question for itself.[96] Following the judgment of the Court of Appeal in *R (on the application of YH) v Secretary of State for the Home Department*[97] the question for the court on judicial review – whether there is a realistic prospect of success – was found to be a question for the court, subject to the principle that the jurisdiction is one of review and not a de novo hearing in that the court can

---

90 See policy document 'Further submissions' in the Asylum Process Guidance, post-decision representations section UKBA website.

91 *R v Secretary of State for the Home Department, ex p Onibiyo* [1996] Imm AR 370, and e g see Laws LJ in *R (on the application of AK(Sri Lanka) v Secretary of State for the Home Department* [2010] 1 WLR 855 '"Realistic prospect of success" means only more than a fanciful such prospect' at [34].

92 Section 94(1A) and (2) set out the 'clearly unfounded' merits threshold, and the remainder of sections 94 and 94A set out the basis for certification on 'safe third country' grounds. Section 96 provides for certification as where there has been an earlier right of appeal which has, or could have if it had been exercised, determined the issues now raised in further submissions.

93 *ZT (Kosovo) v Secretary of State for the Home Department* [2009] UKHL 6 and Lord Phillips in *R(L) v Secretary of State for the Home Department* [2003] 1 WLR 1230 at [56] 'The test is an objective one: it depends not on the Home Secretary's view but upon a criterion which a court can readily re-apply once it has the materials which the Home Secretary had. A claim is either clearly unfounded or it is not'.

94 [2009] 1 WLR 348 (HL).

95 *WM (DRC) v Secretary of State for the Home Department* [2007] INLR 126; *R (TK) v Secretary of State for the Home Department* [2009] EWCA Civ 1550.

96 *KH (Afghanistan) v Secretary of State for the Home Department* [2009] EWCA Civ 1354.

97 [2010] 4 All ER 448.

only consider material which has been before the Secretary of State.[98] The Court of Appeal has now revisited the matter[99] and concluded that the two tests are different and that the scope of review in fresh claim cases is the Wednesbury test subject to anxious scrutiny. However, the distinction may be one without a difference given that the House of Lords in *ZT* was also plainly considering a rationality challenge, see for example Lord Phillips at [23]:

> 'Where, as here, there is no dispute of primary fact, the question of whether or not a claim is clearly unfounded is only susceptible to one rational answer. If any reasonable doubt exists as to whether the claim may succeed then it is not clearly unfounded. It follows that a challenge to the Secretary of State's conclusion that a claim is clearly unfounded is a rationality challenge. There is no way that a court can consider whether her conclusion was rational other than by asking itself the same question that she has considered. If the court concludes that a claim has a realistic prospect of success when the Secretary of State has reached a contrary view, the court will necessarily conclude that the Secretary of State's view was irrational.'

14.40 The Court of Appeal has recently held[100] that it is only if the Secretary of State could be satisfied that nobody would find the applicant credible that she could certify a claim and, if there was any reasonable doubt, the claim could not be described as clearly unfounded. For practitioners the essential task is to demonstrate clearly and specifically what impact the further material has on any previous findings or refusal having regard to any relevant Country Guidance decision. Previous adverse credibility findings are not necessarily fatal to a fresh claim,[101] particularly where the further material emanates from a source independent of the claimant. But there should be a full explanation available as to the provenance of documents specific to the claimant and the timing and circumstances of obtaining them. Where an Immigration Judge has reached his own adverse view of the plausibility of an account in the absence of accurate material relating to the conditions in the country of origin, for example where generically available material does not address the claimant's situation, an expert report if obtainable may be adduced in a fresh claim as a means of rebutting adverse findings. The expert's qualifications and experience should be set out clearly, contain a self-direction as to the expert's duty, and be supported if possible by any judicial endorsement and address in express terms the matters of fact which it is alleged the decision-maker has misapprehended in addition to giving any opinion on prospective risk.

Delay and refusal to issue an appealable decision

14.41 Delay in making decisions concerning the immigration status of persons including families with children is a persistent feature of immigration practice. Delay by the Secretary of State is a relevant, but not decisive factor which may be weighed in the balancing exercise to be conducted under article 8 when considering the right to respect

---

[98] But the court will not shut out further material which is relevant and may build in to the judicial review procedure scope for reconsideration by the Secretary of State and amended grounds in response in an appropriate case. See discussion at para **14.30**.

[99] *R (MN (Tanzania)) v Secretary of State for the Home Department* [2011] EWCA Civ 193.

[100] *R (on the application of MD (Gambia)) v Secretary of State for the Home Department* [2011] EWCA Civ 121; *R (on the application of L) v Secretary of State for the Home Department* [2003] EWCA Civ 25, (2003) 1 WLR 1230 applied.

[101] See Collins J in *R (on the application of Naseer) v Secretary of State for the Home Department* [2006] EWHC 1671 (Admin).

for private and family life.[102] But delay in reaching an immigration decision or regularising immigration status, may have serious adverse effects for claimants, particularly those involving children and those effects have been recognised by the ECtHR as engaging article 8 of the ECHR.[103] The Court of Appeal has recently considered whether the Secretary of State is bound to issue an 'immigration decision' enabling a claimant to exercise a right of appeal and access independent judicial scrutiny of decisions concerning immigration status. In *R (on the application of Daley-Murdock) v Secretary of State for the Home Department*[104] the court decided that it would be contrary to the policy and objects of the 2002 Act to impose an obligation on the Secretary of State when refusing an overstayer's application for leave to remain to make at the same time an appealable refusal decision so as to confer a right of appeal because the list of appealable immigration decisions in section 82(2) makes it clear that Parliament did not intend that overstayers, unlike those who are lawfully in the UK with leave, should have a right of appeal against a refusal of leave to remain. However in *R (on the application of Mirza) v Secretary of State for the Home Department*[105] the court also observed that 'there is no legal justification for routinely putting removal on prolonged or indefinite hold [...] it may follow that an unjustified deferral of a decision on removal, being contrary to law, makes it impossible to justify the disruption of family or private life'.

14.42　For practitioners considering whether a claim for judicial review is merited where a claimant has been subjected to unreasonable delay by the executive in taking a decision concerning immigration status, it is necessary to assess the specific adverse impact of delay on the claimant and any affected third parties including children, whose best interests must now be a specific and paramount consideration in the exercise of any discretion by the Secretary of State.[106]

Illegal entry and the precedent fact jurisdiction

14.43　Decisions to treat individuals as illegal entrants, which have never attracted a right of appeal, have declined in significance since section 10 of the Immigration Act 1999 extended the Secretary of State's powers to effect administrative removal to overstayers and those in breach of conditions attached to their leave. However, illegal entry decisions provide a useful insight into the circumstances in which the court on judicial review has a 'precedent fact' jurisdiction. That means that the court is entitled to conduct its own investigation as to whether the conditions necessary to trigger a power in law in fact exist,[107] by contrast with the classic form of review of executive action. The key authority, *Khawaja v Secretary of State for the Home Department*[108] established that whether a person is an illegal entrant is an issue of precedent fact that the court will

---

[102]　*EB (Kosovo) (FC) v Secretary of State for the Home Department* [2008] UKHL 41, [2008] 4 All ER 28.

[103]　See for example *Mendizabal v France* (2010) 50 EHRR 50.

[104]　[2011] EWCA Civ 161.

[105]　[2011] EWCA Civ 159 at [45]–[46].

[106]　See section 55 of the Borders, Citizenship and Immigration Act 2009 and the important decision of the Supreme court in *ZH (Tanzania) v Secretary of State for the Home Department* [2011] UKSC 4; [2011] 2 WLR.

[107]　Which may include, in an appropriate case, live evidence and cross-examination.

[108]　[1984] 1 AC 74.

investigate for itself in a challenge to a removal decision. Similarly where a claimant seeks declaratory relief that he is a British citizen the court will also investigate the issue in its precedent fact jurisdiction.[109]

ESSENTIAL WEBSITES

14.44

- Aire Centre: http://www.airecentre.org/

- Asylum and Immigration Tribunal practice directions and caselaw: http://www.ait.gov.uk/practice_directions/case_law.htm

- Bail for Immigration Detainees (BID): http://www.biduk.org/

- British and Irish Legal Information Institute: http://www.bailii.org/

- European Court of Human Rights: http://cmiskp.echr.coe.int/tkp197/search.asp?skin=hudoc-en

- Electronic Immigration Network: http://www.ein.org.uk/

- European Country of Origin Information Network (ECOI): http://www.ecoi.net/

- Home Office Country of Origin Information (COI): http://www.homeoffice.gov.uk/rds/country_reports.html

- Home Office Policy Instructions (OEM, IDIs, APIs): http://www.ind.homeoffice.gov.uk/lawandpolicy/policyinstructions/

- ILPA: http://www.ilpa.org.uk/

- Ministry of Justice Civil Procedure Rules site http://www.justice.gov.uk/civil/procrules_fin/menus/rules.htm

- National Archives: http://www.nationalarchives.gov.uk

- Office of Public Sector Information: http://www.opsi.gov.uk/ – legislation and statutory instruments

- Special Immigration Appeals Commission (SIAC): http://www.siac.tribunals.gov.uk/

---

[109] For a useful decision concerning on whom the burden lies as to citizenship where it is asserted that the passport produced in support of such assertion is forged see *R v Secretary of State for the Home Department, ex p Obi* [1997] 1 WLR 1498.

Part 3

APPENDICES

Appendix A

PROCEDURAL GUIDE: CLAIMS FOR JUDICIAL REVIEW

LEGAL BACKGROUND

Claims for judicial review are governed by CPR Pt 54.

A claim for judicial review is a means of vindicating rights in public law. It is defined in the CPR as 'a claim to review the lawfulness of (i) an enactment; or (ii) a decision, action or failure to act in relation to the exercise of a public function'. It is sometimes difficult to tell whether a particular complaint involves a matter of public law or of private law. Frequently, the complaint involves elements of both; where it does, the courts are allowing claimants greater flexibility in choosing their forum. But the distinction between public and private law remains important for a number of purposes.

There are a number of respects in which claims for judicial review differ from private law claims:

- There are short time-limits.

- The claimant requires the permission of the court to bring the proceedings.

- The proceedings are generally conducted without oral evidence.

- There is rarely disclosure of documents.

- Relief is discretionary.

A Practice Direction on Judicial Review accompanies Pt 54. In addition, there is available from the Administrative Court Office a helpful booklet entitled *Notes for Guidance on Applying for Judicial Review*.

PROCEDURE

Availability	Where the substance of the claim is a matter of public law and the remedy sought is as stated above. Proceedings for judicial review are generally not appropriate where an alternative remedy is available, such as a statutory appeal	Judicial Review Protocol, paras 2–4 SCA, ss 29–31 Rules 54.2, 54.3
	Judicial review is available in criminal proceedings save in matters relating to trial on indictment	SCA, s 29(3)
Letters before action	The prospective claimant should write a detailed letter before action, allowing 14 days for the prospective defendant to respond, save where the nature of the claim precludes this. The prospective defendant should write a similarly detailed response. The letters should be copied to any interested parties	Judicial Review Protocol, paras 8–17, Annexes A and B
Venue	Proceedings must be issued in the High Court. A claim for judicial review cannot be transferred to a county court	CLSA 1990, s 1(10) CCA 1984, s 38(3)
	Proceedings should be issued in the Administrative Court Office in the Royal Courts of Justice, London or in the Administrative Court Office at Birmingham, Cardiff, Leeds or Manchester High Courts.	PD 54D
	The claimant or defendant can make an application to transfer the claim to a more convenient venue if the criteria set out in the Practice Direction 54D are met. Similarly the court can transfer a case to a different court centre of its own volition if it appears that the case is more conveniently heard at a different court centre.	

Permission	A claimant needs the permission of the court to bring a claim for judicial review	SCA, s 31(3) Rule 54.4
	The application for permission is generally made on the papers in the first instance	PD54A, para 8.4
	If permission is refused, or is granted subject to conditions or on certain grounds only, the application may be renewed to a judge orally but only if the initial refusal was on the papers	Rule 54.12
	Where a person served with the claim form has not filed an acknowledgment of service in accordance with the rules (see below), he will not be permitted to take part in the renewed permission hearing unless the court allows him to do so, but the defendant may take part in the substantive hearing, providing that he complies with any directions about filing his grounds and evidence	Rule 54.9
	If permission is refused at the oral hearing, the claimant may apply for permission to appeal to the Court of Appeal. Such application must be filed within 7 days of the decision of the High Court. If the Court of Appeal grants permission to apply for judicial review, the case will proceed in the High Court unless the Court of Appeal orders otherwise	Rule 52.15
	If the Court of Appeal refuses permission to appeal, no further appeal lies to the Supreme Court	AJA 1999, s 54

	Where permission is given, the court may give directions. The court will serve the order giving permission, and any directions, on the claimant, the defendant and on any interested party who has acknowledged service	Rule 54.10 Rule 54.11
	Neither the defendant nor any other party served with the claim form may apply to set aside the grant of permission to apply for judicial review	Rule 54.13
Time-limits	The proceedings must be brought promptly and in any event within 3 months from the date when the grounds for the application first arose	Rule 54.5
	Where the claimant seeks the quashing of a judgment, order or conviction, time begins to run from the date of that judgment, order or conviction	PD54A, para 4.1
	If there is undue delay by the claimant, the court may refuse to grant permission or any relief	SCA, s 31(6)
	The claimant must serve the claim form on the defendant and on any interested party within 7 days after the date of issue	Rule 54.7
	An interested party is any other person who is directly affected by the claim	Rule 54.1(2)(f)
	The defendant and any interested party served with the claim form who wishes to take part in the judicial review must file an acknowledgment of service not more than 21 days after the claim form is served on him; and must serve his acknowledgment on the other parties within 7 days after it is filed. It is not served by the court	Rule 54.8

	If the application for permission is refused, or is granted subject to conditions or on certain grounds only, the application to renew the request for permission at an oral hearing must be made within 7 days after the court serves on the claimant its reasons for not (simply) granting permission	Rule 54.12(4)
	An application for permission to appeal to the Court of Appeal against the refusal of permission must be made within 7 days of the decision of the High Court	Rule 52.15
Contents of claim form	The claim form must specify the relief claimed and must include –	Rule 54.6
	the name and address of any interested party;	
	a detailed statement of the claimant's grounds for bringing the claim for judicial review;	
	a statement of the facts relied on;	
	any application to extend the time-limit for filing the claim form;	
	any application for directions; and	PD54A, para 5.6
	It should be accompanied by –	
	any written evidence relied on;	
	a copy of any order that the claimant seeks to have quashed;	
	where the claim relates to a decision of a court or tribunal, an approved copy of the reasons for reaching that decision;	
	copies of any documents on which the claimant proposes to rely;	
	copies of any relevant statutory material;	

	a list of essential documents for advance reading by the court (with page references to the passages relied on); and,	
	insofar as any of the above are not available, reasons why they are unavailable	PD54A, paras 5.7, 5.8
	The claim form should also give details of the claimant's solicitors.	
	Where the claimant seeks to raise any issue under HRA 1998, the claim form must give the particulars required by PD16, para 16.1	PD54A, para 5.3
	Where the claimant seeks to raise a devolution issue, the claim form must say so and must specify the relevant statutory provision and the relevant facts	PD54A, para 5.4
Acknowledgment of service	The acknowledgment of service should state whether the defendant contests the claim and, if so, summarise his grounds for doing so	Rule 54.8(4)
Opposing the claim	The defendant, and any interested party who wishes to oppose or be heard on the claim, must serve detailed grounds and any evidence within 35 days after service of the order giving permission	Rule 54.14(1)
	The claimant must serve any reply within 14 days of service of the defendant's or interested party's evidence	Rule 54.14(2)
	No other evidence is admissible without the court's permission	Rule 54.16
Preparation for hearing	The claimant requires the court's permission to rely on any grounds other than those for which he has been given permission	Rule 54.15

The claimant must give the other parties 7 clear days' notice of an application to rely on additional grounds	PD54A, para 11.1
Any person wishing to apply to the court for permission to file evidence or to make representations at the hearing of the claim for judicial review should do so promptly	Rule 54.17
The court may allow such an intervention and may do so subject to conditions	PD54A, paras 13.1, 13.2
Disclosure is not required unless the court orders otherwise	PD54A, para 12.1
The court may order cross-examination but this is rare	
The claimant must file two copies of a paginated and indexed bundle	PD54A, paras 5.9, 5.10
The bundle, and the claimant's skeleton argument, must be filed 21 working days before the hearing	PD54A, para 15.1
The defendant and any interested party wishing to make representations must file skeleton arguments 14 working days before the hearing date	PD54A, para 15.2

Skeleton arguments must contain –

a time estimate for the complete hearing, including judgment;

a list of issues;

a list of the legal points to be taken (together with any relevant authorities with page references to the passages relied on);

a chronology of events (with page references to the bundle of documents);

	a list of essential documents for the advance reading of the court (with page references to the passages relied on) (if different from that filed with the claim form);	
	a time estimate for that reading; and	
	a list of persons referred to.	PD54A, para 15.3
Transfer	Proceedings which commenced as a claim for judicial review may be ordered to continue as if they had not been commenced under Pt 54	Rule 54.20
	Proceedings which were commenced other than under Pt 54 may be transferred to the Administrative Court	PD54A, paras 14.1, 14.2 Rule 30.5
Agreed final orders	Where the parties agree about the final order to be made in a claim for judicial review, the claimant should file a document (with two copies) signed by all the parties setting out the terms of the proposed order, together with a short statement of the matters relied on as justifying the proposed order and copies of any authorities and provisions relied on	PD54A, para 17.1
	If the court is satisfied that the proposed order should be made, it may make it without a hearing	Rule 54.18
	If the court is not so satisfied, a hearing date will be set	PD54A, para 17.3
Forms	Claim Form N461	
	Application for urgent consideration N463	

Acknowledgment of
service N462
Form N464 Application for
directions as to venue for
administration and
determination
Form N465 Response to
application for directions as to
venue for administration and
determination

Application for permission to
appeal a refusal of permission
to bring claim for judicial
review N161

Appendix B

STATUTORY MATERIALS

SENIOR COURTS ACT 1981

31 Application for judicial review

(1) An application to the High Court for one or more of the following forms of relief, namely –

(a)   a mandatory, prohibiting or quashing order;

(b)   a declaration or injunction under subsection (2); or

(c)   an injunction under section 30 restraining a person not entitled to do so from acting in an office to which that section applies,

shall be made in accordance with rules of court by a procedure to be known as an application for judicial review.

(2) A declaration may be made or an injunction granted under this subsection in any case where an application for judicial review, seeking that relief, has been made and the High Court considers that, having regard to –

(a)   the nature of the matters in respect of which relief may be granted by mandatory, prohibiting or quashing orders;

(b)   the nature of the persons and bodies against whom relief may be granted by such orders; and

(c)   all the circumstances of the case,

it would be just and convenient for the declaration to be made or the injunction to be granted, as the case may be.

(3) No application for judicial review shall be made unless the leave of the High Court has been obtained in accordance with rules of court; and the court shall not grant leave to make such an application unless it considers that the applicant has a sufficient interest in the matter to which the application relates.

(4) On an application for judicial review the High Court may award to the applicant damages, restitution or the recovery of a sum due if –

(a)   the application includes a claim for such an award arising from any matter to which the application relates; and

(b)   the court is satisfied that such an award would have been made if the claim had been made in an action begun by the applicant at the time of making the application.

(5) If, on an application for judicial review, the High Court quashes the decision to which the application relates, it may in addition –

(a)   remit the matter to the court, tribunal or authority which made the decision, with a direction to reconsider the matter and reach a decision in accordance with the findings of the High Court, or

(b)   substitute its own decision for the decision in question.

(5A) But the power conferred by subsection (5)(b) is exercisable only if –

(a)   the decision in question was made by a court or tribunal,

(b)   the decision is quashed on the ground that there has been an error of law, and

(c)   without the error, there would have been only one decision which the court or tribunal could have reached.

(5B) Unless the High Court otherwise directs, a decision substituted by it under subsection (5)(b) has effect as if it were a decision of the relevant court or tribunal.

(6) Where the High Court considers that there has been undue delay in making an application for judicial review, the court may refuse to grant –

(a)   leave for the making of the application; or

(b)   any relief sought on the application,

if it considers that the granting of the relief sought would be likely to cause substantial hardship to, or substantially prejudice the rights of, any person or would be detrimental to good administration.

(7) Subsection (6) is without prejudice to any enactment or rule of court which has the effect of limiting the time within which an application for judicial review may be made.

Amendments—SI 2004/1033; Tribunals, Courts and Enforcement Act 2007, s 141.

THE HUMAN RIGHTS ACT 1998

Scotland – This Act applies to Scotland. For the application of the European Convention on Human Rights (ECHR) to Acts of the Scottish Parliament see the Scotland Act 1998, ss 57(2) and 100.

Introduction

1 The Convention rights

(1) In this Act, 'the Convention rights' means the rights and fundamental freedoms set out in –

(a)   Articles 2 to 12 and 14 of the Convention, and

(b)   Articles 1 to 3 of the First Protocol, and

(c)   [Article 1 of the Thirteenth Protocol],

as read with Articles 16 to 18 of the Convention.

(2) Those Articles are to have effect for the purposes of this Act subject to any designated derogation or reservation (as to which see sections 14 and 15).

(3) The Articles are set out in Schedule 1.

(4) The [Secretary of State] may by order make such amendments to this Act as he considers appropriate to reflect the effect, in relation to the United Kingdom, of a protocol.

(5) In subsection (4) 'protocol' means a protocol to the Convention –

    (a)   which the United Kingdom has ratified; or

    (b)   which the United Kingdom has signed with a view to ratification.

(6) No amendment may be made by an order under subsection (4) so as to come into force before the protocol concerned is in force in relation to the United Kingdom.

NOTES

Amendments: SI 2003/1887; SI 2004/1574.

2 *Interpretation of Convention rights*

(1) A court or tribunal determining a question which has arisen under this Act in connection with a Convention right must take into account any –

    (a)   judgment, decision, declaration or advisory opinion of the European Court of Human Rights,

    (b)   opinion of the Commission given in a report adopted under Article 31 of the Convention,

    (c)   decision of the Commission in connection with Article 26 or 27(2) of the Convention, or

    (d)   decision of the Committee of Ministers taken under Article 46 of the Convention,

whenever made or given, so far as, in the opinion of the court or tribunal, it is relevant to the proceedings in which that question has arisen.

(2) Evidence of any judgment, decision, declaration or opinion of which account may have to be taken under this section is to be given in proceedings before any court or tribunal in such manner as may be provided by rules.

(3) In this section 'rules' means rules of court or, in the case of proceedings before a tribunal, rules made for the purposes of this section –

    (a)   by ... [the Lord Chancellor or] the Secretary of State, in relation to any proceedings outside Scotland;

    (b)   by the Secretary of State, in relation to proceedings in Scotland; or

    (c)   by a Northern Ireland department, in relation to proceedings before a tribunal in Northern Ireland –

        (i)   which deals with transferred matters; and

        (ii)   for which no rules made under paragraph (a) are in force.

3 *Interpretation of legislation*

Legislation

(1) So far as it is possible to do so, primary legislation and subordinate legislation must be read and given effect in a way which is compatible with the Convention rights.

(2) This section –

    (a)   applies to primary legislation and subordinate legislation whenever enacted;

    (b)   does not affect the validity, continuing operation or enforcement of any incompatible primary legislation; and

(c)   does not affect the validity, continuing operation or enforcement of any incompatible subordinate legislation if (disregarding any possibility of revocation) primary legislation prevents removal of the incompatibility.

4 Declaration of incompatibility

(1) Subsection (2) applies in any proceedings in which a court determines whether a provision of primary legislation is compatible with a Convention right.

(2) If the court is satisfied that the provision is incompatible with a Convention right, it may make a declaration of that incompatibility.

(3) Subsection (4) applies in any proceedings in which a court determines whether a provision of subordinate legislation, made in the exercise of a power conferred by primary legislation, is compatible with a Convention right.

(4) If the court is satisfied –

(a)   that the provision is incompatible with a Convention right, and
(b)   that (disregarding any possibility of revocation) the primary legislation concerned prevents removal of the incompatibility,

it may make a declaration of that incompatibility.

(5) In this section 'court' means –

[(a)   [the Supreme Court;]
(b)   the Judicial Committee of the Privy Council;
(c)   the Courts-Martial Appeal Court;
(d)   in Scotland, the High Court of Justiciary sitting otherwise than as a trial court or the Court of Session;
(e)   in England and Wales or Northern Ireland, the High Court or the Court of Appeal.
[(f)   the Court of Protection, in any matter being dealt with by the President of the Family Division, the Vice-Chancellor or a puisne judge of the High Court.]

(6) A declaration under this section ('a declaration of incompatibility') –

(a)   does not affect the validity, continuing operation or enforcement of the provision in respect of which it is given; and
(b)   is not binding on the parties to the proceedings in which it is made.

NOTES

Amendments—Mental Capacity Act 2005, s 67(1), Sch 6, para 43. Amendment: Constitutional Reform Act 2005, s 40(4), Sch 9.

5 Right of Crown to intervene

(1) Where a court is considering whether to make a declaration of incompatibility, the Crown is entitled to notice in accordance with rules of court.

(2) In any case to which subsection (1) applies –

(a)   a Minister of the Crown, or
(b)   a member of the Scottish Executive,
(c)   a Northern Ireland Minister,
(d)   a Northern Ireland department,

is entitled, on an application made to the court in accordance with rules of court, to be joined as a party to the proceedings.

(3) An application under subsection (2) may be made at any time during the proceedings.

(4) A person who has been made a party to criminal proceedings (other than in Scotland) as the result of an application under subsection (2) may, with leave, appeal to the [Supreme Court] against any declaration of incompatibility made in the proceedings.

(5) In subsection (4) –

'criminal proceedings' includes all proceedings before the Courts-Martial Appeal Court; and
'leave' means leave granted by the court making the declaration of incompatibility or by the [Supreme Court]

NOTES

Amendment—Constitutional Reform Act 2005, s 40(4), Sch 9.

6 *Acts of public authorities*

(1) It is unlawful for a public authority to act in a way which is incompatible with a Convention right.

(2) Subsection (1) does not apply to an act if –

(a)   as the result of one or more provisions of primary legislation, the authority could not have acted differently; or
(b)   in the case of one or more provisions of, or made under, primary legislation which cannot be read or given effect in a way which is compatible with the Convention rights, the authority was acting so as to give effect to or enforce those provisions.

(3) In this section, 'public authority' includes –

(a)   a court or tribunal, and
(b)   any person certain of whose functions are functions of a public nature,

but does not include either House of Parliament or a person exercising functions in connection with proceedings in Parliament.

(4) [repealed].

(5) In relation to a particular act, a person is not a public authority by virtue only of subsection (3)(b) if the nature of the act is private.

(6) 'An act' includes a failure to act but does not include a failure to –

(a)   introduce in, or lay before, Parliament a proposal for legislation; or
(b)   make any primary legislation or remedial order.

NOTES

Amendments—Constitutional Reform Act 2005, ss 40(4), 146, Sch 9, Pt 1, para 66(1), (4), Sch 18, Pt 5.

7 *Proceedings*

(1) A person who claims that a public authority has acted (or proposes to act) in a way which is made unlawful by section 6(1) may –

(a)   bring proceedings against the authority under this Act in the appropriate court or tribunal, or

(b)   rely on the Convention right or rights concerned in any legal proceedings,

but only if he is (or would be) a victim of the unlawful act.

(2) In subsection (1)(a) 'appropriate court or tribunal' means such court or tribunal as may be determined in accordance with rules; and proceedings against an authority includes a counterclaim or similar proceeding.

(3) If the proceedings are brought on an application for judicial review, the applicant is to be taken to have a sufficient interest in relation to the unlawful act only if he is, or would be, a victim of that act.

(4) If the proceedings are made by way of a petition for judicial review in Scotland, the applicant shall be taken to have title and interest to sue in relation to the unlawful act only if he is, or would be, a victim of that act.

(5) Proceedings under subsection (1)(a) must be brought before the end of –

(a)   the period of one year beginning with the date on which the act complained of took place; or

(b)   such longer period as the court or tribunal considers equitable having regard to all the circumstances,

but that is subject to any rule imposing a stricter time limit in relation to the procedure in question.

(6) In subsection (1)(b) 'legal proceedings' includes –

(a)   proceedings brought by or at the instigation of a public authority; and

(b)   an appeal against the decision of a court or tribunal.

(7) For the purposes of this section, a person is a victim of an unlawful act only if he would be a victim for the purposes of Article 34 of the Convention if proceedings were brought in the European Court of Human Rights in respect of that act.

(8) Nothing in this Act creates a criminal offence.

(9) In this section 'rules' means –

(a)   in relation to proceedings before a court or tribunal outside Scotland, rules made by ... [the Lord Chancellor] the Secretary of State for the purposes of this section or rules of court,

(b)   in relation to proceedings before a court or tribunal in Scotland, rules made by the Secretary of State for those purposes,

(c)   in relation to proceedings before a tribunal in Northern Ireland –
       (i)   which deals with transferred matters; and
       (ii)   for which no rules made under paragraph (a) are in force,
       rules made by a Northern Ireland department for those purposes,

and includes provision made by order under section 1 of the Courts and Legal Services Act 1990.

(10) In making rules regard must be had to section 9.

(11) The Minister who has power to make rules in relation to a particular tribunal may, to the extent he considers it necessary to ensure that the tribunal can provide an appropriate remedy in relation to an act (or proposed act) of a public authority which is (or would be) unlawful as a result of section 6(1), by order add to –

(a)   the relief or remedies which the tribunal may grant; or

(b)   the grounds on which it may grant any of them.

(12) An order made under subsection (11) may contain such incidental, supplemental, consequential or transitional provision as the Minister making it considers appropriate.

(13) 'The Minister' includes the Northern Ireland department concerned.

NOTES

Amendments: SI 2003/1887; SI 2005/3429.

8 *Judicial remedies*

(1) In relation to any act (or proposed act) of a public authority which the court finds is (or would be) unlawful, it may grant such relief or remedy, or make such order, within its powers as it considers just and appropriate.

(2) But damages may be awarded only by a court which has power to award damages, or to order the payment of compensation, in civil proceedings.

(3) No award of damages is to be made unless, taking account of all the circumstances of the case, including—

(a)   any other relief or remedy granted, or order made, in relation to the act in question (by that or any other court), and

(b)   the consequences of any decision (of that or any other court) in respect of that act,

the court is satisfied that the award is necessary to afford just satisfaction to the person in whose favour it is made.

(4) In determining –

(a)   whether to award damages, or

(b)   the amount of an award,

the court must take into account the principles applied by the European Court of Human Rights in relation to the award of compensation under Article 41 of the Convention.

(5) A public authority against which damages are awarded is to be treated –

(a)   in Scotland, for the purposes of section 3 of the Law Reform (Miscellaneous Provisions) (Scotland) Act 1940 as if the award were made in an action of damages in which the authority has been found liable in respect of loss or damage to the person to whom the award is made;

(b)   for the purposes of the Civil Liability (Contribution) Act 1978 as liable in respect of damage suffered by the person to whom the award is made.

(6) In this section –

'court' includes a tribunal;

'damages' means damages for an unlawful act of a public authority; and

'unlawful' means unlawful under section 6(1).

9 *Judicial acts*

(1) Proceedings under section 7(1)(a) in respect of a judicial act may be brought only –

(a)   by exercising a right of appeal;

(b)   on an application (in Scotland a petition) for judicial review; or

(c)   in such other forum as may be prescribed by rules.

(2) That does not affect any rule of law which prevents a court from being the subject of judicial review.

(3) In proceedings under this Act in respect of a judicial act done in good faith, damages may not be awarded otherwise than to compensate a person to the extent required by Article 5(5) of the Convention.

(4) An award of damages permitted by subsection (3) is to be made against the Crown; but no award may be made unless the appropriate person, if not a party to the proceedings, is joined.

(5) In this section –

'appropriate person' means the Minister responsible for the court concerned, or a person or government department nominated by him;

'court' includes a tribunal;

'judge' includes a member of a tribunal, a justice of the peace [(or, in Northern Ireland, a lay magistrate)] and a clerk or other officer entitled to exercise the jurisdiction of a court;

'judicial act' means a judicial act of a court and includes an act done on the instructions, or on behalf, of a judge.

'rules' has the same meaning as in section 7(9).

NOTES

Amendments: Justice (Northern Ireland) Act 2002, s 10(6), Sch 4, para 39.

Remedial action

10 Power to take remedial action

(Not reproduced)

Other rights and proceedings

11 Safeguard for existing human rights

A person's reliance on a Convention right does not restrict –

(a)   any other right or freedom conferred on him by or under any law having effect in any part of the United Kingdom; or

(b)   his right to make any claim or bring any proceedings which he could make or bring apart from sections 7 to 9.

12 Freedom of expression

(1) This section applies if a court is considering whether to grant any relief which, if granted, might affect the exercise of the Convention right to freedom of expression.

(2) If the person against whom the application for relief is made ('the respondent') is neither present nor represented, no such relief is to be granted unless the court is satisfied –

(a)   that the applicant has taken all practicable steps to notify the respondent; or

(b)   that there are compelling reasons why the respondent should not be notified.

(3) No such relief is to be granted so as to restrain publication before trial unless the court is satisfied that the applicant is likely to establish that publication should not be allowed.

(4) The court must have particular regard to the importance of the Convention right to freedom of expression and, where the proceedings relate to material which the respondent claims, or which appears to the court, to be journalistic, literary or artistic material (or to conduct connected with such material), to –

(a)   the extent to which –
    (i)   the material has, or is about to, become available to the public; or
    (ii)   it is, or would be, in the public interest for the material to be published;

(b)   any relevant privacy code.

(5) In this section –

'court' includes a tribunal; and
'relief' includes any remedy or order (other than in criminal proceedings).

13 Freedom of thought, conscience and religion

(1) If a court's determination of any question arising under this Act might affect the exercise by a religious organisation (itself or its members collectively) of the Convention right to freedom of thought, conscience and religion, it must have particular regard to the importance of that right.

(2) In this section, 'court' includes a tribunal.

Derogations and reservations

14 Derogations

Derogations

(1) In this Act, 'designated derogation' means –

...   any derogation by the United Kingdom from an Article of the Convention, or of any protocol to the Convention, which is designated for the purposes of this Act in an order made by the [Secretary of State]

(2) ...

(3) If a designated derogation is amended or replaced it ceases to be a designated derogation.

(4) But subsection (3) does not prevent the [Secretary of State] from exercising his power under subsection (1) ... to make a fresh designation order in respect of the Article concerned.

(5) The [Secretary of State] must by order make such amendments to Schedule 3 as he considers appropriate to reflect –

(a)   any designation order; or
(b)   the effect of subsection (3).

(6) A designation order may be made in anticipation of the making by the United Kingdom of a proposed derogation.

NOTES

Amendments: SI 2001/1216; SI 2003/1887.

15 Reservations

(1) In this Act, 'designated reservation' means –

  (a) the United Kingdom's reservation to Article 2 of the First Protocol to the Convention; and

  (b) any other reservation by the United Kingdom to an Article of the Convention, or of any protocol to the Convention, which is designated for the purposes of this Act in an order made by the Secretary of State.

(2) The text of the reservation referred to in subsection (1)(a) is set out in Part II of Schedule 3.

(3) If a designated reservation is withdrawn wholly or in part it ceases to be a designated reservation.

(4) But subsection (3) does not prevent the Secretary of State from exercising his power under subsection (1)(b) to make a fresh designation order in respect of the Article concerned.

(5) The Secretary of State must by order make such amendments to this Act as he considers appropriate to reflect –

  (a) any designation order; or
  (b) the effect of subsection (3).

NOTES

Amendments: As amended by SI 2003/1887.

16 Period for which designated reservations have effect

(Not reproduced)

17 Periodic review of designated reservations

(Not reproduced)

18, 19 Judges of the European Court of Human Rights

(Not reproduced)

Supplemental

20 Orders under this Act

(Not reproduced)

21 Interpretation etc.

(1) In this Act –

'amend' includes repeal and apply (with or without modifications);

'the appropriate Minister' means the Minister of the Crown having charge of the appropriate authorised government department (within the meaning of the Crown Proceedings Act 1947);

'the Commission' means the European Commission of Human Rights;

'the Convention' means the Convention for the Protection of Human Rights and Fundamental Freedoms, agreed by the Council of Europe at Rome on 4th November 1950 as it has effect for the time being in relation to the United Kingdom;

'declaration of incompatibility' means a declaration under section 4;

'Minister of the Crown' has the same meaning as in the Ministers of the Crown Act 1975;

'Northern Ireland Minister' includes the First Minister and the deputy First Minister in Northern Ireland;

'primary legislation' means any –
- (a)   public general Act;
- (b)   local and personal Act;
- (c)   private Act;
- (d)   Measure of the Church Assembly;
- (e)   Measure of the General Synod of the Church of England;
- (f)   Order in Council –
  - (i)   made in exercise of Her Majesty's Royal Prerogative;
  - (ii)   made under section 38(1)(a) of the Northern Ireland Constitution Act 1973 or the corresponding provision of the Northern Ireland Act 1998; or
  - (iii)   amending an Act of a kind mentioned in paragraph (a), (b) or (c);

and includes an order or other instrument made under primary legislation (otherwise than by [Welsh Ministers, the First Minister for Wales, the Counsel General to the Welsh Assembly Government], a member of the Scottish Executive, a Northern Ireland Minister or a Northern Ireland department) to the extent to which it operates to bring one or more provisions of that legislation into force or amends any primary legislation;

'the First Protocol' means the protocol to the Convention agreed at Paris on 20th March 1952;

...

'the Eleventh Protocol' means the protocol to the Convention (restructuring the control machinery established by the Convention) agreed at Strasbourg on 11th May 1994.

['the Thirteenth Protocol' means the protocol to the Convention (concerning the abolition of the death penalty in all circumstances) agreed at Vilnius on 3rd May 2002;]

'remedial order' means an order under section 10;

'subordinate legislation' means any –
- (a)   Order in Council other than one –
  - (i)   made in exercise of Her Majesty's Royal Prerogative;
  - (ii)   made under section 38(1)(a) of the Northern Ireland Constitution Act 1973 or the corresponding provision of the Northern Ireland Act 1998; or

        (iii)   amending an Act of a kind mentioned in the definition of primary legislation;

(b)   Act of the Scottish Parliament;

[(ba) Measure of the National Assembly for Wales;

(bb) Act of the National Assembly for Wales;]

(c)   Act of the Parliament of Northern Ireland;

(d)   Measure of the Assembly established under section 1 of the Northern Ireland Assembly Act 1973;

(e)   Act of the Northern Ireland Assembly;

(f)   order, rules, regulations, scheme, warrant, byelaw or other instrument made under primary legislation (except to the extent to which it operates to bring one or more provisions of that legislation into force or amends any primary legislation);

(g)   order, rules, regulations, scheme, warrant, byelaw or other instrument made under legislation mentioned in paragraph (b), (c), (d) or (e) or made under an Order in Council applying only to Northern Ireland;

(h)   order, rules, regulations, scheme, warrant, byelaw or other instrument made by a member of the Scottish Executive[, Welsh Ministers, the First Minister for Wales, the Counsel General to the Welsh Assembly Government], a Northern Ireland Minister or a Northern Ireland department in exercise of prerogative or

other executive functions of Her Majesty which are exercisable by such a person on behalf of Her Majesty;

'transferred matters' has the same meaning as in the Northern Ireland Act 1998; and 'tribunal' means any tribunal in which legal proceedings may be brought.

(2) The references in paragraphs (b) and (c) of section 2(1) to Articles are to Articles of the Convention as they had effect immediately before the coming into force of the Eleventh Protocol.

(3) The reference in paragraph (d) of section 2(1) to Article 46 includes a reference to Articles 32 and 54 of the Convention as they had effect immediately before the coming into force of the Eleventh Protocol.

(4) The references in section 2(1) to a report or decision of the Commission or a decision of the Committee of Ministers include references to a report or decision made as provided by paragraphs 3, 4 and 6 of Article 5 of the Eleventh Protocol (transitional provisions).

(5) [Repealed].

NOTES

Amendments: SI 2004/1574; Government of Wales Act 2006, s 160(1), Sch 10, para 56. Armed Forces Act 2006, s 378(2), Sch 7.

22 *Short title, commencement, application and extent*

(1) This Act may be cited as the Human Rights Act 1998.

(2) Sections 18, 20 and 21(5) and this section come into force on the passing of this Act.

(3) The other provisions of this Act come into force on such day as the Secretary of State may by order appoint; and different days may be appointed for different purposes.

(4) Paragraph (b) of subsection (1) of section 7 applies to proceedings brought by or at the instigation of a public authority whenever the act in question took place; but otherwise that subsection does not apply to an act taking place before the coming into force of that section.

(5) This Act binds the Crown.

(6) This Act extends to Northern Ireland.

(7) ....

NOTES

Amendments: As amended by the Armed Forces Act 2006, s 378(2), Sch 17.

SCHEDULE 1

The Articles

PART I

The Convention

Rights and Freedoms

Article 2

Right to life

1. Everyone's right to life shall be protected by law. No one shall be deprived of his life intentionally save in the execution of a sentence of a court following his conviction of a crime for which this penalty is provided by law.

2. Deprivation of life shall not be regarded as inflicted in contravention of this Article when it results from the use of force which is no more than absolutely necessary:

(a)   in defence of any person from unlawful violence;
(b)   in order to effect a lawful arrest or to prevent the escape of a person lawfully detained;
(c)   in action lawfully taken for the purpose of quelling a riot or insurrection.

Article 3

Prohibition of torture

No one shall be subjected to torture or to inhuman or degrading treatment or punishment.

Article 4

Prohibition of slavery and forced labour

1. No one shall be held in slavery or servitude.

2. No one shall be required to perform forced or compulsory labour.

3. For the purpose of this Article the term 'forced or compulsory labour' shall not include:

    (a) any work required to be done in the ordinary course of detention imposed according to the provisions of Article 5 of this Convention or during conditional release from such detention;

    (b) any service of a military character or, in case of conscientious objectors in countries where they are recognised, service exacted instead of compulsory military service;

    (c) any service exacted in case of an emergency or calamity threatening the life or well-being of the community;

    (d) any work or service which forms part of normal civic obligations.

Article 5

Right to liberty and security

1. Everyone has the right to liberty and security of person. No one shall be deprived of his liberty save in the following cases and in accordance with a procedure prescribed by law:

    (a) the lawful detention of a person after conviction by a competent court;

    (b) the lawful arrest or detention of a person for non-compliance with the lawful order of a court or in order to secure the fulfilment of any obligation prescribed by law;

    (c) the lawful arrest or detention of a person effected for the purpose of bringing him before the competent legal authority on reasonable suspicion of having committed an offence or when it is reasonably considered necessary to prevent his committing an offence or fleeing after having done so;

    (d) the detention of a minor by lawful order for the purpose of educational supervision or his lawful detention for the purpose of bringing him before the competent legal authority;

    (e) the lawful detention of persons for the prevention of the spreading of infectious diseases, of persons of unsound mind, alcoholics or drug addicts or vagrants;

    (f) the lawful arrest or detention of a person to prevent his effecting an unauthorized entry into the country or of a person against whom action is being taken with a view to deportation or extradition.

2. Everyone who is arrested shall be informed promptly, in a language which he understands, of the reasons for his arrest and of any charge against him.

3. Everyone arrested or detained in accordance with the provisions of paragraph 1(c) of this Article shall be brought promptly before a judge or other officer authorised by law to exercise judicial power and shall be entitled to trial within a reasonable time or to release pending trial. Release may be conditioned by guarantees to appear for trial.

4. Everyone who is deprived of his liberty by arrest or detention shall be entitled to take proceedings by which the lawfulness of his detention shall be decided speedily by a court and his release ordered if the detention is not lawful.

5. Everyone who has been the victim of arrest or detention in contravention of the provisions of this Article shall have an enforceable right to compensation.

Article 6

Right to a fair trial

1. In the determination of his civil rights and obligations or of any criminal charge against him, everyone is entitled to a fair and public hearing within a reasonable time by an independent and impartial tribunal established by law. Judgment shall be pronounced publicly but the press and public may be excluded from all or part of the trial in the interest of morals, public order or national security in a democratic society, where the interests of juveniles or the protection of the private life of the parties so require, or to the extent strictly necessary in the opinion of the court in special circumstances where publicity would prejudice the interests of justice.

2. Everyone charged with a criminal offence shall be presumed innocent until proved guilty according to law.

3. Everyone charged with a criminal offence has the following minimum rights:

   (a)   to be informed promptly, in a language which he understands and in detail, of the nature and cause of the accusation against him;
   (b)   to have adequate time and facilities for the preparation of his defence;
   (c)   to defend himself in person or through legal assistance of his own choosing or, if he has not sufficient means to pay for legal assistance, to be given it free when the interests of justice so require;
   (d)   to examine or have examined witnesses against him and to obtain the attendance and examination of witnesses on his behalf under the same conditions as witnesses against him;
   (e)   to have the free assistance of an interpreter if he cannot understand or speak the language used in court.

Commentary

See Chapter 2, Right to a Fair Trial.

Article 7

No punishment without law

1. No one shall be held guilty of any criminal offence on account of any act or omission which did not constitute a criminal offence under national or international law at the time when it was committed. Nor shall a heavier penalty be imposed than the one that was applicable at the time the criminal offence was committed.

2. This Article shall not prejudice the trial and punishment of any person for any act or omission which, at the time when it was committed, was criminal according to the general principles of law recognised by civilised nations.

Article 8

Right to respect for private and family life

1. Everyone has the right to respect for his private and family life, his home and his correspondence.

2. There shall be no interference by a public authority with the exercise of this right except such as is in accordance with the law and is necessary in a democratic society in the interests of national security, public safety or the economic well-being of the country, for the prevention of disorder or crime, for the protection of health or morals, or for the protection of the rights and freedoms of others.

Article 9

Freedom of thought, conscience and religion

1. Everyone has the right to freedom of thought, conscience and religion; this right includes freedom to change his religion or belief and freedom, either alone or in community with others and in public or private, to manifest his religion or belief, in worship, teaching, practice and observance.

2. Freedom to manifest one's religion or beliefs shall be subject only to such limitations as are prescribed by law and are necessary in a democratic society in the interests of public safety, for the protection of public order, health or morals, or for the protection of the rights and freedoms of others.

Article 10

Freedom of expression

1. Everyone has the right to freedom of expression. This right shall include freedom to hold opinions and to receive and impart information and ideas without interference by public authority and regardless of frontiers. This Article shall not prevent States from requiring the licensing of broadcasting, television or cinema enterprises.

2. The exercise of these freedoms, since it carries with it duties and responsibilities, may be subject to such formalities, conditions, restrictions or penalties as are prescribed by law and are necessary in a democratic society, in the interests of national security, territorial integrity or public safety, for the prevention of disorder or crime, for the protection of health or morals, for the protection of the reputation or rights of others, for preventing the disclosure of information received in confidence, or for maintaining the authority and impartiality of the judiciary.

Article 11

Freedom of assembly and association

1. Everyone has the right to freedom of peaceful assembly and to freedom of association with others, including the right to form and to join trade unions for the protection of his interests.

2 No restrictions shall be placed on the exercise of these rights other than such as are prescribed by law and are necessary in a democratic society in the interests of national security or public safety, for the prevention of disorder or crime, for the protection of

health or morals or for the protection of the rights and freedoms of others. This Article shall not prevent the imposition of lawful restrictions on the exercise of these rights by members of the armed forces, of the police or of the administration of the State.

Article 12

Right to marry

Men and women of marriageable age have the right to marry and to found a family, according to the national laws governing the exercise of this right.

Article 14

Prohibition of discrimination

The enjoyment of the rights and freedoms set forth in this Convention shall be secured without discrimination on any ground such as sex, race, colour, language, religion, political or other opinion, national or social origin, association with a national minority, property, birth or other status.

Article 16

Restrictions on political activity of aliens

Nothing in Articles 10, 11 and 14 shall be regarded as preventing the High Contracting Parties from imposing restrictions on the political activity of aliens.

Article 17

Prohibition of abuse of rights

Nothing in this Convention may be interpreted as implying for any State, group or person any right to engage in any activity or perform any act aimed at the destruction of any of the rights and freedoms set forth herein or at their limitation to a greater extent than is provided for in the Convention.

Article 18

Limitation on use of restrictions on rights

The restrictions permitted under this Convention to the said rights and freedoms shall not be applied for any purpose other than those for which they have been prescribed.

PART II

The First Protocol

Article 1

Protection of property

Every natural or legal person is entitled to the peaceful enjoyment of his possessions. No one shall be deprived of his possessions except in the public interest and subject to the conditions provided for by law and by the general principles of international law.

The preceding provisions shall not, however, in any way impair the right of a State to enforce such laws as it deems necessary to control the use of property in accordance with the general interest or to secure the payment of taxes or other contributions or penalties.

Article 2

Right to education

No person shall be denied the right to education. In the exercise of any functions which it assumes in relation to education and to teaching, the State shall respect the right of parents to ensure such education and teaching in conformity with their own religious and philosophical convictions.

Article 3

Right to free elections

The High Contracting Parties undertake to hold free elections at reasonable intervals by secret ballot, under conditions which will ensure the free expression of the opinion of the people in the choice of the legislature.

PART III

The Thirteenth Protocol

(Not reproduced)

SCHEDULE 2

Remedial Orders

(Not reproduced)

SCHEDULE 3

Derogation and Reservation

(Not Reproduced)

SCHEDULE 4

Judicial Pensions

(Not Reproduced)

Appendix C

CIVIL PROCEDURE RULES

[PART 54
JUDICIAL REVIEW [AND STATUTORY REVIEW]]

[Section I – Judicial Review]

[54.1 Scope and interpretation

(1) This [Section of this] Part contains rules about judicial review.

(2) In this [Section] –

  (a) a 'claim for judicial review' means a claim to review the lawfulness of –
    (i) an enactment; or
    (ii) a decision, action or failure to act in relation to the exercise of a public function.
  (b)–(d)…;
  (e) 'the judicial review procedure' means the Part 8 procedure as modified by this [Section];
  (f) 'interested party' means any person (other than the claimant and defendant) who is directly affected by the claim; and
  (g) 'court' means the High Court, unless otherwise stated.

  (Rule 8.1(6)(b) provides that a rule or practice direction may, in relation to a specified type of proceedings, disapply or modify any of these rules set out in Part 8 as they apply to those proceedings)]

Amendments—Inserted by SI 2000/2092; amended by SI 2003/364; SI 2003/3361.

[54.2 When this [Section] must be used

The judicial review procedure must be used in a claim for judicial review where the claimant is seeking –

  (a) a mandatory order;
  (b) a prohibiting order;
  (c) a quashing order; or
  (d) an injunction under section 30 of the [Senior Courts Act 1981] (restraining a person from acting in any office in which he is not entitled to act).]

Amendments—Inserted by SI 2000/2092; amended by SI 2003/364.

[54.3 When this [Section] may be used

(1) The judicial review procedure may be used in a claim for judicial review where the claimant is seeking –

  (a) a declaration; or

(b)   an injunction[(GL)].

(Section 31(2) of the [Senior Courts Act 1981] sets out the circumstances in which the court may grant a declaration or injunction in a claim for judicial review)

(Where the claimant is seeking a declaration or injunction in addition to one of the remedies listed in rule 54.2, the judicial review procedure must be used)

(2) A claim for judicial review may include a claim for damages[, restitution or the recovery of a sum due] but may not seek [such a remedy] alone.

(Section 31(4) of the [Senior Courts Act 1981] sets out the circumstances in which the court may award damages[, restitution or the recovery of a sum due] on a claim for judicial review)]

Amendments—Inserted by SI 2000/2092; amended by SI 2003/364; SI 2003/3361; Constitutional Reform Act 2005, Sch 11, para 1(2).

[54.4 Permission required

The court's permission to proceed is required in a claim for judicial review whether started under this [Section] or transferred to the Administrative Court.]

Amendments—Inserted by SI 2000/2092; amended by SI 2003/364.

[54.5 Time limit for filing claim form

(1) The claim form must be filed –

(a)   promptly; and
(b)   in any event not later than 3 months after the grounds to make the claim first arose.

(2) The time limit in this rule may not be extended by agreement between the parties.

(3) This rule does not apply when any other enactment specifies a shorter time limit for making the claim for judicial review.]

Amendments—Inserted by SI 2000/2092.

[54.6 Claim form

(1) In addition to the matters set out in rule 8.2 (contents of the claim form) the claimant must also state –

(a)   the name and address of any person he considers to be an interested party;
(b)   that he is requesting permission to proceed with a claim for judicial review; and
(c)   any remedy (including any interim remedy) he is claiming.

(Part 25 sets out how to apply for an interim remedy)

(2) The claim form must be accompanied by the documents required by [Practice Direction 54A]].

Amendments—Inserted by SI 2000/2092; SI 2009/3309.

[54.7 Service of claim form

The claim form must be served on –

(a)   the defendant; and

(b)   unless the court otherwise directs, any person the claimant considers to be an interested party, within 7 days after the date of issue.]

Amendments—Inserted by SI 2000/2092.

[54.8 Acknowledgment of service

(1) Any person served with the claim form who wishes to take part in the judicial review must file an acknowledgment of service in the relevant practice form in accordance with the following provisions of this rule.

(2) Any acknowledgment of service must be –

(a)   filed not more than 21 days after service of the claim form; and
(b)   served on –
    (i)   the claimant; and
    (ii)   subject to any direction under rule 54.7(b), any other person named in the claim form, as soon as practicable and, in any event, not later than 7 days after it is filed.

(3) The time limits under this rule may not be extended by agreement between the parties.

(4) The acknowledgment of service –

(a)   must –
    (i)   where the person filing it intends to contest the claim, set out a summary of his grounds for doing so; and
    (ii)   state the name and address of any person the person filing it considers to be an interested party; and
(b)   may include or be accompanied by an application for directions.

(5) Rule 10.3(2) does not apply.]

Amendments—Inserted by SI 2000/2092.

[54.9 Failure to file acknowledgment of service

(1) Where a person served with the claim form has failed to file an acknowledgment of service in accordance with rule 54.8, he –

(a)   may not take part in a hearing to decide whether permission should be given unless the court allows him to do so; but
(b)   provided he complies with rule 54.14 or any other direction of the court regarding the filing and service of –
    (i)   detailed grounds for contesting the claim or supporting it on additional grounds; and
    (ii)   any written evidence,
    may take part in the hearing of the judicial review.

(2) Where that person takes part in the hearing of the judicial review, the court may take his failure to file an acknowledgment of service into account when deciding what order to make about costs.

(3) Rule 8.4 does not apply.]

Amendments—Inserted by SI 2000/2092.

[54.10 Permission given

(1) Where permission to proceed is given the court may also give directions.

[(2) Directions under paragraph (1) may include —

(a)   a stay$^{(GL)}$ of proceedings to which the claim relates;
(b)   directions requiring the proceedings to be heard by a Divisional Court.]

> (Rule 3.7 provides a sanction for the non-payment of the fee payable when permission to proceed has been given)]

Amendments—Inserted by SI 2000/2092; SI 2010/2577.

[54.11 Service of order giving or refusing permission

The court will serve –

(a)   the order giving or refusing permission; and
(b)   any directions,

on –

(i)   the claimant;
(ii)   the defendant; and
(iii)   any other person who filed an acknowledgment of service.]

Amendments—Inserted by SI 2000/2092.

[54.12 Permission decision without a hearing

(1) This rule applies where the court, without a hearing –

(a)   refuses permission to proceed; or
(b)   gives permission to proceed –
   (i)   subject to conditions; or
   (ii)   on certain grounds only.

(2) The court will serve its reasons for making the decision when it serves the order giving or refusing permission in accordance with rule 54.11.

(3) The claimant may not appeal but may request the decision to be reconsidered at a hearing.

(4) A request under paragraph (3) must be filed within 7 days after service of the reasons under paragraph (2).

(5) The claimant, defendant and any other person who has filed an acknowledgment of service will be given at least 2 days' notice of the hearing date.]

[(6) The court may give directions requiring the proceedings to be heard by a Divisional Court.]

Amendments—Inserted by SI 2000/2092; SI 2010/2577.

[54.13 Defendant etc may not apply to set aside$^{(GL)}$

Neither the defendant nor any other person served with the claim form may apply to set aside an order giving permission to proceed.]

Amendments—Inserted by SI 2000/2092.

[54.14 Response

(1) A defendant and any other person saved with the claim form who wishes to contest the claim or support it on additional grounds must file and serve –

- (a) detailed grounds for contesting the claim or supporting it on additional grounds; and
- (b) any written evidence,

within 35 days after service of the order giving permission.

(2) The following rules do not apply –

- (a) rule 8.5(3) and 8.5(4) (defendant to file and serve written evidence at the same time as acknowledgment of service); and
- (b) rule 8.5(5) and 8.5(6) (claimant to file and serve reply within 14 days).]

Amendments—Inserted by SI 2000/2092.

[54.15 Where claimant seeks to rely on additional grounds

The court's permission is required if a claimant seeks to rely on grounds other than those for which he has been given permission to proceed.]

Amendments—Inserted by SI 2000/2092.

[54.16 Evidence

(1) Rule 8.6[(1)] does not apply.

(2) No written evidence may be relied on unless –

- (a) it has been served in accordance with any –
  - (i) rule under this [Section]; or
  - (ii) direction of the court; or
- (b) the court gives permission.]

Amendments—Inserted by SI 2000/2092; amended by SI 2002/2058; SI 2003/364.

[54.17 Court's powers to hear any person

(1) Any person may apply for permission –

- (a) to file evidence; or
- (b) make representations at the hearing of the judicial review.

(2) An application under paragraph (1) should be made promptly.]

Amendments—Inserted by SI 2000/2092.

[54.18 Judicial review may be decided without a hearing

The court may decide the claim for judicial review without a hearing where all the parties agree.]

Amendments—Inserted by SI 2000/2092.

[54.19 Court's powers in respect of quashing orders

(1) This rule applies where the court makes a quashing order in respect of the decision to which the claim relates.

[(2) The court may –

    (a)   (i)   remit the matter to the decision-maker; and

    (ii)   direct it to reconsider the matter and reach a decision in accordance with the judgment of the court; or

    (b)   in so far as any enactment permits, substitute its own decision for the decision to which the claim relates.

    (Section 31 of the [Senior Courts Act 1981] enables the High Court, subject to certain conditions, to substitute its own decision for the decision in question.)]

…]

Amendments—Inserted by SI 2000/2092; SI 2007/3543 (in force from 6 April 2008); Constitutional Reform Act 2005, Sch 11, para 1(2).

[54.20 Transfer

The court may –

    (a)   order a claim to continue as if it had not been started under this [Section]; and

    (b)   where it does so, give directions about the future management of the claim.

    (Part 30 (transfer) applies to transfers to and from the Administrative Court)]

Amendments—Inserted by SI 2000/2092; amended by SI 2003/364.

54.21

(*revoked*)

…

54.22

(*revoked*)

…

54.23

(*revoked*)

…

54.24

(*revoked*)

…

54.25

(*revoked*)

…

54.26

(*revoked*)

...

54.27

(*revoked*)

...

[Section III – Applications for Statutory Review under section 103A of the Nationality, Immigration and Asylum Act 2002]

(*revoked*)

...

Amendments—SI 2009/3390.

PRACTICE DIRECTION – PD54A: JUDICIAL REVIEW

This Practice Direction supplements CPR Part 54 (PD54A)

1.1 In addition to Part 54 and this practice direction attention is drawn to –

- section 31 of the [Senior Courts Act 1981]; and
- the Human Rights Act 1998.

The Court

2.1 Part 54 claims for judicial review are dealt with in the Administrative Court.

> [(Practice Direction 54D ... contains provisions about where a claim for judicial review may be started, administered and heard.)]

...

Rule 54.5 – Time Limit for Filing Claim Form

4.1 Where the claim is for a quashing order in respect of a judgment, order or conviction, the date when the grounds to make the claim first arose, for the purposes of rule 54.5(1)(b), is the date of that judgment, order or conviction.

Rule 54.6 – Claim Form

Interested parties

5.1 Where the claim for judicial review relates to proceedings in a court or tribunal, any other parties to those proceedings must be named in the claim form as interested parties under rule 54.6(1)(a) (and therefore served with the claim form under rule 54.7(b)).

5.2 For example, in a claim by a defendant in a criminal case in the Magistrates' or Crown Court for judicial review of a decision in that case, the prosecution must always be named as an interested party.

Human rights

5.3 Where the claimant is seeking to raise any issue under the Human Rights Act 1998, or seeks a remedy available under that Act, the claim form must include the information required by paragraph [15] of Practice Direction 16.

Devolution issues

5.4 Where the claimant intends to raise a devolution issue, the claim form must –

    (1)   specify that the applicant wishes to raise a devolution issue and identify the relevant provisions of the [Government of Wales Act 2006], the Northern Ireland Act 1998 or the Scotland Act 1998; and

    (2)   contain a summary of the facts, circumstances and points of law on the basis of which it is alleged that a devolution issue arises.

[5.5 In this practice direction 'devolution issue' has the same meaning as in paragraph 1, Schedule 9 to the Government of Wales Act 2006, paragraph 1, Schedule 10 to the Northern Ireland Act 1998; and paragraph 1, Schedule 6 to the Scotland Act 1998.]

Claim form

5.6 The claim form must include or be accompanied by –

    (1)   a detailed statement of the claimant's grounds for bringing the claim for judicial review;

    (2)   a statement of the facts relied on;

    (3)   any application to extend the time limit for filing the claim form;

    (4)   any application for directions ...;

    ....

5.7 In addition, the claim form must be accompanied by –

    (1)   any written evidence in support of the claim or application to extend time;

    (2)   a copy of any order that the claimant seeks to have quashed;

    (3)   where the claim for judicial review relates to a decision of a court or tribunal, an approved copy of the reasons for reaching that decision;

    (4)   copies of any documents on which the claimant proposes to rely;

    (5)   copies of any relevant statutory material;

    (6)   a list of essential documents for advance reading by the court (with page references to the passages relied on); and

5.8 Where it is not possible to file all the above documents, the claimant must indicate which documents have not been filed and the reasons why they are not currently available.

Bundle of documents

5.9 The claimant must file two copies of a paginated and indexed bundle containing all the documents referred to in paragraphs [5.6] and [5.7].

5.10 Attention is drawn to rules 8.5(1) and 8.5(7).

Rule 54.7 – Service of Claim Form

[6.1 Except as required by rules 54.11 or 54.12(2), the Administrative Court will not serve documents and service must be effected by the parties.]

[6.2 Where the defendant or interested party to the claim for judicial review is –

   (a)   the Immigration and Asylum Chamber of the First-tier Tribunal, the address for service of the claim form is Official Correspondence Unit, PO Box 6987, Leicester, LE1 6ZX or fax number 0116 249 4240;

   (b)   the Crown, service of the claim form must be effected on the solicitor acting for the relevant government department as if the proceedings were civil proceedings as defined in the Crown Proceedings Act 1947.

     (Practice Direction 66 gives the list published under section 17 of the Crown Proceedings Act 1947 of the solicitors acting in civil proceedings (as defined in that Act) for the different government departments on whom service is to be effected, and of their addresses.)

     (Part 6 contains provisions about the service of claim forms.)]

Rule 54.8 – Acknowledgment of Service

7.1 Attention is drawn to rule 8.3(2) and the relevant practice direction and to rule 10.5.

Rule 54.10 – Permission Given

Directions

8.1 Case management directions under rule 54.10(1) may include directions about serving the claim form and any evidence on other persons.

8.2 Where a claim is made under the Human Rights Act 1998, a direction may be made for giving notice to the Crown or joining the Crown as a party. Attention is drawn to rule 19.4A and paragraph 6 of Practice Direction 19A.

…

Permission without a hearing

8.4 The court will generally, in the first instance, consider the question of permission without a hearing.

Permission hearing

8.5 Neither the defendant nor any other interested party need attend a hearing on the question of permission unless the court directs otherwise.

8.6 Where the defendant or any party does attend a hearing, the court will not generally make an order for costs against the claimant.

Rule 54.11 – Service of Order Giving or Refusing Permission

9.1 An order refusing permission or giving it subject to conditions or on certain grounds only must set out or be accompanied by the court's reasons for coming to that decision.

Rule 54.14 – Response

10.1 Where the party filing the detailed grounds intends to rely on documents not already filed, he must file a paginated bundle of those documents when he files the detailed grounds.

Rule 54.15 – Where Claimant Seeks to Rely on Additional Grounds

11.1 Where the claimant intends to apply to rely on additional grounds at the hearing of the claim for judicial review, he must give notice to the court and to any other person served with the claim form no later than 7 clear days before the hearing (or the warned date where appropriate).

Rule 54.16 – Evidence

12.1 Disclosure is not required unless the court orders otherwise.

Rule 54.17 – Court's Powers to Hear any Person

13.1 Where all the parties consent, the court may deal with an application under rule 54.17 without a hearing.

13.2 Where the court gives permission for a person to file evidence or make representations at the hearing of the claim for judicial review, it may do so on conditions and may give case management directions.

[13.3 An application for permission should be made by letter to the Administrative Court office, identifying the claim, explaining who the applicant is and indicating why and in what form the applicant wants to participate in the hearing.]

[13.4 If the applicant is seeking a prospective order as to costs, the letter should say what kind of order and on what grounds.]

[13.5 Applications to intervene must be made at the earliest reasonable opportunity, since it will usually be essential not to delay the hearing.]

Rule 54.20 – Transfer

14.1 Attention is drawn to rule 30.5.

14.2 In deciding whether a claim is suitable for transfer to the Administrative Court, the court will consider whether it raises issues of public law to which Part 54 should apply.

Skeleton arguments

15.1 The claimant must file and serve a skeleton argument not less than 21 working days before the date of the hearing of the judicial review (or the warned date).

15.2 The defendant and any other party wishing to make representations at the hearing of the judicial review must file and serve a skeleton argument not less than 14 working days before the date of the hearing of the judicial review (or the warned date).

15.3 Skeleton arguments must contain –

    (1)   a time estimate for the complete hearing, including delivery of judgment;
    (2)   a list of issues;

(3)   a list of the legal points to be taken (together with any relevant authorities with page references to the passages relied on);

(4)   a chronology of events (with page references to the bundle of documents (see paragraph 16.1);

(5)   a list of essential documents for the advance reading of the court (with page references to the passages relied on) (if different from that filed with the claim form) and a time estimate for that reading; and

(6)   a list of persons referred to.

Bundle of documents to be filed

16.1 The claimant must file a paginated and indexed bundle of all relevant documents required for the hearing of the judicial review when he files his skeleton argument.

16.2 The bundle must also include those documents required by the defendant and any other party who is to make representations at the hearing.

Agreed final order

17.1 If the parties agree about the final order to be made in a claim for judicial review, the claimant must file at the court a document (with 2 copies) signed by all the parties setting out the terms of the proposed agreed order together with a short statement of the matters relied on as justifying the proposed agreed order and copies of any authorities or statutory provisions relied on.

17.2 The court will consider the documents referred to in paragraph 17.1 and will make the order if satisfied that the order should be made.

17.3 If the court is not satisfied that the order should be made, a hearing date will be set.

17.4 Where the agreement relates to an order for costs only, the parties need only file a document signed by all the parties setting out the terms of the proposed order.

[SECTION II – APPLICATIONS FOR PERMISSION TO APPLY FOR JUDICIAL REVIEW IN IMMIGRATION AND ASYLUM CASES – CHALLENGING REMOVAL

18.1

(1) This Section applies where –

(a)   a person has been served with a copy of directions for his removal from the United Kingdom by the [UK Border Agency] of the Home Office and notified that this Section applies; and

(b)   that person makes an application for permission to apply for judicial review before his removal takes effect.

(2) This Section does not prevent a person from applying for judicial review after he has been removed.

(3) The requirements contained in this Section of this Practice Direction are additional to those contained elsewhere in the Practice Direction.

18.2

(1) A person who makes an application for permission to apply for judicial review must file a claim form and a copy at court, and the claim form must –

(a) indicate on its face that this Section of the Practice Direction applies; and
(b) be accompanied by –
    (i) a copy of the removal directions and the decision to which the application relates; and
    (ii) any document served with the removal directions including any document which contains the [UK Border Agency's] factual summary of the case; and
(c) contain or be accompanied by the detailed statement of the claimant's grounds for bringing the claim for judicial review; or
(d) if the claimant is unable to comply with paragraph (b) or (c), contain or be accompanied by a statement of the reasons why.

(2) The claimant must, immediately upon issue of the claim, send copies of the issued claim form and accompanying documents to the address specified by the [UK Border Agency].

> (Rule 54.7 also requires the defendant to be served with the claim form within 7 days of the date of issue. Rule [6.10] provides that service on a Government Department must be effected on the solicitor acting for that Department, which in the case of the [UK Border Agency] is the Treasury Solicitor. The address for the Treasury Solicitor may be found in the Annex to Part 66 of these Rules.)

18.3

Where the claimant has not complied with paragraph 18.2(1)(b) or (c) and has provided reasons why he is unable to comply, and the court has issued the claim form, the Administrative Court –

(a) will refer the matter to a Judge for consideration as soon as practicable; and
(b) will notify the parties that it has done so.

18.4

If, upon a refusal to grant permission to apply for judicial review, the Court indicates that the application is clearly without merit, that indication will be included in the order refusing permission.]

PRACTICE DIRECTION –
PD54D: ADMINISTRATIVE COURT (VENUE)

This Practice Direction supplements CPR Part 54 (PD54D)

Scope and purpose

1.1 This Practice Direction concerns the place in which a claim before the Administrative Court should be started and administered and the venue at which it will be determined.

1.2 This Practice Direction is intended to facilitate access to justice by enabling cases to be administered and determined in the most appropriate location. To achieve this purpose it provides flexibility in relation to where claims are to be administered and enables claims to be transferred to different venues.

Venue – general provisions

2.1 The claim form in proceedings in the Administrative Court may be issued at the Administrative Court Office of the High Court at –

(1)   the Royal Courts of Justice in London; or

(2)   at the District Registry of the High Court at Birmingham, Cardiff, Leeds, or Manchester unless the claim is one of the excepted classes of claim set out in paragraph 3 of this Practice Direction which may only be started and determined at the Royal Courts of Justice in London.

2.2 Any claim started in Birmingham will normally be determined at a court in the Midland region (geographically covering the area of the Midland Circuit); in Cardiff in Wales; in Leeds in the North-Eastern Region (geographically covering the area of the North Eastern Circuit); in London at the Royal Courts of Justice; and in Manchester, in the North-Western Region (geographically covering the Northern Circuit).

Excepted classes of claim

3.1 The excepted classes of claim referred to in paragraph 2.1(2) are –

(1)   proceedings to which Part 76 or Part 79 applies, and for the avoidance of doubt –

(a) proceedings relating to control orders (within the meaning of Part 76);

(b) financial restrictions proceedings (within the meaning of Part 79);

(c) proceedings relating to terrorism or alleged terrorists (where that is a relevant feature of the claim); and

(d) proceedings in which a special advocate is or is to be instructed;

(2)   proceedings to which RSC Order 115 applies;

(3)   proceedings under the Proceeds of Crime Act 2002;

(4)   appeals to the Administrative Court under the Extradition Act 2003;

(5)   proceedings which must be heard by a Divisional Court; and

(6)   proceedings relating to the discipline of solicitors.

3.2 If a claim form is issued at an Administrative Court office other than in London and includes one of the excepted classes of claim, the proceedings will be transferred to London.

Urgent applications

4.1 During the hours when the court is open, where an urgent application needs to be made to the Administrative Court outside London, the application must be made to the judge designated to deal with such applications in the relevant District Registry.

4.2 Any urgent application to the Administrative Court during the hours when the court is closed, must be made to the duty out of hours High Court judge by telephoning 020 7947 6000.

Assignment to another venue

5.1 The proceedings may be transferred from the office at which the claim form was issued to another office. Such transfer is a judicial act.

5.2 The general expectation is that proceedings will be administered and determined in the region with which the claimant has the closest connection, subject to the following considerations as applicable –

(1) any reason expressed by any party for preferring a particular venue;

(2) the region in which the defendant, or any relevant office or department of the defendant, is based;

(3) the region in which the claimant's legal representatives are based;

(4) the ease and cost of travel to a hearing;

(5) the availability and suitability of alternative means of attending a hearing (for example, by videolink);

(6) the extent and nature of media interest in the proceedings in any particular locality;

(7) the time within which it is appropriate for the proceedings to be determined;

(8) whether it is desirable to administer or determine the claim in another region in the light of the volume of claims issued at, and the capacity, resources and workload of, the court at which it is issued;

(9) whether the claim raises issues sufficiently similar to those in another outstanding claim to make it desirable that it should be determined together with, or immediately following, that other claim; and

(10) whether the claim raises devolution issues and for that reason whether it should more appropriately be determined in London or Cardiff.

5.3 (1) When an urgent application is made under paragraph 4.1 or 4.2, this will not by itself decide the venue for the further administration or determination of the claim.

(2) The court dealing with the urgent application may direct that the case be assigned to a particular venue.

(3) When an urgent application is made under paragraph 4.2, and the court does not make a direction under sub-paragraph (2), the claim will be assigned in the first place to London but may be reassigned to another venue at a later date.

5.4 The court may on an application by a party or of its own initiative direct that the claim be determined in a region other than that of the venue in which the claim is currently assigned. The considerations in paragraph 5.2 apply.

5.5 Once assigned to a venue, the proceedings will be both administered from that venue and determined by a judge of the Administrative Court at a suitable court within that region, or, if the venue is in London, at the Royal Courts of Justice. The choice of which court (of those within the region which are identified by the Presiding Judge of the circuit suitable for such hearing) will be decided, subject to availability, by the considerations in paragraph 5.2.

5.6 When giving directions under rule 54.10, the court may direct that proceedings be reassigned to another region for hearing (applying the considerations in paragraph 5.2). If no such direction is given, the claim will be heard in the same region as that in which the permission application was determined (whether on paper or at a hearing).

PRE-ACTION PROTOCOL FOR JUDICIAL REVIEW

General note—This protocol came into force on 4 March 2002 – see PDProt, para 5.1.

Introduction

This protocol applies to proceedings <u>within England and Wales only</u>. It does not affect the time-limit specified by Rule 54.5(1) of the Civil Procedure Rules which requires that any claim form in an application for judicial review must be filed promptly and in any event not later than 3 months after the grounds to make the claim first arose.[1]

1   While the court does have the discretion under Rule 3.1(2)(a) of the Civil Procedure Rules to allow a late claim, this is only used in exceptional circumstances. **Compliance with the protocol alone is unlikely to be sufficient to persuade the court to allow a late claim.**

1 Judicial review allows people with a sufficient interest in a decision or action by a public body to ask a judge to review the lawfulness of:

- an enactment; or
- a decision, action or failure to act in relation to the exercise of a public function.[2]

2   Civil Procedure Rule 54.1(2).

2 Judicial review may be used where there is no right of appeal or where all avenues of appeal have been exhausted.

[Alternative Dispute Resolution

3.1 The parties should consider whether some form of alternative dispute resolution procedure would be more suitable than litigation, and if so, endeavour to agree which form to adopt. Both the Claimant and Defendant may be required by the Court to provide evidence that alternative means of resolving their dispute were considered. The Courts take the view that litigation should be a last resort, and that claims should not be issued prematurely when a settlement is still actively being explored. Parties are warned that if the protocol is not followed (including this paragraph) then the Court must have regard to such conduct when determining costs. However, parties should also note that a claim for judicial review 'must be filed promptly and in any event not later than 3 months after the grounds to make the claim first arose'.

3.2 It is not practicable in this protocol to address in detail how the parties might decide which method to adopt to resolve their particular dispute. However, summarised below are some of the options for resolving disputes without litigation:

- Discussion and negotiation.
- Ombudsmen – the Parliamentary and Health Service and the Local Government Ombudsmen have discretion to deal with complaints relating to maladministration. The British and Irish Ombudsman Association provide information about Ombudsman schemes and other complaint handling bodies and this is available from their website at *www.bioa.org.uk*. Parties may wish to note that the Ombudsmen are not able to look into a complaint once court action has been commenced.
- Early neutral evaluation by an independent third party (for example, a lawyer experienced in the field of administrative law or an individual experienced in the subject matter of the claim).
- Mediation – a form of facilitated negotiation assisted by an independent neutral party.

3.3 The Legal Services Commission has published a booklet on 'Alternatives to Court', CLS Direct Information Leaflet 23 ([*www.clsdirect.org.uk*]), which lists a number of organisations that provide alternative dispute resolution services.

3.4 It is expressly recognised that no party can or should be forced to mediate or enter into any form of ADR.]

4 Judicial review may not be appropriate in every instance.

Claimants are strongly advised to seek appropriate legal advice when considering such proceedings and, in particular, before adopting this protocol or making a claim. Although the Legal Services Commission will not normally grant full representation before a letter before claim has been sent and the proposed defendant given a reasonable time to respond, initial funding may be available, for eligible claimants, to cover the work necessary to write this. (See Annex C for more information).

5 This protocol sets out a code of good practice and contains the steps which parties should generally follow before making a claim for judicial review.

6 This protocol does not impose a greater obligation on a public body to disclose documents or give reasons for its decision than that already provided for in statute or common law. However, where the court considers that a public body should have provided **relevant** documents and/or information, particularly where this failure is a breach of a statutory or common law requirement, it may impose sanctions.

This protocol will not be appropriate where the defendant does not have the legal power to change the decision being challenged, for example decisions issued by tribunals such as [the Asylum and Immigration Tribunal].

This protocol will not be appropriate in urgent cases, for example, when directions have been set, or are in force, for the claimant's removal from the UK, or where there is an urgent need for an interim order to compel a public body to act where it has unlawfully refused to do so (for example, the failure of a local housing authority to secure interim accommodation for a homeless claimant) a claim should be made immediately. A letter before claim will not stop the implementation of a disputed decision in all instances.

7 All claimants will need to satisfy themselves whether they should follow the protocol, depending upon the circumstances of his or her case. Where the use of the protocol is appropriate, the court will normally expect all parties to have complied with it and will take into account compliance or non-compliance when giving directions for case management of proceedings or when making orders for costs.[3] However, even in emergency cases, it is good practice to fax to the defendant the draft claim form which the claimant intends to issue. A claimant is also normally required to notify a defendant when an interim mandatory order is being sought.

3   Civil Procedure Rules Costs Practice Direction.

The Letter before Claim

8 Before making a claim, the claimant should send a letter to the defendant. The purpose of this letter is to identify the issues in dispute and establish whether litigation can be avoided.

9 Claimants should normally use the suggested **standard format** for the letter outlined at Annex A.

10 The letter should contain **the date and details of the decision, act or omission being challenged and a clear summary of the facts** on which the claim is based. It should also contain the **details of any relevant information** that the claimant is seeking and an explanation of why this is considered relevant.

11 The letter should normally contain the **details of any interested parties**[4] known to the claimant. They should be sent a **copy** of the letter before claim **for information.** **Claimants are strongly advised to seek appropriate legal advice when considering such proceedings and, in particular, before sending the letter before claim to other interested parties or making a claim.**

4   See Civil Procedure Rule 54.1(2)(f).

12 A claim should not normally be made until the proposed reply date given in the letter before claim has passed, unless the circumstances of the case require more immediate action to be taken.

The Letter of Response

13 Defendants should normally respond within 14 days using the **standard format** at Annex B. Failure to do so will be taken into account by the court and sanctions may be imposed unless there are good reasons.[5]

5   See Civil Procedure Rules Pre-action Protocol Practice Direction paragraphs 2–3.

14 Where it is not possible to reply within the proposed time-limit the defendant should send an interim reply and propose a reasonable extension. Where an extension is sought, reasons should be given and, where required, additional information requested. **This will not affect the time-limit for making a claim for judicial review**[6] nor will it bind the claimant where he or she considers this to be unreasonable. However, where the court considers that a subsequent claim is made prematurely it may impose sanctions.

6   See Civil Procedure Rule 54.5(1).

15 If the **claim is being conceded in full**, the reply should say so in clear and unambiguous terms.

16 If the **claim is being conceded in part or not being conceded at all**, the reply should say so in clear and unambiguous terms, and:

(a)   where appropriate, contain a new decision, clearly identifying what aspects of the claim are being conceded and what are not, or, give a clear timescale within which the new decision will be issued;

(b)   provide a fuller explanation for the decision, if considered appropriate to do so;

(c)   address any points of dispute, or explain why they cannot be addressed;

(d)   enclose any **relevant** documentation requested by the claimant, or explain why the documents are not being enclosed; and

(e)   where appropriate, confirm whether or not they will oppose any application for an interim remedy.

17 The response should be sent to **all interested parties**[7] identified by the claimant and contain details of any other parties who the defendant considers also have an interest.

7   See Civil Procedure Rule 54.1(2)(f).

Annex A
Letter before Claim

Section 1 – Information Required in a Letter Before Claim

Proposed Claim for Judicial Review

1 **To**

(*Insert the name and address of the proposed defendant – see details in section 2*)

2 **The claimant**

(*Insert the title, first and last name and the address of the claimant*)

3 **Reference details**

(*When dealing with large organisations it is important to understand that the information relating to any particular individual's previous dealings with it may not be immediately available, therefore it is important to set out the relevant reference numbers for the matter in dispute and/or the identity of those within the public body who have been handling the particular matter in dispute – see details in section 3*)

4 **The details of the matter being challenged**

(*Set out clearly the matter being challenged, particularly if there has been more than one decision*)

5 **The issue**

(*Set out the date and details of the decision, or act or omission being challenged, a brief summary of the facts and why it is contented to be wrong*)

6 **The details of the action that the defendant is expected to take**

(*Set out the details of the remedy sought, including whether a review or any interim remedy are being requested*)

7 **The details of the legal advisers, if any, dealing with this claim**

(*Set out the name, address and reference details of any legal advisers dealing with the claim*)

8 **The details of any interested parties**

(*Set out the details of any interested parties and confirm that they have been sent a copy of this letter*)

9 **The details of any information sought**

(*Set out the details of any information that is sought. This may include a request for a fuller explanation of the reasons for the decision that is being challenged*)

10 **The details of any documents that are considered relevant and necessary**

(*Set out the details of any documentation or policy in respect of which the disclosure is sought and explain why these are relevant. If you rely on a statutory duty to disclose, this should be specified*)

11 **The address for reply and service of court documents**

(*Insert the address for the reply*)

12 **Proposed reply date**

(*The precise time will depend upon the circumstances of the individual case. However, although a shorter or longer time may be appropriate in a particular case, 14 days is a reasonable time to allow in most circumstances*)

Section 2 – Address for Sending the Letter Before Claim

Public bodies have requested that, for certain types of cases, in order to ensure a prompt response, letters before claim should be sent to specific addresses.

- Where the claim concerns a decision in an Immigration, Asylum or Nationality case:

The Judicial Review Management Unit
[UK Border Agency]
[1st Floor
Green Park House
29 Wellesley Road
Croydon CR0 2AJ]

- **Where the claim concerns a decision by the Legal Services Commission:**

  - The address on the decision letter/notification; and
[Legal Director
Corporate Legal Team
Legal Services Commission
4 Abbey Orchard Street
London SW1P 2BS.]

- **Where the claim concerns a decision by a local authority:**

  - The address on the decision letter/notification; and
  - Their legal department[8]

8   The relevant address should be available from a range of sources such as the Phone Book; Business and Services Directory, Thomson's Local Directory, CAB, etc.

- **Where the claim concerns a decision by a department or body for whom Treasury Solicitor acts** *and Treasury Solicitor has already been involved in the case* a copy should also be sent, quoting the Treasury Solicitor's reference, to:

  [The Treasury Solicitor,
  One Kemble Street,
  London,
  WC2B 4TS]

- **In all other circumstances, the letter should be sent to the address on the letter notifying the decision.**

Section 3 – Specific Reference Details Required

Public bodies have requested that the following information should be provided in order to ensure prompt response.

- **Where the claim concerns an Immigration, Asylum or Nationality case, dependent upon the nature of the case:**
- The Home Office reference number

- The Port reference number
- The [Asylum and Immigration Tribunal] reference number
- The National Asylum Support Service reference number

Or, if these are unavailable:

- The full name, nationality and date of birth of the claimant.

• **Where the claim concerns a decision by the Legal Services Commission:**

- The certificate reference number.

Annex B
Response to a Letter before Claim

Information Required in a Response to a Letter Before Claim

Proposed Claim for Judicial Review

1 **The claimant**

(*Insert the title, first and last names and the address to which any reply should be sent*)

2 **From**

(*Insert the name and address of the defendant*)

3 **Reference details**

(*Set out the relevant reference numbers for the matter in dispute and the identity of those within the public body who have been handling the issue*)

4 **The details of the matter being challenged**

(*Set out details of the matter being challenged, providing a fuller explanation of the decision, where this is considered appropriate*)

5 **Response to the proposed claim**

(*Set out whether the issue in question is conceded in part, or in full, or will be contested. Where it is not proposed to disclose any information that has been requested, explain the reason for this. Where an interim reply is being sent and there is a realistic prospect of settlement, details should be included*)

6 **Details of any other interested parties**

(*Identify any other parties who you consider have an interest who have not already been sent a letter by the claimant*)

7 **Address for further correspondence and service of court documents**

(*Set out the address for any future correspondence on this matter*)

Annex C
Notes on Public Funding for Legal Costs in Judicial Review

Public funding for legal costs in judicial review is available from legal professionals and advice agencies which have contracts with the Legal Services Commission as part of the Community Legal Service. Funding may be provided for:

- *Legal Help* to provide initial advice and assistance with any legal problem; or
- *Legal Representation* to allow you to be represented in court if you are taking or defending court proceedings. This is available in two forms:
- *Investigative Help* is limited to funding to investigate the strength of the proposed claim. It includes the issue and conduct of proceedings only so far as is necessary to obtain disclosure of relevant information or to protect the client's position in relation to any urgent hearing or time-limit for the issue of proceedings. This includes the work necessary to write a **letter before claim** to the body potentially under challenge, setting out the grounds of challenge, and giving that body a reasonable opportunity, typically 14 days, in which to respond.
- *Full Representation* is provided to represent you in legal proceedings and includes litigation services, advocacy services, and all such help as is usually given by a person providing representation in proceedings, including steps preliminary or incidental to proceedings, and/or arriving at or giving affect to a compromise to avoid or bring to an end any proceedings. Except in emergency cases, a proper **letter before claim** must be sent and the other side must be given an opportunity to respond before *Full Representation* is granted.

Further information on the type(s) of help available and the criteria for receiving that help may be found in the Legal Service Manual Volume 3: '*The Funding Code*'. This may be found on the Legal Services Commission website at:

www.legalservices.co.uk

A list of contracted firms and Advice Agencies may be found on the Community Legal Services website at:

www.justask.org.uk

Appendix D

JUDICIAL GUIDANCE

ADMINISTRATIVE COURT GUIDANCE

Notes for guidance on applying for judicial review

1   Introduction

2   What is Judicial Review?

3   What is the Pre-action protocol?

4   Where should I commence proceedings?

5   When should I lodge my application for permission to apply for judicial review?

6   Is there a fee to pay and, if so, when do I pay it?

7   How do I apply for Judicial Review?

8   What do I do if my application is urgent?

9   What is an Acknowledgement of Service?

10   What happens after the defendant and/or the interested party has lodged an acknowledgement of service, or the time for lodging such has expired?

11   What happens if my application for permission is refused or if permission is granted subject to conditions or in part only?

12   What happens if my application for permission is granted?

13   What happens when my case is ready for hearing?

14   What if I need to make an application for further orders after the grant of permission?

15   Can my application be determined without the need for a hearing?

16   What if the proceedings settle by consent prior to the substantive hearing of my application?

17   What if I want to discontinue the proceedings at any stage?

18   Will I be responsible for costs of the defendant and/or the interested parties if my application is unsuccessful?

19   What can I do if I am unhappy with the Judge's decision?

20   Where can I get advice about procedural matters?

Section 1

General introduction

1. These notes are not intended to be exhaustive but are designed to offer an outline of the procedure to be followed when seeking to make an application for judicial review in the Administrative Court. For further details of the procedure to be followed you and your representatives/legal advisers should consult Part 54 of the Civil Procedure Rules (CPR) and the Practice Directions accompanying Part 54.

Section 2

What is judicial review?

2.1 Judicial review is the procedure by which you can seek to challenge the decision, action or failure to act of a public body such as a government department or a local authority or other body exercising a public law function. If you are challenging the decision of a court, the jurisdiction of judicial review extends only to decisions of inferior courts. It does not extend to decisions of the High Court or Court of Appeal. Judicial review must be used where you are seeking:

- a mandatory order (ie an order requiring the public body to do something and formerly known as an order of mandamus);

- a prohibiting order (ie an order preventing the public body from doing something and formerly known as an order of prohibition); or

- a quashing order (ie an order quashing the public body's decision and formerly known as an order of certiorari)

- a declaration

- HRA Damages

2.2 Claims will generally be heard by a single Judge sitting in open Court. The Administrative Court sits at:

- **The Royal Courts of Justice in London** – Room C315, Royal Courts of Justice, Strand, London, WC2A 2LL;

- **Birmingham Civil Justice Centre** – Priory Courts, 33 Bull Street, Birmingham, B4 6DS;

- **Cardiff Civil Justice Centre** – 2 Park Street, Cardiff, CF10 1ET;

- **Leeds Combined Court Centre** – 1 Oxford Row, Leeds, LS1 3BG;

- **Manchester Civil Justice Centre** – 1 Bridge Street West, Manchester, M3 3FX

Where a case is directed to be heard by a Divisional Court (a court of two judges) the hearing will usually be in London.

Section 3

What is the pre-action protocol?

3.1 The protocol sets out a code of good practice and contains the steps which parties should generally follow before making a claim for judicial review. The objective of the pre-action protocol is to avoid unnecessary litigation.

3.2 Before making your claim for judicial review, you should send a letter to the defendant. The purpose of this letter is to identify the issues in dispute and establish whether litigation can be avoided. The letter should contain the date and details of the decision, act or omission being challenged and a clear summary of the facts on which the claim is based. It should also contain the details of any relevant information that the claimant is seeking and an explanation of why this is considered relevant. A claim should not normally be made until the proposed reply date given in the letter before claim has passed, unless the circumstances of the case require more immediate action to be taken.

3.3 Defendants should normally respond to that letter within 14 days and sanctions may be imposed unless there are good reasons for not responding within that period.

NB – The protocol does not affect the time limit specified by CPR Part 54.5(1) namely that an application for permission to apply for judicial review must be made promptly and in any event not later than 3 months after the grounds upon which the claim is based first arose.

NB – You should seek advice as to whether the protocol is appropriate in the circumstances of your case. Use of the protocol will not be appropriate where the defendant does not have the legal power to change the decision being challenged. It also may not be appropriate in circumstances where the application is urgent.

NB – A letter before claim will not automatically stop the implementation of a disputed decision.

NB – Even in emergency cases, it is good practice to fax the draft claim form that you are intending to issue to the defendant. You will also normally be required to notify a defendant when you are seeking an interim order; ie an order giving some form of relief pending the final determination of the claim.

3.4 Any claim for judicial review must indicate whether or not the protocol has been complied with. If the protocol has not been complied with, the reasons for failing to do so should be set out in the claim form.|

Section 4

Where should I commence proceedings?

4.1 Claims for judicial review under CPR Part 54 are dealt with in the Administrative Court.

4.2 Claims may be issued at the District Registry of the High Court at Birmingham, Cardiff, Leeds or Manchester as well as at the Royal Courts of Justice in London. Cases started in Birmingham will normally be determined at a court in the Midland region; in Cardiff in Wales; in Leeds in the North-Eastern Region; in London at the Royal Courts of Justice and in Manchester, in the North-Western Region.

4.3 The general expectation is that proceedings will be administered and determined in the region with which the claimant has the closest connection, subject to the following considerations as applicable:

(1)   any reason expressed by any party for preferring a particular venue;

(2)   the region in which the defendant, or any relevant office or department of the defendant, is based;

(3)   the region in which the claimant's legal representatives are based;

(4)   the ease and cost of travel to a hearing;

(5)   the availability and suitability of alternative means of attending a hearing (for example, by videolink);

(6)   the extent and nature of media interest in the proceedings in any particular locality;

(7)   the time within which it is appropriate for the proceedings to be determined;

(8)   whether it is desirable to administer or determine the claim in another region in the light of the volume of claims issued at, and the capacity, resources and workload of, the court at which it is issued ;

(9)   whether the claim raises issues sufficiently similar to those in another outstanding claim to make it desirable that it should be determined together with, or immediately following, that other claim; and

(10) whether the claim raises devolution issues and for that reason whether it should more appropriately be determined in London or Cardiff.

Can I get Legal Services Commission funding (legal aid) for my application?

4.4 Neither the Court nor the Administrative Court Offices have power to grant funding (previously legal aid). The responsibility for the provision of public funding is held by the Legal Services Commission.

Further information on the type(s) of help available and the criteria for receiving that help may be found in the Legal Services Commission Manual Volume 3: 'The Funding Code'. This may be found on the Legal Services Commission website at http://www.legalservices.gov.uk/.

4.6 A list of contracted firms and Advice Agencies may be found on the Community Legal Services website at http://www.justask.org.uk/. The Legal Services Commission can also provide you with a list of solicitors in your area if you telephone them on 0845 345 4345.

Section 5

When should I lodge my application for permission to apply for judicial review?

5.1 The claim form must be filed promptly and in any event not later than three months after the grounds upon which the claim is based first arose (CPR Part 54.5).

5.2 The court has the power to extend the period for the lodging of an application for permission to apply for judicial review but will only do so where it is satisfied there are very good reasons for doing so.

NB – The time for the lodging of the application may not be extended by agreement between the parties.

NB – If you are seeking an extension of time for the lodging of your application, you must make the application in the claim form, setting out the grounds in support of that application to extend time (CPR Part 54.5).

Section 6

Is there a fee to pay and if so, when should I pay it?

6.1 A fee of £50.00 is payable when you lodge your application for permission to apply for Judicial Review. A further £180.00 is payable if you wish to pursue the claim if permission is granted (Civil Proceedings Fees (Amendment) Order 2008).

NB – If you are in receipt of certain types of benefits you may be entitled to remission of any fee due as part of Judicial Review proceedings. If you believe you may be entitled to fee remission you should apply to the relevant Administrative Court Office using Form EX160 (Application for a Fee Remission) and lodge the application with your claim form.

NB – Cheques should be made payable to HMCS. If you lodge your claim form at the court office in person, personal cheques must be supported by a cheque guarantee card presented at the time the claim form is lodged.

Section 7

How do I apply for judicial review?

7.1 An application for permission to apply for judicial review must be made by claim form (Form N461).

7.2 The claim form must include or be accompanied by:

- a detailed statement of the claimant's grounds for bringing the claim for judicial review;

- a statement of the facts relied on;

- any application to extend the time limit for filing the claim form; and

- any application for directions.

7.3 Where you are seeking to raise any issue under the Human Rights Act 1998, or a remedy available under that Act, the claim form must include the information required by paragraph 16 of the Practice Direction supplementing Part 16 of the Civil Procedure Rules.

7.4 Where you intend to raise a devolution issue, the claim form must specify that you (a) wish to raise a devolution issue (b) identify the relevant provisions of the Government of Wales Act 1998, and (c) contain a summary of the facts, circumstances and points of law on the basis of which it is alleged that a devolution issue arises. Cases involving Welsh devolution issues are expected to be lodged at the Administrative Court Office in Wales.

7.5 The claim form must also be accompanied by:

- any written evidence in support of the claim or application to extend time;

- a copy of any order that you are seeking to have quashed;

- where the claim for judicial review relates to a decision of a court or tribunal, an approved copy of the reasons for reaching that decision;

- copies of any documents upon which you propose to rely;

- copies of any relevant statutory material;

- a list of essential documents for advance reading by the court (with page references to the passages relied upon). Where only part of a page needs to be read, that part should be indicated, by side-lining or in some other way, but not by highlighting.

NB – Where it is not possible for you to file all the above documents, you must indicate which documents have not been filed and the reasons why they are not currently available. The defendant and/or the interested party may seek an extension of time for the lodging of its acknowledgement of service pending receipt of the missing documents.

What documents do I need to lodge?

7.6 You must file the original claim form and witness statement, together with a set of paginated and indexed copy documents for the courts use containing the documents referred to in paragraph 7.5 above (CPR Part 54.6 and Practice Direction 54). You should also file a complete set of copy documents (including a copy claim form and witness statement) in a paginated and indexed set for the courts use. Please ensure you paginate in consecutive page number order throughout your bundle. Also ensure that each page has a page number on it and provide an index, which lists the description of documents contained in your bundle together with their page reference numbers.

7.7 Please note that if your case is of a criminal nature then the Court will require you to lodge two paginated and indexed bundles of copy documents.

7.8 You must also lodge sufficient additional copies of the claim form for the court to seal them (ie stamp them with the court seal) so that you can serve them on the defendant and any interested parties. The sealed copies will be returned to you so that you can serve them on the defendant and any interested parties.

7.9 If you are represented by solicitors they must also provide a paginated, indexed bundle of the relevant legislative provisions and statutory instruments required for the proper consideration of the application. If you are acting in person you should comply with this requirement if possible.

NB – Applications that do not comply with the requirements of CPR Part 54 and Practice Direction 54 will not be accepted, save in exceptional circumstances. In this context a matter will be regarded as exceptional where a decision is sought from the Court within 14 days of the lodging of the application. In such circumstances an undertaking will be required to provide compliance with the requirements of the CPR within a specified period.

NB – If the only reason given in support of urgency is the imminent expiry of the three month time limit for lodging an application, the papers will nonetheless be returned for compliance with Part 54 and Practice Direction 54. In those circumstances you must seek an extension of time and provide reasons for the delay in lodging the papers in proper form.

Who should I serve my application on?

7.10 The sealed copy claim form (and accompanying documents) must be served on the defendant and any person that you consider to be an interested party (unless the court directs otherwise) within 7 days of the date of issue (ie the date shown on the court seal). The Administrative Court Office will not serve your claim on the defendant or any interested party.

NB – An interested party is a person who is likely to be directly affected by your judicial review application.

NB – Please note that under the provisions of the Crown Proceedings Act 1947 service must be upon the Department responsible for the defendant.

NB – Where the claim for judicial review relates to proceedings in a court or tribunal, any other parties to those proceedings must be named in the claim form as interested parties and served with the claim form (CPR 54 PD.5). For example, in a claim by a defendant in a criminal case in the Magistrates' or Crown Court for judicial review of a decision in that case, the prosecution must always be named as an interested party.

7.11 You should lodge a Certificate of Service in Form N215 in the relevant Administrative Court Office within 7 days of serving the defendant and other interested parties.

7.12 The date of deemed service is calculated in accordance with CPR part 6.14 (see methods of service below).

Method	Deemed day of service
First class post, Document Exchange (DX) or other service which provides for delivery on the next business day	The second business day after it was posted, left with, delivered to or collected by the relevant service provider provided that day is a business day; or if not, the next business day after that:
	Posted Monday, deemed served Wednesday Posted Tuesday, deemed served Thursday Posted Wednesday, deemed served Friday Posted Thursday, deemed served Monday Posted Friday, deemed served Monday
	Please note: if the service date falls on a Public Holiday the deemed service date is the first working day following the Public Holiday
Delivering the document to or leaving it at the relevant place	Where it is delivered to or left at the relevant place before 12.00 midnight, on the second business day after that day
Fax	The second business day after completing the transmission of the fax (e g if the fax is sent at 10.30pm on Monday, it will be deemed served on Wednesday)
Other electronic method e g e-mail	The second business day after sending the email or other electronic transmission

| Personal Service | The second business day after completing the relevant step required by CPR 6.5(3) |

NB – The time for the lodging of the defendant and any interested party's acknowledgement of service (21 days) commences from the date that the claim is deemed served upon them.

Section 8

What do I do if my application is urgent?

8.1 If you want to make an application for your application for permission to be heard/considered by a Judge as a matter of urgency and/or to seek an interim injunction, you must complete a Request for Urgent Consideration, Form N463, which can be obtained from the HMCS website or the relevant Administrative Court Office. The form sets out the reasons for urgency and the timescale sought for the consideration of the permission application, e g within 72 hours or sooner if necessary, and the date by which the substantive hearing should take place.

8.2 Where you are seeking an interim injunction, you must, in addition, provide a draft order; and the grounds for the injunction. You must serve the claim form, the draft order and the application for urgency on the defendant and interested parties (by FAX and by post), advising them of the application and informing them that they may make representations directly to the Court in respect of your application.

8.3 A judge will consider the application within the time requested and may make such order as he/she considers appropriate.

NB – The judge may refuse your application for permission at this stage if he/she considers it appropriate, in the circumstances, to do so.

8.4 If the Judge directs that an oral hearing must take place within a specified time the Administrative Court Office will liaise with you and the representatives of the other parties to fix a permission hearing within the time period directed.

8.5 Where a manifestly inappropriate urgency application is made, consideration may, in appropriate cases, be given to making a wasted costs order.|

Section 9

What is an acknowledgement of service?

9.1 Any person who has been served with the claim form and who wishes to take part in the judicial review should file an acknowledgment of service (Form N462) in the Administrative Court Office, within 21 days of the proceedings being served upon them.

NB – Whilst there is no requirement upon you to serve the defendant and any interested party with a Form N462 for completion by them, it is good practice to do so.

9.2 The acknowledgement of service must set out the summary of grounds for contesting the claim and the name and address of any person considered to be an interested party (who has not previously been identified and served as an interested party).

9.3 The acknowledgement of service must be served upon you and the interested parties no later than 7 days after it is filed with the court.

NB – Failure to file an acknowledgement of service renders it necessary for the party concerned to obtain the permission of the court to take part in any oral hearing of the application for permission.

Section 10

What happens after the defendant and/or the interested party has lodged an acknowledgement of service, or the time for lodging such has expired?

10.1 Applications for permission to proceed with the claim for judicial review are considered by a single judge on the papers. The purpose of this procedure is to ensure that applications are dealt with speedily and without unnecessary expense.

10.2 The papers will be forwarded to the judge by the Administrative Court Office upon receipt of the Acknowledgement of Service or at the expiry of the time limit for lodging such acknowledgement – whichever is earlier.

10.3 The judge's decision and the reasons for it (Form JRJ) will be served upon you, the defendant and any other person served with the claim form.

10.4 If the judge grants permission and you wish to pursue the claim, you must lodge a further fee of £180.00 (or a further Application for Remission of Fee (Form EX160) with the relevant Administrative Court Office within 7 days of service of the judge's decision upon you.

NB – If you do not lodge the additional fee, your file will be closed.

Section 11

What happens after permission is refused or if permission is granted subject to conditions or in part only?

11.1 If permission is refused, or is granted subject to conditions or on certain grounds only, you may request a reconsideration of that decision at an oral hearing.

11.2 Request for an oral hearing must be made on the Notice of Renewal, Form 86b, (a copy of which will be sent to you at the same time as the judge's decision) and must be filed within 7 days after service of the notification of the judge's decision upon you (CPR Part 54.11 & 54.12).

11.3 Where the judge directs an oral hearing or you renew your application after refusal following consideration on paper, you may appear in person or be represented by an advocate (if you are legally represented). If you are not legally represented you may seek the court's permission to have someone speak on your behalf at the hearing.

NB – Any application for permission to have someone speak on your behalf should be made to the judge hearing the application who will make such decision as he considers appropriate in all of the circumstances.

11.4 Notice of the hearing is given to you, the defendant and any interested party by the Administrative Court List Office. An oral hearing is allocated a total of 30 minutes of court time. If it is considered that 30 minutes of court time is insufficient, you may provide a written estimate of the time required for the hearing and request a special fixture.

11.5 Neither the defendant nor any other interested party need attend a hearing on the question of permission unless the court directs otherwise.

Section 12

What happens if my application for permission is granted?

12.1 On granting permission the court may make case management directions under CPR 54.10(1) for the progression of the case. Case management directions may include directions as to venue, as to the service of the claim form and any evidence on other persons and as to expedition.

12.2 Where a claim is made under the Human Rights Act 1998, a direction may be made for the giving of notice to the Crown or joining the Crown as a party. In that regard you attention is drawn to the requirements of Civil Procedure rule 19.4A and paragraph 6 of the Practice Direction supplementing Section I of Part 19.

When should the defendant/interested party lodge its evidence following the grant of permission?

12.3 A party upon whom a claim form has been served and who wishes to contest the claim (or support it on additional grounds) must, within 35 days of service of the order granting permission, file and serve on the Court and all of the other parties:

- Detailed grounds for contesting the claim or supporting it on additional grounds and

- Any written evidence relied upon.

12.4 Any party who has done so may be represented at the hearing.

12.5 Where the party filing the detailed grounds intends to rely on documents not already filed, a paginated bundle of those documents must be filed at the Court when the detailed grounds are filed.

12.6 The Court has power to extend or abridge the time for lodging evidence.

Section 13

What happens when my case is ready for hearing?

13.1 When the time for lodging of evidence by the parties has expired, the case enters a warned list and all parties are informed of this by letter.

13.2 Where a direction has been given for expedition, the case will take priority over other cases waiting to be fixed and enters an expedited warned list.

What is the procedure for the listing of a case for hearing?

NB – The procedure is the same whether you act in person or are legally represented.

13.3 Where advocate's details have been placed on the court record, the parties will be contacted by the relevant Administrative Court List Office in order to seek to agree a date for the hearing. You and advocate's clerks will be offered a range of dates and will have 48 hours to take up one of the dates offered. If the parties fail to contact the List Office within 48 hours, the List Office will fix the hearing on one of the dates offered without further notice and the parties will be notified of that fixture by letter. Where a hearing is listed in this way the hearing will only be vacated by the Administrative Court Office if both parties consent and good reason is provided for the need to vacate the fixture, using the adjournment form available from Administrative Court Listing Offices.

13.4 There may be circumstances where you are unable to attend at court on the date fixed to hear your application, ie as a result of illness or accident. If you are unlikely to be able to attend court on the hearing date you must notify the relevant List Office immediately. You should contact the other parties to seek their consent to the adjournment using the adjournment form. If illness is the cause of your inability to attend, a medical certificate should also be provided. Your application for an adjournment will be considered by the Appropriate Officer of the relevant Administrative Court Office. Please note that there is a fee payable for any application to adjourn made within 14 days of the hearing date, unless you are entitled to fee remission, in which case you must lodge an Application for a Fee Remission (Form Ex160) with your adjournment form.

13.5 Where agreement to an adjournment cannot be reached, a formal application for adjournment must be made to the Court (on notice to all parties) using Form PF244 – Administrative Court Office. Please note that there is a fee payable (£75.00) for any application to adjourn made without the consent of all parties, notwithstanding when the application is lodged, unless you are entitled to fee remission, in which case you must lodge an Application for a Fee Remission (Form Ex160) with your application.

13.6 There are occasions when circumstances, outside the control of the List Office, may necessitate them having to vacate a hearing at very short notice. Sometimes this can be as late as 4.30pm the day before the case is listed. This could be as a result of a case unexpectedly overrunning, a judge becoming unavailable, or other reasons. The List Office will endeavour to re-fix the case on the next available date convenient to the parties.

What is the short warned list?

13.7 Whilst the Administrative Court usually gives fixed dates for hearings, there is also a need to short warn a number of cases to cover the large number of settlements that occur in the list. Parties in cases that are selected to be short warned will be notified that their case is likely to be listed from a specified date, and that they may be called into the list at less than a day's notice from that date. If the case does not get on during that period, a date as soon as possible after that period will be fixed in consultation with the parties.

What is a Skeleton Argument and do I need to lodge one?

13.8 A skeleton argument is a document lodged with the court by a party prior to the substantive hearing of any application for judicial review.

13.9 Whilst there is no requirement for a litigant in person to lodge a skeleton argument there is nothing to prevent you from doing so if you wish and if you consider that it would assist the Court.

13.10 If you wish to lodge a skeleton argument you must file it with the Court and serve it on the other parties not less than 21 working days before the date of the hearing of the judicial review or the short warned date, where a case has been 'short warned'.

13.11 The defendant and any other party wishing to make representations at the hearing of the judicial review must file and serve a skeleton argument not less than 14 working days before the date of the hearing of the judicial review (or the short warned date).

13.12 The skeleton argument must contain:

- a time estimate for the complete hearing, including delivery of judgment;

- a list of issues;

- a list of the legal points to be taken (together with any relevant authorities with page references to the passages relied on);

- a time estimate for the complete hearing, including delivery of judgment;

- a chronology of events (with page references to the bundle of documents);

- a list of essential documents for the advance reading of the court (with page references to the passages relied on) (if different from that filed with the claim form) and a time estimate for that reading; and

- A list of persons referred to.

What is a trial bundle and when should I lodge it?

13.13 You must file a paginated and indexed bundle of all relevant documents required for the hearing of the judicial review whether or not you file a skeleton argument. The bundle must be filed with the court and served on the other parties not less than 21 working days before the hearing.

NB – Two copies of the bundle are required by the Court when the application is to be heard by a Divisional Court in London.

NB – The bundle must also include those documents required by the defendant and any other party who is to make representations at the hearing.

Section 14

What if I need to make an application to the court for further orders / directions after the grant of permission?

14.1 Where case management decisions or directions are sought after permission has been granted, application should be made by way of an application under CPR Part 23, using Form PF244 – Administrative Court Office. You will be required to pay a fee for such application (currently £75.00, or £40.00 if all parties provide their written consent to the order being made), unless you are entitled to fee remission (in which case you should complete and submit a form EX160 with you application).

Section 15

Can my substantive application be determined without the need for a hearing?

15.1 The court may decide a claim for judicial review without a hearing where all parties agree (CPR Part 54.18).

Section 16

What do I need to do if the proceedings settle by consent prior to the substantive hearing of the application?

16.1 If you reach agreement with the other parties as to the terms of the final order to be made in your claim, you must file at the court a document (with 2 copies) signed by all the parties setting out the terms of the proposed agreed order.

NB – There is a fee of £40.00 payable on lodging the consent order, unless you are entitled to fee remission (in which case you should complete and submit a Form EX160 with your application).

NB – If you agree with the other parties that a mandatory order etc. is required, the draft order should be accompanied by a statement of reasons (ie a short statement of the matters relied on as justifying the proposed agreed order) and copies of any authorities or statutory provisions relied on. If settlement is reached before permission is considered, the draft consent order must include provision for permission to be granted.

NB – Such a statement is not required where the agreement as to disposal (usually by way of withdrawal of the application) requires an order for costs or a detailed assessment of the claimant's Legal Services Commission costs – in those circumstances the parties should file a draft consent order setting out the terms of settlement signed by all parties.

16.2 The court will consider the documents submitted and will make the order if it is satisfied that the order should be made. If the court is not satisfied that the order should be made, the court will give directions and may direct that a hearing date be set for the matter to be considered further.

Section 17

What if I want to discontinue the proceedings at any stage?

<u>Before service</u> of the claim form etc. on the other parties,

17.1 If you have not yet served any of the parties with the sealed claim form and accompanying documents you may discontinue the proceedings by notifying the Court in writing of your intention to do so. The Court will accept a letter of withdrawal provided that you confirm in writing that you have not effected service on the parties.

<u>After service</u> of the claim form etc. on the other parties,

17.2 Discontinuance of a claim is governed by CPR Part 38. Discontinuance renders you liable for the costs incurred by the other parties until the date of discontinuance.

17.3 There is a right to discontinue a claim at any time, except where:

- An interim injunction has been granted or an undertaking has been given – in those circumstances the permission of the court is required to discontinue the proceedings (an example of this would be where bail had been granted pending determination of the application for judicial review)

- Interim payment has been made by defendant – in those circumstances the consent of the defendant or the permission of the court is required to discontinue the proceedings

- There is more than one claimant – in those circumstances the consent of every other claimant or the permission of the court is required to discontinue the proceedings.

17.4 If you wish to discontinue the proceedings at any stage after the service of those proceedings upon the other parties you must file a Notice of Discontinuance in the requisite form (N279) at the relevant Administrative Court Office and serve a copy on every other party.

17.5 A defendant may apply to set aside the Notice of Discontinuance, within 28 days of being served with it (CPR Part 38.4).

NB – If the parties require any order for costs, then a draft order setting out the terms of the order sought is required. A Notice of Discontinuance would not be appropriate in those circumstances.

Section 18

Will I be responsible for the costs of the defendant and/or the interested parties if my application is unsuccessful?

18.1 The general rule is that the party losing a substantive claim for judicial review will be ordered to pay the costs of the other parties. However, the Judge considering the matter has discretion to deal with the issue of costs as he/she considers appropriate in all of the circumstances.

NB – Costs may be awarded in respect of an unsuccessful paper application. Any application by the defendant/interested party for costs will normally be made in the Acknowledgment of Service.

Section 19

What can I do if I am unhappy with the Judge's decision?

Civil matters

Appeal after refusal of permission

19.1 If you are unhappy with the Court's decision in a civil matter you can appeal to the Court of Appeal Civil Division (with permission of the Court of Appeal (CPR Part 52.15)). Application to the Court of Appeal for permission to Appeal must be made within 7 days of the refusal by the Administrative Court of permission to apply for judicial review.

Appeal after substantive hearing

19.2 In substantive applications, permission to appeal may be sought from the Administrative Court when it determines the claim for judicial review. If an application for permission to appeal is not made at the conclusion of the case, the application for permission to appeal must be made to the Court of Appeal Civil Division within 21 days (CPR Part 52.3 & 52.4).

19.3 Guidance as to procedure should be sought from the Civil Appeals Office, Royal Courts of Justice, Strand, London, WC2A 2LL.

Criminal matters

Appeal after refusal of permission

19.4 There is no further remedy in the domestic courts after a refusal of permission by the Administrative Court.

Appeal after substantive hearing

19.5 If you are unhappy with the Court's decision in a substantive claim for judicial review in a criminal matter, you can appeal to the Supreme Court but only with the leave of the Administrative Court or the Supreme Court and such leave may only be granted if: (a) The Administrative Court certifies that a point of law of general public importance is involved in its decision; and (b) It appears to the Administrative Court or the Supreme Court that the point is one which ought to be considered by the Supreme Court. (see The Administration of Justice Act 1960 s.1).

Section 20

Where can I get advice about procedural matters?

20.1 If in doubt about any procedural matter you can contact the relevant Administrative Court Office, telephone numbers below. Court staff cannot give legal advice as to the merits of a case.

- **Birmingham Civil Justice Centre** – 0121 681 3043 or 0121 681 3181;

- **Cardiff Civil Justice Centre** – 029 2037 6400;

- **Leeds Combined Court Centre** – 0113 306 2578;

- **Manchester Civil Justice Centre** – 0161 240 5313 or 0161 240 5314;

- The Royal Courts of Justice in London – 020 7947 6205 or 020 7947 6655.

PRACTICE STATEMENT (ADMINISTRATIVE COURT: LISTING AND URGENT CASES)

Queen's Bench Division

1 February 2002

[2002] 1 WLR 810

Scott Baker J

2002 Feb 1

SCOTT BAKER J

the lead judge of the Administrative Court, delivered the annual statement of the Administrative Court at the sitting of the court.

1. Nominated judges

There are presently 25 Judges nominated by Lord Woolf CJ to sit in the Administrative Court.

They include two judges of the Chancery Division and two of the Family Division who act as additional judges of the Queen's Bench Division when dealing with Administrative Court cases. A list of those currently nominated is attached at Annex A. The Administrative Court now has regular use of six courtrooms—courts 1, 2, 3, 10, 27 and 28. Routinely there are approximately eight judges allocated to single judge sittings and one or two Divisional Courts sit.

2. Modern judicial review

[His Lordship gave details of the impact of the changes arising from the establishment of the Administrative Court and the coming into force of the Human Rights Act 1998 in October 2000.]

3. Performance of the court in 2001

[His Lordship gave details of the performance of the court in 2001, and continued:]

Waiting times during 2001

The average waiting time for a decision on an application for *permission to apply for judicial review was eight weeks* (from lodging to decision). The average waiting time for a *substantive determination (of all types of case) was 20 weeks* (from lodging to decision). Expedited cases are being listed in a matter of weeks.

Legal representatives should bear these figures in mind when preparing cases. In the light of the performance of the court a short warned list has been reintroduced to ensure the court is fully listed and time is not wasted when cases settle at the last minute. Parties in cases which are short warned will be notified that their case is likely to be listed from a specified date, and that they may be called into the list at less than a day's notice from that date.

Approximately six cases are short warned for each week. If the case does not get on during that period, a date as soon as possible after that period will be fixed in consultation with the parties.

For the benefit of users the current listing policy of the Administrative Court is annexed to this statement (Annex C).

4. Users group

The Administrative Court Users Group provides a useful forum for discussion between the court users, the court staff and the nominated judges. Some of the forthcoming initiatives I am about to announce resulted from those discussions.

I intend for the group to continue to meet each term. I welcome suggestions for the agenda and the feedback which court users are uniquely placed to give.

5. Use of alternative means of resolution

I draw the attention of litigants and legal advisers to the decision of the Court of Appeal in *R (Cowl) v Plymouth City Council (Practice Note)* [2001] EWCA Civ 1935; [2002] 1 WLR 803.

The nominated judges are fully committed to resolving disputes by alternative means where appropriate and are exploring ways of promoting this.

6. Forthcoming initiatives

Pre-action protocol for judicial review

The protocol was published in December 2001 and comes into force on 4 March 2002. Any claims for judicial review lodged on or after that date must indicate that the protocol has been complied with. Reasons for non-compliance must be given in the claim form. The form is currently being reconsidered in the light of the experience of the past 16 months and the comments of users. The revised form will be available on the Court Service website shortly.

Urgent cases procedure

CPR Pt 54 makes no express provision for urgent applications for permission to apply for judicial review to be made orally. As the result of user's concerns I now issue guidance on the procedure to be applied for urgent applications and for interim injunctions. Advocates must comply with this guidance; and where a manifestly inappropriate application is made, consideration will be given to a wasted costs order. The full terms of the guidance and the form for use in this procedure are annexed to this statement (Annex B).

1. The Administrative Court currently allocates paper applications for judicial review on a daily basis and one judge also act as the 'urgent judge'.

2. Where a claimant makes an application for the permission application to be heard as a matter of urgency and/or seeks an interim injunction, he must complete a prescribed form which states:

    (a)   the need for urgency;
    (b)   the timescale sought for the consideration of the permission application, eg within 72 hours or sooner if necessary; and
    (c)   the date by which the substantive hearing should take place.

3. Where an interim injunction is sought, a claimant must, in addition, provide

    (a)   a draft order; and
    (b)   the grounds for the injunction.

4. The claimant must serve (by fax and post) the claim form and application for urgency on the defendant and interested parties, advising them of the application and that they may make representations.

5. Where an interim injunction is sought, the claimant must serve (by fax and post) the draft order and grounds for the application on the defendant and interested parties, advising them of the application and that they may make representations.

6. A judge will consider the application within the time requested and may make such order as he considers appropriate.

7. If the judge directs that an oral hearing take place within a specified time the representatives of the parties and the Administrative Court will liaise to fix a permission hearing within the time period directed.

E-mail addresses for use for urgent post

The Administrative Court Office now has e-mail addresses for *urgent post* . The addresses are not available for formal filing of documents. When using these addresses the office opening hours must be borne in mind and it cannot be assumed that mail sent after 4.30 p m will be opened before 9 a m on the following day. The e-mail addresses are:

For mail relating to paper applications—

Administrativecourtoffice.generaloffice@courtservice.gsi.gov.uk

For mail relating to listed cases—

Administrativecourtoffice.listoffice@courtservice.gsi.gov.uk

For mail relating to court orders—

Administrativecourtoffice.courtclerks@courtservice.gsi.gov.uk

Revised renewal form – judicial review

With immediate effect, when completing the form used for renewing applications for permission to apply for judicial review, claimants must set out the grounds for renewal in the light of the reasons given by the single judge when refusing permission on the papers.

C R S

Annex A

[This Annex contains a list of the judges of the Administrative Court.]

Annex B

[This Annex sets out the procedure for urgent applications to the Administrative Court, in the same terms as section 6 of the practice statement, and the following form for use in that procedure:]

Administrative Court Office Reference Number: CO/

REQUEST FOR URGENT CONSIDERATION

THIS FORM MUST BE COMPLETED BY THE ADVOCATE FOR THE CLAIMANT

THIS FORM AND THE CLAIM FORM MUST BE SERVED BY THE CLAIMANT's SOLICITORS, BY FAX AND POST, ON THE DEFENDANT AND INTERESTED PARTIES

NAME OF CLAIMANT:

Name, address and fax number of solicitor acting for the claimant

Name of counsel/advocate acting for the claimant

NAME OF DEFENDANT:

Date of service of this form and claim form

Fax number served

NAME OF INTERESTED PARTY(IES):

Date of service of this form and claim form

Fax number served

1.   REASONS FOR URGENCY

2.   PROPOSED TIMETABLE

    (a)   The application for permission should be considered within hours/days.
    (b)   Abridgement of time is sought for the lodging of acknowledgments of service.
    (c)   If permission is granted, a substantive hearing is sought by (date).

3.   INTERIM RELIEF

Interim relief is sought in terms of the attached draft order on the following grounds:

SIGNED ADVOCATE FOR THE CLAIMANT

DATE NOTE TO THE DEFENDANT AND INTERESTED PARTIES

Representations as to the urgency of the claim may be made to the Administrative Court Office by fax—0207 947 6802.

Annex C

Listing Policy in the Administrative Court

February 2002

Fixing substantive hearings

Where a case is ready to be heard substantively, it enters a warned list and all parties are informed of this by letter. Some cases require an early hearing date and take priority over other cases waiting to be fixed—these enter the expedited warned list.

Where counsel has been placed on the court record, their chambers are contacted by the Administrative Court list office in order to agree a convenient date for the hearing. Counsel's clerks are offered a range of dates and have 48 hours to take up one of the dates offered. If counsel's clerk fails to contact the list office within 48 hours, the list office will fix the hearing on one of the dates that was offered, without further notice and the parties will be notified of that fixture by letter. Where a hearing is listed in this way the hearing will only be vacated by the Administrative Court Office if both parties consent. Failing that, a formal application for adjournment must be made (on notice to all parties) to the court. The same procedure is followed where a claimant is in person.

Short warned list

Whilst the Administrative Court usually gives fixed dates for hearings, there is also a need to short warn a number of cases to cover the large number of settlements that occur in the list.

Parties in cases that are selected to be short warned will be notified that their case is likely to be listed from a specified date, and that they may be called into the list at less than a days notice from that date. Approximately six cases are short warned for any specified week. If the case does not get on during that period, a date as soon as possible after that period will be fixed in consultation with the parties.

Vacating fixtures

There are occasions when circumstances, outside the control of the list office, may necessitate them having to vacate a hearing at very short notice. Sometimes this can be as late as 4.30 p m the day before the case is listed. This could be as a result of a case unexpectedly overrunning, a judge becoming unavailable, or other reasons. In deciding which hearing has to be vacated, the list office will assess the cases listed for the following day and take the following factors into consideration:

- Which case(s), if removed, will cause the least disruption to the list (the aim is to adjourn as few cases as possible, ideally one).

- How many cases need to be adjourned given the reduced listing time available.

- Have any matters previously been adjourned by the court.

- The urgency and age(s) of the matter(s) listed.

- Where the parties and/or their representatives are based (this is relevant as in some cases the parties travel to London the day before the hearing).

- Whether it is appropriate to 'float' the case in the event of another listed matter going short (cases will not be floated without the consent of the parties).

- The likelihood of a judge becoming available to hear a floated case.

After taking these factors into account, the list office decide upon the case(s) which will have to be refixed and will inform the parties concerned that their hearing has been vacated. The case record will be noted that the matter is not to be adjourned by the court again. The court will also endeavour to refix the case on the next available date convenient to the parties.

Appendix E
FORMS

Judicial Review
Claim Form

In the High Court of Justice
Administrative Court

Notes for guidance are available which explain how to complete the judicial review claim form. Please read them carefully before you complete the form.

For Court use only	
Administrative Court Reference No.	
Date filed	

Seal

SECTION 1 Details of the claimant(s) and defendant(s)

Claimant(s) name and address(es)

name

address

Telephone no. Fax no.

E-mail address

Claimant's or claimant's solicitors' address to which documents should be sent.

name

address

Telephone no. Fax no.

E-mail address

Claimant's Counsel's details

name

address

Telephone no. Fax no.

E-mail address

1st Defendant

name

Defendant's or (where known) Defendant's solicitors' address to which documents should be sent.

name

address

Telephone no. Fax no.

E-mail address

2nd Defendant

name

Defendant's or (where known) Defendant's solicitors' address to which documents should be sent.

name

address

Telephone no. Fax no.

E-mail address

SECTION 2 Details of other interested parties

Include name and address and, if appropriate, details of DX, telephone or fax numbers and e-mail

name	name

address	address

Telephone no.	Fax no.	Telephone no.	Fax no.

E-mail address	E-mail address

SECTION 3 Details of the decision to be judicially reviewed

Decision:

Date of decision:

Name and address of the court, tribunal, person or body who made the decision to be reviewed.

name	address

SECTION 4 Permission to proceed with a claim for judicial review

I am seeking permission to proceed with my claim for Judicial Review.

Is this application being made under the terms of Section 18 Practice Direction 54 (Challenging removal)? ☐ Yes ☐ No

Are you making any other applications? If Yes, complete Section 7. ☐ Yes ☐ No

Is the claimant in receipt of a Community Legal Service Fund (CLSF) certificate? ☐ Yes ☐ No

Are you claiming exceptional urgency, or do you need this application determined within a certain time scale? If Yes, complete Form N463 and file this with your application. ☐ Yes ☐ No

Have you complied with the pre-action protocol? If No, give reasons for non-compliance in the box below. ☐ Yes ☐ No

Have you issued this claim in the region with which you have the closest connection? (Give any additional reasons for wanting it to be dealt with in this region in the box below). If No, give reasons in the box below. ☐ Yes ☐ No

Does the claim include any issues arising from the Human Rights Act 1998?
If Yes, state the articles which you contend have been breached in the box below.   ☐ Yes   ☐ No

---

SECTION 5 Detailed statement of grounds

☐ set out below   ☐ attached

SECTION 6 Details of remedy (including any interim remedy) being sought

---

SECTION 7 Other applications

I wish to make an application for:-

SECTION 8 Statement of facts relied on

Statement of Truth

I believe (The claimant believes) that the facts stated in this claim form are true.

Full name

Name of claimant's solicitor's firm

Signed

Position or office held

Claimant ('s solicitor)

(if signing on behalf of firm or company)

SECTION 9 Supporting documents

If you do not have a document that you intend to use to support your claim, identify it, give the date when you expect it to be available and give reasons why it is not currently available in the box below.

Please tick the papers you are filing with this claim form and any you will be filing later.

☐ Statement of grounds   ☐ included   ☐ attached

☐ Statement of the facts relied on   ☐ included   ☐ attached

☐ Application to extend the time limit for filing the claim form   ☐ included   ☐ attached

☐ Application for directions   ☐ included   ☐ attached

☐ Any written evidence in support of the claim or
application to extend time

☐ Where the claim for judicial review relates to a decision of
a court or tribunal, an approved copy of the reasons for
reaching that decision

☐ Copies of any documents on which the claimant
proposes to rely

☐ A copy of the legal aid or CSLF certificate *(if legally represented)*

☐ Copies of any relevant statutory material

☐ A list of essential documents for advance reading by
the court *(with page references to the passages relied upon)*

If Section 18 Practice Direction 54 applies, please tick the relevant box(es) below to indicate which papers you are filing with this claim form:

☐ a copy of the removal directions and the decision to which   ☐ included   ☐ attached
the application relates

☐ a copy of the documents served with the removal directions
including any documents which contains the Immigration and   ☐ included   ☐ attached
Nationality Directorate's factual summary of the case

☐ a detailed statement of the grounds   ☐ included   ☐ attached

Reasons why you have not supplied a document and date when you expect it to be available:-

Signed _____ Claimant ('s Solicitor)_____

Judicial Review **Acknowledgment of Service**	**In the High Court of Justice** **Administrative Court**	
	Claim No.	
Name and address of person to be served	**Claimant(s)** *(including ref.)*	
┌name┐ 	**Defendant(s)**	
┌address┐ 	**Interested Parties**	

SECTION A

Tick the appropriate box

   1. I intend to contest all of the claim   ☐ } complete sections B, C, D and E

   2. I intend to contest part of the claim   ☐

   3. I do not intend to contest the claim   ☐   complete section E

   4. The defendant (interested party) is a court or tribunal and **intends** to make a submission.   ☐   complete sections B, C and E

   5. The defendant (interested party) is a court or tribunal and **does not intend** to make a submission.   ☐   complete sections B and E

Note: If the application seeks to judicially review the decision of a court or tribunal, the court or tribunal need only provide the Administrative Court with as much evidence as it can about the decision to help the Administrative Court perform its judicial function.

SECTION B

Insert the name and address of any person you consider should be added as an interested party.

┌name┐	┌name┐
┌address┐	┌address┐
┌Telephone no.┐ ┌Fax no.┐	┌Telephone no.┐ ┌Fax no.┐
┌E-mail address┐	┌E-mail address┐

SECTION C

Summary of grounds for contesting the claim. If you are contesting only part of the claim, set out which part before you give your grounds for contesting it. If you are a court or tribunal filing a submission, please indicate that this is the case.

SECTION D

Give details of any directions you will be asking the court to make, or tick the box to indicate that a separate application notice is attached.

If you are seeking a direction that this matter be heard at an Administrative Court venue other than that at which this claim was issued, you should complete, lodge and serve on all other parties Form N464 with this acknowledgment of service.

SECTION E

delete as appropriate

*(I believe)(The defendant believes) that the facts stated in this form are true.

*I am duly authorised by the defendant to sign this statement.

(if signing on behalf of firm or company, court or tribunal)

Position or office held

(To be signed by you or by your solicitor or litigation friend)

Signed

Date

Give an address to which notices about this case can be sent to you

name

address

Telephone no.

Fax no.

E-mail address

If you have instructed counsel, please give their name address and contact details below.

name

address

Telephone no.

Fax no.

E-mail address

Completed forms, together with a copy, should be lodged with the Administrative Court Office (court address, over the page), at which this claim was issued within 21 days of service of the claim upon you, and further copies should be served on the Claimant(s), any other Defendant(s) and any interested parties within 7 days of lodgement with the Court.

Administrative Court addresses

- Administrative Court in **London**

  Administrative Court Office, Room C315, Royal Courts of Justice, Strand, London, WC2A 2LL.

- Administrative Court in **Birmingham**

  Administrative Court Office, Birmingham Civil Justice Centre, Priory Courts, 33 Bull Street, Birmingham B4 6DS.

- Administrative Court in **Wales**

  Administrative Court Office, Cardiff Civil Justice Centre, 2 Park Street, Cardiff, CF10 1ET.

- Administrative Court in **Leeds**

  Administrative Court Office, Leeds Combined Court Centre, 1 Oxford Row, Leeds, LS1 3BG.

- Administrative Court in **Manchester**

  Administrative Court Office, Manchester Civil Justice Centre, 1 Bridge Street West, Manchester, M3 3FX.

Judicial Review
Application for urgent consideration

This form must be completed by the Claimant or the Claimant's advocate if exceptional urgency is being claimed and the application needs to be determined within a certain time scale.

The claimant, or the claimant's solicitors must serve this form on the defendant(s) and any interested parties with the N461 Judicial review claim form.

To the Defendant(s) and Interested Party(ies)
Representations as to the urgency of the claim may be made by defendants or interested parties to the relevant Administrative Court Office by fax:-

For cases proceeding in

London – 020 7947 6802   **Birmingham** – 0121 250 6730

Cardiff – 02920 376461   **Leeds** – 0113 306 2581

Manchester – 0161 240 5315

In the High Court of Justice Administrative Court	
Claim No.	
Claimant(s) *(including ref.)*	
Defendant(s)	
Interested Parties	

SECTION 1 Reasons for urgency

SECTION 2 Proposed timetable *(tick the boxes and complete the following statements that apply)*

☐ a) The application for interim relief should be considered within _____ hours/days

☐ b) The N461 application for permission should be considered within _____ hours/days

☐ c) Abridgement of time is sought for the lodging of acknowledgments of service

☐ d) If permission for judicial review is granted, a substantive hearing is sought by _____ (date)

INDEX

References are to paragraph numbers.